Be B

Centuries of Economic Endeavor

Centuries of Economic Endeavor

Parallel Paths in Japan and Europe and Their Contrast with the Third World

John P. Powelson

Ann Arbor

THE UNIVERSITY OF MICHIGAN PRESS

Copyright © by the University of Michigan 1994
All rights reserved
Published in the United States of America by
The University of Michigan Press
Manufactured in the United States of America
⊗ Printed on acid-free paper

1997   1996   1995   4   3   2

Library of Congress Cataloging-in-Publication Data

Powelson, John P., 1920–
    Centuries of economic endeavor : parallel paths in Japan and
Europe and their contrast with the Third World / John P. Powelson.
        p.   cm.
    Includes bibliographical references and index.
    ISBN 0-472-10547-7 (alk. paper)
    1. Economic history.   2. Japan—Economic conditions.   3. Europe—
Economic conditions.   4. Developing countries—Economic conditions.
I. Title.
HC21.P67   1994
330.9—dc20   94-17693
                                                           CIP

To Cynthia
Beloved daughter, 1955-92
and to Robin, Judy, Ken, Carolyn, Larry, and Tim
with whom she shared her life and love

Contents

List of Appendixes

Preface

This book sums up, but I hope does not end, my forty-year career devoted to studying, teaching, lecturing and advising about economic development, in universities, governments, and international agencies in the United States and in thirty-five countries in Asia, Africa, and Latin America.

Twenty years ago I decided that an understanding of economic development lay as much in history as in economics. The resulting incursion into history forced upon me an observation I had not wanted to find, to wit:

• In the quest to raise vast numbers out of poverty all over the world—known as "economic development"—all that I was proposing to governments had been advocated over centuries: land reform, liberal trade, sound money, realistic exchange rates, stable fisc, enforcement of contracts, adequate public investment, privatization of enterprise, defense of property rights, and economic integration. Yet for centuries in most of the world, these good orders had not been adopted or if adopted, had not lasted.

• Why should the present era be different, I wondered? Why do we expect eastern Europe and the Third World to implement reforms at the behest of consultants like me, or the International Monetary Fund, when most of Asia, Africa, and the Middle East would not adopt these very same reforms despite repeated urging by European governments in earlier centuries?

• Yet some world areas have succeeded in economic development. What distinguishes them? Under what conditions may or may not modernizing reforms become the way of the future in eastern Europe and the Third World?

This book addresses these questions.

xii

Acknowledgments

I am indebted to Wallis Bolz, Clarence Boonstra, the late Kenneth Boulding, Murray Bryce, Joseph Clawson, Martin Cobin, Colin Day, the late Ragaei el Mallakh, Barbara Engel, Steven Epstein, Ray Evans, Herbert Fraser, Jenny Gibson, Patricia Gilmore, Grace Goodell, Elizabeth Herr, Bruce Herrick, Lewis Hoskins, Jerry Jenkins, Tim Kasser, Charles Kindleberger, the late Russell Kirk, Joyce Lebra, Donald Marsh, Philip Mounts, David Murdock, Mark Perlman, Barry Poulson, Gerald Sazama, William Shropshire, Niles Utlaut, J.D. Von Pischke, and James Wescoat for their advice and assistance.

My wife (Robin) and children (Cynthia, Judith, Kenneth, Carolyn, and Lawrence) all read parts of the manuscript and offered useful comments. Cynthia died of cancer while the manuscript was still being evaluated. One of her last questions was, "Has Michigan accepted the book?"

Norma Price and Louise Dudley, professional editors not employed by the Press, read the entire manuscript and offered some excellent suggestions on presentation and style. Debra Armour helped with the organization of notes and secretarial work. The staff of the University of Michigan Press was very helpful in the final preparation of the manuscript and page proofs, especially Laurie Ham, Michael Kehoe, Lorrie Lejeune, and Christina Milton.

Since I did the entire book on my home computer with laser printer, from writing the original manuscript to the preparation of photo-ready copies of page proofs, any errors, whether of fact, reason, or typographical, are my full responsibility.

I am also indebted to the Earhart and Wilbur Foundations for their assistance.

Language

Non-sexist language ("he or she") is used except where it would be verbose, ungrammatical, or indefinite. In deference to non-Christian readers, BCE (Before Common Era) and CE (Common Era) are used instead of BC and AD respectively. "Liberal" and "liberalism" are used in their original senses, implying freedom of trade, thought, politics, and the like, not in the more recent sense of "progressive."

Chapter 1
Durable Economic Development

Why do Japan, western Europe, North America, and Australia and New Zealand lead the world in economic development, and why are their prosperity, infrastructure, and standards of living far, far greater than those of the less-developed zones?

This book offers an answer to this puzzle. Comparing the histories of Japan and northwestern Europe from the middle ages onward, it finds a startling parallel between the two, which has been relatively neglected in explanations of economic development. Then it contrasts the Japan/Europe pattern with the histories of Africa, Asia except Japan, Latin America, and eastern and southern Europe, where the parallel vanishes. Could this divergence explain why development occurred first in Japan and northwestern Europe (and Europe's cultural descendants in North America, Australia, and New Zealand) and less so or not at all elsewhere? Will it also help us understand economic development *in general*?

In both Japan and northwestern Europe, the methods, rules, and instruments of policy and exchange were fashioned primarily by bargaining among the parties concerned: farmers, landowners, producers, and traders. Money and banking, commercial law, rules of the market, corporate enterprise, government bureaucracies, and ultimately parliamentary democracy were created in this way. Let us call these—and others to be added—the *institutions of economic development*. As the parties negotiated with each other and with the sovereign, they built into their systems ways of holding each other accountable for performance and for efficient use of resources, both public and private. On these foundations, economic development took the form of millions upon millions of positive-sum transactions, agreed upon by thousands upon thousands of people and groups, acting separately, often independently of superior authority. While the sovereign attempted to interfere with economic endeavor at all times, for the most part the people resisted, and for the most part the people won.

In the rest of the world, by contrast, economic endeavor and its rules and instruments were conducted or fashioned primarily by the sovereign, using the weight of superior authority and military command. Here the people either could not resist, or they lost. These areas are now the less-developed zones.

Furthermore, in Japan and northwestern Europe, plus cultural descendants of the latter, the institutions of economic development are held in place by a balance of power among interest groups, which have created an *interlocking society.* The institutions so fit into each other, like pieces in a jigsaw puzzle, that none can be displaced without the whole society's unraveling. Because they have vested interests in many of the institutions, groups with a preponderance of power prevent the unraveling. This is why, for example, democratic government is well established in Europe, North America, and Japan. By contrast, in much of the rest of the world the analogous institutions are held together by the military or by elites ruling over a weakened citizenry. They do not interlock. Besides, an unraveling of society in these areas may not be viewed with much alarm by some groups with the power to make it happen.

It is often supposed that Japanese economic development "began" around the turn of the twentieth century and that Japan copied its economic system from the West. Recent scholarship demonstrates that neither of these assertions is completely true. Rather, Japanese economic development had been progressing strongly for almost three centuries before the Meiji Restoration of 1868. Indeed, the Japanese at that time may have been as far advanced as were the British just before their Industrial Revolution. Furthermore, the Japanese had developed sophisticated banking and exchange practices, commercial law, and bureaucracies capable of handling advanced economic policy. Their agrarian system had been modernized. Taking a cue from this scholarship, I will argue that Japan did *not* copy the West. Rather, the Japanese and Europeans were independent progenitors of economic development.

This perspective leads to another remarkable finding: that the common features of Japanese and Western histories, which distinguish them from other societies, date from early medieval times onward, even though Japan and the West are not known to have communicated with each other before the sixteenth century. While these common features have been recognized by some Japanese historians such as Asakawa and Takekoshi, and by a few Western Japanologists such as Hall and Mass, they have been largely ignored by economic historians and development economists in the West.

The initial question in this book, therefore, is why were northwestern Europe and Japan the historic leaders in economic development? The answer to this is of obvious importance to many current world problems. As well as addressing the general question of how to lift vast portions of the world population out of poverty, the argument developed in this book will enhance our understanding of some other crucial questions, to wit:

> • First, can we predict whether the liberalizing reforms currently undertaken in less-developed zones and the Soviet successor states will last over centuries, or whether they will crumble as have so many similar reforms in the past?

• Second, when economists propose sound policies for economic development—such as inflation control, equitable taxes, and realistic exchange rates—why are these proposals so often not implemented by government officials in less-developed zones and eastern Europe, when economic development is presumably their goal?

• Third, when sound policies have in fact been followed for a decade or more, as in Colombia in the 1950s, Guatemala in the 1960s, or Kenya in the 1970s, why are they reversed, when this reversal leads to excessive inflation, unemployment, economic slowdown, and other unwanted consequences?

The ultimate explanation of economic development—I will argue—lies not in economic factors, such as land, labor, and capital, or even in social forces, such as education, religion, and entrepreneurship. Rather, all these will be added when most people learn, as the Japanese and northwestern Europeans did, that it is good business to be just and considerate toward one's neighbors; to solve quarrels peacefully; to be held accountable for the efficient use of resources (both public and private); and to abide by modes of behavior—hereafter called *institutions*—that have been negotiated and agreed by interested parties.[1] Our purpose is to understand a phenomenon—economic development—not to display its economic aspects separately from its historical, sociological, or other aspects.

This book coordinates history with economics. Leaving the other social sciences to others, I do not claim the total picture. But I do argue that the histories of the more-developed zones explain much about how development occurs, and why it has happened more in some places than in others. I address the lay public in addition to my colleagues. Technical jargon will be kept to a minimum and explained.

Economic History and Economic Development

Economic history and economic development are deemed separate subfields of economics. In part, the reason for this paradox is itself historical: economic history was there first. Although classical economists (Smith, Malthus, Mill, Ricardo) did write about development, and although Schumpeter based his business-cycle theory upon it, nevertheless not until after World War II did development rank alongside theory, international trade, money and banking, and others as a recognized subfield.

But surely a more cogent reason why development is not merged with history is that many leaders in less-developed countries, being strongly nationalist, think that the history of more-developed zones has little to say to them. This belief has been seconded by diplomats seeking the support of Third World governments in the cold war; by international agencies lending them money; by economists advising them; and by professors teaching and researching in their universities. All these professionals (I among them) have had reasons to pretend that development was not history.

Two unfortunate results have followed. One is that economic development has become treated largely as a mathematical exercise, manifesting itself in the plethora of growth models whose popularity peaked two decades ago. Underdevelopment was attributed to forces beyond the control of Third World peoples, since it was not diplomatic to blame it on culture. Most models cited lack of capital, both physical and human. President Mobutu of Zaire referred to his country as "underequipped," denying that it was "underdeveloped." The other, more serious, result is that lessons from the historical experiences of the more-developed zones have been neglected. Especially has this been so in policy-making toward eastern Europe and the Third World. Of course, it is not at all certain that history, which occurs over centuries, would influence politicians, whose time span may be until the next election. But there is no excuse for its neglect by all except a few scholars.

The Power-Diffusion Process

The historic contrast between Japan and northwestern Europe on the one hand and the rest of the world on the other lies primarily in the concentration or diffusion of power. In this book, power means the ability to influence or direct the behavior of others.

Power is an economic good, either capital (capable of yielding other products for its possessor) or consumer (enjoyed for its own sake). It has costs and benefits. The costs may be monetary, but they may also lie in other sacrifices, such as the number of companions killed to obtain it. Power is tradable for money or for other goods, and one may hold more or less of it. Thus power shares the major attributes of other economic goods and services.

In the less-developed zones today, the power of the central authorities over economic decisions—on production, prices, the money supply, interest and exchange rates, and others—is far more concentrated than is that of their counterparts in the more-developed zones. It is also subject to fewer checks and balances. Therefore, the answer to questions two and three is already hinted. Powerholders may be unwilling to take socially advantageous measures because these would diminish their power.

Durable economic development is defined as economic growth lasting for a century or more, along with the formation of institutions to sustain the growth. It requires a mechanism by which powerholders either trade their power for other goods or are deprived of it by other persons. The common elements found in the histories of Japan and northwestern Europe both illustrate that process and will help us predict whether current policy toward eastern Europe and the less-developed zones will result in enduring development.

Up to medieval times, power was concentrated everywhere in the world, in ways similar to those found in less-developed zones today. But in northwestern Europe and Japan, over time it became diffused among more and more persons and organized groups. The pertinent question becomes not why power is still concentrated in less-developed zones today but why it became less concentrated in today's more-developed zones.

Power diffusion in Japan and northwestern Europe was initiated in similar ways, and it continued in matching ways for at least seven centuries. In the next five chapters I will show examples of how both societies developed a growing balance of power among economic interest groups and how this balance led toward institutions that were both equitable and growth-promoting. Power diffusion also fostered liberal economic attitudes, along with parliamentary democracy, widespread ownership of assets, and decentralized decision making. These are what led to durable economic development.

More than in other regions, as far back as the twelfth and thirteenth centuries many *corporate economic interest groups* were being formed in northwestern Europe and Japan. At first these included guilds, religious organizations, village assemblies, military bands, and peasant associations. Over the centuries political associations, labor unions, consumer cooperatives, lobbies for industries, farmers' unions, and more were added. Each interest group possessed a structure by which it might negotiate as a body with other interest groups. (By contrast, a *corporate category* is a loose configuration of persons with similar interests but without bargaining capabilities. Definitions of M.G. Smith are used.[2]) A society of many corporate interest groups, possessing the capacity to negotiate with each other, will be called a *pluralist society* in this book. Other types of pluralism—such as many educational systems, religions, and ethnic groups—followed. Therefore, my economic construct for pluralism is consistent with the wider, more popular definition. Corporate interest groups did exist in other parts of the world, but they did not achieve the critical mass necessary for power diffusion.

I have distilled the common features of the Japanese and northwestern European experiences into what I call the *power-diffusion process*, which operated as follows: Beginning in medieval times, lower-level (as perceived by contemporary cultures) interest groups allied themselves with upper-level groups, exacting power in return. For example, as nobility, kings, or church competed with one another, peasant groups might join forces with either side, demanding greater power or freedom if their side won. If their side lost, they would bide their time until the next occasion. These arrangements, across social clusters, will be called *vertical alliances*. Reference will also be made to *vertical communication, contracts, negotiation, bargaining,* and the like. The application of vertical alliances to enhance power is referred to as *leverage*. The power-diffusion process consists in repeated instances of vertical alliances with leverage, hundreds and thousands of times over centuries, with power becoming incrementally more balanced each time. "More" balanced means that lower-level groups gained in their ability to promote or thwart the goals of upper-level groups. In no society has this process led to a complete balance of power, nor would one even know what "complete" would be.

In Japan and northwestern Europe, rather than rely on the sovereign, the interest groups themselves negotiated the institutions to implement new arrangements. These included a monetary system, a legal system, corporations, trading practices, education, and parliamentary democracy. The sovereign's role was secondary, often endorsing what the groups had decided or making decisions that might be countered or revised by the groups. Therefore, the interest groups had vested interests in the institutions, while the sovereign had only a limited ability to subvert them to his own advantage. This restraint upon concentrated power constitutes the principal difference, in the context of durable economic development, between Japan and northwestern Europe on the one hand and the rest of the world on the other.

Curiously, the industrialized powers are now supporting in eastern Europe and the Third World authoritarian methods that they gave up a century or more ago in their own territories. They are encouraging—even bribing—authoritarian governments to impose upon their peoples economic liberalism, modern monetary structures, and private markets, all of which are governed by rules that defy the norms of millions of their citizens. Since these reforms are ahistorical, they may not last for centuries. But more than that, this book will show that all of them have been attempted in authoritarian ways many times, often in the same areas. Why must they be tried again?

Institutions

Institutions that sustain economic development are created slowly in the power-diffusion process. An *institution* is an accepted mode of behavior protected by the culture; it contrasts with an *organization*. The international monetary system is an institution, but the International Monetary Fund is an organization. An organization can be formally established, but an institution comes about only as patterns are repeated so many times that they become respected, trusted, and even demanded. The monetary systems of two countries (or laws, parliaments, and the like) may be organizationally identical but institutionally different. What are those particular institutions that most promote durable economic development, and what causes them to be formed?

Imagine an institution as a balloon floating in many-dimensional space, sustained in its position and shape by interest groups blowing on it from all sides. Some breaths are stronger, some weaker. An institution is durable if, with many groups blowing upon it, the breath of any one or small combination is too weak to affect its location or shape very much. Durable economic development requires durable institutions. But even a durable institution may change character gradually as the groups or their relative powers change.

Any institution is, therefore, a compromise among interest groups weighted by their respective powers. The general rule is: *In an institutional vacuum, a conflict is resolved by a relative show of power among interest groups and individuals. If the event is repeated many times, the manner of resolution becomes an institution, to which future behavior tends to conform. If, however, relative power shifts over time, so also does the institution.* Thus, if the power-diffusion process operates successfully, economic institutions become negotiated by many interest groups whose powers become more diffuse over time.[4]

In any society, each corporate group tries to shape institutions to promote its interests. Organized labor may want not only one set of laws, but also a certain way of lawmaking, management guilds another, and the presidential bureaucracy still another. Efficiency and justice are secondary criteria. In the United States, anti-abortion or pro-choice groups would select judges of the Supreme Court primarily according to the ideologies of the candidates and only secondarily by their general qualifications as jurists.[3] If, however, the pro- and anti- sides are evenly balanced, then the qualifications and integrity of the candidate may swing the vote. Thus the secondary criterion becomes the decisive one in a system of relatively even balance of power. By analogy, all sides, wishing monopolies for their own products, may retreat to a free market for goods and services when power is so dispersed that monopolies for all are impossible. The efficiency of the market—and with it economic development— creeps in serendipitously as everyone's second choice.

If the power-diffusion process progresses, two or more groups may freely negotiate a mode of behavior that does not harm others. If it should harm others, presumably these would exert *their* power to object. The institution is slowly formed as the mode of behavior is repeated many times. The repetition of this process for many institutions will be called a *free market in institutions*. Such a market is delayed if a powerful third party repeatedly abuses the negotiating parties for its own gain.

Since each new institution in a free market is shaped around those already formed, they tend to interlock with each other: none can be changed without changes in many others. This is the interlocking society referred to previously. By contrast, institutions mandated by sovereign powers or by elitist governments tend to be imposed suddenly with little respect for existing institutions. Therefore, they tend not to become interlocking and hence not durable.

Institutions not evolving through balance of power are likely to waste resources in two ways:

First, when power is grossly unbalanced, the dominant group consumes resources extravagantly, either for its own enjoyment or to retain its power. Even with relatively well-balanced power, groups consume resources to retain their influence on institutions, for example by lobbying. But the relatively mild expenditures of lobbies are nothing compared with the egregious waste caused by military repression of opposition groups and violations of their human rights, which are cruel as well. The line between "normal" and "excessive" power is, of course, subjective, often depending on comparisons with social norms elsewhere.

Second, rules that do not reflect the real balance of power will not be fully honored. For example, price controls that defy supply-demand realities may not be enforceable. But evasion is always at some cost, which wastes resources.

This book addresses not only how and why institutions evolved through greater balance of power in Japan and northwestern Europe, but also how and why institutions and morality change with development; how and why institutions promoting development spread from northwestern Europe toward southern and eastern Europe but slowed down as they approached the southern and eastern extremities; how and why they have been less well formed in other parts of the world; but also how and why some of them have begun to appear in the less-developed world today.

Explanations by some institutional economists, such as Buchanan and Tullock, Williamson, and Coase generally refer to events that *follow* those of the present book historically, rather than precede them. These authors deal with the benefits and costs of deriving optimal institutions such as a firm of a certain size and shape. But that process can take place only *after* the evolution of cultural attributes such as to compromise rather than to confront, to resolve conflicts peacefully rather than with violence, and so on. This book explains how those cultural attributes are acquired. Because the contributions of these authors, with whom I do not disagree, fall subsequent to the continuum of my argument rather than upon it, it would be a digression to explain them in this text. Rather, they are summarized in appendix 1.1.

Game theory has been another avenue toward understanding cooperative economic behavior. Through the amplification of games derived originally from prisoner's dilemma,[5] economists have pointed out how persons may discover that their own welfares become maximized not through selfishness but through cooperation and altruism, given their expectations concerning the responses of others to their actions.[6] Concerned with game theory per se only to the extent that repeated plays give rise to institutions,[7] this book suggests that the repetition of successful strategies leads to the expectation that others (even non-players) will behave as the game-players do. Social constraints—institutions—cause them to do so.

Rabin finds that persons are motivated to improve the welfare of those others who do the same for them.[8] (Not "do as you would be done by" but "do unto others as they actually do unto you.") But this leaves the crucial question: Who starts such a virtuous circle, and why? Using the abstract language of game theory, one might expect that a game played in one territory is as good as one played in another. But this is obviously not so. Stripped of the mathematical language, this book explores why games played in some societies are more successful than those in others, leading to greater economic development in the former than in the latter. A further note on game theory is found in appendix 1.2.

Concurrently with the preparation of this book, Douglass North was writing *Institutions, Institutional Change, and Economic Performance* (1990), whose subject matter overlaps with this work. However, institution building by the power-diffusion process differs significantly from North's theory, as will be explained in chapter 5.

A vast literature exists on economic development, covering not only the evolution of institutions but also long waves, why the Industrial Revolution occurred when and where it did, the roles of capital, labor, education, technology, and entrepreneurship, econometric models, and so on.[9] For the most part, these theories and models will not be discussed in this book, whose only subject is why and how the power-diffusion process has generated accountability, efficiency, and other institutions of development more in some regions than in others. Apart from that, I have nothing to add to these theories, and any disagreements I may have with them do not impinge on what I have written here.

Since I respect those theories, I do *not* say: "Pluralism . . . leverage . . . hey presto, economic development!" Nor do I maintain that when power diffusion is added to any or all of these theories economic development is fully explained. The field is much too vast and complex for that. But I do assert that power diffusion is critical to economic development. Development will soon or later fail in all societies where power is concentrated at the center, in an elite that can make economic policies affecting the lives of thousands or millions of citizens, with little input or assent from the large masses of those citizens.

Power Diffusion and Other Ways of Economic Growth

So I argue that the power-diffusion process is essential to durable economic development. Other ways of economic growth, which will be mentioned in this book, are either of limited geographic relevance or are not sufficiently robust to be longlasting. Three of these ways are the following:

First is *chronic growth*, or growth from the gradual accumulation of capital and knowledge. Virtually all societies experience this type. E. L. Jones argues that economic growth is the natural state of humankind, which lapses when it is over-ridden by officeholders who suck income from their positions of power, quite apart from their productive contributions (if any). He avers (and I agree) that this "rent seeking" occurs most of the time.[10] Powerholders do more than seek rent, however. They often believe that by their very positions they understand more about the normal functioning of the detailed economy than do those working on the line. For example, the minister of education—who may be a political appointee with little background in schools—may believe that because of his exalted position he knows more about how to teach third grade than does the elementary school teacher with a lifetime of experience, so he dictates the curriculum. The same will be so for the minister of agriculture vis-à-vis the farmer, the minister of industry vis-à-vis the factory owner, and so on down the line. When these forces coalesce, along with rent seeking, they dampen the chronic growth, which becomes neither as great, nor as consistent, as durable economic development with power diffusion. Zones experiencing only chronic growth have long periods of stagnation—such as Le Roy Ladurie's *longue durée* (for France)—or very slow growth, plodding along for centuries (as in China).

Second is *command growth*, which occurs when a small elite, controlling resources, decrees policies such as forced saving and direct allocation of resources to infrastructure and heavy industry. The erstwhile Soviet Union grew by command for many decades (see chapter 14), as did many less-developed countries. But command growth is inefficient because the commanders do not always make the right choices. As their errors accumulate, growth begins to fail.

Third is *reflected growth*, in which a society copies the institutions of a close geographical neighbor with which it shares a cultural affinity. Spain and Portugal may be examples; they are discussed in chapter 16. Reflected growth dies out the farther it moves, geographically and culturally, from its

source, and its possibilities are not widely extended. Only with power diffusion will economic development—however it was caused—become durable.

Plan for the Remainder of this Book

In summary, durable economic development requires institutions—modes of
behavior—established through long-term negotiations among many interest
groups, none of which is powerful enough to dominate the others entirely.
These institutions were brought about over centuries in northwestern Europe
and Japan through the power-diffusion process, involving pluralism, vertical
alliances, leverage, negotiations, and compromise. In thousands upon thousands of conflicts, no group could impose its will; each learned to settle for
some positive sum short of its ideal. Thus were the rules of market, corporate
enterprise, parliamentary government, financial system, and commercial laws
fashioned and endowed with sustaining power. More important, the various
groups came to value long-term ends more than short-term ones, and they
learned that negotiation and compromise, not confrontation and violence, would
best achieve them. Checks and balances to limit abuse were agreed upon.
Elsewhere in the world, by contrast, institutions that did not contain the necessary checks and balances were imposed by governments upon unwilling
subjects, or by victors in war, or in other authoritarian ways. The short term
continued to be the imperative time span. Confrontation and violence remained
first-choice means of resolving disputes long after they had become obsolete
in the more-developed zones. This book will posit that these differences constitute a significant, though not exclusive, reason why our world today is divided between rich and poor.

Chapters 2 and 3 illustrate the power-diffusion process in Japan, showing how it tended toward liberal institutions. Chapters 4 and 5 will do the
same for northwestern Europe, with comparisons with Japan. In these chapters only enough examples are presented to show the process in operation.
Skeptics will find more in the appendixes. At the end of chapter 5, the power-
diffusion process is summarized. Then the questions are posed: "Why Japan
and northwestern Europe? Why not the rest of the world?"

Chapter 6 will show how commercial law was negotiated more by
the interest groups in northwestern Europe than imposed by the sovereign,
despite the historic centralization of law in England and France. It will make
comparisons with Japan.

Chapters 7 through 21 turn to the rest of the world, showing how the
power-diffusion process did not take hold in most areas, or at least how it was
attenuated, in comparison with northwestern Europe and Japan. Something of
an exception is made for Spain and Portugal, and possibly for Mexico, whose

economic institutions have been influenced by their neighbors to the north. Germany is postponed until chapter 22, since its history has been a mosaic of features from both worlds, more- and less-developed, which have given it a unique character today. These can best be expressed by contrast with all earlier chapters.

Chapter 23 returns to the critical issue. Is the power-diffusion process essential to the less-developed zones and eastern Europe in the twenty-first century? Or will current attempts to institute liberal and efficient institutions by government direction be successful? Is durable economic development a matter for centuries, of which the twenty-first will be only another way station, or can it be made secure in a decade or two? We will sum up what has been learned from our worldwide examination of economic development and look at possible scenarios for the future.

Notes

1. It should not be supposed that these lessons have been learned completely anywhere in the world. It is only that some areas are more advanced than others.
2. Smith 1966:123-25.
3. An "activist" and a "constructionist" Supreme Court are the archetypes, although neither is specifically defined.
4. We cannot and do not need to define balance of power absolutely. We need only note, intuitively, that weaker groups are gaining relative to stronger ones, for example labor unions compared to management, or ethnic minorities compared with ethnic majorities.
5. Two persons, A and B, are caught in the act of committing a minor crime, X, but are both suspected of a major crime, Y, of which the authorities have no proof. They are put in separate cells, unable to communicate with each other. The police make an offer: If A supplies evidence that B committed Y, A will not be charged with X. A suspects that B has been given the same offer. There are three possible outcomes: (1) Neither tells on the other, so they both receive light punishment for X only; (2) Each tells on the other, and they both serve heavier sentences for Y; and (3) A talks but B does not (or vice-versa): A goes scot free, while B is punished for both X and Y. The dilemma lies in each not knowing what the other will do. However, if the game is played many times, and especially if each can choose one's partner, so that A and B trust each other not to talk, then the outcome will be (1), the best in the long run for each. Economists have expanded prisoner's dilemma to many circumstances, in which individuals in their own interests restrain themselves from ambitious undertakings that, if successful, will lead to gains for themselves but losses for others.
6. Economists would refer to this as a Nash equilibrium.
7. A brief description of game theory and its relationship to cooperation in economic ventures is found in "Evo-Economics," *The Economist*, 12/25/93-1/7/94, pp. 93-95.
8. Rabin 1993:1281-1302.
9. For example, this literature includes works by Adelman and Morris; Domar; Etzioni and Etzioni; Fei and Ranis; Harrod; Gillis, Perkins, Roemer, and Snodgrass; Herrick and Kindleberger; Landes; Le Roy Ladurie; Arthur Lewis; Postan; Ricardo; Paul Romer; Rostow; Schumpeter; Maurice Scott; Solow; and Todaro. All these works are cited in the bibliography.
10. Jones, E.L., 1988, especially chapter 3.

Chapter 2
Japan: The Power-Diffusion Process

The Japanese have saved much, and they have organized their corporations along modern lines. Despite business families (*keiretsus*) and government planning, they are mainly liberal: free enterprise and free trading. Corruption scandals in the 1990s have come out in the open and have caused a government to fall. But the real question is why they did all that, while Africans, other Asians, and Latin Americans mostly did not.

To find out, we move back into history. We discover that the Japanese were not nearly so poor in the nineteenth century as Western historians have alleged them to be. To discover why they were not, and how they advanced, we go back to the era in which Japanese economic organization first seemed different from the rest of the world. We arrive at the ninth century.

Pluralism in Early Agriculture

At that time, almost all cultivated land in Japan was organized into *sho-en*, which looked like large, feudal estates. But instead of being ruled by a feudal lord as in Europe, the Japanese had two people at the top: *honke*, or "noble patron" and *ryoke*, or "proprietor." Two centuries later there were other claimants as well: *jishu*, whom Western scholars have dubbed "owner," *ryoshu*, or "non-noble lord;" *azukari dokoro*, or "middle-level manager;" and *zuryo*, or "tax-collecting governor."[1] There were also tenants, free laborers, half-free laborers, and slaves.

The Japanese land system had one point in common with the European manor: almost all who worked the land, other than hired laborers and slaves, had clearly defined legal rights. In Japan the legal right to land was called a *shiki*. There was an owner-shiki, a proprietor-shiki, a manager-shiki at different levels, a tenant-shiki, and so on. In Europe also, the rights were enforceable contracts between lords and tenants. Elsewhere in Asia, as in most of the rest of the world, tenants on conquered land usually could be dispossessed at the whim of the master.

Unlike rights on the European manor, shiki could be bought and sold. In principle they could not be confiscated. Thus every person's rights and obligations were defined with respect to those of every other person: to hold land, to produce crops, to sell them, to pay taxes, and to serve in the military. These relationships may have been violated, but if so the culture was violated too.

We can only speculate on how definable rights to land, which the sovereign could not take away, came about for all classes except slaves in Japan and northwestern Europe, but nowhere else. Let us adopt the axiom that no one gives away rights unless one has to. In our own day, one might assume that workers acquire rights either by law or by alternative opportunity: they must be bid away from other potential employers. If these assumptions were translated into ninth-century Japan, we might suppose that unless peasants received favorable treatment on the sho-en, they would clear and farm their own land instead. But solitary farmers risked capture and enslavement on someone else's property. While this must have happened, it was not the major way in which labor was sought.

Lacking evidence to the contrary, I assume that tenants possessed enough clout—perhaps as organized food growers, military bands, or rebels— so that owners or proprietors could not force them to work as slaves but had to make some agreements with them. Another possibility is that when overlords fought each other peasants would band with one or the other side, demanding rights in exchange for support. We cannot be certain how they obtained their shiki, but we do know that they employed this leverage in later centuries.

The Diffusion of Power

The Emperor, by agreeing to convert his personal political powers—then declining—into public powers, in order to maintain his titular authority, acknowledged a new balance of power.[2]

This quotation might have referred to Taisho democracy in the 1910s. But Jacobs was writing about the Taika reform of 645. From the beginning of Japanese history, authority has been parceled among many claimants.

"Alternative power" has been a feature of all Japanese administrations. Not only did powerholders compromise with each other, but if a lower class could not obtain satisfaction from one source it might go to another. Early emperors shared power with or were dominated by families, such as the Soga and later the Fujiwara. In 1185, the strong Minamoto family, headed by Yoritomo, defeated the ruling Taira family in the Gempei war. In 1192, Yoritomo had himself appointed the first *shogun* ("barbarian-suppressing general") while respecting the dignity of the emperor. His successor shoguns were assisted by a commoner family, the Hojo. Thereafter until 1868, the emperor and shogun existed side by side, with the shogun as the main power. But lords of the land would frequently defy the shogun or vice versa. This was especially so during the Tokugawa era (1603-1868).

A similar pluralism affected social relationships. In the thirteenth century, new officials appeared on the sho-en. They quarreled with each other and with the military. Since no group emerged as the dominant power, they were forced to compromise on both authority over land and the division of its produce.

During the fourteenth and fifteenth centuries the more powerful warriors became lords known as *daimyo*, who captured fiefs and demanded fealty from the peasants. In exchange, the peasants sought secure tenure and rights to agricultural products. From this, a contract feudalism similar to that of Europe replaced the sho-en system.

Ordinary farmers became divided into warriors (*bushi*, later *samurai*) and cultivators. Bushi clustered in castles while cultivators lived closer to their fields, much as was happening in Europe. These peasants formed villages, in which they elected their own officials, managed their own affairs, and collectively negotiated with the daimyo. Mostly they had no obligations other than taxes.

In these ways power became diffused. Laws of the central government were increasingly ignored. In the Onin War (1467-77) the shogunate fell apart, and Japan was divided into hundreds of small states. Even when they were militarily reunited in the sixteenth century, under Nobunaga, Hideyoshi, and then Tokugawa, none of these rulers held absolute control. Each was linchpin presiding over a balance among surviving daimyo, whose legitimacy in turn depended on recognizing the village assemblies.

Leverage

Leverage was the primary force in this diffusion of power. As early as the ninth and tenth centuries, peasants took advantage of the rivalry between governors and powerful families to ally themselves with one or another in exchange for improved work conditions.[3]

In the twelfth century, they capitalized on rivalry among nobles:

The key positions at court were objects of fierce competition among the eligible nobles, who sought allies in the imperial house and the provincial aristocracy below. Warrior groups could ally themselves with noble factions, which, if successful, could reward their members with official titles and immunities.[4]

Wanting firm contracts in place of erratic work, peasants also "could ally with higher authority in an effort to resist a jito [estate steward], or they could attempt to negotiate directly with the jito concerning rates and times."[5]

In the fourteenth century both estate stewards and peasants improved their positions by shifting their vertical alliances in a civil war between the emperor and the shogun. Village autonomy resulted in part from alliances between peasant groups and estate stewards to gain concessions from proprietors.[6] From the fourteenth to sixteenth centuries, organizations known as *ikki*, composed of warriors and farmers, became prominent.[7] While some writers have translated *ikki* as "rebellion," Davis points out that it literally means "of one goal" or "in agreement," and that it applies more to an organization than to an action. Bix reports its meaning as "identity, identical, or the same, as in 'This and that are identical' . . . The solitary band—with corporate bargaining power—was formed expressly to make a decision that was just and unswayed by special interests because it was based on the will of heaven."[8]

Ikki levered their power by vertical alliances with court nobility or military governors. For example, in a rebellion over debt cancellation in the fourteenth century ikki—peasants themselves—would not accept the shogun's offer to forgive peasant debts unless he also forgave those of the court nobility and the greater military houses, with whom they were presumably allied.[9] From the fifteenth century on, the military support of the ikki was increasingly sought by the daimyo. As a result, "on the political stage the power gradually fell into the hands of a lower class of people that had never been recognized in such a circle."[10]

As the daimyo were consolidating their power or losing it during the period of the warring country at the end of sixteenth century, the local gentry (*kokujin*), who had previously dominated the villages, stood in their way. To overcome them, the daimyo joined forces with the villagers, granting them virtual autonomy in exchange for support.[11]

Peasants became "'negotiators' who played fiefs and bakufu [shogunate] against each other to their own advantage."[12] The shogun was particularly concerned to maintain peace on the fief, for even violence that did not affect him directly nevertheless threatened his stability. He often would order the easiest solution to a domainal problem, which sometimes favored the peasant. Especially when violence had already broken out or was imminent, the shogunal court might dictate a decision.[13] In at least one case, a daimyo was ordered by the shogun "to commit suicide for having allowed a peasant uprising to occur in his territory."[14] This precedent would supply a sobering incentive for any daimyo to negotiate with peasants. Occasionally peasants might call on merchants for help in their rebellions. In one revolt rice and iron merchants "gave strong support to the peasants upon whom their trade depended."[15]

In the early nineteenth century, reformers on the fief Mito "recognized the political and economic importance of the lower strata of society and spent a good deal of time and effort cultivating their support."[16] In that same century "the participation of rural commoners in political actions . . . marked a significant departure from the exclusively samurai involvement in the Tempo reforms."[17] When the shogunate modernized its army in response to American pressure in the 1860s, it encountered resistance from the daimyo but recruited peasants, whose standard of living was thereby improved.[18]

All the aforementioned cases are instances of leverage by peasants. But merchants employed leverage as well. As far back as the seventh century, the emperor was taxing merchants heavily. To escape, the merchants joined monasteries, which provided them with "adequate facilities for business, storage, financial assistance and cooperative credit. In return for these benefits traders lent money to the priests who also provided military protection."[19] Each group—merchants and monasteries—enhanced its power vis-à-vis the emperor. Merchants also allied themselves with nobles who granted them court rank and privilege in exchange. Independent trading companies were sponsored by the nobility.[20]

Other groups exercised leverage as well. In the thirteenth century, housemen of the shogun transferred their loyalty to provincial governors or estate stewards to obtain better terms of service.[21] Once towns had become prominent as commercial centers, they shifted their vertical alliances, formally or informally, among daimyo and shogun. "The ports or cities gradually came to overshadow their feudal protectors in economic power. They then entered into political-economic alliances with other feudal lords on their own initiative."[22]

Merchants and peasants advanced not only relative to the shogun but also to the daimyo. For example, the tax and monetary reforms of the early nineteenth century, which were necessary for the survival of almost-bankrupt fiefs, required the daimyo to cooperate with peasants and merchants. The peasants and merchants, of course, exacted their price. "[E]very successful political defense [the daimyo] made of their own position was matched by a corresponding social advance by the top stratum of the peasant and merchant classes."[23]

Rivalry between the fief and growing cities provided leverage for merchants during the Tokugawa period. "[I]t was probably the dire necessity of improving han [fief] finances and the possibility of doing so by playing the han regional economies against the great city markets of Osaka and Edo that drove han authorities into the arms of merchant houses and gave rise to the numerous han monopolies after the middle of the eighteenth century."[24]

In the democracy forged by Japan after the Meiji Restoration, leverage mutated to the form familiar to democracies: parties jockeying for position, making and re-making alliances, and horse-trading. Once a polity and economy become complex, with multilateral issues that can no longer be negotiated among two or three groups face to face, a parliament may become the honest broker among them all. Parliament is, therefore, an organization by which multilateral applications of leverage are institutionalized.

In the first decade of the twentieth century, local bosses would swing blocs of votes to gain party patronage.[25] Toward the end of the second decade, liberal party politicians, academics, a leftist political movement, and journalists joined to promote new strength for the labor movement.[26] All this is leverage in its modern cast. Eclipsed by World War II, these movements are now coming alive again.

The Origins of Compromise

Over their history the Japanese have compromised rather than confronted; negotiated rather than stonewalled; and cooperated rather than going-it-alone, *relative to other societies.* In absolute terms the Japanese many times confronted, stonewalled, and went-it-alone, just as other societies did.

Fairbank, Reischauer and Craig note that the system of taxation and law codes initiated in 670 "were made piecemeal, with pragmatic compromises with existing institutions and the power of the various uji [clans]."[27] Jacobs cites "constant coercion, coordination, and compromise . . . a process repeated many times in Japanese history, first by the estates against the Taikwa imperialists in the court [seventh century], then by the markets, farmers, and soldiers in the structure established by the estates [sho-en], and later by the merchants in the true feudal structure."[28]

Asakawa writes of compromises in private farms (*sho*) arising in the eighth century: "The native genius of the race for adaptability found its expression here in a free division of the various interests and rights relative to land, in their investment in different lands, and in their almost infinite redivision and conveyance . . . the same piece of land cultivated by one person soon giving titles and yielding profits to many."[29]

Social immobility sometimes promoted negotiation and compromise. "The typical azukari dokoro [custodian] of sho-en land was a locally based aristocrat, completely ineligible for the noble status enjoyed by a capital ryoke. . . . The lord and the custodian functioned cooperatively because neither could fundamentally challenge the other's prerogatives. . . . Consociation between persons of disparate status was a cardinal feature of the political system."[30]

A famous compromise occurred in the fourteenth century, after the opposing military forces of the shogun and one of two rival emperors had occupied land to sustain themselves during the civil war. On conclusion of hostilities, the soldiers refused to leave. Peace was established by permanent division of the yearly produce between the absent proprietors and the soldiers.[31]

In an earlier writing[32] I have described the main contestants for land in this period and the juggling of forces and manner of compromise among them. Out of these forces arose the term *wayo*, often translated as "compromise." "Wayo was not a mode of settlement adhering to any specific pattern but merely an expression of detente on any issue of long-standing dispute between jito [estate steward] and shugo [provincial governor]."[33] Sometimes compromise took the form of ignoring obstacles that other cultures might have found humiliating. For example, in the fourteenth century the Chinese insisted that imports from Japan were "gifts" and payment of "tribute" to the Chinese celestial emperor by the "inferior" Japanese. He made "gifts" in return. Japanese traders played the game. When the Ming emperor appointed shogun Yoshimitsu "King of Japan" under Chinese tutelage in 1401, he accepted the title, which in no way affected his prerogatives at home.

The nature of the Japanese as compromisers has been challenged. Najita argues that "the characterization of Japan as a consensual society proceeding along an evolutionary course or, at times, deviating from it, was misleading."[34] Challengers who point to myriad conflicts and much violence throughout Japanese history are correct, but they miss the point: that conflict and violence were mingled with negotiation and compromise more than in most societies; that concessions by victors to vanquished abounded; and that ways were discovered for former adversaries to trust each other and do business once the conflict was resolved.

Negotiation and Compromise in the Tokugawa Era (1603-1868)

When Tokugawa Ieyasu had defeated the other daimyo in 1600 and been appointed shogun in 1603, he divided his foes into categories and granted them privileges. This treatment contrasts, for example, with the total annihilation meted out by Mongols when they overran cities. Ieyasu's leniency occurred not because of his generosity, but because his victory was not overwhelming; his position west of Osaka was precarious, and compromises with defeated daimyo were the pragmatic solution.

Tokugawa villages combined negotiated with imposed institutions. On the imposed side, every individual belonged to a class stipulated by the shogunate: noble (a member of the imperial court), warrior, priest, peasant, or town resident. Class mobility was impossible. On the negotiated side, villagers formed their own associations, resolved their disputes locally when they could, and bargained with the daimyo over taxes. Although technically not allowed to do so, the peasants sometimes took their quarrels with the daimyo to the court of the shogun. Occasionally, they even won their cases—another instance of leverage.

Village government was by elected committee. While the head man was approved by the daimyo, he was elected by the villagers and deemed to represent them, to forward their requests to daimyo or shogun. Asakawa suggests that this arrangement was the genius of Tokugawa Ieyasu.[35] If so, his genius lay only in yielding to existing custom and power, not in discovering a system.

Harootunian finds that the Japanese of the Tokugawa era were resourceful in concealing conflict and claims to power, and that power itself was concealed.[36] But any concealment of power, such as in the shogun-emperor relationship, or any means to prevent an eruption constitutes de facto compromise.

Many have believed that the great peace of 1600-1868 was held together by the power of the Tokugawa shogun.[37] From the mid-seventeenth century on, however, the shogunate was being weakened relative to daimyo, merchants, and financiers. As a sign of weakening, both shogun and daimyo became indebted to merchants. Also, time and again the shogun could not enforce his decrees, such as those controlling prices. His foreign-exclusion command was repeatedly flouted by "outer daimyo" of the west. His attempts to establish monetary standards failed. Peasant rebellions were settled on terms he would not have favored. He continued to exist only by compromising with lower-level officials. For further references to the weakening of the shogunate during the Tokugawa era, see appendix 2.1.

Peasant Rebellions

Yet Japan's history has been studded with peasant rebellions, caused by excessive taxes, forced loans, and demands for bribes;[38] by daimyo and shogun monopolies and controls over prices and trade; by disputes over rights to land; and attempts by the lords to control peasant movement and behavior. Both daimyo and shogun lived in fear of peasants, suspicious of their goings and comings, wondering what harm they would do next, or whether they would defect to other daimyo or threaten the shogunate.

Mostly, rebellions were *not* motivated by demands to change the system.[39] Peasants protested not the levy of taxes, but the amount; not the system of tenancy, but the terms; not the idea of private business, but its monopolies; not the fact of daimyo or shogun control over the monetary system, but their monetary policies. Peasants did not usually try to change an institution, only the parameters within it.

Ikki led many of the protests. They formed their own governing bodies to negotiate with overlords, either nonviolently or in open rebellion. In alliance with "robber gangs, dissatisfied roaming noble warriors and armed monks of the new Buddhist sects, plundering, destroying or burning down store houses of the wealthy or pawn shops, temples or shrines," they forced "the government to issue moratoriums on loans, mortgages, or pawned articles."[40]

Withdrawal was a mode of passive resistance. Peasants would lay down their tools and depart until their demands were met.[41] They would swear oaths to cooperate and defend each other through their village organizations.

Throughout the Tokugawa period, peasants combined negotiation with violence of varying degrees, from riots to military operations. In one example among many compiled by Bix, a revolt at Ueda in 1761 over taxes and servitudes took place in five stages: (1) "mobilization and invasion of the castle town;" (2) "stalemate and confusion;" (3) "recommencement;" (4) "'vertical' discussions, conciliation, reintegration, and repression;" and (5) "public execution of [two peasant leaders], followed by more group discussions throughout the fief."[42] The revolt was settled with a number of concessions by the daimyo, including reduced tribute and less onerous conditions of servitude.

I am indebted to Bix for his meticulous documentation of peasant rebellions throughout the Tokugawa period. Using the same information, however—his own, plus that of other writers such as T.C. Smith and Borton—I come to interpretations different from his. Bix emphasizes the class struggle. To him, concessions were palliative; the village was part of the apparatus of oppression; peasants are eulogized in their struggles, but their lot was not substantially improved in these crucial centuries.[43]

My own interpretation is less marxist: that the Tokugawa village was far from a total instrument of the state; that while it reflected fears that the violence of preceding centuries would recur or that the precarious power balance in outside society might not hold, nevertheless it also reflected a willingness to negotiate and compromise in ways not easily found in many other societies.

Change occurred because each peasant victory, so small in itself, contributed cumulatively to the manner in which Tokugawa society fluidly shifted into modern Japan. But I go beyond the mainstream by suggesting that this characteristic is a major explanation of the remarkable economic growth in Japan today.

GLOSSARY OF JAPANESE TERMS

Applicable to Chapters 2 and 3

azukari dokoro, middle-level manager on a sho-en
bakufu, shogunate
daimyo, feudal lord or lords
han, feudal fief
honjo, landed proprietor
honke, noble patron of a sho-en
ikki, peasant solidarity group, leaders of rebellions
jishu, owner of a sho-en
jito, estate steward on a sho-en
kabu, a kind of guild
kaisha, business corporation
kokujin, village gentry
kabunakama, a kind of guild
kumiai, a kind of guild
nakama, a kind of guild
ritsu, penal law code
ryo, administrative law code
ryoke, proprietor of a sho-en
ryoshu, non-noble lord (lower on the scale than ryoke)
shiki, transferable right (to land, office, employment, etc.)
shikimoku, a legal code, or a compilation of legal questions
sho, medieval farm
sho-en, medieval landholding structure, precursor to feudal fiefs
shogun, military ruler of Japan ("barbarian-suppressing general")
shugo, provincial governor
tonya, a kind of guild
tozama daimyo, an "outer" daimyo, who lived far from Edo, during the Toku-
      gawa period
wayo, a compromise way of life
za, a kind of guild
zuryo, tax-collecting governor

Many of the above terms have no exact English equivalent; these meanings
are therefore approximations.

Notes

1. The translations are inventions of English-speaking scholars and do not correspond exactly. For example, sometimes "owners" were not allowed to live on their own properties.
2. Jacobs 1958:80.
3. Takekoshi 1930:1:40.
4. Kiley 1974:111.
5. Mass 1974:187.
6. Davis 1974:224,
7. Davis 1974:221-247.
8. Bix 1986:142.
9. Davis 1974:229.
10. Takekoshi 1930:2:280.
11. Davis 1974:234.
12. Bix 1986:xxx.
13. Bix 1986:163.
14. Bix 1986:7.
15. Bix 1986:23.
16. Koschmann 1982:89.
17. Koschmann 1982: 94
18. Totman 1982:74.
19. Jacobs 1958:32.
20. Jacobs 1958:120.
21. Hall 1970:103.
22. Jacobs 1958:33.
23. Bix 1986:152.
24. Hall 1970:213.
25. Fairbank, Reischauer and Craig 1978:686.
26. Fairbank, Reischauer and Craig 696.
27. Fairbank, Reischauer and Craig 1978:337
28. Jacobs 1958:129
29. Asakawa 1916:314
30. Kiley 1974:110.
31. Asakawa 1914:109; Duus 1969:63; Grossberg 1981:9; Hall 1970:193; Wintersteen 1974b:211-20.
32. Powelson 1988:179-80.
33. Mass 1974c:165-66.

34. Najita 1982:9.
35. Asakawa 1916:327.
36. Harootunian 1982:25.
37. For example, Max Weber (1964:377) writes of the great power of the shogun.
38. Borton 1968:26ff.
39. Bix 1986:147.
40. Borton 1968:16.
41. In similar fashion, plebeians of Rome are said to have retreated to the Sacred Mount in 793-792 BCE to force the Senate to create magistrates to defend them (Grant 1978:73-74). Some claim this story to be myth.
42. Bix 1986:75ff.
43. Bix pp. xxv-xxxiii.

Chapter 3
Japan: Institutions and Economic Growth

Over the centuries, the power-diffusion process changed Japan's economic development in three ways, to be discussed in the first three sections of this chapter. First, although the authorities (emperor, shogun, and daimyo) tried to mold the institutions of economic growth to their advantage, for the most part they failed. These institutions—markets and business, wage labor, money and finance, and commercial law—were fashioned mainly by the producers, traders, and financiers who used them. Second, the institutions supported phenomenal economic growth in the seventeenth through nineteenth centuries, closely rivaling that of the West. Western authors have not accorded the Japanese adequate credit for this. Third, the power-diffusion process created a basically liberal economy, or one founded on freedom of trade. Japan's current face toward the world, one of government-business liaison ("Japan Inc."), is not a reliable indicator of the degree to which the Japanese economy is culturally liberal. In the fourth section, we will discover that the much-touted "adoption of Western institutions" at the end of the nineteenth century consisted merely of marginal changes in the institutions the Japanese had already created.

The Institutions of Economic Growth

Corporate Business and Wage Labor

The history of business enterprise anywhere is a struggle between those who would participate in it—businesses, customers, suppliers, and creditors—and ruling groups who would set the terms and tax the benefits. In broad generalization, the participants mostly won this struggle in Japan and northwestern Europe, while the rulers mostly won it elsewhere. (By way of exception, in modern democracies, the government in power presumably regulates businesses to assure their compliance with the law and to fulfill public policy. Whether this regulation is self-serving, or answers to special interests, or meets a broad public interest is much debatable, but I do not join the debate here. The period under discussion is pre-democratic, in which the motives of the ruler were primarily self-serving; therefore the generalizations of this paragraph apply.)

As in many other places, in Japan businesses formed guilds at an early stage. Here and elsewhere guilds restricted production, raised prices, and foreclosed opportunities for outsiders. But in the fourteenth century, sur-rounded within Japan by still greater concentrations of power, guilds *opened* opportunity. They spawned wage labor where previously workers had been slaves, serfs, or confined to family enterprises, and they challenged the om-nipotence of shogun and lords. Above all, they were groups of cooperators who trusted each other, compared with an outside Japanese environment in which war, mistrust, and coercion were the norms. Guilds introduced a bi-ased, limited democracy, excluding many while admitting elements previ-ously excluded. Although individuals had joined in corporate bodies before, guilds demonstrated how corporations could engage in economic ventures that individuals acting separately could not.

At the beginning of the sixteenth century, guilds monopolized al-most every branch of trade, setting up barriers under license from the daimyo. Several times rulers —among them Hideyoshi, Nobunaga, and Tokugawa Ieyasu—tried to suppress the guilds but could not do so—another example of diffusion of power.

Guild memberships (*kabu-shiki*) were tradable. Trading shares in a monopoly might increase allocative efficiency because mergers or breakups would be facilitated, to approach an optimum size of firm. They might im-prove organizational efficiency[1] if more efficient managers bought the kabu-shiki of less efficient ones. Modern skills in trading might be traceable to Japanese experience in a market economy, not only in goods but also in rights and shares.

Just as pluralism in offices and shiki extended to all ranks in the sho-en except landless laborers and slaves, so also did guilds proliferate in many ways: in numbers and members; in names, such as *za, onaka, kabu, nakama, kumiai, kabunakama,* and *tonya*; and in titles and types of officials.[2] Some-times and in some places membership was open and in others it was closed. Several times guilds were prohibited by the authorities, only to be reprieved.

Guilds were finally abolished in the Meiji Restoration of 1868. But it was not for whim of shogun or daimyo, who had both been dismissed, or emperor. Rather, guilds no longer served the interests of the groups that had negotiated their founding. These interests were to be better served by corpora-tions (*kaisha*) and civil contracts with ways of business determined by parlia-mentary law and the courts. The same was happening in nineteenth-century northwestern Europe.

Money, Banking, and Credit

Monetary history everywhere is a struggle between those to whom money is a medium of exchange and facilitator of trade and those who seek to gain through manipulating its value. On balance, the former won in Japan and northwestern Europe, while the latter won in most of the rest of the world. (In modern democracies, a stable currency for the public welfare may be the goal of independent monetary authorities. In pre-democracies, stable currencies were the goal of rulers only if they served their own interests).

Japan's money system was created by individual initiative. In the eleventh century, many kinds of coins were traded in exchange houses.[3] Moneylenders and financial agents were found in trade fairs in the thirteenth century.[4] The terms *discount* and *exchange charge* are found in fifteenth-century documents. Reflecting the economic expansion of the fourteenth and early fifteenth centuries, both lords and traders minted new coins, which mingled with coins received in trade with Korea and China. Gold and silver coins appeared for the first time in the fifteenth century.

After an attempt to issue paper money failed because of lack of trust,[5] fourteenth-century shoguns found it easier to gain their wealth by taxing moneylenders. In 1346, they passed special laws, ostensibly to protect lenders from theft, but with the real intent of protecting their own extortions.

The authorities threatened the private monetary system in two ways during the Tokugawa period (1603-1868). First, the shoguns sponsored gold coinage from their territories in the east, whereas silver was more in favor in Osaka and farther west. Several times they attempted to issue new coinage based on gold, or to control the exchange rate in ways that favored gold. But their power depended on the acceptance of gold. Every attempt introduced trading uncertainties from the changing value of money. Second, over and over the daimyo and their samurai tried to milk the merchants. No longer needed as warriors during the Tokugawa peace, the samurai had become civil administrators on the fiefs. As such, they held certain prerogatives over the civilian population, including the merchants. Being of less value to the daimyo than in more warlike times, the samurai had not been awarded salary increases to keep up with the cost of living. Both daimyo and samurai would therefore demand loans from the merchants, now seen as a new source of wealth.

Constraints upon this system operated with vague borders. On one side, the daimyo and samurai could not destroy the goose of the golden eggs by demanding everything the merchants had. From the other side, the merchants could not ignore the daimyo and samurai except at their peril. These officials could swing favors toward obliging merchants and mete out punishments to the others.

Ieyasu, who began the Tokugawa family's 265-year reign, prohibited private coinage, established his own mints for gold, silver, and copper coins, each with a unified value based on a standard Oban with a monopoly of legal tender. Was this a grab for power, or an attempt to facilitate trade and finance for buyers, sellers, lenders, and borrowers? Had power played no role, Ieyasu might have allowed his coins to compete with others for favor. In fact, private coins continued to circulate, tacitly permitted. Accepting what was fact, in 1616 the second Tokugawa shogun, Hidetada, decreed no discrimination against any coinage. Any who discriminated would have their faces branded by burning iron, and all inhabitants of their towns would be fined. It is not clear to what extent this edict was enforced.

In the early years, Tokugawa shoguns were proud of their currency, refusing the opportunity for debasement. But the fourth shogun, Ietsuna, debased after considerable discussion. In response to an empty treasury, his successor, Tsunayoshi, debased further in 1695. Bad money drove out good, and trading circles were confounded by the uncertain value of any coin. The battle between money manipulation as a tax on merchant assets and money as a means of circulation began in earnest.

Sometime in the first half of the seventeenth century, rice merchants began speculating in futures, issuing bills against rice not yet grown. In 1653, the shogun outlawed this practice for the city representatives of the daimyo but not for ordinary merchants. The prohibition failed, and futures contracts and bills of exchange became well established. By the 1680s more than thirteen hundred rice brokers and over fifty money changers were at work.[6]

Early in the seventeenth century an Osaka merchant named Kambei contracted to deliver rice from the fiefs to the city. Clan officials issued him tickets as claims against their rice, and he developed a market for the tickets. They came to be used as money in the rice trade, and loans were made on the basis of them. A prohibition by the shogun in 1627 was disregarded, but when Kambei failed because of a bad harvest he was punished for selling short. The practice ceased, although whether because of the prohibition or for lack of trust is not clear. Takekoshi reports not only the case of Kambei, but also a number of similar attempts at new instruments of credit, which were widely popular but of doubtful legality.[7]

Settlement by bill of exchange also dates to the seventeenth century. Mitsui Hachiroemon, whose house is still a leading Japanese firm, contracted to deliver gold and silver taxes from the fiefs to the shogun's headquarters in Edo (modern Tokyo) within sixty days. He offered bills as receipts for the gold and silver. He then produced finished textiles, shipped them to Edo at less cost than metals, sold them for gold and silver, and redeemed his bills. He gained from both interest and sales.[8]

Two merchants in Osaka—Kikoyo Goroemon and Kinokuniya Tozaemon—printed paper money redeemable in silver in the early 1600s.[9] About 1640, another merchant, Tennojiya Gohei, issued deposit receipts in small amounts. These circulated widely and were copied by other merchants. Convertible paper money soon was issued by daimyo. Money changers acted as regular banks by the 1630s, and parent-bank relationships were established for interbank transfers.[10] Thus, the principal institutions of money and credit known to the West in the seventeenth century functioned in Japan at the same time. Associations of traders were mostly responsible for initiating them. Indeed, "the degree of trust between merchants was widely noted by contemporary writers."[11]

By the eighteenth century, the exchange market operated in the open with regular hours. Bid and ask prices were posted, and check clearing took place through banks.[12] A chain of endorsements was still required, and if any was missing the bill would not be honored. Although merchants did not issue bearer notes, banks did. Whoever received a bill drawn on a bank could present it and receive, instead of a deposit, a "deposit note." This would circulate, but the holder ran the risk of bank insolvency. "Integrity and reliability were the characteristics of the typical Osaka house. Credit was so solid that bills and notes passed freely from hand to hand, and after a long circulation came back to the drawer or maker."[13] Although currency and deposits were not government guaranteed, nevertheless by the late Tokugawa era, the law in Osaka and Edo gave priority to their protection.[14] One can only suppose that this legal protection reflected the high value placed by urban merchants on the integrity of the credit system.

These descriptions of money, banking, and credit demonstrate the power-diffusion process: that before the twentieth century, the financial and monetary system in Japan was fashioned by its common users more than by the authorities. The power of the users to influence finance was greater than that of the government.

Law

As in a monetary system, the evolution of law[15] everywhere is a struggle between those with sovereign power to make it and those who, concerned for their personal, business, and contractual relationships, work out agreements that take on the character of law. In Japan, as in northwestern Europe but not in much of the rest of the world, the latter group mainly won the struggle. (Independent law with a power of its own is characteristic only of modern democracies).

Central law in early Japan was promulgated by the emperor, perhaps at the behest of the families that controlled him. A constitution of 604 proclaimed the supremacy of the emperor. The statutes of Taika (645-52) defined political units and land rights, taxation, and salaries of officials. In 702, the penal and administrative codes *(ritsu* and *ryo* respectively) were set forth. Two comprehensive codes (Taiho in 710 and Yoro in 718) followed.

These codes illustrate laws handed down by authorities in order to control and extort from their subjects.[16] They contrasted with the customary law of the sho-en. As the emperor lost control during military upheavals that culminated in the Gempei War, law enforcement became privatized at the local level. Still, shoguns and daimyo made laws. Only as they ran into countervailing power were they forced to compromise with each other, with ikki, and with peasants. A perusal of Grossberg, who studied the laws of the Muromachi shogunate (1338-1573), yields the following observations, all of which reflect a shift downward in the fulcrum of power:[17]

First, the shogun succeeded in transferring jurisdiction over many cases from the emperor's court to his own.

Second, many shogunal laws appear as moralistic pleas rather than decrees. The shogun would deplore wrongdoing such as seizure of land or failure to repay debt, admonishing his subjects to behave better. The Kemmu shikimoku of 1336, sometimes referred to as a legal code, was more properly a set of questions posed by the shogun to his advisors, and their opinions.

Third, the repetition of many laws, such as on land ownership and debt cancellation, indicates that earlier laws had not been enforced.

Fourth, classes not accustomed to power, such as commoners, priests, and merchants, participated in shogunal justice without being paternalized.

Fifth, disorder ranging from petty violence to open rebellion obstructed law enforcement by the shogun for over two hundred years.

In addition to laws at the shogunal level, each daimyo maintained his own courts. Increasingly, the daimyo claimed new powers of administration.[18] Here on the fief, sho-en customs continued to be a significant source of law, and village affairs continued to be settled locally.

The legal protection of the peasant is probably the most significant contribution of the Muromachi era to power distribution in Japan at that time. Laws refer to returning land to commoners. Grossberg cites Ishii as calling this era "the zenith of commoners' legal rights."[19]

Why did the Muromachi shoguns cede so much power to the daimyo? Why did they defer to the customary laws of the sho-en just as the sho-en were disappearing? Why did they make the peasant's right to land secure? Why did the village remain a significant political unit? Why have some writers referred to this period as "enlightened?"[20]

The probable answer to all these questions is that the shogunate was becoming progressively weaker militarily, while Japan was disintegrating into a loose confederation of separate states, in which daimyo, villagers, shogun, and all their retainers jockeyed for power and made concessions to each other in exchange for support. In this dissolution the seeds of legal pluralism sprouted.

Law expanded and diversified during the Tokugawa era, responding to the growth of guilds, merchants, production, and moneylending, and to changes in agricultural technology and land tenure. Most of the changes took place in villages or on the fief, or through market regulations or guild rules. Thus, they were undertaken mainly in a free market for institutions, albeit with merchants and landowners more powerful than consumers and workers.

The shogun's laws related primarily to preserving the power balance and keeping the peace, resolving conflicts among the estates, suppressing contact with foreigners, meting out punishment, and minting coins. These laws directed a hierarchical society with rigid class distinctions, and with peasants to be kept uneducated "in their place." Nevertheless, the rights of ordinary people were increasingly protected.[21]

Wigmore's (1969) ten-volume study of Tokugawa law leads to the inescapable conclusion that commercial law was developed primarily in the cities and markets, by local agencies including guilds. Citing differences from place to place, he nevertheless finds overall consistency. Primarily, commercial law both formalized customary law and introduced new principles concerning contracts (what constitutes acceptance; how the interests of all parties are protected; when a contract is valid; how its fulfillment is determined; how disputes are settled; damages, discounts, cancellation, and so forth); concerning agency (who is and who is not an agent; how an agent can bind the principle, what an agent can do on his or her own account, and so on); concerning debts (how they are incurred; how they are settled); concerning rules for selling and buying (how earnest money is determined; what constitutes delivery; notices; quality of goods), as well as other elements of modern commercial law.

By the time of the Meiji Restoration in 1868, Japanese law ranked alongside that of advanced nations in comprehensiveness, diversity, and balancing of conflicting interests. If Western law was "copied" by Japan, the changes were marginal.

Conclusion

The foregoing examples of corporate business, wage labor, money and finance, and law have in common that these institutions were fashioned predominantly by negotiation and compromise among the business groups and other individuals who used them. Attempts by sovereign powers (daimyo, shogun, or emperor) to influence or control them were often frustrated by the humble participants.

Economic Growth

That Japan's economic growth rate since 1868 has been greater than that of
the West or of underdeveloped areas is much documented and widely agreed
upon.[22] Though the growth of industry and cities in the Tokugawa period has
been recognized, however, until recently historians have maintained that most
Japanese of that era had a very low standard of living.

Admitting that their evidence was fragmentary, and making highly
qualified observations, Ohkawa and Rosovsky[23] subscribed to the backwardness of Japan during the Tokugawa era (1603-1886). They also asserted that
"modern economic growth in Japan began . . . some time after the middle of
the 1880s."[24]

Some Western writers have been extremely paternalistic toward pre-
Meiji Japanese. In a prime example of insulting nonsense, Hirschmeier[25] wrote
as late as 1964 that "men who had been brought up with the abacus could not
be expected to . . . exercise entrepreneurial initiative." In a generality that is
anti-historic, he also tells us:[26] "The Osaka bourgeoisie—and we may take
this group as representative of the Tokugawa city merchants in general—lacked
most clearly the required set of attitudes, the mentality, for launching modern
business."

By assembling widely fragmented data and analyzing them in detec-
tive-like fashion, however, Hanley and Yamamura[27] challenge such traditional
findings. They conclude that the Japanese economy grew, but at different rates,
throughout the entire Tokugawa period; that commerce and manufacturing
expanded more than did agriculture; that productivity and real wages increased
in commerce and manufacturing; and that because labor moved from agricultural to nonagricultural pursuits the increase in real wages fed back into agriculture.

Hanley further supports these results. "Information on housing and
food, urban water quality and waste disposal, and life styles is examined along
with representative family budgets and two sets of real-wage estimates. The
evidence . . . suggests that the standard of living in mid-nineteenth century
Japan was not only higher than in the 1700s, but relatively high in comparison
to most of the industrializing West."[28]

Yasuba agrees, asserting that in the nineteenth century, "the Japanese
standard of living may not have been *much* below the English standard of
living before industrialization, and both of them may have been considerably
higher than the Indian standard of living."[29] Totman writes of "phenomenal"
growth in Japan during the Tokugawa period.[30] E. L. Jones describes in some

detail the economic growth and cultural changes in Tokugawa Japan.[31] Going beyond the claims of these authors, however, I am suggesting here that the roots of this growth were planted through the power-diffusion process, in the four or five centuries before the Tokugawa family came to power.

Agriculture

Agricultural advances have been reported as early as the thirteenth century. Artisans found employment on private estates, local markets grew, and new strains of rice and other crops such as tea were introduced from China.[32] New irrigation works in the fourteenth century led to new crops and crop products.[33]

Fresh fields and farms were opened up in the Tenwa era (1681-83), and new villages were formed.[34] Writing of seventeenth-century feudal lords, Takekoshi uses language reminiscent of the innovating landlords of England of that same century: "[F]arm districts [were] opened up in many places by feudal lords and other public-spirited men."[35] Rich farmers, and later merchants, undertook public improvements with their own funds.

Traditional forms of cooperation led to new crops and marketing improvements during the eighteenth century.[36] Land reclamation from 1600 to 1862 caused the area under cultivation to increase by 64 percent. Productivity was increased by new draft animals, more fertilizer, more iron in plows and hoes, and the spread of double cropping.[37] Deeper plowing, greater use of fertilizer, and production of cash crops are indirect evidence for increased yields.[38]

Manufacturing, Trade, and Entrepreneurship

Evidence also exists for growth in manufacturing and trade in pre-1868 Japan. Despite the closing of the country to the outside world from 1635 onward, much smuggling occurred, especially in the ports of the western (*tozama*) daimyo. Furthermore, the Tokugawa period saw a great increase in internal trade.

Priests and temples traded with China and Korea during the fourteenth century.[39] In a manner reminiscent of Italian city states of the same era, Buddhist priests invested gold and silver in trade and themselves traveled on the tribute ships. Japanese ships were also engaged in piracy off the Chinese coast. Imports increased.[40] In 1369, the shogun assumed jurisdiction over moneylenders and sake brewers, previously controlled by temples, and sub-

jected them to taxation.[41] Trade must have been gaining in importance for the
shogun to have taken this action.

Evidence of entrepreneurship in manufacturing is abundant from the
sixteenth century on. Japanese shipbuilders immediately copied the big ships
of the Portuguese after they arrived in 1543. Takekoshi calls the Genroku age
(1688-1703) "epoch-making in industrial development"[42] and goes on to cite
entrepreneurs, some by name, who were active in timber, rice brokering, transport, transmission of price quotations, iron manufacture and export, dry goods,
monetary movements and banking, and introduction of commercial crops.
Daimyo tried to attract new industries into their fiefs, just as medieval lords in
Europe did for new towns. The big cities grew, especially Osaka, Kyoto, and
Edo, but also Nagasaki, with new roads for overland transport, and new ship-
ping lines, to connect them.

These historical writings make incredible the picture of underdevelopment and poverty portrayed, without quantitative evidence, in so many
Western writings about nineteenth-century Japan. Scarcely more credible are
the frequent assertions that the major era of economic growth began only
when Japan had been "opened" by the West. The rise of guilds, money and
banking, corporations, and law in the Tokugawa era could not have occurred
had it not been for strong economic growth.

The Growth of Liberalism

Several times before 1868, Japanese central authorities tried to command free
trade when they deemed it to their advantage. Always they failed. Nevertheless, Japan made great progress toward free trade through centuries of negotiation among producers, merchants, peasants, and local authorities, each
wanting monopoly in its own province but each willing to settle on limited
free trade as the compromise. This section sketches that course of history, up
to the Meiji Restoration of 1868.

In contrast to China, "the freedom of the market and the formation of
independent corporate life were distinctive features of [Japanese] feudal economic life."[43] We have seen the free market in land shiki. In contrast to the
slavery of virtually all the rest of the contemporary and earlier world, lands
were reclaimed and irrigated in eighth-century Japan with paid labor by freemen.[44] But Jacobs exaggerates the idyllic situation for merchants. Although
free trade existed in many places, for the most part emperors, shoguns, and
daimyo tried to restrict it to their advantage.[45]

While every group wanted a monopoly for its own products, freedom of trade grew out of merchant alliances with leverage and flight from
restrictions. When merchants fled the emperor's taxing power before the twelfth

century, Buddhist temples offered them sanctuary, provided that they would accept free trade so that none would dominate the others.[46]

The growth of trade offered irresistible temptation to political authorities at all levels to profit from it. Until the mid-fourteenth century the landed proprietors (*honjo*) would erect toll barriers with permission of the imperial court at Kyoto. About 1346, the shogunate passed a law prohibiting these: "Since they create an unpardonable hindrance to travelers going to and from the capital, both new and formerly established barriers must be dismantled immediately."[47]

The shogunate was striking at an important source of revenue of its rival, the emperor. But in 1368, the imperial court relinquished the right of approval to the shogunate (I do not know the circumstances but would presume a show of power by the shogun). The shogunate suddenly favored toll barriers after all.[48] The growth of liberalism was see-saw. Daimyo established barriers at their boundaries,[49] but within their fiefs they abolished monopolies and declared trade to be free and exempt from taxes, in order to attract merchants.[50]

As various authorities erected barriers to tax itinerant merchants, these in turn fought back through guilds. "Under the patronage of a prestigious religious institution, the Kyoto court, or a local feudal authority, to which they paid fees, the guilds succeeded in establishing protection from extortion by other authorities and some degree of local monopoly under which their trade and profession could flourish."[51]

This exercise in leverage brought with it liberalization at one level (freedom from extortion) but restriction at another (guild monopoly). The net result was probably a step toward freedom of markets. Here, then, is a hint that free markets may come about not by atomizing the economy but by balancing monopolies against each other. Sometimes, guilds would buy the toll barriers from local lords so that they might operate them for the benefit of their members.[52]

Among the groups opposing toll barriers were peasants, who were directly affected by higher prices of goods they bought, and landowners, who paid the costs of tolls on other estates. In calling off a stalemated war in 1485, two provincial warlords withdrew their armies and demanded that estates be returned by the governors to their owners and that toll barriers be prohibited. At this point, the local ikki formed a government for a section of the province that they controlled, with a "constitution" that prohibited tolls. When the new provincial governor, who represented the ikki, established tolls to meet a need for funds, a massive peasant rising ensued.[53]

In international trade, bargaining for liberal policies was sometimes rough. When Japanese traders were thwarted by the restrictive policies of

Korea and China, they often took what they wanted by force. The distinction between pirates (*Wako*) and traders was ambiguous.[54] In 1443, the Koreans liberalized their restrictions against the Japanese to lessen the piracy. But tribute ships paid a duty—10 percent in the fourteenth century—upon their return from China.[55] By the sixteenth century, merchant ships traded without government interference.[56]

With the breakdown of the sho-en during the Muromachi era (1338-1568), towns developed and merchants enjoyed increased freedom, just as occurred in the breakdown of feudalism in Europe. Sho-en had attempted to be self-sufficient; towns could not be. "The increased freedom gained by the nonagricultural sector of the Japanese economy had two important repercussions during the Muromachi period: the growth of towns and the attendant urban commercial society and the freeing of merchants and artisans from certain social constraints."[57] As these cities grew, they formed a further interest favoring free trade.[58]

When Nobunaga unified Japan in 1568, he declared trade should be free throughout the islands. All barriers and tolls were forbidden. Perhaps he was just recognizing an already existing situation. Guilds, which had favored tolls, had broken down during the preceding wars. Peasants, merchants, and city dwellers all opposed the tolls and avoided them where they could. Another possibility is that Nobunaga foresaw the rise of trade and industry over the next century and wished to prepare for this by promulgating policies that anticipated Adam Smith, as yet unborn in a country of which Nobunaga probably had never heard. Both these answers possess some credibility. Towns and cities, trade, crafts, and guilds. were growing. Public opinion was swinging toward free trade on a broad front, not only domestically but in foreign commerce as well. No duties were exacted at Nagasaki and Hirado, and taxes on government imports were negligible.[59]

Yet another reason is also probable. The daimyo already had established free trade within the fief; Nobunaga looked upon all Japan as his fief, and therefore free trade represented the shift of power from daimyo to himself. He also abolished guilds, probably for the same reason.

Nobunaga's policies did not last, even though his successor, Hideyoshi, confirmed them by abolishing all road checkpoints to promote transportation. But the daimyo reestablished customs tolls on their fiefs, which were not abolished until 1869.[60] Instead of withering before Nobunaga's command, guilds became the new forces that both promoted and monopolized trade. Nobunaga's commands were one more example of top-down reform not in equilibrium with the power balance below.

In the Tokugawa era (1603-1868), that power balance shifted in favor of merchants. Guild monopolies proved more weighty than toll barriers. Jealous of guild power, the shogun tried once again to legislate liberalism, issuing an edict of 1622: "Commercial transactions must be free, and no one shall act in the contrary or combine to raise prices."[61]

The shogun's law could not be enforced. Peasants were frequently required by law of the domain to sell to monopoly merchants.[62] As new facets of trade and exchange opened, each was entrusted to some monopoly or semi-monopoly group: transport, principally between Osaka and Edo; foreign trade in port cities; exchange houses; and buying and selling of rice. For the most part, these monopoly groups were registered and controlled by the city or the fief, although the shogun attempted from time to time to impose his own regulations.

When the Tokugawa capital was moved to Edo (modern Tokyo), Osaka was released from harassment by the samurai and therefore grew as a commercial center.[63] It outstripped Edo in business talent, wealth, and commercial organization. In another attempt to legislate liberalism, Minister Tadakuni Mizuno (in the Tempo reforms, 1841-43) abolished guilds and all middlemen, ordering that sales should be transacted directly between producers and urban retailers.[64] All exclusive systems were destroyed for twelve years and freedom of the sea was decreed. But middlemen were a necessary link. Not conforming to the reality of the market, the reforms failed and were withdrawn after a period of chaos.

But the liberalism that could not be mandated grew by itself, not by control of monopolies but by their weakening through proliferation, not by enforcement of law but by its evasion, not by central control but by fragmentation of authority. Liberalism was hindered primarily by guild restrictions: price controls and "proper" procedures. But these might be offset by outside traders or simply by the large numbers in some guilds, whose actions were more overlooked than overseen.[65]

In the same era, landholding became increasingly fragmented, with decision-powers becoming dispersed among farmers through compromises among main and branch families. As families were split and parcels divided, paternalist obligations between senior and junior branches gave way to arms-length contracts. Rent was paid in cash instead of services. Parcels were bought, sold, and mortgaged; and a free market in land emerged.[66]

Free markets were also strengthened when attempts to control the rice trade failed. From the late 1680s peasants were selling rice directly to merchants on the fief.[67] This rice would be handled by approved but competitive brokers in each locality.[68] Without actually seeing the rice, successful bidders would sell competitively to distributors, arranging delivery.

However, Tokugawa merchants never were completely free of control by daimyo and/or shogun.[69] The daimyo would organize a monopoly for each product of the fief and sell through special agents in Osaka. Specified "house" merchants were patronized by shogun or daimyo. These merchants acted as agents of the authorities in enforcing rules to their mutual advantage. Perhaps these vertical alliances were precursors to the government-business cooperation of the late twentieth century, sometimes dubbed "Japan Inc."

Still, the unification of the national economy, the proliferation of merchants, and the array of financial instruments increasingly presented the kinds of choices associated with liberal economies. Trade and industry flourished despite harassment by shogun or daimyo. Merchants almost always found ways around obstacles.[70] Eighteenth-century traders without any guild connections usurped guild privileges in the import trade in Osaka.[71] The balance of power, increasingly favorable to merchants, and the gains from competition and evasion of rules were critical forces in the evolution of a free market.

By the Meiji Restoration in 1868, the basis for a liberal economy had been laid. Workers were free and mobile, many producers chafed at guild restrictions, and consumers were more concerned for choice. When the guild system crumbled,[72] no one cared to defend it. Only forty-five years after the chaos of the Tempo reforms, similar reforms had occurred, by agreement, with hardly a murmur. Power had shifted downward.

The Presumed Adoption of Western Institutions

The conventional view in the West is that Japan adopted Western institutions of law, money, banking and financial markets, private farming, a constitution, corporations, and parliamentary democracy at the end of the nineteenth century. The Japanese, however, saw European and American institutions as only marginal changes, if any at all, from the ones they themselves had created. Their most economical course was to upgrade their own institutions by selecting from among the Western.

The selection took place through traditional compromises. Daimyo willingly gave up their fiefs in exchange for provincial governorships. Samurai were pensioned or given new administrative positions. Even the defeated shogun was treated with honor. Peasants were given titles to land. In these ways no one lost. By the end of the nineteenth century, when economic and political life required the consensus of many large groups instead of a few small ones, central-government institutions formalized what had been custom and became brokers for personal and commercial law. It was then that parliamentary democracy began.

Some difficult questions remained. Who would rule the new Japan? The emperor, in whose name the change had been made? The western daimyo, who had masterminded the restoration? Or a parliament? To resolve these questions, the Japanese called on their age-old facility for compromise. "[T]he Japanese tendency toward ambiguity, consensus, and compromise permitted an evolutionary development that moved with remarkable speed along the parliamentary paths blazed long before in England."[73] Power over the purse, conferred by the constitution upon the Diet (Parliament), provided it with leverage in its struggle with the military to achieve democracy. Only if the military had been willing—which they were not—to overthrow the constitution could this leverage have been suppressed.

Some were more ready to compromise than others, and a showdown between the "democrats" and the military seemed likely. Because the power-diffusion process had been mainly run, however, the story of the twentieth century is not part of this book: how Hara Kei led in forging a parliamentary system by repeated compromises with the military elite;[74] social legislation of the 1910s and 1920s; the crisis that led to Taisho democracy in the mid-1910s; realization that the people were sovereign even over the emperor, when the Diet rejected the emperor's command to reverse a vote of no confidence in 1913;[75] the heyday of party government and the advance of labor unions in the 1920s; and how the Japanese government handled the depression of the 1930s. In a tragedy that engulfed the world, the military, whose role had been ambiguous since the restoration and which had never been clearly subject to civilian authority, used its power to edge out democracy in the 1930s, taking extraparliamentary action to start a war in Manchuria. Perhaps—let us hope—World War II was the "last hurrah" of the samurai.

While some power concentration continues even today, nevertheless the concept of accountability is so far advanced that a government could fall in the corruption scandals of the 1990s—something that would have been unheard-of only half a century earlier.

Notes

1. Sometimes known as *x-efficiency*, a term invented by Liebenstein 1978.
2. All these are detailed in Takekoshi's massive economic history of Japan, 1930, in three volumes.
3. Takekoshi 1930:3:18.
4. Grossberg 1981:4.
5. Takekoshi 1930:1:204.
6. Takekoshi 1930:2:247.

7. Takekoshi 1930:2:249ff.
8. Takekoshi 2:278; Wigmore 1969:121.
9. Takekoshi 1930:2:280.
10. Crawcour 1961:351ff.
11. Crawcour 1961:344.
12. Wigmore 1969:119ff.
13. Wigmore 1969:99.
14. Wigmore 1969:127.
15. Elizabeth Herr helped me with the research for this section.
16. I have written more extensively about them in Powelson 1988:175ff.
17. The detailed occurrences that underlie these observations are found in Grossberg 1981.
18. Hall 1970:131.
19. Grossberg 1981:9.
20. Grossberg 1981:13.
21. Wigmore 1969:xxii.
22. For example, Ohkawa and Rosovsky 1973; Patrick and Rosovsky 1976.
23. Ohkawa and Rosovsky 1978:137.
24. Ohkawa and Rosovsky 1978:143
25. Hirschmeier 1964:37.
26. Hirschmeier 1964:43.
27. Hanley and Yamamura 1977.
28. The information is presented in detail in Hanley 1983:183ff.
29. Yasuba 1986:224
30. Totman 1981:219, quoted by E.L. Jones 1988:155.
31. Jones, E.L. 1988: chapter 9.
32. Grossberg 1981:5.
33. Hall 1970:121.
34. Takekoshi 1930:2:199.
35. Takekoshi 1930:3:412.
36. Hayami and Ruttan 1971:35; Braudel 1981:157.
37. Hall 1970:201.
38. Yasuba 1986:217.
39. Takekoshi 1930:1:211ff.
40. Hall 1970:122.
41. Grossberg 1981:10.
42. Takekoshi 1930:2:238.
43. Jacobs 1958:30.
44. Asakawa 1929:193.
45. Tsuchiya 1937:84.
46. Jacobs 1958:32. "So that none would dominate the others" is my supposition, not found in Jacobs.
47. Law quoted in Grossberg 1981:35.
48. Wintersteen 1974:204.
49. Tsuchiya 1937:135.
50. Duus 1969:79.
51. Fairbank, Reischauer and Craig 1978:382.

52. Takekoshi 1930:1:241.
53. Davis 1974:236.
54. Fairbank, Reischauer and Craig 1978:383.
55. Takekoshi 1930:1:219.
56. Takekoshi 1930:2:404.
57. Hall and Takeshi 1977:126.
58. Takekoshi 1930:1:267.
59. Takekoshi 1930:2:282.
60. Fairbank, Reischauer and Craig 1978:505; Ohkawa and Rosovsky 1974:143.
61. Takekoshi 1930:2:489.
62. T.C.Smith 1970:160.
63. Takekoshi 1930:3:42.
64. Takekoshi 1930:2:546.
65. Takekoshi 1930:3:253.
66. Mitsuru 1982:150ff; Powelson 1988: chapter 15.
67. Bix 1986: 10.
68. Takekoshi 1930:3:92; Wigmore 1969:119.
69. Hall 1970:208.
70. Takekoshi 1930:2:471.
71. Takekoshi 1930:2:517.
72. Takekoshi 1930:3:273.
73. Fairbank, Reischauer and Craig 1978:547.
74. Najita 1967; Fairbank, Reischauer and Craig 1978:685ff.
75. Najita 1967:151-53.

Chapter 4
Northwestern Europe:
Power, Pluralism, and Leverage

From the tenth to the twentieth centuries, northwestern Europe, like Japan, moved jerkily toward becoming a pluralist society, of diverse social, political, and economic groups that cooperated with each other to create the material product on which they subsisted and which they traded with other societies.

In the High Middle Ages (tenth through twelfth centuries), power was grossly skewed in favor of kings, lords, and high church officials. Over time, the weaker groups—peasants, craftspeople, financiers, and traders—demanded a greater share of both power and resources. They acquired it by organizing themselves into corporate bargaining groups that made opportunistic alliances with powerful groups contesting each other. In this they were helped by an increase in material output which they controlled. In addition, the weaker groups proliferated, and in numbers they found strength.

To cooperate more efficiently, the groups formed banking, legal, and corporate business systems, rules of the market, and a parliamentary democracy that grew more representative in the nineteenth and twentieth centuries. Each of these advances occurred through negotiation among the groups with the greatest stake in its successful functioning. Unlike in many other places, they were not *mainly* formed or shaped by rulers' decrees.

Although each group strove to create a monopoly in its own field, their inability all to succeed led to compromises. Among these was a tendency toward freeing the market in goods and services. By repeated practice, northwestern Europe came to prefer negotiation and compromise in economic and other disputes, rather than their settlement by warfare, coup d'état, or rulers' fiats. This change is evident in the shift from endemic warfare to periodic wars. The resulting institutional framework, which tended to equate private and social returns,[1] follows closely the one already developed by North and Thomas[2] and by North.[3] The main addition to their theories is the power-diffusion process.

Boundaries of Northwestern Europe

The boundaries of northwestern Europe are not easily delineated, since differences from eastern and southern Europe are only by degrees. Furthermore, any reasonable boundary may differ according to social subsystems. It might be in one place for the land-tenure system and in another for the legal system. As a working compromise, "northwestern Europe" is here defined as the area bordered on the east by the Elbe River and on the south by the Loire or—after the Albigensian Crusades (1208-26)—the Pyrenees and the Alps. The Low Countries, Britain, Ireland, and Scandinavia are included.

These boundaries were cultural as well as physical. Before the thirteenth century, northern Frenchmen did not feel at home in the different social system and language of the south,[4] and less so in eastern Germany. But they could communicate well in London or Cologne. Consequently, they did not move outside northwestern Europe so fluidly as did Mongols, Turks, Chinese, and Africans in their migrations. In the tenth to the fourteenth centuries, however, northwestern Europeans shared many cultural characteristics among themselves, particularly their type of feudalism, which was not found anywhere else in the world at that time.

The Prevailing Orthodoxy

The prevailing orthodoxy[5] holds that population increases in the tenth and later centuries led to more and bigger urban centers with enhanced possibilities for specialization and trade. These in turn spurred agricultural improvements and a higher standard of living. When population began to outstrip land in the thirteenth century, rents and food prices rose, real wages dropped, and improved terms of trade for agriculture versus crafts favored the accumulation of capital by landlords. Higher incomes, new potential for investment, and greater diversity of production caused the feudal system to be dismantled as landlords needed cash for trade and as individual rent-paying farms proved more profitable to them. Excesses in the thirteenth century led to depression in the fourteenth, the effects of which were compounded by plague and war. But growth was resumed in the fifteenth, and northwestern Europe was on its way.

This historical perspective is accurate but incomplete. It does not explain why northwestern Europe moved forward into durable economic development while roughly the same set of events in different places and different eras, such as Tang China, Gupta India, and colonial Mexico did not bring similar results. Missing from the prevailing orthodoxy is the role of power.

The Power-Diffusion Process

From the ninth to the nineteenth century, power in Europe not only became more diffuse but also changed its character. At first, it belonged to individuals as a property right. Power positions were inherited, bought and sold, or granted by the monarch. They were based on military force, religion, and wealth. Toward the end of the period, power belonged more to organizations—such as a senate, business corporation, or labor union, than to individuals. It was grounded on institutions supported by a balance of tensions among groups. Individual power depended on one's position within an institution, which might have been inherited but increasingly was achieved. This shift has taken centuries and is not complete in our own time.

Pluralism, vertical alliances, and leverage were the principal means by which power became diffuse and changed its character in northwestern Europe.

Pluralism

Pluralism on the Manor

Power diffusion can occur only in a pluralist society. In Europe, the first step toward pluralism occurred on the manor. By the tenth century, feudalism in northwestern Europe already differed from that in most of the world:

First, relationships between strata in the hierarchy were defined by contract or custom, down to and including serfs.[6] These were enforceable, mutual obligations. Slavery was disappearing. However, the contracts were not between equals and often were coercive, because the distribution of power was seriously lopsided.

Second, manors were managed by bailiffs and stewards whom the lord had selected from among well-to-do villagers. These bailiffs collected taxes, made rules, organized courts of law for settling disputes, negotiated changes in contractual relationships, and kept communications open between the lord and the peasants.[7] By contrast, in most of the rest of the world except Japan, landlords used military force to collect tribute and had little other communication with peasants.

As early as the tenth century villagers in Normandy elected delegates from regional gatherings to sit in a general peasants' assembly. From this and similar meetings grew up the practice of negotiation over labor services, dues, fees, and rights.[8] Similar events in England have been reported by Hilton:

> The villagers [in England] were indispensable for the running of the business of the manor court. By this date [1381] they were in many places almost completely in control of the enforcement of the bylaws . . . there were innumerable gild organizations run by their members for their own purposes.[9]

Genicot describes the assemblies through which these actions were effected on the continent,[10] and Hogue explains how officials were drawn from the peasantry.[11] Goodell attributes state-formation in Europe to the process of building national institutions out of these feudal contracts,[12] while Postan shows how the lords could not act arbitrarily against the tenants or revoke their privileges.[13] De Tocqueville also wrote of the independence of the peasants,[14] and Kriedte depicts the decentralized nature of European feudalism.[15] In an earlier writing, I have described in greater detail the network of manorial negotiations and communications.[16]

North and Thomas also described European feudalism as contract.[17] But North later took note that "we . . . did not lay sufficient stress on the one-sided nature of the arrangement."[18] I also recognize that the feudal contract was *very* one-sided. But the foot in the door led to changes over the centuries.

Europe's prosperity suffered a temporary reversal in the thirteenth and fourteenth centuries. Malthusian population pressure is the conventional explanation. But to this should be added another: Changes in relationships among economic classes were taking place so swiftly that new institutions to accommodate them, such as free markets and royal justice, could not be negotiated fast enough. In chapter 23, I will argue that the same is likely to happen in the less-developed zones and eastern Europe in the twenty-first century.

Pluralism in the Wider Society

The idea of forming groups for lord-peasant interaction proved contagious, moving from the manor into other areas. Younger sons of lords began to want power of their own, while village leaders wanted alternative lords. Interest groups proliferated.[19]

Beginning at least in the twelfth century, noble families began to indulge themselves with separate, scattered living quarters. Knights previously attached to lords established their own residences. Castellanies broke up. Fewer restrictions upon sons' marriages enabled them to move away from extended families. At the same time, lower classes also were seeking their independence. Some went to towns, while others formed war bands, known as *comitatus*,[20] that were comparable to the Japanese ikki. When such "companies" reappeared in fourteenth-century France, they achieved independent power, employed by lords in their private wars or sometimes by the king.[21]

The formation of new groups is usually explained as the result of increased wealth.[22] True, but wealth creates choices, not mandates, so this explanation is not complete. Scholars in the Annals school of history[23] tell us that communal life in larger aggregations was highly desired in the Middle Ages, but they do not say why.

Beginning with the thirteenth century, a vassal in France might have many seigniors, with gradations of homage. While one seignior was theoretically liege (dominant), in practice it was possible to play one against another, and choices could be made, allowing for leverage, circumstance by circumstance.[24]

The move toward pluralism also was reflected in the church. After the investiture controversies, the clergy felt a corporate identity that distinguished them from both the king and the pope. By the twelfth century neither the bishop nor the parish priest was supreme at his respective level; each was surrounded by other functionaries who shared the power and the decision making.[25]

Commercial towns, known as communes, presumably distinguish medieval Europe from the rest of the world and account in large part for European economic development.[26] Towns were replete with guilds, exchange facilities, and laws favoring merchants. But this conventional distinction, while valid, has been overdone. Towns and trade in many parts of the world rivaled those of Europe in the Middle Ages (see chapters 10 on India and 11 and 12 on China).

The conventional explanation of the growth of commercial towns in Europe is economic: "The urban movement in medieval times was a social phenomenon due primarily to economic causes and one which, in its turn, caused profound changes in the economic structure of the Western world."[27] But the same economic causes occurred at different times in India, Africa, and China, where commercial towns were less vigorous. So this explanation becomes insufficient.

The growth of communes, while economically motivated, also resulted from a trend toward pluralism already in effect on the manor. "The social differentiation brought new groups into being, and the spread of lay culture made these more vocal."[28] Pluralism also became incorporated into the law (see chapter 6). "Feudal lordship units and local political units (vills, hundreds, counties) could, and often did, exist side by side. The vill, the hundred, and the county each had its own governing body, which was a court (in England, 'moot') consisting of an assembly of free men."[29] Pluralism in the emerging towns simply reflected the society of the manor.

Just as peasants were being reclassified into new groups on the manor, so in the towns patricians, guildsmen, professions, ordinary workers, churchmen, and tradesmen of different rankings were accorded different rights and liberties:[30] it was a "community of communities."[31]

The concept of contracts among groups spread from manor to town. This in turn led to a free market in labor, where family, serf, or slave labor had previously dominated. "The work contracts comprise the most ubiquitous and diverse category of notarial acts. . . . Older than the guild or the apprentice-ship system, the work contract existed in oral form for centuries before the first one appeared in writing."[32]

Just as royal jurisdiction was initiated side by side with existing ju-risdiction, so also new town agencies were begun side by side with old ones.[33] To a modern observer, the result might seem confusion. To a medieval partici-pant, it may have provided choice. Although harmony among these groups was an avowed value, controversies nevertheless occurred among subgroups.[34]

Medieval guilds illustrate Olson's implication no. 2: "Stable societ-ies with unchanged boundaries tend to accumulate more collusions and orga-nizations for collective action over time."[35] But once again, a correct analysis proves insufficient. Stable societies with unchanged boundaries in China, In-dia, Africa, and elsewhere did not always have the same results as in north-western Europe and Japan.

Among the groups were labor organizations. These have formed and disappeared since ancient times, but not in lineal progression. Organizations of employers dominated in the medieval period. Peasant revolts were orga-nized as well as spontaneous. Conventionally, each one is treated as specific to the occasion. But the concept of labor organizing may have been reinforced from one occasion to the next, and one group organizing may have inspired emulation.

In the fourteenth century laborers launched organizations to refuse to work unless their terms were met. The plague and the Hundred Years' War displaced many workers, who formed wandering bands capable of bargaining with cities suffering a labor shortage. Members of these bands paid dues, collected treasuries, struck even where it was forbidden to do so, and made alliances for mutual support with similar groups in other territories.[36]

Political and economic pluralism were accompanied by intellectual pluralism. In Bologna in the eleventh century, students grouped themselves into "nations" which in turn combined into two groups, one for north of the Alps and one for the south. Each was a *universitas*, a Roman term for a corpo-rate group.[37] These organizations negotiated with city governments for char-ters. They hired their own professors, who also formed an association. Later the name "university" was applied to the whole company. Such corporations were the precursors to many student and scholastic associations throughout Europe.

Azo, one of the foremost legal scholars at the turn of the thirteenth century, saw in these groups the basis for sovereignty. In an early medieval expression of democracy, he held that the source of the ruler's imperium lay "in the corpus, the universitas, the communitas. Jurisdiction did not descend downward from the emperor but upward from the corporate community."[38]

The growth of nations and nationalism in subsequent centuries is perhaps an extension of this pluralism, for groups banded together under a sovereign for negotiation, compromises, and war making with other nations.

With the dawn of the Enlightenment in Europe, intellectual and literary societies, lodges, and clubs proliferated, becoming a feature of private life in the seventeenth century.[39] They may also have been precursors of the scientific and technical academies associated with the Industrial Revolution and of the political clubs of the French Revolution, such as the Jacobin and the Feuillants.

Thus, pluralism in Europe spread upward, downward, and sidewise in the social scale, just as it did in Japan. The prerogative of making choices became valued on all rungs of all ladders. Over the centuries, the very structure of that scale and of those ladders was altered.

Peasant Leverage

The conventional explanation credits lords with engineering the demise of feudalism. But the lords were not in full command of the manors, and change could not have occurred without the collaboration of the lower classes. Economically, the end of feudalism was a positive-sum move, although powerwise it was not. Instead, power was traded for goods. In their manorial councils and courts, Europeans already possessed the institutions through which this momentous change would be bargained and implemented.

Leverage is the common feature. Peasants allied themselves with groups that, although more powerful than themselves, nevertheless needed peasant support in conflicts with other powerful groups. In this interchange, the power of peasants was enhanced.

The process was already at work at the time of Charlemagne, who "tried to offset the power of the aristocracy by fostering and protecting other classes of the population—notably the common freemen, the free peasantry—who would look to the king as their master and protector and not to their immediate aristocratic lords, as did the servile tenants."[40] In the ensuing centuries, peasants wanting to be liberated from feudal dues would encounter resistance from the lords. Court cases then would decide tenure status. Royal and manorial courts vied with each other for jurisdiction. As each strove to enhance its scope, it might offer more favorable judgments to peasants bringing cases. Instead of bargaining for an improved definition of villein rights, a peasant might ask the court to declare him free.

Peasants were not alone in seeking to better their positions. In the eleventh century, bishops and counts left the French royal household, forcing the king to rely more upon knightly families and villeins for his retainers.[41]

Poly and Bournazel describe the way one such retainer argued before Louis VI that he had been born free, and therefore the king did not have the right to confiscate his possessions as a villein.[42]

The case of Simon de Paris illustrates one way in which peasant status was upgraded. Counted as a villein in his home community at Necton in England, de Paris moved to London, where he became alderman and sheriff. Upon his return to Necton for a visit in 1306, he was apprehended by the lord's bailiff and commanded to become reeve, since as villein he was still in the lord's service. Taken to trial, the jury found that his residence in London had made him a free man. "The influence of the City of London was powerful and Simon was released,"[43] a clear case of leverage provided by Simon's ties with the City.

The church was another source of peasant leverage. In its rivalry with the Holy Roman emperor and the kings of France and England, the church in the twelfth century often favored the peasants. They might become emancipated by joining a crusade or taking holy orders. The church attracted peasants away from other lords by offering more advantageous conditions and freeing slaves on its own domains.[44] Serfs also levered their power by associations with free peasants. The latter cooperated because, in the twelfth century, "the free man living among serfs was always liable to be confused with them."[45]

New towns, in competition with other towns or to gain status vis-à-vis manorial lords, offered freedom to serfs who would register with them and remain for a year and a day. If the manorial lords wished to keep peasants from running off, they had to offer freedom or other advantages.[46] Whichever vertical alliance they chose, peasants were exercising leverage.

Vertical alliances between peasants and bourgeois sometimes enhanced the power of each. "A peasant leader ... Guillaume Karle ... organized a council [in the fourteenth century in France] which issued orders stamped by an official seal, and appointed captains elected in each locality, and lieutenants for squads of ten. ... [His] hope was to win the alliance of the towns in a joint action against the nobles; it was here that the two movements, peasant and bourgeois, came together."[47]

Peasants were the beneficiaries of the battle between nobles and monarch over the right to tax. Had the lords won in France, no peasant would have been free.[48] By establishing its own right to tax, the French monarchy in effect declared the peasants free, albeit paying rents to the lords. Peasant leverage was diminished in the age of absolutism beginning with Louis XIV (1643-1715). But as France approached the Revolution, instances of peasant and bourgeois alliances with upper classes, and leverage, reappear. I will return to these after a digression into England.

In England, tension between monarch and nobility remained fairly steady through the centuries, perhaps a bit higher during the baronial revolts of the thirteenth century, a bit lower after the Wars of the Roses in the fifteenth century, and higher again under the Stuarts.

Peasant leverage also arose serendipitously out of actions by the gentry. The free market in land owes its origin, at least in part, to the desires of gentry to transfer their holdings. Gentry wanting to alien land despite their feudal obligations might do so with court rulings. Once a decision had been made in their favor, legal precedence required that it apply to freeholding peasants as well. I have described this in greater detail in an earlier work.[49]

Instead of deeds, in England unfree peasants held copies of manorial records of their holdings; hence their land was copyhold, and they were copyholders. In the 1550s, when common-law courts began to rule on copyholds, copyholders acquired the same rights as freeholders.[50] The gradual assumption of jurisdiction by royal, or common-law, courts away from manorial courts helped the peasants acquire the right to transfer, a step toward ownership. The difference between freehold and copyhold narrowed so much that manorial records gradually ceased to recognize it.[51] I count this as another instance of leverage, or peasants gaining an advantage through conflict between two greater powers, manorial and royal courts.

Peasant leverage in England was further enhanced by the military needs of the lords. As armies became more mercenary and less feudal-service, lords who needed money to pay soldiers became more willing to yield their arbitrary power over subjects' lands in exchange for money rents.[52]

England's free market in land was coupled with freeing the market in labor. Whereas the "standard holding" was a property of feudalism, once holdings could be transferred, all or in part, the sizes of tracts began to differ from each other, presenting the land manager with greater difficulty in assigning tasks. This helped lead to the emancipation of workers.

Serfs achieved their freedom in diverse ways. Some paid for it; some received it in a charter from the lords, which might enfranchise a whole village; some ran away; some called themselves free and went unchallenged; some won it by court ruling.[53] Some, holding serf land, sold it as free land, and no one challenged them.[54] Some simply rented land and became indistinguishable from free tenants.[55] All these maneuvers illustrate the working of a free market in institutions.

Whatever their method in attaining freedom, English peasants were not alone in their efforts. Merchants and industrialists quarreling with their own landlords lent them support. Friars and priests would favor them for moral reasons. In his opposition to the established church, John Wycliffe supported peasants in withholding tithes from "unworthy" clergymen, as did John Ball, a priest frequently punished for his utterances.[56] All of these actions constituted leverage.

In the High Middle Ages, peasant leverage in England was confined to sporadic arrangements with a few groups, such as rival courts of law or the church. None of these was a faithful ally under all circumstances. Indeed, in the fourteenth century, "Short of the king, their imagined champion, all officialdom was [the peasants'] foe—sheriffs, foresters, tax-collectors, judges, abbots, lords, bishops, and dukes—but most especially men of the law because the law was the villeins' prison."[57]

By the seventeenth and eighteenth centuries, however, vertical alliances and leverage had become institutionalized in two ways. First, the more successful peasants in England had become yeoman farmers, many cooperating with the nobility in agricultural improvements. Others lost out in enclosures, some drifting to the cities to look for employment. The richer ones were acquiring more social prestige than they had enjoyed in earlier centuries.

Second, common interests of peasants and other groups made for longer-lasting relationships. In pluralist societies, over time a greater number of groups finds more interests in common, and bonds tend to continue for longer periods. For example, the guilds supported the Levellers in England, since both protested monarchical authority as civil war approached;[58] both favored opening the enclosures of the fens and the end of servile tenure.[59] In sixteenth-century Normandy the peasants' natural allies were the nobility: "Peasant self-defence had become normal, condoned and even actively supported by the nobility. . . ."[60] According to Mousnier, peasants, merchants, and craftsmen had common interests in opposing royal taxes.[61] Priests sometimes found common ground with "their" peasants in defense of the estates. They may have felt a sense of mission because their literacy made them natural communicators for illiterate peasants.[62]

Back in France, the twilight of the *ancien régime* saw a resurgence of peasant leverage: "[T]he throne saw its interests best served by a landed peasantry with secure tenures, with greater personal freedom, and with regulation by the state of the obligations owed to the seigniors."[63] "Sometimes [in the late eighteenth century], with the support of royal law, peasant communities triumphed over the seigneurial tribunals."[64]

Just before the French Revolution, the concerns of the peasants were swept into a maelstrom of denunciations of a whole society: "[D]iscussion of the plight of the peasantry and criticism of seigniorial privilege were minor themes in the assault upon the old order."[65] The bourgeoisie also exercised leverage in revolutionary France. In the Estates General of 1789, "voting by head raised the possibility that the bourgeoisie would be able to act in concert with allies among the lower-ranking clergy and liberal nobility."[66] In local assemblies to elect the Third Estate for its meeting in Versailles in 1789, master craftsmen usually dominated. However, credible procedures required universal suffrage, including for peasants, who therefore held on to the coattails of considerations more momentous than their own.[67] But there was a limit: suffrage was confined to those who paid taxes.

Peasants often gained from the application to them of benefits for the more powerful that could only be implemented universally. For example, in eighteenth-century France, the justice system needed "to guarantee proper and profitable use of property and talents, so potential aggressors had to be taught that to attack even the most modest of homes, possessions, and persons was fraught with peril. A poor wretch whom some hardy predator had thought to harass with impunity might receive assistance from a personal enemy of the plaintiff."[68]

Instances of peasant leverage could be found throughout northwestern Europe. In Zurich during the Reformation, the Catholics in power and their evangelical challengers competed for the loyalty of the peasants. "Peasants played off the abbot against his rivals by offering their allegiance to any power that gave the best promise of satisfying their rural grievances."[69] In seventeenth-century Netherlands, workers and lower middle class citizens found the Prince of Orange to be their defense against urban patricians. "[T]he Swedish peasant had never been a serf. In part, this was because the monarchical state, an enemy of the nobility, intervened on the peasants' side."[70] The same was so in Finland.

Rising nationalism in the eighteenth and nineteenth century often boosted the peasants' position, for peasants were needed in the struggle against foreign overlords. The Irish struggle for independence was carried on mainly by urban interests, but early in the twentieth century it resulted in land for the peasants.[71]

With the blossoming of democracy and parliamentary horse trading, small-farmer support (the word peasant is no longer appropriate in the twentieth century) has led to political concessions. For example, in 1980, President Valéry Giscard d'Estaing announced a development program for southwest France to woo the farmer vote for the admission of Spain to the Common Market.[72]

In these many ways, vertical alliances and leverage were a principal means of enhancing the power of peasants from the tenth century to the present day. Evolution toward free markets in both land and farm labor was part of the process. All this unfolded step by step, mainly in a free market for institutions.

Peasant Rebellions

Like Japan, northwestern Europe from the fourteenth century into the eighteenth was studded with peasant rebellions. As in Japan, many of these rebellions were on-and-off outbreaks, combined with negotiations. As in Japan,
most peasant violence was put down, in some cases brutally, with execution
and torture. As in Japan, negotiations frequently were fruitful, and peasant
power was enhanced, often through the leverage of vertical alliances. As in
Japan, many authors have commented on the reasonableness of peasant demands.[73]

     As in Japan, peasants for the most part did not insist on radical changes
in political or landholding structures, the Diggers in England being an
exception. "The objectives of all these protesters were strictly limited, and
those who wished to turn such violent upheavals as the Jacobite rebellions [of
eighteenth-century Britain] into national revolutions were disappointed."[74]
Mainly, peasants sought specific improvements in their work conditions, such
as lower rents, fewer work days a week on seigniorial farms, exemption from
specified work details or payments, greater mobility, and political freedom.

     The best known of peasant rebellions are the French Jacquerie of
1358, the English peasant revolt of 1381, the Zurich revolt of 1489, the German Peasants' War of the 1520s, the English Pilgrimage of Grace of 1536,
Ket's rebellion in England in 1549, violence by the Diggers and Levellers in
England in the seventeenth century, and the Irish tithe war of 1831-38. In
other years, violence ranged from sporadic to endemic. The generalizations
of the preceding paragraph are supported by the histories of these rebellions,
which can be found in encyclopedias.

Leverage by Other Groups

Peasants were not the only ones who enhanced their power by leverage.
Throughout the period under review, rivalries among king, nobility, town governments, and church spurred vertical alliances among many groups, such as
rear-vassals (vassals of vassals), merchants, traders, and laborers. For example,
Philip II of France (r.1180-1223) "played off clergy, feudal lords, and town
authorities against one another, favoring especially the towns, to which he
granted considerable self-government, and the great merchants, to whom he
granted trading privileges and monopolies."[75]

     In the thirteenth century, a rear-vassal might take a complaint against
his seignior to the king for settlement. If the king were in any kind of rivalry
with the seignior, the rear-vassal might win. Hughes de Lusignan complained

to Philip II that John, his seignior, had married Hughes's fiancée. As king of England, John was a rival of Philip's. Philip took advantage of this complaint to call John to account, for John was Philip's vassal for his lands in France. Upon his failure to appear, Philip confiscated John's French lands.[76] In a similar episode in the fourteenth century, citizens of Beauvais in France, which had been a bishopric for centuries, complained against their grand seignior, the bishop. Endorsing their complaint, the king granted the town the title of commune.[77]

The powers of towns and villages relative to nobility, clergy, and king were further strengthened as Philip IV of France (r.1285-1314) called upon them in national assemblies to support him in his fight with the pope over taxation and his struggle with the Knights Templars over power. The first Estates General in 1302 was one of these assemblies.

In these many ways, leverage was applied by middle-class groups as well as peasants, not always successfully and sometimes to concentrate power. But for the most part, the power of weaker groups grew relative to stronger ones, and thereby the diffusion of power was promoted. Further historical references to the use of leverage by groups other than peasants appear in appendix 4.1.

Other Ways of Diffusing Power

Even without vertical alliances, economic development and the diffusion of power were mutually reinforcing. As private agriculture, towns, and markets enhanced production and trade, power became still more diffuse and institutionalized. Increased trade in the eleventh and twelfth centuries diminished the power of kings to control it. Earlier a king would travel, with an itinerant court, to render justice throughout his kingdom. As economic life became more complex, he could no longer do this efficiently. So local decision-making expanded. For example, Henry II of England (r.1154-89) lacked a police force and could raise only temporary armies of knights.[78]

The growth of towns brought new classes—merchants and craftspeople—who could bargain for rights from lords and kings without allying themselves with other groups. Their strength lay in the material wealth they could create and share with those who bestowed the privileges.[79] "[T]he middle classes as a body were accorded a higher, more responsible position."[80]

E. L. Jones has argued that the shift to "money fiefs" as opposed to "service fiefs" occurred when lords, who previously had consumed only the produce of their lands, now needed cash for imports. Therefore, they demanded cash rents from their peasants, who could pay only by selling their products.[81] While this may be so, it is not clear why the lords could not raise cash by seizing peasant produce, as had been their wont, and selling it themselves.

More likely, the peasants were becoming traders on their own account, leaving the lord no choice but to demand his share in cash. If this is indeed what happened, it would signal increasing power of peasants relative to lords.

The growth of corporations also helped disperse power. "A corporation could easily avoid rendering customary feudal services and payments. A corporation never rides out fully armed and prepared for battle in the service of an overlord."[82] Local dynasties, a legacy of the Hundred Years' War, limited the powers of French kings Charles VII (r.1422-61) and Louis XI (r.1461-83) in ways that had not been possible under Philip IV (r.1285-1314). The *baillis* and *sénéchaux* sent out as local officials by Henry II (r.1547-59) and other kings were generalists, whose power was eclipsed by specialists in water and forests, and the like.[83] "The process of land reclamation [in the Netherlands, c.1600-1750] established a set of drainage institutions that gave peasants some voice in local affairs and a vehicle to secure cooperation in improvement schemes."[84] Further references to nonleverage ways by which weaker groups enhanced their power relative to stronger ones are listed in appendix 4.2.

Middle Class Power: Its Effect on War

By refusing to fund them, parliaments and estates decreased the capacity of kings and princes to make war. The military prowess of the ruler was not always to the advantage of the middle classes. Partly because of this, European wars became periodic rather than endemic. Thus, the dispersion of power promoted institutions of trust in two ways: (1) through the demand for them as such by the middle classes, and (2) through the diminished capacity of rulers to destroy them by war.

Balance of Power

Balance of power emerged in Europe in three senses.

First was the political-international. From the sixteenth to the nineteenth centuries, under pressure primarily from England, the major European governments gave up the quest for individual dominance and strove instead for balance, such that no country might overwhelm the others militarily.[85]

Second was the political-national. As parliamentary democracy evolved in northwestern Europe, political groups sought to ensure that no ruling faction should dominate all others. Thus came the countervailing powers of executive, legislature, and judiciary; multiparty government; and the division of authority among bureaucratic departments and offices.

Third was a less well-known balance of power among interest groups. But "balance" must be understood intuitively, for measurement would run afoul of the vague borders of groups and the problems of weighting. Should groups be weighted according to the size of their membership or by their organizational purposes—social, political, economic, and the like—some being deemed, subjectively, more important than others? Furthermore, balance does not mean *equal* power. It means a set of tensions by which unequal groups nevertheless inhibit each other's excesses.

Compare a labor union in North America, able to stand off employers and bargain for a favorable settlement, with one in Latin America that must accept its government's verdict.[86] In the former, labor power is balanced against employer power; in the latter it is not. Since no way exists to measure the power of one group relative to the other, the balance of power of interest groups must be understood intuitively.

Balance of power is an abstract concept learned through experience, in which balance in one arena may foster its acceptance in others. Just as the twentieth-century concept of equality among races (say, blacks and whites in the United States) may later extend to other ethnic groups and to gender, so also in earlier centuries, the balance of military power among European countries may have strengthened the idea that power should be balanced among executive, legislative, and judicial branches. These two types of balance may have increased the acceptance of balance among interest groups; say, between peasants and nobility or laborers and employers. Alternatively, the causation may have occurred in a different order, or they may all have been mutually reinforcing. Finally, the relative balance among interest groups probably encouraged bargaining for positive-sum, or efficient, solutions, which are the essence of durable economic growth.

Institutions of Economic Growth

The major institutions of economic growth in northwestern Europe—such as money and finance, law, corporations, labor organizations, and parliamentary democracy—were created through an emerging free market of ideas,[87] even though each institution was to some extent limited by monarch or government. Although coin was minted by the sovereign, the financial system was mainly one of promissory notes and banking instruments arranged by traders and financiers. Although guilds controlled or were controlled by town governments, they also were shaped by merchant and producer groups. Business organizations ranging from the Hanseatic League to the giant staples, the royal monopoly trading companies, and the modern corporation, all were molded by producing and trading groups, though often in concert with a government. Because the history of these institutions is well known in the West (unlike the history of Japanese institutions), they are mentioned only cursorily here.

Each of these organizations has wanted a monopoly over its own products, and some for awhile succeeded. But monopolies for all were impossible. Bargaining among them—towns with other towns, guilds with other guilds, merchants with competing merchants, bankers with other financiers, employers with unions—led toward a market in goods and services which, while not completely free, was relatively so compared with that of less-developed zones.

All these institutions are sustained by a balance of tensions among the groups supporting them. No government is capable of emasculating them or even of changing them significantly. The European Union is today being fashioned by negotiation among *somewhat* equal partners. No one group can indefinitely dominate the monetary system, manipulating it to transfer product to itself, although governments or businesses may do this for awhile. Nor can any group totally command the pricing and marketing policies of business corporations. Even the strongest "monopoly" is subject to competition, if not for its own products at least for substitutes or for the consumer's money. Nor does any one group control the law. All these institutions contain some built-in accountability, either to others or to the constraints of the market. For the most part, this degree of accountability is unique to Japan and northwestern Europe and its descendants (North America, Australia, and New Zealand). Only a few elements of this system are found outside those areas.

Notes

1. North 1981:5.
2. North and Thomas 1973.
3. North 1981, 1990.
4. Strayer 1992: chapter 1.
5. Representative authors of the "prevailing orthodoxy" include Habakkuk (1958), Postan (1966), and North and Thomas (1973).
6. Bloch (1961, English translation) is the principal author to discover this relationship, although Weber 1964:374 (originally *Wirtschaft und Gesellschaft*, 1922 and 1925), among others, had mentioned it earlier.
7. Hilton 1973:216; 1978:9.
8. Berman 1983:555-56; Hilton 1973:70-71, 74-75.
9. Hilton 1973:216.
10. Genicot 1966:733-34.
11. Hogue 1966:133.
12. Goodell 1980:298.
13. Postan 1966:611.

58   *Centuries of Economic Endeavor*

14. de Tocqueville [1856] 1955:47.
15. Kriedte 1983:16.
16. Powelson 1988:53-65. There I quote other authors than those mentioned above: Barraclough 1946:148; Berman 1983:321ff; Bloch 1966b:170; Brenner 1976:55; Geiger 1973; Gregg 1976:90; Wunder 1978:55.
17. North and Thomas 1973:31, 61, 79, 92.
18. North 1981:130.
19. Tuchman 1984:39.
20. Black 1984:55.
21. Tuchman 1984:269.
22. Duby 1988b:57.
23. For example, Chartier 1989.
24. Gilles 1986:104.
25. Berman 1983:107, 212.
26. Geiger 1973. Van Werveke 1963:3-41 stresses these essentials in medieval European towns but does not compare them with the rest of the world.
27. Van Werveke 1963:40.
28. Holborn 1959:100.
29. Berman 1983:300.
30. Gilles 1986:114.
31. Berman 1983:394.
32. Epstein 1991:78.
33. Black 1984:46.
34. Black 1984:71.
35. Olson 1982:74, 124.
36. Tuchman 1978:69, 286, 365.
37. Berman 1983:124.
38. Berman 1983:292.
39. Chartier 1989:17.
40. Barraclough 1976:30.
41. Poly and Bournazel 1991:187-88.
42. Poly and Bournazel 1991:189.
43. Hibbert 1987:30.
44. Berman 1983:320.
45. Braudel 1982:257.
46. Blum 1957:810.
47. Tuchman 1984:177-78.
48. Brenner 1985:56.
49. Powelson 1988:67-76.
50. Harvey 1984:328.
51. Harvey 1984:331.
52. Rosenberg 1986:120.
53. Hibbert 1987:29.
54. Harvey 1984:347.
55. Gregg 1976:290.
56. Hibbert 1987:35-6.
57. Tuchman 1984:373-74.

58. Black 1984:126.
59. Gregg 1961:71.
60. Nicholls 1984:110.
61. Burke 1984:76.
62. Nicholls 1982:115.
63. Blum 1978:197.
64. Furet and Ozouf 1989:688.
65. Blum 1978:305.
66. Richet 1989:537.
67. Lefebvre 1947:59.
68. Castan 1989:47-48.
69. Broadhead 1982:162.
70. Braudel 1984:254.
71. Clark 1979:263.
72. *New York Times*, 10/19/1980.
73. For example, Nicholls 1984·120, dealing with peasant risings in Normandy; Braudel 1982:257, writing of several rebellions; Blum 1978:197, 206, on France; Broadhead 1982:162, with reference to Zurich.
74. Hibbert 1987:478.
75. Berman 1983:464.
76. Gilles 1986:118; Barber 1992:289.
77. Mousnier 1974:590.
78. Berman 1983:407, 450.
79. Rosenberg and Birdzell 1986:55.
80. De Tocqueville 1856/1955:85.
81. Jones, E.L., 1981:86.
82. Hogue 1966:74.
83. Sicard 1986:218.
84. de Vries 1976:70.
85. This quest for balance of power is well known and requires no explanation here. Every attempt to destroy it, such as by Louis XIV, Napoleon, and Hitler, was met by a combination of other powers.
86. Although government may intervene in labor disputes in both the United States and Latin America, in the former case intervention is the exception while in the latter area it is the usual condition for all major disputes. The minister of labor may supervise the negotiations, declaring some strikes legal and others illegal, or approving the settlements. Poblete and Burnett (1960) provide a concise history of the Latin American labor movement.
87. Their histories have been amply written by economic historians and are well known in the West. I do not repeat them here.

Chapter 5
Compromise in Northwestern Europe

Europe was far from a compromising, negotiating society in the tenth century. From ancient times to at least the fifteenth century, quarrels produced more violence than reconciliation; war was endemic; power was a dominant value, intransigence the regular order. Indeed, violence and the quest for power were among the principal forces deterring European economic development. By the twelfth century, changes were evident, although many of these qualities have remained in some parts, even to the present day.

But it is necessary to explain the candles, not the darkness. This chapter summarizes in five short sections the major historical experiences in negotiation and compromise that occurred from the Middle Ages to the present day: in economics and trade, taxation, jurisdiction and power, religion, and intellectual discourse. Northwestern Europe moved from a position of intransigence and violence toward one of negotiation and compromise in all these areas. Finally, we will summarize the power-diffusion process and explore possible reasons for its occurrence only in northwestern Europe and Japan.

Economics and Trade

European traders were already cooperating with each other by the twelfth century. Merchant vessels were owned by "companions," each with his own space on board. "The little community would decide on the voyage and the sailing date, each member being responsible for stowing his own goods, helping or being helped by his neighbour."[1]

In England, the first part of Edward I's reign (1272-92) was a golden age for compromise and negotiation among king, barons, ecclesiastics, and burghers, undertaken through the Parliament, which was becoming institutionalized. During this period, major legislation was enacted to compromise between the new commercial attitude that land should be freely sold and the old feudal custom of a vassal holding unalienable land of a lord. I have described this more fully in a previous work.[2] The rights of merchants and traders, as well as those of barons (landowners), negotiated in Magna Carta of 1215, were renegotiated and reconfirmed throughout the thirteenth century. Among other things, safe conduct was provided for foreign merchants in England, even those from enemy countries, provided that English merchants received equivalent protection in their lands.[3] In his studies of medieval charters for artisan businesses, Epstein found a wide range of negotiations and compromises not fully evident in the charters themselves,[4] a testimony to a free market in institutions.

By the twelfth century in France, judicial proceedings involving merchants were decided by their peers. Town administrations were more concerned for compromise solutions than for punishment or vengeance.[5] Peace was recognized as important to the welfare of the town.

In choosing between guild monopolies and privileges on the one hand and free competition on the other, medieval guilds often sought a middle way: regulated competition to reward effort without threatening established houses excessively. "Even the most restrictive guild practices prescribed rules for competition rather than abolish it. Throughout Europe groups of artisans chose this middle way that granted a measure of security and at the same time rewarded individual effort."[6] This compromise tended toward the free market, even though merchants were far from fully ready for it.

Cooperation in medieval European villages is a much-repeated theme. The following are only a few examples from a vast literature. The strip system in feudal agriculture made it "in each man's interest to work in cooperation with his neighbour."[7] Also, "it was natural that the spread and development of the village community should make the farmers co-operate more and more."[8] Earlier, cooperation had been essential to defense, not only against Viking, Magyar, and Saracen invasions, but also against depredations by neighboring lords or their tenants.[9]

Trade agreements incorporating reciprocal rights were drafted in German cities at least since the thirteenth century. The "bargaining" was not always peaceful: the Hanseatic League raised an army and defeated Denmark in 1380. Reciprocal arrangements were negotiated among cities to protect the rights of nationals, both commercial and legal. In the fifteenth century, the Merchant Adventurers of England negotiated trading arrangements with Amsterdam and later with Hamburg and towns in the Netherlands. In the sixteenth century, the British negotiated agreements for their companies to operate in other countries, notably Russia and Turkey.

In the early eighteenth century, it was commonly believed that to destroy the trade of one's neighbor was one way to gain trade for oneself. "Yet already before the end of the [Seven Years'] war there was evidence that the merchant interest was less confident of the virtues of war as an instrument of policy."[10] Lenient terms to France after the war, and the ensuing British prosperity, helped lead to the concept that the prosperity of another nation is to the advantage of one's own.

The most-favored-nation principle was incorporated into trade agreements as early as the seventeenth century, but the nineteenth was the century for major liberalization, notably with the Cobden treaty between England and France in 1860 and the Franco-Prussian (Zollverein) treaty of 1862, each of which reduced duties reciprocally and contained a most-favored-nation clause. These were the precursors of the reciprocal trade agreements of the twentieth century and thence of the European Union.[11] The General Agreement on Tariffs and Trade (GATT) and the World Trade Organization represent the highest degree of economic compromise achieved by humankind by the end of the twentieth century, though not—it is to be hoped—the highest in all time. Seven years of struggle, dotted with confrontations, threats, and hardline brinksmanship, yet also with yielding and recognition of potential gains, marked the historic agreement of December 1993, concluding the Uruguay Round. Further historical references on negotiation, cooperation, and compromise on economics and trade in Europe appear in appendix 5.1.

Taxation as Leverage

In much of the medieval world, and in some places for centuries thereafter, taxation was tribute collected by force. In Britain, by contrast, from the twelfth century onward, the ruler could tax only with the consent of his bourgeois and noble subjects, who in turn had to deal with their peasants. That pattern later became the norm in other European countries.

In 1258, Henry III of England, weakened by civil war and bankrupted by an ill-advised military foray into Sicily, called upon his barons for funds. They made their cooperation contingent on his accepting a body of counselors who prepared the Provisions of Oxford, which specified the authority of Parliament.[12]

Thenceforth taxation became a matter of negotiation. Centuries later, in the Great Contract of 1610, James I agreed to restrain his extravagance in return for an appropriate income guaranteed by Parliament.[13] Under Charles II, Parliament withheld taxes that the king would allegedly use to promote "Popery" and absolutism.[14] All these arrangements strengthened the concept that higher authorities could be held accountable.

The course was similar in France. "French kings . . . established their power to tax income and property through a process of negotiation and conciliation that extended over several centuries. . . . During the twelfth century, subjects in different towns in the kingdom agreed to pay periodic tallages . . . in exchange for the king's written pledge to maintain a stable currency during his lifetime."[15] In similar vein, Webber and Wildavsky describe the further evolution of taxes through negotiation between kings and representatives of taxpayers.[16]

Jurisdiction and Power

Conflicts over jurisdiction and power were common to Europe throughout the period under review.[17] But a relative cultural shift occurred, away from sheer power and toward trade and wealth as the most meaningful objectives sought by rulers, as well as a shift from insistence on total victory to willingness to make a compromise peace. Foremost among the early conflicts were those over who should rule, with what powers, and over what territory.

In an effort to end joint kingships and to decrease the violence of competing claimants to the throne, in the late ninth century the West Saxon kings decided on succession by will or family agreement. While the kingship would go to only one candidate, family property would be divided so that all relatives were satisfied.[18] By the twelfth century in France, younger brothers were being recognized through the granting of *apanages*, princely domains in which they would rule while remaining under the titular authority of the king.[19] All this was an improvement over the succession battles of the later Roman Empire.

About 1200, a large number of allodial landholders in France (those not subject to feudal lords) wanted to upgrade their status by assuming noble titles and converting their houses into small castles. The neighboring nobility opposed this move, fearing a challenge to their prerogatives. In an "unprecedented compromise,"[20] the titles and rights to build small castles were granted in exchange for subjecting the land to the feudal jurisdiction of the neighboring nobility.

In the perennial conflict between state power and regional jurisdiction, Philip II (r.1180-1223) validated local administrative organizations but appointed his own men from Paris to administer them. He strengthened the church while enforcing royal rights over the clergy. These compromises probably reflected a realistic appraisal of the balance of power among king, church, and provincial authority. They remained in effect for generations.

Both Henry III (r.1216-72) and Edward I (r.1272-1307) of England claimed the right to appoint their own officials and advisors, but the barons, prelates, knights, and burghers insisted that their consent was essential to new laws and taxes beyond what was customary. Each recognized the rights of the other in a "working compromise" and "uneasy truce."[21]

Although burghers were classified as "rich" and "poor" in town documents in Germany of the fourteenth century, equality between them, in conducting the town's business and in a common justice, was frequently sought in practice. Power sharing was agreed in compromises in Augsburg in 1340 and Strasburg in 1334.

The powers of the king of England, still unsettled at the time of the Restoration (1660), were defined gradually, by negotiation, in the Convention of 1660 and with the "Cavalier Parliament."[22] Parliament "had demonstrated a capacity for adaptation and an ability to carry on the government of the country in very difficult circumstances."[23] Further historical references to compromise on jurisdiction and power are found in appendix 5.2.

Religion

Frederic Maitland, historian of law, wrote in 1898 about an earlier era:

> Everywhere we see strife and then compromise, and then strife again, and at the latest after the end of the thirteenth century the state usually gets the better in every combat. . . . The rulers of the church, therefore, had to tolerate much that they could not approve in the name of the church. They could give and take without any sacrifice of first principles. . . . Popes, and popes who were not weaklings, had taught them by precept and example that when we are dealing with temporal powers we may temporize.[24]

The greatest religious crisis of medieval times—the Gregorian reformation and the investiture struggle (1075-1122)—was settled everywhere by compromise, eventually. The controversy between Pope Gregory VII and the Holy Roman Emperor Henry IV led to a long civil war in Germany, not settled during the lifetime of either. In England the dispute was mainly between Anselm of Canterbury, devotee of Pope Urban II, and Kings William II and Henry I. Both were settled by heroic compromises. In England, the Synod of Westminster in 1107 recognized Henry's right to reconquer Normandy from his brother Robert, while Henry gave up his right to invest the clergy. Anselm in turn agreed to do homage to Henry. In Germany a similar conflict was settled by the Concordat of Worms in 1122, with the clergy doing homage to the emperor, Henry V, for their secular responsibilities but receiving their spiritual authority from the pope, Calixtus II. An image of the conflict returned with the confrontation between England's King Henry II and Thomas Becket, culminating in Becket's murder in 1170.

The disputes ranged much more widely than those settled at Westminster and Worms, however. They played into the wars between the Hohenstaufen and the pope, which involved the French and the English as well, from Frederick I's first invasion of Italy (1158) through the battle of Bouvines (1214) to Tagliacozzo (1268).[25] Warfare and other violence were endemic, but "ultimately compromises were reached on a whole range of issues involving not only the interrelationship of church and state but the interrelationship of communities within the secular order—the manorial system, the lord-vassal unit, the merchant guilds, the chartered cities and towns, the territorial duchies and kingdoms, the secularized empire."[26] Even the Henry-Becket controversy ended in compromise—albeit too late for Becket—in that the pope and the king agreed on two separate legal jurisdictions and set the boundaries between them.[27]

With the possible exception of the French Revolution, the wars of religion of the sixteenth century marked the greatest period of civil bloodshed and internal hatred in French history. To end these wars, France's Henry III (r.1574-89) proposed Protestant Henry of Navarre as a compromise successor provided that he became Catholic. The peace that followed under Henry IV (r.1589-1610) called for an utmost attempt at compromise between Catholics and Protestants, whose bitterness toward each other had been nurtured for decades.[28] A *parti des politiques* was formed "to subordinate religious conflicts to a national interest and to a *raison d'état*. [But] this happened only after the turn of the [seventeenth] century."[29] The revocation of the Edict of Nantes by Louis XIV in 1685, depriving Protestants of their civil liberties, was a temporary setback in an irreversible trend toward freedom of religion.

The wars of religion are not yet over in Europe. Perhaps by imagining the struggles of Northern Ireland—or even the Middle East—as somehow encompassing virtually the entire continent of Europe, present-day observers may obtain some idea of the impact of these wars and of the power ethic on the European economy. Surely the ultimate settlements by compromise were essential to the economic advances of Europe. So will they also be, ultimately, to the economic health of Ireland and the Middle East. (The compromises of 1993-94 in the Middle East will be discussed in Chapter 20). Further historical references on negotiation and compromise in religious matters are found in appendix 5.3.

Intellectual Discourse

The art of negotiation and compromise applies not only to economic, political, and religious affairs but also to ideas and intellectual discourse. The harmonizing of reason with faith—antithetical in many cultures, including some Western fundamentalist sects—was a principal goal of scholastic philosophers in the Middle Ages. The idea that reason could help understand faith and that free will did not conflict with divine order had been introduced by Boethius as far back as the sixth century CE. It was carried on by the Scholastic method from the twelfth to the fifteenth centuries. Thomas Aquinas (1224/5-74) was one of its principal exponents.

This method depended on dialectical reasoning, which might be construed alternatively as a foundation for scientific thinking and a basis for intellectual compromise. In *Policraticus* (1159), John of Salisbury tried "to put together in a comprehensive way theories, texts, and examples from the most diverse and contradictory sources—Plato, Aristotle, Cicero, Seneca, Virgil, Ovid, the Old Testament, the New Testament, the church fathers, the Roman lawyers, . . . the canon lawyers, and others—and to attempt to synthesize them. . . . John found a method of actually achieving synthesis through the use of concepts which combined contradictory norms by abstracting their common qualities."[30] The belief that all of these documents were sacred and absolute, yet the need to synthesize them and resolve internal conflicts, surely provided excellent training in compromise.

One example of the synthesis of opposites was the conflict between hereditary succession and election of kings. John of Salisbury proposed a compromise in which the eldest son would be the presumed heir but confirmed by election. In so suggesting, he anticipated another compromise not agreed upon until centuries later in the West: the existence of a "public power" distinct from both the ruler and private society.

The very Scholasticism that Hegel eschewed in the nineteenth century may have been the ancestor of his philosophy of thesis-antithesis-synthesis. This harmonization of opposites is surely a part of that period in Western history called the Enlightenment. Shapiro writes of "a common set of assumptions about the nature of truth, the methods for attaining it, and the degree of probability or certainty that may be attributed to the findings."[31] She shows how this common set cuts across natural science, religion, history, law, and literature in the West. Wilson associates the Enlightenment with universalism: the view that one's own moral sentiment should be extended to encompass persons of other races, cultures, and nationalities than one's own, which he finds to be peculiar to the West.[32] He also points, with some marvel, to the way in which the ideas of philosophers such as those cited here were extended to the common citizenry, embracing their everyday actions, instead of being confined to the writings of an elite group of thinkers.

Confrontation and Intransigence

The tendency toward negotiation, compromise, and cooperation among pluralist groups was neither linear nor unbroken. European history is full of examples of confrontation and intransigence. Henry II and Thomas Becket each set forth demands knowing the other would not accept them.[33] In 1419, Henry V of England insisted on sovereignty over Normandy and Aquitaine, a condition neither the Duke of Burgundy nor the Queen of France could accept.

Talks were fruitless.[34] Events leading to and during the English civil war and the war itself revealed many instances of misunderstanding, mistrust, polarization of ideology, and intransigence.[35] "Almost without exception, contemporaries attached long-term significance to their struggles and described them as confrontations between monarchy and Parliament."[36] While the issues of the civil war could not be surmounted at the time, however, they were all resolved by compromise within the next century.

Although the French Revolution did contain compromises, on balance intransigence was the rule. The legislature changed hands and composition several times, and those whose opinions fell from favor often had their heads fall as well, especially during the Terror from 1792 to 1794.

Liberalism lost in the European revolutions of 1848, with many of its proponents mercilessly hanged. Yet virtually all they had fought for—nationalism, independence of artisans from guilds, freedom for workers, the end of serfdom, more attention to education—were put into place before the end of the century, mainly by negotiation, compromise, and legislation. Most of these reforms were achieved by the very leaders who had opposed them in 1848 or by their political heirs.[37]

Confrontation and violence have not disappeared from Western culture. Rather, negotiation and compromise have grown *relatively* stronger, over the centuries, as principal means of resolving conflicts. The same has been true among the Japanese. But other societies—Middle East, African, and Latin American—have not followed this pattern to the same extent. It is because of their centuries-long experience in conflict resolution, and not only their economic power, that Western Europe and the United States are called on as arbiters in other conflicts, such as those of the Middle East.

Summary of the Power-Diffusion Process: Common Elements of Japan and Northwestern Europe

Let us now summarize the power-diffusion process as it operated in the histories of Japan and northwestern Europe from the Middle Ages to at least the nineteenth century.

1. The economic systems of both regions in the Middle Ages were based on contract feudalism,[38] in which lords and tenants performed specific assignments for each other. This contrasts with the rest of the world, where feudalism was mainly by conquest, with tenants subject to whims of the lords, unable to gainsay them in their extravagant demands. Contract feudalism emphasized the *concept* of contract, which ultimately led to its counterpart concept of private property and then to free markets.

2. Taxes were increasingly collected by agreement with middle-class contributors, granted in return for their right to monitor government expenditures.[39] While medieval peasants paid dearly and mostly had no choice, nevertheless from time to time they too bargained, as part of a peasant rebellion. The fact of agreement, if only by members of parliament or the estates in Europe or the village councils in Japan, reinforced accountability. In other parts of the world, taxes were collected mainly as tribute and often by military force.

3. The earliest legal and monetary systems of both areas were initially derived, for the most part, by agreements among the groups that used them, acting as corporate bodies. For example, commercial law was agreed upon by groups of bourgeoisie and their customers, while monetary instruments were free contracts between issuers and holders.[40] In other world areas, by contrast, these systems were mainly dictated by sovereign powers.

4. In northwestern Europe and Japan, lower-ranking corporate groups levered their power by allying themselves with upper-ranking groups. For example, peasants, though intrinsically weak, would swing the balance in a conflict between nobility and royalty, demanding greater power for themselves in return. Vertical alliances with leverage over the centuries constitute the power-diffusion process, which became a principal reason why power is more diffuse in northwestern Europe, its cultural descendants, and Japan than in the less-developed zones today.

5. By vertical negotiation and compromise, the corporate interest groups of Japan and northwestern Europe offered economic benefits to each other. By contrast, in the rest of the world economic "cooperation" was principally forced by elite groups upon politically-weak, unorganized peasants and artisans.

6. Because of all the aforementioned factors, the art of negotiation and compromise grew in both Japan and northwestern Europe, relatively to brute confrontation, stonewalling, and military force. This art facilitated the creation and modification of institutions of economic growth, such as the legal system, the monetary system, trading rules, corporations, and parliamentary democracy.

7. Likewise, endemic warfare gave way to long periods of peace in both societies.[41] Prosperity, economic growth, and institutional change were concentrated in these periods. The concept of taxes by permission of the parliament helped limit endemic warfare. The king could no longer engage in war on his own, and parliament did not always find the king's wars to be to its advantage. Periodic wars—those with clear beginnings and endings—did continue, however.

8. Not only did power become more diffuse over the centuries, but its nature changed. The bases of power shifted away from the military and religion and toward economic and political institutions. For example, over time a king and his army or a priest and his clergy lost power over social action, relative to corporate groups such as labor, the senate, and political lobbies. Personal power came to depend on one's position within such institutions more than on brute force or fear of God.

9. Market freedom was the result of these negotiations conducted through these behavioral norms. In the rest of the world, market freedom either did not evolve or was mandated by authorities and did not last long.

Because of pluralism, vertical alliances, and leverage, lower classes gained greater access to resources in Japan and northwestern Europe than did their counterparts in the rest of the world. They also held their leaders, and each other, more accountable for the efficient use of resources through free-market institutions. This access and freedom, brought about through a *culture* of negotiation and compromise, constitute keys to Japanese and northwest European economic development. North American and Australian/New Zealand development are descended from the northwest European and are not covered separately in this book.

A Warning

None of the propositions in the preceding section is absolute. All are subject to exceptions and mixtures with their opposites. While the power-diffusion process conduces to negotiation and cooperation up and down the social scale, and to peaceful resolution of conflicts, the opposite— confrontation, violence, misunderstanding, and institutional destruction—also are found throughout European and Japanese histories. The violence in inner cities in the United States is an example. Nor is the power-diffusion process totally absent in today's less-developed areas; the verdict is relative only.

In the chapters on Europe and Japan, the power-diffusion process has been explained with a small number of examples. The same number could probably be found for less-developed areas. The difference lies in the fact that hundreds, maybe even thousands, of instances occur in the histories of northwestern Europe and Japan, some of which are found in the appendixes. Very few occur elsewhere. The scholar who wishes to challenge the power-diffusion process may consult the appendixes to examine the relative occurrences. Readers who wish only to understand the process may be content with reading the text.

Relationship to North's Theory of Institutions

Concurrently with the present volume, Douglass North was writing *Institutions, Institutional Change, and Economic Performance* (1990), which covers similar territory. While the two books are complementary, there are significant differences. Page numbers and other parenthetical references in this section refer to North's book.

Elements Common to the Two Books

1. "History matters" (vii). Neoclassical economic theory assumes the existence of institutions of information, contract, enforcement, and others, which allow the economic model to function efficiently. It is deficient in not recognizing alternative patterns of economic intercourse in areas where these institutions do not exist. It also fails to explain how the requisite institutions have been historically shaped.
   2. A major purpose of institutions is to reduce transaction costs.
   3. With minor exceptions, free markets are more efficient than centrally directed institutions. Institutions that tend to equate private with social costs and private with social benefits[42] also tend to be efficient. The question is: "What creates *efficient* institutions?" (137)
   4. We both specify the importance of contract and property in economic institutions.

Elements of North's Theory Not Found in the Present Book

1. North distinguishes between informal and formal institutions, and he deals with theories of enforcement and transaction costs. None of that material is covered in this book. Rather, I agree with North's theses on these points.
   2. In explaining the rise of institutions, North relies on *path dependency*, a concept that he credits to David (1975) and Arthur (1988). Because of some circumstance—geographical, accidental, or other—two societies make slightly different early choices. Each initial choice implies a different choice of the next institution, and so on into increasingly divergent paths. One path may be more efficient than the other, but by the time this efficiency is recognized the marginal cost of changing is greater than the marginal benefit.
   3. "Institutions change, and fundamental changes in relative prices are the most important source of that change" (84). North is right in that such changes bring about new technologies, and these in turn imply dif-

ferent ways for people to deal with each other: advanced communications, for example. While accepting this, I suggest still more important ways by which institutions change, according to the power-diffusion process.

Elements of the Present Book Not Found in North's Theory

1. While not denying the roles of technology and prices, I explain institutional change more importantly in terms of culture, such as the willingness of a people to compromise rather than to confront and to seek peaceful resolution of conflict rather than to choose war as a first resort. North recognizes culture (37, 42), but he does not address the source of cultural differences. The power-diffusion process suggests that they arise largely (though not exclusively) when a society happens into some circumstance in which the dominant group is forced, for its own survival, to negotiate with groups it deems inferior. Repeated practice and the increasing recognition of positive sums cause the two (or more) groups to behave with constraints that become institutionalized. This experience, more than relative prices, technology, or other economic conditions, can explain the difference between northwestern European and Japanese institutions on the one hand and those of the rest of the world on the other.

2. In this book, power is treated as an economic good, with both costs and benefits. It may be a capital good (to produce other goods for the powerholder) or a consumer good (to be enjoyed for its own sake). North also mentions power (21), but he adheres to the idea of *economic* utility/productivity and costs, while I accept *cultural* variables as having their own utility/productivity and cost functions as well. For example, the cost of power includes the mental anguish from losing it.

North illustrates path dependency by contrasting England with Spain in the sixteenth century. England had become a relatively centralized state while Spain was not unified. England had developed a Parliament that reduced rent seeking, while Spain possessed an extravagant bureaucracy, and so on (112-16). For these reasons, each government reacted differently to the common fiscal crisis brought about by widespread warfare. "In [England], it led to the evolution of a polity and economy that solved the fiscal crisis and went on to dominate the Western world. In [Spain], in spite of initially more favorable circumstances, it led to unresolved fiscal crises, bankruptcies, confiscation of assets, and insecure property rights and to three centuries of relative stagnation."[43] So far so good, and I agree with North's path-dependency analysis. But surely

Spain's Philip II (r.1556-1598), with his almost absolute power, could have solved his fiscal crisis through his current institutions *if he had wanted to.* Rather, Philip valued his power over his subjects[44] in Spain, Portugal, and the Netherlands more than he valued fiscal responsibility. He also wanted to humble France and the Ottoman Empire. So he made an *economic* choice between two goods—power and fiscal responsibility—when he could not afford both. To me, this choice, *and Philip's power to make it,* were the major factors in Spain's fiscal crisis and all that followed from it (see chapter 15). With power already more diffuse in England, his rival Elizabeth I (r.1556-1603) did not have to waste resources defending hers.

3. If successful, the power-diffusion process leads, over centuries, to a sufficient balance of power among interest groups, but precisely what constitutes "sufficient" is impossible to quantify or specify. Labor must not be "too" weak vis-à-vis management, exporters not "too" weak vis-à-vis domestic producers, and so on. The diffusion of power has led to a constellation of forces more balanced in northwestern Europe and its cultural descendants and in Japan today than in the rest of the world. This balance holds a relatively efficient institutional structure in its place. North comes closest to this point when (123) he quotes Colson (1974:59): "The communities in which all these people live were governed by a delicate balance of power, always endangered and never to be taken for granted." But he does not show how this balance is obtained or held.

4. North writes: "Third-party enforcement means the development of the state as a coercive force able to monitor property rights and enforce contracts effectively, but *no one at this stage of our knowledge knows how to create such an entity."* (59, italics mine). While no one knows how to command such a state to exist, the power-diffusion process does explain—in part—how northwestern Europe and Japan achieved such a state. Each decision leading toward it was taken for its own specific reasons, and the contract-enforcing state was the serendipitous result.

Conclusion

North's volume is helpful to the present book, for it carries the theory of economic institutions into important areas that I did not touch. I wanted to concentrate on vertical alliances, pluralism, leverage, accountability, and power diffusion.

The principal difference between North's theory and my own is that North has not broken the "economics barrier" and therefore bases his analysis on *economic* goods and services, and their prices and technologies. In the present book, by contrast, cultural artifacts—including power—are deemed to be economic goods. They, too, may be analyzed within the economics matrix. Once these are included, the formation of institutions follows logically, through repeated transactions based on individual perceptions of benefits and costs. The benefits may be selfish or altruistic. The costs may be self-centered or may include social values, such as environmental protection. But benefits and costs must be perceived by each individual separately, while the transactions are negotiated institutionally. All this is complementary to North's path-dependency theory and in no way disputes it.

Why Northwestern Europe? Why Japan?

Why did the power-diffusion process happen only in northwestern Europe and Japan? Throughout this book, I will speculate on any proposition for which no provable reason is apparent. Let us consider two possibilities—land scarcity and relative lack of trade—which may have initiated contract feudalism, the first step in the power-diffusion process in these two areas.

Land Scarcity

In mainstream economic theory, development is promoted by the availability and mobility of factors of production. This book takes a contrasting view, that the relative *lack* of land and the relative *immobility* of labor in the tenth to thirteenth centuries may have helped initiate the power-diffusion process, and hence durable development, in Japan and northwestern Europe.

In the tenth to thirteenth centuries in northwestern Europe and in the sixteenth century in Japan, specific peasants bonded with specific lords[45] for want of alternative land. Each group could not have survived without the other. By negotiating across the social scale, and by requiring accountability of each group to the other, this bonding may have set the power-diffusion process into motion.

In Japan, land was limited by the islands. In northwestern Europe it was scarce because to the north lay cold territory, to the west the ocean, to the south the mountains and settled areas of the Mediterranean, and to the east the Germans. None of these was an impenetrable barrier, but each inhibited migration. By contrast, land stretched in abundance across eastern Europe, China, south Asia, the Middle East, Africa, and the Americas, where vast movements of peoples were possible. Lords who did not agree with peasants could wipe them out or force them to leave, replacing them with serfs or slaves from war. Peasants too severely oppressed would escape or die. Thus only in northwestern Europe and Japan did specific lords and specific peasants stay with each other long enough to form groups and negotiate. I will refer to this phenomenon as "peasants and lords not being able to *escape* each other." Its result was labor by contract instead of slavery. The word "escape" will be used in this sense frequently in the remainder of this book.

The culture of contract facilitated the free market for labor, as opposed to serfdom and slavery. Epstein shows how this came about among urban guilds in Europe.[46] Outside northwestern Europe and Japan, slavery, which was associated with land abundance, continued much longer. Who would be willing to work for another if alternatively one's own land might be free? Unable to hire workers, would-be employers would enslave them by force. The choice probably depended on which was cheaper, free hire or slavery. In the land shortage of northwestern Europe and Japan, free hire was ultimately selected because tenants—in possession of land by their settlement upon it and having some power and minds of their own—became cheaper to hire by contract, or their product cheaper to buy, than either was to seize and control.

While land shortage and one-on-one bonding of peasants and lords appear to me valid reasons for starting the power-diffusion process in northwestern Europe and Japan, they may not be the full explanation. Similar conditions occurred in ancient Rome and Greece, where the same process did not result. Helots (serfs) of Sparta in the fifth century BCE, and their counterparts in other Greek and Roman city-states, also bonded one-on-one with their patrons, and land was in short supply.[47] Spartan patrons and helots also could not escape each other. Yet pluralistic groups and vertical negotiation did not emerge. The major difference that I see is that these ancient patrons had conquered their serfs instead of making agreements with them and were far more cruel— they tortured them routinely—than were medieval Europeans. While violent rebellions occurred in Sparta, they were brutally suppressed, and never were lords and peasants close enough to each other to negotiate. Perhaps Roman lords in the fifth century CE became more humane toward their serfs because they needed each other to defend themselves against a collapsing government that had been tyrannical toward both. I am left thinking that while land shortage is a logical hypothesis partially explaining the start of the power-diffusion process in northwestern Europe and Japan, its fruition depends also on other reasons for establishing vertical trust. This will become more clear in subsequent chapters, on areas where the power-diffusion process was aborted.

The land abundance in early North America and in Australia and New Zealand does not negate this hypothesis, which relates only to the *start* of the power-diffusion process in northwestern Europe and Japan. By the time the Western hemisphere and South Pacific were settled by Europeans, the power-diffusion process was already far advanced for them.

Lack of Trade: The Goodell Thesis

While long-distance trade was prevalent over all the world, the geography of northwestern Europe and Japan was less conducive to it in medieval times than that of the Mediterranean states, the Middle East, or India. In the latter areas, lords escaped bonding with specific peasants. They still needed peasants, but if they killed or drove off one set of them, gold earned directly from trade or from taxing its passage enabled them to survive until they could find another. In northwestern Europe and Japan, by contrast, the scant opportunity for trade forced specific lords and specific peasants to depend more closely on each other. This second cause of lord-peasant bonding is called in this book the "Goodell thesis."[48] Goodell wrote about Persian lords along the silk route, but her thesis would apply elsewhere as well.

Other Reasons for European Economic Development

Speculation on land shortage and the Goodell thesis as possible causes of the power-diffusion process in northwestern Europe and Japan in no way precludes the many other theories of economic development that have been posited for Europe, such as through institutional remnants of the Roman Empire, through preservation of knowledge by monasteries, and through population growth. The purpose of this book is to add to existing thought, not necessarily to replace it.

From Contract Feudalism to the Free Market

Those who minimize the importance of contract feudalism argue that the power gap between peasants and lords was so great and peasants so oppressed that mutual agreements benefited them little. Unequal though these contracts were, they nevertheless started a cumulative process in which contracts became less unequal over the centuries.

But the free market in all goods and services did not come quickly. Indeed, it is far from complete today. As national health programs are instituted in western Europe and North America in the twentieth century, the first thought of virtually all politicians and their constituents has been that governments must manage them. They will only be disabused of this idea if programs fail through lack of accountability, improper management, and power to tax—developments that may require decades to reveal themselves. Production and price controls have remained for many goods and services, even in northwestern Europe, its cultural descendants, and Japan—rent controls and minimum wages, for example. Only over centuries did the idea of a free market spread, and only over future centuries will it evolve further. Always the free market was nobody's first choice; every group preferred a monopoly for its own product or wished to make major decisions alone. Only when monopolies became clearly unavailable to all, and only as the powers of all bargaining groups began to be felt, and only after centuries of negotiation mixed with warfare, did free markets emerge. Product by product, their immediate cause was economic efficiency, which later became explicated in general by Adam Smith.[49]

Notes

1. Braudel 1979:362.
2. Powelson 1988:70-73.
3. Berman 1983:293.
4. Epstein 1991:62.
5. Gilles 1986:113.
6. Epstein 1991:100.
7. Hibbert 1987:21.
8. Bolin 1966:646.
9. Koebner 1966:46.
10. Wilson 1967:537.
11. Other references to economic compromises include those between Edward III and the merchants (Cannon and Griffiths 1988:225); new leaseholding arrangements between innovating landlords and tenants in England in the seventeenth century (Brenner 1985:49); and cooperation among Dutch towns in the seventeenth century (Braudel 1979:180).
12. Hogue 1966:62.
13. Cannon and Griffiths 1988:360.
14. Miller 1987:245.
15. Webber and Wildavsky 1986:180.
16. Nevertheless, the Estates often bargained badly in France, compared to England. Sometimes they gave up the power to approve taxes by approving them in perpetuity. The English parliaments were more cautious. In addition, the French Estates did not meet from 1614 until 1789.
17. Berman 1983:75, citing Stephen White 1978:301-2.
18. Cannon and Griffiths 1988:38.
19. Gilles 1986:123.
20. Barthelemy 1988:416.
21. Hogue 1966:57.
22. Miller 1987:184.
23. Cannon and Griffiths 1988:402.
24. Maitland 1898:56-57, cited in Berman 1983:261.
25. This history is too well known to require repetition here. For a recent, insightful analysis, see Barber 1992, especially Chapter 4.
26. Berman 1983:107.
27. Berman 1983:268.
28. Sicard 1986:181.

29. Holborn 1959:251.
30. Berman 1983:279-80.
31. Shapiro 1983:3.
32. Wilson 1993:191-221.
33. Berman 1983:257.
34. Seward 1987:130.
35. Miller 1987:67.
36. Cannon and Griffiths 1988:389.
37. Robertson 1952:412.
38. To the best of my knowledge, the term *contract feudalism* was first used by Bloch (1961). It has been widely accepted in the literature on feudalism.
39. This statement applies more to England and Germany than to France, more to France than to Japan. But some elements of it were true for all northwestern Europe and Japan. See the appropriate chapters.
40. *Monetary systems* here includes promissory notes, bank currency, and other instruments issued by private persons. The coin of the realm was usually minted by the sovereign, or else private parties could submit their metals for minting, by paying a seignorage fee.
41. This statement applies from the late seventeenth century on for England on its own soil; from the seventeenth century on for Japan, and from 1815 on for continental Europe. I do not count the Crimean War, Franco-Prussian War, and the Balkan wars as endemic.
42. Private costs are those paid for by a producer; social costs are all costs to a society, including private costs plus damage suffered by others than the producer, such as pollution of streams or acid rain. An analogous distinction is made for private and social benefits.
43. North 1990:113.
44. Philip married Elizabeth's predecessor, Queen Mary, neither for love nor to make his economic institutions more efficient. He did so to extend his power.
45. I use *lords* and *peasants* generically. In fact, each group had many subdivisions.
46. Epstein 1991.
47. Grant 1992:85-91.
48. After Goodell 1980, who I believe originated the idea.
49. I do not propose that a free market exists totally anywhere today—all is relative. Indeed, "today" is but one point of historical evolution.

Chapter 6

Law as an Institution of Economic Growth:
Europe Compared with Japan

> Doom very evenly: doom not one doom to the rich, another to the poor; nor doom one to your friend, another to your foe.[1]

Pluralism in law is a feature of the more-developed world. It consists of multiple jurisdictions, relationships among them, appeals, checks and balances, and distinctions between public and private law and among judicial, legislative, and executive functions. This pluralism was crafted over centuries by negotiation and compromises among many interest groups.

In the less-developed world by contrast, law often "belongs" to power groups. Although the organizations of law may be similar to or even copied from those of the West, the institution is not. Power groups make laws by executive decree, manipulate the parliament, interpret and selectively enforce laws according to their interests, and make arrests or seize property and persons without regard to law. This contrast is presented starkly for emphasis. While qualifications and exceptions abound, they are insufficient to devalue the general distinction. In the power-diffusion process, law plays a significant role in the resulting efficiency or inefficiency of economic enterprise.

Law and the Power Group

From medieval times on, European kings might make law but they also had to obey it, at least in principle and often in practice. Henry II of England (r.1154-89) wrote down both the capabilities and the limitations of royal power.[2] Ptolemy of Lucca wrote that "Political rulers are bound by laws and cannot proceed beyond them in the pursuit of justice."[3] Louis XI and Charles VIII of France each "imposed rules upon himself and recognized limits to his power, those limits being the customs of the country."[4]

"The king had to beg and pray, as Maitland put it, for he could not command and punish."[5] John of Salisbury, who protested professional specialization in royal and ecclesiastical bureaucracies, declared in *Policraticus* in the twelfth century that "the military class has general responsibility to maintain laws against abuse by the monarch."[6]

According to Berman, "belief in a 'fundamental law,' to which governments must adhere or risk overthrow as despotisms is characteristically Western."[7] Cannon and Griffiths suggest that it descends from Roman and Christian law, which "served, on the one hand, to develop the power of kings and, on the other, to direct—even to limit—their actions."[8] The church played a major role in curtailing the power of kings. As far back as 390, Ambrose, bishop of Milan, had declared that the emperor is "within and not above the church."[9] It is hard to believe that the precept of a legally-limited monarchy would endure over the centuries if contemporary circumstances did not continually re-inforce it.

This good order has not been perfected anywhere. In the United States, even though President Nixon was forced to resign in 1974, other high-level usurpers or evaders of the law have escaped punishment, when the reputation of a high office—not the officeholder—was thought likely to suffer unduly. The Iran-Contra hearings in the 1980s are an example of this principle.

When a ruling group persistently dictates law in its own interests or flouts it, then—in addition to human suffering—resources are wasted and economic development retarded. Bribery, property seizures, suppression of competition, and diversion of public funds all are characteristic of much of the less-developed world today.

When the power-diffusion process operates, law may first "belong" to power groups, which violate it to their advantage, but the pressure of newly forming groups causes law to have power of its own. It becomes like the institution described on page 7—a balloon being held in position by the breaths of the power groups that sustain it—none being strong enough to alter its course substantially. Ideally, none will destroy the legal system just to win a single case. Finally, as the groups tend toward balance of power, the law tends toward equality for all corporate beings, personal and artificial.

Max Weber presumed that "modern capitalism has need, not only of the technical means of production, but of a calculable legal system and of administration in terms of formal rules."[10] These two needs are mutually re-inforcing. Economic growth may proceed while law is still captured by a power group; for a modern example of this, see chapter 21 on the "Four Dragons." Ultimately, however, an independent law must prevail, or the power-diffusion process will be slowed and economic development delayed.

Law in the Middle Ages

In both northwestern Europe and Japan, early law was of two types. First, it was custom: that which has been done from time immemorial. Customary law kept a society functioning smoothly, settling disputes rather than seeking abstract justice. Decisions, made in the courts of rulers or local authorities, centered on fact-finding and punishment, not around contract and enforcement. Punishment usually required the violator to compensate the victim.

Second, law was promulgated by decrees of those in power, whose primary aim was to maintain their power. This law concentrated on land ownership, taxes, treason, lèse majesté, and other insult to authority. Punishment was brutal, torture, mutilation, and death being common. This was the law that Henry II centralized in England in the twelfth century.

The origins of customs often remain unknown, but presumably they come from some intratribal balance of power and are not determined solely by the chiefs. Cantor writes that Germanic customary law resided in the *Volk*, and that even the chief could not invent laws. British law was derived from the German in this respect.[11] However, because the chiefs and elders administer it and because there is no legal process independent of them, it is reasonable to presume that even customary law "belongs" to the power group.

For a long time Europeans believed law was either "divine" or "natural" or both. Divine law comes direct from God, usually with priests or tribal chief or king as intermediary. Natural law conforms to nature as perceived by people. Over the centuries, law has become more recognized as "positive," or determined by enactment or judicial procedure.

Under the centralization of law by Henry I (r.1100-1135) and his grandson Henry II (r.1154-1189), "the royal government sought to exercise a general supervision over the workings of the local courts [which] remained community courts."[12] The law itself was composed by local officials responsible to the king. Over the centuries, however, this common law of the courts replaced the king's capture of the law.

Likewise on the continent, law originally captured by the king increasingly leaked into the domains of judges and scholars. About 1080, when Italian legal scholars discovered a vast collection of documents from Emperor Justinian, whose code had been published about 534 CE,[13] they were tempted to consider these the long-sought universal law. Law schools sprang up in many cities, the most famous in Bologna in the twelfth century, and "Roman law" thereafter applied in many places.

Philip II of France (r.1180-1223) found himself threatened by this law, which he interpreted as enhancing the power of the Holy Roman (German) emperor. He obtained a papal bull forbidding Roman law in Paris, but increasingly it spread to local jurisdictions.[14] His successors, however, discovered the usefulness of Roman law in centralizing power in the king. By the sixteenth century it was dominant in the south of France, although supplemented by court decrees and customary law. Customary law still dominated in the north.[15] As in England, so in France, law that early on purported to centralize power in the monarchy moved increasingly into the domain of lower-level legists and scholars.

Nor did the studies end with Roman law. In a heroic example of compromise, the jurists reconciled and synthesized Hebrew theology, Greek philosophy, and Roman law into legal systems useful to principalities and emerging nations. All this happened despite the fact that Greek philosophy and Roman law were not acceptable to Hebrew culture, nor Roman law or Hebrew theology to Greek culture, nor Roman culture to Hebrew theology.[16] Into this melting pot they also stirred principles from the customary laws of widely differing European tribes.

Thus, the laws of northwestern Europe originated in a compromise among customary laws of many tribes, plus manorial law, royal law, church law, Roman law, and Greek philosophy. This pluralist origin helped law become a power in its own right, because those who came before any court had a vast array of precedent from which to choose. This complexity in turn made rulers more dependent on jurists, who, adopting professional standards, began to value law as independent doctrine.

As feudalism waned and economic development proceeded, a distinction had to be worked out between public and private law. Today, this line divides administrative and constitutional law on the one hand from laws concerning the rights between private persons on the other. The Romans understood the difference, but Germanic tribes, such as Burgundian, Frank, and Lombard, did not.[17]

The borders between private and public power, possessions, and behavior had all eroded by the Middle Ages. In a document by Charles the Bald in 856, in which the king and several subjects agreed on an undertaking, it is not clear whether the obligations of each were contract or public law, and surely the difference had not occurred to those participating.[18] Europeans of the Middle Ages did make a distinction, however, between the laws of the kingdom and the laws of the family. Presumably the laws of the family would be adjudicated by the *paterfamilias*, supreme within his domicile. Only the community beyond the family was governed by custom. Thus the family rather than the individual was the economic actor, capable of suing and being sued.

The ruler's law was an antagonist, against which the private person defended oneself: "[F]riendships formed a bulwark against 'the law,' which insinuated itself wherever it could, manifesting its power when successful through a symbolism of penetration."[19] This is still the law of the powerful, not yet yielding to a balance of forces.

Two incidents in the early fifteenth century in England illustrate the bending of a general law to suit a particular circumstance. In the first case, Henry IV (r.1399-1413) refused to allow statutes that would make piracy illegal, because to do so would limit the rights of British ships to attack the French, who were supplying his Scottish foes. Henry V (r.1413-22) reversed this stand by demanding statutes to outlaw the piracy that was damaging English trade with Burgundy, with whose duke he was allied in the war against France.[20] Neither Henry expressed a principle against piracy per se. In the second case of expedient law, Henry V, hoping to win the loyalty of "his" subjects in Normandy, introduced sound English currency in place of the debased and uncertain coinage from many parts of France.[21] Thus sound money was a matter of momentary political advantage, not a value in itself. Each Henry, IV and V, used his power to make a decision responding more to the exigency of the moment than to any consistent principle.

Only over subsequent centuries did merchants gain power relative to the king so that laws against piracy and for sound money became institutionalized and universally applicable. By the time of the English civil war in the seventeenth century, the king could no longer legislate to suit his whim. He had to pay some attention to his subjects, albeit not yet to the most humble of them.

Comparison with Japan

Chapter 2 summarizes how, from the first shogun in 1192 until the Meiji Restoration in 1868, power over the law was contested among the shogun, officials such as shugo and jito, ikki (peasant warriors), and later on daimyo (feudal lords) and merchants. Each of these lower groups captured law where it could, ignoring the shogun if it could.

Among the similarities with northwestern Europe is the continuing contest between centralized and local law. The two areas waged this contest in different ways. Whereas feudal law declined with centralization of government in Europe, in Japan it was strengthened, probably because a feudal chief, Yoritomo, overcame the emperor in the thirteenth century, taking power by issuing orders over a domain where his only rights were by military conquest.[22] He then imposed feudal law on local areas at the expense of customary and domain law.[23] In northwestern Europe, by contrast, the kings and lords compromised on power sharing, an exogenous difference (one with no more fundamental explanation), but possibly a reason why European economic development preceded Japanese.

In the thirteenth century, the Hojo family—the power behind the shogun—drew up the Joei formulary as a codification of feudal law.[24] This set forth the duties of local officials and distinguished them from the shogunal court.

Pluralism in Law

"In the West, the competition and cooperation of rival limited jurisdictions not only required each to systematize its law but also gave each the basis for doing so."[25] Each jurisdiction became bound by the laws of the others: a "system of plural jurisdictions."[26]

Legal pluralism was evident in northwestern Europe early in the Middle Ages.[27] King Aethelstan encouraged nobles, clergy, and commoners in London to combine in making city law in the 920s or 930s.[28] The multitude of jurisdictions in the twelfth century forced compromises on which courts accepted which cases. While ecclesiastical courts accepted those where secular law had "failed," nevertheless they voluntarily placed restrictions on their own jurisdiction.[29] Feudal princes, ecclesiastics, and monarchs not only staked out their territories, but they delegated authority to others reporting to them, creating a patchwork of jurisdictions.[30]

From the eleventh to the thirteenth century, however, England and France moved toward centralized government and centralized law. However, this centralization refers to the scope of jurisdiction, not to all lawmaking. From the thirteenth until the seventeenth century, the royal jurisdiction was extended in England, but the law itself was increasingly fashioned by towns, merchants, sellers of land, and financiers, who argued their cases in both town and royal courts. By the early fifteenth century, Parliament was the primary lawgiver for national issues in England (coinage, war, treason, religion, piracy, taxes for the king) while local authorities administered most commercial law and local disputes. Land was adjudicated on both levels. Few statutes were "'officially' sponsored (what today might be called a 'government bill,')"[31] other than requests for taxes to finance the king's war with France.

From the twelfth century on, "legislation and its enforcement came to be a central feature of the monarchy, binding peoples to respect and obey their king's authority . . . [L]aw codes were stressing royal rights, royal justice, and royal control in a monarchy where the balance between the king and the community as the fount of law and the dispenser of justice was being perceptibly altered in favour of the king."[32] Likewise, "Gregory VII [pope 1073-85] asserted for the first time the power of the pope to 'create new law in accordance with the needs of the time.'"[33] This centralization may have been the result of military victories, such as the Norman conquest in England, Philip II's unification of France, and Gregory's struggle against Emperor Henry IV.

In France, the king rarely interfered with customary law of localities before the sixteenth century, but thereafter Louis XIII and XIV extended their authority persistently.[34] Only in the eighteenth century, as France was being swept into the Revolution, did the tendency again turn toward decentralization.

Even as law was being centralized, however, local jurisdictions and interest groups took actions of their own to gain command over certain aspects of it, in particular merchant law. The concept of civil disobedience, peculiar to the West and Japan, may help explain how local initiative came about. In their famous "heresy" of the fourth century, the Donatists declared that no Christian need participate in church ceremonies under an unworthy priest. In the eleventh century reformist Cardinal Humbert found that although the laity should not interfere in affairs of the church, nevertheless no parishioner was required to take sacraments from an immoral priest.[35] Since the king was responsible to the law but there was no court to try him, in the twelfth century Gratian argued that citizens were morally obliged to disobey unjust laws.[36] But if ordinary people could be civilly disobedient, they must have held some power vis-à-vis the church or the king.

Gratian's view was echoed by other scholars, such as Eike von Repgau, Beaumanoir,[37] Thomas Aquinas, Althusius,[38] and Azo.[39] Thomas Becket tested this principle in his dispute with Henry II of England.[40] Mario Salamonio (about 1450-1532) wrote that "the ruler is a contractual partner in the state [like partners in a mercantile venture]; and, if he breaks the law, the state is dissolved—inequality of conditions break up a partnership."[41] All these writers, who viewed the situation as contemporaries, wrote in terms of a *moral* society. Serendipitously, however, they reveal that military vassals, town officials, and others *could* hold the king in check. Passive resistance to taxes was extensive in thirteenth-century England,[42] as it was in the Poujadiste movement in France in the twentieth century.

The medieval concept that the king was subject to his own laws was sorely tried by later kings, both in England and on the continent, but it has never been utterly violated. James I (r.1603-25) agreed that he was subject to the law, but he insisted that he was the judge of his actions. "The obligation to keep within the law was a matter of the king's own conscience, knowing that God would punish any transgressions."[43] Charles I (r.1625-49) "never broke the letter of the law, but his law officers stretched his powers to a point where the letter of the law was far removed from its spirit."[44] During his trial, he said: "If power without law may make laws, I do not know what subject he is in England that can be sure of his life."[45]

By their civil disobedience, men like John Hampden, John Lillburne, Walter Udall, and William Penn "laid the foundations for the English and American law of civil rights and civil liberties."[46] Royal Judge Jenkins and

Presbyterian John Maynard went to the Tower of London in civil disobedience.[47]

In France, the same principles applied despite the recentralization of authority under Louis XIII (r.1610-43) and his successors. Louis and Richelieu avoided relying on the king's absolute authority as much as they could. Even Louis XIV did not conceive of himself as above the law. But the king exercised justice "retained" (*retenue*), or all the powers that he had not specifically delegated.[48] However, "French constitutional ideas were essentially ambiguous. On the one hand, writers [of the seventeenth century] stressed the king's absolute authority to legislate and tax at will, limited only by his obligation to observe the fundamental laws. . . . On the other, it was argued that he should respect France's customs and traditions. . . He should respect the privileges of provinces, towns, courts and other groups."[49]

Not all Western jurists and philosophers agree on the legitimacy of disobedience. Spinoza, for example, wrote that "the individual justly cedes the right of free action, though not of free reason and judgment; no one can act against the authorities without danger to the state . . ."[50]

Comparison with Japan

As in Europe, the Japanese legal system of the thirteenth century conformed to the pluralist society already forming. Each jurisdiction—emperor, court nobility, shogun, sho-en, and temple—had its own courts. As in Europe, it was possible for a plaintiff to move from one to the other. If the lower courts did not give satisfaction, cases could sometimes be appealed upward, to the emperor or—increasingly—to the shogun.

Beginning about the thirteenth century, independent farmers and warriors carved out their own spheres of autonomy outside the sho-en. But the multiplicity of jurisdictions was of a different quality from the European. In northwestern Europe, the law of one jurisdiction was likely to be accepted in another, and jurists made an effort to reconcile them. In Japan, the competition was fierce. Instead of attempting to reconcile different kinds of law, the jurisdictions tried to capture it, each unto itself. By mid-fifteenth century, shogunal law was increasingly ignored.

Yet in Japan, as also in Europe, local law became well developed. The evidence is cited in chapter 2, from authors such as Wigmore and Henderson. In each case, the balance of power was the underlying reason. Also, where Europe began to distinguish private from public law, the fifteenth-century shoguns developed a rough division between civil and criminal law.[51]

As in Europe, civil disobedience occurred in Japan, expressed by the ikki. Bix writes of peasant resistance during the period 1590-1884:

When local officials failed to act in the interests of the majority, or when they were overly enthusiastic in enforcing fief policies of tax exploitation, peasants formed autonomous groups outside their reach. These would threaten to break off the village's relationship to the state, that is, to withhold labor and tribute payments.[52]

In both northwestern Europe and Japan, pluralism and centralization developed side by side, without contradicting each other. The kings of England and France and the shogun of Japan all fine-tuned and intensified their legal systems on their levels, with more distinctions in law and greater specialization in their courts. They all wanted to extend their authority downward. Each of them was stopped by "lesser" authorities, who were also filling out their law and their legal institutions. On the "lower" levels, law was increasingly in the hands of towns, guilds, and other regional organizations, and it was influenced by ikki and other organizers of peasant rebellions. By the seventeenth century in both northwestern Europe and Japan, the boundaries between central and local law had become reasonably clear.

Laws for Production and Trade

From the start towns established their own courts and made their own laws. . . Already in the early towns the rule of law . . . was widely adopted as a constitutional principle. This was partly because the town judge was often appointed by the lord, and townsmen were therefore keen to insist that he give sentence according to their own laws.[53]

In northwestern Europe laws of apprenticeship, hiring and contract, buying and selling, transporting commodities, insurance, property, leasehold, chattels, and borrowing and repayment grew out of medieval court cases and decrees by town patricians and sometimes by the lord. For the most part, however, the lord left town law alone, partly because he did not have the power to influence it and partly because it was not in his interest to do so. So long as the town brought prosperity and taxes to his manor, he was content.

Town patricians and guildmasters composed the rules. Their concerns were to feed the town, which had to survive famines; to produce goods of sufficient quality to sell in available markets at "fair" prices; to create and protect monopolies; and to employ and train labor. These were the precursors to modern legal and economic principles. On the one hand, townspeople conceived of competition negatively, to be avoided; they did not extend equal rights and privileges to all citizens; status was by birth; "fairness" was a concept of the ruling classes; many disputes were settled within the guild to the advantage of the master; and quarrels with neighboring towns were bitter.[54] "Merchants regularly paid fines for breaking every law that concerned their business, and went on as before."[55]

On the other hand, "fair prices" were debated publicly; the concept of the "public good" underlay decisions;[56] some disputes were tried in town courts—outside the guild—with citizen jurors free to decide;[57] courts became more orderly, with written records[58] and judgments based on precedent; and disputes with neighboring towns were often—not always—settled by negotiation, not war.

In France, the decentralization of law was promoted under Henry II when he "created a consular jurisdiction at Toulouse in 1549; this practice would be extended to different trading sites within the kingdom."[59] Judges and consuls were elected by local merchants. In 1673, after consulting other merchants and jurists, a merchant named Savary prepared a merchants' code for France, which simplified rules that up until that time had become entangled in details. This code continued in use for over two centuries, and many of its provisions were adopted in the Commercial Code of 1807, under Napoleon.[60]

Until the eighteenth century, commercial law in England was primarily adjudicated by town courts. Only toward the end of that century had royal courts acquired the expertise to act in "disputes over insurance, bills of exchange, ships' charters, sales contracts, partnership agreements, patents, arbitrations, and other commercial transactions to make English courts and law seem a factor contributing positively to the development of English commerce."[61]

These examples have three elements in common. First, laws on trade and economics were forged by the participants—guilds, towns, merchants, and craftsmen—with the cooperation of the lord of the manor or the king and his bureaucracy. Second, although discriminatory early on, over the centuries the laws tended toward equal treatment of all participants. Third, and most important to the power-diffusion process, the changes were not sudden. Mainly they were negotiated, as hundreds of positive-sum moves, in a free market for institutions. Royal authorities cooperated, but generally they did not dictate.

From Simple Laws to Complex

Compared with later centuries, early medieval law in northwestern Europe and Japan was simple, conforming to the simple nature of the economy. It relied much on "the concept of the good-faith purchaser (whose rights in the goods might exceed those of the seller), symbolic delivery of goods through transfer of documents, implied warranties, the binding character of informal agreements, and joint ventures."[62] Thomas Aquinas spoke of "just purchases, sales and suchlike, without which men cannot live together," as "derived from the law of nature."[63]

Over time, the increasing complexity of the economy had to be matched by complexity in the law. Instead of specifying how to deliver a cow, the law often required "the coordination of an intricate sequence of activities by people far removed from one another in space and time."[64] This complexity was matched by increasing popular knowledge of the law and greater willingness to act upon that knowledge.[65]

These complex forms would have been impossible or grossly inefficient had they been worked out from *tabula rasa* by a central bureaucracy. Only when they were crafted, piece by piece, by those intimately knowledgeable could they sustain complex economic development. Popular knowledge also required successive experiences over time. Both complexity and popular knowledge increased as part of the power-diffusion process, for neither would have been possible under concentrated power.

Comparison with Japan

Chapter 2 described how law was made by Japanese merchants and financiers through village and town agreements that they themselves adjudicated. They appealed to daimyo and shogun only for disputes they could not settle among themselves. While the shogun considered his laws to be supreme, beginning around the fifteenth century he was increasingly unable to enforce them.

Upon unifying the country in the sixteenth century, Hideyoshi opened free trade and made the highways safe for the first time in centuries, under laws to which all were bound.[66] But this centralized law was both partial and transitory. The burst of finance and trade that characterizes the Tokugawa era once more returned commercial lawmaking and dispute settlement to those engaged in manufacture and commerce.

Notes

1. The Laws of King Alfred, ruled England, 871-901, cited in Berman 1983:65. From Webster's dictionary: "Doom: To judge; to estimate or determine as a judge." *Archaic.*
2. Berman 1983:458.
3. *De Regimine Principum*, book 4, chapter 1, cited by Black 1984:80.
4. Maurois 1948:101.

5. Berman 1983:68.
6. Hogue 1966:87.
7. Berman 1963:175.
8. Cannon and Griffiths 1988:34.
9. Ozment 1980:140.
10. Weber 1958:25.
11. Cantor 1993:98.
12. Cantor 1993:316.
13. Berman 1983:121-22.
14. Gilles 1986:72.
15. Miller 1987:37.
16. Berman 1983:3.
17. Rouche 1987:421.
18. Barraclough 1976:96.
19. Duby 1988a:8.
20. Allmand 1992:318.
21. Allmand 1992:319.
22. Asakawa 1933:123-25.
23. Asakawa 1933:112.
24. Hall 1970:92.
25. Berman 1983:224.
26. Berman 1983:292.
27. Sicard 1986:165.
28. Epstein 1991:40.
29. Berman 1983:215, 222-3.
30. Black 1984:51.
31. Allmand 1992:322.
32. Cannon and Griffiths 1988:66.
33. *Dicatus Papae*, chapter 7, quoted by Berman 1983:202.
34. Sicard 1986:165.
35. Cantor 1993:255.
36. Berman 1983:293; Berman 1977:923.
37. Berman 1983:536; Gilles 1986:82.
38. Black 1984:139.
39. Berman 1983:407.
40. Berman 1983:269.
41. Black 1984:85.
42. Webber 1986:179.
43. Miller 1987:32.
44. Miller 1987:119.
45. Cannon and Griffiths 1988:385.
46. Berman 1983:31.
47. Gregg 1961:183,198.
48. Sicard 1986:207.
49. Miller 1987:127.
50. *Theologico-Political Treatise*, chapter 20.

51. Grossberg 1981:8.
52. Bix 1986:xxxii.
53. Black 1984:48.
54. Gregg 1974:91.
55. Tuchman 1984:38.
56. Black 1984:66-70.
57. Epstein 1991:202.
58. Epstein 1991:63.
59. Sicard 1986:220; my translation.
60. Sicard 1986:167.
61. Rosenberg and Birdzell 1986:116.
62. Berman 1983:534.
63. *Summa Theologiae*, Ia IIae, q.95 a.4, cited by Black 1984:35.
64. Haskell 1985:557.
65. Brewer and Styles 1980:15.
66. Takekoshi 1930:544.

Chapter 7
Africa: Trade, Entrepreneurship,
Pluralism, and Leverage

North Africa, the Middle East, India, and China all have led the world at separate times in economic development and science. By the fourteenth century, all these areas—and sub-Saharan Africa as well—were trading vigorously both at home and with the rest of the world. They all exhibited resourceful entrepreneurship, innovative systems of money and corporate enterprise, and capital formation. All therefore possessed the basic requisites for economic development found in conventional theories. Yet by the eighteenth century these same areas had become the most underdeveloped, while northwestern Europe led the world. The next six chapters address the reasons for the turnaround. We start with Africa.

The Early Promise

Trade

Herodotus reported that in 500 BCE horse-drawn chariots were crossing the Sahara from the Fezzan and from southern Morocco.[1] In the eighth century CE the king of Ghana derived a major portion of his revenue from taxes on trade, mainly in gold but also salt.[2] Before the eleventh century, Soninke traders in West Africa were more at home on trade routes than in their agricultural way of life.[3] In the fourteenth century, "Zimbabwe was the political and religious centre of a mighty trading state with connections as far distant as China."[4]

African trading networks prospered on into the period of European influence. "The growth of trade in the seventeenth and eighteenth centuries along the routes leading from the interior [of the Sahel] to the [Atlantic] coast caused the migration of Muslims, traders, and *ulama* (Islamic religious authorities) westward, and the establishment of new Muslim settlements."[5] These routes also converged with a trading network that the Dyula, African forest traders, had developed since the fifteenth century, to connect the Sahara with the southern savanna and seacoast.[6]

In southern Africa in the eighteenth century, "the Tsonga were developing sophisticated entrepreneurial skills and were reaching out to exploit the trading opportunities of an immense arc, from Uteve in the north to the Venda in the Zoutpansberg and the Pedi on the high veld, and southward, through the length of Natal, as far away as the Xhosa."[7] In the early nineteenth century, the Chokwe "established their own long-distance caravan system, with their own routes, carriers and leaders. Once they had launched into the business of carrying, the Chokwe began to rival the old entrepreneurs."[8]

"Hundreds of ad hoc arrangements and adjustments during the eighteenth and nineteenth centuries [in the central Zaire basin] resulted in the complex and diverse commercial institutions observed by the Europeans in the late nineteenth century. [T]rade crossed the boundaries between the inland populations and the river people by two methods: formal markets, and informal ties between individual traders."[9]

Entrepreneurship

Schumpeter (1936), McClelland (1961), Hagen (1962), Gillis et al. (1987:26-28) and many other authors cite entrepreneurship as essential to economic development.[10] All the great movements across African soil were entrepreneurial: the Berbers migrating westward during prehistory, the southward jihads dating from the Almoravid conquests of the eleventh century to the eastward movements of the Fulani and the Sultanate of Sokoto in the nineteenth. So also were the establishment of trade routes spanning the Sahara in two directions and forming an intricate cobweb across central and southern Africa, concentrating on the Zaire and Zambezi Rivers.

Entrepreneurship was vital to the great empires of Ghana, Mali, Songhai, Kongo, Loango, Luba, Lunda, Mwene Matapa, Rozvi, Mozambique, Bunyoro, and Buganda. As they were formed, trade routes were reshaped, tributary states founded, new production initiated, and imperial business houses established. Alliances were made with the Portuguese on both sides of the continent and with the Arabs to the east, leading to trade as far as the Americas and China.

Agricultural innovation also dates to ancient times. Experimentation and innovation occurred in the Ptolemaic period (332-30 BCE) in Egypt, with a tripling of agricultural output in the Fayyum and the introduction of new viticulture.[11] Extension services today might contemplate how quickly the Africans introduced new crops, such as maize and cassava, from the Americas in the seventeenth century, with no outside agency to teach them other than the traders who sold them the seed.[12]

Crops spread rapidly up and down the west coast in the seventeenth century. "The trade in agricultural products [in Zaire] was given impetus by the introduction of cassava, which replaced millet, yams, and plantains as the staple crop in most areas. . . . By 1698 it was the staple food at the Pool [in the Zaire River], and from there it spread upward and inland."[13]

Crops spread even farther, into Luba-Lunda territory in the center. "A leader called Ntatatkwa ascended the fertile Fipa plateau after migrating from Buluba. In a typical charter myth, he and his people are said to have introduced the cultivation of millet, with its need for cooperative labour, and iron working."[14] From middle Africa, American crops spread into the east. The Kalenjins of present-day Kenya adopted "new ideas in agriculture from the peoples to the west. Both maize and tobacco were introduced into the Kalenjin-speaking parts of the western highlands from the Bantu and Luo to the west . . ."[15]

The swell of trading caravans led to the need for foodstuffs along the way. Lacking manpower—for the bulk of their males were off trading—the Nyamwezi introduced slaves to grow crops along their routes from Central Africa in present-day Tanzania to the coast. "The coastmen introduced new foods such as rice, cassava, pawpaw and citrus. Tutsi with large herds of cattle also came in great numbers and settled in various parts of Unyamwezi."[16]

Similar events in what is now southwestern Uganda led to increased specialization in the eighteenth century, with commercial agriculture supplementing subsistence and the appearance of traders and craftspeople. Cloves in Zanzibar and cocoa in Ghana are other examples of entrepreneurial burst. In 1840, Omani *imam* Sayyid Sa'id moved his capital from Oman to Zanzibar. He experimented with several commercial crops and settled on cloves. Setting up forty plantations himself, he persuaded his fellow Arabs to establish even more.[17] Cocoa plantations in Ghana were founded, at the end of the nineteenth century, by two migratory groups, the Adangbe-speaking Shai and Krobo, and the Twi-speaking Akwapim. Hill has documented the migrations,[18] and Hunter has written about their cooperation in determining land-ownership patterns.[19]

Agricultural entrepreneurship continues into our own time. In 1981, Nichodamas Manomano, a Zimbabwean farmer, "with careful cultivation practices that he learned in a course for so-called master farmers . . . raised more than 100 bushels of corn an acre . . . where yields as low as 35 and even 15 bushels an acre are commonplace . . . [H]is output was little short of miraculous."[20]

Nor has entrepreneurship been confined to agriculture. "Increasingly [in the seventeenth and eighteenth centuries] one can discern the impact of individual personalities, technological advances, and intellectual or ideological innovations. [I]ndividuals are known through their exploits and achievements recorded in tradition, or through second-hand reports of foreigners."[21]

A network of trading villages in the Congo from 1500 to 1891 also exemplifies nonagricultural entrepreneurship. Harms[22] shows how the family and labor system adapted to new circumstances such as the slave trade; how younger people formed satellite villages; how financing was obtained; and how long-distance ventures were undertaken by cooperating families. "In response to the expanding regional and international trade, many of the people living along the upper Zaire abandoned fishing as their primary occupation and took up commerce. Many fishing villages became trading centers."[23] Although using canoes instead of sailing ships, shells and copper instead of bank notes, and oral instead of written contracts, nevertheless these joint ventures are reminiscent of Italian city states of the fifteenth century.

Still another example of entrepreneurship is the growth of city-states and Canoe Houses in the Bight of Biafra (modern Nigeria) in the eighteenth and nineteenth centuries. Descent-based families formed themselves into trading societies, radically changing their character by obtaining workers through marriage and slave purchase. Although initially expanded to supply slaves to European traders, these houses traded widely in other commodities as well. Houses combined to form villages, composed of chiefs, elders, age sets, and other political organizations.[24] "The remarkable expansion of the slave trade in the eighteenth century provides a horrific illustration of the rapid response of producers in an underdeveloped economy to price incentives."[25]

Among the Loango in central Africa in the seventeenth century, "the level of locally inspired economic exchanges went far beyond the bounds of a 'subsistence-oriented' trading system. . . . Many of the goods produced required a high degree of entrepreneurial specialization. . . . By the 1660s the Loangans had a well-organized copper-producing enterprise."[26]

In the eighteenth century the Chokwe of eastern Angola created a new trading empire by moving northward into the less sparsely settled Congo basin. There they took up wax production, responding to a thirtyfold increase in demand from Benguela and Luanda. When the Portuguese abolished the royal monopoly of ivory in 1834, the Chokwe produced less wax and hunted more elephants. Investing the proceeds in women slaves, they expanded their agricultural output. Then they diversified into rubber tapping. Once again responding to price signals, they established long-distance caravans for ivory. "In the short space of fifty years the Chokwe had risen from being a small, remote, forest people to being one of the most dynamic economic forces in central Africa."[27]

The Yao of the interior behind Mozambique equaled the Chokwe in a stunning advance during the eighteenth century "by responding immediately and intelligently to the rapidly changing market conditions of the coast, which were at once the source of raw materials of the continent and the provider of exotic goods that were desired by the Yao and other Africans of the interior."[28]

All these examples attest to the entrepreneurial genius of the Africans, indicating that the explanation for African underdevelopment lies elsewhere than in any presumed lack of entrepreneurship. Further historical references to Africa as a trading continent are listed in appendix 7.1.

Aborted Institutions

African progress toward economic development was similar to that of northwestern Europe and Japan in many ways, even before these two areas had come into extensive contact. Trading organizations, corporations and guilds, monetary systems, and law were all forming. Yet none of these institutions reached the complexity of its European or Japanese counterparts.

Money and Credit

In the earliest known times, money and credit instruments were more advanced in Egypt and the Maghrib than in Europe or Japan. In the Ptolemaic period (from 332 until 30 BCE), both private and royal banks in Egypt received money on deposit and paid it out on order; they also traded foreign exchange. Although banks did not lend at interest, much lending occurred outside banks.[29]

Nor did the banking tradition die with the Roman Empire. By the eleventh century, North African banks were issuing credit instruments similar to bills of exchange in Europe, and promissory notes circulated, their value depending on the reputation of the issuer.[30] Mamluk times in Egypt (1250-1517) saw a stable dinar and ample silver coinage.[31] In sub-Saharan Africa, on the other hand, money consisted mainly of cowrie shells, beads, and other natural objects right up until colonial times. In the eighteenth century tribute and debts in some areas were settled in slaves.[32]

The inconvenience of different currencies in different territories was resolved both by exchange houses, operated privately, and by adoption of copper or brass rods as international currencies, like gold in European trade. Birmingham associates the advanced economy of Loango in the eighteenth century with its copper currency,[33] as does Harms with the Upper Zaire region in the nineteenth century.[34]

Africans also used credit. But before the twentieth century and in some places even today, it was usually limited to one's own ethnic group or to people the creditor knew personally.[35] The Fulani would borrow only from others in their lineage,[36] while the Yoruba had a credit union (*esusu*) for deposits and loans.[37] One of the principal functions of secret societies among the Ibo peoples "was to regulate credit and provide sanctions for the recovery of debts. This was very effectively carried out."[38] Muslims also would make loans, for God's wrath would fall upon those who did not repay them.[39] Credit might be extended by Europeans on the Atlantic coast[40] or by Asians on the Indian Ocean coast. Europeans would give "trusts" (credits) to Niger delta kings with which to buy slaves and provisions in the interior.[41] In West Africa, "the large farmers, though sometimes temporarily in debt themselves, stood as creditors at the head of an extensive network of financial relations, and frequently advanced money (usually on a seasonal basis) to the smaller farmers in the locality."[42] Sayyid Sa'id borrowed from Indian financiers to plant his cloves in Zanzibar.[43] Sometimes strong African states would borrow from weaker ones on terms set by the former. For example, Asante leaders borrowed in the Upper Niger in the seventeenth century.[44]

Sub-Saharan African states did not develop promissory notes, paper currency, modern banks, or investment houses, nor did they create money markets and accounting systems to facilitate large-scale capital formation. Furthermore, some societies assigned different currencies to consumption and investment, impeding a flow of resources from one to the other.[45] Why did the history of financial instruments pause before these institutions were created?

Corporations

Guilds—or something similar—arose in both northern and sub-Saharan Africa. They were even known in Ptolemaic Egypt.[46] The idea of a corporate body making decisions and holding assets and liabilities also was understood. "[A] guild could be held corporately liable for default in tax-payments by one of its members."[47] Mabogunje found evidence of a guild system well developed among the Nupe of northern Nigeria around the eighteenth century or earlier that was "in many respects comparable to that of medieval Europe."[48]

The Canoe Houses of the Ibo functioned in some ways like European and Japanese guilds. The head of a house could tax the members. "In political terms he became a member of the King's council—the successor of the village assembly—which decided on internal and external relations. . . . All members belonged directly to the head's trading organization or depended on him for recommendation to European merchants."[49] Old houses spawned new ones. The head of a new house depended on the old house for political status but traded independently.[50]

Age sets, secret societies, and clans have been among the bodies organizing African economic activities. All these have been traditional to peoples spanning the sub-Saharan continent. Like the guilds of Europe and Japan, they were socially integrative, with trading only one of their functions. Age sets of the Mande people and secret societies in eighteenth-century Nigeria "constituted forums for resolving conflicts which arose within the ruling class or at least within the ruling class of a broad ethnic community; they set values for all citizens through educational programmes; and they regulated economic activities."[51]

By the nineteenth century, many trade organizations existed in West Africa, but their influence over prices and competition was slight. Rather, their greater success lay "in representing the interests of their members in negotiating with state authorities, and in helping to enforce regulations regarding weights and measures, and laws governing debt, contract and agency."[52]

Despite these vertical negotiations, these groupings did not grow into trading communities like the East India Company or into modern corporations with limited liability, diversified debt instruments, and shareholdings, nor did they expand into investment banks and stock exchanges.

Why Were These Institutions Aborted?

Before examining why these institutions were aborted, some commonly presumed explanations of economic development or its lack must be set aside: population growth, the nature of trade, and literacy. Others are slavery and colonialism, which will be considered in the next chapter.

Population

According to the demographic theory, population growth spurred Europe's development in the eleventh to thirteenth centuries. Africa's population increased little before the twentieth century. Colin Clark's figures show European population increasing by 23 percent per century during the critical period, 1000 to 1340 CE, while that of Africa went up by only 10 percent per century.[53]

The demographic theory proposes that population growth induced new towns, specialization, and trade in Europe, and that these in turn led to economic development. In Africa, however, new towns, specialization, and trade grew in the absence of strong population growth and without leading to substantial economic development. Since the middle portion exists without either the presumed prerequisite or the presumed effect, the demographic theory is incomplete.

External versus Internal Trade

Other observers point to Europe's external orientation—its explorers and overseas traders—whereas Africa either turned inward or relied on other countries' ships. But Japan did much the same as Africa, at least during the Tokugawa period (1603-1868). Furthermore, no good theory explains why outward trade should be superior to inward. If greater opportunities directed Africans toward trade within Africa, economic development would require them to turn that way.

Literacy

Still other observers have suggested Africa's illiteracy as an impediment to economic development. This proposition requires more insight than is at present possessed on why *any* society becomes literate, such as the ancient Egyptians, Arabs, Romans, Greeks, or Chinese.

Illiteracy might have held sub-Saharan Africans back in their quest for monetary and corporate systems, but their innovativeness in other ways makes it hard to believe that they could not have invented literacy, numeracy, and accounting had they needed them. Nothing in the African systems of trade and finance would suggest any necessity for these inventions. Therefore, they probably did just as well without them, at least until late in the nineteenth century.

Slavery and Colonialism

Many see slavery and colonialism as the reasons for the aborted development of the institutions of economic growth. Surely these disastrous events played their part, as will be discussed in the next chapter. But even before the swell of European slavery and much before colonial conquest, Africans were showing signs of falling behind the powerful economic growth occurring in northwestern Europe.

Failure of the Power-Diffusion Process

The institutions of economic growth—law, money, corporations, wage labor, and the like—may have been aborted because they were handed down as rules or organizations by the centralized state and were not formed primarily through the interaction of many groups at a grass-roots level. For the most part, the state was governor, producer, trader, executive officer, and judge, with no separation of powers. Although local goods were sold on free markets, labor and capital often were stolen or kidnapped when family resources proved insufficient. This occurred whether the state/producer/trader was a small city-state as among the Hausa, or a Canoe House as among the Ibo, or in tribes or clans acting like states, or in great empires with conquered people. The simplicity or complexity of states, the amount of their power, and the size of their bureaucracies correlated mainly with trade. In many cases, the state rose or fell with trade.

"State" in the African context can be much different from the Western concept. Writing about West Africa of the seventeenth to nineteenth centuries, Obayemi distinguishes between mini-states and mega-states. The former are lineages "united to form the community. [They are] characterized by a number of settlements at varying distances from one another distributed all over its territory."[54] The latter are empires established by some groups or clans conquering others.

According to Obayemi, long-distance trade was the principal reason for forming megastates in western Africa, for trade and kingship were "closely linked." Probably "the power of the kings derived in some way or other from their involvement in the development of local and probably also long-distance trade in the area."[55] Usually there was no stipulation against long-distance trading apart from the state, and private trade organizations existed by the nineteenth century. On balance, however, the synthesis of economic organization and the political state has been overwhelming and remains so today.

Almost always the power of the chief of state was primordial; economic advantage was secondary. Security was a principal factor. Unless one carried the magic of the Muslim, it was simply not safe to transport goods long distances without the protection of the state. It is sometimes suggested that chiefs were constrained by tribal custom. While this may be so to some extent and in some places, more frequently their power was overwhelming, their cruelty great, and they themselves defined custom.

> The cruelty of the chiefs is a byword among the Mambwe; they emphasize the power and authority that the chief held over their lives and property in the past . . . [H]is power to take a man's life was his most significant characteristic.[56]

Illustrations of the dominant role of the state in trading are plentiful. Ancient Egypt serves as a prototype:

> The Ptolemaic government [was] one of the most efficiently run and most rigidly hierarchical bureaucracies ever devised; an administrative regime whose *raison d'être* was the enrichment of the monarchy through a highly organized and tightly controlled economy. . . . The administration was staffed by a host of officials and bureaucrats, recording and regulating the activities and obligations of the king's subjects, down to the last detail of the enforced labour which every able-bodied male was forced to perform . . .[57]

When Gray argues that innovative leaders rather than historical determinism influenced the history of seventeenth-century Africa, he lists rulers rather than private citizens as those contributing to economic and technological advance. "Increasingly one can discern the impact of individual personalities, technological advances, and intellectual or ideological innovations. . . . Iyasu I of Ethiopia, Mai Aloma of Bornu, Garcia II of Kongo and Queen Nzinga of Matamba, or Herry from the Cape, are all clearly recognizable."[58]

"States in the Yoruba/Aja group [in the seventeenth and eighteenth centuries] exercised wide powers over money and trade. Having developed a monetary system based on cowries, the state treasury controlled the inflow and circulation of currency. Foreign trade was exclusively under the administration of the central government. . . . Local production and distribution also came to some extent under central control."[59]

"In some parts of Africa the development of long-distance commerce was accompanied by the growth of states to control and regulate trade. In the Zaire basin, however, the micropolities that dotted the area remained largely independent of one another. . . . Each market was under the control of a market chief, usually the inland chief who controlled the land on which the market was held."[60]

In the Mossi states of West Africa, 1500-1800, agricultural "surpluses passed, by various forms of taxation, to the local chiefs, who were able to maintain courts, often small-scale replicas of that of the king, and to equip and train a number of their kin as cavalrymen who could be mobilized in time of war."[61] "In 1600 the *maloango* was a powerful king whose influence extended not only over his own kingdom of Loango, but also over the whole [Atlantic] coast from St. Catherine in the north to the smaller kingdoms of Kakongo and Ngoyo in the south. . . . Internal trade was conducted through the king, whose government collected taxes and used the unconsumed surplus for commercial exchanges."[62]

"Much trade in eighteenth-century southern Africa took place as tribute, conducted by royal embassies:"[63] Trade in the Luba Empire in central Africa in the early nineteenth century was "a vertical exchange, with producers paying a part of their produce in kind to the chief and receiving in return material rewards derived from tributes of others. Such a system did not encourage horizontal trade between producers, and did not lead to the emergence of full time traders. . . . On the other hand, when outside traders established links with Luba leaders, these rulers were immediately in a position to go into business as monopolist entrepreneurs. . . ."[64]

Other illustrations of state dominance in trading abound. Mabogunje writes that lands seized by the Fulani in the twelfth and thirteenth centuries became property of the state. "When the Yoruba/Aja peoples decided that family enterprise was not strong enough to meet the European challenge," he goes on, "they decided on a strong central monarchy."[65] Horton describes how stateless societies evolved into states by rulers co-opting economic resources and enterprise.[66] Wilks and Hopkins both write of ownership of mining by chiefs.[67] Marks and Gray tell how, once the royal court's needs were satisfied in Butua, no one was allowed to industrialize further, possibly to reduce any threat to the ruler. In addition, Rozvi trading expeditions were considered official embassies; only influential persons could participate. Birmingham explains how Lozi and Kongo kings controlled their empires' economic resources.[68] Alpers tells of the concentration of wealth in the ruling Tutsi of Rwanda, with the Hutu becoming little more than serfs. He also explains how Buganda gained its superiority over Bunyoro in the eighteenth century by making trade a royal monopoly.[69] Chanock writes that in Malawi and Zambia in the nineteenth century, "chiefs claimed a control over the right of movement and settlement of persons."[70] According to Marks and Gray, the northern Nguni chiefs monopolized the cattle and ivory trade in the nineteenth century, and the Xhosa chiefs dominated it in their region.[71] Wilks explains that the Asante managed state enterprises.[72] According to Birmingham, in the Lunda Empire in the eighteenth century "control of the country's external economy became a central function of royal authority."[73] Among the Ngonde, according to Alpers, the ruler of the Kyungu dynasty represented all his people in the initial dealings with traders, and from this he increased his economic power by controlling the ivory export trade.[74] Hopkins tells of official traders transacting business for the state in the kingdoms and city states that are now Nigeria.[75] Richmond tells how Mohammed Ali, Ottoman viceroy of Egypt in the early nineteenth century, required that all crops be delivered to the state at prices fixed by it.[76] Unomah and Webster tell how interior rulers in eastern Africa controlled trading movements by protecting them militarily.[77] Marks and Gray explain how slave ownership by Loango chiefs in the nineteenth century led to their control over land and trade. They also describe how the Tswana chief "held supreme religious, judicial, legislative and executive power over his people, and controlled trade." [78] These examples support the generalization that African states have dominated production and trade from early centuries, often to the exclusion of other groups or private enterprise.

Political and military power determined economic strength as much as the other way around. Thus northern African states—Egypt and the Maghrib—were both more powerful and more prosperous than those south of the Sahara. The empires of Ghana, Mali, and Songhai rose and declined with the great trade routes of the Sahara. Ethiopia identifies with the Red Sea trade, while Arab states along the east coast and on Zanzibar depended for their nationhood on trade with India and China. This trade helped form empires in the interior, such as Lunda, Bunyoro, and Buganda, to link with the Indian Ocean as well as with the Atlantic.

The central African forests—Cameroon and its interior, where land was abundant and geographic facilities for trade scant—were the home of stateless peoples, who did not engage much in economic enterprise. Farther south, where the Congo River system linked central Africa with the Atlantic coast, other great trading empires arose: Kongo, Loango, Bobangi, Luba, and Lunda, to mention only some. As the land base narrowed into a cone and the Zambezi and Limpopo rivers offered more transportation, new trading states were formed, such as Zimbabwe, Mwene Matapa, Butua, Rozvi, and Mozambique.

The link between trade and state must not be overstated. Sometimes trade tended to break states apart rather than glue them together. For example, the Kanuri Empire, "ruled by kings of international fame . . . rested on an unstable balance between centralizing and disintegrating forces."[79] It broke down in civil war.

Laroui even argues that "throughout the history of the Maghrib, maritime trade, though often regarded as a mark of prosperity, has gone hand in hand with a *weakening* of political authority"[80] (italics mine). This undocumented statement—even if true for the Maghrib—does not represent the generality for *non*maritime trade in the rest of Africa.

While statehood in England, France, the German princedoms, and Japan also depended on trade, the very identities of these countries, their nationalities, and their geographies, were not as intimately tied to international trade as were those of the African states. Independent traders in Europe and Japan arose as a counterpoise to the state.

Reasons for the Failure of Power Diffusion

The state's central role in trade, along with its primordial concern for power and security, stifled diffusion of power in Africa and retarded economic development for the following reasons.

First, no effective way existed to transfer land and other physical property from less efficient to more efficient uses. Sovereignty was not distinct from land ownership. Alienation of land to individuals within the tribe usually required the chief's permission. Outside the polity it would have been an unthinkable cession of sovereignty.

Second, no independent labor market developed. Since the productive power of people was oriented toward the state, no need existed for a free labor market. Slavery and marriage were employed to move labor from areas of its abundance to those where it would be more productive. Neither is an efficient means of allocating labor.

Third, no easy way existed to tell when consumer preferences changed. Goods to be consumed were supplied mostly by domestic agriculture and what the chief decided to import. Therefore, changing utilities, including propensity to invest, could be stifled.

Fourth, not enough independent groups formed to challenge the authorities and to compete with them. Without such challenge and negotiation, the cultural *capability* to negotiate and compromise on economic matters did not mature enough to lead to complex economic ventures. While Africans were very good at compromise within their clan and other small circles, they did not extend this facility to wider economic circles.

Fifth, for all the aforementioned reasons, traders did not ordinarily write modern contracts, did not have the markets in which to fulfill them or the law courts to enforce them, and did not trust each other sufficiently to want to engage in these activities.

Sixth, confrontation and war became the principal means of "resolving" disputes; the term is in quotation marks because—as Bozeman suggests[81]—disputes were not expected to be resolved in a Western sense. They might only be contained, indefinitely.

The foregoing assertions raise more questions, even more controversy, than they solve, because they are all relative. Central authority did have its offsets, such as a titled nobility or tributary groups far enough removed to act independently, or the inability of the government to control all behavior. Nevertheless, these propositions reflect the overwhelming generality about most of Africa for most of known history before colonialism. Further historical references to African state domination over trade, land, and other resources are listed in appendix 7.2.

Power and Leverage

Two reasons for the state's strong power over production and trade may be advanced. Both are speculative. First, in the wide open spaces of Africa, until the twentieth century peoples enjoyed both long-term migrations and short-term escapes from each other. Second, following the Goodell thesis mentioned in chapter 5, through widespread trade which they controlled, chiefs became so wealthy that they did not have to negotiate with their subjects.

Not until the late nineteenth or the twentieth century did most Africans encounter the land shortage that elsewhere had forced cooperation across cultures or groups whose survival was otherwise threatened. Although some

African societies developed a sort of vassalage, no contract feudalism like that of Japan and Europe emerged, and few vertical alliances were formed. Institutions of trust, such as financial, monetary, and legal systems, were aborted, partly because no further advances were needed for the types of commerce in which Africans were engaged and partly because the essential culture of negotiation had not been sufficiently developed.

While evidence of some incipient pluralism with the possibility of leverage has been found, such instances do not slide off the pages of African histories as voluminously as they do from those of northwestern Europe and Japan. Nevertheless, the scant evidence must be examined to see why a crucial threshold was not reached, to put the power-diffusion process into motion.

In Egypt of the first century CE, "counteractive institutions and practices developed—alternative authorities strong enough to force the government to encourage co-operation rather than to coerce. Such strength, of course, needed an economic base; . . . the church had such a base, both in totality and in its constituent parts, particularly the monasteries which are excellent examples of such institutions offering protection to their inmates."[82] This leverage might have improved the balance of power between church and monarchy, in the direction of pluralism, had not Egyptian institutions later been compromised by anarchy throughout the Roman Empire, including Egypt.

Wolfe writes that "the maintenance of power [in North Africa in the fourteenth century] depended on keeping control of the region through its elite, and on effective alliances with pastoral groups able to defend the caravan routes and oases in the hinterland. Contesting control meant forming alliances with disaffected tribal segments and enlisting the cooperation of disgruntled urban merchants and artisans."[83] Instead of gradually enhancing their status through such vertical alliances, however, the "disgruntled" sectors bided their time until they could seize power for themselves. With insufficient stability in the central government, the power-diffusion process was not at work.

In the sixteenth century, Portuguese traders settling in the Kongo formed vertical alliances to play off the interests of Kongo and Portugal, alternatively. But they seem merely to have retained their status rather than enhancing it through leverage.[84]

In Dahomey, Oyo, and Benin in the eighteenth century, power was diversified with checks and balances upon each authority. "The *olu* of Warri boasted of his independence from the *oba* of Benin, but his own power was limited by that of three nobles. . . . [T]here was competition for place and power among the various dignitaries, . . . the power of the *oba* was whittled down relative to that of the collective nobility, the titled elite interposed between the *oba* and the rest of his subjects.[85] Since this kind of pluralism is reminiscent of northwestern Europe and Japan, why did subject groups, such as slaves and common freemen, not offer their support to the nobility or the *oba* or the *olu* in their conflicts with each other, in exchange for greater privilege? In the absence of any evidence that this occurred, one can only speculate either that the elite groups in competition were sufficiently united in their subjection of lower classes or that the lower classes sensed too low a probability of success, especially if they should ally themselves with the losing group.

Birmingham writes how "the economic and political growth of Luba began to weaken" about 1870, with "constant feuding between royal factions."[86] One may question why lower classes did not take advantage of these divisions to make vertical alliances. Possibly successful leverage requires alliances with relatively stable stronger groups; otherwise, the risk of losing is too great. By this time, Luba was not a stable society.

The failure of economic development may ultimately lie in geography, especially the greater availability of land in Africa. The high fluidity of interest groups, and indeed of whole societies in Africa, was not conducive to vertical alliances with leverage. Migrations, state formation and dissolution, capture and enslavement, the quick rise and fall of states, new empires and their breakup, all impeded the essential stability, in contrast to northwestern Europe and Japan. Thus, circumstances did not force Africans to negotiate and compromise beyond the clan or tribe. As a result, the power-diffusion process did not occur, and the requisite institutions for durable economic development did not take root.

Notes

1. EBMa 1974:19:762.
2. EBMa 1974:19:761.
3. Levtzion 1976:146.
4. Barraclough 1984:166.
5. Levtzion 1975:218.
6. Levtzion 1975:182.
7. Marks and Gray 1975:408.
8. Birmingham 1976:237.
9. Harms 1981:71-72.
10. Schumpeter 1936; McClelland 1961; Hagen 1962; Gillis et al 1987:26-28, and many more.
11. Bowman 1986:101.
12. Gray 1975:8.
13. Harms 1981:52.
14. Alpers 1975:500.
15. Alpers 1975:494.
16. Unomah and Webster 1976:297.
17. Unomah and Webster 1976:273-76.
18. Hill 1959:14-28.

19. Hunter 1972:85-109.
20. Lelyveld, in *New York Times*, 10/10/1981.
21. Gray 1975:8.
22. Harms 1981. Harms is an anthropologist who lived among the Bobangi, collecting his evidence from whatever written or archaeological records existed, but largely by oral history, not only among the Bobangi but also among fishermen from other tribes.
23. Harms 1981:5.
24. Rodney 1975:261.
25. Hopkins 1973:105.
26. Birmingham 1975:345-46.
27. Birmingham 1976:238.
28. Alpers 1975:525.
29. Bowman 1986:113.
30. Udovitch 1979:268-70.
31. Lewis 1988:188.
32. Fisher 1975:101.
33. Birmingham 1975:345.
34. Harms 1981:85.
35. Hopkins 1973:64.
36. Horton 1976:99.
37. EBMi 1974:10:829.
38. Rodney 1975:264.
39. Hopkins 1973:64.
40. Hopkins 1973:109.
41. Alagoa 1976:359.
42. Hopkins 1973:239.
43. Unomah and Webster 1976:285-7.
44. Rodney 1975:324.
45. Harms 1981:165.
46. Bowman 1986:110-11.
47. Bowman 1986:112.
48. Mabogunje 1976:24.
49. Alagoa 1976:343.
50. Rodney 1975:261.
51. Rodney 1975:280.
52. Hopkins 1973:57.
53. Clark 1968:64.
54. Obayemi 1976:205.
55. Obayemi 1976:258.
56. Watson 1958:161, cited in Chanock 1985:33.
57. Bowman 1986:56.
58. Gray 1975:8.
59. Rodney 1975:239.
60. Harms 1981:71-73.
61. Wilks 1976:421.
62. Birmingham 1975:348.
63. Marks and Gray 1975:403.

64. Birmingham 1976:250.
65. Mabogunje 1976:27.
66. Horton 1976.
67. Wilks 1976:427; Hopkins 1973:47.
68. Birmingham 1975:381, who cites Mainga 1973.
69. Alpers 1975:478-81.
70. Chanock 1985:168.
71. Marks and Gray 1975:438.
72. Wilks 1976:449.
73. Birmingham 1975:372.
74. Alpers 1975:514.
75. Hopkins 1973:62.
76. Richmond 1977:63.
77. Unomah and Webster 1976:303.
78. Marks and Gray 1975:417.
79. Abdullahi Smith 1976:171.
80. Laroui 1977:187.
81. Bozeman 1976.
82. Bowman 1986:86.
83. Wolf 1982:38.
84. Birmingham 1975:331.
85. Rodney 1975:240.
86. Birmingham 1976:251-52.

Chapter 8
Africa: Warfare, Slavery, Colonialism, and Law

War and Violence

> But fundamentally it was endemic war, waged for millennia in all parts
> of the [African] continent, that set the norm of the territorial fluid state.
> ... [W]ar itself and preparation for war summed up the purpose of the
> masculine life.[1]

This same quotation would have applied to northwestern Europe or Japan in
the Middle Ages, for war was a legitimate means of resolving conflicts in both
those areas. The change in Europe was gradual: conflict resolution was transferred over centuries from the military to the courts, bargaining tables, and
embassies. It is hard to tell how the legitimacy shifted in Japan, for peace was
suddenly imposed by Tokugawa Ieyasu after the Battle of Sekigahara in 1600.

"Legitimacy" means that war or other violence is an ordinary way to
resolve conflicts, as acceptable as collective bargaining or the courts. Legitimacy is displayed in two ways: by repetition—war continues for decades or
even centuries—and by ease of initiation—whether war is a first resort or a
last one. A modern example is the street gangs in American cities that appear
to accept violence as a legitimate first-resort means of winning conflicts.

In Africa, inter-societal war was a first-resort means of resolving conflicts outside the family or clan, until peace was imposed by colonial powers
in the latter part of the nineteenth century. Violent force was the weapon of
choice to gain labor (by enslavement) and capital (cattle). While peaceful
transactions may have taken hold in some places after independence in the
1960s, in others the tradition of legitimate violence has returned.[2]

The Universality of War and Violence

That war was almost continuous in North Africa from the seventh to fifteenth
centuries is no surprise, for it was then endemic to the entire world. Examples
of long-term hostilities include the Arab sweep across the Maghrib and on
into Spain; the conflict of the Kharijite Movement in the eighth century;[3] the
violent struggles for power among North African states and tribes in the tenth
and succeeding centuries;[4] wars between the Fatimids and the Umayyads in
Egypt in the eleventh century;[5] the military conquests of the Almohad and

Almoravid Empires in the eleventh and twelfth centuries;[6] and the beginnings of the jihads that in ensuing centuries swept down the west coast of Africa.

The historical record of war becomes more extensive in the sixteenth century. By demolishing the Songhai Empire in 1591, the Moroccans added a hostile force that intensified the turmoil in Jenne, Timbuktu, and other trading centers.[7] Songhai already had been weakened by civil wars earlier in the century, arising out of nepotism and succession disputes.[8] Kano and Katsina, city states in what is now Nigeria, had their first recorded war in the second half of the fifteenth century; wars between them continued throughout the sixteenth.[9] In Bornu (now eastern Nigeria and Chad) Idris Aloma was expanding southward into Mandara, Bagirmi, and Kwararafa, destabilizing regimes by shifting support for rival candidates.[10] In the Niger delta, communities initiated drum praise names to show their approval of piracy, head-hunting, and slave raids.[11] Beset by succession disputes, the Mwene Matapa dynasty in south-central Africa both raided and was raided by its neighbors.[12] "The seventeenth century was, par excellence, a century of warfare for western Hausaland. It had also been a century of rapid power build-up."[13] Tubu and Tuareg nomads raided trans-Saharan trade, and Tuareg and Bornu fought repeatedly.[14] Nasr al-Din, leader of the Zawaya, launched extensive jihads in 1673, attacking the Hasan to the south.[15] He dislodged and incited the Torodbe and the Fulani, who both continued the jihads southward and eastward. Peaceful when they could trade manure with local people for supplies, the Fulani waged war under other circumstances. By the end of the eighteenth century they had overthrown most Hausa states and were threatening Mandara, Bagirmi, and Bornu.[16] In Hausaland, "frequent wars [led] either to a stalemate or very transient dominance of one state over another."[17] "In Oyo's sphere, military encounters persisted throughout the seventeenth and eighteenth centuries."[18]

Farther south, the revolt of Sohio against Kongo and the Angola (Portuguese)-Kongo wars, which lasted fifty years, led to the end of the Kongo monarchy in 1655.[19] At the southern end of the continent, Nguni chiefly families split into rival lineages, which sometimes negotiated their differences peacefully but more often went to war.[20]

Toward the east, Arab states were frequently in conflict with Portuguese and Turks in the seventeenth century. No sooner had the Portuguese been forced out of Mombasa in 1698 than a series of internecine wars erupted among Arab rivals.[21] In the interior, Buganda conquered her neighbors over a two-century period but then was afflicted by wars of succession that coincided with rebellions of tributary states.[22] Farther east, Kikuyu, Kalenjin, and Masai engaged in frequent warfare and traded cattle raids. "[T]he dealings between the Masai and their neighbours varied from chronic warfare to peaceful market contacts and inter-marriage."[23] In Ethiopia the Galla attacked the Gondar

Empire from all directions, and other wars broke out in the eighteenth century.[24] In Madagascar "war took place between clans, and, more frequently, between kingdoms; there were frequent periods of insecurity."[25]

The nineteenth century opened upon continuous warfare. "Civil wars, anarchy, perpetual robbery and violence lasted for over a century"[26] in Fouta Djallon (modern Guinea and Sierra Leone). "In Morocco there were many succession struggles, and "revolt can almost be described as endemic."[27] "[T]he jihad movements engulfed the whole breadth of the Sudan."[28] Mohammed Ali of Egypt set about to conquer Palestine and Syria, with wars from 1811 until the European powers stopped him in 1841. In Ethiopia, the "era of the princes" (*Zamana Mesafent*) led to decades of disorder. "Kings were enthroned and dethroned at the whims of governors, who fought among themselves for the position of *ras* of the kingdom. . . ."[29] Inter-personal offenses, strictly punished, could result in warfare among clans. In Malawi, "an offence resulted in 'nothing more or less than war or death of the criminal,' fighting could take place between relatives, and slaves exchanged as compensation."[30] In Lunda, "the empire had constant difficulty in defending its northern border, which never lay far from the *mwata yamvo*'s capital."[31] Among the Zulu, "service in the age-regiments and participation in actual warfare served as the *rite de passage*, marking the transition from adolescence to adulthood."[32] In approximately 1820, King Shaka of the Zulus launched a devastating series of wars, known as the *mfecane*, whose domino effects displaced tribes as far north as Lake Victoria.

War as Inhibitor of Institutions of Trust

Quite apart from the destruction of human and physical capital, war inhibits economic development because it displaces peaceful ways to resolve conflicts and to form institutions of trust. The references cited in footnote 2 tell of immense human suffering as societies were weakened or destroyed. But that is not all. The society itself is the framework within which institutions of trust are created. Councils of chiefs *did* resolve some internal conflicts and might have evolved into modern parliaments, but if these councils are destroyed along with the society they cannot become mediators for more intricate questions of business contracts.

References to the destruction of whole societies in Africa are legion. Formed in the thirteenth century, the Kanuri Empire, "ruled by kings of international fame," was brought down by wars lasting throughout the fourteenth century. A "rapid succession of rulers" and "disregard of proper succession procedures"[33] do not create a stable background for bargaining over economic privileges. "The period [1600-1790] witnessed the decline or temporary eclipse of most of the major states first encountered by the Portuguese: Benin, Kongo, Ndongo, Matapa, and Ethiopia. But against these . . . there were many other examples of growth."[34]

When such instability prevails, gaining wealth by loot may be less costly than by economic enterprise, when the risks of each are taken into account. The conquest of the western Sudan by the sultan of Morocco in 1591 was "envisaged from the start as a source of taxes and loot—taxation of the salt mines and control of the gold mines."[35] Alternative ways to prosperity— agriculture and crafts at home and Mediterranean trade—were less appealing. When his venture failed over the ensuing decades, the sultan's state collapsed. Likewise, in the sixteenth century, "the mai's [Idris Aloma of Bornu] revenue was obtained solely from the booty of his campaigns, the most important commodity being captives whom he could barter for horses with the North African merchants."[36]

When the institutions of economic development are not integral to the culture, their appearance in fledgling form is weak. In the Upper Zaire basin in the eighteenth century, family enterprises would grow, but often the younger generation, wanting to "break free from the master's control were opposed by military might."[37] A developing society must be sufficiently fluid so that enterprises adapt and sometimes split, but it must also be sufficiently cohesive that they do not do so as a regular working process. The example from Zaire reflects a failure of cohesiveness: stability imposed by force, hardly a situation favoring the nurture of institutions of trust.

In Malawi and Zambia during the late nineteenth century, Chanock emphasizes "not state building and proto-modern institutions with law and judging as an essential feature, but localism, parochialism, lack of government, arbitrary alteration of status, violence between and within communities, as well as bargaining and local consensual arbitration.[38]

From all these examples, one might suppose that for centuries Africa was so swept up in warfare and violence that it would be impossible for normal polities and economies to function. Yet we have seen that Africans showed high entrepreneurial skills and engaged in extensive, long-distance trade. Two possible explanations occur to me:

First, despite endemic warfare, there were long periods of peace in particular places. For example, "the century before 1875 was marked by conspicuous stability in the heart of Central Africa, and by long uninterrupted reigns at the courts of the Lunda kings. . . ."[39]

Second, and probably more meaningful, because the legitimacy of warfare puts it on a par with collective bargaining and modern courts in more industrialized areas, like these it was written into the calculations of risk and enterprise. By occupying the place of negotiation, compromise, and contract, warfare in Africa made those methods seem less necessary. However, the trans-action cost of warfare must have been ultimately greater than that of negotia-tion.

Warfare can resolve only simple conflicts, such as over territory, suc-cession, trade routes, and rights to industry. By conquering, one cannot force others to become partners in great trading companies, to join in contracts, to allocate capital efficiently, to give and receive promissory notes, to issue trust-worthy money or bank accounts, to acquire financing from distant places, or to cooperate in inventions and research. By continuing to rely on warfare to resolve conflicts, Africans approached a dead end. Economic development lay on a different path, which they had not taken. This is an example of North's path dependency theory. [40]

Slavery and the Labor System

> "Slavery" in Africa is simply one part of a continuum of relations which at one end are part of the realm of kinship and at the other involve using persons as chattels. "Slavery" is a combination of elements, which if differently combined—an ingredient added here or subtracted there— might become adoption, marriage, parentage, obligations to kinsmen, clientship and so forth.[41]

The complexity of slavery is matched by the complexity of the free market in labor. There are degrees of slavery, which shade into family labor and free labor.

Despite the vagueness of boundaries between them, some labor sys-tems have nevertheless been mainly free and others mainly slave. Why? With professional ethnocentrism, economists have tended to reason that the choice was made by weighing benefits and costs based on relative scarcity of factors of production. Amplifying a model applied to Russia by Kliuchevsky, Domar hypothesized that a high land/labor ratio would bias a society toward slavery, provided a government would enforce the system. If land were free, then free men would find their own farms. Only by government-enforced slavery would large owners acquire labor.[42]

An abundance of land is part of the reason for slavery. By confining himself to Europe and America with their relatively stable governments, how-ever, Domar did not ask why slavery occurred in stateless societies in Africa. He also presumed there were owners of specific pieces of land, without con-sidering migratory societies in which land is held in common and holdings "migrate" with the society. Nor did he inquire why landowners unable to hire labor because of the abundance of land might not use the market to obtain what they needed from free farmers, instead of slavery to make those same farmers produce it.

The answer does not lie solely in relative availabilities of land and labor. Rather, in fifteenth-century Russia, as in tenth-century Europe and Japan and eighteenth-century Africa, strong people forced the weak to provide their sustenance, in exchange for defending the weak against other strong people who would have done the same to them. Since the Russian landowners had nothing to offer free farmers except this "protection," the alternative to slavery was surely not a free market at all. Instead, after "free" peasants had grown their food, the czar's henchmen might have taken what they wanted rather than buy it. The results of free farming and slavery would have been the same.

Loss of population in the American slave trade, cruel and destructive as it was, probably did not inhibit Africa's economic development over the long term. The resurgence of European population after the Black Plague (1348), which wiped out a quarter of the people within five years, and the Thirty Years' War (1618-48), which killed up to fifty per cent of the population in some parts of Germany, demonstrate the ability of peoples to overcome such tragic losses and to revive economic activity. Both Clark (1968:64) and Hopkins (1973:121-2) estimate that the slave trade merely offset the natural increase in population. Curtin (1969) shows that it deprived Africa of much less labor than had previously been thought.

The dislocation rather than loss of populations, the warfare to capture slaves, and interference with other kinds of trade were the major sources of economic harm. Slavery inhibits efficient allocation of resources by melding labor to land and capital. Laborers move only to occupations more attractive to their owners, not to themselves. Therefore this movement responds to the productivity of land and capital, not of labor. All these effects were already in process before the Europeans initiated the American slave trade.

Slavery did not immediately end in Africa when colonial authorities gave the command. Only when a cash market for many products, including wage labor, appeared attractive to large numbers of people did it become increasingly difficult for slave owners to keep their labor. Since these owners did not see an immediate benefit to themselves, they resisted cash markets and gave in only when they had no other choice.

Whether slavery is *economically* efficient—a question much debated among Western economists—is irrelevant here. The very existence of slavery, with its relationship to warfare, violence, and confrontation, has inhibited the growth of complex institutions of economic development. In this broader sense it is inefficient, regardless of benefit-cost calculations for plantations in the ante-bellum U.S. South.[43]

In sum, slavery is historically the normal system for acquiring labor in all early societies, including European, Japanese, and African. The question is not so much why the Africans retained it as it is why the Europeans and Japanese gave it up. Because of its inefficiency, the retention of slavery by Africans is another element explaining their retarded economic growth. Further references on slavery as a labor system appear in appendix 8.1. References on the transition from slavery to cash labor are in appendix 8.2.

Colonialism

Conventionally, the debate over colonialism centers on three issues. First, did the colonial powers seize more assets, such as land, than they supplied, such as infrastructure, credits, and other benefits? Second, did they pay fair prices for primary products purchased? Or, by seizure and unfair prices, did they decapitalize Africa? Third, did they discriminate against Africans, refusing them access to markets and resources available to Europeans?

The historical facts are well known, and the debate is increasingly sterile. The colonial powers did indeed seize land. Whether they supplied equivalent assets will be questioned forever. They paid for their primary products, usually with market prices, but whether these were "fair" will never be resolved. They did not decapitalize Africa, but they did discriminate, refusing Africans access to resources available to Europeans.

Whatever the impact of these events, they do not explain continued poverty in Africa today. Except in South Africa, the land was restored decades ago, and if colonial-style discrimination has not vanished by now it is because present-day forces keep it alive.

But colonialism had another impact, more serious, more negative, and more longlasting. It displaced African groups that might have learned to negotiate, compromise, and contract with each other, imposing conflict resolution through its own organizations. It removed some prerogatives from chiefs while granting them others greater than those chiefs had ever known. Although power concentration was already endemic, colonialism strengthened it, making it harder to overcome in the postcolonial period.[44]

By the tenets of Western economics, the old African ways were inferior to the colonial set. Neither war nor the melding of land and labor through slavery nor beads as money nor economic decisions by chiefs is an efficient way to conduct an economy. Land registers, free markets, commercial and central banking, and Western law are much superior. What the colonial powers did not understand, however, was that land registers and law courts and central banks and parliaments are *organizations*, not institutions, and an institution cannot be imposed from outside.

But even worse, whatever progress Africans might have been making in the direction of appropriate institutions was cut off. This is illustrated in the following subsections, where the colonialist governments' handling of land tenure, the monetary system, and public administration are considered. Law will be treated in the next major section.

Land Tenure

While the boundaries of European countries had been determined over centuries by war, negotiation, compromise, and treaty, Europeans drew those of Africa in one fell swoop in Berlin in 1884-85, with no African participation. They cut boundaries down the middles of tribal territories, thus setting up irredentist wars that continue today. They set up power statuses among Africans that tend today to perpetuate the very wars the Europeans were trying to end.

Europeans imposed upon Africans the distinction between sovereignty and ownership of land. In virtually all the colonies where they settled as farmers, Europeans declared themselves landowners by the legal instruments of their own governments. Vicious as these seizures were, they may have been no more so than earlier seizures by other Africans. But there was a major difference. Before colonialism, land taken by conquest could be regained by conquest. With colonialism, however, the military power of the conqueror was so great that seizure was "final." Thereafter, land transactions would be settled by the laws of the conquerors,[45] at least until independence in the 1960s.

In an earlier publication, I have outlined traditional African land systems, with examples from different peoples.[46] These systems differed greatly among tribes and nations, some with provision for "migrating" land (land patterns that remained the same, each piece relative to the others, as the tribes moved), some with maternal and some with paternal inheritance, some with maternal inheritance but husband control, and so on. Bohannan has described spatial concepts of land tenure that are strange to a person of Western orientation.[47] Usually a tribal chief would assign land to families, who would live in compounds, a man and a hut for each of his wives. The chief might allocate land to strangers who had come to live in the village, or he might periodically reallocate land among families according to need.

Maximum economic development requires that these customary features change to fee-simple ownership and free alienation, so that land may move to its most efficient uses.[48] In many African states, therefore, land tenure was changed to fee-simple ownership, partly by the colonial powers and partly by the successor independent governments.

But the Western ethic that land use should be determined by the farmer, not the chief, is not widely accepted in Africa. Many chiefs, now become political officers, took much land for themselves. Some land was put into state-sponsored "cooperatives," which facilitated state control.

Could African land tenure have evolved otherwise? (The "might-have-beens" of history are treacherous, but sometimes unavoidable.) The essential groups were already in place, which might have allied themselves with each other to bargain with chiefs over land use: clans and families, age sets among warriors, village elders, nobility in some societies, neighboring villages, or even nations. Ownership is a bundle of rights over cultivation, enjoyment of product, taxation, marketing, and the like, which might have been negotiated piecemeal or in differing combinations. All this was cut off by colonialism. Because European governments endorsed the sovereignty of chiefs, when in fact many checks and balances had been developed by the Africans (see Powelson 1988), colonialism left the African state and its rulers with much greater power over land than they had previously held. In the next chapter I will show how this concentration of power has impeded current economic development.

The Monetary System

Credit systems existed in pre-colonial times. But instead of linking with these systems, the colonial powers started from scratch, as if none of them existed. Branches of foreign banks, and the home-country central bank, were employed. Transfers, even between neighboring African countries, passed via London or Paris, often requiring weeks in transit. Usually Africans did not use these banks, not because they were legally barred but because access was made difficult. A recommendation from a "reliable person" may have been necessary to open an account. In Egypt, an indigenous private bank for industrial and commercial development was established in 1920,[49] but it was an exception, and it did not function in sub-Saharan Africa.

A new currency was introduced—rupee in East Africa, franc in French territories. The old currency—beads or copper bars or shells or whatever—was not recognized by the colonial powers and could not be exchanged for the new. A common way to introduce the new was to impose a hut tax payable only in currency, then to offer Africans cash jobs to earn the money to pay it.[50] New stores with new goods tempted them to want the new money. The old currencies died out, and holders lost their value.

Nothing prevented the Africans from using traditional lines of credit, however, whose survival through the colonial period shows they are well and strong. But the traditional lines were discouraged from developing into modern banking and were never integrated into the imposed system. For example, local moneylenders normally could not resort to city banks for, say, seasonal agricultural credit. By preempting the various functions, city banks prevented African moneylenders from evolving into banks themselves, as European goldsmiths had done two centuries earlier. African creditors and debtors acquired limited experience with the institutions of modern banking and held little stake in them.

Public Administration

Competing hypotheses are offered about why the European powers occupied Africa: (1) for the wealth they could extract, (2) for strategic and military purposes, and (3) for trade. While all of these probably operated, in the cases of Britain, France, and Holland the third seems most persuasive, with a lesser bow to the second and little credibility to the first. British documents reflect the primary interest in trade and protecting the route to India. Unfortunately, in the European mind the Africans did not possess the requisite commercial laws, the banks, and the courts for trade or even a social basis for creating them. So the colonial powers founded these themselves. They could not do so, however, without becoming the government.

This is not a whitewash or even a charitable assessment. The colonial governments contravened their own morality, invariably giving themselves the benefit of any doubt. They took land and property as they wished. They paternalized the Africans, denigrating their systems without understanding them, and setting them aside wholesale. When they created their own legal and financial organizations, they allowed Africans access to them only insofar as this was convenient to the Europeans.

Popular opinion in the Western world holds that however they may have suffered under colonialism, Africans at least were educated or trained in European ways. They learned how modern institutions function, so that upon independence they might undertake their own trade, their own banking, their own adjudication, and their own parliaments.

Let me suggest differently. These organizations were not negotiated by groups with relatively balanced power. Instead of operating as they do in the industrial world, they became instruments by which the African power groups continued to seek their own advantage. As new wine (organizations) in old bottles (institutions), they retarded economic development rather than advancing it. Specific examples will be given in the next chapter. Let us now relate how preexisting power imbalances were cast into concrete under colonialism.

Europeans did not want to be bothered with petty disputes among Africans. They set out to confine their own administrations to matters affecting trade, finance, and the general peace, as well as the agriculture of their own settlers.[51] Although in principle the Parliament in London or Chamber of Deputies in Paris was the ultimate authority, for all practical purposes the local governor (European) held absolute power. In British East Africa, the district officer considered himself both ruler and paternalistic advisor of African chiefs. He was "responsible for law and order in his district, for the collection of revenue, and a host of statutory duties which . . . made him . . . a township authority, a registrar of marriages, a licensing authority, and an agent of the Administrator-General."[52]

Thus, the colonial governors were increasingly sucked into detailed decision-making on local affairs, affecting even how the Africans conducted their family lives. Two main forces were at work: (1) the desire for power on the part of low-level European functionaries who in no way could reach such authority at home, and (2) in Africa, economic and social systems that were so intertwined that intervention in one area led inescapably to another, and so on deeper and deeper. The colonial powers found themselves doing things they had never intended to do, and paying for them.

Perhaps the trap into which the colonial powers fell will be better understood by comparison with a modern example. History was repeated in 1993 when the United States and United Nations invaded Somalia for the humane reason of supplying food to starving people. They stepped into cultures that they did not understand; they were increasingly sucked into local disputes; they waged war and took on some of the attributes of a colonial government.[53]

In some ways, the colonial governors usurped powers previously held by African chiefs. But in other ways, they conveyed powers upon African rulers that these had never held before. For example, they partitioned jurisdictions, creating new chiefs or even kings.[54] Sometimes chiefs would persuade their European mentors to legalize powers they said were "customary" when this was not true or what was "customary" was in dispute or evolving.

As in Europe and elsewhere, empires in Africa had been forged by war. But also as in Europe and elsewhere, the wars were rarely absolute. Always the kind of society to which conquered people were attached was in some way negotiated, along with their rights. But the military power of the colonial conquerors was overwhelming, the racial differences obvious, and their sense of apartness so keen, that they launched a new kind of absolute authority. Vertical alliances with leverage were impossible. It was this authority, not the imperial rank, that African rulers would inherit upon independence.

Law

By definition, the origin of customary law is not known. But precolonial African law was not all "customary." Indeed, it had plural origins that might rival the European. The Almoravids introduced Islamic law at least as far back as the eleventh century, and Warf Djabi, ruler of Takrur—later part of the Mali Empire—helped carry it into sub-Saharan Africa.[55] Omani traders and settlers brought it to the east African coast. This law existed side-by-side with tribal laws. "[I]n several . . . respects Somali customary law and Islamic law are . . . closely related."[56] In Zanzibar, Islamic law operated alongside European law.[57] Among the Ibo, secret societies made laws for their communities.[58] By settling disputes among trade houses, they must have contributed to commercial law.

Multiple jurisdictions in multiple empires brought as many kinds of law as they did judges. In the sixteenth-century Matapa kingdom south of the Zambezi River, "legal cases were heard regularly on the six holidays in every thirty days, and the ruler's judicial function was of considerable importance."[59] Hindu law drifted into eastern and southern Africa. The rulers of Saharan states felt a responsibility for justice and internal security to promote their long-distance trade.[60] Justice was performed by Muslim *qadis*.[61] While Islamic law in principle is immutable, in fact it has changed with the times. Although no record of trade cases exists, it is not difficult to suppose that participating traders might have negotiated with judges.

Yet Chanock points out for Malawi and Zambia in the nineteenth century:[62]

> Power was obviously a crucial factor in what was "customary" compensation and it could be randomly exercised, as is clear from the recollections of a woman from Karonga: "People do that in our land. If a man has a claim on another and it is not settled, he seizes goods or children, and he who has been made to suffer innocently must go and beg the accused until he gives satisfaction."

With scattered sources, inadequate in total, only a partial understanding of law in the precolonial era may be gained. Probably a chief or judicial officer had considerable discretion in resolving disputes by customary or other law; he was influenced by his council; and together they tended to favor prestigious persons, including their own families. While the chief was to some extent constrained by custom, nevertheless he had the power to define "custom" and even to modify it.

Why the Europeans felt African Law
was Inadequate

Following are ten ways in which European powers may have found African
law wanting.

1. African concepts of "binding" differed both among communities
and from the European concept. Africans did have a concept of commitment, but it depended on personal relations, oaths, and sanctions: "courts
are found not to insist on enforcing contractual obligations, but aim instead at settling the underlying dispute."[63]

2. The fragmentation and fluidity of African societies implied diverse judicial processes, often unreconcilable. This diversity would dis-
courage trade or agreements over territories of disparate jurisdictions.[64]
In particular, there was no way to adjudicate land across jurisdictions.

3. "African society traditionally did not recognize the distinction
between private and public law."[65]

4. Checks and balances to which Europeans were accustomed at home
often did not exist in Africa, since legislative, judicial, and executive
functions were usually combined. However, it was sometimes possible
to appeal decisions to higher authorities.[66]

5. "Indigenous African law is generally unwritten . . . because of its
predominantly illiterate environment. . . . The African governments, their
jurists and social scientists, do not regard their recordings or restate-
ments as codes. . . . They have no statutory effect."[67]

6. African law tended to be exhortatory and moralistic. "Large parts
of the judgements of the Lozi courts read like sermons . . . 'the judges
cite not past court decisions but actual instances of upright behavior. . . .
[L]aw . . . is instantly exhibited in the conformity of upright people to
norms.'"[68]

7. The Europeans were accustomed to greater clarity of boundaries
between jurisdictions, responsibilities of individuals, and scopes of authority, than were the Africans.[69]

8. Historians debate whether African judgments were based on neu-
tral legal principles or on the easiest way to restore peace, or both.
Bozeman writes that "African courts are concerned above all with the
restoration of order, social equilibrium, and the status quo."[70] But Mensah-
Brown disputes this.[71]

9. Because Africans did not always use judicial precedent, it was
difficult for Europeans to know what the law was.[72]

10. Perhaps the greatest chasm between European and African concepts of law is the African predilection for the supernatural and magic.[73]

Law under Colonialism

All of the above "inadequacies" were common to both European and Japanese law in earlier centuries. In both northwestern Europe and Japan, the law evolved into its modern form by negotiation among many groups, whose results were enacted by parliaments or in judicial decisions. With colonialism, however, African history took an irreversible turn.

As the colonial powers "preserved" African customary law, they took a paternal interest in it. They tended to view an evolving law as if it were immutable. Ignoring African ways of mediation and change, they frequently wrote down what they considered customary law to be. "Under the Natal law no. 19 of 1891 the native code became a legally binding enactment, and the living Zulu customary law, with all its virtues, was discarded and replaced by a rigid, written version of what the Administration wanted the Zulu customary law to be: thus submitting a lifeless, written image of Zulu customary law for the living reality of it."[74] Thereafter, the law was changeable only in European ways, through parliamentary enactments or court decisions, and not in ways familiar to Africans.

Thus, colonial law was dichotomized: one part—revised "customary"—for the Africans and another part—modern—for the Europeans. But the modern part always overruled the customary. By applying modern law, therefore, native judges in native courts might modify or overturn "custom," without referring the matter to a tribal meeting where anyone might speak one's mind.[75] In this way, the colonial government unwittingly increased the powers of the African judges.

As some Africans took on European ways—adopted Western clothing and were educated in Europe—they objected to being subject to native courts, with their livelihoods decided by untrained judges whom they considered inferior to themselves, and themselves being denied appeal.[76] Although African courts were gradually phased out after World War II, the position of these Africans was not fully resolved until independence.

In sum, the negative impact of colonialism on law was twofold. First, by imposing Western organizations for law and other public functions, it denied Africans the experience of negotiating these or others for themselves. Courts, juries, and judges, even to their British-style robes and wigs, sprouted on African soil and remained on into independence. Second, in many countries the prerogatives of local and tribal chiefs were emasculated under colonialism, and the power concentration in the central city continued into independence. By both contorting, preserving, and enhancing an existing power imbalance, colonialism had postponed the urgency to negotiate modern institutions. Upon independence Africa retreated into its earlier, power-skewed political processes now buttressed by a façade of modern economic and political organizations. These were turned into implements of even greater power concentration for the rulers. This evolution in no small way contributes to the present chaos in African economies.

Notes

1. Bozeman 1976:124.
2. For a few selected references to negative impact of warfare on trade and industry during African history, see Abir 1975:550; Alpers 1975:533; Birmingham 1976:239, 267; Fisher 1975:123, 127; Harms 1981:75, 83, 96; Hunwick 1976:282; Laroui 1977:155; Levtzion 1975:152, 179, 199-215; Levtzion 1976:144; Shinnie 1965:140; Unomah and Webster 1975:278; and Wilks 1976:439. For a few selected references to negative impact of warfare on agriculture during African history, see Birmingham 1976:234; Hopkins 1973:143, 218; Horton 1976:100; Laroui 1977:274; Richmond 1977:67; Rodney 1975:300; and Stevens 1966:105.
3. Laroui 1977:97.
4, Laroui 1977:283.
5. Laroui 1977:146.
6. Laroui 1977:168.
7. Gray 1975:2.
8. Hunwick 1976:293-94, 298.
9. Hunwick 1976:274-76.
10. Fisher 1975:130.
11. Curtin 1976:352.
12. Marks and Gray 1975:385ff.
13. Adeleye 1976:586.
14. Fisher 1975:105.
15. Levtzion 1975:200.
16. Fisher 1975:106ff.
17. Adeleye 1976:594.
18. Rodney 1975:229.
19. Birmingham 1975:336-42.
20. Marks and Gray 1975:429-35.
21. Alpers 1975:532.
22. Alpers 1975:478ff.
23. Alpers 1975:491.
24. Abir 1975:564-71.
25. Deschamps 1976:394.
26. Suret-Canale and Barry 1976:499.
27. Johnson 1976:99.
28. Levtzion 1975:216.
29. Rubenson 1976:57.
30. Chanock 1985:194.
31. Birmingham 1976:227.
32. Omer-Cooper 1976:324.
33. Smith, Abdullahi 1976:175.
34. Gray 1975:6.
35. Laroui 1977:257.
36. Hunwick 1976:268.

37. Harms 1981:156.
38. Chanock 1985:18-19. He refers to Roberts 1976:80, 81, 141 (reference in my bibliography is to revised edition, 1979) and 1973:295.
39. Birmingham 1976:229.
40. See chapter 5, pp. 70-73.
41. Miers and Kopytoff 1977:23, quoted in Chanock 1985:161.
42. Domar 1970:18-31. He cites V. Kliuchevsky, *Kurss russkoi istorii*, Moscow 1937.
43. Fogel and Engerman (1974) found slavery to be profitable to U.S. plantations.
44. I am indebted to my student Henry Christian Bierwirth, who with his research helped me develop this idea.
45. Some accommodation was made for tribal ownership, analogous to Indian reservations in the United States. Other than that, even land left in African hands was to be adjudicated according to European laws.
46. Powelson 1988: Chapter 20.
47. Bohannon 1963:101-11.
48. This assertion is disputed, but I prefer not to join the argument here. I base my statement on classical economic theory as well as on the recent misfortunes of socialist economies.
49. Richmond 1977:200.
50. This process is described in a novel by Huxley (1964).
51. For British East Africa, these generalizations rely principally on Morris and Read 1972.
52. Morris and Read 1972:19.
53. This is attested to by many newspaper articles, among them Mitchell, Alison, "Marines in Somalia Try to Rebuild a Town Council," *New York Times*, 1/18/93; Schemo, Diana Jean, "Marines Search Somalis' Homes for Arms but find 'Hatfields and McCoys,'" *New York Times*, 2/16/93; "U.S. Envoy Warns a Somali Leader," *New York Times*, 2/24/93; and Lewis, Paul, "U. N. Asks Arrests of Somali Killers," *New York Times*, 6/7/93.
54. Chanock 1985:34.
55. Levtzion 1976:129.
56. Anderson 1956:73.
57. Anderson 1956:71.
58. Rodney 1975:265.
59. Marks and Gray 1975:389.
60. Levtzion 1976:145-46.
61. Hunwick 1976:292.
62. Chanock 1985:164.
63. Bozeman 1976:242-43.
64. Phillips 1956:92; Alpers 1975:482.
65. Poirier 1956:156. My translation from the French.
66. Schapera 1956:103.
67. Mensah-Brown 1976:23-25.
68. Chanock 1985:30, citing Gluckman 1972.
69. Chanock 1985:32; Van Velsen 1957:83,82.
70. Bozeman 1976:243.
71. Mensah-Brown 1976:30.
72. Mensah-Brown 1976:33-34. There are, however, some instances in which precedents were used (Gluckman 1955:253).
73. Bozeman 1976:228.
74. Holleman 1956:232.
75. Barnes 1967:164, cited in Chanock 1985:41.
76. Morris and Read 1972:135-36.

Chapter 9
Africa Today

Out of the 45 black African nations [in 1990], just four—Botswana, The Gambia, Mauritius and Senegal—allow their people to vote, choose their leaders and express themselves freely. Twenty-three countries are military dictatorships where no political parties are admitted. The rest are one-party states ruled by dictators for life.[1]

Compared with the rest of the Third World, African economic development since World War II has lagged sorely. Since the early 1960s, per capita income in sub-Saharan Africa has grown by only 0.6 percent per year, and its 450 million people have produced about the same as Belgium's ten million.[2]

Centralization of Power

Upon assuming nationhood, African rulers concentrated power in single-party national governments. Mostly, tribal chiefs were stripped of their authority. Usually local governments were denied the power to tax. They were left dependent on the central government for both their financing and their policies over roads, schools, and the like,[3] repeating a pattern of the power concentration that had been characteristic of Africa for centuries.

Agriculture

In a previous publication, my co-authors and I studied agriculture in five African countries (as well as others elsewhere): Algeria, Egypt, Somalia, Tanzania, and Zambia.[4] Because the detailed stories, with data, are found in that book, my summary here is brief. In each of the five cases, the central government attempted to manage agriculture from the capital city. All applied price and production controls, which tended to reduce output.

Algeria and Tanzania forced farmers to join "cooperatives."[5] In Tanzania the army burned their huts to keep them from returning home. In both countries the "cooperatives" were a means by which the agricultural surplus was extracted by the government, through price controls and forced sales to state marketing agencies. The philosophy was altruistic—government helping its people—but the results were not. Production languished because farmers, inadequately rewarded, abandoned their farms or decreased production.

In Egypt a single minister carved out a government fief for himself, from which he forced farmers to grow cotton and sell it to the government at low, virtually subsistence prices. The government in turn exported it at a profit to itself. Other price and production controls hampered farming, leading to underfed people and food riots.

In Somalia the central government tried to settle nomads on lands that could not support settled farming. Interclan warfare has been an even greater disaster, leading to widespread starvation that caused military intervention by the United States and other countries in 1993.

In Zambia, all land was declared to belong to the state, and restrictions were placed upon the farmers.

African tribes have been accustomed to storing food in time of surplus, to cover themselves for inevitable famines. Today, governments extract surpluses through taxes or forced sales, spending the proceeds—often to line the pockets of politicians—so there is nothing left to ward off famine.

State export monopolies introduced into West Africa in World War II by the British became lasting instruments by which governments have forced farmers to sell crops to marketing boards, with profits on foreign sales going to the government rather than to the farmers.[6] This practice has been common in East African countries as well. In 1983, a Mozambican government congress admitted "that agricultural policy had overemphasized the benefits to be gained from huge state farms to the detriment of subsistence farmers."[7]

The United Nations Food and Agriculture Organization says most African countries adopted policies that gave farmers little incentive to grow more food than their own families could eat. Instead, these policies lured many farmers, the backbone of African economies, to cities. There, they stopped farming and started eating imported food, purchased with overvalued currency and foreign aid money. In those years, food imports rose tenfold.[8]

Shortly after seizing power in Ethiopia in 1977, Chairman Mengistu Haile-Mariam announced a land reform in which all farms were nationalized, "cooperatives" established, and farming put under the control of the government. Seven years later:

> [S]ince this Government came to power in a coup, virtually no land has been irrigated and little has been done to correct environmentally destructive agricultural practices. . . . Cutting of forests and overgrazing by livestock have been widespread. Also, the low prices paid by the state-owned Agricultural Marketing Corporation have discouraged farmers in still-fertile regions from producing a surplus or selling whatever surplus they produce.[9]

A high government official who defected from Ethiopia in 1987 reported that "chronic food shortages, civil war, political unrest and famine are the order of the day. . . . Thousands have disappeared or have been summarily executed without trial. Millions of peasants are being uprooted from their homes and villages to implement a policy of regimentation of the rural population and collectivized farming."[10]

In Malawi "the country's agricultural 'miracle' has bypassed the majority of the rural population, subsistence farmers, who suffer some of the highest child malnutrition death rates in east and central Africa."[11]

In Tanzania, President Julius Nyerere in 1976:

> abolished the country's 2,500 local cooperative unions, arguing that many were corrupt, inefficient and politically uncontrollable. In their place, he established . . . parastatals, that were given legal monopolies. . . . These companies ran up big deficits and quickly soaked up most of the country's investment capital. According to the World Bank, 90 percent of capital expenditures in agriculture between 1975 and 1982 went to the parastatals. By 1982, 11 crop-marketing boards had lost a total of more than $200 million.[12]

Bruce and Dorner have shown how complex registration procedures of the Zambian Land Board have generated uncertainty and interrupted cultivation.[13] In Zambia also, "the monopolizing of the handling of maize—the major marketed crop—has inhibited the growth of enterprising merchants, who could provide merchandising, transport, and handling facilities, and the national growth of cooperative marketing."[14]

Virtually all these authoritarian policies have been partially or wholly reversed in the liberalism that swept the Third World after the downfall of socialism in the early 1990s. In 1991, the Mengistu government in Ethiopia fell, and by 1993, farms were again private. Nyerere retired in Tanzania in 1985, and gradually the restrictions on farmers have been removed at the behest of the International Monetary Fund. Agricultural output has increased significantly. While most Western observers have rejoiced at these events, let us be soberly reminded that they may all be overturned by a new sweep of ideology when new people take power.

Industry and Government Enterprises

Upon independence, the unique power held by many rulers enabled them to appropriate the profits of industry. Their modes of organization wasted resources grossly. Such plums could hardly go unchallenged by their rivals. But the only "opposition" was other people like themselves, who might seize power if they could. Loyalty of the military was often the crucial asset.

Such a chasm lay between these groups and weaker ones—tribal chiefs and councils, age sets, or newly forming business organizations and labor unions—that none of the latter could hold the rulers in check. Because they were powerless, these groups could not make vertical alliances or enjoy the leverage known to their Japanese and European counterparts some centuries earlier.

The power groups organized industry in two ways. One was private enterprise in which they were themselves the principal stockholders, the other parastatal enterprises reporting to ministries occupied by themselves. Nationalized or state-owned banks could be forced to lend money to the former; taxes and government borrowing would finance the latter. Resources of each could be diverted to oversize salaries or contracts with private enterprises in which the power groups held interest. Since both the private enterprises and the parastatals were often monopolies, they possessed considerable latitude in pricing and profits. If contracts were awarded outside the power group, "commissions" would be charged.

Both kinds of enterprises also financed themselves with loans and grants from foreign governments and international agencies. The international agencies would make these loans because their existence depended on it: they were designed to promote "development" in the Third World. By international agreement, they were precluded from operating in any country without government approval. Thus, their only alternatives were to comply or go out of business. Foreign governments also contributed, to win the political or cold-war support of the Third World countries.

The inefficiencies of industry and parastatal enterprises are illustrated by the following reports:

[In Algeria] a plan to make state-owned factories more profit-minded and independent from government is badly stalled. Managers worry that they will be ousted if they do not churn out profits, while government officials fret that profit-minded managers will lay off their friends and relatives placed in cushy jobs.[15]

Many respondents [in interviews undertaken by Hickock and Gray in Mali and Senegal] cited pervasive doubts in the community as to the long-run solvency of government-run enterprises, including banks, and expressed the view that distancing the latter from public control, even if the government retained substantial equity, would boost confidence and raise deposits. . . . In 1981, 85% of outstanding bank credit in Mali had been extended to state enterprises, which were paying a real rate of interest of zero (9.5% nominal rate, roughly equal to the rate of inflation).[16] [In Senegal] 27 companies completely operated by the state and 75 quasi-public concerns, all of which together employ 25,000 people, [use] four times the manpower that some critics say is needed in these enterprises.[17]

Many World Bank reports have described the abuse of parastatals in Africa, for example in Tanzania[18] and Zambia.[19]

Zaire's economic woes may be dated at least to 1973 when President Mobutu launched "Zairianization," under which European-owned businesses were seized and given to Zairians for token compensation. Many of the businesses went to the President's family and cronies, and within two years, Zaire's economy had shrunk by 15 percent. The new owners often had no idea how to manage their holdings. When Mobutu was forced in 1975 to invite the Europeans back to run the businesses, there was often not much left to run.[20] By 1992, the Zairian economy was in shambles, with foreign enterprises having left, their plants looted by soldiers who had not been paid for months; schools, hospitals, and many local businesses closed; the president holed up on a yacht in the Zaire River, protected by his military and too fearful to enter Kinshasa. The people were subsisting mainly on cassava, which provides calories but few nutrients. At the moment of writing (1994), Zaire appears to be an impending case of mass starvation.

Just as agriculture has been liberalized after the collapse of socialism, so also are many government industries being privatized in African countries. It is too early to say whether these moves will be successful. A privatized enterprise need be no more efficient or progressive than a public one, however, if it is a monopoly controlled by the same elite that operated it under a government name.

The Structures and Policies of Intervention

Upon independence, African governments wanted all the trappings of modern states: executive offices, ministries, central banks, courts of justice, and parliaments. Once again confusing the organizations with the institutions, international agencies and governments of more-developed countries supplied the expertise and often the financing for these. Carbon copies of organizations from the more-developed world were set up wholesale in Africa. Without the checks and balances of their home countries, they became a source of power and enrichment for the elite.

Attached to these structures were instruments of monetary and fiscal policy, conceived step-by-step in more-developed countries to combat depression, inflation, and balance-of-payments deficits. But the same instruments, without built-in checks, might *create* depressions, inflation, and balance-of-payments deficits when these would be to the advantage of the policy makers.

The ways to abuse these organizations are well known: (1) money creation, preferentially for the elite; (2) low interest rates with credit also rationed to the elite; (3) overvalued exchange rates coupled with import permits granted to select people; (4) government monopolies, or—when privatized—private monopolies; (5) permissions for economic activity granted to favorites and denied to others; (6) expropriation of private assets for government enterprises from which the elite will benefit; and (7) loans from abroad for projects that the elites can milk.

None of these abuses can be documented or studied systematically. All Westerners exposed to the inner workings of African governments know they exist,[21] but explicit references would expose friends or violate confidences. They are not mentioned in economists' growth models or in assessments of economic plans. Rather, they are referred to obliquely in the reports of international agencies. Reports of journalists may be the best source of information on them.

Budgetary control is often loose. Ministries may be allowed to spend up to the limit of their budgets without question. If they reach that limit in the middle of the fiscal year, parliament must pass supplementary allocations or the government will stop. If many ministries do the same, the matter becomes routine, and budgetary control is virtually useless. While I was economic advisor in the Ministry of Finance and Planning in Kenya (1972-74), budgetary supplements were passed regularly.

Governments frequently say they will correct these deficiencies, and their statements are publicized in international agency reports. But enforcement is another matter. For example, in 1977 the World Bank reported that the "Government [of Zambia] has taken a number of important steps to control the growth in recurrent expenditures,"[22] including greater controls over spending by the various ministries. But the data from then on indicate that the promise was not kept.[23]

Probably not all rulers have gained personally from these practices. Former presidents Julius Nyerere of Tanzania and Kenneth Kaunda of Zambia are well known for honesty and sympathy for their people—"Familyhood" (*Ujamaa*) was the slogan in the former country and Humanism in the latter. But they had in common with others the belief that good results would come only if they or persons of their choosing were in power. Even if not corrupt themselves, they could not control an overstaffed bureaucracy whose members seized and granted privileges.

The economic and political manipulations have in many cases exceeded any potential for achievement, either perversely for the enrichment of the elite or positively for economic development. Ultimately, even the elites skim off less than they could in a growing economy. Therefore, only power for its own sake can explain their actions.

Commands that one day institute price controls and the next day rescind them; that one day require permission for this and the next day for that; that order street-vendor stalls and shanty towns to be bulldozed, then allow them to be built up again; that call for the construction of towers and conference centers or the largest cathedral in the world—all these are manifestations of power as a consumer good, rather than as a capital good dedicated to further production either for its holders or for the community at large. Further references to the concentration of state power and centralized, often capricious decision-making in Africa are found in appendix 9.1.

Warfare and Violence

Just as power is wanted for its own sake, so are warfare and violence still in many places the legitimate means of resolving disputes. One may even argue that warriors want war for its own sake, as indeed was the case with European knights in the Middle Ages.

Since independence, the principal wars in Africa (in alphabetical order) have been (1) Algeria versus Morocco over the former Spanish Sahara;[24] (2) the rebellion in Angola, largely by the Ovimbundu people against the government;[25] (3) Tutsi-Hutu chronic violence and massacres in Burundi and Rwanda, (4) civil war in Chad and the invasions by Libya;[26] (5) three wars in Ethiopia, involving Tigrean, Eritrean, and Somali rebels;[27] (6) civil war in Liberia; (7) rebellion and guerrilla war in Mozambique;[28] (8) the war for independence of Namibia;[29] (9) the Biafra war in Nigeria; (10) civil war in Somalia; (11) civil war in Sudan;[30] (12) various civil wars in Uganda, plus one war against Tanzania;[31] and (13) several mutinies by armed forces in Zaire.

It is difficult to judge whether war continues to be a legitimate means of settling disputes in Africa. First, in the past century, some areas have had years of peace, earlier enforced by colonial powers and now continued by independent governments. Second, instances of warfare in Africa may be matched by cases elsewhere, such as the Arab-Israeli wars, violence in Northern Ireland, the United Nations/Iraqi war of 1991, and the Balkan war that began in 1991 and shows no sign of ending at the time of this writing (1994). Third, one cannot compare the intensity of, say, World War II, with its nuclear bombs, against the endemic struggles in Africa, where fewer people are killed at a time but where the contest goes on and on and on.

Yet certain wars have characteristics similar to those of endemic warfare over the centuries. The Ethiopian-Eritrean war (now presumably settled), the civil war in Sudan, the intertribal violence of Uganda, the inhuman massacres of the Mozambican war, the Tutsi-Hutu chronic violence, the Angolan war (even with its occasional truces and presumed final settlement), and the interclan wars of Somalia, all smack of the endemic African wars of the nineteenth century and earlier. They are also reminiscent of the European Crusades, the Hundred Years' War, the Wars of the Roses, the wars of religion in France, and the Thirty Years' War. All continued for a decade or more, those of Ethiopia and Angola for three decades; all sides are hard-line, reluctant to negotiate (except perhaps where militarily defeated as in Ethiopia); and the wars are waged with intense cruelty and even genocide, as in the cases of Angola, Ethiopia, Somalia, and Mozambique.

Some individuals make a career of warfare and would not easily find places in civil society. The Black Prince, son of Edward III of England, is a fourteenth-century example.[32] Jonas Savimbi of Angola might be one today. Given the presence of many such persons, a culture of warfare is entrenched.

On the positive side, Gluckman and Newman suggest a tendency away from violence and toward compromise among the Barotse:

> Gluckman's masterful work on the law of the Barotse of Northern Rhodesia (Zambia) showed that in "multiplex societies," where people are bound by multiple social and economic interdependencies, conflict is particularly disruptive and cannot be tolerated if the community is to survive. Barotse judges are therefore oriented toward reconciliation and devoted to "mending" broken ties, not simply punishing offenders. "Multiplexity" therefore explains the character of the Barotse judicial process.[33]

This judgment would support the hypothesis that negotiation and compromise are born when a society reaches a stalemate in which it would not otherwise survive. But the scant evidence suggests that such situations are not yet widespread in Africa today. Further examples of modern, endemic African wars and the cruelty and suffering they have engendered are listed in appendix 9.2.

Summary for Chapters 7, 8, and 9

Throughout its known history, Africa has not been lacking in trade and entrepreneurship. Early on, Africans formed states and empires, business companies, laws, courts, judiciary procedures, and money. But none of these grew into complex institutions like those of northwestern Europe and Japan. Instead, the organizations of today were imposed by colonial powers or by national elites in imitation of the industrial world.

Because land was abundant relative to labor and because power groups gained from extensive trade, African elites were not forced to negotiate their differences with lower classes. While many interest groups did form, the great chasm between rulers and ruled made it less likely that weaker groups would improve their conditions through vertical alliances and leverage.

Before the nineteenth century, few Africans needed literacy to record contracts or laws, nor did they require a free labor market. Labor and capital continued to be appropriated through war, slavery, marriage, and cattle raids. War was a legitimate means of carrying on conflicts that were never expected to be settled in a European sense.

Economic planning by elite groups after independence is the modern manifestation of power concentration over centuries. This concentration was unwittingly strengthened by the colonial governors, as it was also after independence by foreign economic advisors such as myself. The nation state further reinforces it, as have so-called "socialism" and "cooperatives." All these reduced further the likelihood of pluralist economic development.

The foreign powers and international agencies that today urge free markets and privatization of industry and agriculture seem not to grasp that the Western concept of these proposals would constitute a complete turnabout in Africa's centuries-long history, not just a change in direction. The understanding by African power groups will be different. For them, the old institutions will continue somehow, through the new organizations. We will return to that dilemma in chapter 23.

Notes

1. Ayittey, George B.N., in *Wall Street Journal*, 3/28/90.
2. World Bank 1989.
3. Examples of the concentration of power in the central government of all African states are legion. Here are a few references culled from a much longer list: for Algeria, Ibrahim, Youssef M., in *New York Times*, 11/27/88; for Botswana, University of Wisconsin, Land Tenure Center *Newsletter* No. 68, July-September 1980; for Equatorial Guinea, Brooke, James in *New York Times*, 11/01/87; for Ghana, Rule, Sheila, in *New York Times*, 06/09/85; for Ivory Coast, Cowell, Alan, in *New York Times*, 04/21/82, also 11/2/83, 11/15/87, 11/19/89, 2/25/90, and 3/3/90; for Kenya, Perlez, Diane, in *New York Times*, 2/14/91 and 3/10/91; for Liberia, Rule, Sheila, in *New York Times*, 6/5/85, also 6/10/84, 6/11/84, 6/5/85, 7/3/85, 4/13/86, 8/15/89, and 1/31/90; for Mozambique, *Wall Street Journal* 12/30/80; for Nigeria, *New York Times* 11/21/82,2/12/83, 1/18/84, 10/2/85, 3/4/86, 6/22/88, also Brooke, James, in *New York Times*, 8/11/88; 6/4/89 and 1/14/90; for São Tomé, Brooke, James, in *New York Times*, 3/6/88; for Tanzania, Morris and Read 1976:264; for Zaire, *New York Times*, 8/09/81, 8/10/81, 8/16/81, 8/30/81, 6/18/82, 6/06/83 (article on torture), 10/06/83, 10/25/83, 04/13/86, 12/14/86, 2/04/87, 2/08/87; Brooke, James, in

New York Times, 9/29/88; Greenhouse, Steven, in *New York Times*, 5/04/88, also 5/24/88; for Zambia, Moseley, Ray, in *Chicago Tribune*, taken from *Boston Globe*, 9/25/81.
4. Powelson and Stock 1990.
5. In quotations, because these were not voluntary associations agreed upon by members.
6. Bauer 1972:372-74.
7. Cowell, Alan, in *New York Times*, 6/03/83.
8. Hardin, Blaine, in *Washington Post*, National Weekly Edition, 9/1/86, p.6.
9. May, Clifford, in *New York Times*, 11/18/84.
10. Dawit Wolde Georgis, in *Wall Street Journal*, 11/12/87.
11. Battiata, Mary, *Washington Post*, in *International Herald Tribune*, 9/13/88.
12. Frankel, Glenn, *Washington Post*, from *Boulder Daily Camera*, 11/23/84.
13. Bruce and Dorner 1982.
14. World Bank 1977.
15. Greenhouse, Steven, in *New York Times*, 10/12/88.
16. Hickock and Gray 1981:65, 68.
17. Guptie, Pranay B., in *New York Times*, 9/17/80.
18. World Bank 1983:50.
19. World Bank 1977, main report p. 88, and annex 12-3.
20. Greenhouse, Steven, in *New York Times*, 5/23/88.
21. I have myself seen them in my work as economic advisor.
22. World Bank, Zambia: *A Basic Economic Report*, no. 1586b-ZA, Washington, D.C., 10/3/77, p. 83.
23. International Monetary Fund, *International Financial Statistics Yearbook* 1989:760-1, and March 1992:586.
24. *New York Times*, 9/8/80, 7/4/81, 11/19/81, 4/8/85, 1/15/89, *New York Times Magazine*, 4/27/80.
25. *New York Times*, 9/16/79, 12/25/84, 12/31/84, 1/31/86, 11/23/86, and 9/12/88.
26. *New York Times*, 3/19/86, 6/16/87.
27. *New York Times*, 12/4/80, 6/23/83, 11/25/84, 1/6/85, 1/17/85, 12/3/87, 3/22/89, 9/10/89, and 1/7/90.
28. *New York Times*, 10/4/81, 11/1/82, 11/18/84, 11/25/84, 6/30/85, 7/1/85, 12/30/85, 5/18/86, 12/8/86, 1/12/87, 1/22/87, 2/1/87, 2/19/87, 8/30/87, 10/7/87, 1/25/88, 2/18/88, and 5/11/88.
29. *New York Times*, 1/6/81.
30. *New York Times*, 5/4/86, 8/21/86, 10/12/86, 1/3/88, 10/3/88, and 12/6/88.
31. *New York Times*, 8/26/80, 8/27/80, 11/16/80, 4/7/81, 7/14/83, 6/23/86, and 9/15/86.
32. "War provided him with his *raison-d'être*" (Hallam 1987:269).
33. Newman 1983:3, citing Gluckman 1955.

Chapter 10
India

Though each has its individualities, India and Africa possess many common features accounting for the failure of the power-diffusion process. In both areas before the nineteenth century land was plentiful and migrations common. India and Africa each traded vigorously over long distances in early history, the Africans within their continent and the Indians across continents. Despite the existence of private trading and production, nevertheless in both India and Africa the state—through tribal chieftains and rulers—dominated production and the ownership of assets and enjoyment of income. (It still does.) Endemic warfare ravaged both continents for long periods. (It still does.) Each experienced a colonialism that deprived the subject peoples of opportunity and land and also endowed indigenous rulers with powers they never had held before. When colonialism ended, the land was returned but the power imbalance remained. Finally, although each had its local governing organizations—tribe and village—historical references to vertical alliances or to economic negotiations between villagers and overlords are not so numerous in India and Africa as in northwestern Europe and Japan. We may speculate that the land abundance and alternative income through thriving trade in earlier centuries, along with the power imbalance under colonialism, constrained communication between rulers and underclass, and that this communication failure blinded both sides to the positive-sum cooperation and complex institutions that might have led to durable economic development.

A Trading and Entrepreneurial Society

Even more so than Africa's, India's history is rich with trade and entrepreneurship. Unlike Africa, India's precolonial past also includes literacy, high-level science, written law, and banking.

In the second millennium BCE India already traded internationally. It became an entrepot, where goods were exchanged between Western and oriental shippers. Guilds were registered with town authorities, and a money economy evolved, spawning financiers and bankers. But there are also evidences of concentration of power. The uniformity of weights and measures, common script and seals, "all indicate some measure of political and economic control and point to the great cities of Mohenjo-dara and Harappa [2500-1700 BCE] as their centres."[1]

Even in the era of political disunity (184BCE to 320CE) trade extended as far as Rome and China,[2] and "revenue from trade contributed substantially to the economies of the participating [Indian] kingdoms."[3]

In the fourth through eighth centuries CE monasteries in southern India were centers of learning. Mathematicians had calculated both pi and the length of the solar year. High-quality gold coins were circulated. Legal texts were written and formal judicial procedures practiced.[4] India was a jewel in Britain's trading sphere from the seventeenth century right up until its independence. "Growing demand for cotton revolutionized the Indian export trade after 1835."[5]

India had a head start on Africa because of its location at the center of the East-West trade routes. Early on, Indian legal and monetary systems were more advanced than African and at least on par with European. But they still did not become fully modern. Being largely elite-managed, they did not reflect the interests of the groups they presumably served, so they were not institutionally capable of negotiating the many positive-sum moves that were physically possible. Ultimately, they were supplanted by British systems that also did not serve the interests of non-elite Indians.

Village Organizations

Although village organizations existed abundantly in India,[6] peasants did not negotiate vertically to the same extent as did their counterparts in northwestern Europe and Japan. In an earlier writing, I have documented the existence and nature of village organizations,[7] which I summarize here.

Before the British, Indian land was held on three or more levels: (1) the sovereign or conqueror, whose objective was to receive taxes and maintain security; (2) the intermediate official, called zamindar, jagirdar, or other name, whose purpose was to collect taxes, keep his share, and pass the rest on to the sovereign; and (3) the village, which often held land in common, whose purpose was to allocate plots among villagers, feed itself, and pay taxes. Often layer (2) was actually many layers and many privileges, in a complex pattern of rights and obligations based on seemingly infinitesimal, changing distinctions among land uses. The pattern was so complex that the British did not truly understand it in all the years of their overlordship. More detail on the enormous variation in agrarian relations is found in Kumar.[8]

Wade writes of the Indian village as a corporate group. "Indian villagers are emotionally dependant on and derive their identity from groups—and in that sense are not individualistic." He also describes "a complex web of patron-client ties within the village and stretching upwards to higher levels of politics and administration."[9]

The most convincing explanation of the failure of village organizations to negotiate vertically and of the difference between India and Europe is
pathetically expressed in a passage by an Indian author:

> None of the major struggles in Indian history had for its object the exercise
> of rights within the village, but the exercise of rights over the village. They
> were conflicts between overlords of various grades for the right or power to
> get a payment from the peasant, not to seize his land. European history, on
> the contrary, reveals a conflict between the peasant and the manorial lords
> because the latter not only demanded a share of the produce, but desired to
> retain a particular method of cultivation—by forced labor—or to introduce
> new methods of cultivation (enclosures, large-scale farming). The Indian
> conflict was between lords who were concerned not at all with the method
> of farming, but to draw an income from the peasantry. . . . The issue was
> always between different claimants of the sword, the village and the peas-
> antry remaining throughout the passive subject of conflict, the booty over
> which the rival powers fought each other.[10]

Other authors reinforce this sentiment. I quote from my previous
work:[11]

> Metcalf writes that after the Gupta fell, village organizations took form,
> with distinctions among cultivating castes. Tribes slowly migrated across
> the fertile Gangetic plain, "observers of the great struggle that raged over
> their heads between imperial dynasties and local powerholders." . .[12]
> In the south, where rival empires existed precariously, village orga-
> nizations became highly developed, but not at all in the European-Japa-
> nese mold. . . . The agrarian organization before the eleventh century is
> little known. By that time, however, well-organized villages were emerg-
> ing, which Stein[13] calls "nuclear areas of corporate institutions." Two
> types predominated: the *brahmadeya* (each one a group of villages con-
> trolled by a Brahman organization) and the *periyanadu*, an extended lo-
> cality controlled by organizations of commoners (*Sat-Sudras*).

The brahmadeya consisted of groups of settlements that Brahmans
assembled and managed, taking themselves a share of output. The periyanadu,
covering a wider territory, was governed by corporate groups of farmers or
merchants or both.

Although some historians argue that Indian "feudalism" is enough
like its European and Japanese counterparts to merit that term, others point to

the crucial difference of contract.[14] Peasants and overlords in Japan and northwestern Europe forged a binding relationship, with obligations on both sides, enforceable in courts of law. Indian peasants and lords had no such relationship.[15] When the cultural distance between lords and peasants was so great, when peasants had no legal rights to land but instead had been told for hundreds of years that they were less than the dirt beneath their feet, they would not be so bold as to think of vertical alliances or negotiating. A British assessment of tenancy in Bengal in the eighteenth century reports that "the zamindars, in general, did not enter into agreements with the ryots [peasants]; they collected what they could, and the impositions were 'numerous and unascertainable.'"[16]

I have found a few references to "contract" for land use, but usually they were between persons of high rank, not between high-status and low-status people. Or they may have been passed down by authorities or arbitrated by outsiders instead of by peasants through their own committees. For example, *miras* were group-controlled resources found in irrigated villages in southern India in the nineteenth century. Shareholders, primarily Brahman or high-caste peasants, would "take disputes outside their community for arbitration, and intercommunity squabbles naturally required an authority outside of but respected by many distinct shareholding assemblies. Officers of the state undoubtedly served this role."[17] Finally, the caste system precluded negotiation between high- and low-level people. A Brahman did not talk to an untouchable.

Hence the organizations to carry on economic transactions were—as in Africa—mainly managed by rulers, including the Mughal emperor, the rajas, the Brahmans, the zamindars, the British East India Company, the British government, and later the Government of India.

Three Possible Reasons for Lack of Contracts

Three reasons may explain why Indian villagers did not enjoy binding contracts with their superiors: abundance of land, international trade, and persistent warfare.

Abundance of Land

A religious divine of Delhi (c.1454) . . . cites the example of a peasant who needs to have seed, a pair of oxen, and tools or implements. Possession of land is not included among the essential implements. Clearly, our divine was living in a period of land abundance.[18]

Historical sources on India are replete with references to migration and land abundance. Ludden writes that migration "accelerated and expanded after 1300" and describes how "land was abundant and labor scarce . . . anyone with family labor could find land to cultivate for at least a meager subsistence."[19]

In eighteenth-century Bengal, "the *pattas* [deeds of lease] granted to the *paikashi* ryots generally contained a limitation in point of time; where they regarded the terms as unfavourable they migrated to some other place."[20] In Khandesh, villages would be periodically deserted and later revived with new cultivators.[21]

Villagers all over India sometimes negotiated with their overlords in good times. They were "not mere passive observers." But "when the situation worsened, they 'voted with their feet' and left for better conditions."[22] Thus land availability set a limit on bargaining, which was not normally forced by lack of alternative.

A British government report of 1820 refers to waste land being granted to speculators, with the hope that it would "not only draw back the Natives of Candiesh who have retired to Guzerat and other Countries, but even attract new settlers, from places where the population is overabundant."[23]

Contrary evidence is found in some places. In sixteenth-century Delhi, land was "almost fully under cultivation."[24] Kerala has long been densely populated. Kumar quotes the Arab explorer Ibn Battuta as remarking that in fourteenth-century Malabar "there is not a foot of ground but what is cultivated." Yet Kumar also writes of South India: "When population grew, or when the rains failed, men would migrate to other areas seeking permanent or seasonal employment."[25]

From these scattered references, one may conclude that land was sufficiently abundant in much of India that—unlike in northwestern Europe and Japan—lords and peasants were often (but not always) physically mobile and could escape each other. They did not need a binding, one-on-one relationship.

International Trade

Adapted to India, the Goodell thesis would appear as follows: During the first millennium CE, the lords of India could earn their wealth by trade. While they had to rely on tenants for their food, nevertheless they did not need to make contracts with any specific tenants. They could either expel an obstreperous group or make conditions so miserable that the group would leave. Landlords would tide themselves over with gold from trade until new peasants were co-opted.

In view of India's intensive participation in international trade during the early centuries CE, the Goodell thesis appears plausible, but more research would be required to find specific instances of it. In any event, the proposition that lords and tenants did not normally form vertical alliances does not rely on the Goodell thesis, so there is no need to prove it or disprove it for India.

Persistent Warfare and Violence

India's major wars include the Arab invasions of the eighth century; the Ghaznavid conquest of the late twelfth century, which began the main Muslim period; the overthrow of the Ghaznavids by the Ghurids; the ensuing wars of the Delhi Sultanate (thirteenth to sixteenth centuries) with its factional intrigues, battles against the Mongols, and the subduing of Hindu kingdoms; the power struggles of the Khaljis (1290-1320), Tughlug (1320-1416) and Sayiid (1414-51) dynasties; Timur's invasion of 1398; the Mughal initial conquest of the sixteenth century and its continued warring to subdue Hindu kingdoms; in the south, the power seizures and rivalries under the Bahmani kingdom (1347-1527) and its rivalry with the Vijayanagar Empire (1336-1646); Marathan rebellions against Mughal encroachment in the south and their own expansion in the eighteenth century; and finally the European colonial wars, fought among British, French, Dutch, and Portuguese, but involving the Indians.

Far more disruptive are the many succession disputes, violent overthrows of petty states, and the almost continuous, often low-level, warfare. Eleven historical citations on such violence are found in appendix 10.1. This endemic violence produced unstable and fluid ruling groups, just as was the case in Africa. In northwestern Europe and Japan, by contrast, the durability and cohesiveness of high-level competing groups had made vertical alliances possible.

As in Africa, there were periods of peace in India. But—again as in Africa—these were neither long enough nor pervasive enough to alter the underlying properties. As in Africa, this violence did not stop entrepreneurship, capital formation, or trade. But it did put a cap on the institutions of durable economic development, which can reach the necessary complexity only when their participants come to trust each other through continuous peaceful relations.

Endemic violence was temporarily suppressed by the British occupation. After independence in 1947, it erupted again over the whole subcontinent: between Hindus and Muslims as Pakistan was created; three succeeding wars between India and Pakistan; the communal riots in various states in 1978; fighting between Muslims and Hindus in 1982;[26] bombings by militant Sikhs in 1982;[27] massacres in Assam in 1983,[28] which broke out again in 1989;[29] Hindu-Sikh warfare in 1984, including the Hindu assault on the Sikhs' Golden Temple with 41 victims of torture;[30] clashes with Ghurkas demanding a state of their own;[31] the assassination of Prime Minister Indira Gandhi in 1984;[32] battling between Bengali immigrants and Chakra tribespeople in Bangladesh in 1987;[33] "hundreds reported killed each year" in Bihar;[34] new assassinations in 1985 with violence in the Punjab in 1986;[35] warfare of Tamils of India and Sri Lanka versus Buddhist Sinhalese throughout the 1980s;[36] the assassination of M.M. Farooq, senior Islamic leader in Kashmir in 1990;[37] Hindu-Muslim riots in 1990 over a Hindu plan to erect a temple on the site of a mosque in Ayodha, and the destruction of that temple;[38] the assassination of Prime Minister Rajiv Gandhi in 1991,[39] and fighting on the Kashmir border.[40]   Also:

> Indian paramilitary forces and local police officers fought here today with thousands of students and other demonstrators demanding an end to a new policy reserving more jobs to some lower-caste Indians.[41]

> [A] recalcitrant voter or two may be gunned down as an example to others. . . . This newfangled system of voting can be settled best by violence; violence alone proves a point dramatically and irrefutably.[42]

Caution must be exercised in assessing Indian warfare, however. We do not know how to measure violence. All wars are different, and endemic violence is always to a degree. Nor is the threshold between violence and nonviolence known at which vertical alliances, leverage, and trust become possible. Europe and Japan also had their share of warfare. Violence erupts also in the industrialized world: rioting and burning in Washington, D.C. in 1967 and in Los Angeles in 1992, for example. The bombs dropped on Nagasaki and Hiroshima in 1945 and the United Nations/Iraqi War of 1991, with an economy destroyed, an estimated 100,000 killed and many more uprooted, and a country driven to poverty, starvation, and ethnic hatreds, shows that the United States still is ready to employ violence. Vicious and terrible though these events were, however, U.S. economic growth was not interrupted. Rather, a different kind of violence—continuous, on the inter-personal level, all-pervading, and therefore endemic—inhibits the institutions of economic growth in Africa and India.

The wars in northwestern Europe and Japan ceased to be endemic during the centuries of rapid economic development. Even without exact measurement, the far greater intensity and frequency of inter-personal violence in Africa and India today puts it in a different class from the violence of the more developed countries.

Colonialism

As in Africa, European colonial governments—this time primarily the British—unwittingly elevated Indian elites to powers they had never held before. This they did by mandating organizations and relationships copied from their home country, but whose checks and balances had not evolved in India. As in the case of Africa, powerful Indians, appointed to positions in these organizations, behaved with the aggressiveness of their time-honored institutions, not limited by the constraints of English institutions.

In the seventeenth century, when sovereign boundaries were looser than they are today, the British East India Company dotted the coast with trading points, or "factories." Recognizing that rulers dominated economic enterprise, it bought and sold through the Mughal emperor or territorial rulers. This policy worked for a century, but contradictions gradually emerged.

First, the British East India Company became involved in local wars. The Mughal emperor was trying to assume paramountcy over many autonomous rulers, to make them lose hereditary rights and depend on him.[43] The company reinforced his power by doing business with him.

Second, the company fought other Europeans for trade jurisdiction. These wars overlapped rivalries among Indian rulers, who would ally with one or another European power. Not being clear whether it was a private business or a representative of the crown, the company increasingly resembled a feudal lord.

But an obsolete feudal lordship in Britain differed from its living counterpart in India. In the latter, mutual obligations did not exist or were not clearly defined. When the company became zamindar under the Mughal Empire by buying rights over cities in 1698, it began to assign lands and collect rents on behalf of the Mughal emperor. Uninhibited by legal restrictions, British officials grabbed powers they could never have acquired at home. Parliament found this to be "corruption."

Third, dismayed at this corruption, in 1784 the British Parliament assumed the political but not the business functions of the company. After a bloody rebellion in 1857, the British Government took these over as well.

Fourth, the British tried to remodel Indians after themselves. An influx of British agencies—banks, law courts, and the like—was easy. But the landholding system became its nemesis.[44]

Out of the bewildering array of land and tax rights, the British tried to establish private ownership. They selected the zamindars and certain other claimants as the most likely to imitate the "innovating landlords" of seventeenth-century England. In a series of "settlements," they made these the private owners. But "innovating landlords" did not materialize. Instead, the new landowners had a more powerful weapon over their tenants than ever before. Previously, there might have been some custom or obligation that would mitigate excessive taxation or dispossession or cruel treatment, or the tenants might have held some incipient leverage, if for example some other overlord, an enemy of their immediate rent collector, would protect them. But naming the zamindar as the landowner protected by the British government removed whatever minimal leverage the peasants possessed. The new owners demanded maximum rent with minimum outlay. Perhaps in time they would have perceived that improved agricultural output through investment and cooperation with tenants would have yielded just that. But in a world in which possession had never been secure and the stability of workers never assured, immediate payoffs were preferred.

A further explanation may lie in a cultural difference touched upon by Neale, who writes that the British, in acting as if the Indians responded culturally as they themselves would have, failed to grasp different values that Indians placed on money and power: "more Englishmen were willing to trade in more power for money while more Indians were willing to trade in more money, or goods, for power. . . . To the Englishman, the route to power lay in public administration or in parliamentary politics. [To the Indian, on the other hand, it lay in control over people.] Since villages were often split by faction fights, the political Indian needed to increase the unity of and the numbers in his faction. The ideal position for an Indian interested in power was to be a leader of the dominant faction of the dominant caste in a village."[45] But tenants selected on the basis of who would bring the most power might not be the same as those who would produce the greatest output. These observations reinforce the hypothesis that a shift in relative values—from power to material wealth—correlates with durable economic development.

Law

Religious and political hierarchies define social distinctions and allocate privileges in premodern societies. The caste system has always performed this function in India. With Brahmans as the highest caste for millennia, one may presume that the law was made by Brahmans for Brahmans. Even before the first millennium CE, rules were being compiled in the sacred writings, which were intended to cover every aspect of life, including the economic.

Hindu law traditionally originates in the Vedas, at uncertain dates about 1500-1200 BCE. But these writings were sacred hymns, not laws, and they did not apply to non-Hindu Indians, such as Christians, Jews, and Muslims. Rather than judicial precedent, the sacred writings were guides to behavior, which kings and judges would take into account in their legal decisions. Subsequent scholars—virtually all Brahman—elaborated and interpreted them, in a series of writings collectively known as Dharmasastras, which might differ according to region. The "duty of the King to give justice lies within the whole concept of a dharmic ideal."[46]

In addition to this top-down law, early village law, the *kula*, was probably negotiated by "cultivators, barbers, traders, artisans, herdsmen, and so forth. . . . [L]ater literature shows that these lower classes also had their group organizations or guilds for regulating their own affairs. . . . [T]hese inferior classes had guild usages which were binding on them irrespective of any reference to the sacred law."[47] Indeed, many commercial disputes were resolved in villages without being brought to the king or Brahmans. Principles of this law were studied by scholars and written down in manuals.

Like that of Europe and Africa, Indian law has multiple origins. First are the Vedas and the Dharmasastras, which are specifically Hindu.[48] Second is Muslim law, the shari'a, based on the Koran. Third are many ad hoc arrangements by local kings, such as trading rules in ports visited by European ships. Fourth is the kula, or village law. Finally, European laws—mostly British—were added to the mix.

Before the British occupation, no known attempt was made to reconcile the disparate laws into a single system, as had occurred in northwestern Europe. Hindu and Muslim laws could hardly be integrated, for they sprang from different divinities, and the Koran was presumably immutable. Only the third and fourth types—ad hoc arrangements and kula—were drawn up by agreements among participating parties, and these might be swept aside by the next conqueror.

Thus elitist and religious law overwhelmed lawmaking on lower levels, in contrast to the cases of northwestern Europe and Japan, which tended toward agreed or negotiated justice. "Many disputes [in India] could not be brought by the aggrieved parties, but were promoted suo motu as the outcome of the king's officers' enquiries, including espionage."[49] However, contrasts based on this quotation must be made with caution, for early European and Japanese courts also would not consider family disputes, whose judgment belonged to the head of the family. Nevertheless, the path from "unequal contract" to "impartial law," however imperfectly completed in the West and Japan, was not undertaken at all in India until modern times.

Sen-Gupta[50] attributes the following law to Visna, a god of the Vedic period: "If the seller fails to deliver the goods to the buyer who has paid the price, the seller is liable to repay the price with interest and to pay a fine of

100 panas." He attributes the following law to Yajnavalkya, a semi-legendary sage of approximately the same period: "The time allowed (to the vendee) for the examination of seeds, iron, beasts of burden, jewels, females, and milch beasts, is ten days, one day, five days, seven days, one month, three days, and a fortnight respectively."[51] Other similar laws are also attributed to gods. If one supposes that these laws were written by Brahman scholars rather than by gods or ancient sages, however, they spring from elitist morality rather than the haggling of the marketplace.

A further inconvenience must have been the obvious inconsistency—even flagrant hypocrisy—between high moral qualities enunciated in the writings and the persistent, permeating violence and inhumanity practiced over centuries. Virtues such as "truth, abstention from injuring, freedom from anger, humanity, self-control, uprightness, abstention from theft, [and] ritual purity"[52] are the ideal of many religions. That qualities so distant from observed behavior should be considered standards of judicial procedure diminishes the credibility of the law itself.

A still further inconvenience of Indian law was the abrupt change with each conqueror. The Muslim period had an advantage for trade, in that for the first time all of northern India was subject to the same laws,[53] but also a disadvantage, in that the sudden abandonment of traditional laws must have led to some confusion.

Both the capriciousness of conquest and the distance between ideal and practice would imply that laws were interpreted in ways to preserve hierarchy and privilege rather than in the "equal justice" to which European visitors were aspiring in their own lands. The British dilemma was that laws they might impose would not be enforced, while Indian laws did not protect trade and production to the degree they wanted. Their modus vivendi was, as in Africa, to allow indigenous legal principles to continue for local disputes but gradually to introduce British laws of ownership and contract through statute and judicial precedent.

As in Africa, however, three adverse elements crept in. First, British courts did administer local law, Hindu for Hindus and the shari'a for Muslims. Not only were they unfamiliar with these laws, but they assumed them to be static. In writing them down, they both stopped their natural evolution and adjusted them to their own custom.[54] Second, laws imposed by outside authority are not accompanied by the checks and balances established when the same laws evolve through negotiation and parliamentary debate. The gap between lawgivers and subjects was vast.[55] Third, without these checks, Indian judges and civil servants gained authority they had never known before. That authority did not emerge full blown until after independence, however, for until then it was suppressed by the racial arrogance of British officials.

Paying little attention to the needs of the multitude, during the nineteenth century the British prepared codifications based on English law in many branches: "criminal law, civil and criminal procedure, evidence, contract, and succession."[56] Morris and Read call this a "remarkable achievement," but Mensah-Brown finds that all the British attempts to reform Indian law failed.[57] Only after independence was a Hindu legal code written by the new government, in 1955-56.

Is the Indian legal system today able efficiently to resolve disputes arising out of economic matters? If scholars have addressed this question, I have not found their works. Perhaps the Union Carbide case will offer some clue.

In December, 1984, a gas leak at this company's plant at Bhopal resulted in 2,000 deaths, with many more thousands seriously injured.[58] This accident prompted discussion as to whether damage suits should be tried in the United States, since India's courts might not be capable of handling them. Few if any damage claims were filed, for to do so is not the custom in India:

Even without Bhopal litigation, the country's chaotic district and high courts labor with a backlog of a million cases, many of which will drag on unresolved into the 1990s. The notion that India could handle the Bhopal suits "is ludicrous," says Salman Khurshid, a Delhi lawyer who has studied and taught in England.[59]

Money

In many respects, the Indian financial system of the thirteenth century resembled those of Europe. Although coins were minted primarily by monarchs (as in Europe and Japan), private credit was extensive. Guilds and other merchant associations possessed links beyond Indian borders. Some specialized in money exchange and lending. Merchants used commenda-style arrangements similar to those of the Italian city states.[60]

Indian traders had known money at least since Roman times. Gold coins were minted by the Kushan (from about 78 CE) and Gupta (320-540 CE) monarchs. By the eleventh century, money circulated in all parts of the subcontinent. Coinage by the Sultanate of Delhi, begun in 1193, helped develop an international credit network.

The currency of the Mughal Empire (1526-1761) became one of the most highly reputed in the world, with uniform, standardized issues and coinage open to everyone who brought bullion to an authorized mint. Seigniorage fees were small, so the exchange value of coins approximated the market value of the metal. Prices fluctuated among gold, silver, and other metals.[61] Nonmetal and base-metal currencies were used for small trade, including copper, cowries, badam (an inedible bitter almond from Persia), lead, iron, tin, and seeds.[62] European trading companies also issued coins, often authorized by territorial rulers in southern India, where Mughal control was looser.[63] Presumably Indian rulers made these accommodations—for which contemporary African rulers saw no need—because India was in the center of the trade routes, and coins and credit arrangements were needed for trade. Metal had to come from abroad for these coins.

Why India did not grow into one of the world's greatest financial centers, rivaling Britain and Holland, is unexplained. The European powers did nothing to prevent it. Indeed, a source of coinage in India might have been to their advantage. A major reason for this lack of development may have been the failure to diffuse power in India, with the result that the monetary system was heavily adapted to the collection of taxes rather than to the needs of trade.

Probably the main need of coins for Mughal and territorial rulers was to buy the goods of war; taxation was the way to obtain the coins; and, because of India's location and exposure to European technology, demanding coins rather than produce was a more apt means of taxing.[64] Perlin elaborates on the relationship of money to taxes in the Mughal period. First, "big urban bankers had become closely involved with the activities of tax-collectors in many parts of India."[65] Second, even when taxes were paid in kind, other charges on a peasant's income required coin: "contracts between absentee and residential right-holders, the huge range in size of different accumulations of rights, and the complexity of organization of the larger households, would have allowed considerable flexibility in choice as to the medium of collection."[66] Thus the relationship between coins and taxes is not simple. Rather, coins played their part in a complex set of economic transactions, in which surplus extraction from the peasantry was the dominant motif.

Contemporary Europeans, on the other hand, had long since passed the day when surplus extraction from the peasants was their primary reason for minting coins. By the seventeenth century, world power and trade were so intermixed that it is impossible to distinguish European motives. Whichever the case, by Gresham's era sound coinage was valued by enough of the many interest groups—traders of many countries, manufacturers, farmers large and small, the Queen of England and the King of France—that they converged on stable money (though they did not always achieve it) for reasons far beyond taxes. It was different in Japan, where Tokugawa rules were trying to suppress international trade. But it was also different in India, and this difference may have been a reason why India did not remain what it once was, the dominant trading power of the world.

Not only was gold coinage advanced in India by the seventeenth century, but so also was the private credit market:

> Country moneylending involved both professionals and potentially anyone retaining an annual surplus: managers of rights, administrators in their private capacity, soldiers, wealthy right-holders and the better-off peasantry. . . . Borrowers also included a considerable range of different occupations and statuses, . .[67]

Such a rich mixture of groups and institutions was already integrated into a total system, through which international flows of specie must have related directly to the money supply for all activities of the country, each one to be supplied according to its needs and the rate of interest. This in turn probably led to multiple expansions of bank money, common also to the more-developed countries. The ultimate development is a central bank, the Reserve Bank of India, created in 1935. Although India missed its opportunity to become a world financial center, nevertheless its monetary system is today modern and efficient.

Yet some disturbing factors—to be elaborated in the next section—can be traced to Mughal times. Efficient as the credit system was, the records show that in the Mughal era it was biased toward supplying resources to leading families.[68] It was built mainly upon the demands of both the central government and dispersed foci of local power and upon the need to fulfill a vast network of obligations, rather than as a source of credit for economic entrepreneurship. It could be as efficient and modern as any in the world, but it would serve the imbalance of power. The same is so today.

In sum, the money system in India had all the inherent possibilities of becoming a modern rival to that of northwestern Europe. That it did not do so reflects the fact that money follows culture, not the other way around. Like its legal and fiscal systems, India's monetary system is built on the skewness of power, the failure of vertical negotiation and leverage, the unforgiving land-tenure system, and the continued dominance of authorities over underclasses. The system revolves around perpetuating these imbalances rather than maximizing domestic production and international trade.

India Today

India's real gross domestic product increased, on average, by 4.39 percent per year for twenty years, 1970-90. With population growth averaging 2.16 percent per year during the same period, the per capita increase in gross domestic product was about 2.23 percent per year, a respectable rate by world standards. Increases in agricultural output, thanks in part to the green revolution, have been spectacular; periodic famines appear to be past. Unlike many Third World countries, India has not incurred excessive foreign debt. Finally, the monetary authorities have controlled inflation to a modest average of 6 to 9 percent per year since independence.[69] "[India] is increasingly emerging as a major industrial and military power. . . an increasingly modern, powerful and self-sufficient industrial nation that manufactures everything from video recorders to fighter aircraft."[70]

By the major economic indicators, India is on its way toward becoming a more developed nation. Yet it scarcely complies with the power-diffusion process. Have we therefore uncovered a flaw in that process?

Not necessarily. Had we been analyzing Russia under Peter the Great, Turkey during the Tanzimat of the nineteenth century, or China in the early 1950s according to the precepts of mainstream economics, we might have concluded that any of those areas had "taken off" into sustained economic growth. Yet all of them faltered.

There are today a few signs that India may be at the threshold of acquiring the early elements of a power-diffusion process. First, land is running short. While the afflictions of population explosion are well known, it carries one bright spot. Indians can no longer migrate away from their human relations; there is no more place to go. Second, interest groups are forming, to put peaceful pressure upon "superiors" for a change in institutions.[71] There are signs of vertical negotiation, not just horizontal. Third, there is some awareness of the need for a free market in goods and services.

But the positive signs are—so far—overwhelmed by a sea of negatives. First, although privatization of industry is rife in the 1990s, nevertheless the central government is hanging on to its control over the economy. "Businesses must obtain permission to enter markets or leave them, to build new factories or close old ones, to import or export."[72] "[N]ot only must a minister be propitiated before he will issue a license, allot a house, or award a pension, but so must every clerk through whose hand the relevant file passes. . . ."[73] Second, violence is as strong as ever. In many areas it remains a legitimate means of resolving conflicts. Third, most proponents of free markets in goods and services, whether Indians or the international community, are content that these should be imposed centrally and do not understand why central authorities do not always perceive the advantages. They do not yet grasp that free markets will become durable only if, as institutions, they are formed in free markets for institutions.

India's economic problems, much analyzed elsewhere,[74] are only summarized here. First and foremost, poverty—both rural and urban—is grinding and intense.[75] Second, business enterprise is high-cost and inefficient. Private producers are protected from international competition, and government enterprise incurs heavy subsidized losses.[76] Privatization can hardly be expected to yield efficiency under these circumstances. Third, price and production controls favor the wealthy few, while limiting or closing opportunities for the many poor. Fourth, the spectacular agricultural progress is largely limited to water-abundant lands of wealthier farmers. In other farms, agriculture has been stagnant for a century or more. The vast majority of India's rural population lives in the less-favored areas; many are landless sharecroppers. Fifth, government employment is excessive and largely nonproductive. Some predict that without major policy changes, India's vaunted economic progress will be short-lived.

On the assumption that the Government of India is motivated to promote the "general national welfare," economic advisors are proposing some or all of the following steps: (1) Continue to sell ("privatize") unprofitable government enterprises or make them otherwise accountable so that they operate at a profit. Close those where this is impossible. (2) Eliminate price controls. (3) Reduce unnecessary bureaucracy, to bring government accounts into balance. (4) Both the rate of inflation and the foreign deficit should be diminished by appropriate interest and exchange-rate policies. Although price rises and balance of payments are not chronic problems, they have been worsening of late. (5) A major land reform is essential to agricultural improvement.

Land reform exemplifies the technical possibility of a positive-sum move on which the parties refuse to agree. Because the "overriding constraint is the unfavorable ratio of land to population in the rural areas" and "extreme inequalities in the distribution of ownership,"[77] and because sharecropping does not supply incentive to do labor-intensive agriculture, Frankel concludes that land reform is a prerequisite to increased peasant incomes. Large owners (50 acres or more) farm small, scattered plots on which they are "rarely able to realize the maximum return [because the size is] less than the optimum area for the efficient cultivation of the high-yielding varieties." Although Frankel maintains that an increase in output is physically possible with known technology, she explains convincingly that achieving it is impossible under existing tenurial arrangements. But changing the tenurial arrangements is also impossible, she says. The central government cannot command it. This decision is reserved constitutionally to the states, whose governments are controlled by the landowners. Nor can it arise from below, for the beneficiaries are too weak to demand it effectively. Though pessimistic for the immediate future, she ends with the vague hope that a democratic land reform will sometime occur.[78]

Frankel does not follow up her cogent observation, however, that a positive-sum solution—increased agricultural output—is physically possible with known technology. So, if all parties would gain through some distribution of the increment between landowners and peasants, why cannot they agree to do it and to divide the gains? One of Frankel's explanations is that "some landowners simply have no interest in land development or in maximizing output from their holdings. Under existing tenurial arrangements, they have reliable income effortlessly by collecting rent and interest on loans."[79] Still, it seems unreasonable that landowners would not wish to increase their rents through increased productivity. The marginal utility of income surely has not reached zero for them.

Several possible explanations come to mind, for the failure of greater landlord-peasant cooperation to increase output for mutual advantage. Owners might fear that any seemingly positive-sum move would enable peasants to seize their lands violently. Or they might believe that consolidating fragmented holdings would reduce their political prowess, which depends on an extensive presence. Or they might not want to recognize lower-caste peasants as legitimate bargaining agents. Or they might feel that any change is a risk they do not want to take. Reassuring them on these matters might require communication with the lower castes and some trust, both of which are lacking. Whichever of these may be the case, the owners appear unwilling to trade power for goods.

These are speculations, all of which imply that lack of trust in vertical relationships is still a barrier. The power-diffusion process would be initiated only when the landowners are forced to negotiate with peasants because some circumstance requires them to do so for their very survival.

Conclusion

India's economic achievements, compared with, say, those of Africa, are explained primarily by geography—its location in the center of East-West trade routes—but this happy circumstance has not been enough to realize the promise of the highly advanced industrial and financial society that might have been predicted in the thirteenth century.

Probably because of another geographic circumstance—the abundance of land until the present century—Indian groups have rarely been forced to communicate and negotiate vertically with each other. Numerous invasions and chronic warfare are another explanation. International trade (according to the Goodell thesis) may be still another. With the ability to escape each other, Indian elites and commoners have followed the age-old pattern, that power will not be yielded in favor of vertical cooperation, and free markets will not be agreed upon as second-best for everyone, until there is no other path for survival.

Some Indian elites join foreign governments, international agencies, and academicians in believing that decentralized power and freedom of enterprise can be imposed by government mandate. For example, two newspaper sources proclaimed:

> India's Rajiv Gandhi Moves to Reform Government, Industry. He Lowers Barriers to Trade, Shuffles Senior Officials, Tackles Vast Bureaucracy.[80]

> Prime Minister Gandhi, promising voters a decentralization of power, wants to make elected village councils compulsory all over India, and has introduced a constitutional amendment to bring about "panchayat raj," or "power to the panchayats." The slogan is plastered on walls everywhere he goes.[81]

"What the lord gives, the lord may take away." Gandhi's promises were no guarantee that he or his ministers or successors would not subsequently retract what he had granted. He never had the chance to implement his long-term plans anyway; he was assassinated in 1991.

Foreign and international agencies may well be repeating the mistakes of the British when they support "centralized decentralization," morally or financially. In so doing, they help elites gain power they had never held before, and they make the peasants more beholden to the rulers, just as the British did, and for the same reason: so they will mold their country into a world of foreign choosing.

The current semblance of liberalized economy and economic advancement will not survive unless the interest groups now forming can exert enough power to hold the rulers accountable for their use of resources. In this, the emergence of democracy may be a great boon. That a government can be voted out of office and will not come back by coup d'état, as it might in some countries of Latin America or Africa, provides these groups with a powerful bargaining tool.

So far, however, they have not used it well. Unless they do, India will share a fate similar to other historic instances of command development, which were also abetted by foreign powers. Only with the advance of new, pluralized forces, already weakly evident, will the poorer segments of India escape their centuries of grinding poverty.

Notes

1. EBMa 1974:9:339.
2. Wolpert 1977:70, 74, 78.
3. EBMa 1974:9:345.
4. Wolpert 1977:92; Lewis 1988:185.
5. Ludden 1985:139.
6. Ludden 1985:35.
7. Powelson 1988:chapter 16.
8. Kumar 1982, chapter II.
9. Wade 1988:4,5. For support, he cites Hofstede 1980 and Kakar 1981.
10. Shelvankar 1940:102, cited by Desai 1954:3.
11. Powelson 1988:194.
12. Metcalf 1979:3.
13. Stein 1969:180.
14. EBMa 1974:9:363.
15. Powelson 1988:195.
16. Banerjee 1980:262.
17. Ludden 1985:89. The descriptions of mirasidars are on preceding pages.
18. Habib 1982:48.
19. Ludden 1985:42, 81.
20. Banerjee 1980:261.
21. Gordon 1979:74.
22. Gordon 1979:78.
23. Gordon 1979:75.
24. Habib 1982:48.
25. Kumar 1982:207, 29.
26. Banks 1990:284-5.
27. "Sikhs Raise the Ante at a Perilous Cost to India," *New York Times*, 11/7/82.
28. Hazarika, Sanjoy, "The Benaglis in Assam: How a Tragedy Evolved," *New York Times*, 2/24/83; "Ethnic Slaughter in Assam Abating, but Not the Fears of the Survivors," 3/28/83; and "Peace Fragile in Assam Year After Massacres," 2/26/84.
29. Hazarika, Sanjoy, "Scores Killed in Ethnic Violence in Northeast India," *New York Times*, 8/13/89.
30. Articles by William K. Stevens in *New York Times*, 3/27/84. 4/3/84, 4/8/84, and 5/23/84. Also Hazarika, Sanjoy, "41 Torture Victims Found at Sikh Shrine," *New York Times*, 8/7/88.
31. Weisman, Steven R., "Indian Tea Region Yields Bitter Harvest of Unrest," *New York Times*, 10/3/86.
32. Charlton, Linda, "Assassination in India: A Leader of Will and Force," *New York Times*, 11/1/84.
33. Weisman, Steven B., "Murderous Feuds Threaten Unity of South Asian States," *New York Times*, 4/26/87.
34. Weisman, Steven R., "India's Corner of Misery: Bihar's Poor and Lawless," *New York Times*, 4/27/87.
35. Weisman, Steven R., "In Punjab, the Young are Particularly Restless," *New York Times*, 6/29/86.
36. Weisman, Steven R., "Sri Lanka: A Nation Disintegrates," *New York Times Magazine*, 12/13/87.
37. Banks 1990:289.
38. Encyclopedia Britannica *Book of the Year* 1991:430.

39. Spaeth, Anthony, and Greenberger, Robert S., "Assassination of Gandhi Ends Political Dynasty That Shaped India," *Wall Street Journal*, 5/22/91.
40. Hazarika, Sanjoy, "Kashmir Dispute is Souring India-Pakistan Relations," *New York Times*, 1/31/90.
41. Hazarika, Sanjoy, "2 Die as Upper Castes Fight Allotment of Jobs in India," *New York Times*, 9/26/90.
42. Desai, Anita, "India: The Seed of Destruction," *The New York Review*, 6/27/91.
43. Hasan 1969:19.
44. Powelson 1988: chapter 17.
45. Neale 1969:8-10.
46. Derrett 1973:10.
47. Sen-Gupta 1953:8-9.
48. "Although Hindu law had its origins in India, it is not the law of India any more than Islamic law is the national law of Muslim states. It is the law of a community which in southeast Asia observes Hinduism or a philosophy of life known as Brahmanism" (Mensah-Brown 1976:53).
49. Derrett 1973:13.
50. Sen-Gupta 1953:272-73.
51. The fact of six commodities but seven time spans is an apparent error in the author's rendition.
52. Derrett 1973:22-23.
53. Lewis 1988:183.
54. Derrett 1973:22-23.
55. Derrett 1973:25.
56. Morris and Read 1972:110.
57. Mensah-Brown 1976:55.
58. Banks 1989:275.
59. Stewart, James R., "Why Suits for Damages Such as Bhopal Claims are Very Rare in India," *Wall Street Journal*, 1/23/85.
60. Lewis 1988:186.
61. Prakash 1987:173.
62. Perlin 1987:240.
63. Prakash 1987:188.
64. Prakash 1987:204.
65. Perlin 1987:278.
66. Perlin 1987:279.
67. Perlin 1987:280-1.
68. Perlin 1987:282-3.
69. Data in this paragraph are calculated from International Monetary Fund, *International Financial Statistics* Yearbook 1989:412-3 1992:406; March 1992:282-4; and May 1993:280-1.
70. House, Karen Elliott, and Kann, Peter R., "India, though plagued by poverty, emerges as major world power, *Wall Street Journal* 8/8/84.
71. See, for example, "Organized Interest Groups," in Divekar 1978, chapter 5. The formation of interest groups is also reported in *New York Times*, 8/14/81, 1/17/82, 1/20/82, 6/15/82, 10/29/84, 7/26/88, and 6/28/89.
72. Passell, Peter, "India's Slow-Growth Path," in *New York Times*, 3/18/87.
73. Desai, Anita, "India: The Seed of Destruction," *The New York Review*, 6/27/91.
74. For example, World Bank 1990a and 1990b; also Lucas and Papanek 1988. For newspaper articles on industrial progress and entrepreneurship, see *New York Times*, 8/2/81, 2/24/83, and 8/6/83.

75. For newspaper articles on population and poverty, see *New York Times*, 2/19/82. 8/8/84, and 4/27/87.

76. For newspaper articles on overcentralization and inefficiency, see *New York Times*, 7/28/81, 1/14/82, 1/17/82, 2/20/82, 7/16/82, 8/15/82, 9/16/84, and *Wall Street Journal*, 4/11/88.

77. Frankel 1979:154.

78. A democratic land reform did occur in the state of Kerala. Although the state government was labeled "communist," the reform did not follow communist precepts. Land was confiscated from large owners and divided in private property among the middle classes. Many remained landless. This reform is described in Powelson and Stock 1990: chapter 10.

79. Frankel 1979:158.

80. Sterba, James P., "India's Rajiv Gandhi Moves Fast to Reform Government, Industry," in *Wall Street Journal*, 2/14/85.

81. Croisette, Barbara, "Village Councils Reborn (Gandhi Gets There Late)," *New York Times*, 6/28/89.

Chapter 11
China: The Puzzles of History

China has puzzled economic historians in three related ways: why it became the world's leading economic power during the Sung dynasty (960-1279 CE); why it traded so vigorously with Japan and southeast Asia and all the way to Africa; and why it turned inward beginning with the Ming dynasty in the fourteenth century, abandoning both international trade and leadership in economic development. This chapter will describe the failure of the power-diffusion process, which may have contributed to an explanation of these puzzles.

Trade and Entrepreneurship

Chinese trade was robust as far back as history records. The state of Ch'i was a trade center in the seventh century BCE. From there, imports of bronze and iron were distributed widely.[1] Merchants were accumulating fortunes as far back as the fifth century BCE and probably earlier.[2] International trade expanded especially in the Early Han dynasty (206 BCE-9 CE).[3] By 110 BCE, when Han armies had secured the Silk Roads, caravans of several hundred persons set out frequently from Chang'an to the West.[4]

In the southern kingdom of Shu Han (221-263 CE), wealthy merchants sold grain, metals, and timber, buying medicaments and other products from Tibet.[5] Trade caravans traveled to and from China through Sinkiang in the third century. In the sixth century CE, the Sui emperor Yang Ti constructed canals to provide grain for the capital, Loyang, and to open new markets in the northeast and south.[6] These were the precursor of the imperial canal system of a few centuries later. Trade with south Asia in the sixth and seventh centuries helped bring Buddhism to China. Monasteries became repositories of capital and centers of production. Caravans were bringing luxury goods from western and central Asia in the seventh century. Foreign colonies became integrated within a Chinese network spreading throughout the country. Inland trading centers mushroomed, with warehouses, counting-houses, and crafts.[7] Trade in tea developed between south China and Chang'an.

Medieval towns in China have the reputation of being administrative centers, not primarily for trading. Geiger characterizes all Asian city states except Hong Kong and Singapore in this way,[8] but this may be a Western bias. If indeed Chinese cities served mainly the imperial court and the army, nevertheless great markets were held next to town walls, especially for trade with nomads of the north.[9] Private workshops and probably foundries were connected with these markets.[10]

By 1100, China had developed "the most advanced form of economic life to be found in all of Eurasia."[11] Agricultural productivity was increasing through imported strains of rice, new reservoirs and dams, more irrigation, and canal construction and improvement. Industry was expanding in the north, with coal consumption increasing faster than it did in England right after the Industrial Revolution.

The Southern Sung dynasty (1127-1279) awakened a new interest in foreign trade by sea. It negotiated treaties on behalf of merchants,[12] much as the English monarchs would do three centuries later. The Mongols (1280-1368) also traded widely.[13] The Ming (1368-1644) built a huge fleet that traded abroad for decades before it was suddenly retired.[14]

Although China may have reached its overall economic zenith under the Sung, progress continued in specific fields. An agrarian revolution occurred under the Ming, with improved irrigation technology, new strains of rice and other foreign crops, and crop alternation. Industry expanded, and new markets were opened. During the eighteenth century textile plants and dyeing and calendering factories grew; division of labor became more intricate; and copper and lead mining expanded. "We hear of many men who started out with one loom and later ended up with over forty looms, employing many weavers."[15] And "when the Manila galleon set up its link with New Spain across the Pacific, Chinese junks hurried out to meet it."[16]

Despite these entrepreneurial qualities, and despite centuries of pioneering in agriculture, industry, and trade, hindsight tells us what might not have been seen at the time: that during the Ming and especially the Qing (1644-1911) dynasties, the Chinese economy lost its vigor in all its branches.

Centralization and Power

The Chinese economy stagnated in part because it was subject to a powerful, oppressive imperial office and bureaucracy. The bureaucrats appear to have been motivated mainly by desire for power, for they often did not profit much, materially, from their interventions. Although the following restrictions applied at different eras and places, and although there were exceptions, nevertheless the restrictive spirit pervaded historical time.

Craftsmen, a hereditary caste, were held in low esteem, were required to work for the emperor, and they were placed in humiliating circumstances with their clothing, hairstyle, and housing carefully monitored and ridiculed;[17] they could change occupations only with imperial permission. City markets were controlled by the government,[18] with crippling restrictions on traders. Foreign trade was monopolized by the bureaucracy and placed on a tributary basis.[19] The Tang and Sung rulers restricted trade to a few ports chosen for ease in collecting duties.[20] Industry above a small-factory level was mostly controlled by government officials, for whose benefit it was directed. The Ming dynasty intervened to the extent that it could in the personal as well as economic lives of its subjects. Although land was held privately and peasants could determine what to grow and how to grow it, nevertheless they were burdened by rents and taxes so heavy as to consume the investable surplus. Their land was subject to impulsive confiscation.[21] Wars and rebellions frequently despoiled their efforts. These conditions lasted until the establishment of the People's Republic in 1949.

The greatest, most capricious, and most continuous interference in the market process has been through price and production controls, which were often carried out by government officials to whom the supervision of local markets had been entrusted. Close state intervention—down to the individual factory level and into the details of everyday operation—is a commonplace throughout Chinese history, even to the present day. I have found hundreds of references to it in various history books, of which the following, chosen because they span centuries, are only a few:

[Shang Yang , 361 BCE] instituted a strict system of rewards and punishments, forced all persons into "productive" occupations, set up a system of mutual responsibility and spying among the people [in an] effort to bring all the territory of the state under the direct control of the central government.[22]

[In the third century BCE] an archaic and murderous bureaucratic state that destroys the individual in its search for an impossible precision where all deviance from the state's norms will be obliterated.[23]

The law did not protect any individual member from arbitrary action by his gild [during the Sung dynasty, 960-1279]; so the ruling authority was able to control the gild by controlling its leading members. . . . All the conditions and assumptions that led to gild power in Japanese and European society were absent in Chinese society, where powerful and independent gilds could not operate.[24]

Government itself [under the Sung dynasty] could now become more thoroughly centralized than before and both its domestic commerce and its foreign trade much better organized.[25]

[During the Ming dynasty, 1368-1644] each province was under a collegial group of officers who represented the same threefold administrative, military, and supervisory functions as in the capital. A governor was eventually added as a coordinator at the top of each province. The administrative hierarchy was also watched . . . by censors on tour.[26]

The gathering of power into the emperor's hands was a continuing tendency during the Yüan, Ming, and Qing periods (1279-1911).[27]

A statute of 1699 had given the rights of copper purchasing to the merchants from the Imperial Household, instead of leaving those rights in the hands of private merchants . . . . [T]hese rights were granted also to the textile commissioner of Nanking who was one of the emperor's trusted bondservants. This means that the textile factories were not only a case of direct state control in their specific field of activity, but that, at least during the Ch'ing period, the state could control other sectors of the economy through them.[28]

Under the [Qing] empire [1644-1911], state intervention in the economic field was determined by different motivations, depending on the sector, such as the control of those activities considered particularly dangerous for social order, the control of certain products of particular importance, the possibility of obtaining considerable fiscal income, and the importance of certain interventions in terms of "public" affairs.[29]

Further references to centralization and state power in China are found in appendix 11.1.

Absolutism had its exceptions, however. At all times it was subject to the incomplete ability of the emperor to control his people. This was the case especially before the Sung dynasty. The Confucian tradition counseled the emperor not to intervene below the level of the *hsien* (county). (He did not always keep this counsel.) In the third century BCE, "the emperor was a completely powerless figurehead,"[30] while warring feudal lords possessed power as imperious as that of an emperor but in their own territories. In a debate reminiscent of ideological splits today, the first century BCE squared off "modernists," who favored both absolutism and government control of the economy, against "reformists," who found it "improper for the government to compete with members of the public for monetary profit." [31] After the An Lu-shan rebellion of 750 CE, territorial lords tended to eclipse the emperor. [32]   In the Republic of China, 1912-49, the president frequently could not control outlying areas.

In principle, absolutism won out in the tenth century. But it was always subject to what the emperor could enforce. "[T]he Sung dynasty was marked by the growth of despotism, which culminated in the Ming dynasty."[33] Under the Mongols, "China was so large and complex a society that the lower-ranking civil servants had to be allowed to continue with their jobs if government was to function at all. In fact, the Mongols do not appear to have set up a rigidly centralized government in China, as was once thought." [34] Under the Ming, "administration was now more authoritarian than in the Sung period, but the small bureaucracy . . . continued to rely on considerable self-government within the society."[35]

Still, central management of the economy was the dominant theme, and if there was a discrepancy between official law and what could be enforced, the uncertainty of that alone would weigh upon the economic actors. The contrast with Japan and northwestern Europe is enormous.

Land and Labor

For long periods peasants were on the move. Sometimes they migrated to escape war, at other times to flee excessive taxes or rents, massacres, or physical abuse by their landlords. At still other times they were impressed into military or other settlements. Lords had their lands pulled out from under them with changes in *their* overlords—the emperor, provincial aristocracy, or bureaucracy—so that peasants were frequently faced with new masters. Whatever the circumstances, long-term relationships based on vertical alliances and trust among classes, such as developed in Japan after the sixteenth century and in northwestern Europe earlier, may have been difficult or impossible at all times in China.

The number of historical references to land abundance and "escape" by different classes is legion. Twenty-six citations, extracted from a much larger literature, appear in appendix 11.2. They include also references to the migratory nature of labor and small amount of communication among social classes.

Except for the directed immigration into Sinkiang under the People's Republic, the references to large movements of people and sudden changes in overlords taper off in the eighteenth and nineteenth centuries. Wars and rebellions, of which the most serious was the Taiping Rebellion of the nineteenth century, did displace people. Peasants in Henan province migrated to escape drought, landlordism, and taxes as late as the 1920s.[36] But population increase was making land less available. Farm sizes decreased, so that by the twentieth century China was a country of peasant farms of only a few acres, without great extremes in size. I have expanded on the evolution of Chinese land tenure in a previous publication.[37]

In sum, the history of Chinese land and peasantry approximates more the histories of Africa and India than those of northwestern Europe and Japan in the following ways. First, the availability of land made great migrations possible. Second, since the third century BCE, Chinese lower classes lived directly under the purview of the emperor, theoretically with no feudal lords "protecting" them as in Europe and Japan. In practice, however, the peasants often—even usually—had gentry patrons. Third, frequent changes in these patrons, through either conquest or slavery, typified China, Africa, and India more than they did northwestern Europe and Japan. For all these reasons, vertical alliances with leverage, and the institutional arrangements of northwestern Europe and Japan—such as rules delineating the rights of peasants, craft guilds, towns, lord-peasant contracts, and manorial courts with peasant participation—did not take shape so strongly in China.

In several ways, however, the distinctions between China on the one hand and Japan and northwestern Europe on the other are neither simple nor clear-cut. First, Japanese and Chinese cultures intersected, in land law, religion, and Confucian concepts of authority. Second, difficulties in communication over great distances diminished imperial power in China and increased that of local warlords, whose rule sometimes approximated the daimyo of Japan or the manorial lords of Europe. Third, local initiative in making contracts, promoting crafts and industry, and developing market and legal systems is found in both China and Japan. Sometimes it was encouraged by the imperial office, and sometimes it could not be suppressed. Fourth, crafts and industry were held in low esteem in both China and Japan, and to a lesser extent in Europe. Fifth, wars, which created impossible conditions for trust and contract, were common in all the areas mentioned and were devastating in Japan in the sixteenth century and in large parts of Europe in the seventeenth century.

However, these are all minor exceptions to the overwhelming generality, that vertical communication and bargaining, through which the rights of lower groups might have become stronger and more clearly defined over the centuries, occurred far less in China than in northwestern Europe and Japan.

Pluralism

Interest groups that created pluralist societies in Japan and northwestern Europe usually had their counterparts in China: peasant and village societies, guilds, clans, corporations, and student associations. Unlike those of northwestern Europe and Japan, however, the Chinese groups normally did not become foci of independent power. The gap between them and the imperial bureaucracy and military was so great and communication across it so scarce that vertical alliances and leverage were rare.

Corporate groups in China centered mainly in the family or clan. These were sometimes fluid organizations, which could be molded through adoptions or liaisons. But clans and families served more the common purpose of a rigidly hierarchical society than they acted as bargaining entities.

Chinese peasant organizations approximating the village associations to which Hilton and Berman referred in Europe do not crop up in the literature. The European associations negotiated with the lords over rights and obligations; they even sued the lords in court and sometimes won.[38] Perhaps Chinese peasant associations such as the White Lotus and the Taiping come closer to the Japanese ikki, with their warrior caste. But Chinese peasant rebellions were more often all-out violent war than the intermittent fighting and mutual concessions characteristic of Japanese peasants and lords. The crucial difference seems to lie in whether groups are deemed to be generically hostile or are seen as presenting opportunities to cooperate.[39] Eberhard concludes that "at all times, down to the present, Chinese governments looked with suspicion at any organization other than the family (the basis of Chinese society to 1949), because such an organization could become a centre of power and hence a threat."[40]

Whereas European guilds dominated many a city government by the fourteenth century, and whereas Japanese guilds were the prime force in organizing production in the Tokugawa era, in China guilds were insignificant until the nineteenth century. Then craftsmen "began to organize in guilds of an essentially religious character. . . . No guild, however, connected people of the same craft living in different cities. . . . Thus, guilds failed to achieve political influence even within individual cities."[41] "The Chinese gild (*hui*) was predominantly a local association, intent on monopolizing the handicraft activity of one community.'[42]

Only in the eighteenth century, when the Chinese government needed some vehicle for negotiating with British traders in Canton, did it authorize merchant organizations. Only then were the restrictions that had humiliated craftsmen and artisans gradually lifted. From their Chinese name *kung-hang* ("officially authorized merchants"), the British called these guilds the Cohong.[43]

Perhaps the closest the Chinese came to wider merchant confederations were regional associations (*hui-kuan*), also of the eighteenth century. "Such associations united people from one city or one area who lived in another city. People of different trades, but mainly businessmen, came together under elected chiefs and councillors."[44]

In sum, the guilds existed only when authorized by government; they did not grow into independent political foci, able to negotiate with government or other corporate groups besides foreign merchants; and they did not serve as prototypes for further corporate entities capable of bargaining with each other. In medieval Europe and Japan, the creation of new corporate categories became the vehicle for social mobility. In China, by contrast, "it was impossible to change one's status by creating new corporate categories. There was only one standard way to achieve privileged status: to become a member of the corporate intellectual elite (whether Confucian, Nationalist, or Communist) or submit to it."[45]

Leverage

Many instances of potential leverage are found throughout Chinese history, but none (that I could find) so functioned as to enhance the power of lower classes.

During the "Spring and Autumn" period (722-481 BCE), when the emperor was "first among equals" of many lords, the nobility frequently called for peasant support in their struggles with the emperor or other nobles.[46] While the peasants received material goods in exchange for support, they did not achieve an increase in status or power. Instead, by crushing the aristocratic class totally in the fourth century BCE,[47] Shang Yang, principal minister of the Qin state, removed all possibility of leverage by weaker groups. There was no rival of the emperor with whom to form a vertical alliance. In the third century BCE the nobility used their peasants as soldiers, to fight their rivals. They even induced peasants to immigrate into their domains, to increase both their armies and their taxes.[48] But again we have no indication of peasants demanding increased privileges or power in exchange for military help.

Fairbank, Reischauer and Craig tell us of "menaces" to the Han emperor, such as families of empresses or pastoral peoples of the north,[49] but peasants did not lever their power by allying with these, probably because "society seems to have been made up of [only] two main groups: taxpaying peasants and rich landowners."[50] The communication gaps were too great for vertical alliances and leverage.

The Tang rulers (618-906) used imperial servants to counteract the power of the nobility.[51] Rivalries among cliques in the emperor's court were conditions that might elsewhere have led to vertical alliances and leverage.[52] Under the Hongzhi emperor (1487-1505) rivalries occurred between the gentry-bureaucrats and the eunuch-bureaucrats, but they were resolved in favor of the former.[53]

As the Mongols were destroying the Sung, many gentry—fearful of peasant rebellions—made common cause with the invaders.[54] As objects of hostility by each group, however, the peasants could hardly have allied with either one.

Disputes among landlords and communities over water rights and financial responsibilities in Ming hydraulic systems might have enabled peasants to swing their weight to one or the other of the disputants. But this did not happen, possibly out of fear, or possibly because as newly arrived outsiders they had no status with the alternative groups. Instead, tenants supported their own landlords. "Common peasants and tenant farmers seem to have been used as rank and file for purposes of intimidation or when it was intended to create a *fait accompli.*"[55]

In none of these situations did peasants increase their power or status in exchange for support for a stronger group, as was the case in northwestern Europe and Japan. We can only surmise a reason: Not only the vastness of the cultural and communications gaps but also the embryonic, unorganized nature of the corporate groups always prevented vertical alliances. The geographical shifting among both gentry and peasant farmers would have interfered with one-on-one relationships. Thus weak and stronger groups did not learn to negotiate and compromise vertically.

The same conditions have applied during the People's Republic. Before 1989, foreign observers had noted, with some wonderment, that the Chinese government at least three times turned criticism on, and when it became excessive turned it off, like water from a spigot. Such were the cases of Mao's Hundred Flowers speech of 1956,[56] of Democracy Wall in 1979,[57] and of a four-week flurry of protests in November-December 1986. In all these cases, by encouragement or at least tolerance on the part of the authorities, protest groups mounted posters, made speeches in public places, and were featured on television. But the authorities and the protest groups did not sit down to serious talk.

Some might suggest that the Confucian ethic of loyalty and authority enabled the government both to turn the protests on with confidence and to turn them off with obedience. Perhaps. But I see another twist. After centuries of little communication between "inferiors" and "superiors" in the traditional hierarchy, no expectation exists on either side for down-to-earth diplomacy. Goldman has suggested that the officials used student protests to make their own points of disagreement in their inner circles: While students put up posters, officials debated similar themes behind their walls.[58] Chinese of different classes were accustomed to talking "past" each other, with communication rubbing off indirectly, to the extent that it did at all.

In April 1989, Beijing students began street protests not authorized by the government. By May, they had occupied Tiananmen Square in the heart of Beijing, next to government offices. Millions were marching in many

Chinese cities, defying martial law and calling for "democracy." In Beijing, they were organized into their own "mini-government: a secretariat, a printing office, a financial affairs ministry, a propaganda ministry, a liaison ministry, a picket squad, a special action squad, a small loud-speaker broadcast station, a pharmacy and three clinics."[59] But they had neither a program nor a definition of democracy nor ambassadors to the government. No reports of even secret talks leaked out. Protesters and government officials were "escaping" communication with each other. On June 4, soldiers shot their way into the square, killing an unknown number of students and taking others into custody. The protests ceased abruptly.

Over centuries, powerful and weak had "escaped" each other in similar ways, carrying on their transactions by power or force, speaking broad generalities and millennial ideas but with few vertical alliances and little negotiation, compromise, or leverage on concrete issues. They had failed to create the social structures by which Chinese people might bargain with one another to convert to a "modern" society in the twenty-first century.

War and Violence

As in virtually the entire world, warfare dominated China's early history. Unlike Europe and Japan, but like Africa and India, endemic warfare has not materially decreased in recent centuries. Violence continues to be a legitimate means of resolving disputes.

Peasant Rebellions

As in Europe and Japan, peasant rebellions dotted the centuries. But the Chinese rebellions tended to differ from those of Europe and Japan in four ways:

First, some European rebellions occurred under improved conditions for the peasantry, such as the English Peasant Revolt of 1381. The plague of 1348 and ensuing years had increased the bargaining power of the reduced number of peasants, whose strength incited them to redress long-standing grievances. By contrast, Chinese rebellions grew out of excruciating hardship. For example, the Yellow Turban Revolt of 184 CE arose from the great struggles of the cliques against each other. Peasants had been drafted into the fighting, and their houses and crops were destroyed.[60] Likewise, "the continual warfare of the military governors, the sanguinary struggles between the cliques, and the universal impoverishment which all this fighting produced"[61] led to famine in Chekiang in 860 and in Hopei in 874, which in turn unleashed rebellions. Other peasant armies joined in uncoordinated violence. The war devastation of the tenth century led to a number of popular uprisings in the north.[62] When the dikes of the Yellow River burst in 1351, peasants drafted to repair them revolted at the ensuing hardships.[63] Early in the sixteenth century, oppressive taxation led to revolts in Sichuan.[64]

Second, European and Japanese rebellions often arose with specific demands: the status of the peasants as villein or free; recognition of freedom of religion; or work terms and schedules on feudal manors. In China, peasants usually did not voice specific demands or sit down with rulers or bureaucracy to negotiate terms. Rather, their revolts were general explosions arising from frustrations. There was no Wat Tyler who could approach the Chinese equivalent of Richard II close enough to grab the reins of his horse.

Third, Chinese rebellions often expressed deeply religious or millennial principles, more akin to Islamic jihads or purification movements, such as the Wahabbi or Almoravid, than to European wars of religion. Best known among these is the formidable Taiping rebellion, started in 1851, "influenced by Christian ideas but more so by Chinese traditional thought."[65]

Where Chinese rebellions did have political aims, they were frequently grandiose, such as the restoration of the Sung dynasty, the intention of some in 1351.[66] The White Lotus society wanted the abdication of the Manchus and restoration of the Ming. Two centuries later, the same society looked for a return of the Buddha to end the suffering. The Taiping also fought for a radical restructuring of the social order into a Christian kingdom. All these rebellions did not reach down to earthy issues between lords and peasants, such as land tenure and labor terms, which were common to the northwest European and Japanese rebellions.

Fourth, Chinese rebellions possessed an element of continuity over time and/or space. The secret White Lotus society, dating to the thirteenth century, sponsored numerous rebellions. A serious one at the turn of the nineteenth century "consisted of uncoordinated roving bands using hit-and-run guerrilla tactics."[67] The Society itself lasted into the twentieth century. The Taiping Rebellion continued for fourteen years, despoiled seventeen provinces, and took about 20 million lives.[68] Some European rebellions, such as the German Peasants' War of 1525, did range over wide territories, but with more limited and more specific goals.

Wars for Land and Power

In more ways than the peasant rebellions, with a few exceptions Chinese have lived most of their history under threat of violence and war. War did not occur at all times and all places, but always violence threatened to erupt for land or power.

Periods of peace occurred at the beginning of every major dynasty since the Tang (618 CE). But these periods—which helped define the dynastic cycle as prosperous in its early years—always came to an end within one to two centuries. Unlike Europe and Japan, no tendency can be seen toward diminution of war or war-related instability in the nineteenth and twentieth centuries.

The Shang dynasty (1766 to about 1122 BCE) existed "in a more or less continuous state of war."[69] The succeeding dynasty, Zhou (1122-221 BCE) "had to hold in check the subjugated but warlike tribes of Turks and Mongols who lived quite close to their capital,"[70] while other feudal lords were continually rising against them. Around 750 BCE any internal cohesion had broken down. In the period of the warring states (481-221 BCE) feudal lords eliminated each other until only the Qin remained. The Qin dynasty (221-206 BCE) is considered the first Chinese empire; the country is named after it. The Qin period was characterized by unremitting threats by nomad tribes from the north. Succession struggles and rebellions by nobles culminated in the murder of the second Qin emperor in 206 BCE, bringing an end to the dynasty.

During the Early Han dynasty (206 BCE-9 CE) some degree of political stability was achieved. Nevertheless, uprisings by feudal princes and kings continued; quixotic alliances against the emperor were common. The Han invaded western Korea in 108 BCE, and under Wu Ti (r.140-87 BCE) they moved into southern China. The drain on resources from maintaining occupation forces so far from home base devastated the imperial finances. The northern empire of Hsiung-nu was a constant threat until it collapsed in 58 BCE. Rivalries in court cliques and palace intrigues during the first century BCE led to the usurpation of the throne by Wang Mang in 9 CE. Wang Mang's brief "empire" (9-23 CE)—characterized by "reforms" that did not last—was punctuated by a great popular uprising by the "Red Eyebrows," which was put down. Harassment of the Hsiung-nu, now Chinese vassals, goaded these northern tribes into rebellions. Vast armies were concentrated in the north, at great expense and at the cost of territories lost.

During the Later Han dynasty (23-220 CE), intrigues by palace cliques brought steady disintegration of the government from 80 CE onward. Provincial generals fought bloodily with each other, and the peasant rebellion of the Yellow Turbans took place. At the same time, the northern threat continued.

When the Han dynasty crumbled in 220, China became divided into a number of kingdoms and dynasties until it was unified again by the Sui dynasty in 580. During this "first division," constant struggles occurred among Chinese cliques and between Chinese gentry and alien nobility in the north. This was a period of massive migration. A great popular rising in the south, around the year 400, was bloodily suppressed. Incessant fighting continued on the borders. "For nearly three hundred years the southern empire had witnessed unceasing struggles between powerful cliques, making impossible any peaceful development within the country."[71]

Attempts by the first Sui emperor to resettle population in his home area in the north brought rebellions in the south. Continuous wars were waged against the Turks, who defeated the Chinese in 615. Expeditions were undertaken into Nam Viet (Vietnam), Tonking, and Taiwan, along with costly and futile campaigns in Korea (612-14). These foreign wars led to risings against the second Sui emperor, which in turn led to his murder in 618 and the beginning of the Tang dynasty.

Internal fighting continued until the Tang were firmly established in 623. The Turks invaded all the way to the Tang capital in 624, but thereafter peace was established. This, however, was balanced by war with the Tibetans, during which China lost Sinkiang. The internal stability and military strength of the early Tang marked two centuries of increased prosperity, but armies on the frontier and campaigns against Islam were expensive. Korea was conquered in 640. The Uighurs dissolved from 832 onward, as did the Tibetan Empire from 842.[72] A series of revolts rocked the dynasty from 755 until its fall in 906.

In the "second division" of China (906-960), ten southern kingdoms fought with each other; any one might ally with a northern power against the northern dynasty. Threats continued from the Turks and the northern empire of Khitan. The northwest became depopulated from ruinous external wars.

China was again reunited by the Northern Sung dynasty (960-1127). From 960 to 979 "in northern China there was constant warfare, and everywhere it was a period of insecurity and sweeping social change."[73] Thereafter, a great period of prosperity began, along with an unusual period of peace. "But there was constant and bitter factional strife between those who wished to rationalize government. . . and this weakened the Sung state."[74] Sporadic wars with the Khitan ended with the payment of an annual tribute to them after 1004. The independence of the Juchen from the Khitan in 1114 released the former to fight the Sung, whom they subdued quickly, bringing an end to the northern dynasty. The Sung retreated to the south, where they set up a new capital.

The Southern Sung dynasty (1127 to 1279) again launched a period of internal stability, though sporadic fighting occurred against the Juchen. But in 1233 the Sung allied with the Mongols to defeat the Juchen. However, the Mongols attacked the Sung and ended the dynasty.

The Mongol (Yüan) dynasty (1280 to 1368) marked another period of relative external peace, with wars confined to the frontiers of Burma, Annam,

Cambodia, and Java. Two attempts to invade Japan were defeated by typhoons. However, the great internal suffering that the Mongols inflicted on the Chinese led to internal revolts beginning in 1325, which destabilized the dynasty and ultimately ended it.

The early Ming dynasty also ushered in a period of relative internal stability and—once the Mongols had definitely been defeated in 1425—external peace. Coastal piracy by the Japanese, one campaign against the western Mongols in 1449, and a rebellion to secure the independence of Annam punctuated this peace. Misrule and extravagance by the emperors led again to uprisings from 1512 on, which became more serious in the seventeenth century. In 1517, Portuguese traders built a fortress on an island off Canton. "Hindering trade and flouting Chinese law, these semipirates were accused of robbery, blackmail, and buying Chinese children from Chinese kidnappers."[75] Intrigues by court cliques and murders threatened the dynasty from within. Border threats increased after 1521, with incursions by the Mongols and, later on, the Manchu. Wars with Annam, Burma, and Thailand continued from 1544 to 1604. Insurrection broke out in every part of China.[76] The Manchus and Mongols united to take Korea in 1637, and the Manchus drove on into Peking in 1644, ending the Ming dynasty.

After some mopping up of recalcitrant Ming, the Qing dynasty of the Manchus ushered in another period of internal peace and stability, which lasted until late in the eighteenth century. Some wars occurred on the northern border in the late seventeenth century, leading to the Treaty of Nerchinsk with Russia in 1689, China's first modern treaty with a Western power. A few disturbances with the Mongols occurred from about 1690 to 1720. Aside from these, plus some border skirmishes, the eighteenth century until 1774 was an unusual period of peace.

Popular risings began in Shantung in 1774, followed by the White Lotus rebellion (1775-1804). Rebellions broke out with greater frequency during the nineteenth century: Taiping (1850-64), which nearly overthrew the dynasty; Nien (1856-68); and several Muslim risings (1855-73). The intrusion of Europeans, with the Opium War (1840-42), Russian intervention (1858), Anglo-French attack on North China (1860), and war with Japan and the loss of Taiwan (1894) revealed Chinese weakness vis-à-vis Western technology and military strength. The Qing dynasty was overthrown by Hupei army troops in 1911.

The Republic of China (1911-1949, but still existing on Taiwan) led quickly into civil war between the northern and southern governments, until 1927. Even as that war was raging, China was fragmented into spheres of warlord influence. "The typical warlord army had no roots among the local people but was a scourge among them, exacting taxes, living off the villages, feared and despised."[77]

Chiang Kai-shek's campaign against warlords had scarcely ended when the Communist revolution began, to last from 1927 to 1949, with an intermission to fight the Japanese. In 1931, the Japanese invaded Manchuria and went on to occupy major seaports and some internal centers in China. This war mixed into World War II, and the Japanese were defeated only in 1945. The Communist revolution resumed, with the Nationalist Government driven to Taiwan in 1949. In the People's Republic (1949 to date) peace was interrupted by the Cultural Revolution of 1968. Mao's concept of "continuous revolution"[78]—a struggle against capitalism for twenty-five years (if not forever)—smacks of endemic warfare being considered a legitimate means of conducting economic relations. Chinese reforms begun after the death of Mao in 1976 may have been delayed by the tensions arising out of the Tiananmen Square massacre in 1989.

Over the centuries, those not directly participating in wars were disastrously affected, through loss of livelihood and the push to migrate. Right down to the Cultural Revolution and the Tiananmen Square massacre and on into today, no Chinese has been safe from the violence of government or its challengers. Military solutions have always been, and still are, considered a legitimate way to resolve disputes, at least among the powerful. Furthermore, they tend to be implemented through the confrontation of extreme but vaguely worded positions and to conclude with total victory or defeat, not compromise.

Such endemic violence is not consistent with commitments to intergroup cooperation, saving and investment, and long-term ventures. The fact that such commitments were widely made in earlier history is a testimony to the natural vigor of trade and entrepreneurship everywhere, but only up to a certain point. That these commitments did not pass the threshold of sustained economic development is attributable to Chinese circumstance.

Notes

1. Eberhard 1977:60.
2. Loewe 1985:258.
3. Eberhard 1977:85, 89.
4. Loewe 1985:265.
5. Eberhard 1977:112ff.
6. Eberhard 1977:172.
7. Eberhard 1977:183.
8. Geiger 1973.

9. Eberhard 1977:54.
10. Hulsewe 1985:231.
11. Lewis 1988:107.
12. Lewis 1988:13.
13. Lewis 1988:178.
14. Lewis 1988:199.
15. Eberhard 1977:256.
16. Braudel 1981:454.
17. Eberhard 1977:193.
18. Fairbank, Reischauer and Craig 1978:105.
19. Jacobs 1958:34.
20. Fairbank, Reischauer and Craig 1978:136.
21. I have supplied many examples of this in Powelson 1988: chapter 14.
22. Fairbank, Reischauer and Craig 1978:55-56.
23. Spence 1987:1.
24. Jacobs 1958:107.
25. Lewis 1988:9.
26. Fairbank, Reischauer and Craig 1978:185.
27. Fairbank, Reischauer and Craig 1978:227.
28. Santangelo 1985:283.
29. Santangelo 1985:287.
30. Eberhard 1977:48.
31. Loewe 1985:255.
32. Eberhard 1977:191.
33. Li 1977:xlviii.
34. Morgan 1986:110.
35. Rozman 1973:41.
36. Thaxton 1982:375.
37. Powelson 1988: chapter 14.
38. Berman 1983:555-6; Hilton 1773:70-71, 74-75.
39. Karl Marx, for example, would find them generically hostile; to Alexis de Tocqueville, cooperation was a possibility.
40. Eberhard 1977:192.
41. Eberhard 1977:207-8.
42. Jacobs 1958:38.
43. Fairbank, Reischauer and Craig 1978:255-56.
44. Eberhard 1977:208.
45. Jacobs 1958:142.
46. Hsu 1965:90.
47. Li 1977:lx.
48. Eberhard 1977:49.
49. Fairbank, Reischauer and Craig 1978:60.
50. Fairbank, Reischauer and Craig 1978:61-62.
51. Wolf 1982:53-4.
52. Eberhard (1977:266) writes of the Ming, but the same must have been so for other dynasties.
53. Grimm 1985:42.
54. Eberhard 1977:247.
55. Will 1985:321.
56. MacFarquhar 1974:51-6.

57. Reported in sporadic newspaper articles during 1979. In *New York Times*, these culminated with James P. Sterba, "Peking Closes Democracy Wall, Banishes Posters to Remote Park,"12/7/79
58. Goldman, Merle, "How China's Leaders Use Student Protests," *New York Times*, 1/1/87.
59. Wu Dunn, Sheryl, "In Quest for Democracy, Mini-Government is Born," *New York Times* 5/31/89.
60. Eberhard 1977:99-100.
61. Eberhard 1977:193.
62. Eberhard 1977:215.
63. Eberhard 1977:247.
64. Eberhard 1977:271.
65. Eberhard 1977:302.
66. Eberhard 1977:247.
67. EBMi 1974:10:656.
68. EBMi 1974:9:774.
69. Eberhard 1977:17.
70. Eberhard 1977:29.
71. Eberhard 1977:166.
72. Eberhard 1977:192.
73. Barraclough 1984:126.
74. Barraclough 1984:126.
75. Fairbank, Reischauer and Craig 1978:244.
76. Eberhard 1977:278.
77. Fairbank, Reischauer and Craig 1978:758.
78. MacFarquhar 1983:29.

Chapter 12
China: Institutions and Reform

Now that we have seen what aspects of China's historical development hindered the power-diffusion process, we will examine the roles of law, money and banking, and the labor system as representative institutions. We then will summarize the failure of power diffusion in China and look for signs of hope that it may eventually occur.

Law

Law more than any other institution of economic growth characterizes the vast divide between rulers and people in China. The present section begins with a list of observations on the nature of Chinese law, followed by a short subsection for each observation.

> • The main purpose of Chinese law is to preserve state power, not the rights of the individual.
> • Traditional Chinese law sees little or no distinction between criminal and civil. It is more concerned with penalties than with righting civil wrongs. Thus rules and judgments regarding trade, sales, and production were not part of the legal system before Western ways were copied after 1912.
> • Merchants and landowners have made contracts throughout Chinese history. With the rulers considering commercial matters too far beneath them to interfere, these contracts have been expanded—through a free market in institutions—into informal rules of commerce composed, written, and enforced by guilds and trading organizations. They resulted in a paralegal system, sufficiently complex and sophisticated to permit high levels of economic interaction.
> • Inequality and hierarchy have been legalized, with different rules applying to persons of different rank. This discrimination still applies today.
> • For much of Chinese history, only government officials were allowed to know the official law. If commoners knew the law, it was believed that they would become litigious and defy authority. This concept changed with the Ming dynasty, but the present rulers still do not go out of their way to see that their laws are widely understood.

• Although the Chinese early adopted the principle that the ruler must obey the law, nevertheless law in China is so centered around the ruler—much more so than in northwestern Europe or Japan—that he can change it at will or set it aside momentarily. Therefore, his obedience to law becomes meaningless.

• Codes and statutes were highly developed in early centuries. Their principal purpose was to inform provincial magistrates on the content of the criminal statutes they were expected to enforce. Common law, or the use of precedents, has been rare.

• A class of professional lawyers emerged but slowly and with great difficulty. Although professionalization of the law has advanced in the twentieth century, it is limited by the government's arbitrary actions and evasions.

• Unlike northwestern Europe and Japan, the basic nature of Chinese law has not changed much over the centuries. Principles from the Shang dynasty (1766 to about 1122 BCE) still govern the legal actions of the People's Republic.

All nine of these points reinforce the proposition that little of the power-diffusion process has been at work in China over the centuries. Appendix 12.1 lists historical references to China's legal system, particularly regarding state power and criminal versus civil law.

State Power

[T]he emperor—the only authority which can be formally considered as the source of legality, if indeed legality may be said to exist. [I]t has never been possible to speak, in China, of *the law* in the sense in which that term has been applied in the Western juridical tradition, to actual positive laws.[1]

Dividing the world's legal models into three types—ethical, religious, and realistic—Yan Meng characterizes the Chinese as ethical: rule by *Li*, legal thought, and rule by *Fa*, law. These were later joined, to become rule by *Li-Fa*, virtue with law.[2]

Confucius (551-479 BCE) described the Chinese system as "ethical" because, as an intellectual seeking government position, he needed to please his masters.[3] His system validated the cruel, hierarchical, stifling code of behavior already adopted by the warlords of his era. Fifteen centuries after Confucius, Chu Hsi also wrote that "law (*li*) was the guide and rule for man, an ethical norm, preferred and good."[4]

Although the emperor's authority had already been deemed absolute for one thousand years, its formalization is associated with the Legalist School attributable to Shang Yang (about 390 to 338 BCE), who became an advisor to Duke Hsiao of Qin. He persuaded the Duke "to institute a series of wide-ranging reforms to promote state control, centralization of power, and economic and military expansion."[5] When Qin had conquered its rivals in 220 BCE and founded the first unified Chinese empire, it adopted these laws. Vandermeersch refers to Legalism as "pseudo-law, which had nothing to do with the idea of right, [but which] was formulated purely and simply as an instrument of government . . . rule imposed upon its subjects by the state administration."[6]

One characteristic of state control has been that the same officials arrest, seek evidence, prosecute, determine guilt or innocence, and pass sentence.[7] In principle, this was not always so. For example, "Sung legal institutions are noteworthy for the relatively thorough appellate reviews they provided and for the effort, reflected in this organization, to insure a separation of judicial from police functions."[8] But the ease with which alleged traitors and revolutionaries have received "summary justice" belies the continuation of these Sung practices.

Henderson contrasts the Ming Chinese with Japanese judges of the Tokugawa era. Ming judges were bound "to protect the absolute authority of the emperor to legislate and to ultimately decide all major cases on appeal. In contrast, the Tokugawa legal system (*bakuhan*) was the epitome of delegated judicial decision making: the 'judge' in each tiny domain was the court of first and last instances for most cases . . ."[9]

But during the Qing dynasty in China (1644-1911):

> Forced to kneel abjectly before the Emperor's high bench, flanked by guards wielding bamboo staves, whips, and other instruments, precluded from presenting his own witnesses, and denied the services of a professional advocate, the accused had no meaningful opportunity to defend himself.

> This Ch'ing procedure reflected the view that law and legal institutions serve principally as instruments for maintaining the power of the state rather than enhancing the sense of security of its citizens.[10]

This purpose of law has continued right into the late twentieth century. During the Cultural Revolution of 1968 "enemies" of the state were quickly exiled to the country. After the Tiananmen Square massacre of 1989, "enemies" were imprisoned or executed.

Through judicial decisions and reviews, law in the West has evolved along with changing mores. In China, by contrast, mores are expected to conform to the law. "Rectification denotes the coordination of the reality of the social situation with the definition of that situation in law or other codes."[11] More recent rectification campaigns, to bring public morality into line with state decisions, were carried out in 1957[12] and 1984.[13]

Criminal versus Civil Law

> Law for the Chinese people is not an autonomous body of rational rules and precedent which is applied uniformly to all classes in society; it is merely a tool to bring the recalcitrant members of society who are not open to moral suasion into line with established mores. Thus from earliest times law was deemed to be primarily criminal and administrative in character.[14]

Formal Chinese law has excluded private trade, possibly for the reasons that Yan Meng mentions. Other reasons might be: First, the communication gap between the imperial bureaucracy and merchants was so great that disputes among the latter would neither be brought to exalted places nor even understood there. Second, the bureaucracy already exercised the only authority it needed, to milk society economically and keep it peaceful politically. Its means were licenses, taxes, usury, prices, bailments, weights and measures, and monopolies in mining and grain deliveries and storage.[15] Other disputes, for example over contract performance among private traders, may have been deemed inconsequential.

The exclusion of private trade from formal law led to certain anomalies. In the Sung dynasty, a civil case might last indefinitely because lower courts did not have the authority to resolve it, yet appeal to the imperial court was forbidden because it might not be important enough.[16]

Contracts

Another anomaly was contracts. The intractability of hierarchical relationships made vertical contracts (those between social classes) difficult. Yet contract existed from early days. By studying bronze inscriptions Creel discovered contracts as far back as the beginnings of the Zhou dynasty in 1028 BCE: "as early as 3,000 years ago Chinese were making contracts, litigating disputes, and enlisting others as advocates of their causes."[17] Creel reports that "this very early concern with private contracts is quite surprising as compared with later practice."[18] But the cases he reports concern only disputes among royal officials over sales and among gentry over land.

Some vertical contracts may have existed during the Early Han dynasty: "All 'gentry' families owned substantial estates in the provinces which they leased to tenants on a kind of contract basis."[19] Rents were about half the produce. However, it is not clear that these were true contracts, in which tenants bargained over their political or personal status vis-à-vis lords, as they did in European and Japanese feudalisms. Given the high rents, it may be doubted that they acted from any strength at all.

By the Ming dynasty (1368-1644), the land contract became more like the European of a few centuries earlier and the Japanese of the same period.[20] But there is no indication of tenant associations or bargaining in the European or Japanese modes. The only redress for breach of contract could be to walk away from it, to "escape," if one could. The dynastic convulsions and peasant rebellions were so severe that contract could hardly have been the governing force in the tenant-landlord relationship.

Although no commercial law was adjudicated in ordinary courts, toward the end of the nineteenth century merchant guilds on Taiwan employed "contract forms and substantive contract rules which incorporated mechanisms of self-enforcement and self-execution directly into the contracts themselves"[21] for members of the same guild. These contracts, studied by Brockman, contained well-defined terms, agreed informally within the guilds. Because they had no judicial system to interpret and enforce them, "the parties were careful to specify their reciprocal rights and obligations in the contracts themselves" and to generate "out of trade practices and usages a number of well-defined rules which provided for a determination and allocation of the rights and obligations of the parties on the occurrence of certain contingencies." Thus these contracts expanded into a sort of commercial law, privately administered. Before the twentieth century, however, neither imperial nor provincial nor other courts would resolve disputes between members of different guilds, and—possibly because of continued warfare, state interference, or other unsettled conditions—the guilds and other merchant associations did not negotiate the rules across trades.[22]

In sum, even before the nineteenth century the Chinese possessed rudimentary types of negotiation and commercial contracts. Their formation, arranged by the participating parties, resembles a free market for institutions. However, they did not progress into impartial, enforceable law as a power in itself. Nor did the Chinese afford legal protection and equality among groups of different political or social status. Rather, "the enforcement of these contracts depended on the types of informal community pressures and social controls that have been shown to operate in cohesive communities in the absence of a formalized legal system."[23]

The adoption of modern legal practices during the Republic did little to change this situation, since the new lawyers were ill trained and lacking in practice. With the advent of the People's Republic in 1949, any commercial law that had been negotiated by businesspeople through their guilds became emasculated as state law came to dominate all society, including the economy.

Hierarchy and Inequality

Probably the most conspicuous single Confucian influence on imperial Chinese law is the principle of legalized inequality. Prior to the revolution of 1911, Chinese law endlessly differentiated its treatment according to individual rank, relationship, and specific circumstance.[24]

[O]nly an educated person, . . . a member of the gentry, could claim that his action should be judged by the decisions of Confucius.[25]

Even today, in the People's Republic, persons of different statuses continue to be judged differently. Children of political opponents are stigmatized legally and judged harshly. The big question is not the existence of legalized inequality, which is common to all early societies, but why it did not diminish in China over the centuries, as it did in northwestern Europe and Japan.

Ignorance of the Law

In the sixth century BCE, "Tzu-ch'an, prime minister of the state of Cheng, was strongly criticized for publicly promulgating its penal code. The critic contended that after learning the exact content of the penal law (*hsing*) the people would never again be bound by the principles of correct social behavior (*li*) but would have constant recourse to litigation."[26]

This principle may have operated continuously for over a millennium. It appears again in the Sung dynasty (960-1279), when copies of laws were intended only to guide government officials.[27] Private individuals were forbidden to print or copy them.[28]

There is no way to analyze why this restriction continued as long as it did or why the first Ming emperor reversed it in the fourteenth century. It became one more way in which communication and cooperation on economic matters were restricted. Even today, questioning of the law by ordinary persons is not provided for in any courts.

Emperor-Centered Law

For ten centuries from approximately 1000 BCE, "the emperor was bound by the law code; he could not change it nor abolish it."[29] Confucius wrote that the emperor and all nobility should in their lives exemplify virtue before their people.[30]

Throughout imperial China, however, the question of the emperor's obeying the law hardly arose. The emperor was both the source and interpreter of law, and his actions would determine what the law was. Each time a new dynasty was established, the first emperor would justify the overthrow of the old by its illegal or unjust behavior. The first Qing emperor, for example, declared that he was defending the pure principles of the Ming dynasty against their abuse by the latest emperors.

In the same vein, after the death of Mao Zedong in 1976, certain high officials, including the Gang of Four, advocates of Mao—one was his wife—were charged with violating the law and the principles of the revolution. (There are many cases, in the less developed zones, when a change of president will bring violent or serious action against the preceding incumbent). Often the law is distorted for political ends; this is the diametric opposite of equality before the law whatever the rank of the person.

Codes and Statutes

Law codes existed continuously during the Spring and Autumn period (722 to 481 BCE), with new ones frequently compiled on the basis of old.[31] Statutes came even earlier; the Zhou (1122 to 221 BCE) adopted some of those of its predecessor dynasty, the Shang (1766 to about 1122 BCE). At least until the Qin dynasty (221-206 BCE) every aspect of daily life had its rules, imposed by land statutes, storehouse statutes, working statutes, and others.[32]

Every dynasty drew up its own code, usually an adaptation of that of the preceding dynasty. The Qin code was copied by the Han and was revised by every Han emperor.[33] The Tang code, covering every aspect of private and public life, is the most complete feudal legal document extant.[34] Inherited by the Sung, it was "a comprehensive legal system that furnished a model not only for subsequent Chinese dynasties but also for the early rulers of Korea, Vietnam, and Japan."[35]

Attempting to combine Chinese codes with their own traditional laws,[36] the Mongols drew up the Great Yasa code in 1206. The Ming codes of 1397 and 1585 honored imperial statute as "sacred and immutable."[37] The statutes of the Qing code of 1646 were virtually identical to those of the first

Ming code. "It was preeminently an instrument for state building and the preservation of the social order, being essentially a compendium of rules, directed to district magistrates and their superiors, for the punishment of persons who hindered the operation of government."[38]

Professionalization

Creel has found some evidence that in the Spring and Autumn period (722-481 BCE) contestants in legal cases were represented by advocates.[39] But this is a far cry from evidence of a legal profession.

During the Sung period, there emerged "for the first time theoretical discussion and legal rules concerning the interrogation of defendants, the right to appeal, the training of judges, the evaluation of testimony."[40] Those participating in these discussions might be labeled proto-lawyers. This was approximately the same period in which legal scholars were emerging in Europe.

Eberhard suggests that "if these rules were really applied in practical life, the judicial system of China can only be called very progressive and modern, if compared with Europe at the same time."[41] But he has missed a major point: that the Chinese system was handed down by an elite class, while the European—even if more rudimentary—was founded on a depth of discussion and negotiation among scholars turning professional.

"[T]here were no advocates or lawyers permitted in Sung courts. There were, however, others who became involved in the administration of justice. These were classified into three categories according to social rank: officials, clerks, and commoners."[42] But all these individuals, as Miyazaki goes on to explain, were officials of the bureaucracy. When the reformer Wang An-shih promoted judicial knowledge and examinations (about 1070 CE), these too were for officials only. Private scholars or professional advocates did not exist. "The judicial process was an important responsibility of a highly articulated centralized bureaucracy that was staffed by officials generally selected on the basis of merit demonstrated in passing examinations that tested knowledge of the Confucian classics and literary skill."[43] Indeed, "in the hope of restraining an increasingly litigious populace, the general use of advocates was prohibited."[44]

Before 1912, the only group that might be called legal scholars were those who prepared private interpretations and compilations. For a people that produced significant historians of dynasties, however, it might seem odd that few private compilations of the legal statutes of those dynasties were written. Instead, there are "no more than occasional compilations, often prepared by scholars acting in a private and unofficial capacity, and they are invariably incomplete."[45] The most famous among these is Shen's private commentary, written about 1715. This and others like it were intended to help the Qing local magistrates, who had to interpret tersely written imperial laws without much help from the bureaucracy. But Chang Chen, who studied 9,000 entries from contemporary judgments, found no more than twenty-one references to Shen's commentary.[46] By 1822, provincial officials were told not to rely on it.

An embryonic legal profession did emerge after the Republic of 1912. At that time "a professional lawyer class was allowed to develop as part of the paraphernalia of modernization. [But by] 1922 China was . . . overrun by ill-trained, self-aggrandizing practitioners. . . ."[47] Even today, despite greater education possibilities both at home and abroad, and despite the existence of lawyers, China does not possess a modern legal profession.

Slow-Changing Law

In 1911, the new Republican government promulgated criminal and civil codes, the former taken largely from the Qing code and the latter written by a Japanese scholar. In 1931, the Legislative Yuan of the Nationalist government wrote a new constitution, together with civil and commercial codes, to modernize Chinese laws. Laws on contracts, sales, leaseholds, negotiable instruments, bills of exchange, agencies, bailments, and partnerships and corporations were copied from those of other countries. Ownership of property was defined and protected.[48]

In 1949, the Central Committee of the Communist Party declared the constitution and all the laws and statutes of the Nationalist government (Guomindang) void. The People's Republic started its laws from a clean slate.[49] Local laws were abolished, and all new laws were those of the centralized state. From 1949 through 1952, 376 legal documents were issued by the Central People's Government Council, the Central People's Government Administration Council, and various ministries and commissions. New constitutions were written in 1954, 1975, and 1978. All together, these transformed the economic and political organizations, captured ownership of property for the state, and defined the economic relationships of all persons.[50]

Despite this "clean sweep," observers from outside China, and more recently from inside as well, have commented on the consistency from ancient to modern legal practice, for example, "the persistence of China's a-juridical system in the political practice of the People's Republic [in that all organs of government are] subordinated to the leadership of the Party."[51] Other ancient principles, still practiced, include shaming criminals through public viewing and placards, self-criticism, and punishments lasting for three generations.[52]

In sum, modern organizations were decreed by both the Nationalist government and the People's Republic. But new behavior was not negotiated from new balances of power. Hence the old institutions governed much the same kinds of action as before. Except for extra-legal commercial "law" negotiated and enforced by guilds, law has in all centuries been for the benefit of the ruling powers, who were the ones to create it. At no point in Chinese history has official law been made by those who are subject to it.

In 1993, the head of the pro-democracy party in Hong Kong tried to file a case against an official of Beijing's preparatory working group for the takeover of Hong Kong. The case was turned down by eighteen leading law firms, which did not want to offend a defendant with the proper connections. This condition bodes no good for the enforcement of "property rights, contracts, and free speech" in a Hong Kong absorbed by the Chinese.[53]

Money and Banking

As in Japan and Europe, the history of money and banking in China has been a struggle for control between private entrepreneurs and the state. As in Japan and Europe, in most eras there has been a mixture of responsibilities and power between these two sectors. But in China, the state competed more successfully against private interests than did its counterpart in Europe or Japan. Therefore "the financial administration in China [has] from ancient times been an essential aspect of the machinery and of the functions of the central power."[54] The state today is able to use—and abuse—the monetary system in ways that could not be employed in northwestern Europe and Japan.

Although private coins circulated in the early years, they were prohibited in 186 BCE and again in 112 BCE. Thereafter with only a few exceptions, coinage was a monopoly of the state, to the extent that this could be enforced.[55] Exports of coins were frequently prohibited, although they might occur clandestinely.

Private money did have an early beginning. In the third to sixth centuries CE, merchants deposited both goods and money in Buddhist monasteries.[56] In the eighth century there were "shops dealing with gold, silver, and commodity vouchers issued by the government against monopoly goods like salt and tea. Part of the business of these shops was to issue promissory notes and to remit money to distant places. They accepted deposits, but it is not clear whether they made loans."[57]

Beginning in the ninth century, merchants began to use drafts. In response to the high cost and danger of transporting coins, in the tenth century these drafts were circulating as prototypes of paper money, and a private banking system began to link wholesale trade.[58] Paper money was first issued by merchants in Sichuan in 1024.[59]

Only in the eleventh century did China begin to follow a significantly different path from northwestern Europe and Japan. The Sung emperors captured the monetary system. Paper money was made a state monopoly.[60] Both in response to burgeoning international trade (or as a stimulus to it) and to its own explosive budget (mainly military), the Sung minted more coins than any other dynasty.[61] "The state budget increased from 22,200,000 [pieces of money] in 1000 to 158,800,000 in 1021."[62] State-issued paper money proliferated; the government would redeem it only at a discount of 3 percent, which also added to the treasury. Private paper issues, known as *hui-tzu*, circulated but were forbidden and taken over by the Southern Sung dynasty, which issued money as an imperial monopoly.[63]

Imperial extravagance during the Mongol (Yüan) dynasty provoked the export of metallic money. When not enough was left inside the country, the government printed large quantities of paper currency. These quickly depreciated, and confidence of the public was lost. Soon the government would no longer accept its own money at face value.[64] To bolster it, in 1262 it forbade the use of copper, gold, and silver as media of exchange, making its paper currency the sole legal tender.[65] (This was the money known to Marco Polo.) Since the prohibition had to be repeated, probably it was not very effective.

Under the Ming dynasty, paper currency continued to be issued but was declared inconvertible. Finally worthless, it was abandoned in 1450.[66] Silver in bars and ingots had increasingly circulated since Sung times, and Chinese also used gold in trading with Japan.[67] But copper cash was now restored as the basic money. Thus the Chinese state dominated money issues, using them for its own purposes, mainly for war and court extravagances, while inhibiting, though not completely preventing, private merchants from issuing currencies useful to their trades.

Approximately 1700, notes issued by local banks began to supplement metallic currency,[68] and the Qing government did not stop them. "From the eighteenth century on, native banks organized by Shansi bankers began to establish a network covering the major cities of the empire."[69] These were supplemented by private notes in the nineteenth century, issued not only by banks but by other businesses.[70] The reserves behind them were limited because both government itself and top-ranking officials hoarded much gold and silver, thus keeping this money out of productive circulation.[71] There was no direct link between public reserves and private money, as had developed in Europe and Japan.

As foreign traders arrived more frequently in China in the nineteenth century, they complained about the chaotic nature of the currency: small and counterfeit coins, many with lower than stated metallic content; debased official coins; and many notes by issuers of unknown credit rating, whose exchange rates were unclear.[72] In the mid-nineteenth century the government again issued paper currency, this time to finance the war against the Taiping. Not being convertible, these notes rapidly lost value.[73]

Foreign banks began to fill the gap, beginning in 1865 with the Hong Kong and Shanghai Banking Corporation, a British concern. Foreign silver currency circulated, mainly the Indian rupee before 1893 and the Mexican peso before 1903. The Chinese silver dollar circulated thereafter.[74] The Imperial (later Commercial) Bank of China became the first modern Chinese bank, founded in 1897.[75] True to historic tradition, however, Chinese banks of the early twentieth century financed mainly the government; hence they congregated in the capital, Peking.[76] Foreign trade was mainly financed by foreign banks.

In 1935, a new monetary system was put into place, with the currency of three government banks—the Central Bank, the Bank of China, and the Bank of Communications—becoming legal tender and the Central Bank controlling monetary policy.[77]

The close relationship between banking and government has been continued in the People's Republic. A new State Bank, also known as the People's Bank, was formed in 1948. Private banks were nationalized in 1952 and placed under its purview.[78] During the Mao period, banks were no more than government agencies for transmitting funds to and from government and among entities fulfilling plans of the central government, communes, or village or production brigades.

With post-Mao liberalism, some reforms were undertaken in the late 1970s. These included:

(1) transforming banks into profit-oriented business enterprises whose employees are eligible to earn bonuses; (2) allowing lower-level bank branches to make some reallocations among different categories of loans, as long as they meet aggregate targets; and (3) letting banks that attract more deposits than planned or speed up the turnover of their loans use the proceeds to make additional loans of their choice. . . . The most important measures have been the decentralization of the credit management system and the establishment of domestic trust and investment organizations.[79]

These reforms merit four comments. First and foremost, they are changes in *organizations*, not institutions. While shifting a few formalities and channels, participants behave in the new organizations much as they did in the previous ones. Second, the reforms are modest, revealing more about the remaining central control than about what has been liberalized. Third, they were passed "down" by central authorities. They did not arise from banking officials protesting, with some clout, to the government concerning their needs. Fourth, the banks have no more power than before, no position from which they can defend their gains if the government should try to take them away again. Thus, "bank branches in practice still may not be independent from local government authorities and finance bureaus. In particular, some branch banks may still be forced to continue providing credit to inefficient enterprises that should be closed down."[80]   In addition, "involuntary loans [were] exacted by the central government from the provinces starting in 1981 as well as to a lesser extent [by] the sales of treasury bonds."[81]

Unchecked power over the monetary system led, in the 1980s, to artificially low interest rates and excessive credit extension to state enterprises, which in turn led to an inflation in the neighborhood of 20 to 30 percent.[82] In an address before a conference of economists in Shanghai in 1988, Milton Friedman argued for a rapid end to the inflation as a condition for effectively operating a market economy.[83] Given the power configuration, however, the government could not have adopted a Western banking system in the 1980s or 1990s even if its top officials had all wanted to. It could not have stopped the rampant inflation without denying credit to hundreds, possibly thousands, of inefficient factories dotting the countryside. Massive bankruptcies and unemployment would have followed. In addition, local party bosses, who had been subsidized for decades, could not suddenly be cut off unless they had lost their political following in other ways first. Either of these events would have triggered at least a local rebellion.[84] The idea that simple changes in monetary and fiscal policy will contain an inflation is Western. It does not reflect reality in China.

The Labor System

In one sense, China has always had a free market in labor. In another sense, it never has. In the first sense, for more than two thousand years, labor has normally been compensated in cash, and workers have been officially free to move.[85] In the second sense, under the empire, the state always had the right to corvée labor; until the sixteenth century, craftsmen were virtual serfs; slavery existed until the twentieth century; wages in kind or food and lodging have been common. Under the People's Republic, labor mobility has been restricted, with workers assigned to tasks and wages determined by committees assessing work done or political points earned ("Redness") rather than by negotiation. Although Deng liberalism brought improvements in 1977 and thereafter, the greatest labor freedom has come—at all ages—from circumventing government restrictions.

In the period BCE and the early centuries CE, laborers of lower rank were subject to many kinds of corvée, required by local officials, landowners, or the imperial government. Sometimes a specific amount was required per year, at other times the demands were ad hoc. Holders of higher rank were exempt. In the Shang dynasty (1766 to about 1122 BCE), "there were no free men: nobody was free, but the higher a person was in the social scheme, the more freedom he had."[86] In the Qin government (221-206 BCE), the labor force contained "two distinct groups of people: statute labourers on the one hand and hard-labour convicts on the other. . . . Statute labour was performed by all men between the ages of fifteen and sixty; no service was imposed on the higher aristocratic ranks."[87]

As in Africa, slavery was often the product of war, and some wars were waged specifically to seize slaves. Much of the raiding back and forth with the Hsiung-nu tribes to the north occurred for this reason, on both sides.[88] Although slavery "faded out slowly over the centuries," nevertheless "some of the larger ethnic groups living in areas where they were still the majority, remained under restrictions into the twentieth century."[89]

The Mongols used Chinese slave labor to build their palaces.[90] In the early fifteenth century dikes on the Han and Yangtze rivers were rehabilitated with conscript labor.[91] The Ming (1358-1644) and Qing (1644-1912) required artisans to be listed in "yellow registers" from which corvée labor was drawn for imperial factories. They also sent slaves from the imperial court.[92] Under the Qing, "enslavement by the state was inflicted as an aggravated form of punishment for heinous offenses. In exceptionally serious cases, it was imposed not only on the offender but also on his relatives."[93] These practices do not differ greatly from slavery elsewhere in the world during those centuries.

But in China, labor restrictions continue, today. To curb urban sprawl, the Government of the People's Republic in the early 1960s required that persons might move into any city only with government permission. This was "the most rigid urban policy in the world. . . . At Wuhan Iron and Steel Company . . . boys inherit jobs from their fathers; fathers retire in favor of their sons."[94]

Confronted with new information that unemployment was approximately 20 percent of the nonagricultural labor force, the government in 1979 began urging local authorities to establish "collective" (as opposed to state-owned) enterprises, into which hundreds of thousands of workers were placed.[95] Possibly these enterprises, so hastily formed, may have been among those which ten years later required inflation-fueling subsidies.

When the government revealed in 1980 that 196,000 scientists and technicians were unemployed, more than the number graduated by the universities in a year, state enterprises were pressed to hire them. But the *People's Daily* reported that hirings were slow.[96] In 1980, a bureaucrat in Changchun, where automobiles are produced, observed to a foreign reporter: "We have to take on inefficient, untrained young workers, whom we could do better without, just to give them jobs."[97] But Eyster, an international business consultant, reported in 1984 that "it is gradually becoming possible, albeit not yet common in China, to change jobs if dissatisfied. Thus, party control over job assignments is weakening . . ."[98] In 1987, Gargan wrote of "an inability to efficiently absorb people highly trained in Western management and technological specialties. Biologists and economists, chemical engineers and physicists, all with foreign degrees, are relegated to jobs that have little, if any, relation to their education."[99]

In the wake of the Tiananmen Square massacre of 1989, the government announced that to rekindle Communist values, "most college graduates will have to work for a year or two in villages or factories before being permitted to enter graduate school."[100]

All these illustrate a continued deep state intervention in labor assignments and little faith in the free market as allocator of workers among potential employments.

Failure of the Power-Diffusion Process

In sum, the People's Republic brought no essential change in the power structure, only in the personalities who hold power, the titles they wear, and the organizations through which they wield it. The same lack of communication holds between rulers and ruled as has held for centuries.

Deng Xiaoping's liberalization policies began only after Mao Zedong's death in 1976 and only after the consolidation of Deng's power. The commune was dismantled, and farmers were allowed to grow what they wished and sell it in the free market. Grain output jumped from 305 million tons in 1978 to 407 million tons in 1984.[101] But even these policies came as central directives. No farmers' lobby had pressured for them. Rather, Deng and his companions in power had decided—from on top—that increased agricultural output was essential to China's economic health and to their own continued power, and that liberalization was the way to bring it about.

The increase in agricultural output tapered off in 1984-87, possibly because the government did not invest sufficiently in the farms.[102] It dropped to around 3 percent per year in the early 1990s. The government has complained that farmers are not producing enough grain. But the officials might have foreseen this result when they liberated prices for products other than grain and allowed farmers to choose their own crops outside a certain grain quota. Naturally, they shifted away from controlled grain into liberated crops.

Furthermore, although the government has allowed certain private trading, it has kept major industries and communications under its control.

This decision led to an exhortation by Friedman: "The way to expedite the transition in China is to proceed with privatization as rapidly and on as wide a scale as possible."[103] If agriculture is free and industry is not, Friedman noted, the farmers cannot buy the quantity and quality of industrial goods they need. Cheung is even more emphatic: "It is time for China to consider the creation of private property by mandate."[104] A far cry from the timely negotiation of institutions through the power-diffusion process!

As the present "dynasty" (that is, the Republic, whether Nationalist or People's) approaches the end of its first century, it has been rent several times, just as seriously as were the dynasties of imperial China: first by the north-south civil war, next by the battles of Sun Yat-sen and Chang Kai-shek versus the warlords, next by the Nationalist-Communist civil war, next by the Japanese invasion and occupation, next by the Taiwan-mainland dichotomy, next by the Great Leap Forward, next by the Cultural Revolution, next by the succession struggle after Mao, and now by the massacre of Tiananmen Square and the struggle for power between Deng liberals and the hardliners, which continues into the 1990s.

In not understanding that the very *structure* of society is mandated from on top, just as it was during three thousand years of the empire, many foreign observers today are making the same mistakes as did the British, French, and Russians during the nineteenth century. Some believe that if, by central mandate, Chinese organizations were suddenly patterned after Western ones, and if the Chinese followed monetary, fiscal, and trade policies like those of Western nations, they would behave as Westerners or Japanese do. The efforts of U.S. lawmakers to persuade their own government to put sanctions on the Chinese if they do not liberalize their polity fails to take account of the *inability* of any Chinese government to do so in a lasting way, quite apart from its unwillingness. By suggesting that liberalism be mandated, foreign observers encourage not liberalism, but mandate.

A list of decisions taken by the central government either to strengthen its own power or to manage the economy and society in ways its leaders thought best, without much discussion by individuals or groups affected, appears in appendix 12.2.[105] References to inefficiencies in the Chinese economy are listed in appendix 12.3.[106] References to liberalization by government mandate are found in appendix 12.4, while reports of reversals of liberalization are in appendix 12.5.

What Hope for China?

Nevertheless, signs can be detected that the free market is arising from below. As individuals have undertaken new businesses without the blessing of the authorities, and private enterprises have proved themselves more efficient than those of the state, power becomes decentralized willy-nilly. The state is simply unable to control the countryside, nor can Beijing mandate events in the south.

Some futurists are now predicting that China will become the great power of the twenty-first century. Gross domestic product has increased in the neighborhood of 12 percent per year in recent years[107] and industrial growth sometimes over 20 percent.[108] Industry is growing "miraculously" in the south—the real growth in Guangdong was 12½ percent from 1979 to 1992,[109] and the *economic* border between Hong Kong and China has been all but erased, even before the colony reverts to China in 1997. A CIA report in 1993 found that the Chinese economy rivaled that of Japan and was growing at 13 percent a year.[110] "Factories keep careful track of costs, pay their employees by the piece rate and use complex systems of incentives to increase production."[111] Even in agriculture some experimental reforms are being done privately.[112]

New economic arrangements are being worked out. For example, "collectively owned enterprises sometimes blur the distinction between state and private sectors because they sometimes are run partly by village or township governments. In any case, they tend to operate on market principles and are much more entrepreneurial than Government-run enterprises."[113]

These new arrangements would not be possible if they were not organized by groups—corporations, farmers, village authorities, or other—who work out the local conditions. (Not enough study has been done to identify them.) At some point these groups will *have* to negotiate with higher authorities over money and finance, property rights, and legal guarantees. It will take years of study by social scientists to determine what groups are involved, how they are negotiating, and what arrangements are made.

Paul Kennedy cautions against excessive optimism, since population growth may offset the economic advances, and if it does not the advances will engender intolerable environmental problems.[114] My own cautious optimism comes not from ignoring these problems nor from extrapolating the extraordinary gains of the early 1990s but from the possibility that lower-level interest groups may be forming and that Chinese society may soon reach the crisis where the elites *must* negotiate with them or not survive.

Most who agree with Kennedy's warnings would deem population and environment to be challenges to the central government. But I would argue that these afflictions will be alleviated only by inter-actions of the newly-forming groups, with the government as arbiter but not as power. Such is the history of Japan and the Western world. Nor need they be solved in the immediate future; Japan and Europe took centuries. While the cautious optimism of many observers depends on the government's success in managing the society, my optimism depends on its failure.

Notes

1. Vandermeersch 1985:3.
2. Yan Meng 1988:1:1.
3. Confucius has not always been popular with the rulers, however. The first Emperor, Shih Huang Ti (ruled 221-206), ordered his books to be burned. In the twentieth century, Mao Zedong, who likened himself to Shih Huang Ti, was equally unappreciative of Confucius.
4. Jacobs 1958:162.
5. Li 1977:xiii.
6. Vandermeersch 1985:14.
7. Or so Brockman (1980:84) described the legal duties of the local magistrate in Taiwan, at the end of the nineteenth century.
8. Miyazaki 1980:72.
9. Henderson 1980:281.
10. Cohen 1980:7.
11. Jacobs 1958:97.
12. Fairbank, Reischauer and Craig 1978:918.
13. Wren, Christopher, "China Purging Radicals and Incompetents from Party Ranks," *New York Times*, 7/8/84.
14. Yan Meng 1988:2:4.
15. Brockman 1980:85.
16. Miyazaki 1980:66.
17. Cohen 1980:9.
18. Creel 1980:34.
19. Eberhard 1977:69.
20. Eberhard 1977:258-59.
21. Cohen 1980:14.
22. Brockman 1980:83.
23. Brockman 1980:82.
24. Bodde 1980:137.
25. Eberhard 1977:78.
26. Miyazaki 1980:59. One senses a bit of the same in American society today, in which litigiousness—or trigger-like resort to the courts—is criticized as being more prevalent, yet less ethical, than friendly compromise. For example, see Geyelin, Milo, "More Judges Punish Frivolous Litigants," *Wall Street Journal*, 7/20/90.
27. Cohen 1980:12.
28. Miyazaki 1980:58.
29. Eberhard 1977:80.
30. Cohen 1980:10; Creel 1980:38.
31. Creel 1980:34.
32. Yan Meng 1988:1:2.
33. Eberhard 1977:78.
34. Yan Meng 1988:1:8.
35. Cohen 1980:11.
36. Yan Meng 1988:1:8.
37. Chen 1980:170.
38. Cohen 1980:13.
39. Creel 1980:41.

40. Eberhard 1977:222.
41. Eberhard 1977:222.
42. Miyazaki 1980:69.
43. Cohen 1980:11.
44. Cohen 1980:12.
45. Vandermeersch 1985:6.
46. Chen 1980:171.
47. Cohen 1980:6.
48. Wang 1934:6.
49. Wu 1986:2.
50. Wu 1986:7-8.
51. Vandermeersch 1985:24.
52. Yan Meng 1988:2:10.
53. Crovitz, L. Gordon, "Hong Kong Lawyers: Profiles in Kowtowing," *Wall Street Journal*, 8/4/93.
54. Bastid 1985:51.
55. Yang 1952:16, 37-38; Hulsewe 1985:228.
56. Eberhard 1977:136.
57. Yang 1952:7.
58. Yang 1952:2; Eberhard 1977:197.
59. Lewis 1988:108.
60. Yang 1952:9.
61. Yang 1952:38.
62. Eberhard 1977:213.
63. Yang 1952:55.
64. Eberhard 1977:242.
65. Yang 1952:2, 63. By exception, at the end of the thirteenth century the government rewarded two ex-pirate generals for transporting grain through dangerous seas by allowing them to print notes. This privilege was revoked in 1303 (Yang 1952:66).
66. Fairbank, Reischauer and Craig 1978:187.
67. Takekoshi 1930:2:405.
68. Yang 1952:2.
69. Yang 1952:7.
70. Yang 1952:69.
71. Yang 1952:4-5.
72. Brockman 1980:109.
73. Yang 1952:68.
74. Lin 1936:5.
75. Yang 1952:85.
76. Yang 1952:90.
77. Lin 1936:78.
78. Hsiao 1971:17.
79. Byrd 1983:125-28.
80. Byrd 1983:124.
81. Byrd 1983:126-27.
82. Dorn 1989:564. But Chinese economists have told me that these official estimates are probably too low: some guessed as high as 50 percent or 60 percent, including prices in the black market.

83. Gang 1988:32.
84. These points were made to me by a Chinese professor of economics at a reception following the Friedman talk at Fudan University, Shanghai. When I asked him why he did not mention them in the question period, he replied that he would not dispute such a well-known economist as Friedman.
85. Yang 1982:3.
86. Eberhard 1977:20.
87. Hulsewe 1985:226.
88. Eberhard 1977:73-74.
89. Eberhard 1977:207.
90. Eberhard 1977:240.
91. Will 1985:309.
92. Santangelo 1985:273, 279.
93. Meijer 1980:328.
94. Kronholz, June, "In China, Rigid Rules Curb the Urban Sprawl Afflicting Third World," *Wall Street Journal*, 6/14/83.
95. Wang, John, "China's Jobless Youth: A Mounting Problem," *New York Times*, 9/30/79.
96. Butterfield, Fox, "Skilled Manpower Wasted, China Says," *New York Times*, 12/14/80.
97. Oakes, John B., "China's People Problem," *New York Times*, 8/29/90.
98. Eyster, Patricia, Letter to the Editor, *New York Times*, 11/11/84.
99. Gargan, Edward A., "For Chinese, A Mismatch of Job Skills," *New York Times*, 12/12/87.
100. Kristof, Nicholas D., "China is Planning 2 Years of Labor for Its Graduates," *New York Times*, 8/13/89.
101. Butterfield, *New York Times*, 11/15/87, quoting Nicholas Lardy.
102. Butterfield, Fox, "Mao and Deng: Competition for History's Judgment," quoting Nicholas Lardy, *New York Times*, 11/15/87.
103. Friedman 1989:573.
104. Cheung 1989:595.
105. Many more examples have appeared in recent newspapers, but space does not permit them all to be cited.
106. Once again, many more examples than those listed have appeared in recent newspapers.
107. Predicting a "bust," however, *The Economist* (5/29/93) finds the very fact of such unsustainable increases to be an ill portent.
108. Wu Dunn, Cheryl, in *New York Times*, 5/19/93.
109. Kennedy 1993:185.
110. Weiner, Tim, "C.I.A. Says Chinese Economy Rivals Japan's," *New York Times*, 8/1/93.
111. WuDunn, Sheryl, "Village in China finds Road Paved with Gold," report on the village of Daqiuzhuang, *New York Times*, 1/10/92.
112. Sutherland, Daniel, "How China's Economy Left its Comrade Behind," *Washington Post Weekly*, 9/2/91.
113. "China's Divided Economy," *New York Times*, 12/18/91.
114. Kennedy 1993: chapter 9.

Chapter 13
Russia: Trade, Entrepreneurship, and Institutions

Socialism in the Soviet Union collapsed in the 1980s and 1990s because the economy could not sustain the minimum quality of life that the people had come to demand. Seventy years of experiment were required for this lesson. But another lesson is not yet learned: that underlying the economic collapse is the failure to create an interlocking society, with checks and balances on the enormous power that has been concentrated in the center since at least the thirteenth century. Current Western and international proposals to resuscitate the successor states, through economic measures and financial bolstering, serve only to prolong the power imbalance.

Trade and Entrepreneurship

Lack of entrepreneurship is not the problem. Throughout their history, Russians, Ukrainians, and neighboring peoples have excelled as both traders and entrepreneurs.

While the Kievan state of the tenth and eleventh centuries was based largely on conquest, agriculture, and land, its international reputation was made by commerce from the Baltic to the Black Seas.[1] After defeating the Khazars, Kievans traded to the far corners of Islamic territory.[2] Constant warfare[3] and a shift in Mediterranean routes from north-south to east-west after the First Crusade (1096-99)[4] led to the demise of the Kievan state, but Novgorod quickly filled the gap. Then Mongol rule reopened the north-south routes, enabling northern Russia to trade again with the Black Sea. By 1270, Italian merchants had formed colonies in Kaffa and Tana, trading as far as Turkestan and central Asia.[5] New towns such as Itil and New Sarai became commercial centers in an extensive Mongol trading empire.[6] Contrary to popular belief, the Mongols were "more interested in developing commerce than in despoiling their subjects."[7] Trading prospered when the Russians took Narva in 1585, opening relations with French and Dutch sellers of wine and manufactured goods.[8] The British plied routes to ports on the White Sea, to avoid their enemies in and around the Baltic.

Entrepreneurship also flourished. Although risking confiscation of land and liberty if they fell out of favor with the tsars, medieval seigneurs established industries, using serf labor. By the eighteenth century peasants were cooperating with seigneurs in these ventures. "An exceptional number of large peasant-owned factories were concentrated in the villages of Ivanovo in Vladimir Guberniia, and in Pavlovo and Vorsma in Nizhnii Novgorod."[9]

Even in the Soviet period, private plots consistently outproduced collective farms.[10] Upon the collapse of the Soviet Union, "private entrepreneurs, inventive economists, and capable administrators have sprung up as if they had been lying in wait since the region's short period of capitalist independence between the two world wars."[11]

But in Kievan times foreign trade was done chiefly by the rulers,[12] and thereafter industry was principally undertaken by tsars, high nobility, and later Soviet bureaucrats. The failure of these rulers and elites to develop an interlocking society with bourgeoisie and farmers is a principal historic reason for Russian backwardness, and it remains so today. A study of the institutions of economic development, starting with the law, supports this assertion.

Law

"Russian social and legal institutions emerged from a background very similar to those of the West. . . . a social order not essentially different from that of the Germanic peoples . . . they produced an essentially similar law."[13] But Russian law did not adopt, and in practice it still has not adopted, the Western concept that the king is subject to his own laws. While law became centralized in both the West and Russia, that centralization possessed a different quality in each place. In the West, the rulers dispensed justice through their courts, but they became obliged to respect precedent and to explain the logic and justice of their decisions. In Russia, the tsar and his bureaucracy ruled capriciously, composing the law themselves and not being bound by western-style constraints.

Until the nineteenth century, Russian law was not commented upon, re-written, or argued and modified by scholars, lawyers, merchants, and others, as was law in the West. Instead, except for local law beyond his reach, the tsar or his bureaucracy were the prime makers of law. In its organizations, however (as opposed to its institutions), the Russian legal system became modernized over the centuries. Courts and an infrastructure were created, usually intended to copy the West. Especially in the times of Ivan the Terrible, the early Romanovs, Peter the Great, and Alexander II, efforts were made— by command from the center—to convert Russian law into that of a "Western" society. The same is happening at the end of the twentieth century. Few are asking why it is necessary to perform this task so many times.

From the Tenth to the Sixteenth Centuries

The principal sources of early Russian law are the *Primary Chronicle* and the *Russkaia Pravda* (Russian Law). The *Chronicle*, a history of Kievan Russia probably written by a monk about 1100, "when speaking of pre-Christian times, often referred to the 'Russian law', the customs, usages, traditions, etc. of the Russian tribes."[14] It also contained the earliest known legal texts.[15] The *Pravda*, written by Kievan Grand Prince Yaroslav about 1015-36 and expanded by his sons in 1072, covered rules on the property of princes and their servitors. It also compiled lists of penalties to be paid by perpetrators to victims as compensation for injuries.[16]

While law may at first have been based on tribal custom, nevertheless its codification and enforcement were the province of the prince. In Africa "customary" law was interpreted by tribal chiefs and colonial authorities in ways convenient to them. The same was so in Russia, where "each prince or landlord administered customary law on such principles as seemed good to him. There was no 'common law' for the Russian land and no judges appointed by central authority to dispense even-handed justice."[17]

Berman characterizes medieval Russian law as "five hundred years behind the West. . . . The development of Russian law from the eleventh to the fifteenth centuries is in many ways a recapitulation of Frankish legal development from the sixth to the tenth centuries."[18] Lawrence is more pithy. While the West philosophized upon and fine-tuned Roman law to apply to its own cultures, Russia, he says, was left with "nothing but third-hand epitomes of Justinian."[19]

In search of reasons, let us first examine Novgorod.[20] Because of Novgorod's charter of self-government granted in 1019 and its subsequent trade with the West and connection with the Hanseatic League, this northern city would seem the most likely part of Russia to develop commercial law similar to that of the West. Indeed, "the powers and revenues of the prince of Novgorod were strictly limited by custom and enshrined in a contract between townspeople and the prince."[21] In addition, "the straightforward business methods of the merchant princes of the north contrasted with the tortuous ways of other Russian traders."[22]

Secondary sources pay scant attention to drawing up and enforcing contracts on joint ventures, investment, and trade; security for delivery and quality of merchandise; debt repayment; and the like. Instead, the emphasis is on the subordinate relationship of merchants to the prince. For example: "Generally inclined to monetary fines, the Novgorod code also included provision for restoration of losses incurred by the victim. But, like its Muscovite successor, Novgorod took care to compensate the emerging bureaucracy for the myriad tasks associated with litigation . . ."[23] Disputed contracts, inheritance cases, and quarrels over land were brought before the prince's court.[24]

Possibly the primitive legal development simply mirrored the Hanseatic League and all of northern Europe, which lagged behind the Italian city states in commercial and financial law, contracts, and the use of accounting. Why this should be, no one has explained.

Berman puts some of the blame on the Mongols. He argues that the "conquest of Russia and most of Eurasia by the Mongols in the thirteenth century, and their domination for almost 250 years, exercised a deteriorating influence of the first magnitude upon Russian legal development."[25] The *Yasa* (law code) of Ghengis Khan (r.1206-27) called for "absolute and unqualified obedience" and "assigned to each person a specific position in service to the state, from which he could not depart without penalty of death."[26] Yet the Mongol khans also promoted trade throughout their far-flung empire. Why would they not perceive the necessity of decentralized commercial law as requisite to that trade?

Furthermore, Russian law did recover and become institutionalized in the centuries right after the Mongols, and many of the processes known to the West were introduced, such as "higher and lower courts, procedures for impaneling a jury, for appeal, and for obtaining bail, a recognition of 'conflict of interest' as applied to a judge, . . . rules of evidence, and authenticating transcripts to assure that a rational format had been followed in conducting a trial."[27]

These organizations (not institutions) had been imposed from on top rather than negotiated from below. Also, true to historical form, the sophisticated machinery of the 1497 law code (*Sudebnik)* "was devoted almost exclusively to the role of state officials and detailed a juridical apparatus over which the Moscow grand prince reigned."[28]

An English visitor in the 1580s wrote of the Russian "ruler controlling legislation, appointment of officials, conduct of diplomatic relations, war and peace, and even all final decisions in matters of law."[29] Some western "authors believed these codes played a very small part in the administration of justice and one doubted their very existence."[30]

By 1568, Ivan's own great Law Code had been openly pushed aside. "Fear not the law, fear the judge," warned a contemporary Russian proverb; and once in prison even for a misdemeanor a man might languish "until his hair hung down to his navel." Just about everyone in the system received kickbacks, from magistrate to bailiff, and it is said that a petitioner or litigant couldn't even get into court without paying off the guard.[31]

This description differs from English law under the Tudors and Stuarts only in degree and direction, but the degree and direction are momentous.

The Seventeenth and Eighteenth Centuries

In 1649, Alexis, the second Romanov tsar, prepared the *Subornoe Ulozhenie*, a codification of all existing Russian law. This code clarified two major points: first, the supremacy of the tsar in all matters of law, and second, the complete subjection of peasants to serfdom.

Five quotations from different historians affirming these purposes and describing the cruel punishments of the tsar and are found in appendix 13.1.

It was against this background that Peter I, later known as the Great (r.1682-1725), set about reforming Russian society including its laws. An Austrian visitor of the time wrote that "each new monarch makes new laws; for in a country governed despotically, nothing but the sovereign's pleasure has the force of law."[32] Since the 1649 *Ulozhenie* had been prepared hastily, in three weeks, Peter made several attempts to revise it, a task not completed when he died in 1725.[33]

The changes that he did make failed, for the reasons mentioned by Berman:

> This was an attempt to incorporate into the Russian social order, at one stroke, a public-law system similar to that which had been developed in Western Europe over centuries. The attempt was bound not to succeed for two reasons . . . the basic principle of autocracy was preserved intact [and] the absence of a decent system of private law on which to build.[34]

Law was further divorced from practical and personal applications during the eighteenth century under Anna, Elizabeth, and Catherine II, when it was pegged to the cameralism of "enlightened despots." This "scientific" interpretation of society was transplanted to Russia from the court of Frederick the Great of Prussia. "The new law codes transformed the law into a consistent, uniform framework for interpreting individual relations in a quantitative manner and established rules and procedures for the regular and mechanical application of the statutes."[35]

In 1766, Catherine called an assembly of more than five hundred representatives of social estates, to "explain the needs of their communities and participate in the drafting of a new law code. [However] No law code emerged, nor did the assembly reach any conclusive point in its deliberations."[36] A commission appointed by Catherine in the following year, to respond to petitions from urban groups, was dismissed when its deliberations took an "overly liberal and critical turn."[37] Thus law, like other social relations, became subject to the belief that the sovereign and her bureaucracy, knowing what was best for her subjects, might interpret and mold the law to fit the occasion. Conflicts over land resulted in "bitter lawsuits, . . . with one party taking the law into his own hands, sure of his superior strength or of protection from patrons and officials won over by bribes. . . . The legal system offered no real protection: there was no civil code, since the code of Tsar Alexis . . . had been rendered largely obsolete by the changes wrought by Peter the Great. . . . The personalization of authority was incompatible with regular legal procedure."[38]

The Nineteenth Century

In pursuit of his liberal reforms, Tsar Alexander I (r.1801-25) in 1809 instructed his minister, Mikhail Speransky, to prepare a new Statute on State Laws. In 1830 his task was complete, with forty-two volumes of laws enacted since 1649. These were compiled into a new code in 1833, complete with commentaries, the "first systematic presentation of law as a whole in all Russian history."[39] Speransky revised the bureaucracy into "something of a compromise between an oligarchic system and a bureaucratic system."[40]

In the following three decades, "the beginnings of a Russian legal literature appeared. A class of Russian jurists emerged, educated abroad in the capitals of Europe."[41] Finally, beginning with Tsar Alexander II (r.1855-81), the Russian legal system became westernized. A comprehensive reform of 1864 copied many of the principles of a western system, including courts independent of the bureaucracy, local courts, justices of the peace, oral pleadings and testimony, and trial by jury.[42] These reforms helped to supply "a legal system capable of dealing with modern commercial relationships and institutions impartially, swiftly and predictably."[43]

All these reforms took place "from above," by the bureaucracy and its legal scholars, with no participation by peasants and workers and little by business groups or independent scholars. While they may have formed a framework in which spectacular industrial advances occurred from 1890 to 1914, the laws did not attend to peasant needs arising out of the emancipation of 1861. Except for major crimes, peasants were judged by a separate system (*volost* courts). Furthermore, from 1885 on the government restrengthened its control over the judiciary.[44]

Peasant land, peasant mobility, and peasant economic choices were still woefully inadequate and not justiciable. The demands of a rebellious group, the Peoples' Will (*Narodnaia Volia),* which was composed of intellectuals rather than peasants, could not be handled by any court. Terrorism—including the assassination of Alexander II in 1881—was the chosen route. The legal system proved incapable of handling the crises that gave rise to the

Bolshevik Revolution.[45] Berman's summary of the situation shows that the power-diffusion process had not been at work at all in the law:

> [T]he Bolshevik Revolution . . . forces us to consider two hypotheses . . . the first . . . that legal development, brilliant as it was, took place only on the surface of Russian life, that it was not actually an incorporation of the fundamentals of Western law into the Russian tradition, but largely an adoption of Western forms without the substance, and that it did not penetrate into the consciousness of the Russian people as a whole, particularly the peasants.[46]

Thus, it constituted "old institutions in new organizations."

The Soviet Union

Although not all at once, Soviet law adopted the institutions of the prerevolutionary period in the following ways:

First, the Soviet Union continued a religious conception of the state. The rulers "take responsibility for both the political and spiritual life of their subjects and expect from them not only respect but also worship."[47] Placing dissidents in psychiatric hospitals in the 1970s, so condemned by the West, may have reflected a belief that their maverick nature was indeed something akin to mental illness.

Second, "Soviet criminal law has built on the nineteenth and early twentieth-century reforms."[48] "The emphasis on community action to correct the offender and bring him back into harmony with the group has echoes of the . . . cultural tradition of collective responsibility for individual misconduct."[49] In this way Soviet law was similar to Chinese, as described in chapter 12.

Third, under Stalin, the Soviet worker did not have the right to move freely from one location to another or to quit one employment for another, without permission of some authorities. This limitation was partially relaxed later.

Fourth, work requirements of Soviet citizens were the responsibility of the state. According to the 1961 edict of the Russian Soviet Republic on parasitism, which is applicable to nonworking people, "adult able-bodied citizens who do not wish . . . to work honestly according to their abilities . . . shall be subject . . . to resettlement in specially designated localities . . . with confiscation of the property acquired by non-labor means, and to obligatory enlistment in work at the place of resettlement."[50]

Fifth, "the management, use, and disposal of the property of the household are in the members as a whole; in the absence of unanimity, . . . a majority vote of the adult members is decisive."[51]

Sixth, "man is conceived to be in need of education, guidance and training to make him better-disciplined, more honest and hard-working, more conscious of his social obligations."[52] This educational role of law was stressed in political literature and speeches. "Soviet labor law . . . protects, guides, and trains both management and labor, educating them in discipline and self-discipline, inculcating in them a sense of their mutual rights and duties."[53]

Seventh, legal accountability for the use of resources entrusted to business managers or others was not a primary virtue.

Thus Soviet law was perceived as an instrument through which the state would guide the economic, social, and political actions of its citizens. While law respected the humanity of the person more than in earlier centuries and was enforced with less cruelty, nevertheless in the aforementioned functions it had not changed substantially since Ivan the Terrible or Peter the Great. It was not perceived as a means to guarantee rights to personal liberty or to own or alien possessions or to make contracts or to enforce agreements or to move freely about the country.

The Situation Today

It is too early to say how law will develop in the successor republics, but there is no reason to expect a quantum leap into Western precepts. Principles of law similar to the Soviet have ruled through Russian history at least back to the thirteenth century, if not before; they have been imposed by an elite upon its subjects and are still so imposed; they are not necessarily the laws which would have emerged from free negotiation among independent groups; and finally, by restricting the inventiveness and entrepreneurship of individuals and the accumulation of capital, they have retarded economic development and continue to retard it.

The Monetary System

The Russian monetary system before the twentieth century reflects its primary purpose: to finance consumption by the elite. By contrast, credit instruments arose in northwestern Europe and Japan mainly to finance private trade. For trade in Kievan Russia, foreign coins were sufficient. Thereafter, as production and trade were suppressed by wars and invasions and also were dominated by the central government, they required only the coins of the tsars.

In all societies, heavy consumption borrowing by the elites marks the transition from a subsistence to a market economy. In northwestern Europe, kings, nobles, and princes borrowed in the thirteenth to sixteenth centuries, as did daimyo and shogun in Japan. But in these areas, towns and trade were also growing, so the same instruments that financed borrowing by the rulers also financed production and trade.

Unlike Japan and northwestern Europe, Russia's early monetary system did not depend mainly on money changers, lenders, and private credit instruments, although these existed. Instead, the earliest "system," in the ninth century, was simply the use of foreign currencies. Later, under the tsars, coins were struck and persistently depreciated. (The same happened in northwestern Europe and Japan.) In the sixteenth century, the government recoined foreign money, extracting a 100 percent profit. A paper assignat was issued by Catherine II in 1769, which quickly depreciated and lost its convertibility in 1777, in a set of events not much different from those of the French Revolutionary government fifteen years later. A silver ruble was proclaimed in 1810 and was made the standard unit in 1839, with a fixed value in convertible paper currency. But in 1841, new "credit notes" were issued; paper issues multiplied during the Crimean War; and convertibility was suspended. Only with the advent of the gold standard in 1897 did Russia obtain a stable currency.[54] As late as the early eighteenth century, the seignorial estate was financing its luxury consumption primarily by taxing the serfs and secondarily by the sale of agricultural product. Then it turned more to borrowing.[55]

If overwhelming indebtedness for consumption was characteristic of the Russian gentry, and if loans were extended but not repaid, then surely the concept of credit for productive enterprise, which requires repayment, could not have been well advanced. We have seen how the balance of power between merchants and daimyo in Japan and between elites and bourgeoisie in Europe resulted in consumption and production loans competing with each other for available savings. In Russia before the twentieth century, merchants and industrialists had little power vis-à-vis the gentry, so consumption by the latter mainly won.

In 1754, the Russian government established and then owned and managed the State Loan Bank for the Nobility and the State Commercial Bank. The former lent to the nobility on land mortgage while the latter financed trade in the port of St. Petersburg,[56] but the commercial bank lent to favorites rather than merchants with bankable projects, and it was closed for mismanagement in 1786. In the same year, the Bank for the Nobility became simply the State Loan Bank. Its purpose was political. Needing the support of the nobility, Catherine wanted to preserve them as a class by protecting their estates from loss to outside creditors. Therefore, the State Bank presumably absorbed much of the available credit, channeling it into consumption by the nobility.

A new State Loan Bank of 1797, together with other state-organized financial agencies, lent mainly to the government's favorites at low rates, who in turn re-lent at much higher rates. Thus the financial system became a private estate for the benefit of a few. A State Commercial Bank founded in 1817 to discount notes of merchants and industrialists found little business in these lines. In 1854 its assets were transferred to the Loan Bank and thus made available for consumption by the gentry.[57]

During the 1850s, the banks were compelled to pay 4 percent interest on new deposits created in the Crimean War inflation. Little opportunity was afforded to invest these funds, however. Furthermore, a group of favorites developing railroads received government guarantees for bond issues at 5 percent, while the government ordered the banks to reduce their interest rates to 3 percent. As deposits fled for more profitable investment in joint-stock companies, the government temporarily banned the formation of these companies. These moves derailed economic development and emasculated the banking system. "The banks had in their portfolios nothing but 'frozen' assets consisting of long-term loans to the nobility and of loans to the government."[58]

During most of the nineteenth century, the state itself was a major borrower from the State Bank, so much so that it forced "the State Bank to use its resources otherwise earmarked for commercial operations in order to support the Treasury accounts." Therefore, the claim by historians and economists that the Treasury contributed to the development of the banking system can be applicable only to the period of the 1890s and afterward.[59]

Modern banking "was a strictly post-emancipation [1861] phenomenon, . . . there was hardly any tradition of banking (except for land banks) providing loans to an economy that was diversifying and industrializing, where capital was scarce relative to the economically advanced countries of Western Europe."[60] In 1860, the old state banks were closed and a new State Bank was formed, with the burden of discharging the obligations of its predecessors. Before 1890 it had few funds for loans to business.[61] But in 1864 it did establish the first joint-stock bank, the St. Petersburg Private Commercial Bank, owning one-fifth of its capital. Thirty-one other joint-stock banks were formed from 1864 to 1873, but few from then until 1890.

From 1890 until 1914, Russia experienced unprecedented economic growth, paralleled only by Germany at that time. In 1912, a French economist who followed Russia closely gave the following opinion. "If things develop in the major European countries as they have between 1900 and 1912, Russia will, toward the middle of the present century, dominate Europe politically as well as from the economic and financial point of view."[62] To finance this spurt, joint-stock companies were formed during the 1890s imitating German commercial banks. At first they discounted commercial paper but quickly expanded to ordinary lending on current account. By 1908-14 the balance in lending had shifted from state banks to private commercial banks.[63] They obtained their finance from the savings of peasants, workers, and private and government lower-level employees, as well as from foreign banks and the Russian state bank.

Both the spurt in economic growth and the surge in private banking ended with World War I and the Bolshevik Revolution. Specie payment was suspended in 1914, and note issues were expanded. Gold disappeared from circulation. All banks were nationalized in 1917.[64]

During the Soviet period, the banks served the state and its enterprises, including the collective farms. Both the government and its enterprises borrowed from the banks to finance their deficits. Although inflation broke out immediately after World War II, it was held in check primarily by price controls and rationing.

However, the government continued to increase its deposits and to print currency for its own use, thus transferring goods and services to itself and its enterprises. During the 1970s and 1980s, the quantity of rubles greatly increased, compared with the goods and services available to the public. The eruption of this latent inflation is a current concern of officials in the successor states, as they contemplate freer markets. In the meantime, Russians have been holding three kinds of currencies: foreign exchange; government coupons available to those with special privileges, such as workers abroad; and rubles, with little purchasing power.[65] The principal problem is that during the decades of government as the sole financer of wealth, a diversified financial market to attract private saving, with instruments representing differing degrees of risk and maturity, has not been needed.

Just before the end of the Soviet Union, Feldstein summarized these problems as follows:

• "[T]he Soviet public has too much financial wealth relative to the annual production of goods and services."

• "[T]he Soviet interest rate is far less than the currently expected rate of inflation. . . ."

• "[T]hey must create a more complete financial market, . . . offer the Soviet people an opportunity to exchange their cash balances for deposits bearing an interest rate that reflects expected inflation." But "creating financial assets that are attractive enough to absorb excess cash balances won't be easy because successful financial markets depend on the credibility of contractual obligations. A government that has lied to its public for decades isn't a credible issuer of bonds. . . ."[66] In addition, he might have added, the bonds would be a dead-weight burden on the government, for they would not be counterpart to productive assets.

Corporate Groups

In the thirteenth century, Novgorod presented many of the same characteristics as towns in the West. "Through its *veche* or town meeting, the people elected their chief officials by direct democracy, much as in the ancient city-state republics of Athens and Rome. But sovereignty resided in the town itself."[67] Political action was taken by corporate bodies.[68]

In the West, the modern corporation grew out of guilds (along with other sources such as Roman corporations). But guilds were not a feature of either Novgorod or any medieval Russian towns.[69] "The economic historian of Novgorod, Nitikinsky, affirms that in that city 'there was never any trace whatever of western European guilds, a view supported for other cities by his contemporaries. The leading economic historian of the Soviet period concluded that 'during those centuries when craft guild organizations flourished in western Europe, they made no progress whatever in Moscow, though Pazitnov finds the evidence weak.'"[70] Most likely, guilds did not arise in Russia until the nineteenth century, at just the time they were becoming obsolete in the West. Thus they could not perform the function that they did in medieval western Europe, as foci of cooperation among workers, guildmasters, and town patricians.

Kaser attributes the lack of guilds to the Mongols, whose practices were continued by Russian tsars: "The 'Tatar yoke' made its imprint upon entrepreneurship by its fiscal imposts," many of the terms for which in present-day Russian are of Tatar origin.[71] Once again, however, censure of the Mongols—who were powerless after the fifteenth century—seems misplaced. The question is not how guild suppression began, but why it continued—probably because subsequent rulers preferred more subservient organizations and had the power to attain them. They arranged their "inferiors" in a rigid hierarchy because nothing forced them to do otherwise.

With the bourgeoisie sidelined and the church dominated by the tsar, from the fifteenth century on, the active political classes were the tsar and his bureaucracy and nobility of different levels. The great gulf in communication between peasants and merchants on the one hand and the upper classes on the other left little opportunity for vertical alliances with leverage, so lower-group identities withered.

Although Catherine II attempted to form trading companies to encourage manufacturing, the social and economic agencies capable of carrying out her policies did not materialize. Groups either to fulfill these functions or to be counterweights to the government were not allowed to form.[72] Instead, the separation of merchants, who might manufacture, from nobles, who monopolized agriculture, was in principle complete. (The same separation did not exist in England, at least by the sixteenth century, and in France it was not complete.) Any local initiative to change this was suspect, under both Catherine and Paul. These two monarchs set up "corporations" of nobility, similar to "orders" in the West, with charters that were highly paternalistic, reserving to the crown the right to arbitrate among them.[73] A Free Economic Society, established in 1765, debated peasant bondage but played no political role.[74] As a result, private initiative was limited to certain individuals, mainly landowners, who acquired enormous power over their territories and their serfs. Local governments of the type emerging in the West did not form. There was still no prospect for the dispossessed to establish corporate groups or to exercise leverage.

Change nonetheless crept in at the beginning of the nineteenth century, when the "corporations" of Catherine and Paul began to demand social roles. Masonic lodges and secret societies were privately forming, along with "cultural circles" both inside and on the periphery of the university. At first these promoted the culture and scholarship of an intellectual elite.[75] They also made contact with the West, whose new ideas helped them turn to the political and the economic.[76]

During the Napoleonic wars, these groups came into touch with peasants and urban workers and discovered that they were reasonable people after all.[77] Their first political action was to reject the crown's paternalism and to advocate a greater role in civil society for "little people." The Decembrist rebellion of 1825 was a brief attempt by intellectual elites, plus military officers who had served in France, to increase their power vis-à-vis the monarchy. Although it failed, two trends were now in motion. First, nongovernment elitist corporate bodies were in Russia to stay. "The government's stubborn refusal to allow the generation of 1815 to fulfill its dreams of civic action drove some members of that generation to organize secret societies."[78] Second, those elitists replaced the monarchs in their paternalistic attitude toward peasants.

They remained in that role at least until the 1890s. Intellectuals were largely responsible for drawing up the conditions of peasant emancipation in 1861, which I have described in an earlier publication.[79] University students, influenced by imported socialist ideas, organized rebellions such as by the People's Will (*Narodniki*) in the 1870s. Peasant rebellions "required previous consultation and organization of the participants."[80] But grass-roots organizations—of the peasants themselves—that genuinely negotiated peasant interests and exerted peasant leverage have not been formed. Perhaps, however, they are among the new groups emerging today.

The same has been so for business groups. "A middle class of the kind the West has known since the end of the Middle Ages did not exist in Russia before about 1860."[81] Only about 1913 did "a few representatives of the commercial and industrial bourgeoisie . . . take an active role in public life [forming] associations and parties."[82]

Labor unions were legalized in 1905 and were freed from legal encumbrances in 1917 by Aleksandr Kerensky, head of the provisional government after the February revolution.[83] During the New Economic Policy (1921-28) collective bargaining was encouraged and collective contracts introduced. All these "benefits" to labor were decreed "from on top," not bargained for by workers. Under the ensuing Soviet system, therefore, no corporate power existed to defend them. Unions became state organizations, reporting to the same officials as the management.[84] Free collective bargaining was restricted under the first Five-Year Plan (1928-33). Collective contracts were discontinued in 1935. Nominally reintroduced in 1947, they were designed primarily for the state "to play a parental role in the Soviet industrial plant."[85]

Until the collapse of the Soviet economy in the 1980s and 1990s, therefore, corporate groups had *never* played in Russia or the Soviet Union the political roles common in the West for centuries. With that collapse and with the reform announcements by Mikhail Gorbachev (last President of the Soviet Union) and Boris Yeltsin (first President of newly independent Russia) in 1989 and 1990, however, private-interest groups suddenly began to proliferate, and workers began to take control of unions. Popular fronts, associations of entrepreneurs, alternative parties, political action groups, are sprouting everywhere.

30,000 to 50,000 clubs and organizations—with their own causes, constituencies and communication channels, which make up the fabric of the "post-Communist" civic society [are forming].[86]

More than 60,000 informal social and political groups have sprung up around the country; at the same time, assorted non-political groups concerned with ecological or historical preservation have increasingly been adopting their own political platforms and asserting themselves in areas where the party is losing influence.[87]

Tolz has catalogued many interest groups and presented case studies of some. She says that such groups had been forming, clandestinely, since at least the beginning of the Soviet Union, but that in the 1980s they began to proliferate.[88] Additional references to the formation of interest-groups in the successor states are found in appendix 13.2.

However, the mere existence of corporate groups with political and economic objectives is not enough for the power-diffusion process. They also must display sufficient clout so that other power groups respect them as potential cooperators or adversaries; they must have sufficient cohesion to appoint emissaries to bargain with the power groups; and they must learn to ally with power groups for leverage. In Russia, all this is for the future, if indeed it happens at all.

Politics in the 1990s

Toward the end of 1991, President Yeltsin of Russia swept up the remaining organizations of the erstwhile Soviet Union and attempted to promote his own liberalizing economic plans. While he consulted international organizations, seeking and being promised assistance from the Western powers and the International Monetary Fund, he continued to ignore the interest groups within his own country.

As Yeltsin squared off against parliament in 1993 to determine who was the primary leader of Russia, voters expressed overwhelming confidence, while demanding new parliamentary elections.[89] Later that year, he disbanded the parliament, which refused to leave its building but instead impeached the president, electing a new one.[90] For a few days Russia had two presidents, in a scene reminiscent of fifteenth-century Europe, when at one point the church had three popes and at another France had two kings. In October Yeltsin called on the troops to attack parliament and arrest its members.

During that month, we witnessed an extraordinary spectacle: Western governments cheered while the Russian parliament was emasculated and power was concentrated in one man—the president—who promptly suspended the high court.[91] He also banned opposition organizations and newspapers. fired political opponents,[92] and dismissed an elected local governor, showing he could do so for all governors if he wished. An impartial observer ("visitor from Mars") might have been astonished that instead of standing up for a division of powers among executive, legislative, and judicial branches, the world's democracies supported the engrosser of absolute power. While expressing a vague wish for democracy in Russia, the President of the United States was more eager for the immediate conflict to be won by free markets (Yeltsin) over Communism (parliament). Probably his reasons were political—the security of the United States—rather than economic or altruistic. Furthermore, Yeltsin began to waver on his free-market stand in less than a year. Most serious of all, the roles of popular groups—businesspeople, farmers, and other interests—were not considered, either within Russia or by international circles.

Notes

1. Lawrence 1978:39.
2. Lewis 1988:64.
3. EBMa 1974:16:40.
4. EBMa 1974:16:41.
5. Lewis 1988:156.
6. Lawrence 1978:58.
7. EBMa 1974:16:43.
8. Bobrick 1987:168,328.
9. Blum 1961:300.
10. Wadekin 1982:97.
11. Keller, Bill, "The Baltic Republics Are on the Road to Capitalist Socialism," *New York Times,* 8/6/89.
12. Blum 1961:20.
13. Berman 1963:188-89.
14. Feldbrugge 1977:5.
15. Feldbrugge 1977:2-3.
16. Berman 1963:192.
17. Lawrence 1978:85.
18. Berman 1963:191.
19. Lawrence 1978:39.
20. Novgorod will be considered at greater length in chapter 21.
21. Lawrence 1978:69.
22. Lawrence 1978:71.
23. Kaiser 1980:91.
24. Kaiser 1980:103.
25. Berman 1963:193.
26. Berman 1963:195.
27. Bobrick 1987:46.
28. Kaiser 1980:3.
29. Kleimola 1977:29.
30. Butler 1977:69.
31. Bobrick 1987:222.
32. Korb 1863:186-87, cited by Butler 1977a:69.
33. Berman 1963:206.
34. Berman 1963:203.
35. Raeff 1984:30.
36. Milner-Gulland 1989:109.
37. Raeff 1984:91.
38. Raeff 1984:80-81.
39. Berman 1963:208.
40. van den Berg 1977:218.
41. Berman 1963:212.
42. A more extensive listing of the reforms is found in Berman 1963:213-4 and in Raeff 1984: 177-86.
43. Wagner 1976, cited in Kaser 1978:465.
44. Kaser 1978:465.

45. Hazard 1977:237.
46. Berman 1963:216-17.
47. Berman 1963:228.
48. Berman 1963:237.
49. Berman 1963:297.
50. Berman 1963:292.
51. Berman 1963:261.
52. Berman 1963:298.
53. Berman 1963:351.
54. Arnold 1937:3-5.
55. Blum 1961:390-91.
56. Arnold 1937:6.
57. Arnold 1937:7-8.
58. Arnold 1937:8.
59. Kahan 1989:58.
60. Kahan 1989:54.
61. Arnold 1937:17.
62. Théry 1912, Preface.
63. Kahan 1989:49.
64. Arnold 1937:30, 53.
65. Taubman, Philip, "In Soviet Shopping: Rubles, Coupons, and Real Money," *New York Times*, 7/22/87.
66. Feldstein, Martin, "Why Perestroika Isn't Happening," *New York Times*, 4/21/89.
67. Bobrick 1987:241.
68. Lawrence 1978:70.
69. Bobrick 1987:29.
70. Kaser 1978:430.
71. Kaser 1978:426.
72. Raeff 1984:66.
73. Raeff 1984:100.
74. Milner-Gulland 1989:109.
75. Raeff 1984:134-35.
76. Raeff 1984:136.
77. Raeff 1984:137.
78. Raeff 1984:142-43.
79. Powelson 1988:115-17. This publication also covers the landholding system, cooperative communities (*mir*), and peasant emancipation, which are not subjects of the present book.
80. Kahan 1989:192.
81. Lawrence 1978:196.
82. Raeff 1984:217.
83. Berman 1963:216.
84. Berman 1963:346.
85. Berman 1963:354.
86. Broder, David S., "Passing the Torch—Soviet Style," *Washington Post Weekly*, 8/6-12/90.
87. Petro 1990:115.
88. Tolz 1990:1.
89. Schmemann, Serge, "Russians Appear to Hand Yeltsin a Victory in Vote," *New York Times*, 4/26/93.

90. Melloan, George, "Yeltsin Triumphs, but Some Bills Will Come Due," *Wall Street Journal*, 9/27/93.
91. *Wall Street Journal*, 10/08/93.
92. Schmemann, Serge, "Yeltsin Uses Decrees to Curb Dissenters," *New York Times*, 10/6/93.

Chapter 14
Russia: Five Centuries of Authoritarian Reform

Russia has been an authoritarian society since at least the sixteenth century. The major decisions on land tenure, use of labor, prices, and production have always been made by a small elite, who have foreclosed the participation of others. Unlike northwestern Europe and Japan, this condition has been continuous, down to the present day. It was not interrupted by the emancipation of serfs in 1861, nor by the Bolshevik Revolution of 1917, nor by glasnost and perestroika in the 1990s, nor by the end of the Soviet Union in 1991.

In chapter 5, I speculated that land scarcity may underlie the origins of the power-diffusion process. Let us turn to the vast expanse of space, which allowed Russians to avoid vertical communication and negotiation in the Middle Ages. Ever since then wars, escapes, and migrations over the centuries may have made unnecessary the pluralism of northwestern Europe and Japan and prevented the power-diffusion process from starting—until perhaps now.

Abundance of Land

Abundance of land led first, to free occupation by free labor in the tenth to fifteenth centuries, and second, to the birth of coerced rather than contract feudalism in the sixteenth.

In Kievan Russia, during the tenth to thirteenth centuries, land holdings were often acquired by simple occupation. Upon the decline of the Kievan Federation, princes of the Oka-Volga triangle "invited peasants to settle as free renters holding directly from the prince, offering them long exemptions from all obligations, light dues when they did have to start paying them, communal autonomy, and freedom of movement."[1] The freedom of landholding during the Mongol period of the fourteenth and fifteenth centuries also implies abundance: "there were no restrictions on the right to own land."[2]

Paradoxically, the same forces that gave rise to peasant freedom in the tenth to the fifteenth centuries contributed to enserfment in the sixteenth. Prior experience with contract feudalism had been lacking. When economic circumstances required greater organization of labor, this was undertaken by the powerful rather than arranged by contract. Domar recognized this causation: "Thus both ingredients for the development of serfdom—a high land/labor ratio and the government's determination to create a class of servitors—were present."[3]

Land abundance, with its possibility for peasants to escape their misery through migration, is a Russian theme right up to the end of the nineteenth century.[4] In contrast to the feudalism of western Europe, therefore, the peasant in Russia was relatively free before the sixteenth century, being able to move and to hold his own property. Just as feudalism was being dismantled in the West, however, it was tightened in the East.[5]

Anticipating Goodell, Feldbrugge also argues that the "hierarchy of reciprocal feudal relationships" that developed in the West, "providing a delicate balance of power, and of rights and duties, between various social classes," did not arise in Kievan Russia in part because of "the importance of trade."[6] But he does not explain this further, in the manner of Goodell.

Dukes suggests that peasants were free in the Middle Ages because an authoritarian government, which had not yet evolved, was a prerequisite to feudalism.[7] Blum believes that feudalism was delayed because the nobility could not enforce it until they had won their struggle with the princes and the towns, to become "the class on which the throne depended."[8] This happened in the sixteenth century. Also, "an urban bourgeoisie strong enough to act as a countervailing force to the nobility did not emerge in eastern Europe."[9] For this reason, the peasants missed the opportunity for leverage through vertical alliance with town power.

All these explanations are likely correct and are not inconsistent with each other, but they do not explain why no urban bourgeoisie evolved, or why the nobility won out over princes and town, or why the nobility did not foster industry on their own estates. The answers lie at least partly in the vastness of the Russian land. Communication was difficult, and all these classes could escape rather than understand each other. They failed to envision the opportunities of cooperation. Power concentration, persistently attenuated in the West, was reinforced in the East. Therefore, agricultural progress, so vigorous in the Kievan era, tapered off in the centuries following. Neither landlord nor peasant was motivated to improve.[10] The search for power by nobles and tsar, which depended on quantity of land and numbers of peasants rather than on output, overwhelmed any attention to agricultural development. The peasants, whose land was periodically redistributed by the commune (*mir*), had no incentive to improve it. Further historical references to the abundance of land in Russia are found in appendix 14.1.

The Authoritarian State and Reform from Above

Possibly the watershed in establishing authoritarian government occurred in 1564 when Ivan IV, the Terrible, partitioned the country into crown lands (*Oprichnina*), mainly the prosperous northern and commercial territories, and the nation at large (*Zemschina*), ruled by a boyars' (aristocrats') council.

This move "openly transformed him into a despot. It allowed him absolute power over the life and property of any disobedient subject 'without advice of council.'"[11] In the Oprichnina he unleashed imperial guards sworn to total obedience, who had license to torture, maim, or kill at their pleasure. Many nobles were executed, their lands seized and given to favorites. With its economy shattered by this experience as well as the costly Livonian war, the Oprichnina was reintegrated into the greater state in 1572. Whoever mentioned its name thereafter would be sentenced to death.

With few corporate groups forming until the nineteenth century, reforms in the political and economic system have always been undertaken "from on top." The first reforms of Ivan IV, beginning in 1549, spanned the entire political and judicial systems, affecting all administration and the church as well. The new legislation was designed entirely to increase the revenue of the state.[12] His second wave of reforms, after 1557, gave greater self-rule to local communities in exchange for support in the Livonian war.[13] None of these substantially improved conditions or privileges of lower classes. Instead, military and financial reforms were linked to social dependence.[14]

Likewise, in the sixteenth century, the Shuiskys and the Belskys bid for popular support by transferring criminal proceedings to local governments; however, the new local police could employ the same methods as the central government—torture, execution without trial—and no benefit resulted for most citizens.[15]

The seventeenth century saw a peculiar combination of increased knowledge of liberalism by Russian elites, yet a strengthening of their social control. Visitors and growing trade supplied them with an intellectual and even emotional attachment to Western goods and philosophy. Instead of converting the upper classes to liberalism, however, this enlightenment widened the gap between them and common people who had not been so exposed.[16] Peasant rebellions were brutally suppressed; the tsar imposed a new religious orthodoxy which the "Old Believers" would not accept; every Russian was defined as a servitor of the state; and military expansion into the Ukraine provoked a chasm between conquerors and conquered.

In this setting, Peter the Great (r.1682-1725) set out to "westernize" his country in a comprehensive "reform from above." Visiting the Netherlands and England, he observed modern factories and technology, was deeply impressed by them, and returned to Russia to order them installed there. However, he paid no attention to the fact that Western workers were freely hired, while the Russians he sent into his factories were serfs. He mistook physical structures, technology, and processes for economic development, failing to understand its institutional foundations and social relations.[17] When Peter abolished the separate patriarchate and took personal control of the church,[18] one possibility of vertical alliance and leverage for the lower classes—rivalry between the ruler and the church—which had been available in the West, was foreclosed in Russia.

The "enlightenment" of the elite, and the chasm between it and more humble Russians, continued throughout the eighteenth century. Clendenning describes the educated foreigners who visited the court of Catherine the Great; the government's initiative to survey the empire for data on economic development and capital formation; the modernizing scientific culture; the questionnaire on the nation's productive forces sent out by the Free Economic Society in 1766; the translation of books; and other ways by which the empress followed a program just as determined and just as authoritarian as that of Peter.[19]

Indeed, Catherine's reforms in the eighteenth century bore a grim similarity not only to those of Peter but also to those proposed by foreign advisors in Russia today. The economic problems of Catherine's time were much the same as confronted by leaders of the successor states to the Soviet Union. Substitute "bureaucracy" for "nobility," "peasantry" for "serfdom," "foreign exchange" for "precious metal and silver coins," and "foreign advisors" for "Shakovskoy" in the following quotation concerning Catherine's society:

> [T]he Commerce Commission's list of acute problems was lengthy: oppressed and poor capital markets, private and public ignorance of foreign commercial and trading mechanisms, poor infrastructure and a totally inadequate distribution system, paucity of credit facilities in major Russian towns together with a rapacious governmental policy toward acquiring precious metal and silver coins, undefined status of both the nobility and serfdom's role in the expansion of commerce, and too few enforceable laws regulating the wealthy merchantry *vis-à-vis* poorer members of that class. . . . Shakovskoy felt that the speedy removal of all trading obstacles would allow Russian merchants to act more efficiently and effectively against foreign competition.[20]

The eighteenth-century reforms brought neither total power for Moscow nor pluralism.[21] Peter the Great and the major empresses that followed him (Anna, Elizabeth, and Catherine II) all tried to maintain absolute power while undertaking economic programs that would have required voluntary cooperation by many.[22] Their dynamism affected the tsars who followed them. Paul (r.1796-1801) made "some tentative steps toward social reform."[23] All these reforms were organized from above, with no participation from lower classes.

Alexander I (r.1801-25) "called together an idealistic group of friends with whom he began to plan a new age."[24] He "dreamed of erecting a theocratic order on earth through God-chosen rulers and a fraternal community of nations."[25] His subsidies of commercial development and his protective tariffs were aimed at creating a state-dominated industry. [26] While the abolition of serfdom and other changes were discussed, Alexander's main achievement—besides his resistance to Napoleon—was a reform of the bureaucracy. But both the proponents (young idealists) and the opposition (older traditionalists) came entirely from the upper classes.[27] These elites talked much of abolishing serfdom and modernizing to imitate the West, just as Harvard and Stanford economists are now telling the government of Russia how to privatize industry. Evidence is scant or lacking that either the intellectuals of the early nineteenth century or the Harvard and Stanford professors of today communicated with or called for the cooperation of serfs (today, farmers) or other working classes.

"Old institutions in new organizations" applies particularly to the peasant emancipation of 1861, under Alexander II (r.1855-81). Having described this in detail in an earlier writing,[28] I merely summarize it here. In the 1830s, a small group of intelligentsia in the government of Nicholas I, "disgusted by society's materialistic values and above all by the newcomers to the public stage: entrepreneurs, merchants, and bureaucrats, . . . fervently desired symbiosis with the people, the Russian peasantry."[29] But there was no way for them either to bring the peasantry into the discussions, nor did they probably understand peasant wishes themselves. Feeling strongly the loss in the Crimean War and the backwardness of Russia compared with the West, Alexander and his intellectual advisors prepared a proclamation freeing the serfs on all imperial and noble lands. Unlike the dismantling of feudalism in northwestern Europe and Japan, the serfs did not negotiate with the lords. Indeed, they had nothing to say about the terms of their "freedom."

The freed serfs individually received no land in private property. Instead, a quantity of land slightly less than they had been accustomed to farm was split off from the estates and granted to "rural societies," a new legal entity roughly equivalent to the communes (*mir*), on which peasant social and political life had been based for centuries. The government lent the rural societies the money to pay the landlords 80 percent of the value of the land taken from them, the landlords losing the other 20 percent. But the peasants were required to pay for the land assigned to them, even though they did not own it outright, over a period of forty-nine years at 6 percent interest. Their inability to do so bound them to the rural society as tightly as they had previously been bound to their lords. They could not leave without permission of the elders.

Berman believes that some element of democracy was introduced by emancipation because "the reform of local government emphasized the fact of the peasantry's newly acquired citizenship. In each county, representatives were elected by the private landowners, by the peasant commune, and by the townspeople."[30] But McKee argues that the appearances were deceiving: the peasants could not vote, their representatives were frustrated by their narrow sphere of action, and the tsar usually rejected their demands.[31]

The loss of the Crimean War stimulated government concern for industrial development. But reforms in the late nineteenth century, seemingly aimed at promoting industry, in fact strengthened the tsar. These included investment in internal transportation, specifically the railroad, stabilization of the ruble, and tariff protection for new industries.[32] "[T]he government, by taxing the income of consumers, . . . deprived Russia of an alternative pattern of production, thus usurping for itself the role of an active participant and stimulant of this process."[33] Also, "only a minute part of its budget expenditures went directly for the purposes of developing the industrial sector. . . . Russian tariff policy was as much revenue oriented as protection oriented, the upward tendency in tariff rates being stimulated as much by fiscal needs as by the clamor for protection from imports. . . . [T]he burden of taxation to support the Russian political regime appears to have been the chief obstacle to a more vigorous industrial development of Russia."[34] Raeff reports that "paradoxically, reforms intended to introduce modern economic relations and European political institutions . . . ended by reinforcing the power and moral authority of the autocrat."[35] Finally, the cultural chasm between rulers and elites on the one hand and the "little people" on the other has continued into the twentieth century. Educated officials communicated but rarely with lower classes, and only in limited ways. The imperial court did not take full advantage of the capabilities of its civil servants.

It is not surprising that such reforms would lead to a twenty-five year spurt in economic growth (1890-1914). But this was command growth. It would have been surprising if the bureaucracy that ordained this spurt had lasted long enough to sustain it, however. Furthermore, the main goals of emancipation were not met. Peasant revolts and agricultural stagnation, capped by loss of a war to Japan, brought the government to the same awareness in 1905 as that of the tsar in the 1850s: the polity and economy were backward, compared with western Europe. The reaction was the Stolypin reform, by which farms were allocated in outright ownership to the peasants. This reform— once again by decree, without peasant participation—released the peasant from the commune and provided for private property,[36] but it was not until 1911 that the full legislation was in place. Delayed by surveys and questions of who would get what, the reform was implemented but slowly and died with World War I and the 1917 revolutions.

In assessing the Stolypin reform favorably, Klebnikov wrote in the context of reform in the 1990s:

> The lesson of Stolypin's reforms is that given economic freedom, even backward peasants can become entrepreneurial and politically conservative. Simply put, privatization pays. But economic reform should be undertaken boldly: Vacillation leads to economic deterioration and political polarization. If he is serious about economic reform, Mr. Gorbachev needs a prime minister like Stolypin.[37]

But Klebnikov did not consider whether reform by decree rather than vertical negotiation today would once again contribute to the power ethos that destroyed the Stolypin reforms in a revolution.

The history of Soviet authoritarianism is well known: the forced collectivization of 1927 through 1930, the terror-famine, and the purges of the 1930s, in which millions died;[38] the successes of industry and agriculture during World War II; the problems of both industry and agriculture during the 1980s, which led to the virtual collapse of the economy in the 1990s and ultimately to the end of the Soviet Union.

In summary, this section has emphasized the continuity of Russian history. The authoritarian society of Ivan the Terrible led to the idea of reform from above, implemented by Peter the Great, Catherine the Great, Alexander I and II, Stolypin, Lenin and Trotsky, Stalin, Khrushchev, Gorbachev, and now Yeltsin. Common to all these was and is domination by the elites, lack of pluralism and vertical negotiations, plus well-meaning foreign advisors who tried (and still try) to convert Russia into an image of themselves. Further historical references to the Russian authoritarian state are found in appendix 14.2. References to the concentration of power are found in appendix 14.3.

The Reforms of the 1990s

Pressed by the economic decline mentioned at the beginning of the preceding chapter, in the late 1980s the government of the Soviet Union proposed radical economic reforms from above, which—like the political switch—conformed to Western values. Western observers also urged bold, surgical moves. The following two quotations reflect the dominant Western theme:

> Still, it is unlikely that dramatic improvements in economic performance will come through policy changes and partial reforms; therefore the ulti-

mate logic of developments is on the side of a shift toward more radical reforms.[39]

Over the next few months one can hope to expect a flurry of decrees and draft laws that taken as a whole will resemble the plans that Mr. Abalkin [a cautious free-enterpriser] had rejected as too risky.[40]

Roberts stated the proposition more boldly: "Privatization, especially in the context of a system that is failing, cannot be done in piecemeal fashion."[41]

When Gorbachev visited Stanford University in 1990, he was greeted with a professor's ready-made plan for privatization, with the manner in which ownerships would be distributed spelled out in detail.[42] Angell, a Federal Reserve governor, declared that monetary reform is prerequisite to market reforms. He presented a further plan for the new currency of the Russian Republic in 1992.[43]

Feldstein outlined the essential elements of Soviet economic reform, again with detailed steps such as checking the disintegration of the market; ending the budget deficit; decontrolling prices; increasing the interest rate; and ending subsidies.[44] McKinnon agreed but placed tax and monetary reform in the key positions, without which none of the market reforms would be possible.[45]

The *New York Times* summarized the reforms proposed by American Sovietologists as price decontrol—"Markets can work only if prices reflect realistic value"—monetary reform—"Price decontrol can work only if excess rubles are eliminated"—and fiscal reform—"Monetary reform can work only if Government deficits are controlled."[46]

All these plans assume, without foundation, the existence of Western-style institutions, not just organizations. None of them analyzes how each provision might be distorted in ways familiar to Soviet society. For example, private monopolies would supplant public ones, vouchers might be distributed to friends, price control would become political and erratically enforced, and so on.

One might more likely expect that it would be citizens of Russia and the other republics rather than Westerners who would propose a set of reforms to be mandated by despots. Indeed they have been doing so. While Andrei Sakharov, celebrated Russian dissident, complained of the excess power granted to Gorbachev,[47] nevertheless in a speech before the Congress of People's Deputies in 1989 he outlined a Decree on Power that could only be implemented by concentration of authority in the Congress.[48] Even Sakharov did not understand that democracy means dispersing power over various branches of government, not taking absolute rule from the executive in order to vest it in a Congress.

Former President Gorbachev also had his "total plan." At the end of 1989, he began announcing a radical, structural change: First was the relinquishment of some government controls.[49] Next, some private property ownership was permitted, along with the right to own small businesses.[50] After much criticism that these piecemeal changes were not enough, in September 1990 he and President Yeltsin of the Russian Republic announced a 500-day plan that would accomplish most of the reforms proposed by Western economists and even more, except that some price controls would remain. Exactly what would happen in the first 100 days, the next 150 days, the next 150 days, and the final 100 days was carefully spelled out. In fact, none of it occurred.

To implement the plan by decree, Gorbachev demanded and received virtually dictatorial powers from the legislature. But before the end of the year, his presidency, the legislature, and the government of the Soviet Union all had ceased to exist. Yeltsin proposed a similar plan for Russia in 1992, which was endorsed by the International Monetary Fund and seven Western nations, which promised to contribute a total of $24 billion in aid to the Russian Republic alone.[51] In 1993, they promised an immediate $3 billion. But promises are not contracts; in April 1994 the I.M.F. did vote $1.5 billion for Russia.[52]

Declarations that "all reforms must take place at once" reflect the ethnocentrism of Westerners who understand their own societies but who have forgotten their history. But that is not all. Evidence that Western governments do not understand Russian culture at its grass roots has also begun to surface. A poll of the Russian Academy of Agricultural Sciences in 1990 showed that 83% of collective farm workers opposed private property.[53] American economist Robert McIntyre has shown that the combination of private and collective farming in eastern Europe has been much more successful than Westerners acknowledge and is not easily given up.[54] In 1994, communist parties claimed a resurgence of adherents throughout Europe. If free-market reform is *not* what most Russians want, can it be imposed upon them?

The Twenty-First Century: A Possible Scenario

Time will not stop. So what would happen instead of liberal reforms? The following is one of many possible scenarios.

The central plan of Russia or any other republic will fail because the institutions to implement it cannot be put into place. The rulers cannot force all civil servants to banish corruption and privilege; they cannot force local governments to respect the free market; they cannot force bankers to make loans based on probability of profit rather than personal favoritism; they cannot force local elites to promote competition instead of monopoly; they cannot force businesspeople to cooperate in forming corporations for complex economic activity; they cannot force stock and bond issues to be honest; and most of all, they cannot force the governments of all regions of Russia to live in peace with each other—and even less so the other successor states. Too many whose cooperation would be essential would fail to execute this or that part of the plan. Thereafter, the economy would fail. Food would not be delivered to cities, the ruble would be worthless, barter would abound, thousands would starve, and ethnic groups would battle each other (as some are already doing). Foreign governments might intervene to alleviate the suffering, or stop the fighting, as best they could.

The closest historical precedent would be the fall of the Roman Empire. Strongmen would take over both factories and collective farms. The farms would continue as before but in a sort of manorial economy equivalent to the post-Roman. Political units different from the present ones might emerge. Peasants would commend themselves to protectors, possibly the same directors of collective farms, who would organize food production and create local currencies, possibly with their own promissory notes. The most crucial need would be for food distribution, so agriculture and transportation would assume top priority. City workers would flee to the country, at least until urban industry and services could be restored to employ them, and food distribution systems put into place.

Feudalism would not be repeated, however. The French *longue durée* of centuries would not be necessary. Entrepreneurial individuals would come out of the woodwork, seeing how to profit from whatever the circumstance. They would quickly form groups to build factories, or take over abandoned plants, and organize trade. Modern technology, always available, would be adopted as soon as the need for it was felt. Entrepreneurs would negotiate with the strongmen, both on the manors and in the cities, for protection and privilege, much as medieval bourgeoisie established towns. Since they would know about banking systems, they would form banks which, by agreement with each other, would develop exchange and transfer mechanisms. Local assemblies would sit, to work out rules of local government. Merchants would write and implement their own agreements, which would later be adopted as laws by local governments. Legal scholars would appear, and universities, not completely abandoned, would teach skills borrowed from the West. The local governments would issue new currencies to supplement the private issues of merchants and bankers.

Workers would bargain for wages. Although they would try to do so, strongmen would not be able to restrict labor mobility. Workers would move in ways the medieval serf could not, and wage labor would be quickly adopted. Unions would form, and contracts would be hammered out.

At every stage, the strongmen—mostly parasites—would try to suck the blood of new enterprises to their own benefit. Workers, peasants, and bourgeoisie who were adversely affected would either rebel against them or form unions or other syndicates to oppose them, sometimes forming vertical alliances with rival strongmen for leverage. In a few places, they might turn those strongmen into productive citizens, perhaps even entrepreneurs, like the samurai of Japan.

There is no reason immediately to expect a unified central government to emerge either in any republic or for a combination of republics. Most likely, local jurisdictions would join, ethnic groups with their kin, to form larger political aggregates. There would be wars over territorial boundaries.

It is not necessary to flesh out details. The ideas of the power-diffusion process have been expressed by example. But after an initial pessimism, this is an optimistic scenario. It is alternatively possible that centuries of bloodshed would elapse before a social consensus could be reached. Historical precedents exist for many scenarios, optimist and pessimist. But the central plan endorsed by seven industrial nations and the International Monetary Fund is not among them.

Notes

1. Blum 1957:818.
2. Blum 1961:73.
3. Domar 1970:25.
4. Lawrence 1978:169, 203.
5. Powelson 1988:chapter 8.
6. Feldbrugge 1977:27.
7. Dukes 1977:107.
8. Blum 1957:836.
9. Blum 1961:609.
10. Blum 1961:327.
11. Bobrick 1987:196.
12. Bobrick 1987:103.
13. Bobrick 1987:161.
14. Rieber, Alfred J., "His Dreadfulness, the Czar" (book review of Bobrick 1987), *New York Times Book Review*, 11/8/87.
15. Bobrick 1987:66.
16. Raeff 1984:1-33; Lawrence 1978:167.
17. Raeff 1984:40-41.
18. Raeff 1984:47.
19. Clendenning 1985:443-71.

20. Clendenning 1985:453-54.
21. Raeff 1984:57-87.
22. Lawrence 1978:170.
23. Raeff 1984:113.
24. Lawrence 1978:173.
25. Holborn 1964:437.
26. Raeff 1984:119.
27. Raeff 1984:125-26.
28. Powelson 1988:115-17.
29. Raeff 1984:167.
30. Berman 1963:213.
31. McKee, Margaret, "In Russia of 1800s, Reform Benefited the Czar," Letter to the Editor, *New York Times*, 8/26/89.
32. Kahan 1989:91.
33. Kahan 1989:94.
34. Kahan 1989:96,99,105.
35. Raeff 1984:182.
36. Powelson 1988:117-19.
37. Klebnikov, Paul, "The Man Who Saved Russia . . . with Capitalism," *Wall Street Journal*, 7/24/90.
38. Lewin 1968; Conquest 1986.
39. Hewitt 1984:11.
40. Hewett, Ed. A., "Prognosis for Soviet Economy Is Grave, but Improving," *New York Times*, 2/25/90.
41. Roberts, Paul Craig, "Private Property Is the Solution," *Cato Policy Report*, vol. XIII, no. 1, January/February 1991:1.
42. Moore, Thomas Gale, "A Privatization Program for Gorbachev," *Wall Street Journal*, 5/30/90.
43. Angell, Wayne, "My Plan for a Russian Currency," *Wall Street Journal*, 3/26/92.
44. Feldstein, Martin, "Back in the U.S.S.R. as the Storm Clouds Gather," *Wall Street Journal*, 9/14/89.
45. McKinnon, Donald I., "Can the Soviet Economy be Saved? Maybe—with Tax Reform," *Wall Street Journal*, 12/7/89.
46. "Moscow Reforms: Turning Radical," editorial, *New York Times*, 4/4/90.
47. Keller, Bill, "Sakharov Warns of Peril in New Soviet Setup," *New York Times*, 11/2/88.
48. Sakharov, Andrei, "A Speech to the People's Congress," *New York Review of Books*, 8/17/89.
49. Gumbel, Peter, "Soviet Premier Offers Modest Economic Plan," *Wall Street Journal*, 12/14/89.
50. Hays, Laurie, "Soviet Legislators Vote to Permit Some Private Property Ownership," *Wall Street Journal*, 3/7/90; and Keller, Bill, "Soviets Approve the Right to Own Small Businesses," *New York Times*, 3/7/90.
51. *New York Times*, 4/1 and 4/2/92.
52. Ifill, Gwen, "Seven Wealthy Nations Agree to Speed up Russian Aid Plans," *New York Times*, 7/9/93; Greenhouse, Steven, "I.M.F. Gives Russia a Vote of Confidence: A $1.5 Billion Loan," *New York Times*, 4/21/94.
53. For reports of the poll, see "Half a Russian Loaf," *The Economist*, 12/8/90:58.
54. McIntyre, Robert, "Why Communism is Rising from the Ash Heap," *Washington Post Weekly*, 6/20-26, 1994.

Chapter 15

Spain and Portugal:

Institutions, Pluralism, and Leverage

In the High Middle Ages, Iberia (Spain and Portugal) possessed advanced monetary and legal systems. Most peasants could move about freely. Rivalry among kings, nobility, and church offered potential leverage to peasants and bourgeoisie, just as they did in northwestern Europe. The power-diffusion process was beginning to work. Seeing little advantage in trying for the English throne rather than that of Castile, John of Gaunt preferred Castile. (He lost.)

By the sixteenth and seventeenth centuries, however, Iberia was "refeudalizing" along the lines of eastern Europe. Kings, nobility, and church had formed a solid front precluding vertical alliances and leverage from humbler subjects. With state intervention in virtually all economic activity, peasants and bourgeoisie were left out of major decision making. In economic growth, Spain and Portugal dropped well behind northwestern Europe. Instead of the power-diffusion process, the model characteristic of less-developed zones was now at work.

Suddenly, at the end of the twentieth century, another reversal occurred. Iberian economic growth accelerated. Spain and Portugal joined the European Economic Community (now the European Union) and began to adopt the institutions of the West. But in the mid-1990s, the economy is again beginning to stagnate. Was the acceleration only temporary, or will it resume?

The Declining Likelihood of Vertical Alliances and Leverage

Possibilities of alliance with leverage were available to Iberian peasants in the eleventh century, but they were not enduring. For example, peasant villages in western Castile and León "dissatisfied with the protection and services of their overlord might switch their allegiance to another defender."[1] By the twelfth century, however, this switching was limited to other gentry families within the same lineage, and two centuries farther on it was hardly possible at all.

By the fifteenth century, lands seized in the Christian Reconquest from the Moors had so strengthened the Castilian nobles that they appeared to be challenging the monarchy.[2] Why did not this competition provide opportunity for vertical alliances to lower classes, who might have swung their weight from one to the other in exchange for improved conditions? Possibly because the rupture between nobility and monarchy did not last. Buoyed by precious metals from the Americas, the monarchs increasingly "bought off" both the nobility and the church, much as the ruling house in Saudi Arabia buys off its potential opposition today. Hence there remained no independent upper power with which the bourgeois and peasants might ally: "between peasants and nobles there was nothing resembling a middle class."[3]

In still another example, by the twelfth century the *cortes* (parliaments) of Iberia were either similar to or more advanced than the parliaments of northern Europe. "[T]he first medieval parliament representing the three principal estates of society met in León in 1188, antedating the first parliamentary assemblies in all other European kingdoms."[4] This cortes "already included representatives of the people, besides the members of the clergy and the nobility who used to assist the king whenever he required their advice."[5]

But the lower classes did not take advantage of this cortes to enhance their bargaining power. From the fourteenth century on, as Castile expanded into most of Spain, its cortes became weaker relative to the king, although its Catalonian counterpart managed to retain some vitality. As a result, Castilian towns and peasantry could not defend themselves well against royal taxation. "Thus there did not develop in Castile the union of the lower nobility and upper middle class that later formed the backbone of the English parliament."[6]

By the sixteenth century, the cortes of Castile consisted only of the third estate. "Their function was only to vote taxes."[7] Even this capacity gave them no power. Virtually always they rubber-stamped the monarch's requests. "During the seventeenth century [its] powers, already minimal, lapsed completely.[8] The role of the Portuguese cortes declined similarly.[9]

The decline of the cortes reflects how the monarchs in both Spain and Portugal learned to "escape" negotiation with the middle and lower classes. The money stream from the New World relieved them of the necessity to appeal to the cortes for taxes and allowed the nobility to be exempt. For much of Iberian history, therefore, the nobility, seeing where their bread was buttered, joined the monarchs on the same side of conflicts. The same was so for the church, which was usually in the pocket of the king, although conflicts with the pope occurred. "Nowhere did the church come under more outright secular political domination than in Spain."[10] Hence the quarrels with both nobility and church, that supplied the bourgeois and peasants of northern Europe with potential for vertical alliances and leverage, were less pronounced in Castile and Portugal.

In Aragon, Catalonia, and Valencia by contrast, "the cortes possessed more authentic privileges and greater means of evading government control."[11]

This was in part because the rugged country, the distance from Valladolid (seat of the Castilian court) and the proximity to France of Aragon and Catalonia had given the rulers a certain independence, confirmed in their "privileges" (*fueros*). It was also because with fewer resources these territories were less likely to produce treasure than were the foreign settlements of Castile. (Castile did contend with Aragon for territories in Italy, however.) The relative insulation from the oppressions of Castile may have liberated Catalonia for its greater economic development today.

Power

By the time of the Habsburg monarchs (beginning in the sixteenth century), power was vested absolutely in the king. This did not mean that the king ruled unchallenged or all by himself but that he maintained tight control over a bureaucracy to which decisions on taxes, war and peace, laws, prices and trade, and investments were entrusted, and the American treasure "bribed" the military, nobility, and church to support him. The limitations imposed on him were mainly those of financial and economic necessity and external military pressure, in contrast to northwestern European countries where they arose also from domestic interest groups. The aristocracy in the sixteenth century "had surrendered its feudal role to the demands of absolute monarchy and was now content to serve the crown in the subordinate fields of war, diplomacy, and viceregal administration."[12]

A refeudalization similar to that of eastern Europe took place in Iberia during the sixteenth and seventeenth centuries. It did not happen everywhere, for feudal obligations were dismantled in some parts just as they were being strengthened in others. For example, revolts in Catalonia had brought down feudalism as far back as 1486, when the Sentence of Guadalupe provided personal freedom for peasants.[13] But northwestern Europe and Catalonia, not the rest of Spain, were the exceptions to a general refeudalization in eastern and southern Europe.[14] The refeudalization took place more in the Iberian south than in the north, promoted by divisions of lands taken from Moors during the Reconquest and by strengthening the symbiosis of monarchy and landed aristocracy. It became a principal feature in the consolidation of landed estates that still marks southern Iberian agriculture today.

The following quotation shows the paternalism by which southern nobles depended upon the crown, together with the political defense the crown needed from the nobles. Vertical alliances with leverage to the lower classes by dividing these two was impossible.

> Nobles had to get royal permission to marry, to alienate their patrimony, to mortgage their estates, in short to do anything that might weaken their

class. For the crown regarded the nobility, somewhat naively, as a reserve of talent at the service of the country.[15]

The royal government took total control over all but the most local production. Trade with Asia, Africa, and the Indies (America) was licensed by the state through the *Casa de Contratación* in Spain and the *Casa da Guine* and *Casa da India* in Portugal. It was conducted in royally sponsored caravans for defense against pirates, mainly English. Gold and silver mined in America was the property of the king, to be shared with miners on terms set by the king, although much of it escaped because restrictions could not be enforced. High taxation and state regulations strangled both agriculture and industry far more in Iberia than they did in northern Europe. The middle class did not develop in Iberia.[16]

A paternalistic style cut across all society, resembling Chinese Confucianism though unrelated to it by origin. Extended families were ruled by the eldest male member; the lord of the land made decisions for aristocratic farms, with which peasant farmers complied. The upper society believed that authority and status rather than experience or knowledge led to correct decisions. For example, the *Mesta*, a privileged society of sheep owners, had drovers' rights across Spain twice a year from the thirteenth to the nineteenth centuries. Crops were demolished by these runs, while gains from them were shared with the crown. No one in authority questioned the inefficiency that they wrought upon food production and the hardships upon small farmers.

The sixteenth century—era of Charles I[17] and Philip II—marked the apogee of royal power. From then until the nineteenth century the monarch was theoretically absolute, but military exhaustion, loss of the Netherlands, inability to control distant territories such as the New World, weak kings, absolute rule exercised by southern nobles over their territories, and rivalries with the pope introduced confusion over the real power center. Both the kings of Spain and Portugal began to rule through "favorites" (*validos*) who theoretically acted on their behalf.[18]

A comparison with the rest of Europe is not so simple. Favorites and prime ministers throughout Europe had in common that they were chosen for the job rather than born into it, and therefore they opened the way for administration by competence rather than birth. But the range was wide, from England, whose emerging prime ministers in the seventeenth and eighteenth centuries mainly represented Parliament, through France, whose Richelieu, Mazarin, and others shared power with the king, to Spain and Portugal, whose favorites like Olivares and Pombal ruled almost absolutely in place of the king. Power in Iberia was equally or more concentrated than in France, where in turn it was more concentrated than in England. The king's relationship with his valido and his bureaucracy was therefore not one of give and take among independent-thinking intellectuals, such as was developing in England. Instead, it was one of subservience and paternalism among members of a closed circle.[19]

As a result of all these factors, the kings of Spain and Portugal remained absolute rulers long after the age of absolutism had begun to die in northwestern Europe. Industry and trade were monopolized by the crown and its cronies; wealth was gained by milking more than by production, not only in Iberia but also in America and Italy; countervailing groups and political pluralism were contained; no religious revolt comparable to the Reformation emerged; the Inquisition suppressed innovative thinking; and agricultural as well as industrial productivity lagged. Especially in Portugal, a few elite families continue to monopolize industry, even today; and a poor, Third World type of peasantry has persisted, especially in the south of both countries. In all these respects, Iberia has resembled eastern Europe and less-developed zones more than western. Further historical references to the concentration of power in the Iberian monarchy and state are listed in appendix 15.1.

The Great Divide

Just as in eastern Europe, medieval peasants and lords in Iberia failed to negotiate, compromise, and make contracts vertically. Once again, land abundance and the alternative of long-distance trade may have been the inhibitors.

Land Abundance

Vast tracts of land characterized most of Iberian history,[20] yet to the peasants little was available. Instead, the main lands were monopolized by gentry for merino sheep, which required little labor. By contrast, small plots of agricultural land were farmed by landless tenants, who, although juridically free, did not have much choice of lords, for one was like another. The huge supply of destitute labor possessed little bargaining power. Spanish lords did not bargain much with peasants because they did not have to. They could always expel the peasants and find new ones, or they could convert to sheep raising with little need for peasants.

The absence of contract feudalism in Iberia also is attributed in part to the Reconquest, which began in the ninth and tenth centuries. With land regained from the Muslims, Iberian soldiers were mustered out as free peasants. For protection they committed themselves to lords in an institution known as *behetría*, "by which the peasants themselves elected the seignior and also had the right to replace him should they decide that he was not serving the community."[21]

At first glance, behetría would seem to provide a powerful weapon for the peasantry in negotiating to elect a lord. But it did not do so, for two reasons: (1) The wars of Reconquest and to hold the Netherlands and Italy, akin to the Russian wars of expansion, created a semimigratory society, in which lords and peasants did not easily settle into one-on-one relationships. (2) Since behetría was looser than the vassalage of northwestern Europe, the peasants and lords were not bound to each other. Peasant soldiers receiving land as a one-time award did not at the same time engage organizationally in a balance of power with negotiations that would enable them to participate fully in the economic decisions by which they were ruled.

Colonization in America and Italy continued the land abundance. In Sicily and Naples as in Mexico, Peru, and Brazil, settlements were more closely akin to those of Iberian feudal estates than to the plantation/industrial colonies of northern Europeans. Lack of interclass communication diminished the prospects for leverage by the lower classes. Possible exceptions were Catalonia and the Basque country, which in some ways appeared to belong more to northern Europe. Further historical references to land abundance in Spain and Portugal are listed in appendix 15.2.

Long-Distance Trade

The ways in which the Spanish elites enforced and milked their monopoly over trade and industry included price controls; heavy taxation, especially of precious metals from America; confinement of international trade to the port of Seville and the *Casa de Contratación*; discrimination in privileges in favor of Castile, as opposed to Aragon, Catalonia, Portugal, and the others.

The haunting question is: Why were the monarchs unaware, *for centuries*, of the great potential *to themselves* of permitting greater freedom to business venturers? Even if their primary objectives were war, national aggrandizement, and personal power, could they not have understood that greater resources to achieve these would have resulted from fewer restrictions and less taxation of industry and trade? Could they not have worked out institutions by which they themselves would share in this surplus, *together* with lower classes? Possible answers are:

First, without being compelled to compromise with other classes, the very vision of positive-sum gains lay beyond the horizon of the Iberian monarchs. For example: "Ferdinand and Isabella had no intention of rescuing the crown from the aristocracy *merely to subordinate it to the towns*" [italics mine].[22] The crown could not imagine any other arrangement than its own control. Likewise, Philip II and his successors could see no potential gain from integrating Portuguese merchants into the Spanish trading network during the dual monarchy (1580-1640): "By royal decree the Portuguese were explicitly denied the privileges of Spanish nationality, especially the privileges of trading to the Spanish possessions."[23]

Second, the monarchy was aware that greater freedom to producers and traders required sharing its power with them. Monarchs do not always foresee the greater economic output that comes with freedom to trade, but if they do, they do not always value it as highly as their power to suppress it. When power is factored in as a desideratum, mercantilism has its logic.

In sum, the weak formation of pluralism with leverage for the lower classes is attributable to the solidarity of monarchy, nobles, and church and the great communication divide between them and the bourgeoisie and peasants. Six historical citations are supplied in appendix 15.3. Without being forced by threat to survival into acting in their own *economic* interests (as opposed to power interests), the power group would not do so.

Interest Groups

Interest groups did arise—guilds, labor unions, peasant associations, and employer associations—but they neither evolved nor functioned in the same ways as in northwestern Europe.

Guilds

In northwestern Europe and Japan, guilds supplied management and negotiation skills for a contract labor system. In Iberia, by contrast, the nascent guild system was so burdened by royal restrictions that it failed to blossom until the sixteenth century. Nor did municipal governments jump to its defense. Rather, guilds were first formed in the fifteenth century under the tutelage of kings who saw in them ways of extending royal control.[24]

Guilds grew in numbers and power in the sixteenth and seventeenth centuries. They imposed the same restrictions for which guilds everywhere have been notorious: price controls, divisions of markets, control over labor, and limitations on production. However, as these restrictions were diminishing in northwestern Europe they were being strengthened in Iberia. "Guild organization, with its defensive mentality and the values placed on hierarchy and seniority, maintained a rigid framework around production"[25] in the seventeenth century.

Even as guilds were being dismantled in northern Europe in the nineteenth century, they were still gaining power in Iberia. Not until late in that century, and on into the twentieth, did freedom of corporate enterprise begin to find a place in Iberian economic culture.[26] Further historical references to guilds and corporations are listed in appendix 15.4.

Labor Unions

In 1349, Pedro IV of Aragon prohibited workers from forming associations, while appointing a commission to set their wages.[27] From then until the nineteenth century, references to Iberian labor organizations fade out of the historical literature.

Unions increased in Iberia in the nineteenth century, just as they did in northwestern Europe. But unlike northwestern Europe, they were effectively contained until late in the twentieth century. More pointedly, the independence of labor unions has never been complete: they became instruments of royal or dictatorial (Franco or Salazar) control.

The first labor associations of Spain were organized in the 1830s, as reflections of socialist and Fourierist ideas from elsewhere in Europe.[28] They were legalized in Spain in 1887-90[29] and in Portugal in 1911.[30] Their principal uncertainties have been (1) whether their purpose is to transform the political system (revolutionary, anarchist/syndicalist) or whether they exist mainly to bargain for wages and working conditions; and (2) whether they operate independently or rely for their gains on association with a sympathetic government.

Franco's syndicates were "instruments for controlling labor and for giving employers an edge in bargaining power."[31] Under Salazar in Portugal, unions "became instruments of government policy. . . . Most of the labor associations were made compulsory, while internal regulations restricted freedom of self-government and closely defined their powers in dealing with the *gremios* [employer associations]."[32] Obviously, unions that either depend on governments to negotiate for them or are political tools of those governments are not independent actors. They become estranged from the employers with whom they might otherwise bargain for positive-sum gains.

Peasant associations

Until the sixteenth century, peasant associations and rebellions bore a weak resemblance to those of northwestern Europe. Peasants sometimes banded together, formed alliances with higher-ranking groups, and exerted leverage. Some examples: (1) "by 1448, the crown had granted *remences* [Catalan peasants performing feudal obligations] the right to form local peasant syndicates to represent their claims and try to work out a settlement with the landlords."[33] (2) In 1462, Catalan peasants allied with the crown and some of the nobility in a ten-year war against the clergy and other nobility.[34] (3) A revolt by Galician peasants in 1465 was supported by the king, who wished to diminish the power of the landed gentry.[35] (4) In 1640, a Catalan uprising, aided by the French, occurred as part of an attempt at provincial autonomy. It was put down.[36]

Unlike the peasant movements in northwestern Europe and Japan, however, these occurrences did not become institutionalized into self-sustaining peasant organizations, associated with individual manors, possessing a corporate life, and capable of carrying on regular negotiations.

The division of peasants according to ethnicity and religion—such as Moriscos and Christians—and the tendency of Moriscos to move fluidly to Africa and back impeded their ability to organize. In Valencia, Moriscos were "protected" by landlords to whom they "belonged." Because they were hated by Christians from the outside, they were in a weak position to bargain for privilege or freedom, even with their landlords. Several rebellions by Moriscos were put down. In the mass expulsion of 1609, the Morisco problem was finally "solved" with a disruption of peasant-landlord communications throughout Spain, but especially in Valencia and Granada.

Despite a few victories in the fifteenth century, peasant rebellions were mostly put down in all centuries. By the seventeenth, peasant power had been so reduced by consistently unsettled conditions, and the nobility and the monarchy had forged such a firm alliance that all opportunity for peasants to split the upper-level groups to their advantage had disappeared. Further historical references to peasant associations and peasant rebellions are found in appendix 15.5.

Legal and Monetary Systems

In the early Middle Ages Iberia was at least on a par with northwestern Europe in legal and monetary systems, and in some respects ahead. Only in the fifteenth and sixteenth centuries did its forward motion begin to stall. With all trading so closely mandated by the crown in both Spain and Portugal, and with merchants held in such low esteem, there was little scope for private traders, financiers, town politicians, business managers, and legists to create money, instruments for contracting, and law. In all these respects, Spaniards and Portuguese depended on the crown.

Law

The roots of law in thirteenth-century Iberia were similar to those of northwestern Europe.[37] Furthermore, law was decentralized. "The Spanish realms were a vast accretion of overlapping fueros. . . . Castile, the most unified realm, had eight separate legal codes in 1492."[38] Canon law, several codices of Castilian law, Roman law, and Portuguese legislation were all in use by the thirteenth century.[39] The same was so for Portugal.

Trading on the great divide between the king and his humble subjects, however, the monarchy captured the law. Philip II possessed a "high sense of justice" and "concern for the impartial administration of law. But he also believed that his sovereignty gave him the right to execute private and secret justice, beyond the cognisance of any authority except God. This belief led him to acts of savagery and arbitrary despotism."[40] "'If it be my pleasure,' declared Philip in 1555, 'I shall annul, without the cortes, the laws made in the cortes; I shall legislate by edicts and I shall abolish laws by edicts.'"[41]

In Portugal, magistrates living in the king's court extended themselves downward into local jurisdictions, as *ouvidores*, who reported to the king.[42] "Under Alfonso IV even the local judges had to be confirmed by the king, and the administration of justice was firmly monopolized by the crown."[43] In 1512-21 a new code, the *Ordenaçoes Manuelinas*, brought a "tendency for a greater centralization under a stricter control by magistrates closer to the monarch."[44]

In both Spain and Portugal, the Inquisition was a device to concentrate power in the monarchy, by giving it a legal instrument to use capriciously against its enemies. It meted out its punishments heavily to the merchant class, which—in both political power and decision capacity—paid the main cost of the power accretion by the monarchy.

Often the law did not conform to surrounding reality, and therefore it was violated. "Although the export of bullion was prohibited by law [in the seventeenth century], the law was ignored, because the Spanish market and the Indies trade itself needed foreign manufactures."[45] But evading the law was not the ideal solution, for bribes and concealment could be expensive. There was always the risk of the law being capriciously enforced by a political foe.

In 1829, a uniform commercial code was worked out[46] for the first time in Spain, and in 1885 it was rewritten.[47] By then, Spain was in the era of parliamentary government. The big question is whether the laws enacted by parliament were the ones that would have been negotiated by representatives of producers, merchants, and their customers, or whether the law was mainly fashioned by political actors from their own power. Both Spain and Portugal had skipped the era in which commercial law might have been fashioned by direct negotiation among the parties concerned.

Portuguese law codes of 1832 and 1842 and constitutions of 1911 and 1933 seesawed between centralization and decentralization and tended to set up legal forms not necessarily followed in practice. The constitution set up a presidential regime with voting, but "Salazar's thirty-six year premiership transferred power to the government and reduced the President to almost nothing."[48] When the law of the land is specified in one way and enforced in another, it is difficult to know what the law is and what behavior is legitimate.

Thus, after an experience of the Middle Ages similar to that of the rest of Europe, Spain and Portugal entered the twentieth century with the laws of production and trade still captured by the state.

Money and Banking

In form, the early banking systems of Iberia were similar to those of northwestern Europe: private banks and money changers, and royal coinage subject to depreciation. Once again, the similarity was greatest in the thirteenth and fourteenth centuries, and once again greater in Catalonia[49] and the Basque country than farther south. After that, as all but the most local trade became regulated or monopolized by the crown, the monetary system too became oriented toward the crown.

In Portugal in the twelfth and thirteenth centuries, "an organized exchange between the country and the town grew up. . . . [E]ach demesne started sending most of its production to the nearest town. A generalized monetary economy naturally came into existence."[50]

As political centralization, expansion in the New World with its inflow of precious metals, and wars encompassed the combined monarchy of the sixteenth century, it turned toward the banking system for assistance in all these. In so doing, it inextricably confused the fiscal and monetary systems. It mopped up both the resources and the administrative capabilities of the banking system, making them less available for the private sector, and it monetized the state debt.[51]

The wars of the sixteenth century led the Spanish financial system, public and private, into disasters that spread to the Netherlands and Italy as well. With no state bank to create money, both Charles I and Philip II taxed the resources of the Netherlands to the full extent they were able. They also relied on financial markets such as Genoa, Augsburg, and Antwerp, and on German financial families such as the Fuggers and Welsers.[52]

Although sixteenth-century trade was vigorous—fairs and activity in the port cities rivaling northwestern Europe—nevertheless it all depended on massive infusions of money from America, from merchant bankers within Spain and on loans from abroad. When these sources dried up, the Spanish monetary system was near collapse. Public finance was a Ponzi-scheme, with high interest rates but ultimate loss of investment. The monarchy defaulted on its debts in 1557, 1575, 1627, and 1647. The Portuguese government declared bankruptcy in 1560 and 1605.[53] After the 1627 default, Genoese bankers refused to lend more to the king.[54] Philip IV responded by minting great quantities of vellon (debased copper currency). Inflation, heavy in the sixteenth century, was stabilized during 1611-20 but was set loose again in the mid-seventeenth century.[55] "In 1680, the new government imposed drastic revaluation. Prices fell nearly 50 percent in two years, but the new money supply was totally inadequate for commerce and finance, and much of the economy ceased to function."[56]

Merchants and private banks did not step into the gap, probably for two reasons: First, the fiscal and monetary systems had become so intertwined that it was impossible for one to function independently of the other. Whatever shadow monetary system merchants might have initiated would have been sucked into the conventional fiscal/monetary system. Second, the fiscal system—and therefore the monetary system—was in such disarray that there was no unit of value to which merchants could adhere with the trust of their clients.

Monetary and fiscal instability, with ebbs and flows, continued for two centuries. In 1820, "the treasury lay in a state of total disarray and the debt increased steadily."[57] Out of this disarray, Kindleberger finds that "Spanish financial history may be said to begin with the American War of Independence, when Spain joined France on the side of the colonies against Britain."[58] At that time, the Banco de San Carlos was formed, popularly known as The Bank of Spain. A major purpose was to finance provisions for the military. Another Bank of Spain, formed by private shareholders in 1847, was authorized to issue money for all of Spain in 1851. Its first mission was to provide funds for the state.[59] Thus a "significant obstacle to industrial progress was the close interdependence between the State and the nation's financial institutions, which caused the public and private sectors to compete for the limited funds available . . . The State had a number of advantages over the industrial sector." [60]

Restrictive banking laws of the mid-nineteenth century were eased as the century progressed. A law of 1848 discouraged private banks, but two laws in 1856 eased the restrictions. Finally, in 1869, private banks were allowed to develop freely.[61] In 1874, the Bank of Spain was granted a monopoly of currency issue.[62] From 1898 to 1914, as the government decreased its borrowing, finance became increasingly private. But in 1962, during the Franco regime, the Bank of Spain was nationalized; a government Institute of Official Credit was set up to supervise five nationalized credit institutions; and private banks were required to choose between commercial and investment financing.[63]

In many respects, government controls over Spanish banks resemble those in other countries, such as in reserve requirements and maintenance of sound balance sheets, but the Spanish regulations have been more pervasive.

Interest rates have been regulated, and government has intervened directly in banking operations. The close relationship between crown or state and financial institutions has not died easily. In Portugal, on the other hand, at least until 1974 the "private sector was dominated by some 40 great families. . . . Within this elite group, the top ten families owned all the important commercial banks, which in turn controlled a disproportionate share of the national economy."[64] Thus the power concentration continued in both countries: in Spain in the state, and in Portugal in a small number of families.

Summary

In the High Middle Ages, Spain and Portugal compared favorably with northwestern Europe in economic organization, parliaments, law, and a monetary system. Agriculture and industry were on a par with the northern areas, but peasants were more mobile and feudalism was "looser" than in northwestern Europe. For the most part it was not contractual.

During the sixteenth century, the positions shifted. Compared with northwestern Europe, power in Iberia became more concentrated. With solidarity among the monarchy, nobility, and Spanish church, vertical alliances and leverage were foreclosed for the lower classes. Whereas in northwestern Europe both peasants and bourgeois were increasingly setting the terms of economic intercourse—with freer markets in both towns and international trade—in Spain and Portugal these powers became increasingly concentrated in the monarchy, which used them and abused them to promote its own wealth and power. Peasants became bound to their lords, with but little or no opportunity to negotiate any of their terms. War for national aggrandizement was a constant theme. Economic inefficiency, waste, and low incomes were the legacy.

Only in the nineteenth century did Iberia seem to reflect some of the institutions from northwestern Europe. But power concentration remained the dominant theme, whether in the monarchy or—in the twentieth century—in the dictatorships of Franco and Salazar. Yet surprises lay ahead.

Notes

1. Payne 1973:1:69.
2. Lynch 1981:1:5.
3. Lynch 1981:1:13.
4. Payne 1973:1:81.
5. Marques 1972:99.
6. Payne 1973:1:150-51.

7. Lynch 1981:1:49-50.
8. Payne 1973:1:8, 311.
9. Marques 1972:298.
10. Ozment 1980:188.
11. Lynch 1981:1:9. See also Barber 1992:362.
12. Lynch 1981:1:112.
13. Brenner 1985:35.
14. Payne 1973:1:328.
15. Lynch 1981:2:140.
16. Marques 1972:265.
17. Charles I of Spain was also Charles V of the Holy Roman Empire.
18. Payne 1973:2:27.
19. Payne 1973:2:290.
20. Lynch 1981:1:119; Barber 1992:341.
21. Harrison 1978:8.
22. Lynch 1981:1:5-6.
23. Rich 1967:328.
24. Payne 1973:273.
25. Lynch 1981:2:160.
26. Payne 1973:384.
27. Epstein 1991:239-40.
28. Payne 1973:601.
29. Payne 1973:125.
30. Marques 1976:29,139; Payne 1973:560.
31. Baklanoff 1978:14.
32. Marques 1976:182.
33. Payne 1973:165.
34. Payne 1973:166.
35. Payne 1973:175.
36. Payne 1973:313-14.
37. Berman 1983:513.
38. Melko and Hord 1984:41.
39. Marques 1972:99-100.
40. Lynch 1981:1:183.
41. *Cortes de los antiguos reinos de León y de Castilla*, v. 677, cited by Lynch 1981:1:207.
42. Marques 1972:98.
43. Marques 1972:99.
44. Marques 1972:187.
45. Lynch 1981:2:183.
46. Payne 1973:494.
47. Payne 1973:494.
48. Marques 1976:190.
49. Payne 1973:103.
50. Marques 1972:94.
51. Payne 1973:293.
52. Lynch 1981:1:59
53. Marques 1972:278.
54. Braudel 1982:398.

55. Lynch 1981:2:7.
56. Payne 1973:321.
57. Payne 1973:428.
58. Kindleberger 1984:146.
59. Payne 1973:598.
60. Harrison 1978:42-43.
61. Aceña 1987:110.
62. Aceña 1987:109-10.
63. Aceña 1987:37.
64. Baklanoff 1978:108.

Chapter 16

Spain and Portugal:

Economic Development by Reflection

The surprises are that the economies of both Spain and Portugal grew strongly from 1959 until the 1990s. How can that progress be explained, in view of the failure of the power-diffusion process in earlier centuries? Let us look for answers by examining the earlier backwardness and the later growth, for agriculture and industry separately.

Agriculture

Iberian agricultural backwardness persisted right up until the second half of the twentieth century. During the nineteenth century, greater output was caused mainly by increases in cultivated land, not much by productivity growth.

Growing food might have been more profitable than raising sheep to both peasants and landowners if they had worked out the institutional arrangements for it. Sometimes this happened. From 1450 to 1550 the Portuguese reclaimed land and introduced new crops, especially maize.[1] While these shifts occurred from time to time, until the eighteenth century they were unusual. The rulers might also have gained greater tax revenues through increased agricultural output, had they taxed it less. Both farmers and peasants could have earned more, too. But periods of attention to agriculture, as opposed to sheep raising, were not typical, and taxes were consistently extortionary, so agricultural output and productivity lagged behind industry, and agriculture and industry both lagged behind their counterparts in northwestern Europe. Although data are not reliable before the nineteenth century, historical references for earlier centuries confirm this observation.[2]

An increase in agricultural production in the eighteenth century responded to increase in population, some relaxing of restrictions, a relative shift from pasture to food growing and from subsistence to market, and increased land under the plow following the disentailment of private estates and the sales of church lands.[3] Nonetheless, productivity increased little if at all. Instead, rents were boosted and tenants forced off the land. In Galicia, "rents were raised and cultivation units persistently subdivided until thousands of relatively high-priced but uneconomic minifundia had been created."[4]

Farm productivity throughout the European continent also stagnated before the agricultural revolutions of the seventeenth and eighteenth centuries. But Spain, along with Russia, was the last of European countries to begin its agricultural revolution.[5] Tortella presents tables on agricultural output and yields in Spain compared with other European countries. His conclusion is that "the growth of output [in the nineteenth century] did not at all constitute an 'agricultural revolution'—far from it. . . . Spanish yields were very low at the beginning of the twentieth century; this implies that growth in output had only been possible because of a parallel expansion in cultivated land."[6]

The usual explanation of this retardation includes enormous taxation, the concentration of land ownership in a nonproductive nobility, the destructive practices of the *Mesta*, persistent wars, and the neglect of home production because of wealth from the New World. Accepting all this, one still may ask: So long as increases in output and productivity were physically possible with available technology—and certainly they were—why could not *some* institutional arrangements have been worked out between landlords and peasants or between *Mesta* and farmers that would have realized the possibilities, to the benefit of both parties? Why was a potential positive-sum move not made?

The answer might lie in risk. The great communication divide between landowners and peasants, the persistent denigration by landowners of the qualities of peasants, the belief that they were good for nothing except digging and hoeing, and the sheer terror of the lords about peasant rebellions probably prevented the parties from negotiating rent, tenancy, credit, and other arrangements that elsewhere fomented spectacular increases in agricultural productivity.

Until about 1950, Spanish agriculture scarcely kept up with population growth,[7] but the spread of mechanization has led to an outstanding increase in the years since then.[8] The share of the labor force in agriculture fell from 42 percent in 1960 to 23 percent in 1974. During those years, output increased on average 3.4 percent per year.[9] Was mechanization a one-time boost that will taper off? Or were other forces at work?

Industry

> The decline of Spain in the seventeenth century is not difficult to understand. The fundamental fact is that Spain never developed to begin with.[10]

This summary verdict by Carlo Cipolla, a noted historian, which would apply equally well to Portugal, is blamed on Iberia's wealth from the New World. The massive inflow of specie set in motion a series of economic events—such as inflation and overvalued currency—that in turn encouraged Spanish consumption of imported rather than locally produced goods. Thus the incentive for local industry was lost, and the result was "bottlenecks in . . . the productive system (in particular, lack of skilled labor, standards of value unfavorable to craft and trade activities, the guilds and their restrictive policies). The increase in demand stimulated some growth . . . [but] a large part of the demand was met by foreign goods and services."[11]

In partial confirmation, another historian finds the traditional picture of utter collapse to be overdrawn, while at the same time confirming weaknesses "in the three major growth industries of the period—textiles, metallurgy, and shipbuilding" and losses of trade "to the English, the French, and the Dutch."[12] Import prohibitions, intended to foster industry, instead cut off essential supplies and limited export markets as well. "Spain either took foreign imports or went without manufactures altogether."[13]

The industrial slowness continued through the eighteenth century.[14] Valencia was an exception, whose driving force probably came from outside Spain. "The eighteenth century witnessed spectacular progress in the Valencian silk industry."[15] The explanation that massive inflows of specie and mercantilist economic policies delayed industrial development is correct but not sufficient. Despite all the American wealth and the collaboration of producers and banks such as the Fuggers and the Genoese, Spain was still short of the goods that Charles I and Philip II needed to conduct their wars in Europe. If there was a physical possibility of a positive-sum move—acquiring greater output with available resources—why were the economic policies and institutional arrangements not discovered and implemented, if only to meet the needs of war? Why were not the shipyards of Bilbao, the iron and steel industry of the Basque country, and the textile plants of Seville and Catalonia put to work more effectively? The failure of guild and industrial organizations to mobilize labor, to delineate rules to make and enforce contracts, to fashion modern corporations, and to develop an adequate money and credit system inhibited the integration of mining, shipyards, textiles, and other industries with their sources of labor and supplies.

Two examples, albeit from a later period: "The Ley de Sociedades por Acciones of 1848 (Joint Stock Company Law of 1848) . . . prohibited the creation, without government authorization, of joint-stock companies. [Only in 1856] new legislation facilitated the consolidation of capital and the creation of joint-stock companies."[16] Also, "two of the most striking aspects of the relative backwardness of Catalan industry [at the turn of the twentieth century] were the almost complete absence of joint-stock companies and the limited recourse to borrowing of industrial enterprises."[17]

Signs of industrial growth appeared early in the nineteenth century, which different historians evaluate differently. Harrison writes of cotton textiles as a "prime mover" in the mid-nineteenth century. He finds Catalonian industry strong at the beginning of the century but disappointing later, and railroads unprofitable because of industrial "backwardness."[18] But Baklanoff notes "impressive achievements" by 1900: "an iron and steel complex in the north, a textile industry in Catalonia, European leadership in the production of many metals, a small but expanding chemical industry, a flourishing wine trade, and an infrastructure that promoted the flow of goods, thus facilitating urban life."[19]

The most exhaustive studies of Spanish industry in the nineteenth century are those of Nadal and Carreras. Under the title, *The Failure (Fracaso) of the Industrial Revolution in Spain, 1814-1913*,[20] Nadal finds that from 1831 to 1874 Spain underwent an industrial revolution similar to, and possibly stronger than, that of contemporary northern Europe, stimulated primarily by disentailment, which concentrated wealth in a few capitalists at the expense of peasant farmers.[21] But it did not last, Nadal asserts, because the ownership and profits were too concentrated; no mass market accompanied it; and industrial demand was not enough to stimulate increases in agricultural productivity or urban employment. He concludes that "the transformations related to industrialization in Spain do not reach the significance and depth that they reach in other places."[22]

Carreras's data support Nadal's conclusions. For the century 1831-1935, Spanish industrial output grew by an average of 2.85 percent per year. With population growth averaging 0.67 percent, the per capita average annual increase was 2.17 percent. But the growth was concentrated in the period 1831-60, when it averaged 4.7 percent per year, with wide fluctuations. In those years, Spain compared favorably with France and Britain. In the rest of the century, however, Spain lost relatively to eight other European countries.[23]

Industrial growth continued during the twentieth century, especially under the Primo de Rivera dictatorship in the 1920s,[24] but it decreased with the depression of the 1930s and made little headway in the first two decades of the Franco dictatorship, beginning in 1939. Authors agree that this slowness was caused both by the autarkic policies of the Spanish government and the fact that industrial Europe and the United States isolated Spain to show displeasure with the Franco government.

Early in the Franco regime, industry was in some ways as centrally controlled as under Philip II. The policies of the National Institute of Industry "often seemed to reflect little more than the private whims of its directors."[25] Beginning with 1959, however, the Franco government was better received by and was itself more receptive to the rest of the world. So too in 1963, the Portuguese government under Antonio Salazar adopted a more open position. The Spanish dictatorship ended with Franco's death in 1975, and a democratic government ensued. The Salazar/Caetano regime was overthrown by a military coup in 1974, and a democratic government liquidated Portugal's remaining overseas empire.

From 1960 to 1990 Spanish gross domestic product (GDP) grew at an average of 4.58 percent per year in 1985 prices, while the Portuguese equivalent grew by 4.53 percent per year.[26] These are substantial percentages. Does this abrupt installation of democracy-cum-economic growth, without prior negotiation and inter-group compromise, negate the need for power diffusion?

Reflected Economic Development

In no way does the Iberian experience negate the force of the power-diffusion process as found in northwestern Europe and Japan. The economy turned sour in the 1990s. So which was temporary: the spurt of 1960-90 or the turndown of the 1990s?

The fundamental social structure has not changed. An attempted military coup in 1981, although it failed, shows that Spain is not a true democracy, economic or political, and the requisite balance of power is not yet in place. Economic growth began to taper off in 1991,[27] and the economic record from 1990 to 1994 (using the latest available information at the time of writing) is not good: "Gone are the vibrant growth and heavy investment that turned [Spain's] economy into one of Europe's most dynamic in the mid-1980s. . . . For now, all that remains is painful recession, a stubborn 21 percent unemployment rate—Western Europe's highest—and a bloated public sector."[28] Heavy government spending on social programs—far more than richer European countries can supply—plus a requirement that businesses give lifetime employment contracts, as well as charges of corruption, all hint at the lack of accountability charcteristic of less developed zones.[28]

Let us speculate first on reasons for the phenomenal growth during the preceding three decades and then on the reasons for the 1990 downturn.

Spain and Portugal have much in common with northwestern Europe. They are part of the Judeo-Christian tradition, as well as the Islamic. We have seen how the cortes (parliaments), law, and money and banking of the twelfth and thirteenth centuries were similar to institutions farther north. The Catholic religion, monasteries as repositories of learning, and recognition of the pope were all common points. Associations with the Habsburgs and Spanish domination of the Netherlands meant that Iberia was European. Trade skirmishes of the Portuguese with England, Netherlands, and France in Asia, and the wars of Charles I and Philip II brought both countries into contact with the north. Spaniards could hardly help seeing how commercial systems functioned in the Netherlands and France. Autarkic though they were, economic policies of Olivares in Spain were often similar to those of his arch-rival Richelieu in France. Governments in Spain continued this tradition.[29] For centuries Portugal was a trading partner of England, and English pirates preyed on Spanish ships.

Dynastic marriages and attempts at them, such as the ill-fated trip to Spain of England's future Charles I, must have provided a cross-fertilization of ideas. The Bourbon family of France started the dynasty that presides over Spain today, and the Napoleonic occupation must have further let Spaniards and French know how each other lived. Although Iberia is not usually associated with the Enlightenment, and although the Index inhibited, nevertheless writings from northern Europe infiltrated, such as treatises of the physiocrats and other reformers.[30]

Contacts accelerated in the nineteenth century. The Spanish industrial revolution paralleled that of northern Europeans (except England) in the mid-nineteenth century. Only later did it fail. Land reforms of that century mirrored those in northern Europe. "The law of May 1855, with a few exceptions, provided for the sale of all lands held in mortmain, including the common lands of the municipalities."[31] As in eastern Europe, however, these reforms did not lead to equitable land distributions or modern farming.

Economic liberalism, spreading in northwestern Europe, was copied in nineteenth-century Iberia. Foreign investment was welcomed into Spain from 1850 to 1913.[32] The Restoration governments (after 1874) tended at first toward free trade, with a Franco-Spanish commercial treaty in 1882.[33] Even the increase in tariffs by Conservative Spanish governments in 1891 and 1906 may have been influenced by German policies of that time. Three French credit companies were formed in Spain in the nineteenth century.[34] Technological improvements flowed freely across the Pyrenees. A Barcelona mill brought in the Watt steam engine,[35] and the Bessemer process for the conversion of non-phosphoric ore into iron was introduced into Vizcaya in 1856.[36] By 1882, the Siemens process had also been adopted in Vizcaya, and an Anglo-Basque shipbuilding consortium, Astilleros del Nervión, operated in 1888.[37]

Radical and socialist ideas also came from the north. "The growth of peasant self-consciousness in southern Spain was the consequence of the spread of anarchist ideas. These were imported into the Peninsula in 1868 by Bakunin's envoy."[38] Labor organizations reflected those elsewhere in Europe.

Interest groups, fundaments of a pluralist society, increased slowly in the eighteenth and nineteenth centuries. Most were similar to counterparts in northwestern Europe.[39] In the mid-1760s the nobility and church helped form agricultural societies. By studying publications of physiocrats and others, they brought agricultural improvements from northern Europe. "The Council of Castile received a number of petitions from towns and villages . . . who wished to set up their own Economic Societies."[40] (Note, however: They had to petition to do so).

In the nineteenth century, chambers of commerce and employers' associations, such as the Factories Commission, an agency of mill owners, and the Lliga de Defensa Industrial y Mercantil,[41] were formed in Catalonia. These groups proliferated in the twentieth century, to include the Portuguese Industrial Association, the Commercial Association of Lisbon,[42] the Unión Ibero Americana in Bilbao, Lliga Regionalista of Catalonia, Fomento de Trabajo Nacional,[43] Liga Marítima Español, Hullera Nacional, Central Siderúrgica de Ventas, Asociación Patronal de Mineros Asturianos, and many more. "With Primo de Rivera's dictatorship, the proliferation of these interest groups reached an apex."[44] The formation of political parties during the republics has increased the pluralism.

But pluralism has been limited, in that the interest groups represented mainly business, whose ownership continues to be concentrated in the elite families. Labor unions were repressed during most of this century. In 1904, peasant associations appeared in Old Castile, amid a wave of strikes,[45] but for the most part they have been ineffective, and the agrarian problem in the south remains.

Let us define *reflected economic development* as the *gradual spread of the institutions of economic growth into neighboring areas of related culture*. The Spaniards saw how successfully these institutions functioned farther north, and they copied them. Even during the Franco regime, Spain came to "reflect" northern Europe. The French system of indicative planning was copied, "down to the designation of the smallest bureau."[46] From 1957 on, tourism was promoted as a principal element of economic growth.

With all this cultural affinity and history, it is not surprising that by 1959 "an important segment of the Spanish business community favored some kind of association between their country and the European Economic Community."[47] Spain and Portugal both joined the EEC (now the European Union) in 1986.

But how have the *institutions* adapted? How can countries with the autocratic, hierarchical background of Spain and Portugal, with a persistent great divide between peasants on the one hand and business/government on the other, with a tradition for suppressing grass-roots, liberal institutions, with few vertical alliances and little pluralism or leverage within its history, suddenly blossom into modern European countries with high rates of economic growth?

It is not yet certain that they can. If the Iberian economies succeed, the explanation is surely that all categories of Spaniards and Portuguese have become over the centuries sufficiently familiar with northern European institutions to know how they function and to learn to put their trust in each other through these institutions. If they fail, however—and the news as of publication of this book (1994) is not optimistic—the reason must be that power diffusion and accountability have not advanced far enough. While we can identify the factors behind success or failure, we have no way to weight them, to predict which will be the outcome.

How far, geographically, will institutions be reflected? While those from northern Europe may have drifted into Iberia, they have not crossed the straits of Gibraltar. Is this because of cultural differences with Africa? Insufficient communication? Not enough trust? European institutions not wanted in Africa? Belief that economic development can be accomplished in other ways? Or is Africa excluded by an ethnocentric Europe? All of these, or a mixture, are possible. Power on the other side of the Mediterranean has remained concentrated; the state continues to interfere massively in economic endeavor; vertical alliances and leverage for lower classes are scant, and economic growth is limited. That slight waterway is a formidable dividing line.

Advances in Iberia before 1990 bring hope that distance-reducing technology may some day spread economic development by reflection. If so, the bitter experiments and wars of northwestern Europe and Japan may not be the price for the rest of the world. But the Iberian experience is recent, and most recently it has seemed tenuous. The turndown of the 1990s has revealed the familiar characteristics of underdevelopment: corruption, bloated budgets, lack of accountability, and high, stubborn unemployment. In a phenomenon that spans centuries, one must be wary of the events of one or a few decades, pre- or post-1990.

Notes

1. Marques 1972:168.
2. For example, Payne 1973:276, 278, and 293.
3. Harrison 1978:31.
4. Payne 1973:378-79.
5. Bairoch 1973:460, 472.
6. Tortella 1987:50.
7. Harrison 1978:157.
8. Harrison 1978:161.
9. Baklanoff 1978:58.
10. Cipolla 1980:250.
11. Cipolla 1980:251.
12. Lynch 1981:2:166.
13. Lynch 1981:2:166.

14. Payne 1973:382.
15. Harrison 1978:15.
16. Aceña 1987:109-110.
17. Harrison 1978:71.
18. Harrison 1978:9, 16, 63.
19. Baklanoff 1978:7.
20. Nadal 1975.
21. Nadal 1987:63.
22. Nadal 1987:63.
23. Carreras 1987:75-86.
24. Carreras 1987:86; Harrison 1978:141.
25. Harrison 1978:162.
26. Calculated from International Monetary Fund, *International Financial Statistics,* Yearbook, 1990, pp. 596-97 and 652-53, and March 1992, pp. 442 and 486.
27. International Monetary Fund, *International Financial Statistics,* Yearbook, 1992, p. 643, and May, 1993, p. 484.
28. Gumbel, Peter, and Vitzhum, Carla, "Spain's Economic Boom Turns into Bust," *Wall Street Journal,* 6/4/93. Also, Valente, Judith, and Vitzhum, Carlta, "With Boom Gone Bust, Spain's Social Agenda Still Haunts Society," *Wall Street Journal,* 6/13/94.
29. Harrison 1978:14.
30. Harrison 1978:11.
31. Harrison 1978:28.
32. Baklanoff 1978:7.
33. Harrison 1978:69.
34. Harrison 1978:46.
35. Harrison 1978:59.
36. Harrison 1978:56-57.
37. Harrison 1978:74-75.
38. Harrison 1978:107.
39. Harrison 1978:11.
40. Harrison 1978:10-11.
41. Harrison 1978:32, 37, 83-84.
42. Baklanoff 1978:110
43. Harrison 1978:85, 96.
44. García Delgado 1987:152-53.
45. Harrison 1978:109.
46. Harrison 1978:155.
47. Baklanoff 1978:25.

Chapter 17
Mexico and Central America

Nowhere in Latin America is the power-diffusion process greatly in evidence. In Mexico, however, a case can be made for reflected development in the manner of Spain. Although the countries of Latin America are disparate, nevertheless certain common characteristics make it possible to generalize from a sample. I have selected Mexico, Guatemala, and Nicaragua to be covered in this chapter, and Peru, Brazil, Argentina, and Chile in chapter 18. Instead of alphabetical order, we will examine these countries from north to south.

Mexico

History

The settlement of Mexico and Peru in the sixteenth century continued the tradition of Christian Reconquest in Spain, with Indians replacing Moors as dependents of the conquerors. Landholding was the focus of master-worker relations. Both others and I have written about this earlier,[1] so my summary here will be brief.

Upon arrival in Mexico, the Spaniards discovered an Aztec feudal system similar to their own, with an emperor (Montezuma, or Moctezuma), priests, warriors, free workers, serfs, and slaves. They replaced the emperor with a Spanish viceroy. Finding the Indians unwilling to work for Spanish money,[2] the Spaniards conscripted them for mines and farms through tribute labor, debt servitude, and "protection" by the church. Rebellions were virtually always suppressed, leaving an immense chasm between conquerors and conquered that still affects boundaries between the in-groups and out-groups found in Mexico today.

At no point did the lesser groups approach a degree of power that might have enabled them to negotiate with their "masters" as did the serfs and workers of northwestern Europe and Japan. They did not normally form independent unions that might have activated vertical alliances. Money, laws, and parliamentary "democracy" were handed down from on top. Today the Congress is mainly a rubber stamp for the Institutional Revolutionary Party (PRI), the home of the in-group, although the PRI is increasingly challenged by opposition groups. Marriages, inheritances, and immigration have blurred the distinction between Indians and Spaniards. Thus the border between in- and out-group is no longer clear, and some mobility is possible. Nevertheless, the dichotomy is real.

Despite the war of liberation from the Spaniards, the reforms of Benito Juarez, the dictatorship of Porfirio Díaz, and the Revolution of 1910-17, at no time did Mexico encounter a survival crisis that would have forced the in- and out-groups to cooperate, with some power or leverage for the latter.

During the period of oil prosperity (roughly 1972 until the "oil glut" of 1986-88) many enterprises were nationalized,[3] including the banks (1982) and all the corporations whose stock they owned. Public expenditures grew. Because of oil money, prospects for economic improvement, enhanced public services, and growth of infrastructure were widely predicted, but they fell short of expectations. Rather, new access to enterprises and their financing must have led to payoffs to well-placed officials of the in-group. Thus errors and omissions in the Mexican balance of payments show large debit balances in 1977 and 1978 and again from 1981 through 1985.[4] Surely these represent clandestine imports of goods and exports of capital, such as to buy land in the United States, by those who had illicitly acquired the funds. The arrogance of the government is also expressed in the following: "'We are going to break the power of the transportation middlemen because we have our own trucks, boats and even planes,' explained Mr. Ovalle, who is coordinator of Copalmar [a government agency operating in rural areas]."[5]

While many explain these events as "corruption" or "exploitation"— therefore illegitimate or illegal—more likely they continue the conquest tradition of unclear boundaries between "public" and "private." Mexicans of the in-group have looked upon their positions as private property, from which they may legitimately earn rent. So also did the landowner or government official in Iberia in the fifteenth and sixteenth centuries, as well as the conquerors in Mexico and Peru in the same era. Octavio Paz has described the "patrimonialist system," by which "the head of government—prince or viceroy, *caudillo* or president—directs the State and the nation . . . as though it were his own household."[6]

Foreign economists have naively fit into this system, bolstering the power of the already powerful. As late as 1982, statist policies were being touted from Cambridge, England:

> Strict controls on imports. Foreign exchange curbs. Big budget deficits. Nationalization of the banks. Vast foreign borrowings. They are all part of a radical economic experiment under way in Mexico, an experiment put into place by Mexicans but one that reflects the startling ideas of a group of economists here at Cambridge University.[7]

Further references to centralization and the concentration of power in Mexico are listed in appendix 17.1. References to the lack of accountability appear in appendix 17.2.

The Liberalization of the 1990s

This historic spiderweb of interlinked power, of private claims to public assets and positions, and of paternalism up and down a rigid hierarchy, is the
milieu of a remarkable economic experiment in the 1990s. If the leaders have
their way, the Mexican economy, polity, and social structure will suddenly do
a volte-face.

Although this turn was in principle planned by representatives of the
farming, labor, and business sectors, who agreed on two pacts—one for economic solidarity and one for stability and economic growth[8]—nevertheless
the whole arrangement was orchestrated from on top. Two earth-shaking moves
were declared: privatization of government enterprises and a free-trade treaty
with the United States and Canada. The nationalized banks have been returned to private ownership. Altogether some nine hundred government-owned
enterprises were privatized from 1986 to 1991,[9] although the largest and most
basic, such as steel, electricity, and petroleum remain in state hands. Foreign
investment, previously discouraged by restrictions, is suddenly welcome. Tariffs
were greatly reduced even before the treaty. Drastic cuts in expenditures significantly decreased both the government deficit and the rate of inflation.
Some writers have been citing Mexico as "a model of economic modernization [that] the United States would do well to emulate . . ."[10] The results have
been immediate and spectacular. Both gross domestic product and employment have increased. Although the slowness of Mexican reporting makes it
impossible to have up-to-date official data, private estimates put the growth
rate at about 4 percent a year.[11]

Is Mexico reflecting the institutions of development of the United
States as Iberia may have reflected those of northwestern Europe? Will the
free trade treaty be analogous to the entry of Spain and Portugal into what is
now the European Union? Or is the whole event a temporary aberration—
imitated organizations thrust into unchanging institutions—to be reversed when
a new administration comes into power? The case for the former is that Mexican businesspeople have long been associated with the United States and know
its institutions well. Through the *Partido de Acción Nacional* (PAN), they
have long been opposing the statist policies of the *Partido Revolucionario
Institucional* (PRI). Perhaps there has been a shift in political balance rather
than a radical cultural change.

The case for the latter is that in Mexico, as in Russia, the reforms did
not swell up from below. They are motivated by economic failure and the
need for foreign assistance to maintain the current government and bureaucracy in power. Liberalization—the price of this assistance—will be resisted
or reversed once the new financial assets have been guaranteed and debt reduction achieved. It is hard to believe that the centuries of chasm between in-

and out-groups and the millions of interconnected power relationships can suddenly be set aside in favor of an impersonal market economy.

In neither Russia nor Mexico has widespread consensus emerged that the new institutions are advantageous to diverse interest groups. Nor can weaker ones ally with more powerful for leverage. Businesspeople and farmers have little influence in making the policies. Rather, the two most recent Mexican presidents, Miguel de la Madrid and Carlos Salinas, and Donaldo Colosio, the PRI candidate who was assassinated in March 1994 and his replacement Ernesto Zedillo, were all educated in the United States and brought with them the liberal economics they learned there. De la Madrid and Salinas seized the presidency in questionable elections and used its power to impose reforms in the face of a weak Congress and poorly organized opposition. This procedure contrasts with Spain, where membership in the European Union is widely favored by middle groups.

The president of Mexico is not all-powerful. He depends on a party apparatus spread wide throughout the country, at local as well as national levels. The PRI has co-opted the important interest groups, such as heavy industry, manufacturers, *caciques* (local strongmen), and labor unions. Thousands of persons belong to this in-group, which has marginalized the army, the church, dissident workers, peasants, and consumers in general. It also has aborted independent groups such as splinter unions. With its frequent internal quarrels suppressed, a fabricated unity is maintained against the out-groups. Therefore, we do not know to what extent internal opposition to the reforms may exist. Those in favor of reform have prevailed, and others may have gone along because they did not want either to be expelled from or to upset the system.

One of the out-groups is the peasants, of whom the PRI boasts to be the nominal champion. In Mexico's agrarian reform of 1917 and thereafter, lands were confiscated from large owners (*hacendados*) and distributed to peasants, either as private properties or collectives (*ejidos*). However, as conditions for receiving land, the peasants acceded to government controls. These included co-optation of peasant leagues within the political structure, allocations of credits, forced delivery of merchandise, pricing restrictions, government participation in ejido management, and authorizations required before ejido lands might be transferred. Permissions, exemptions from requirements, and granting of credits depended on bribery or political obeisance. In these circumstances, many farmers saw agrarian reform "as a mere change of masters, and they preferred an individual and well-known patron to an abstract and all-powerful state as their landlord."[12]

In an earlier writing,[13] my co-author and I described a number of cases in which the government offered credit or other supplies on favorable terms to some ejidos and other growing areas while denying them to others.

The criteria were willingness to do the bidding of the government-controlled Ejido Bank, buying inputs and selling crops at government-set prices, and/or political support for the PRI. The government spent vast sums for irrigation to benefit "politically correct" farmers in the northwest, but benefit-cost studies showed that these amounts would have been more profitably directed to smaller farms in the central region and the Caribbean coast.[14]

> "They have to come to us first if they want land," says an official with the peasant confederation. "Even if they get land, they have to come to us to get water. If they get water, they still need credits and fertilizer. The party will never lose control of the countryside."[15]

The announcement at the end of 1991 of a proposed law to expand private farming was met with widespread consternation among collective farmers, just as their counterparts in the former Soviet Union are far from agreed on the end of collective farms there. When a Mexican government official told ejido farmers in Telpancingo that the government would soon allow them to rent or sell their land, the reply was: "Was the revolution worth nothing? What did all those people die for? There is nobody, not even the President of the Republic, who can take away our land!" [16]

This event underscored the paternalistic, top-down nature of the Mexican reforms, which "modernize" the economy against the will of large segments of the population. Unwittingly, Pedro Aspe, minister of finance, reflects the ingrained paternalism when he writes: "[T]he authorities must communicate with the various sectors and tell them what is being attempted, hear their comments, and outline for them the costs and benefits of the measures being taken."[17] The tenor of Aspe's remarks—indeed, his whole book—reveals a government that must determine and control the path by which economic liberalism is to be achieved, down to an expectation of the manner in which private enterprises, including banks, will organize and manage themselves, and that will teach these methods to "lesser" people who would not otherwise understand them. All this contrasts with both the power-diffusion process and reflected development, in which demands for land and other reforms are initiated and shaped by the parties directly concerned for them.

The impoverished underclass is deepseated and longlasting; it will not quickly be elevated by the North American Free Trade Agreement. The peasant rebellion in Chiapas in 1994 reveals both the deep schism in Mexican society and the paternalistic response of the government. Instead of learning what credit institutions, venture capital, and training the peasants might negotiate with a sympathetic government, "officials promised new food programs, farm credits and other aid to fight the crushing poverty of the region."[18]

Taking place as this book goes to press, the negotiations differ from the earlier European/Japanese models in three respects. First, in Europe and Japan peasants were usually represented by their own members, albeit the more prominent ones. Second, European and Japanese peasants usually negotiated for attainable changes directly related to their productive capacities and well-being, not for largesse by manorial lords or daimyo. Third, in Europe and Japan the peasants usually tried to minimize state intervention in their lives. In Chiapas, by contrast, the principal negotiator is a masked man known only as "Subcomandante Marcos," whose command of several languages and intellectual discourse distinguishes him from peasant culture. In addition to land repartition—an achievable goal—Marcos has demanded the resignation of the President of the Republic and all state governors, on the grounds of electoral fraud.[19] Correct though he may be in this judgment, nevertheless to waste negotiating strength on such millennial expressions hardly serves the peasants well. Finally, government promises for "speedy rural electrification; more housing; health clinics and schools,"[20] and other social benefits will, if kept at all, make the peasants more beholden to the state instead of releasing them from official pressures.

In contrast to agriculture, the privatization of industry in the 1990s appears to be popular and taking hold. The telephone company, however, sold to a consortium including foreigners, was permitted to retain a monopoly until 1996. At the time of writing, any prediction on industry is subjective: whether privatization and free markets will represent changing organizations that fail when they confront unyielding institutions, or will follow the Spanish model of reflecting institutions from the north. In the first scenario, privatized companies would receive monopoly guarantees or other favors as yet unreported. They would exhibit inefficiencies similar to the government enterprises that they replaced. The telephone monopoly would be extended, for example. However, the second scenario may occur instead, because the PRI is more vulnerable than ever before. Its weakness is reflected in the ousting of three state governors by opposition protests; the PRI was unable to protect them. Possibly the survival crisis is being approached, or the government is too weak to co-opt the entrepreneurial forces now being unleashed, like Beijing versus China's southern provinces. In that case, the privatized companies might be reorganized and increasingly run by capable managers.

In either event, the belief of many observers from more-developed zones that simple shifts in monetary, fiscal, tariff and foreign exchange policies or the adoption of a free-trade treaty with the United States and Canada will tilt the course of employment, production, and inflation is an ethnocentric illusion. Instead, such policies may further concentrate power in the government.[21]

While development by reflection is a real possibility, nevertheless it is more likely that the volte-face required for a liberalized Mexico to initiate durable economic development will prove too much of a historical jump. Mexico did not have a nineteenth century like that of Spain, and too much history remains on the other side. A free market in goods and services promotes economic development only when the powers of participating groups are reasonably well balanced, so that no newly empowered group may distort prices and production or command others to yield undue favors to it.[22] That day has not yet arrived in Mexico.

Guatemala

To consider the precariousness of Mexico's liberal conversion in the 1990s, one need only look at its neighbor, Guatemala. This country maintained a stable currency, at 1 quetzal to the dollar, for decades ending in 1970 with only slight devaluations to 1980, a liberal foreign exchange and investment policy, a declining percentage of government revenue from import taxes,[23] and a satisfactory rate of economic growth: 5.43 percent, or 2.47 percent per capita, annual average from 1960 to 1980.[24] Inflation (consumer price index) averaged only 0.82 percent per year from 1960 to 1970, though it increased to 9.97 percent for the next decade.[25] Government expenditures were addressed to infrastructure, education, and agricultural improvement, and not especially to nationalized industries as in Mexico. The government deficit averaged less than 1 percent of GDP during the decade of the 1960s. Beginning in 1980, however, the economy worsened. From 1980 to 1990 economic growth averaged only 0.91 percent per year, or a decline of 1.94 percent per year per capita. Prices rose by 11.14 percent per year average, and the quetzal declined by 13.47 percent per year.[26] The government deficit, as percentage of GDP, was rising in the 1970s, and its average in the eighties reached 2.5 percent.

What had happened? First, a growing population of landless farmers, mainly Indians, provided the political reason for guerrilla violence. Active since the 1960s, these guerrillas stepped up their campaigns in the countryside. Land ownership was highly skewed: in 1970, 75 percent of the land was owned by 2 percent of the farmers. Productivity was high on large estates, mainly for export crops: coffee, sugar, and cotton (earlier bananas), but low productivity characterized crops for domestic consumption,[27] and malnutrition plagued the poorer farmers. Second, violent and probably fraudulent elections and a coup d'état brought military presidents between 1978 and 1984. To "pacify" the countryside, the military drove villagers into compounds.[28] Hundreds of tortured and mutilated bodies began to appear on the roads, and Guatemala was severely criticized abroad for violating human rights.

In 1986, a civilian president was elected who was widely alleged to have milked the treasury, appointed cronies, and enriched himself.[29] "Where has all the foreign aid gone?" wrote a Guatemalan economist, president of Francisco Marroquín University. "Nobody seems to know. Statistics are seldom published. Those that are published are carefully drawn up so as to confuse both economists and the laymen."[30] In 1993, with the aid of the military, the president suspended the Congress, only to be deposed himself by that same military.

The Guatemalan experience illustrates an important principle: that decades of "solid" economic growth are not durable if they are not grounded in a pluralistic society with countervailing powers. The prediction is therefore reinforced, that liberalization-from-above, as in Russia or Mexico or elsewhere, may not last.

Guatemala is what may be called a *sectioned society*, or an extreme case of economic dualism. A sectioned society is one in which an in-group attains its own maximum welfare, producing and trading among its members and with foreigners, without any need to communicate with a large portion of the out-group. Enough unskilled labor is co-opted by the in-group to sweep the streets, haul the garbage, and perform other menial tasks, but no more than is essential. Aside from these, the in-group would do just as well or better economically if the out-group did not exist. It can even run a high level of economic growth all on its own, like a separate country. In this case, macrogrowth data for the country tell little about its true development.

Classical economic theory would say that such a society cannot reach a stable equilibrium (one that no force would alter) and remain sectioned. The neglected group would offer its labor cheaply. Because the marginal rate of substitution is high in many processes,[31] previously marginalized labor would be used instead of capital. Ultimately, the marginalized group would be absorbed into the modern economy. But this has not happened *for centuries* in Guatemala and in some other Latin American countries. Why not? Because power is an economic good, with a utility and a cost. Fear and mistrust of the out-group, and the prospect of losing power to them, are among the costs to the in-group. The marginal revenue to the in-group from doing business with the out-group may be less than the perceived marginal cost, including the risk of losing power. In that case, the in-group would maximize its welfare by ignoring the out-group completely, and no force would be initiated to alter this circumstance.

Of course, the boundary between in- and out-groups is never hermetically sealed. The former does employ members of the latter, and it is possible to cross. But mobility is difficult enough to validate the concept of the sectioned society.

The vicious equilibrium can be broken in only two ways. One is what happened in northwestern Europe and Japan: that the out-group—by increasing its capabilities, by forcing the in-group to bargain with it, and by forging vertical alliances with leverage—may negotiate changes in institutions favorable to it. The second is that the out-group may become so violent and "obnoxious" that the cost to the in-group of ignoring it is increased beyond endurance. The first way activates the power-diffusion process; the second way repeats the Chinese dynastic cycle.

In the 1990s, the threat to survival—which leads to negotiation and compromise—does not appear to have been reached in Guatemala. Whether the government or the guerrillas win, another power imbalance will ensue. Thus, another turn of the power cycle would appear to be the more likely event.

Nicaragua

In 1979, the Nicaraguan dictator Anastasio Somoza was overthrown by revolutionaries calling themselves Sandinista. The Sandinistas remained in power until voted out of office in 1990. Much of the world looked upon these governments as diametrically opposite, but they are similar in critical respects. These similarities, which derive from Spanish authoritarianism, are mostly antithetical to durable economic development.

The Land System

Land, the primordial asset of any agrarian society, has been insecurely held by Nicaraguans and always subject to expropriation by authorities. Under both the Spanish conquest and nineteenth-century independence, land was divided into large estates producing for export, which were appropriated by the Spanish-descended elite, while small, low-productive farms were left for indigenous and poorer people. The confiscations happened in much the same way as in Spain during the Reconquest and in Mexico thereafter.[32]

> In 1934, the Somoza family owned no land. By becoming president in 1937, General Somoza established his family as the ruling dynasty. By 1946, that family held almost a monopoly on coffee and beef exports and on domestic milk production. [By the end of the Somoza period in 1979, virtually all the land in large estates was held by Somoza or his sympathizers.][33]

While the Sandinistas confiscated land of the Somozas and their friends, they were just as authoritarian as were their predecessors. Confiscated farms were turned into "cooperatives." I use quotations because these were mandated by the government, not formed by tenant initiative. Small-scale farmers, whose land was not confiscated, were "encouraged" to join "cooperatives"[34] by offerings of cheap credit, fertilizers, and other inputs, which would otherwise be available only at prohibitive prices if at all. Some large-scale export plantations remained private, but they had to sell their product to the government at controlled prices. By these methods, virtually all land came under the control of the Sandinista government, just as it had been under the Somozas.

While the peasants were permitted free choice over some crops, other crops were forcibly procured by official purchasing agencies at low prices specified by the government. In particular, all export crops were delivered to these agencies. By collecting crops from its members and turning them over to the state, the "cooperative" became like a state purchasing bureau rather than a representative of member interests. It squeezed the peasants by forcing them to sell their crops at less-than-market prices while buying their inputs, such as seed and fertilizer, from government agencies at high prices.

Like the Guatemalan government, the Sandinistas forced some peasants off their traditional lands and penned them up in compounds. The Miskito Indians had farmed on family plots, although families helped each other at harvest. The Sandinistas tried to abolish this system in favor of their own "cooperatives." The intervention was violent, and about ten thousand Indians were moved to fenced-in compounds "for fear of subversion."[35]

The government did distribute some land titles,[36] but these did not include freedom to plant and sell crops where and for what prices the owner is able, and to sell, buy, mortgage or bequeath the land. Since the economic value of private land is the capitalized value of its earnings, which on most "cooperatives" was little or negative, these titles had little or negative value.

In these ways the land system under the Sandinistas was similar to classical ownership as exemplified by the Somozas. Neither showed signs of the power-diffusion process.

Accountability

The Somozas ran Nicaragua like a personal fief, granting permissions to do business or to own land, and controlling the money and credit system at their will. Political enemies were exterminated; for example Sandino himself. The Somozas were accountable to no one.

Nevertheless, they maintained a relatively stable and growing economy. The currency (córdoba) held a constant value throughout the 1960s and was only slightly depreciated during the 1970s. Inflation was less well controlled: consumer price increases averaged 10 percent per year during the

1960s and 16 percent during the 1970s as civil war intensified. The government accounts were approximately balanced throughout the 1960s but became deficitary in the 1970s. International payments were approximately balanced most of the time. Gross domestic product in 1985 prices increased by an average of 3.6 percent per year, or 1.0 percent per capita, from 1960 to 1979.[37]

As in Guatemala, these data are deceptive. Nicaragua was also a sectioned society. The Indians on the Caribbean coast and poorer farmers scattered throughout the country were marginalized. The Overseas Development Council gave Nicaragua a Physical Quality of Life Index (PQLI) of 66 out of a possible 100 rating points in 1980 (a composite index based on life expectancy, infant mortality, and literacy), ranking it eighth out of the ten Latin American countries measured.[38]

Probably stability was maintained because a stable economy benefited the elite who lived off exports. Economic growth was confined to a few, who perceived a possible loss of power if they dealt more efficiently with the marginalized groups. The affected liberalism and stability, therefore, were not the result of interest-group interaction of a power-diffusion process.

Nor was the Sandinista government any more accountable than was that of the Somozas. No group could counter or even question its decisions on land, credit, nationalization of businesses and banks, or emission of money. It controlled prices capriciously, one time holding them down and the next suddenly raising them. The luxury homes confiscated from the Somoza family and cronies were assigned to Sandinista officials, who treated them like private property, refusing to give them up when voted out of office. They also kept vehicles and other government property.[39] Government accounts were carelessly maintained.[40] Just as Somoza considered his National Guard his "private property," so also did the Sandinistas continue to control the "national" army even after they had left office. Mass graves of their political foes were discovered after the Sandinistas were no longer in power.[41]

At first, the Sandinista economy showed some recovery from the civil war. GDP rose by 3.33 percent average per year, 1979-84, while declining by 0.36 percent per capita per year. Then it dropped precipitously, by 3.94 percent per year, 1984-88, or 7.30 percent per capita per year.[42] In an earlier volume, my co-author and I showed data from several studies of the decline in output of specific crops.[43] Per capita output has fallen by one fourth since 1980, while average living standards have been cut by more than 60 percent, according to a recent study compiled by foreign economists and underwritten by Sweden.[44]

Proponents and opponents of the Sandinista government have different explanations for the economic disaster. The former attribute it to the contra war, the latter to the economic policies of the government: nationalization of industries and banks, price controls, management of agriculture from the capital city, and inflationary creation of currency. Both explanations are consistent with a confrontational society, whose basic structure and economic policies are decided by power and war rather than by negotiation and compromise. They also reflect an authoritarian government that arrogates all major economic decisions to itself.

Although it had the power to create an egalitarian society, for example by redistributing land in small-farm private ownership, the Sandinista government chose not to do so. Instead, it believed that structure and policies fabricated by its own officials would be superior to those determined by free markets in either institutions or goods and services. Upon departing from office, both the Somocistas and the Sandinistas left the national treasury empty.[45]

Lack of Pluralism

During neither period could Nicaragua be termed a pluralist society. Under the Somozas, the boundary between government and employer organizations was not clear. Collectively, the state and employer organizations controlled exports and imports. The Investment Corporation channeled both national and foreign resources, while the Institute of Foreign Trade regulated trade balances and prices. Cotton and coffee commissions reported to the government. Important unions were government-controlled.[46]

Under the Sandinistas, major businesses and banks were nationalized; unions too were government-controlled. Illegal until 1984, strikes were permitted as part of a new flexibility preceding the elections of that year, but the first strike to be called was halted.[47] In 1988, a strike was declared illegal and strikers dismissed.[48]

Break-the-System

A *break-the-system* mentality is one in which some individuals or groups are willing to destroy a significant element of the legal system, monetary system, parliamentary democracy, or the like, to win a point of specific interest to them. This contrasts with a social structure created by vertical alliances, pluralism and leverage, in which each interest group has a vested interest in the portion that it negotiated: merchants in commercial law, legists in other law, bankers in the monetary system, and so on. When a society is also interlocking, with mutual accountability among groups, then no part of the system may be destroyed without an adverse impact on other parts. As a result, groups develop vested interests not only in their own parts but in the total system.

This does not infer that an interlocking society will not change, only that changes are negotiated piecemeal.

Where a culture forebears from break-the-system, groups allow themselves to lose particular conflicts rather than win them in anti-systemic ways. In chapter 6, we saw how the law might take on a power of its own, because most groups (not all) would prefer to lose a case, or would be required to, rather than destroy the law. But when a group—say, government or military—bends or destroys the law to win a particular point, then it does not have a vested interest in that system of law.[49] If other groups allow it to do so, either through weakness or lack of interest, the society is not interlocking, at least with respect to the law.

Break-the-system also applies when institutional behavior is different from organizational expectations. Under the constitution of 1974, enacted by the Somoza government, the president could not be re-elected, and legislative authority belonged to a bicameral congress. In practice, however, any "independent" president was a figurehead reporting to the Somoza clan, and the legislature was a rubber stamp. (The same was so during the Trujillo regime in the Dominican Republic).

The Sandinistas carried on the system of bending the law to suit their authority. They sometimes forbade rivals to participate in political campaigns,[50] and they supported mobs that broke up demonstrations by rival candidates. "If you are going to vote for the mobs, you are going to vote for the people" (President Ortega).[51]

When Somoza was overthrown, the entire system changed abruptly. When the Sandinistas left office, the nation also became convulsed over its basic structures more than over its policies.

In summary, this section makes three propositions on the continuity of historical tradition in Nicaragua from the colonial period to both Somoza and Sandinista times:

• Land, always subject to confiscation, continued to be so under both Somocista and Sandinista governments.

• Power over economic matters has always been concentrated in the government, and disputes have tended to be met by confrontation, or "stonewalling," more than by negotiations. Persons in power have not been accountable for their actions, a condition begun in the colonial period and continued under both Somocista and Sandinista governments.

• Significant elements of the political system are so lightly valued that they are willingly sacrificed in order to win individual points. This characteristic, break-the-system, has been common to all Nicaraguan governments, including Somocista and Sandinista.

Further references to land, accountability, and break-the-system in Nicaragua are listed in appendix 17.3.

Notes

1. Powelson 1988:chapter 18.
2. Chevalier 1963:67.
3. Junco, Alejandro, "Mexico's Private Sector Reels Under Government Control," *Wall Street Journal*, 6/29/84.
4. International Monetary Fund, *International Financial Statistics*, 1990 Yearbook: 514-5. The same figures may be found in other editions.
5. Riding, Alan, "Mexico, Flush with Oil, Remembers its Rural Poor," *New York Times*, 9/21/80.
6. Paz 1985:167.
7. Rattner, Steve, "Mexico's Cambridge Connection," *New York Times*, 10/24/82.
8. Aspe 1993:22.
9. Moffett, Matt, "Two Mexican Airlines Go Separate Ways After Their Sale by State in Privatization," *Wall Street Journal*, 11/22/91.
10. Shelton-Colby, Sally, "What We Could Learn from Mexico," *Washington Post Weekly*, 11/26-12/2/90.
11. Moffett Matt, "A 1980-Style Boom is Just Now Reaching an Awakening Mexico," *Wall Street Journal*, 12/18/91.
12. Meyer 1984:447.
13. Powelson and Stock 1990:chapter 3.
14. Reynolds 1970:145.
15. Frazier, Steve, "Mexican Farmers Get Grants of Small Plots, but Output is Meager," *Wall Street Journal*, 6/14/84.
16. Golden, Tim, "The Dream of Land Dies Hard in Mexico," *New York Times,* 11/27/91.
17. Aspe 1993:59.
18. Golden, Tim, "Mexican Rebels are Retreating; Issues are Not," *New York Times*, 1/5/94.
19. "Entra el diálogo en fase crítica, *"El Diario de Coahuila*, 2/27/94. Other newspapers would carry the same story, but I happened to be in Coahuila at the time.
20. "Score One for the Indians," *Time*, 3/14/94.
21. Pazos, Luis, "Mexico's Worsening Binge," *New York Times*, 7/3/85.
22. This should not be taken as opposition to a free trade treaty, which I strongly favor. Even if little is gained by it economically, nevertheless the opening of possibilities for new interest groups may spur the power-diffusion process.
23. Inter-American Development Bank, *Economic and Social Progress Report in Latin America*, various annual issues; for example, 1970:230.
24. Increase in gross domestic product.
25. Economic growth and price index changes were calculated from International Monetary Fund, *International Financial Statistics*, Yearbook 1990:386-87 and March 1992:260-61.
26. Same source as preceding footnote.
27. Inter-American Development Bank, *Socio-Economic Progress in Latin America*, 1970:227.
28. Chavez, Lydia, "Guatemala Tries to Win Over 5,000 Indian Refugees," *New York Times*, 11/20/83.
29. Manning, Michael, "The New Game in Guatemala," *The New York Review*, 10/25/90.
30. Monterroso, Fernando, "Foreign Aid Inhibits Market Ideas in Guatemala," *Wall Street Journal*, 11/03/89.

31. Loehr and Powelson 1981:174-7. In this work we assembled a large number of studies (done by others) of technologies that demonstrated the high likelihood of substitutability of capital and labor.
32. Powelson 1988:chapter 18.
33. Quoted from Powelson and Stock 1990:323. Data from Deere and Marchetti 1981:46.
34. Kinzer, Stephen, "Sandinistas Make Ceremony of Freeing Former Rebels," *New York Times*. 9/26/83.
35. Reuters, in *New York Times*, 6/8/84.
36. Simons, Marlise, "Nicaragua Hastens Land Redistribution as Pressures Mount," *New York Times*, 7/19/83.
37. All data in this paragraph are taken from, or calculated from, International Monetary Fund, *International Financial Statistics*, Yearbook 1990:
   542-43.
38. Overseas Development Council, *U.S. Foreign Policy and the Third World, Agenda 1982*:162.
39. Asman, David, "Sandinistas Clean Out Before They Clear Out," *Wall Street Journal*, 3/16/90; Branigin, William, "An 11-Year House Party Ends for the Sandinistas," *Washington Post Weekly*, 4/23-29/90.
40. Kinzer, Stephen, "For Nicaragua, Soviet Frugality Starts to Pinch," *New York Times*, 8/20/87.
41. Uhlig, Mark A., "Sandinistas Accused as Burial Sites are Unearthed," *New York Times*, 8/5/90; Shea, Nina H., "Uncovering the Awful Truth of Nicaragua's Killing Fields," *Wall Street Journal*, 8/24/90. These reports were confirmed by America's Watch, a human rights organization, in a letter by Aryeh Neier, Executive Director, in *Wall Street Journal*, 9/14/90.
42. Calculated from International Monetary Fund, *International Financial Statistics*, Yearbook 1990:544-45.
43. Powelson and Stock 1990: 344-51.
44. Passell, Peter, "For Sandinistas, the Newest Enemy is Hard Times," *New York Times*, 7/6/89.
45. Uhlig, Mark A., "Sandinistas are Blamed for Financial Shambles," *New York Times*, 5/1/90.
46. EBMa 1974:13:62.
47. Kinzer, Stephen, "First Nicaraguan Strike since the 1979 Revolution is Halted, at Least Temporarily," *New York Times*, 8/27/84.
48. Kinzer, Stephen, "Leftists Defy Sandinistas as Labor Strife Hits Peak," *New York Times*, 4/18/88.
49. An exception for civil disobedience, which is part of the Western tradition, was discussed in chapter 6.
50. Kinzer, Stephen, "Sandinistas Move to Outlaw Rivals," *New York Times*, 8/23/84.
51. Kinzer, Stephen, "Sandinista is Favored but Runs Hard," *New York Times*, 10/30/84.

Chapter 18
South America

We continue our examination of Latin America with a sampling of countries in South America, moving roughly from north to south, to cover Peru, Bolivia, Argentina, and Chile.

Peru

Because the culture gap between elites and lower classes in Peru has been so vast, the power-diffusion process has never worked. Instead, fear and mistrust have minimized the possibilities for vertical alliances, pluralism, and leverage.

History

From the time of the Spanish conquest in 1531-33, Peru has been a dual society. The Spanish invaders and their viceroys and hidalgos (minor nobles) took lands from the Inca, converting the people into serfs and the lands into haciendas. (The Inca had earlier done the same to other Indian peoples.) I have described the evolution of the land-tenure system in an earlier work.[1] As serfs bound by indebtedness or other sanction, the Indians could not participate in the market economy. Mostly they did not use money other than chits at the hacienda store, nor did they have access to credit, legal, or democratic institutions. To go into business for themselves was unthinkable. Many did not even know they were Peruvians. Substantial changes in these conditions were evident only after the 1960s.

Some intriguing earlier potential for Indians to make vertical alliances with leverage occurred, but they were not acted upon. Randall writes of a "crown policy [in the sixteenth century] designed to limit the income available to individual colonists. Such a policy was necessary to prevent the development of an independent nobility, which might compete with the Spanish monarchy for control of Peru." She also writes that "in 1565 an attempt was made to limit the abuses of the *encomenderos* [noble Spaniards to whom Indians had been "entrusted"] by appointing government officials—*corregidores de Indios*—in the provinces where encomenderos had wide powers."[2] Could not the Indians have sided with either the crown or the nobility or corregidores to lever their power in these struggles? The question is almost ludicrous, even though this is what peasants in northwestern Europe and Japan did. In Peru for the Indians, as in Spain for the Moriscos, the cultural chasm was so great that communication with upper classes on fundamentals was not feasible. Hence the leverage available in northwestern Europe and Japan was closed off in Peru, as it had been also in Spain.

Until the 1960s, Peru had experienced chronic growth based on nine-teenth-century liberalism.[3] In the 1890s "the economic performance of Peru was impressive."[4] Spanish financial, legal, and parliamentary institutions had been transplanted for the use of the elite. Exports—primarily copper and other minerals, guano, sugar, and cotton—were the engine. Labor from the marginalized sector was cheap, and foodstuffs were extracted or imported sufficiently to feed the formal economy. Technically, there was room for posi-tive-sum moves by which agricultural productivity might have been increased, and the hacendados might have shared the increment with tenants. But to do so would have been risky, even unthinkable, because it might have given the tenants enough power to upset the imbalance. Hence there was neither agri-cultural revolution nor "innovating landlords." Income distribution was highly skewed.[5]

A change—hardly a turnabout—began after World War II. Perhaps because of a worldwide move toward independence of less-developed coun-tries, increasing manifestation of discontent among lower classes everywhere, and growing nationalism, Indians escalated the demand to restore their lands. Land invasions multiplied. Marxist students rioted in favor of radical changes. Guerrilla actions broke out in the sierra. The coup of 1968, in which a "new" military drawn largely from the underclasses announced great impending changes in favor of Indians and other poor, intensified the commotion.

This military government, and civilian governments thereafter, be-came new elites in an equally dual society. Although glorifying the Indians and acting in the name of the poor, they allowed neither of them any more share in decision-making than had their predecessors. Labor unions were co-ordinated by the government's own Confederation of Workers of the Peruvian Revolution. If they failed to conform or struck illegally, they were abolished, as happened to the teachers' union in 1973.[6] Virtually all businesses were declared to be "social property," to be managed by the state or (in theory) by the workers.[7]

The land reform of 1968—which my co-author and I have described in an earlier work[8]—expropriated the large estates, but instead of dividing them into small farms in private ownership, the government organized large communal farms under different guises, called Agrarian Production Coopera-tives and Agricultural Societies of Social Interest. In principle, these organi-zations were to be run by their members, but the government decided to make all important decisions until the land had been paid for by the peasants—an impossible task reminiscent of Russian "emancipation" in 1861.

This "Peruvian experiment"—declared to be neither socialist nor capitalist—was coordinated by a transitional government agency, the *Sistema Nacional de Apoyo a la Movilización Social*, or SINAMOS (*sin amos* means "without masters"). Reminiscent of the marxist dictatorship of the proletariat, SINAMOS would provide political support until a "government of popular organizations" might be assembled. In fact, however, SINAMOS was highly criticized by groups across the political spectrum, from extreme left to extreme right. In a 1973 pamphlet, SINAMOS itself conceded that "few times in the recent history of Peru has an organization been more violently attacked by traditional groups of all distinctions."[9] The probable explanation is that these groups had played no part in creating SINAMOS and therefore had no vested interest in it.

The state controlled the peasants using ways common to many less-developed countries: through bank credit and through "a centralized agency to control all public enterprises in the food industry . . . The *Empresa Pública de Servicios Agropecuarios* . . . [was made] the sole legal food importer and exporter."[10] In 1977, the concept of social property—clearly unworkable—was abandoned, in preparation for a constitution of 1979 and an elected government in 1980.

Even thereafter, poor choices, failure to communicate adequately with workers or to entrust management functions to the out-group, inefficient state-run enterprises, and lack of government accountability, as well as guerrilla warfare by a formidable organization known as Shining Path (*Sendero Luminoso*) were all causes of Peru's economic collapse of the 1980s. Shining Path appears to be a small but vicious group of intellectuals that does not represent the urban poor or the peasants. Instead, it has tried to co-opt them by threats, "taxation," and violence or by murdering their leaders. Controlling vast parts of the country, it has forced peasants to produce cocaine for the foreign market, with which it finances its domestic operations. With the deterioration of legal exports—even sugar has had to be imported—the community experiments in coastal plantations failed. Toward the end of the 1980s these lands were parceled into private farms.

De Soto's Studies

Hernando de Soto has studied the Peruvian economy in two parts, the informal and the formal. It is a dual society, not a sectioned society in the sense of Guatemala and Nicaragua, since the two parts interact more closely. In scholarly investigations, de Soto and his students have mapped out the "informal economy, defined as all transactions not conforming to legal procedures."[11] In this shadow world he found that housing, production, trade, and transport were organized by persons excluded from legitimate institutions, who there-fore had to agree on their own rules. In earlier sections, these are referred to as the "out-group," primarily peasants. But they may also be urban traders and even industrialists.

Two findings from de Soto's studies support earlier propositions in this book. First, "enormous entrepreneurial energy [is found] in the popular classes." In 1984, according to the de Soto studies, 38.9 percent of the GDP was produced in the informal sector, where 61.2 percent of all labor time was worked.[12] Second, for "ordinary" people—those without political connections or enough funds for bribes—doing business legally is impossible in a country that has not undergone the power-diffusion process. Land, credit, and protec-tion of the law are not available to them. When de Soto asked his students to organize a small garment-producing company, they had to "spend 289 days on bureaucratic procedures to fulfill the eleven requirements." The total cost of permissions and bribes was "$1,231—thirty-two times the monthly living wage."[13]

The informal sector, de Soto's studies found, compiles its own laws and "courts" to enforce them, its own assemblies approximating parliamen-tary democracy, its own landholding systems (through land invasions),[14] its own informal credit mechanisms (often by handshake), its own procurement methods, and its own sales and other contracts. His findings on informal credit are consistent with those of Goodell[15] and Tun Wai,[16] who discovered that "moneylenders"—so much reviled in the formal literature—are a vital link in the deprived segments of less-developed zones. The informal sector operates in a free market for institutions because that is all it has.

De Soto's studies are seconded by Dietz and Moore,[17] who found that the urban poor in Lima formed associations for common enterprises among themselves and also negotiated with national authorities when specific ques-tions arose. But none of these authors, nor other sources available to me, tell of corporate groups created for an ongoing relationship with the authorities on such issues as land tenure, the ability to make economic decisions, or prop-erty rights.[18] Vertical negotiations are rare.

The Present Crisis

From 1980 until a few months before publication of this book, Peru's economy had been doing poorly. From 1960 to 1980, gross domestic product at 1985 prices had increased by an average of 4.58 percent per year, or 1.85 percent per capita per year. But from 1980 to 1990 it increased by only 0.45 percent per year, for a decline of 2.10 percent per capita per year. During those same ten years, consumer prices rose by 170 percent per year on average; in 1990 they increased seventy-five-fold. From 1989 to 1990, the government deficit soared from 5.2 million to 202.3 million new soles. The current account of the balance of payments was in deficit every year except three from 1971 to 1990, inclusive.[19]

Suddenly in 1992, President Alberto Fujimori, with the support of the military, disbanded Congress and government offices and began to rule by decree. Complaining that Congress could not agree on his or any proposed economic reforms, nor could the present government adequately confront the Shining Path, he "portrayed his drastic moves as the only way to save Peru's democracy."[20] He arrested the leader of the Shining Path, summarily tried and executed hundreds of suspected guerrillas (some of them probably innocent), obtained "voter approval of a new constitution that eases investment restrictions and curbs labor privileges [and] has set off an effervescence in the investment community."[21] Peru's economy has done a sudden turnabout: as of early 1994 it was the "fastest growing in the Americas." Opinion polls among urban groups showed that his moves were highly popular, as the middle- and upper-class people once again turned to the "savior on horseback" to confront groups with which they could not communicate.

Why did Peru, with chronic development and reasonable stability for decades, suddenly in the 1980s become destabilized? Will the surprising turnabout in 1993-94 last? Although the timing is not easily explained, the destabilization itself should not be surprising. In a dual society, with narrow participation in the formation of economic and political institutions, the equilibrium of tensions among plural groups, which elsewhere sustains free markets and economic development, does not arise. Peru and Guatemala, with their high economic growth for decades and then sharp reversals, should give pause to all who are encouraged by Mexico's top-down reforms of the 1990s and the sudden economic growth that is attached to them. Those who think President Fujimori can bring lasting change might also contemplate the immensity of history.

Prospects

Is Peru reaching the survival crisis, which might motivate wider participation by interest groups? Not many corporate bodies exist that are capable of negotiating with the government for change in underlying rules. The informal institutions found by de Soto and Dietz and Moore are democracy at the grassroots level, such as has been seen in Asian villages for centuries. But they are not the kinds of bodies that have historically precipitated a power-diffusion process. Additional references on state power and lack of government accountability in Peru are listed in appendix 18.1.

Brazil

History

Authoritarianism has been the mode in Brazil ever since the first Portuguese settlement. At first it was embodied in the feudal estates (captaincies) exerting control over "their" Indians.[22] Both for defense and because of failures in settling the captaincies, a central government was established by the Act of 1548. It "gave Brazil unity, a bureaucracy, a capital, a leader, continuity in government. . . . As in [Portuguese] India, however, all the governors belonged to the top aristocracy."[23] In the fifteenth century, the Portuguese king confiscated land from the nobility and church, then declared "himself the owner of all lands discovered overseas. Having won these goals, he instituted a royal monopoly of international trade."[24] This eclipse of nobility and church by the monarchy inhibited vertical alliances and leverage by lower classes just as it had also done in Portugal. The communication gulf between Portuguese settlers and Indians foreclosed them completely at that level.

Authoritarian government was manifest in many ways. "The official policy of the crown was always to centralize learning and force everyone to study in the mother country."[25] In the eighteenth century, "The Overseas Council (*Conselho Ultramarino*) attempted to regulate in detail the life of the colony, so that many small administrative details had to be confirmed by the Council in Lisbon."[26] In 1702 the construction of a new road to Minas Gerais was stopped by the crown, because taxation of the gold trade would be easier if there were fewer roads.[27]

"Portugal [in the eighteenth century] wanted to limit the Brazilian trade to what Portugal could provide. To maintain that trade, Brazilian manufacture was discouraged. In 1785, textile factories were prohibited in Brazil, and those already in existence were ordered to be closed."[28] Power concentration in Brazil was therefore an extension of that in Portugal.

The power-diffusion process has never been at work. The Indians did not form village associations to challenge their feudal lords in the captaincies of the sixteenth century, nor did they ally themselves with those lords or the crown, to gain advantage from conflicts between these two. The miners of Minas Gerais did not negotiate corporately with the crown over terms and taxes, nor did an independent labor movement arise to negotiate its own terms free of government support or intervention. Producers and merchants did not draft laws of trading and ownership for passage by the legislature, which would promote security of investment and stability of production. Bankers did not create an alternative currency when the government failed to provide a sound one.

Power diffusion might have been expected from immigrant workers in the nineteenth and twentieth centuries, because the central government depended on their support. Instead of forming their own bargaining groups, however, these poorer people looked to the government for their patronage. They favored the paternalistic *Estado Novo*, populist government of Getulio Vargas in the 1950s, which aped the Salazar regime in Portugal.[29]

All this while, the interior remained wide open, with bloody struggles for land between European settlers and indigenous peoples. This struggle continues, still bloodily, today. Historically, land abundance had made it unnecessary for contestants to form corporate groups to seek solutions to land problems. In the case of Indians versus European descendants, the cultural gulf has been too wide, just as it had been between Moriscos and Portuguese in Iberia. The lack of trust—and therefore the perceived risk—was too great. These propositions apply as much today as they did at any time in history. Additional references on state power and lack of accountability in Brazilian history are found in appendix 18.2.

The "Brazilian Miracle"

The first decade of the military government that took power in 1964 were heady years for the Brazilian economy. Real GDP grew by an average of 8.63 percent per year, or 6.41 percent per capita, from 1963 to 1975. Consumer price inflation was high also, at an annual average of 27 percent. These years were the heyday of Latin American theories—since discredited—that "structural inflation" was essential to economic growth.[30] With newly printed money the government would transfer resources to itself as prime investor.

The military entrusted governing functions, including economic, to high-level professionals popularly known as "the technocrats." Left largely on their own because the military did not understand either economics or bureaucratic governing, they became "accountable to no one."[31] For example, by their decision facilities were built in the early 1980s that would produce more electric power than the country would need for the next twenty years. Many other state enterprises were founded.[32] Mainly, the growth was fueled by borrowing from abroad. Brazilian foreign debt grew rapidly.

The Brazilian Miracle did not last. From 1975 to 1980 growth slowed, to 6.47 percent annual average, or 3.57 percent per capita, still a creditable rate. Then Brazil went into recession, with an average drop of 2.43 percent per year, or 4.54 percent per capita, for three years, while inflation raged at an average of 76.26 percent per year. Growth resumed for the four years until 1988, with an average increase of 5.92 percent, or 3.80 percent per capita, in real GDP. Inflation from 1989 to 1991 reached 165 percent per year. From

1987 to 1990 growth slowed to zero or negative, and negative per capita.[33] The military government ended in 1982, and thereafter ineffective civilian presidents, highly interventionist, presided over the deteriorating economy.

The Brazilian Miracle illustrates that command growth is possible for short periods, even decades. But governments that command it either make mistakes, or—as in the Brazilian case—finance it and manage it in ways that cannot be sustained.

The Present Crisis

In 1989, a new President of Brazil—Fernando Collor de Mello—instituted sweeping, radical reforms in the face of inflation and a deteriorating economy. These included a floating exchange rate, freezing of large savings accounts, substantial tax increases and extension of the tax base, forced purchase of shares in state companies, closing of two dozen government agencies, and phasing out of import controls. A "super-economics ministry" was established to monitor the changes.[34]

Economists were divided three ways on these reforms. To some, they were badly needed and overdue, to combat inflation, curb the excesses of irresponsible government, and create free markets. To others, they were capricious, inequitable, discouraging to investment, and economy-stopping. To still others, the reforms did not coordinate orthodox stabilization policies with complementary policies in product markets, labor markets, and financial markets (the idea was right; the choice of policies wrong).

I suggest still another perspective. That such sweeping changes were decided upon by one person reveals a noninterlocking society. Affected groups were "policy takers," not policy participants. It matters little what the policies were, since the conditions of their making were such that they could—and probably would—be reversed at any moment. The resulting capriciousness makes sound business planning impossible. Indeed, Collor was impeached and removed from office for corruption in 1992 and a new era of government intervention began, with no abatement in the charges of corruption.

Argentina

History

Based on the usual criteria of economics, an observer in 1890 would have been hard put to predict whether Argentina, Canada, or even the United States would be the most economically advanced country of the western hemisphere one hundred years later.[35] Argentine output was increasing; farms were prosperous; the standard of living was high; and immigrants from Europe came to seek a better life. Some called Argentina the Australia of the western hemisphere.[36]

But the power-diffusion process was not at work. The Argentine "problem" dates back to Iberian ways of dealing with conquered Moors. In Argentina, even more so than in Spain and Portugal the land was so vast that Indians could not be captured as serfs; they were exterminated instead. Over the nineteenth century, the lands were doled out to European settlers, often in reward for military services of conquest. The result was a small but powerful landowning oligarchy, which also monopolized the cattle and beef industry, but whose government was unstable because of struggles for dominance among the oligarchy, especially between Buenos Aires and the outer provinces. These rulers manipulated prices, tariffs, and production rules in their favor.[37] They were served by cowboys of mestizo or European origin (*gauchos*), whom they rewarded but who gained no political status. After about 1850, immigrants from the poorer levels of Europe, especially from Italy, engaged in tasks considered "beneath" this elite, such as manufacturing. By the 1880s "the governmental machinery of the entire nation revolved around the person of the president. The legislators were usually subservient to the governors to whom most of them owed their election. . . . The governors were in turn almost the personal agents of the president."[38]

Change set in toward the end of the nineteenth century, when the immigrants had grown sufficiently numerous to contest the landed aristocracy. Their main political party—the Radicals (*Unión Cívica Radical*, or UCR)—incorporated within itself the idea of *intransigence*: no alliance or compromise with other parties or other groups. Indeed, until 1971 that word was part of the official name of one branch of that party.

Argentina is a prime example of failed power diffusion. Intransigence was made into a political precept, a matter of pride for standing on one's principles. As far back as 1877, certain Republicans "opposed all pacts or agreements between parties"[39] even though President Avellaneda had warded off civil war by a temporary "Conciliation of Parties." Hipólito Irigoyen, the major figure of the Radicals from the 1890s until 1930, declared himself intransigent. "In 1897 he was willing to see the UCR torn in two and almost disappear; he would not relinquish his position of intransigence"[40] (an example of break-the-system). The Organic Charter of the UCR of Buenos Aires province included this injunction: "There shall be excluded all accords or transactions that might impede, at the present and in the future, the integral application of the principles that form the program of this party."[41]

Yet for four decades the Radicals refused to divulge their program in advance, only when they applied it. Rather, they spoke in generalities, declaring themselves the moral renovators of Argentine society. Their only specific platform was for universal suffrage and provincial and municipal autonomy. Leandro Alem, their first leader, gave the party "a messianic fervor; to him the basic mission of the UCR was the reformation of Argentine morality."[42] By the 1890s, "Irigoyen had become convinced that he—and only he—could rescue the Argentine nation."[43] This behavior exemplifies our theses of centralization, elitism, and paternalizing as inhibitors of durable economic development. The Radicals won the election of 1916 and remained in power until the government, falling apart under a senile Irigoyen in 1930, was removed by the military. The Radical program, once it had come to light, was reformist and interventionist but not radical: to nationalize the petroleum industry, to establish minimum wages, to introduce restrictions on hours of labor for women and children, to initiate some price controls, to call for pensions, and to pass an inheritance tax.

All these are found to some degree in the more-developed countries of Europe and North America. But in Argentina, the beneficiary groups have been more confrontational in defending their positions and more prone to violence, kidnapping, and governmental overthrow than have the analogous groups in the more-developed zones, even counting labor violence in the nineteenth century, such as the Homestead strike of 1892.

The landed aristocracy of the nineteenth century was uncommunicative and overbearing with respect to lower classes, especially immigrants. When other groups came to power, they were equally so with all who disagreed with them. The result has been violence, corruption, government overthrow, capriciousness, and intransigence. These are the principal causes of underdevelopment in a nation that mostly sees itself as European and cannot understand what has happened to it.

Three Historic Properties

The failure of durable economic development in Argentina stems from three historic properties:

  • Power for its own sake—not just for the economic advantage it brings—is demanded by competing sectors of the elite. Not trusting the political parties, many in the military believe that stability and peace depend on themselves as fallback. These leaders deem themselves defenders of the fundaments, not just purveyors of policy.
  • Regardless of statements affirming democracy, every group in power has both favored and sustained an interventionist state. This has been true under military and civilian governments, both conservative and radical, including Peronist. All sectors of society endorse this precept, and

all solutions or modus vivendi are designed accordingly. A politically or economically liberal course is beyond the horizon.

• Confrontation characterizes the political process. In a study of ruling groups, Imaz concluded that there is no longer an "elite" in Argentina, for those who govern include persons of all classes, from descendants of immigrant laborers to the traditional landowning aristocracy. But because of differing backgrounds, these groups do not trust each other, they communicate imperfectly, and they make impossible demands upon one another.[44] Under such circumstances, a minor incident may be exaggerated into a serious crime. For example, in 1983 the president of the Central Bank was indicted for treason because he had negotiated an agreement with the International Monetary Fund.[45]

The "dirty war" of the 1960s illustrates a tendency toward break-the-system. Both the Montoneros (revolutionary group) and military government abandoned legality to gain their antithetical ends. Radical revolutionaries kidnapped and murdered industrialists. The military responded by kidnapping, torturing, or murdering 9,000 persons suspected of subversion.[46] Often these were university students who had presumably done no more than express themselves, and whose parents were left wondering what had become of them.[47] Other references to confrontation and break-the-system in Argentina are found in appendix 18.3.

Yet all three historic properties must be qualified. Occasionally one hears proposals for decentralization and liberalization. Sometimes there are political compromises. After an unsuccessful military coup against him in 1987, President Raúl Alfonsín visited the rebel barracks to negotiate a peaceful settlement.[48] America's Watch interpreted the limited prosecutions of the military for "dirty war" crimes to be a compromise preserving the peace[49]—a sentiment disputed by many. Despite these exceptions, the balance lies with the confrontational ethic in Argentine political behavior. Government inefficiency, corruption, wage and price control, and improvident monetary and fiscal policies are the legacy of these historic properties.

While mainstream economists, foreign governments, and international agencies agree that these maladies are the basic problems, their error is threefold. First, they call inefficiency, corruption, and poor policies "structural" when a still more fundamental structure—the three historic properties—underlies them. Second, they call for their resolution by fiat or "structural adjustment," to be undertaken by the same authorities who gave rise to the problems in the first place. Third, by finding a "way out" of financial problems, outside agencies relieve the home government of the necessity to compromise. The International Monetary Fund becomes the scapegoat for unpopular policies not reached by internal agreement. But a scapegoat does not last forever, and when it is gone the problems it allowed to be evaded return in greater force.

The Failure of Reform

Reforms of all the abovementioned conditions are urged by foreign and international agencies and are made conditions for assistance. Yet decade after decade, promise after promise, little happens. It is not that the government has not tried to reform; it is that it *cannot* do so. The historic properties have left it interconnected with interest groups that stonewall more than dialogue, command more than compromise, and insist that their demands be met by central authority.[50]

When the government tried to divest nationalized enterprises in 1989—a program still under way at the time of this writing—potential purchasers demanded monopoly rights. Because a monopoly commands a selling price greater than that of a competitive enterprise, the government—sorely in need of funds—is tempted to accede. The result would be the same excessive prices charged privately instead of governmentally,[51] by companies whose privilege would depend on continued central authority.[52] Industrialists exploit every political means, including bribery, to continue their subsidies.

Pressures to end such subsidies and move toward a free market were widely heard during the economic decline of the 1980s.[53] Yet in 1991 the U.S. ambassador to Argentina complained to the press because he could not get the ear of the president—about delaying red tape and demands upon American companies for bribes in order to receive import licenses and other permissions.[54]

The authoritarian ethos is exemplified by an incident in 1984, when the Argentine government bypassed a mission of the International Monetary Fund to seek approval of the managing director for its austerity plan.[55] Apparently the government believed that IMF authority would rule, just as top government authority rules in Argentina, not grasping that the Fund's culture could not allow this bypass; for unlike in Argentina, the IMF management would not ordinarily undercut its own staff.

All this leads Mexican writer Octavio Paz to describe Argentina as "the great tragedy of Latin America" and Harvard economist Nick Eberstadt to call it "the most dramatic case of a country heading back from the First to the Third World."[56] More cases of state power and the failure of accountability are found in appendix 18.4.

Chile

Chile has challenged us in the 1990s with the question: Can a brutal, military dictatorship that brooks no opposition and tortures its opponents decree a lasting free-market economy, bypassing the power-diffusion process? General Augusto Pinochet, who took power by coup in 1973, introduced free-market policies and privatization of industry by executive decree. He did away with the many permissions similar to those that de Soto found to be strangling industry in Peru.[57] As a result, the country prospered during his presidency, 1973-90: real GDP grew at an average of 3.07 percent per year, or 1.36 percent per capita, compared with a sharp decline during the preceding administration of Salvador Allende. Employment and incomes increased, and consumer goods again appeared on the shelves.[58] Chile took the grape export market from Argentina, where it had been damaged by frequent policy shifts, overvalued currency, and taxation of agricultural exports.[59] One columnist saw similarities with the free-enterprise spirit of Australia and New Zealand.[60]

Because of popular pressure, Pinochet restored democracy in 1989. His successor, Christian Democrat Patricio Aylwin, pledged to maintain most of the economic policies, including "low tariffs, export-oriented growth, the private social-security system, private ownership of the recently-privatized companies, a balanced budget and an independent Central Bank."[61]

Some are now speculating that sixteen years of Pinochet prosperity were enough to institutionalize balanced budgets, privatization, a stable monetary system, and a liberal economy. Political opponents, it is argued, have now become convinced. Recalling that command liberalization has failed in the past—many times—I am less sanguine about Chile's prospects. In order to judge, let us examine whether elements of the power-diffusion process are present in Chile's history.

History

Chile was settled by Europeans, principally Spaniards, who wanted to farm rather than seek precious metals. The Chileans did not conquer the Araucanian Indians but learned to live with them. Chile did develop an aristocracy capable of seizing land and forming a dual society—landowner and laborer— based on ethnic origin, however.

Possibly because of land abundance in the nineteenth century, and possibly because of the language-culture communication gap, the elite were not forced into vertical alliances or negotiations with poorer classes on land tenure, wage systems, or other economic institutions. (The gap was diminished by intermarriage with Indians but never eliminated). These institutions, along with law, monetary systems, and parliamentary democracy, were handed down to the indigenous people by the European elites.

Throughout much of the nineteenth century, Chile was a prosperous, liberal European-style democracy, with growing industry and exports of fruits, and later nitrates (chronic growth, similar to Peru).[62] But as in Argentina, a rural-to-urban demographic shift in the 1890s brought new class conflicts. President José Manuel Balmaceda, an aristocrat-turned-defender-of-the-poor, exacted new business taxes, opposed foreign investment, and instituted government-led, inflationary economic development. He was overthrown in 1891 in a civil war led by the navy, which advocated the traditional free market.

From 1891 to the present day, the gap has widened between conservative businesspeople and landowners on the one hand and radical defenders of the poor on the other. These constituencies became the National and other parties of the right versus leftist parties such as the Movement of the Revolutionary Left. The Christian Democrats occupy an unstable center, from which they have more often sided with the left than the right. Despite political polarities, these disparate groups are similar in crucial respects.

First, they are confrontational, each with respect to the other and often among themselves. Balmaceda "lost the support of important groups and eventually his congressional majority through his vacillating and imperious behavior and their unwillingness to compromise."[63] Military intervention in 1924 limited President Arturo Alessandri's attempts at agrarian reform, after which a military president (Carlos Ibañez) dictated agrarian reform and modern labor laws in 1927. Allende's agrarian reforms of the 1970s were similar in one respect to those of the Roman tribune Tiberius Gracchus in the first century BCE. Each used unusual, albeit legal, methods to obtain his ends, which alienated potential supporters.[64]

Hirschman argues that the chronic inflation afflicting Chile from the 1890s up to his time of writing in 1963 was caused by the inability of groups to agree on a financial policy of benefit to all.[65] The splits within the left during the Allende period resembled Irigoyen's intransigence in Argentina. Seemingly minor differences exploded, as when the ruling coalition was rent in two because Allende and his agricultural minister could not agree on whether to expropriate smaller farms. Diehl suggested that Pinochet's government could last for so long because opponents could not agree on a replacement.[66]

Second, despite the rhetoric of the left, neither group has endowed the dispossessed with any real political power. Presidents Balmaceda, Aguirre Cerda (1938), Ríos (1972), and Allende were all members of the upper classes "assisting the poor" without allocating any important government posts or decision-making functions to them.

Third, each group has violated law. Balmaceda unconstitutionally extended existing laws when Congress refused to pass election laws in 1891.[67] Jacques Chonchól, the agricultural minister, illegally occupied small farms during the Allende period (1970-73). Pinochet set aside the law with his human-rights abuses. Retaining power over the military after ceding the administration to Patricio Aylwin, he protected his soldiers: "If anyone touches any of my men, the state of law is over."[68]

The Pinochet administration demonstrated, decisively, that the free market in goods and services is associated with economic growth. But this book is concerned with *durable* economic development, not momentary growth. With Chile's divisions, confrontations, and communication gaps, one cannot be sanguine over the longevity of Pinochet's or Aylwin's achievements.

Conclusion

The seven countries studied in this chapter and the preceding one carry certain similarities, which can be found in other Latin American countries as well.

First, they continue the Iberian heritage. The land abundance of the Christian Reconquest in Iberia was replicated in Latin America, and the communication gap with the Moors was translated into one with American Indians. A sectioned society—probably more prevalent in Guatemala and Nicaragua than in the other countries—is an extreme example of this condition, and a dual society somewhat less extreme.

Second, they are all elite managed, with a sharp distinction between ruler and ruled. The latter participate in the political process only as a protesting opposition or boisterous cheering section.

Third, institutions of economic transactions—law, commercial system, money system, parliamentary democracy—were imposed by the elite and may be violated at the convenience of the elite. Break-the-system is a common practice.

Fourth, except possibly in Mexico, violence and military overthrow are viewed as a legitimate means to resolve conflict. In each other country, the military stands ready to assume power when civil authority fails. But the military's record of incompetence in economics does not augur well for a stable, prosperous society when it is in power.

Fifth, each country shifts back and forth between free markets and centrally imposed, economy-distorting regulations. Any one shift, such as toward liberalism in Salinas's Mexico or Pinochet's Chile, should not be taken as a new historical era, in view of other times and places where liberalism was imposed from above—such as by Nobunaga, Hideyoshi, and Tokugawa Ieyasu in Japan or by Houphouët-Boigny in Ivory Coast—and what happened to them. Colombia in the 1960s ("showcase" of the United States foreign aid program) is an example from Latin America, not covered in this book. Consider also the decades-long economic growth under liberalism in Guatemala, Peru, and Chile, and how in each country it was interrupted.

None of the societies considered in these two chapters is interlocking; none supplies the milieu for interorganizational trust and stable, intergroup cooperation. Therefore, entrepreneurial impulses are not easily translated into durable economic development. Instead, one must expect sporadic, discontinuous growth for the indefinite future.

Notes

1. Powelson 1988:234-39.
2. Randall 1977:4:27, 29.
3. Randall 1977:4:70. For definition of chronic growth, see chapter 1.
4. Randall 1977:4:137.
5. Randall 1977:4:62. For income distribution, 1963-73, see Webb 1977.
6. Cotler 1975:74.
7. Fitzgerald 1976:34; Knight 1975:350-401; Inter-American Development Bank, *Economic and Social Progress in Latin America*, various years, for example 1974:400.
8. Powelson and Stock 1990: chapter 14.
9. Dietz 1980:175.
10. Powelson and Stock 1990:279.
11. De Soto's work comes in two volumes, one intended to present the findings to a wide audience, and the other a scholarly report, with data, of the research results. These are listed in the bibliography as de Soto 1989a and de Soto 1989b, respectively.
12. de Soto 1988:5.
13. de Soto 1989a:134.
14. I described the organizations of one such system in a land invasion in Colombia, where I interviewed the invaders (Powelson January 1964).
15. Goodell 1986, 1990.
16. Tun Wai 1976, 1977.
17. Dietz and Moore 1979.
18. Dietz and Moore 1979.
19. All data in this paragraph are from International Monetary Fund, *International Financial Statistics*, Yearbook 1990:582-83 and March 1992:426-29.
20. Kamm, Thomas, "Fujimori Shuts Down Peru's Congress, Risks Isolation, Deepening Social Chaos," *Wall Street Journal*, 4/7/92.
21. Moffett, Matt, "Peru's Progress: Fujimori has Tamed Terrorism and Inflation but Means Still Rankle," *Wall Street Journal*, 2/22/94.
22. Ajayi and Crowder 1976:311.
23. Marques 1972:365.
24. Powelson 1988:247.
25. Marques 1972:367.
26. Randall 1977:3:65.
27. Randall 1977:3:32.
28. Randall 1977:3:68.
29. Cehelsky 1979:120.
30. The main authors of these theories are Sunkel 1958 and Pinto 1960,1973. An explanation in English is found in Grunwald 1961. My own critique of structural inflation, a negative one, is found in Powelson 1964:176-80 and in Loehr and Powelson 1981:330-33.
31. Kilborn, Peter, "Brazil's Economic 'Miracle' and Its Collapse," *New York Times*, 11/26/83.
32. Hoge, Warren, "Brazil's Economy—After the Miracle," *New York Times*, 7/17/83.
33. Data in this paragraph are from International Monetary Fund, *International Financial Statistics*, Yearbook 1990:250-51 and March 1992:134-37.
34. Banks et al. 1990:79.
35. Lewis, Flora, "Argentina Cries for Itself," *New York Times*, 5/15/90.
36. Smithies 1965:17; Dyster 1979:91.

37. Powelson 1988:240-46.

38. Snow 1965:6, who cites Matienzo 1917:214.

39. Snow 1965:5.

40. Snow 1965:22.

41. Article I, Section 26, cited in Snow 1965:22.

42. Snow 1965:17.

43. Snow 1965:20.

44. Imaz 1964, esp. chapter 12.

45. Schumacher, Edward, "Argentina's Chief Banker is Held; Pressure Grows to Renounce Debt," *New York Times*, 10/4/83.

46. As estimated by a government commission in 1984. See Chavez, Linda, "Argentina Detailing Army's 'Dirty War,'" *New York Times*, 9/21/84.

47. The most vocal of the victims was journalist Jacobo Timerman, who wrote several articles, such as "Return to Argentina," *New York Times Magazine*, 3/11/84, and at least one book, *Prisoner without a Name, Cell without a Number* (1981) about his captivity in the "dirty war." See also Dionne, E.J., Jr., "Timerman Hoping to Identify his Torturers," *New York Times*, 12/13/83, and Schumacher, Edward, 3 articles in *New York Times*: "In Argentina: Mothers of the Missing Vow They Won't Give Up," 12/31/83; "Argentine Torture: One Who Looked On," 1/28/84; and "Timerman Visits 'Cell without a Number' in Argentine Suburb," 1/20/84.

48. Christian, Shirley, "Visit by Alfonsín Peacefully Ends Argentine Mutiny," *New York Times*, 4/20/87; Cohen, Roger, "Argentina Chief's Halt to Army Trials is Risk Taken to Curb Discord," *Wall Street Journal*, 5/19/87; and Christian, Shirley, "Argentina Moving to Limit Human-Rights Trials," *New York Times*, 5/30/87.

49. *New York Times*, 8/13/87.

50. Editorial, *New York Times*, 5/31/89.

51. Priest, George L., "Will Argentina Simply Replace One Monopoly with Another?" *Wall Street Journal*, 9/22/89.

52. Solo, Tova Maria, "Argentina Tries Cosmetic Surgery on a Sagging Economy," *Wall Street Journal*, 8/31/90.

53. Truell, Peter, "Argentina Tries to End Subsidies to Industries that Drain the Nation," *Wall Street Journal*, 5/31/88.

54. Christian, Shirley, "Bluntly Put: It's Graft: U.S. Envoy Speaks Out," *New York Times*, 1/16/91.

55. Schumacher, Edward, "Argentina Bypassing I.M.F. Staff," *New York Times*, 6/11/84; Farnsworth, Clyde H., "I.M.F. Seen Unlikely to Accept Plan" and Schumacher, Edward, "Defying I.M.F., Argentina Sets Austerity Plan," both in *New York Times*, 6/11/84.

56. Cohen, Roger, "After a Long Decline, Argentina is Striving to Revive Economy," *Wall Street Journal*, 11/12/86.

57. Cohen, Roger, "All Latins Should Try Chile's Homemade Growth Recipe," *Wall Street Journal*, 9/30/88; Christian, Shirley, "Chile's Privatization Pleases Investors," *New York Times*, 7/20/87.

58. Only once during this period did the economy falter: in 1979-81 when the peso was tied to the dollar, becoming so overvalued that investment and employment fell. The error was corrected in 1982, and growth resumed. See Schumacher, Edward, "Economic Ills Shake Chilean Regime," *New York Times*, 12/8/82, and Schwank, Lucy, "Unintended Lessons from the 'Chicago Boys,'" *Wall Street Journal*, 12/23/83.

59. Graham in *Washington Post Weekly*, 2/22/88.

60. Cohen, Roger, "All Latins Should Try Chile's Homemade Growth Recipe," *Wall Street Journal*, 9/30/88.

61. Gressel, Daniel, "Chile's Successful Transition to Democracy," *Wall Street Journal*, 12/29/89.

62. Kirsch 1977.

63. Blakemore 1974:60.

64. Unable to persuade Congress to pass a new agrarian reform law to create state farms, Allende stretched the existing law, making several dubious interpretations. Gracchus misused his position as tribune to promulgate new land laws without senatorial approval.

65. Hirschman 1963:209.

66. Diehl, Jackson, "In Chile, Too Much Democracy is Perpetuating the Dictatorship," *Washington Post Weekly*, 10/5/84.

67. Blakemore 1974:60.

68. Orsinger, Christopher, "In Chile, a Stillborn Democracy?" *New York Times*, 3/11/90.

Chapter 19
The Middle East in History

What would be the advantage of one huge Muslim state? I asked. "Power," Tamimi [an officer of the Muslim Brotherhood] replied without hesitation. "Power comes from unity. . . ." The first objective of power, he explained, was self-defense. . . "The second thing is to be able to protect one's resources. . . The third advantage is that when you are powerful you can impress other nations."[1]

The countries of the Middle East live in the power-syndrome era. The elites value material wealth mainly as a way to achieve power, rather than the other way around. Power derives from military and religious sources instead of from a broad base comprising individual capabilities and institutional positions other than military or religious.

The Middle East is here defined as the Byzantine and Ottoman empires and Turkey, the Arabian peninsula including Lebanon and Palestine/Israel, and Iran. Some references are to Egypt and the Maghrib, which geographically belong in North Africa but may be politically in the Middle East.

Except in Israel, an enormous cultural chasm separates the rulers—imams, generals, sheiks, monarchs, and autocratic presidents and their retinues—from the rest of society. This is so even though the most humble subject may have audience with the king, as in Saudi Arabia. Capriciousness and fear undermine the trust that elsewhere sustains the contracts, cooperation, and investment of economic development. In Israel a similar chasm lies between Jews and Arabs, whether citizens or not.

European and North American powers, along with Israel, view the rest of the Middle East in the perspective of their own past. Americans and their allies waged the Iraqi war of 1991, repeating their military victory in World War II instead of conceiving a political structure based on compromises like those being forged in the European Union. Israel, with a part-European heritage, visualizes the rest of the Middle East in nineteenth-century European terms: of land possession, boundaries, and military security rather than the incipient melting of borders in post-World-War-II Europe. While many suppose that all this will change with the 1993-94 agreements between Israel and the Palestine Liberation Organization, an observer of the power-diffusion process must approach any one event with caution.

Imposing one's own obsolete past on other peoples is not without historical precedent. Britain tried, but failed, to structure India in terms of its own, then-archaic feudal system. European colonialists in Africa endowed

African chiefs with outmoded feudal powers borrowed from Europe, greater than those chiefs had ever known before. The Spanish and Portuguese transplanted their feudalism to Latin America, melding it into indigenous forms.

The Golden Age and its Decline

From the seventh to twelfth centuries, however, the same Middle East—with largely the same Arab peoples and social structures—was a leader in world trade and development, rivaling the Chinese of the time and far ahead of Europe. Historians have marveled that the Arabs, so advanced in commerce, science, and literature from the sixth to twelfth centuries, failed to generate an industrial revolution.

Even before Muhammed, a Quraysh family chain of agreements had opened up highways to commerce. During the Abbasid period (750-936), Baghdad was the great center for international trade, being surpassed by Cairo thereafter.[2] Partnerships and contracts similar to those of the Italian city states, such as commenda, were widely used. Top officials, including sultans, invested in trade just as the English Queen Elizabeth I was to do centuries later. Just as in Europe, new cities were founded: Basra, Kufa, Fustat, Qayrawan, and later Baghdad.[3]

From the ninth century on, philosophical readings became popular, with special emphasis on Aristotle. Advances were achieved in astronomy, geography, mathematics, alchemy, and medicine.[4] Traders brought science and technology from China. Much of the knowledge underlying the medieval Renaissance in western Europe had been transmitted by the Arabs, from both the ancient world and the Far East.

While the Arabs absorbed and preserved the knowledge of East and West, however, they contributed little themselves. Their leading role in trade was eroded after the eleventh century. Conventional reasons for the failure of the Middle East to capitalize on its head start include the following:

First, although the Byzantine emperors did make trade treaties with neighboring rulers, such as the Kievan Russians and the Hamanid emirs of Aleppo, they also discouraged or forbade their merchants to trade in distant places.[5] Jealous of rivalry by their own entrepreneurs, they left trade to outsiders, such as Russians, Arabs, and Italians. But they also feared these outsiders. For example, Kievan merchants could enter Constantinople through only one gate, in parties of fewer than fifty.[6]

Second, the arrival of the Seljuk Turks in the Arabian peninsula in the eleventh century, and then the European Crusades, deteriorated the prospects of merchants.[7]

Third, raids by nomads interrupted the long-distance caravans. For example, in the eleventh century, "the Hilalian Arabs undermined the rural prosperity of much of the eastern Maghreb and interrupted caravan routes leading to Egypt and the Sudan."[8]

Fourth, advances in shipbuilding and greater safety initiated the superiority of sea travel about the eleventh century, compromising land routes across Persia and Arabia.

Fifth, attempts to establish continuous trading routes were repeatedly thwarted by wars. For example, Iran's expensive campaigns against Egypt in the thirteenth century for routes to the Mediterranean irreparably damaged the trading of both countries.[9] The control of Constantinople by Western Christians (1204-1361) depleted its merchant class, leaving the Italians to dominate Byzantine trade until 1453.[10]

Sixth, although Mehmed II (r.1451-81) established a large free trade area,[11] to be extended by further Ottoman conquests, nevertheless the close, central control exercised by the sultan over all human endeavor contributed to stifling trade.[12]

Seventh, the capitulations (special privileges) forced upon the Ottomans by the European powers, starting with the French in 1536, hindered the development of local merchants.

Eighth, the Portuguese blockade of trade routes through the Middle East to Europe in the sixteenth century was the last straw. Thereafter, the Europe-Asia trade took place predominantly by sea, around the African coast and through the Indian Ocean.

These conventional explanations, while no doubt correct, once again raise further questions. Why did the Byzantine and Ottoman emperors and sultans so mistrust their merchants, and why did they milk them rather than cooperate to mutual advantage? Why did they not negotiate more treaties to permit overland trade to Asia, to the extent that it was cheaper than sea trade around the southern tip of Africa? Why did they go to war over trade routes instead of promoting peaceful competition?

The Middle East is a classic case of the failure to diffuse power. Land abundance, nomadism, and military conquest may have been prime causes. Arab and other states came to dominate or be dominated by powers of different ethnic origin and/or geographically distant from themselves, for example the Ottomans over the Arabs. Vertical alliances with leverage were unthinkable in such an atmosphere, as were also the negotiations, compromises, and contracts necessary for complex economies. Feudalism was by conquest rather than contract, and the communication gap between peasants and government was, and still is, huge.

Land and Power

As far back as history is known, the Middle East has been governed by "divine" or religious rulers responding to God, the Torah, and/or Islam. Although their powers have not been unlimited, at any point they have been stretched to the limits possible under momentary circumstances. At no point have these limits become institutionalized, so that power might become more diffuse from generation to generation. Citations exemplifying this concentration of power appear in appendix 19.1.

Early on, power became concentrated through control of land. One of the salient, but most misunderstood, of contemporary issues, is that power is *still* tied to land. Indeed, landed power underlies the Arab-Israeli confrontation. In an earlier writing,[13] I outlined the history of land tenure in the Middle East, with examples, so here I summarize and generalize. The following major differences in land relationships are found between northwestern Europe and Japan on the one hand and the Middle East on the other.

First, at least by 1066, the major ethnic and land relationships were settled in northwestern Europe. The Angles, Saxons, Scandinavians, Danes in England, French, Germanic, Iberian, and Italian peoples were roughly where they remained thereafter. Wars over land pushed back and forth, not unidirectionally. In Japan also, the people in any one place were ethnically homogeneous. In the Middle East, by contrast, some ethnic groups overpowered others continuously for centuries:[14] Arabs over Egyptians and the Maghrib, Turks over Arabs, Ottomans over other Turks, and ultimately European powers over most of the Middle East and North Africa.

Second, century after century, the principal source of revenue in the Middle East was coercive taxes on land, and the principal use of capital was for military conquest. Privileged groups (janissaries, sipahis, ulama, and others) controlled the land and forced the collections. Taxes were so heavy that few people outside the elite could accumulate capital, and the elite squandered their capital on luxuries and war rather than devoting it to economic development. In northwestern Europe and Japan, by contrast, the growing power of peasants and then of bourgeoisie, relative to kings and lords, encouraged the accumulation and productive use of capital.[15]

Gulfs between peoples therefore transcended the simple dichotomy of peasant and noble. Extending rigidly to all classes, they diminished the social, political, and economic interchange and mobility of both people and capital. The Ottomans divided subject peoples into millets (communities). Distinct ethnically, religiously, geographically, socially, and politically, they would be less threat to the power group. But this division inhibited trade, credit flows, and other communication, at just the time that European merchants were traveling to fairs throughout their continent and Italian bankers were lending in France and England. Hierarchical schisms did exist in northwestern Europe and Japan as well, but to a far lesser degree.

Third, the distinction between sovereignty over land and private ownership of it; between religious, private, and royal land; and between taxes and rent, that evolved in northwestern Europe and Japan was fuzzy in the Middle East.[16]

The early Arab conquests yielded private land to the conquering soldiers, while some land was retained by former owners who paid new taxes, but later rulers found reason to transfer much of that land to the state. Ottoman rulers seized land conquered from the Byzantines on behalf of the state and therefore of themselves. The government at Istanbul often seized back land it had granted as fiefs.[17] Since religious property (*waqf*) was taxed more leniently, private estates were converted legally into waqf but exploited as if they were still private.

Some private holdings remained—for example, truck farms in or near villages—but there was a cycle. After a conquest, lands were engrossed and small farmers pushed off. Then small farms would be re-created to supply villages, possibly by fragmentation through inheritance. So the cycle ensued until the next conquest. It was hardly a condition to promote continuous economic development of agriculture or accumulation of capital for industry.

On the larger estates, labor by peasants was committed under contract, sometimes by sharecropping. But the peasant was more servile than in medieval northwestern Europe and Japan. Opportunities for vertical alliances were nil. "The hostility of the peasants to the great landowners can be seen in a number of episodes related by the chronicles."[18]

Fourth, not all was negative. "New canal systems were undertaken by the early caliphs; deserted farms were rehabilitated; and the culture of cotton, olives, and silk reached high standards. Knowledge was interchanged with the crusaders, who brought such products as sesame, millet, rice, lemons, apricots, and scallions. [But these positive features were overwhelmed by the negative.] Techniques of cultivation did not greatly change, and crops and infrastructure fell far short of what was being introduced into Europe during the Middle Ages."[19]

Interest Groups and Potential for Vertical Alliances

Groups to defend economic pursuits did exist, but they did not have the strength, depth, numbers, and quality of negotiation to figure in a power-diffusion process. Corporations, guilds, and towns dot Middle Eastern history,[20] but they were more pawns of central authority than independent associations, more aborted aspirations than balancers of social interests. The soldiers and the *ulama* (religious authorities) were corporate groups but were not available to merchants as foci for vertical alliances and leverage. Rather, in all of Ottoman history, the communication chasms among such groups was so great, and their direct reporting to the sultan so controlled, that all such negotiations were virtually impossible.

Organizations called *futuwwa* have unclear histories. They "consisted of fairly large solidarity groups, mainly, but not exclusively, recruited from the poorer classes and the young, and of males only. They readily adopted an attitude of hostility to the rich and powerful, at times when authority was poorly enforced, in violent disorders."[21] I have found no evidence, however, that the futuwwa negotiated with the groups they opposed in the Japanese-northwestern-European sense. Probably the power and communication gaps between them was so great as to rule this out, leaving violence as their only perceived outlet.

Occasionally one finds an apparent leverage that fails upon scrutiny. In their attempt to counterbalance the power of large landowners, tenth-century Byzantine emperors restored the preemptive rights of small owners over the abandoned land of their neighbors.[22] In the nineteenth century, the Ottomans promoted private ownership of land by Egyptian felaheens to counterbalance the power of nomads whom they considered a threat.[23] In both these cases the mirage of an alliance gives way to a view of emperors or sultans deciding in their own interests how to "support" weaker groups without the latter articulating their aspirations through their own organizations.

Instances of playing off one power against another, however, are commonplace. For example, Selim and Bayazid, sons of Suleiman the Magnificent, fought each other for the succession in 1558-59, each one bribing warrior gangs to fight for him.[24] Although the gangs were "groups" and the action might have constituted leverage, the event did nothing to enhance the power of weaker classes.

In contrast to their relative independence in Europe and Japan, business corporations and guilds were controlled by central authorities in both the Byzantine and Ottoman empires and to a lesser extent in Iran. In European guilds prices were fixed mostly by the merchants for their own profit, in Byzantium and the East mostly by the state because it would benefit from a controlled, taxable economy. The consumer may have gained more from government patronage in the East, but in the long haul the state was a fickle protector. By contrast, disparity of interests among producers in the West provided greater likelihood of subsequent pluralism and leverage.

Historical citations illustrating the central control over guilds and other corporate forms are listed in appendix 19.2.

Money, Banking, and Finance

In the sporadic information on this subject from medieval Islamic literature or documentary sources, we encounter extensive and ramified banking activities, *but we do not encounter banks.* That is, we cannot identify
any autonomous or semiautonomous institutions whose primary concern
was dealing in money as a specialized, if not exclusive, pursuit. Banks
do not make their appearance in the Islamic Middle East until compara-
tively recently, and, partially at least, as a result of economic and political contact with premodern Europe.[25] (Italics in original)

Udovitch goes on to argue that the "notion of deposit is completely foreign to
the Islamic Middle East. In Islamic law, deposit is a custodial contract, . . . [a]
conception [that] stands in sharp contrast to that prevalent in the medieval
West, where the depository not only kept the funds entrusted to him but also
had the right to use them for a variety of commercial purposes."
   The usual explanation of this difference is the anti-usury laws in Islam, which extended the prohibition beyond "making money from money"
into all profit from risk: "the prohibition of *riba* ["usury plus"] required that
there should be absolute equality in the amounts bartered and that there should
be immediate delivery on both sides."[26] Such an interpretation violates the
free-market "positive-sum game," in which each party separately assesses its
own values, believing that what it receives is more valuable to itself than what
it gives. Riba was deemed a violation of God's command.
   The difference with the West is neither compelling nor clear, however. The Koran permitted legal fictions to avoid the prohibition of riba much
like those of the West to avoid the prohibition of interest. Merchants in the
Abbasid period (750-936) employed capital that "was not theirs alone. Whether
they had entered into partnership agreements, or had received goods on
commenda (*qirad, mudabara*), they thus combined their own resources with
those of others, with the object of widening their business activity and spreading the risk."[27] They invented letters of credit and promissory notes. The
hawala, or payment of debt through the transfer of a claim over large distances, was common in the eighth century.[28] There is no persuasive evidence
that Islamic traders were more deterred by the proscription of usury than were
their Christian counterparts. Indeed, the vast free trade area (Dar-es-Islam)
opened up by the conquests of the seventh and subsequent centuries encouraged widespread use of Islamic money and trading documents that rivaled
those of the West and that spread throughout the Islamic area.[29]
   Still, these relationships did not develop into modern banks issuing
their own currency. Udovitch speculates that this was because Middle Eastern

financing was confined to a limited group: "the inordinate prominence of status and personal relations in their operations."[30] True banking requires wider, more impersonal circles. Udovitch is correct, but the failure did not lie with banking alone. Rather, the limitation of all economic activity to persons with status swept all the institutions of economic growth, including the banks, into its orbit.

Law

Islamic law is religious law. Every early society conforms to its own religion and usually does not distinguish among religion, culture, and law. Does an early society choose its religion to justify institutions already selected, or does it select its institutions according to pre-received religious values, or is the causation mutual?

Islamic law has asserted its divine nature to legitimize the power of "divine" rulers. The same was so with European and Japanese laws. But the divinity of kings ended in England with its civil war, in France with its 1789 revolution, and it probably ended in Japan with the Taisho crisis of 1913[31] and, if not then, certainly after World War II. Several Middle Eastern rulers still draw on their divine mandate, however.[32] In this, the "will of God" is simply the will of the rulers. This assessment in no way impugns the religious sincerity of the makers of Islamic law, who may have fervently believed that they were responding to the will of God. Many Christian lawmakers have believed similarly.

Islamic law did not begin this way, however. "At an early period, the ancient Arab idea of *sunna*, precedent or normative custom, reasserted itself in Islam. Whatever was customary was right, whatever their forefathers had done deserved to be imitated."[33] "The Qur'an makes little distinction between law and morality or religious ethic."[34]

In this early law, legal privileges were in principle available to all equally,[35] and different schools developed in different places. Since customary law is the antecedent of most law, including European, Japanese, African, and Indian, there was as yet nothing distinctive about Islamic in this respect. But in the first century of Islam (seventh century CE), judges (*qadis*) began to examine whether customary law conformed to the Koran and to adjust it where it did not. "As a result [of these interpretations, or *ijtihad*], the popular and administrative practice of the late Umayyad period was transformed into the religious law of Islam [the *Shari'a*]."[36] Some conventional ("Western") critiques of how Islamic law inhibits economic development are shown below.

First, Islamic law is inflexible, because in the tenth century "future jurists were denied the right to use their independent effort or *ijtihad* and instead were bound by the doctrines of *taqlid*, or 'imitation,' to follow the rules laid down by their predecessors. . . . Islamic law was denied the opportunity to emerge as a law of Contract and remained crystallized as a law of contracts."[37] *Ijma'*, the result of *ijtihad*, did tolerate different schools but also became "a prohibitive and exclusive principle. . . the infallible expression of God's will, [whose violation was] to be guilty of heresy!"[38]

Second, "A contract in Islamic law is simply a legally recognized undertaking." It may be binding only on one party, for example a marriage contract. Thus a contract may be enforceable only by the more powerful person (e.g., a man, not a woman), or uncertainties may be decided in favor of the more powerful (e.g., landowner rather than tenant).[39]

Third, definitions of trading and partnership are strict, not allowing for circumstances different from those comprehended by the law. For example, a contract usually must fit within four fundamental principles: sale, hire, gift, and loan. Those that do not are not readily protected. Restrictions limit the scope of potential transactions. For example, in partnership "as far as possible the partners should make contributions of the same nature."[40]

All the aforementioned reflect how— unlike in the West and Japan— law from the beginning of Islam to the present day has not been created through negotiation by merchants, industrialists, financiers, peasants, and workers. It has not been forged by politically independent judges following precedents in court cases. Nor has it been fashioned by independent legal scholars, separate from government or religion. Instead, Islamic law represents primarily the interests of those powerful persons who either created it themselves, in the name of God, or appointed the judges who did so.

The law has not been totally rigid. Circumstances change; technologies change; new situations arise. Enterprise and trade cannot take place without risk or interest charges. In one way or another, judgments have allowed for these circumventions. Still, they remain circumventions, not evolution of legal thought. It is said that if one understands Islamic culture one may behave in ways to protect oneself. Still, the uncertainties of a law that changes de facto but not de jure surely inhibit innovation and investment.

Reform

The history of the Middle East is dotted with reforms, or discontinuous change. For the most part, the reforms were brought about by a cohesive group such as a government or sultan and were not negotiated by all affected parties. Middle Eastern reforms are roughly of two types: (1) those intended to purify Islam when it has become too worldly; and (2) government undertakings to modernize political and economic institutions.

Some of the first group were negotiated by participants, for example those of Sufi orders with voluntary membership of believers. These may behave peacefully and spiritually and have no political aspirations. But other groups have "purified" Islam coercively, overthrowing regimes to establish themselves as curators of government and religion. The latter include the Assassins, Almoravids, Almohads, Fulani warriors, Wahabbis, and today's fundamentalists who violently attack in Algeria, Egypt, Iran, and other parts of the Middle East (and even in New York).

Unlike the restructuring in Meiji Japan or the gradual formation of banking and legal institutions in the West, reforms of political and economic institutions in the Middle East have been administered mainly from above. Therefore, either they have been reversed when their progenitors passed on, or the reformed organizations have housed unreformed institutions. Here are a few examples of these reformers.

John of Cappadocia

In 535-36, John of Cappadocia, minister for Emperor Justinian, tried to end corruption and purchase of offices, to cut down on expenditures, and to squeeze out duplicative activities.[41] His problem, common to many societies, was that the system he tried to reform had not been constructed for its logic and efficiency but had been decreed in response to the relative muscle of prominent persons, and the balance of power had not greatly changed. In particular, Theodora, Justinian's empress, took the side of the wasteful officials and had John dismissed and his property confiscated. Despite a subsequent restitution, John was later exiled. He was allowed to return, much chastened, only after Theodora's death. "Many of John's administrative reforms were abrogated by his successors, and the centralized, uniform, tidy empire of his dream—and Justinian's too—was never realized."[42]

Mahmud Ghazan Khan

Fearing that the Il-Khan (Mongol Empire in Iran) economy was being undercut both through decreased food production caused by landholders abusing peasants and through improper handling of money and taxes, Emperor Ghazan Khan (r.1294-1304) decreed comprehensive reforms: "the rates and methods of payment of taxes were prescribed; the *Yam* [postal service] system was reorganized; the coinage and weights and measures were reformed; the activities and payment of Islamic judges, *qadis*, were regulated; incentives to encourage the recultivation of land that had fallen out of use were offered; and the problem of finding an appropriate way of paying the army was tackled."[43]

Ghazan did not act out of sympathy for the peasants: "If it is expedient, then let me pillage them all. . . . Let us rob them together."[44] But he limited landowners' rights, in order to encourage peasants not to abandon the fields (which would have been a case of peasants and lords escaping each other).[45]

But at best, Ghazan's success was doubtful. "The moment control was relaxed there was a tendency to relapse into the old habits, and thus it was a constant struggle to restrain officials from committing extortion against those under their power."[46]

Selim III and Mahmud II

In 1792, the Turkish Sultan Selim III decreed reforms, called *nizam-i-cedid*, to eliminate corruption and bureaucratic inefficiencies: "regulations dealing with administrative, fiscal, and military affairs . . . essentially a programme of modernization and Europeanization of the Turkish machinery of government. . . . His reforms ran into opposition from the powerful conservative forces in Turkish society, the military and religious establishments, the corps of Janissaries and the 'ulema.'"[47]

Findley argues that these reforms, along with those of Mahmud II (r.1808-39), marked the beginning of Turkish modernization.[48] A window to the West was opened through a new foreign ministry and ambassadors to other countries. A new scribal system would lead to a government bureaucracy of a Western model. The Gulhane Decree of 1839 "contained legal innovations of epoch-making importance," including "the effacement of the centuries-old dichotomy of rulers and subjects and the opening of a new age of equality."[49] But Findley also notes that Mahmud "insisted on the sultan's dominance over the course of change."[50]

Mahmud abolished the medieval janissaries but restructured the bureaucracy to bring it more tightly under his control. Attempts to centralize tax collections did not succeed because, unable to afford adequate salaries, the government could not replace the tax farmers. "He failed . . . to abolish bribery and confiscation and to pay salaries regularly."[51]

The Tanzimat

After Mahmud's death in 1839, his sons and their successors continued his reforms for thirty-seven years, under the name *Tanzimat*, derived from a root meaning "order." Education, law, government bureaucracy, and land tenure were restructured after Western precepts.[52] But the Tanzimat was much different from the centralization of law and government in France or England of the tenth to thirteenth centuries. That occurred alongside independently evolving guilds, land tenure, money and credit, commercial law, and parliamentary consultation. In Turkey, on the other hand, Western imitations were decreed without the same history, checks, or balances.[53]

The land law of 1858 was intended to identify owners responsible for taxes, to prevent illegal conversion of religious into private property, and to prevent massive agglomerations such as single owners of whole villages. But the code did not take account of many controversial aspects of landholding, such as collective ownership and share tenancy; nor did it foresee ways of avoidance, such as peasants registering lands in the names of others, more powerful than they, to avoid taxes.[54]

The Tanzimat ended in 1876 with the overthrow of the sultan and the writing of the first Ottoman constitution. In this, "the right to continue legislating by decree was nowhere denied [the sultan], and his freedom to veto laws passed in the parliament . . . was without check."[55] The succeeding sultan, Abdulhamid II (r.1876-1909) "dismissed the parliament, which had met in March 1877, and suspended the constitution in February 1878. Thenceforth for forty years he ruled from his seclusion at Yildiz Palace in Istanbul, assisted by a system of secret police, an expanded telegraph network, and severe censorship."[56]

The White Revolution in Iran

The revolution that overthrew the government of Iran in 1979 was directed against a shah who had accomplished one of the most daring, all-inclusive land reforms in history, giving the peasants not only his own lands, but also those of all large landowners; who had opened the educational system to all, building new universities and greatly increasing the number of students; who had westernized the legal system, taking justice out of the hands of the church (the *ulama*) and establishing secular courts; who had emancipated women, removing the veil and opening equal opportunities in employment; who had initiated a literacy corps to reduce illiteracy from 80 percent of the population to 60 percent in fifteen years; who had greatly increased the number of hospitals and doctors, providing free medical care to the poor; who had professionalized the civil service and the army; who had promoted farming cooperatives and given technical assistance and funds to small farmers; who had helped agricultural and industrial output increase by averages of 9 percent and 16.8 percent respectively, per year for fifteen years; and who had overseen an increase in consumption per capita from $131 per year in 1959 to $416 only fifteen years later.[57] Because small farmers no longer paid feudal rents and because there were more jobs in industry and higher wages, surely income was more equitably distributed during the shah's reign than it ever had been earlier.

But Shah Mohammed Reza Pahlavi's White Revolution failed; he was overthrown and his reforms reversed. Here are some likely reasons. First, the shah imposed the revolution himself, backed by an army financed by oil revenues; parliament was a rubber stamp. Second, he rode roughly over his political opponents, jailing, executing, and probably torturing. Most serious of all, he crossed swords with Shi'ite Muslims, whose institutions owned much of the expropriated land.[58] In all these ways, he created opponents who ultimately became more powerful than he was.

Reform From Above

All the reforms cited here take their place historically alongside others imposed from above upon a cultural complex ill-suited to receive them: those of Wang Mang and Wang An-Shih of China, Peter I and Catherine II of Russia, the European imperialists in Asia and Africa, and the socialist countries of the twentieth century.

Underlying the failures of all these reforms were three principles. First, they attempted to restructure their countries according to the imaginations of the rulers or, for Turkey, in the image of the West. In the case of Turkey and the shah's Iran, they tried to "Westernize" in the absence of complementary institutions like those of the West. Second, they were decreed by rulers or sultans with little incentive to enforce them, for in most cases their own powers would have been diminished. Third, and most important of all, they were not undertaken through negotiations with all persons who might be affected by them, nor could they have been, because those persons were not organized into corporate groups. These three principles are summarized into one: Countries living in the power-syndrome era cannot suddenly become images of those in which the power-diffusion process has run for centuries.

Notes

1. MacLeod, Scott, "In the Wake of 'Desert Storm,'" *The New York Review*, 3/7/91.
2. Cahen 1970:523. Trade in the Islamic world is also described in Chaudhuri 1985.
3. Cahen 1970:512.
4. Encyclopedia Britannica 1978:82-85.
5. Lewis 1988:58, 60.
6. Lawrence 1978:28.
7. Cahen 1970:536-37.
8. Lewis 1988:104.
9. EBMa 1974:9:858.

10. Lewis 1988:155.
11. Parry 1976:50.
12. Babinger 1978:451.
13. Powelson 1988: chapters 11 and 12.
14. Laroui 1977.
15. Powelson 1988:138.
16. Powelson 1988: chapters 11 and 12.
17. Parry 1976:128.
18. Cahen 1970:519-20.
19. Powelson 1988:147.
20. Cahen 1970:514.
21. Cahen 1970:529.
22. Ostrogorsky 1966:217.
23. Granott 1952:252.
24. Parry 1976:128-29.
25. Udovitch 1979:255.
26. Coulson 1984:16.
27. Cahen 1970:525.
28. Udovitch 1979:263.
29. Lewis 1988:37.
30. Udovitch 1979:272.
31. If a specific date is to be given, it might be in February 1913, when the Japanese Diet rejected a command by the emperor to withdraw a motion of no confidence against the prime minister, and it was not punished for disobedience. See Najita 1967:151.
32. Coulson 1968:54, cited in Mensah-Brown 1976:42.
33. Schacht 1970:543.
34. Mensah-Brown 1976:43.
35. Cahen 1970:515.
36. Schacht 1970:549.
37. Coulson 1984:17.
38. Mensah-Brown 1976:44.
39. Coulson 1984:18, 22.
40. Coulson 1984:23. 27.
41. Browning 1987:50.
42. Browning 1987:51.
43. Morgan 1986:169.
44. Morgan 1986:167.
45. I have described Ghazan's land reforms in Powelson 1988:136-37.
46. Lambton 1953:92.
47. Richmond 1977:33.
48. Findley 1980:33, 126-150.
49. Findley 1980:146.
50. Findley 1980:113.
51. Davison 1963:30.
52. Details are found in Davison 1963.
53. Findley 1980:220.

54. Davison 1963:99.
55. Findley 1980:226.
56. EBMi 1974:1:15.
57. All data in this paragraph are from Lenczowski 1978.
58. Gage, Nicholas, "Basis of Iranian Conflict: A Mishandling of Modernization," *New York Times*, 12/22/78.

Chapter 20
The Middle East Today

No substantial change has occurred in the *institutions* of power, paternalism, and the legitimacy of violence in the Middle East over the centuries. Instead, the major changes have involved the *organizations* and the rulers. A possible exception may be the historic agreements between Israel and the Palestine Liberation Organization in 1993-94. But one happening does not make an institution, so one must wait to see how these pacts influence the behavior of all groups in both societies.

In 1991, when President Saddam Hussein of Iraq torched the oil fields in Kuwait despite his claim that it was a province of his own country, unleashing an oil slick intended to damage Saudi Arabia's water supply, he was following a tradition of centuries. In the eighth century, enemies would cut the main line of an irrigation system to reduce a people to tributary status.[1] After the ninth century, nomads "organized themselves into a confederacy which seems to have been inspired by the radical religious Shia propaganda [and] raided both Syria and Iraq, made pilgrimage routes unsafe, and even plundered the Holy Places of the Hejaz."[2] By the eleventh century, "a strong religious element [was] attracted to frontier war zones by the Moslem tradition of the *jihad*, or holy war."[3] War and the exorbitant taxation to finance it were factors in the decline of the Byzantine Empire.[4]

In the Middle Ages, similar institutions of power, paternalism, and legitimate violence existed almost everywhere, including northwestern Europe and Japan. Before the fifteenth century war was general. European cities played "dirty tricks" on each other to steal trade. The Crusades were the jihads of Christian Europe. Japan underwent its period of the warring country in the sixteenth century.

However, differences between Europe/Japan and the Middle East, already incipient in the thirteenth century, became more pronounced after the sixteenth. Chronic war ceased in Japan under the Tokugawa shoguns in the seventeenth century; it stopped in England after the Wars of the Roses in the fifteenth century and on the Continent after the devastating wars of religion and French-Habsburg wars in the seventeenth.[5] Here are a few possible reasons why chronic warfare has continued historically in the Middle East:

First, invading warriors from Asia (Turks, Mongols, Timur) despoiled the Middle East for centuries after they no longer menaced western Europe.

Second, disputes between nomads and settled populations, mostly over land, continued in the Middle East long after western Europeans had settled into the localities where they remain today.

Third, as the Ottoman Empire came to predominate in Anatolia and the Arabian peninsula, subject populations became geographically separated from their overlords, were classified into a strict hierarchy, and were forced to pay tribute through intermediaries (janissaries, sipahis, other military land-holders). They were in no position to bargain or to make vertical alliances to exert leverage. Slavery remained a major source of labor longer than it did in Europe.

Fourth, the peoples of the Middle East remained conscious of their identities as clans and tribes while the peoples in Europe were associating themselves with nation states. Even today, President Hafiz al-Assad of Syria surrounds himself only by his own tribe, the Alawites; President Saddam Hussein of Iraq trusts only his close relatives; and the Emir of Kuwait and king of Saudi Arabia admit only their families, albeit extended, to public office.

Fifth, rulers in the Middle East continue to exercise a paternalistic style toward their subjects. King Fahd of Saudi Arabia conducts *majlis*, or open sessions, in which any subject may make any petition. Often these petitions, involving money, are granted. In this way the subjects remain directly dependent upon their lords, much as in medieval Europe and Japan, instead of upon an impersonal economy.

Lambton illustrates the fourth and fifth points for Iran:

The country is still largely administered on a personal basis. The rise of one group is liable to result in a change of officials right through the administration, often followed by a working off of old scores and personal vendettas. . . . The struggle between the various groups and interests is the keynote of Persian society, and . . . power and money are ends in themselves. . . .

The position is further aggravated by the rivalry between factions, *which has been a characteristic feature of Persian life throughout history*, and has contributed in no small measure to the country's misfortunes (italics mine).[6]

All these forces have militated against the development of contracts, commercial law, advanced systems of credit, and the other institutions of durable economic development. That these unfavorable conditions continue today is illustrated by the following snippets from recent events (in alphabetical order by country).

Iran

Iranians are deeply divided on fundamental structure, not simply on current policies. One faction "expresses the hope that economic growth can be nurtured with international cooperation and free enterprise."[7] But this group is overwhelmed by Shi'ite religious forces, who favor economic planning—although what type is not clear—and strongly oppose intercourse with the outside "Godless" world.

> [To the mullahs] Western ways were decadent, suspect, threatening. . . . Perhaps the most virulent display of this hostility was the campaign by the "makhtabi" that began last winter to purge Western-educated technocrats from the Government. Makhtabi means, roughly, "doctrinaire" and was used to indicate a fierce Islamic piety.[8]

Iraq

Iraq, too, is deeply divided—into tribes, clans, religions, and peoples. Political divergences are based on tribe, clan, and religion, not (as in Japan and the West) on policies. The Kurds in the North have been in rebellion, either open or suppressed, for decades. Evidence of the annihilation of Kurdish villages and torture of their people may be sufficient to bring genocide charges against the Iraqi president, Saddam Hussein.[9] The Shi'ites in the South have opposed the minority Sunni government in Baghdad. That government is sustained by force, brutality, and fear: "The Iraqi President sits at the center of a web of power so carefully spun that a twitch at the periphery triggers a swift and deadly strike. Around him are only those with whom he has blood ties—of relationship or shared killings."[10]

Israel

> More than 90 percent of Israel's land area is owned by the state. The state bureaucracy reaches into every corner of Israeli life, administering a complex web of prerogatives, subsidies, protections, trade barriers and the like that stifle individual initiative and creativity. Because of capital controls and the economic dominance of nationalized banks, capital allocation is woefully inefficient. With the myriad permits required, merely building a house can be at least a two-year project, which sharply boosts

the cost. The government designates who can grow what fruit and woe to the individual who owns more than three lemon trees without special permission. Even the size and shape of doughnuts baked for Purim are specified by the government.[11]

Because of its diversified origins, Israel does not fit easily into the Middle Eastern mold. The antecedents of its government—parliamentary democracy—are European, as are its economic institutions, such as banking and commercial law. So also is its tradition of openness: Israelis may speak their minds without fear; they may leave the country if they wish. Like other Middle Eastern countries, however, Israel is rent into factions: Sephardim (Jews from the Middle East, North Africa, and Spain), Ashkenazim (Jews from northern Europe), and Arabs. Like other Middle Eastern countries, Israelis live in fear for their personal security; their economy is heavily burdened by military expenditures; and industries and land are largely owned by the state.

The dispute over land is another discordant force. "At the core of the argument is the disagreement between Palestinians who insist that land ownership is a function of possession and Israelis who determine ownership using laws left over from the Jordanian and Ottoman eras."[12] In this quotation, the two sides do not start with an impartial law, previously formed, as the source of judgment. Instead, they choose the law that most sustains their predispositions. A single dispute may determine or overrule institutions such as law.

Up to the historic agreement of September 13, 1993, between Israel and the Palestine Liberation Organization, this problem was not resolved (and still is not). Mistrust—belief that the other side would not honor its commitments—and even hatred and vengeance were the strongest barriers in a situation where *economic* positive-sum moves would otherwise abound. As this book goes to press, Jericho and the Gaza strip are handed over to PLO administration. Repeated violence and assassinations threaten, however.

Future historians will question why the agreement should have occurred in 1993, and not at the end of Israel's war of independence in 1949. Had each been willing to compromise then, vast human suffering and economic losses would have been avoided. Part of the answer must be that in 1949 and thereafter, each side overestimated its likelihood of winning. But surely there is more. Claiming the land was, to each, a religious duty, to be upheld regardless of cost or consequence. This kind of religious stand—which is also found in France of the sixteenth century, in Germany of the seventeenth, in Northern Ireland today, and in many other places and times—is part of the power and confrontation ethics. Power, whether religious or not, is valued more highly than material wealth, even than life. Still, why did each "give up" in 1993, and not in 1983 or 1973 or some other date?

United States pressure may have played a part. Acting in the tradition forged over centuries in Europe, the United States combined diplomacy, bribery (foreign aid), and war (with Iraq) to press Middle Easterners toward the bargaining table. But even if this were a main cause, the question remains: Why 1993? The reason probably is that only in 1993 had each side reached the survival crisis. For the Palestine Liberation Organization, "what had once been one of the richest liberation movements in history appeared on the verge of collapse."[13] Disputes among the Arab countries had disillusioned erstwhile supporters, in particular the Saud family, and sources of finance dried up. Without these, the PLO could no longer finance schools, hospitals, and other amenities in occupied territories, so its grass roots support withered. Only by turning to Israel could it avoid decimation by rival groups. For Israel, annual increases in GDP per capita had declined from almost 5 percent (1968-78) to about 1.25 percent (1980-93).[14] Much of that product was dissipated on the military, and government finance was in shambles. Costs of the occupation of the West Bank and Gaza were growing enormously; the *intifada* (six years of rock-throwing attacks by Palestinians) showed no sign of abating; the kibbutzim were failing; and, in the mind of the government, collapse was imminent. If the pact does not hold, surely another survival crisis is not far off.

The pact is hardly unique to history. Indeed, it is just one instance of what has been repeated throughout the world: a major *political* event, whose side-effects will enhance economic development. The agreement was made only when two would-be monopolists (in this case over land) finally became aware that they could no longer survive without a compromise. If the pact is effective, the economic development of Israel, Jordan, and the West Bank will be promoted.

But if that happens, development will be the serendipitous result, not the object. Durable economic development, *wherever it has been initiated,* is the serendipitous result of seemingly disconnected events. This pact alone will not ensure durable economic development in the Middle East. Other Middle Eastern countries must feel the survival crisis first. Only after many additional negotiations and compromises will an institution be formed, if it is at all.

Lebanon

A country once noted for its capacity to accommodate sharply divergent political and religious cleavages, Lebanon in the past 15 years has become a microcosm of virtually every tendency for conflict within the strife-torn Middle East.[15]

The recently ended civil war evokes two observations. First, Lebanon's economic development became absorbed into the troubles of the surrounding community.[16] One part has been occupied by Israel and the other dominated by Syria. Second, the earlier compromise between Christians and Muslims, who shared the government, constituted a clean-cut cleavage, not the complex ties of an interlocking society. Once again, the confrontation ethic and communication chasm have replaced contract and compromise, laying bare how precarious even decades of peace and prosperity may be.

Saudi Arabia

Unlike Iran, Iraq, and Syria—whose governments survive by threat and violence—the Saudis have bought the support of their people with petrodollars and paternalism. Theirs is command development extravagantly financed. "Cost is no object. The Government pays Saudi farmers more than three times the world price for wheat. The Government also picks up the tab for machines, fertilizer and irrigation pumps and supplies no-interest loans of up to $6 million. Moreover, the natural gas used to generate electricity on the farms is free."[17] Material progress has been forced by the government, not built up by the actions and agreements of a business class or farmers.[18]

The extended families play the reverse role of investment banks in the West. Instead of acquiring capital for one venture by selling security issues to many capitalists, they disperse the funds of one capitalist into many ventures.

> [E]ach Saudi is conscious of belonging to a family, clan or tribe whose prestige and wealth he shares by virtue of his name. If his connections are tribal he can, through the tribe's elders or chiefs, make direct contact with the king and tap the considerable government and personal subsidies. . . .
> Put crudely, it is fairly easy for the Government of the kingdom to buy off its citizens through the mechanism of the extended family—and the Al-Saud do this consciously.[19]

The stability of the Saudi system, however, has depended on two forces, neither of them secure. The first is continued oil revenue. The second is that the all-powerful family will not be successfully challenged by some outsider. Not only did the president of Iraq try to challenge it in 1990, but also there are factions within Saudi Arabia which, attracted by the power and the wealth, might pull down the family Saud.

Since 1980, moreover, Saudi Arabia's prospects have varied from uncertain to waning. The volume of petroleum exports decreased to an index of 27.4 in 1985 (1980=100) before it rose erratically to 75.5 in 1991.[20] Monetary reserves fell from $23,746 million to $11,903 million during the same period. The current account of the balance of payments, which had topped at a strong positive $23,025 million in 1975, went to a deficit of $4,107 million in 1990. GDP (1985 prices) declined by an average of 0.36 percent per year from 1980 to 1991, while population increased by 3.55 percent per year, for a drop in GDP per capita of 3.81 percent per year. Problems with Islamic fundamental militants have disrupted government, universities, and the legal profession.[21] The Saudis have decreased their aid to other Islamic countries, and it may be for economic as well as political reasons that they cut off the Palestine Liberation Organization. It is too early to say that the survival crisis has hit Saudi Arabia, but there are signs.

Syria

Even today, a bold economic historian might predict that Syria would lead the Middle East in economic development. "For centuries, Syria was the crossroads of ancient trading routes. As a result, Syrians were sophisticated traders and cultured artisans who saw themselves as the heart of a larger Arab world."[22] The Syrian economy is probably the most liberal and Westernized of all the Middle East.

Yet Syria remains a poor country. No economic innovation, no new technology, scant capital formation, emanates from Syria. This paralysis is most likely explained by the brutalization of all who, by their initiative or incipient power, might be perceived as threats to the rulers.

> Because of the atmosphere of pervasive insecurity, anyone who is anyone in Syria has his own team of bodyguards. These men prey on the populace at large, stopping cars and breaking into homes with impunity. . . . From 1980 through 1982, it was routine for the Defense Brigades and the Special Forces to seal off towns or quarters of cities and comb through the areas house by house; looting and rape were common. Anyone deemed suspect could be put up against the wall and shot, along with his family.[23]

> Syrian tanks are methodically leveling vast areas of Hama, the nation's fifth largest city, as they continue to battle rebels led by Moslem fundamentalists. . . . Tanks backed by artillery and as many as 12,000 troops, Baath party militiamen and plainclothes intelligence officers have reduced much of the ancient part of the city to rubble. . . .[24]

One explanation of this attack might be that the government was simply putting down a rebellion. But another, more sinister, is that this military overkill was intended for revenge and to instill fear. It is reminiscent of the Mongols who annihilated cities that resisted them or the Romans who destroyed Carthage in 146 BCE, sowing salt over the land so it would never again be productive.

Turkey

Beginning with the reforms of Kemal Ataturk after World War I, the democratic organizations of Turkey, both economic and political, have been tightly controlled by the state.[25] The struggle between left-wing reformers and proponents of "order," including a military government from 1979 to 1982, has foreclosed nationwide negotiations about either institutions or policy.

Although the democratic constitution of 1982 was approved overwhelmingly in a ballot, it was not the result of participation or compromise among popular groups. Torture in Turkish prisons is reported frequently,[26] along with periodic violence by and against Kurds and Armenians.[27] Freedom of speech is frequently infringed.[28] Encumbered by political disputes and without the mellowing of policy through interest groups, the economy is languishing, and inflation is periodically severe.

Why the Middle East?

Because of the abundance of land and nomadism; because of the many invasions; because of conquering and subjection; because of their geographical location amid the international trade routes—for all these reasons Middle Eastern societies have not encountered the survival crisis that affected northwestern Europe and Japan. That crisis, however, may be beginning in Israel, Palestine, and Saudi Arabia today. These countries are not close enough to Europe to absorb economic development by reflection. The only development they can try is by command.

Oil, believed by some to be the "answer" to Middle East development, will delay it instead. The ability of European parliaments and estates in the Middle Ages to withhold funding for wars diminished the greed of princes for power and helped turn wars from endemic into periodic. But so long as rulers have a direct source of funding, uncontrolled by any other group, their power is unabated. This is what oil has done to the Middle East countries that are sufficiently "blessed" to have it. While it may finance some economic development, this advantage is outweighed by the uneconomic decisions, extravagance, lack of accountability, and the wars that power-cum-finance makes possible.

Oil and land are merely the manifestations of Middle Eastern problems, whose deeper causes lie in the confrontational society, the absence of pluralism and hence of the possibility of vertical alliances, and deficiency in institutions of trust.

Notes

1. Peisker 1964:327.
2. Lewis 1988:33.
3. Lewis 1988:34.
4. Lewis 1988:127.
5. Wars happened from time to time thereafter, but they were hardly chronic.
6. Lambton 1953:264-65.
7. Ibrahim, Youssef M., "Clerics and Politics: Why There Are No 'Moderates' in Iran," *New York Times*, 2/26/89.
8. Kifner, John, "Iran: Khomeini Seems to Be Force that is Holding the Regime Together," *New York Times*, 9/6/81.
9. The accumulated evidence for genocide is outlined in Miller, Judith, "Iraq Accused: A Case of Genocide," *New York Times Magazine*, 1/3/93.
10. Horowitz, Tony, and Brooks, Geraldine, "Wielding Power: Family Ties and Fear Keep Saddam Hussein in Firm Control of Iraq," *Wall Street Journal*, 1/27/90.
11. Melloan, George, "Israel's Economic Malaise Clouds 'Aliyah' Hopes," *Wall Street Journal*, 3/5/90.
12. Chartrand, Sabra, "Who Owns the Land, Arab or Settler?," *New York Times*, 4/8/89.
13. Marcus, Amy Dockser, "Israel and PLO Agree to Mutual Recognition in a Historic Accord," *Wall Street Journal*, September 10, 1993.
14. Calculated from International Monetary Fund, *International Financial Statistics*, Yearbook 1992 and August 1993.
15. Banks 1990:369.
16. In chapter 21 we will discover that this is a common occurrence in the histories of small states.
17. Martin, Douglas, "Plowing Those Petrodollars into Farming," *New York Times*, 1/24/82.
18. Martin, Douglas, "Saudi Arabia's New Capitalism," *New York Times*, 2/21/82.
19. Lacey, Robert, "How Stable Are the Saudis?" *New York Times Magazine*, 11/8/81.
20. All data in this paragraph are taken or calculated from International Monetary Fund, *International Financial Statistics*, Yearbook 1993, and August 1993.
21. Ibrahim in *New York Times*, 5/13/93.
22. House, Karen Elliot, "Assad's Formula: Syria, Stern at Home and Abroad, Leaves Economy Fairly Free," *Wall Street Journal*, 12/29/88.
23. Reed, Stanley, "Syria's Assad: His Power and His Plan," *New York Times Magazine*, 2/19/84.
24. Kipfner, John, "Syria is Levelling its Rebelling City," *New York Times*, 2/21/82.
25. Banks 1990:652.
26. Laber, Jeri, "Human Rights in Turkey: Is the Glass Half Empty or Half Full?" *New York Times*, 7/13/84; News report (author not mentioned), "Study Says Torture in Turkish Jails Continues," *New York Times*, 3/30/86; Kamm, Henry, "Change in Turkey Clouded by Trials," *New York Times*, 8/10/86; Laber, Jeri, "Cruel and Unusual Punishment," *New York Review*, 7/20/89.
27. Dionne, E.J., Jr., "Armenian Terrorism: A Bitter History of Frustration and a Tangle of Motives," *New York Times*, 8/1/83; Haberman, Clyde, "For Turkey and Kurds, Fragile Reconciliation," *New York Times*, 11/3/89.
28. Howe, Marvine, "Turkey Moves to Tighten Curbs on Newspapers" and "Turkey Enacts New Press Curbs," *New York Times*, 8/29/83 and 11/13/83, respectively.

Chapter 21
Novgorod, Italy, and the Four Dragons

Four "dragons"—Hong Kong, Singapore, South Korea, and Taiwan—seem to defy the power-diffusion process. All have experienced rapid economic growth under autocratic governments with concentrated power. They are hardly pluralist societies. Their market freedoms are the *first* choices of their rulers, not the last choices after centuries of compromise and negotiation. Contrasted with the disasters of economic planning and socialism in other countries, the four dragons reinforce the belief that market freedom, whether commanded or negotiated, lies at the heart of economic growth.

Whether their economic development is durable, however, remains to be seen. The four dragons as independent states are still young. To predict their future, we turn again to the past. In Novgorod and the Italian city-states of the Middle Ages, we find common features with the four dragons. We also have the hindsight of history.

Each of these small-state economies, including the four dragons, was shaped by an administrative aristocracy under the loose tutelage of a sponsor or ruling state. The sponsor or formal ruler intervened but little. The aristocracy composed the laws, regulated the monetary system and banks, enforced justice, and often controlled prices, wages, and other economic transactions. It did all this through an "old-boy" network, with favors for favorites and little regard for impartial law or justice.

For Novgorod the formal ruler was the Prince of Kiev (later of Novgorod). For the Italian city-states, the Holy Roman Emperors or popes or kings of Spain were the formal rulers. When these cities became their own sponsors, they were gobbled up by European powers. For Hong Kong and Singapore, Britain was the imperial power. For South Korea and Taiwan, the sponsor was the United States after World War II. In each case, the ruler or sponsor prevented other powers from emasculating its client. For example, China could not capture Taiwan.[1]

Each of these small states possessed some elements of the power-diffusion process. In Italy that process advanced farther than in the others considered here. But in each case, it did not advance far enough for sustained, high-level economic development. Whereas the ruling elite of most less-developed countries have milked agriculture and industry through state ownership, price controls, and forced purchases and sales, the aristocracy of the city-states of this chapter could not do so. With limited "backyards" for agriculture (Singapore has none) and with a small domestic market for home industry, they had no other source of prosperity than to export. To survive, they were forced to deal with the international market, which they could not control. Hence liberal international investment and market policies were their only options.[2]

The power positions occupied by the rulers of Novgorod and the Italian city-states were not checked by the countervailing powers of other groups. As a potential source of wealth, power was a plum to be seized when the ruler or sponsor weakened or lost interest. The ensuing wars or civil unrest damaged or destroyed the institutions of trust on which the free market was based. Is this the future for the four dragons?

Often a neighboring power seized the small state. For Novgorod, this was Muscovy in 1478. For the Italian city-states it was Spain, France, the German and Austrian emperors, the pope, and finally the unified state of Italy. For Hong Kong and Taiwan, it threatens to be China; for Singapore and perhaps Korea, a widened Asian common market. In each case, the small state's economy would end up no more nor less advanced than that of its absorber.

With some modifications, this history extends to other small states, that are not considered here. Belgium, Luxembourg, and the Netherlands were fought over by greater powers—England, France, Spain, and the Habsburgs. Their independence was a second choice for each of these powers, acceptable only because the tutelage of any one of them was unacceptable to its rivals. These small states also participated in the power-diffusion process by which the northwestern European economy was formed, and their prosperity and freedom ended up being about equal to that of their neighbors. The Swiss and German city-states, independent in the sixteenth century, are now about as prosperous as the rest of Switzerland and Germany. Ancient city-states, such as the Greek and Mesopotamian, also became absorbed into their neighbors, whose economic affluence or lack of it they mirrored. The Hausa city-states, sadly underdeveloped, are now part of Nigeria.[3]

Novgorod

From its ninth-century beginnings, Novgorod was a trading city. A class of boyars (landed nobility) sprang probably from peasants and craftsmen, to wrest control from the distant Kievan prince. The prince granted them self-government in 1019,[4] and an uprising in 1136 gave them the right to choose or expel the prince.[5] Boyar government regulated trade.

During the twelfth and thirteenth centuries Novgorod acquired a vast fur-trading empire, with political control to the White Sea in the north and the borders of Vladimir-Suzdal in the east. Under its own prince Alexander, it defeated the Swedes and the German Teutonic Knights. By paying tribute to the Mongol khan, it escaped the destruction wrought upon Muscovy and Kiev.

Astride the Baltic-Black Sea route, Novgorod became one of the greatest trading centers of eastern Europe in the thirteenth century. It was a hub with spokes radiating to the Baltic, Byzantium, Central Asia, and Russia. As the eastern-most station (*Kontor*) of the Hanseatic League until 1494, it lodged thousands of foreign merchants. From the seventeenth century on, it is hardly mentioned.

No explanation is needed for Novgorod's importance as a trading center. Early societies have always traded when geographic and other conditions were favorable. The question is why Novgorod and surrounding territory did not move on to become an advanced industrial economy, replete with the institutions of economic growth.

The city was divided into five "ends," each under an administrative officer and each controlling one fifth of the outlying empire. No one knows whether the end administrators and other officials were independent powers or were accountable to the boyars; whether merchants influenced the officers of the ends or the boyars; whether the *veche*, or general assembly, was subject to the people or a tool of the boyars; or whether the people through mass meetings affected economic and political policy.[6] Any citizen group could constitute a veche merely by ringing a bell.

Probably the struggles between prince and boyar did not supply opportunities to the peasants or merchants for leverage. The prince lost handily, retaining formal dignity but forfeiting authority. Archaeology has shown that in some quarters—not all have been excavated—merchants lived on the property of the boyars. Probably they were subject to them. The boyars also had co-opted the church, offering land and perquisites to both clergy and monasteries in exchange for loyalty.

Whenever a new office was created, such as *tysyatskiya* (mayor of each of the five ends), it was ultimately controlled by the boyars. Vertical alliances and leverage for merchants or peasants probably did not arise out of the bitter power struggles among the boyars representing the different ends. The boyars compromised finally, forming a Council of Lords in the thirteenth century, as an aristocratic parliament.[7] After sifting the evidence of different historians, Birnbaum concludes that merchants and tradesmen did influence public policy by sheer numbers and economic weight.[8] But this is conjecture. Nothing in the literature suggests that guilds or other associations bargained for trading rules, a monetary system, or commercial law.

With a hierarchical rather than a pluralist order, no serious challenge to boyar power arose, so the power-diffusion process would have been weak. Possibly the threat of invasion by Poland-Lithuania, Suzdal, and Muscovy cowed the lower classes into yielding more power to the boyars, just as the Turkish threat later compromised the power of the estates in Germany. Whether the Russian tsar Ivan III viewed Novgorod as a plum for its great wealth, or whether his appetite for conquest would have led him to take it anyway, is not known. Novgorod was taken, and its rebellions against conquering Muscovy led to massacre by Ivan IV in 1570.

From the seventeenth century on, Novgorod's wealth and power dwindled, as a result of numerous forces: its earlier wars with Muscovy; its capture by the Swedes, 1611-19; the decline of the Hanseatic League; and the Thirty Years' and Great Northern wars. The balance of economic power in a pluralist society had failed, not only in Novgorod, but also in the territories surrounding it: Russia, Sweden, Poland-Lithuania, and eastern Germany.

So long as the administrative aristocracy remained in power, Novgorod prospered. But free markets, mobility of labor, and a welcome for investment were the choice of the boyars and were not culturally ingrained in the surrounding communities nor sustained by a balance of power among groups. When the boyars lost control, the basis for economic growth crumbled.

The lesson from Novgorod is not that economic development requires governments of liberal tendency, such as the boyars. Instead, the lesson learned elsewhere is that *sustained* liberal tendency comes not from the presence of a power endorsing it but from countervailing forces whose *balance* tends toward it, even if no one group would choose it independently.

The Italian City States

History

In the fourteenth and fifteenth centuries, city-states in northern Italy—such as Florence, Genoa, Milan, and Venice—were the leaders in European economic development. They traded in all corners of the European-explored world and created the most advanced laws, financial instruments including money, and commercial contracts outside the Islamic countries. Their money exchanges and banks extended throughout Europe; they financed kings and governments as well as traders. Yet the Industrial Revolution did not take place in Italy. While these cities are today more prosperous than those in Sicily and the south, nevertheless they have long been outperformed—as money markets, industrialists, and traders—by northern states such as England, Holland, and Germany.

The city-states passed through four periods between the eclipse of the Roman Empire and the unification of Italy. In the first, from the sixth to the late eleventh century, they were mainly under the tutelage of bishops or other feudal lords.

A second period began when the Holy Roman Emperors invaded them from the eleventh to the thirteenth centuries but ran into opposition from the pope.[9] By playing off pope against emperor, the city-states gained leverage that brought them functional if not formal independence.[10] They became communes ruled by consuls of their own selection. They expanded their suzerainty over surrounding agricultural areas, from which they acquired food. Instead of opening the way for growing alliances and leverage, however, the power contest of local magnates versus the *Popolo*—merchants, guilds, and other commoners—and the church brought instability. Wars damaged trade. The rivalry between supporters of the pope (Guelfs) and those of the emperor (Ghibellines) widened into bitter personal feuds. The only way a city could keep order was to appoint a *podestà* from another city, free of local rivalries, to rule, with a term of six months or a year. Rivalry was too extreme, mistrust too great, for vertical alliances and leverage.

Bringing on the third period, in the thirteenth century, the city-states invited landed lordships (*Signorías*) to contain their violence by ruling them. These noble families perceived that outward-oriented trade and finance were their quickest route to wealth. Despite wars among these families and with outside powers, this period, which lasted until the sixteenth century, brought on the Renaissance: Italy's greatest florescence economically, financially, and culturally. Besides the great painters and inventors, notable individuals and achievements included Machiavelli, the Medici family in Florence, the first book on double-entry accounting since the ancient Egyptians, insurance, and the *commenda* and other financial instruments.

In the fourth period, from the sixteenth to nineteenth centuries, industry and trade declined as the city-states lost their competitive advantages vis-à-vis northern Europe. Their hierarchical societies, with concentrated wealth, left little possibility for a broad consumer market.[11] They switched "ownership" from one European power to another many times. Finally, in the nineteenth century, they were absorbed into an Italy that is now one of the weaker members of the European Union.

Pluralism, Compromise, and Leverage

During the second and third periods, elements of the power-diffusion process were at work. Corporate groups of many types emerged:[12] church, family and lineage, magnates, civil servants of the commune, neighborhood associations, merchants and artisans including guilds, money changers, notaries and lawyers, business partnerships, university students, professors, outlaws, youth gangs, artificial kinship groups through baptism, organizations of cities such as the Lombard League, and many more. Some of these combined into larger groups with corporate identities, such as the Popolo. Occasionally groups of workers would be gathered, normally for some specific grievance, but they were usually suppressed.[13] "Everyone in the highly urbanized and sociable Italy of this period had the opportunity, the obligation, or desire to join one or another informal group."[14]

Probably these groups were formed for protection. "Beyond the limits of the home and the family there existed a strange world that many people considered too dangerous to confront alone. Confraternities, corporations, and other structured institutions offered the necessary support."[15] But the groups were not always clearly bounded. Clients hung on to powerful patrons, supporting them and drawing on them when either of these was opportune. So how did this particular complex of groups arise, and why were they not brutally suppressed as groups have been in other cultures, such as in South Africa during most of the twentieth century?

The answer would seem to be that the relative power of the groups represented their relative abilities to threaten other groups or to cooperate with them for mutual benefit, and that some kind of tenuous, ever-changing equilibrium of tensions kept them alive. This balance probably arose out of geographic and historical conditions in which contending parties could not benefit from either escaping each other or stonewalling each other, so they decided on a precarious modus vivendi.

Examples of cooperation and compromise abound. The Peace of Constance in 1183 marked a compromise with the emperor, which yielded greater independence for the Lombard League of cities. The Venetians did a juggling act, keeping on good terms with the Western and Eastern Empires and (sometimes) with the Turks once the latter had taken Constantinople in 1453.[16] The consuls of the communes frequently mediated quarrels over restrictive rights claimed by different groups.[17]

Examples of vertical alliances and leverage are also found. After 888, both bishops and cities obtained rights by supporting one contending king rather than another.[18] After the Magyar-Saracen attacks of the tenth century, none of the four great aristocratic families could prevail over the others without the support of bishops, who must have made concessions for the families' patronage.[19] "Emperor Henry IV [a foe of Pope Gregory VII] gave charters of liberty and self-government to the Tuscan cities of Lucca and Pisa in order to help them win their freedom from Gregory's friend and supporter, the Countess Matilda."[20]

Italian kings and Ottoman emperors granted licenses to merchants to open markets in towns or beneath their walls,[21] thereby promoting free trade. To gain their support in a contest with the Holy Roman Emperor, early in the twelfth century the bishop of Milan granted nonnoble citizens their own place in the feudal hierarchy, and thus began the commune of Milan.[22] Venice, Genoa, and Pisa helped the armies of the First Crusade, and "with each new victory they demanded and obtained new privileges."[23] In Genoa, a "disturbance in

1265 shows that the Popolo was able to play a role in politics only when summoned to do so by one of the city's most prominent families."[24] The actions of the signori "always conformed to the fundamental principle of strengthening the weakest classes, weakening the most powerful, and maintaining themselves by machiavellian balance of power between the various classes and the various groups in the state."[25]

In all these actions, and many more, it would appear that the power-diffusion process was at work. It did not advance far enough, however, to prevent the city-states from being still ruled by powerful families when the fourth period began. That fact, along with their prosperity and the absence of strong defenders other than themselves, made them targets for the European conquerors.

Decline of the Italian City States

By the seventeenth century, both commerce and manufacturing were declining. Economic historians point to these causes: inability to compete with Dutch manufactures in price or quality; high wages that inhibited competition; price, production, and trading controls imposed by guilds; monopolies that raised raw materials costs; failure to keep up with textile fashions such as the new draperies in northern Europe; heavy and irrational taxes; wars in Europe; Andrea Doria linking Genoese finance to the Spanish monarchy, which soon became bankrupt; and invasions and occupations of the city-states by European powers.[26]

Having located the "causes" and illustrated them, economic historians usually stop. But all these "reasons" must have been symptoms and not ultimate causes of decline. Why did the rulers of the seventeenth century allow the Dutch to out-compete them when those of the fifteenth century had not? Why were guild restrictions more severe than earlier? Why did monopolies develop? Why were taxes, wages, and materials costs too high? Why did not Italian artisans invent the new fabrics? How did Andrea Doria obtain so much power?

Despite their pluralism, leverage, and tendency toward compromise, the Italian city-states had not yet met the crisis in which groups such as labor, merchants, and patricians *must* cooperate with each other to survive. Patricians such as the Medicis had enacted liberal economic policies vis-à-vis foreigners (though not for the home market) because they perceived these to be in *their* best interests, not because they were forced to do so by tensions from other groups. They had promoted contracts and a more advanced financial system for the same reason, and they had shared some of the resulting wealth with merchants, laborers, and farmers because that was the least costly policy. Although some merchants joined the inner circle, at no point did laborers and farmers acquire a piece of the political action. Their demands were voiced only through a few unsuccessful rebellions and rioting.

If an elite group has charge of all the important governmental and economic processes—the laws, the monetary system, price and production quotas or controls, the military and war making—with no countervailing authority, then the outcome depends on the personal wills of the rulers. If they want the free market, so be it. If they do not, so be that! A change in rulers will bring capricious changes, even though the new policies may come about only over centuries. Finally, if some small group is able to extort product from another, through control of the market, either it or some successor will ultimately do so.

The imaginative thinking of the fourteenth- and fifteenth-century rulers, which made the city-states the most modern economies in the world, did not erect the interlocking society that would maintain the same policies over ensuing centuries. When foreign conquerors and ultimately the government of a unified Italy, not so clear-thinking as their forbears, decided that *their* best opportunities lay in anti-market controls, they enacted them. From these ensued all the "causes" of decline that economic historians have perceived.

The Four Dragons

The twentieth century may turn out to have been for the four dragons what the thirteenth was for Novgorod and the fifteenth was for the Italian city-states.

The success of the four dragons is legendary.[27] Especially from 1960 to 1990, their gross national products increased enormously by world comparisons; their income distributions have come closer to equality than anywhere else in the world; and their poor have been better served than have the poor of any state-organized society. Their miracle has also spread to Indonesia, Malaysia, and Thailand. If Japan is added to this group, their collective gross domestic product has grown by an average annual rate of 5½ percent from 1965 to 1992.[28]

All this has been achieved in relatively free-market economies, open to foreign investment, with few price and wage controls or supports, and relatively low taxes. Adam Smith, come home to southeast Asia! Monetary and fiscal policy has been expansive. A few investments have been subsidized, sometimes with inexpensive credit. Exchange rates have been slightly biased toward exporting, not for mercantilist reasons but in the belief—apparently correct—that exports are an engine of economic growth.[29] This small degree of government intervention in the economy contrasts with a far greater kind in Latin America, Africa, and south Asia. The four dragons—plus Indonesia,

Malaysia, and Thailand—therefore demonstrate once again the power of the market and of sound policies: "they got the economic fundamentals right, with low inflation, sound fiscal policies, high levels of domestic saving, heavy investment in education; and they kept their economies more open to foreign technology than most other developing countries."[30]

Why did they do all this? Without any structural pressures forcing them, these policies were *chosen* by extraordinary individuals—farseeing, civic-minded, and with little corruption. Their main economic-political pressure was a negative one: they did not have a "backyard" to milk. But these same individuals have created paternalistic, authoritarian societies. Labor unions, though tolerated, are discouraged and powerless.[31] For the most part, laws were not composed by democratic forum; the monetary system was not designed by compromise between lenders and borrowers; no equilibrium of power emerged among groups. Hsiao and Hsiao have described the highly-authoritarian nature of the Chinese refugee government in Taiwan and how it sorely paternalized the native Taiwanese, with whom communication was sparse and whose language they could not speak.[32] Indeed, the four dragons are not nearly so pluralist as were the Italian city-states. Does their success disprove the power of the power-diffusion process?

No. The power-diffusion process is one of centuries, not decades. So, do we predict that the four dragons and other southeast Asian states will go the way of Novgorod and the Italian city-states? The argument against this is that unlike the thirteenth and fifteenth, the twenty-first century will be one of global economy. The pluralist society of the four dragons is the world, not just their own territories. The countervailing forces to keep them "straight" are the industrial powers, their suppliers, and their customers. Would this contrast lead to different parameters for the four dragons from those of Novgorod and the Italian city-states? It might, if the rulers of the four dragons are forced into negotiation with the surrounding community of southeast Asian states, to open a wider free-trade area. The competition from each power might hold the others accountable for efficient use of resources. The advantages of large-scale technology in both industry and services and the need for more labor would be the motivating forces. The process of creating this association might even be one of power diffusion as new interest groups vie for authority and influence.

But the idea that we are a global economy and they—Novgorod and the Italian city-states—were not is chronocentric.[33] Novgorod and the Italian city-states existed in their globes, not ours, with mutual benefits possible through free-trade associations. Only mistrust, jealousy, and power hunger prevented Muscovy, Poland-Lithuania, and Germany from forming an economic association with Novgorod, or the Turks or Austrians from forming one with Venice. In all these cases, no checks and balances limited the administrators of home or neighboring territories. The same is so in the four dragons today. Would the holder of power in Singapore share it with his counterpart in Taiwan or South Korea, if necessary to form a free-trade union? Do they trust each other? Historically, the holder of such power relinquishes it, or cautiously begins to trust others, only when survival is otherwise at stake.

Contemporary occupants of power in the four dragons may perceive that their interest lies in the free market and export promotion, provided they command it. But the balanced forces to maintain this are not present. Successors—for no predictable reason—might initiate opposite policies, such as those found in most African countries today. And if they might do so, some successor ultimately will.

A happy long-range outcome is therefore not necessarily in store for the four dragons. If their success continues over centuries, it will be only because they become absorbed into wider areas of balanced tensions and more equalized power, as happened to the Benelux countries and the Swiss and German city-states. It is into all of southeast Asia that one must look to predict the future of the dragons. Perhaps Beijing will soon reach the survival crisis; perhaps its southern provinces will mix with Hong Kong, and ultimately Taiwan, to spread the liberal ethic. Taiwan already shows signs of liberalizing its polity, even though the Chinese have opposed some of these steps. These areas might reflect upon each other. This is the optimistic scenario, and it might happen.

In the meantime, however, Western economists and policymakers who take a centuries-long view would do well to be concerned about the authoritarian natures of the four-dragon governments instead of supporting them just because they have momentarily chosen policies approved by the West.

Notes

1. But it will capture Hong Kong, because Britain did not consider the benefits of retaining this colony to be worth the cost. Prediction: the same will happen to Taiwan, for similar reasons.
2. But not at home. For the most part, they retained controls over the domestic market.
3. See Griffeth and Thomas (1981) for a description of premodern city-states.
4. Bobrick 1987:241.
5. Birnbaum 1981:86.
6. Birnbaum (1981) sets forth these unclarities clearly.
7. Birnbaum 1981:86.
8. Birnbaum 1981:77
9. Venice is an exception, free from the empire earlier.

10. Barber 1992:253.
11. Herlihy 1977:15.
12. More information on groups in the Italian city-states is found in Berman 1983, Black 1984, Blomquist 1979, de la Roncière 1988, Duby 1988b, Epstein 1991, Herr 1988, Lopez 1979, Luzzatto 1961, and Tuchman 1978.
13. For example, the revolt of the Ciompi in 1378 (Epstein 1991:232; Tuchman 1978:366). Also: "Around Siena (ca. 1400) sharecropper families appear to have been organized as small corporations, with labor, debts, harvests, and stores all managed, controlled, and divided up by the father" (de la Roncière 1988:208).
14. de la Roncière 1988:167.
15. de la Roncière 1988:165.
16. Luzzatto 1961:51.
17. For example, a dispute over fishing rights between the monastery of Morimond and the fishermen's guild in 1179 (Epstein 1991:66).
18. Barraclough 1976:102.
19. Barraclough 1976:102-3.
20. Berman 1983:388.
21. Luzzatto 1961:57.
22. Luzzatto 1961:67.
23. Luzzatto 1961:73.
24. Epstein 1991:195.
25. Cipolla 1971:428.
26. Wilson 1977:33; de Vries 1976:26.
27. For details on the economic successes of the four dragons, see Balassa and Williamson (1987), Corbo et al. (1985). Many other sources treat individual countries, of which the following are only a partial list. For Hong Kong, see Hong Kong Institute of Economic Science (1984); Leeming (1975); Rabushka (1979). For Korea see Amsden (1989); Burmeister (1987); Cole (1971); Hamilton (1986); Hasan (1976); Haejoang (1981); Hayami (1979); Hou (1983); Kim Kwang Suk (1979); Kim Hyong Chun (1971); Lee (1979); Lim (1988); Mason (1980); Suh (1975); and Park (1980). For Singapore see Mirza (1986); Rodan (1989); and Ong (1978). For Taiwan see Fei (1979); Hayami (1979); Gold (1986); Ka (1986); Kuo (1981, 1983); Li (1988); Simon (1983).
28. World Bank 1993, cited in *The Economist,* 10/2-8/93.
29. Balassa and Williamson 1987:7.
30. *The Economist,* 10/2-8/93.
31. Balassa and Williamson 1987:16.
32. Hsiao and Hsiao, in Kuark, 1994.
33. "Chronocentric," not in the dictionary, means "placing undue emphasis on one's own time period."

Chapter 22
The German "Miracle"

Why did Germany develop later than northwestern Europe? Why did it catch up so rapidly at the end of the nineteenth century? Why is it the leading economic power in western Europe today?

Germany uniquely straddled East and West. Its "Eastern" characteristics—Brandenburg is a model—were relative freedom for peasants in the twelfth to fifteenth centuries but refeudalization in the sixteenth and seventeenth. Its "Western" characteristics—in, say, the duchies of the Rhine and the southwest—embraced contract feudalism, political action by peasants, and the estates as bargaining agencies with princes. Saxony combined "Eastern" and "Western" traits. While for the most part "Eastern" characteristics were found in the east and "Western" in the west, nevertheless both sets permeated Germany to different degrees and in different combinations, so no strict geographical division is possible.

Weakened towns and docile guilds reflected "Easternness," while Hanseatic and Rhineland towns, trading internationally, testified to "Westernness." Easternness gained when the Hanseatic towns failed to develop institutions of banking and accountability comparable to those of northern Italy; when the princes dominated the towns and the peasantry; when wars of religion lasted a century longer than in France; and when the estates declined in the eighteenth century, making way for the "enlightened" absolutism of Frederick the Great, Maria Theresa, and the princes.

Yet in other dimensions Germany was always a "Western" pluralist society. Her history is replete with compromises that belie the stereotype of Prussian curt command. In the Estates General bourgeois and nobles negotiated taxes with their dukes and princes, just as British and French did with their kings. Multiple princedoms were pluralist by definition, with negotiation and compromise as well as wars among them. The Holy Roman Emperor was sometimes a skilled diplomat (though often not), mediating quarrels among the princes and between princes and estates. Bourgeoisie and princes occasionally (but not often) sided with peasants in their revolts. The Concordat of Worms in 1122 and the religious Peace of Augsburg in 1555 were masterpieces of compromise equal to any in Europe. By refusing taxes for the princes' wars, the estates promoted peace and, incidentally, economic development.

Germany serves admirably to facilitate comparisons with both the "Easternness" and the "Westernness" of the other regions we have discussed. Easternness inhibited the power-diffusion process; Westernness promoted it.

German Openness before the Sixteenth Century

In the High Middle Ages, Easternness and Westernness vied with each other. Vertical alliances, pluralism, and leverage among power groups (Westernness) began with the dismemberment of the Carolingian Empire in the ninth century and the formation of German dynasties in the tenth. Easternness predominated during the ensuing era, and the operation of the power-diffusion process was delayed. For example, contract feudalism was weak. "In Germany . . . the dukes threatened the direct royal administration of the counts and under feudal law accepted the privileges *but not the obligations* of vassalage"[1] (italics mine). In defense, the monarchy allied itself with the church against the dukes:[2] In the tenth and eleventh centuries, "in return for ecclesiastical support, the crown lavished much of its wealth on and delegated the exercise of many of its prerogatives to the church,"[3] hence the *Holy* Roman Empire.

Yet this grant of power allowed the church to challenge the monarchy, just when the latter was also threatened by dukes. To protect himself in the ensuing civil war, Henry IV (r.1056-1105) depended on dukes, princes, lesser nobility, and the towns. He even called briefly for support by the peasantry. In that vertical alliance, he was either desperate or before his time. Probably his "policy of increased reliance on and co-operation with the rising towns, and even with the peasantry, was too revolutionary for his son [who overthrew him]. Henry V (r.1105-25) determined to come to terms with the aristocracy, intending thereby to secure the backing of a united Germany for the struggle with the papacy."[4] Had he succeeded in unifying the upper classes, he would have closed one route toward vertical alliances with lower groups— hence delayed the power-diffusion process.

He did not succeed. In the investiture controversy, Henry IV had tried to depose Pope Gregory VII but was in turn excommunicated and forced to do penance at Canossa in 1077. After bitter civil war, with some dukes favoring the pope and others Henry, and even with shifting alliances, the final solution was engineered by the princes: a landmark compromise of 1122, in which powers were divided between emperor Henry V and Pope Calixtus II.[5] The princes gained power in the process, including the right to elect the emperor[6]—a classic case of vertical alliance and leverage. Some towns took advantage of the controversy also to form vertical alliances and exert leverage. "[T]he people of Worms formed a *conjuratio* in 1073 and were granted liberties by emperor Henry IV, to keep them on his side. Mainz followed suit in 1077. Other charters were granted by princes, to keep towns on their side."[7]

Despite these early exercises in leverage and compromise, over the longer haul the princes forced the emperor into policies inimical to the cities.[8]

Towns and the peasantry were ultimately losers. As power became concentrated in the princes, there was no alternative authority strong enough for the peasants and bourgeosie to seek a vertical alliance. Easternness was winning.

Why did towns in Germany submit to the authority of the princes, while those in the West were gaining concessions from their lords and while in England the bourgeoisie was becoming vertically allied to one or another faction, as in the fights between Edward I and his barons? Why was the peasantry only a bit player in Germany, whereas in the West it was bargaining its way upward on the manor?

Again land abundance may be an answer. The openness of eastern land may have had two consequences: first, vast estates conducive to powerful princes and free-roaming peasantry, and second, the *Drang Nach Osten*[9] (drive to the east) of the twelfth and thirteenth centuries.[10] The lands to which Germans moved were thinly populated, by Slav peasants who were living in "oppressed serfdom without either fixed standards of dues and services or protection against arbitrary ejection, and [who] had no incentive to undertake work which could only benefit their lords."[11] These are the conditions I have described as "Eastern."

The German colonists had contract and freedom. Indeed, looking back from the twentieth century one might have predicted that this new era would enhance peasant power and promote democracy, efficient production, trade, and entrepreneurship. Instead, it led to new serfdom and the landlordism of the Junkers (eastern lords over vast territories).

In the *Drang Nach Osten*, the German peasants had all the opportunities that modern economists associate with development, but they were geographically removed from power elites other than those who had engineered the settlements. Although free and industrious, they gained no experience in vertical alliances or bargaining with leverage. Without the experience of bargaining, these peasants of the east were easy prey to the refeudalization of the sixteenth century. Unexposed—not inoculated—to the disease of feudalism, they succumbed massively when it hit. They were in an analogous position to Chinese peasants today, to whom "superior" powers have conceded freedom in land and market but have denied the right to negotiate for their rules. Also analogous is the position of nationals of less-developed countries upon which international agencies are imposing economic freedom for which they have not bargained.

In sum, Germany before the sixteenth century manifested some elements of the power-diffusion process, including group formation and compromise. But these were outweighed by liberal individualism, mainly in the east, in which the basis for contract feudalism was avoided. The peasants did not learn how to form alliances, bargain, or exercise leverage. By being free, they missed learning how to become free.

Beginnings of the Power-Diffusion Process: Fifteenth to Seventeenth Centuries

Westernness crept in about the fifteenth century, however, not with peasants, but with the estates. These included clerics, nobility, and upper-level bourgeois, who gained power by classical leverage until the seventeenth century. First, they intervened in succession disputes among princes. In exchange for ruling in favor of one or the other, they exacted privileges for themselves. Second, German princes did not have the power to collect taxes by military action, as (for example) sultans did in the Middle East. Instead, they depended on the estates to vote payment. This the estates would do only if they sensed a mutual interest, for example in defense against the Turks. Often they refused to finance military adventures whose only benefit would be to the prince. Thus they unwittingly contributed to five of the characteristics of durable economic development: vertical alliances (or ability to refuse them); negotiation and compromise; accountability for the use of resources; promotion of peace; and dispersion of power. This occurred in both west and east, but more so in the west. (The same was happening in England as Parliament learned to hold the king's wars in check.)

The concessions by princes to the estates included participation in budget preparation, foreign policy-making, and declarations of wars; regulation of princely borrowing and terms of repayment; settlement of religious disputes; determining the size of the army; trying law cases; and auditing the prince's accounts. Accountability for the use of resources as a cultural attribute was promoted in these interchanges. While the princes could incur debts without the consent of their subjects (provided they could find willing creditors), for redemption they needed taxes, which only the estates could provide.[12]

Emperor Maximilian I (r.1493-1519) was faced with some German states, such as the Swiss, that did not want to belong to the Holy Roman Empire at all. Others wanted to enhance their power relative to that of the emperor. Maximilian's Great Committee of the Reichstag was the forum where he or his advisors "could present secret or delicate information, such as an audit of the income from the Common Penny (tax) in the king's hereditary lands, information that had been demanded by the estates as a prerequisite for the release of funds from the Frankfurt treasury.[13]

Many more examples of the increasing power of the estates, relative to princes and emperor, are available in the historical literature.[14] Far from being exceptions, they reflect the generality of a changing balance of power. More historical references to vertical alliances, pluralism, and leverage during the high period of the estates appear in appendix 22.1. References to the accountability demanded of the princes and dukes are listed in appendix 22.2.

Interest Groups Before the Nineteenth Century

In the thirteenth century, the road toward pluralism in Germany paralleled that of the West.[15] Not only were estates forming, but also guilds. The statutes of the clothiers of Cologne in 1247, one of the earliest, hinted at a much longer prior history.[16] Unlike in the West, German guilds did not rule cities. But a sharp distinction is not possible: "Recently admitted members from the craft guilds soon became patricians themselves, eager to defend their special rank and interests."[17]

The Hanse, recognized as a single unit by England in 1281, was "a confederation of merchant guilds, though in fact not all of the member towns had such guilds. The authority of the towns remained dominant over the *Kontore* [permanent trade settlements of the Hanse] and the individual merchant guilds."[18]

The Hanse was not the only league of cities. In the fifteenth century, smaller estates that could not attend the Reichstag because of the expense formed "regional federations which facilitated the provision of services and prevented domination by more prominent neighbors."[19] The League of the Rhine and the Swabian League were among these. In addition, *Kreise* (Circles) were formed by provincial political entities. "[T]he principle of association, already operative in the *corpora* of the Reichstag, appeared in the Empire at large."[20]

> All of the princes and representatives [at the Reichstag of 1497-98] were persons with long experience in negotiation and consultation in the context of various assemblies and corporate bodies. Political federations, alliances, coinage leagues, judicial unions, clerical assemblies, territorial assemblies, even *ad hoc* groupings for the arbitration of single cases: all these combinations were familiar to virtually any fifteenth-century German estate.[21]

The Reformation also gave rise to interest groups. Originally noted for preaching obedience to secular authority, nevertheless "Calvinism took root in countries in which corporate ideas were represented by politically conscious classes who were willing to fight for their way of life."[22] In the Peasants' War of 1524-26 "peasants formed regional organizations or 'groups,' such as the 'lake group' around Lake Constance (*Seehaufe*), and these groups formed a 'fraternal union.' A corresponding military organization was created; colonels and captains were elected. . . . The peasants built up some sort of central organization but continued to deal with the individual governmental authorities of the territories."[23]

But the Peasants' War was brutally suppressed. While the peasants did negotiate with their lords, and while their demands were for specific improvements in their condition rather than a change in the over-all system, nevertheless their interaction with "superiors" did not advance to the same degree as in northwestern Europe and Japan.

The Period of Absolutism: Seventeenth and Eighteenth Centuries

About the seventeenth century, Easternness once again prevailed. The balance of power among estates, princes, and interest groups did not persist, nor did power extend downward to the peasantry. Instead, the dukes, princes, and ultimately the king of Prussia wrested power from towns, estates, guilds, and other interest groups in the seventeenth and eighteenth centuries. Indeed, the estates were essentially moribund before the end of that period. The process was gradual, with reverses and different timetables among principalities. On balance, however, it seemed that the power-diffusion process was running backward.

Towns in the east were first subordinated to princes in the fifteenth century; in the sixteenth they lost in competition with Poles and Russians in the Baltic as well as with British, Flemish, and Scandinavian merchants.[24] One reason was that in their quarrels they did not receive the same support from lords and royalty, either military or economic, as had their northwestern competitors. Also, "there was a constant menace of private war or brigandage in many parts of Germany and towns suffered severely from the persistent hostility of the nobles. To the ordinary expenses of municipal administration were thus added the costs of conducting an independent foreign policy and of maintaining urban armies."[25] Wars accelerated the decline of the towns and the estates, not only by the physical destruction of resources but mainly by the panic that forced estates to vote defense money for the princes and the emperor, thus depriving themselves of bargaining power.[26]

Even in southern and western Germany, peasants had not gained the leverage enjoyed by their counterparts in France or, more so, in England. They were especially weakened by the destruction of farmland and population in the wars of the seventeenth century.[27] "The immediate effect [of the Thirty Years' War] was . . . a dramatic deterioration of agricultural practices. . . . The average herd size plummeted."[28]

Yet the sixteenth- and seventeenth-century wars cannot be the leading cause of the decline of towns and estates relative to the princes, or even of the loss of bargaining power, if only because the decline had begun earlier. Furthermore, other wars have not had the same effect elsewhere. Surely the

Wars of the Roses and the Hundred Years' War derailed the economic development of England and France respectively, but they did not lead to absolute monarchies (only royal attempts at them); they did not reverse the growth of urban commerce; and they did not slow the evolution of parliaments or *parlements*. Why should the Thirty Years' War do those things in Germany?

The East-West Divide

Historians frequently have cited the Elbe River as the line in the historic East-West divide. The Elbe marked the boundary where the *Drang Nach Osten* began. Nevertheless, all assert that "Western" characteristics gave way *gradually* to "Eastern" as one moved from the Atlantic to the Urals. Even the German frontiers, western and eastern, were fuzzy dividers.

Land tenure was the most salient feature of the divide. Princes of the west tried to prevent the consolidation of great estates under the euphemism *Bauernschutz* (peasant protection), whose real purpose was to tax peasants directly rather than through noble lords.[29] The nobility of the east, on the other hand, accumulated vast estates and enserfed the peasants.

A second difference lay in the more extreme subordination of towns in the east than in the west. It might be argued that proximity to western trade gave western towns an edge. The margraves of Brandenburg and other princes broke the political resistance of towns in the east, while western towns—powerful because of the Rhine trade—could resist.[30] Yet geography cannot be a major explanation of the East-West divide. In earlier centuries, Lübeck had been a thriving head city for the Hanseatic League, whose prime trading routes had extended as far east as Novgorod. The obstacle of sailing around Denmark was surmounted. The geography remained unchanged as eastern cities declined relative to western.

As a third difference, the power of princes in the west increased relative to that of the nobility while that of their eastern counterparts declined. For example, in the mid-1550s, the towns of Cleves-Mark (in the west) pressured their duke to tax the nobility, who had been traditionally exempt.[31] The same occurred in other western principalities. Carsten contrasts the Saxon nobility (Saxony is considered mainly "western" despite its central location) with northern and eastern territories in this respect.[32]

The East-West divide is much discussed in historical literature, but no explanation for it is proffered. One might be that because of the land abundance and *Drang Nach Osten*, easterners did not form vertical alliances leading to the institutions of negotiation, accountability, compromise, and leverage between lower (peasants and bourgeois) and upper (nobles, princes, and clerics) classes to the same degree as occurred in western Germany. Therefore, these classes did not perceive the positive-sum gains that would have been possible by greater cooperation. The eastern bourgeois did not hold the nobility and princes in check to the same extent as did their counterparts in the west.

In the west, the stronger organizations of the bourgeoisie and estates shifted political weight to the surviving princes in exchange for privileges for the middle classes. The nobility gained through its membership in the estates, but relative to the east its victory was diluted by power-sharing with princes and bourgeoisie. Thus the power-diffusion process worked more strongly in western Germany than in eastern.

With towns weaker, guilds probably did not develop so strongly in the east as in the west. I find no historical evidence of this (or of the contrary), however, other than the demise of the Hanseatic League in the seventeenth century. Historians do not usually write about what did not happen.

With such divisions, Germany was not ready to join western Europe in the eighteenth century. On the contrary, the westward creep of Brandenburg-Prussia, with its assimilation of other German states and the absolutism of Frederick the Great (r.1740-86) brought Easternness toward the west. The inefficient state control of industries that this entailed, along with agricultural serfdom, trade restrictions and tariffs among German states as well as with the outside world, and the proliferation of wars, all caused German backwardness before 1815.

Law

Like law in northwestern Europe, German law sprang first from the customary laws of tribes. In the thirteenth century it was developing along pluralist lines similar to northwestern Europe. Merchant-determined law is exemplified by the Hanseatic League, which established its own courts and its own law in the Kontore cities, by agreement with the urban governments.[33] As was the case farther west, the ruler in Germany had to abide by his own laws.[34]

But after the thirteenth century, the influence of princes and the emperor seems greater than that of independent scholars, businesspersons, and interest groups. Historical references tell more about princes interpreting customary law or disputing the emperor's jurisdiction than they do about merchants crafting their own laws in the towns. This is especially so in the east.

In the *Drang Nach Osten*, laws were promulgated by rulers, such as Charles IV, Casimir III, and Louis of Hungary. Royal courts were established to subject the nobility to the king. "*The Statutes of Casimir the Great* (1347) and the *Majestas Carolina* are a monument to their efforts; Stefan Duchan also promulgated a code of laws, the *Dusanov Zakonik*, in 1349."[35] Often these rulers brought their laws with them. "The urban law of Magdeburg was adopted by hundreds of towns not only in eastern Germany but far into Poland, Bohemia, and Hungary, establishing everywhere trial by jury and the right of appeal to Magdeburg."[36]

The princes of the fifteenth and sixteenth centuries also wanted to codify custom. Unlike in France, however, where tribes had been melded for centuries by Frankish rule, in Germany "the different peoples, or 'stems', had their own distinctive legal codes."[37] This would seem to make for pluralism. By selecting among diverse customs, however, rulers seized the opportunity to define law in their favor, mainly by establishing Roman law.

From the sixteenth through the eighteenth centuries, the development of law was mainly a contest of jurisdiction among the estates, the princes, and the emperor's Aulic Council. The possibility of shifting cases from one jurisdiction to another provided leverage similar to that described in chapter 6 for the West and Japan. For example, litigants who would lose in the duke's courts might take their cases to the Aulic Council. But the courts did not necessarily recognize each other's verdicts; the Aulic Council usually (but far from always) upheld the prince; and implementation often depended more on relative power or political favor than it did on law.

The differences with northwestern Europe are subtle, for rulers from that part also put their royal stamp on the law and also ruled from power or politics. However, from the melding of different sources a distinctive "French law" and "English law" did emerge apart from the royal patrons. Partly because of the demise of the estates and the weakness of towns, on the other hand, German law turned out to be mainly that of the different princes and the emperor.

This evolution did contain elements of custom, negotiation, compromise, and leverage. The verdicts often were founded on concepts of humanity, justice, and tribal custom, and the judges were usually legal scholars, albeit not independent of rulers. These benign considerations do not allay the paternalism, however, which helped sanction the absolute monarchy of the eighteenth century.

Money and Credit

The historic East-West division extends also to banking, although the boundaries are not so clear. Until the nineteenth century, the German banking system was systemically more primitive than that of the Netherlands and England. But its evolution in the south and west was similar to that of Western Europe, while farther north and east the Hanseatic League actively discouraged both banking and credit. Indeed, "there was a general distrust of credit

among the Hansa."³⁸ A bank founded in Lübeck in 1410 was at first successful, but it closed upon the death of its founder in 1449. A new bank went
bankrupt in 1472, and thereafter no further attempts were made.³⁹

Yet banks were growing in the south in the same century. Just as in
northern Italy, "banking firms had a marked family character. Almost all consisted of a small number of associates, who were close relatives or members
of the same family clan—witness the Medici in Italy and the Welsers in Germany."⁴⁰

Bergier argues that banking initiative shifted from Italy to southern
Germany in the fifteenth century, for three reasons: (1) an agricultural surplus
in southern Germany had fostered urban growth; (2) a location equidistant
from Europe's great trading centers, and (3) the presence of metals.⁴¹ These
reasons are valid, but one wonders why the banking initiative did not also
shift to the north and east, where each reason had its counterpart. Surplus
products were also traded; heavy goods might have matched the agriculture
of the south; the rivers and the Baltic provided trade arteries perhaps as useful
as the central location of the south; and lumber and furs were a source of
wealth analogous to the metals of the south. Yet banking did not grow in the
north and the east as vigorously as it did in the west and the south.

Lacking a satisfactory answer from historians, one may speculate
that the deficiencies of banking in the north and east have the same explanation as those in law and governance: that land abundance and the ability to
escape negotiation, compromise, and accountability had created greater sus-
picions of trading and financial partners than had occurred in the south and
west. This contrasting evolution was part of the differing relationships between estates and princes. In all of Germany, the monetary system was controlled not by commercial bankers but by princes and the emperor, both of
whom debased coins to their own profit.⁴²

The multiplicity of currencies of different Kreise and princedoms
hampered trade but opened possibilities of gain for those who could manipulate. "All territories saw in their local mints a source of quick profit from
cheap coin, whilst claiming that their colleagues and neighbors were even
greater villains."⁴³ Coinage manipulation is a zero sum gain, however: as
princes gained, merchants and consumers lost. Presumably the merchants of
the west—with their greater influence in the estates—were better able to protect themselves from princely and imperial manipulations than were those of
the east.

Why was there no common currency for the German principalities,
comparable to the pound in Britain? Surely the advantages of monetary cooperation must have been seen by both princes and merchants. Probably the
answer lies in the unwillingness or inability of the princes to trade their power

over money for the commercial advantages increasingly available in the West. (The same reluctance faces European countries today, in the European Monetary Agreement.) Before the nineteenth century, the shift in the nature and role of power was not so far advanced in Germany as it was in the West. The creation of a national currency and central bank in the nineteenth century is explained only in the larger scope of freedom of trade and the consequent political unification.

The Nineteenth Century

The nineteenth century marked the fulfillment of all the forces we have discussed. Westernness moved to the east. Many new interest groups were formed; old ones (like guilds) disappeared. The new political-economic complex resulted from the bargaining among the new interest groups. Old-line autocrats, like Metternich, passed on.

The biggest struggle occurred between the eastern Junkers and the Western businesspeople, who sometimes had interests in common and sometimes did not. But Junkers were ultimately reconciled with the businesspeople, as were also employers with workers, and politicians with the nascent socialist and union movements. A modern banking system was assembled, mainly by copying the West,[44] in much the same way that Japan would copy Germany at the end of the century. The Western banking system succeeded because Germany (like Japan later on) was ready for it, in ways the Third World, Russia, and China are not yet ready today.

Prime Minister Otto von Bismarck breathed the next-to-the-last gasp of Easternness. His authoritarianism excluded Austria from the German union when its presence would have provided a wider trading area conducive to economic development. He preferred his own power to a socially advantageous move for all Germans. But Bismarck did have the intelligence to give way when he could not win. Compromising with the workers, quite against his own will he introduced the most advanced social welfare system in Europe of his day. He also gave way when the kaiser discharged him in 1890. The final (we hope) gasp of authoritarianism was reflected in the two World Wars.

Germany has surged as the industrial dynamo with all the elements of the power-diffusion process: negotiation, accountability, and capabilities of institution-building. With examples ("reflection") from the West, the nineteenth century became the historic time when these cultural attributes coalesced in internal free trade and unification, which in turn sparked rapid development. History has overemphasized Bismarck as leader and Prussian wars with Denmark, Austria, and France as unifier.

When the stubborn localism of the princes abated, and the intransigence of the Junkers toward free trade, land reform, and peasant liberation[45] finally gave way, the floodgates of economic liberalism and durable development were opened. The east resumed its Easternness after World War II, with the Democratic Republic, but in 1990 it returned to the West. Germans now face the immense task of absorbing the east, but the essential elements are in place.

Conclusion

Although the Easternness of early centuries diminished the power of both peasants and towns, nevertheless the shifting alliances among power groups—nobles, princes, ministeriales (who were the bureaucrats of the princes), dukes, and the church—supplied practice in pluralism and leverage in both parts of the country. Therefore intergroup negotiation did not need to be "invented" when it was extended by vertical alliances of these groups with craftspeople and peasants, weakly from the sixteenth century and strongly in the nineteenth.

Nineteenth-century progress is explained by western and southern Germany's long experience with Western characteristics; by a nudge from Napoleon that assisted the land and administrative reforms of Prussian civil servants Stein and Hardenberg; by a rise in the power of nonguild merchants, promoting the Zollverein (free trade area) and other reductions in trade barriers; and finally by Bismarck's being reluctantly pushed from his cherished absolutism (Easternness) toward compromise and negotiation (Westernness). The revolutions of 1848 and unification of 1870 were *reflections* of change rather than driving forces.

The two World Wars were a throwback toward Easternness: the paternalism and absolutism of earlier centuries. The Iron Curtain was no political accident but a reenactment of ten centuries of geographic division between east and west. Shorn of its eastern half, Germany fully joined the West only after World War II. In 1990, it laid claim once more to its eastern territories, but the fate of that experiment lies yet in the balance.

Notes

1. Holborn 1959:19.
2. Barraclough 1979:32.
3. Duggan 1974:151.
4. Barraclough 1979:128.
5. Concordat of Worms. See Barraclough 1979:132-33 for details.

6. Berman 1983:485.
7. Berman 1983:375.
8. Holborn 1959:24.
9. Hitler revived this term during the 1930s in his campaign for *Lebensraum*.
10. Barraclough 1947:256.
11. Barraclough 1947:257.
12. Fryde and Fryde 1963:518-19, with reference to *Monumenta Germaniae Historica, Leges*, II, no. 305, p. 240.
13. Rowan 1974:47-48.
14. See especially Carsten 1959, who cites may of them.
15. Braunthal 1965:3.
16. Epstein 1991:86.
17. Holborn 1959:66.
18. Epstein 1991:134.
19. Rowan 1974:48.
20. Gross 1974:14.
21. Rowan 1974:50-51.
22. Holborn 1959:259.
23. Holborn 1959:172.
24. Barraclough 1947:346.
25. Fryde and Fryde 1963:542.
26. For examples, see Barraclough 1947-7:337, 376-77; Miskimin 1975:114; and Holborn 1964:28.
27. Kriedte 1983:69,74-75.
28. de Vries 1976:60.
29. de Vries 1976:61.
30. Carsten 1959:258.
31. Carsten 1959:272.
32. Carsten 1959:195.
33. Herr 1988:7.
34. Tuchman 1978:315.
35. Barraclough 1984:140.
36. Carsten 1959:192.
37. Barraclough 1976:106.
38. Herr 1988:14. See also Dollinger 1964:206.
39. Dollinger 1964:205.
40. Bergier 1979:121.
41. Bergier 1979:116-19.
42. Benecke 1974:137.
43. Benecke 1974:138.
44. The banking history of Germany is well described in Kindleberger 1987: chapter 7.
45. The nineteenth-century land reforms of Prussia and the Habsburg lands are covered in Powelson 1988:103-9.

Chapter 23
The Twenty-First Century

Power Diffusion versus Conventional Thinking

As the twenty-first century approaches, Western thought on economic development appears to be coalescing on two separate ideas, expressed in the following two quotations:

> The triumph of the West, of the Western *idea*, is evident first of all in the total exhaustion of viable systematic alternatives to Western liberalism.[1]

> Central Europe's turnaround may ... be as much a matter of political courage and political will as of investments and of economics.[2]

The first quotation announces the triumph of liberalism over socialism in what Fukuyama chronocentrically[3] calls "the end of history." The free market, he avers, has been found to be the most efficient, fair, and humane way of conducting economic affairs. Since this is now obvious, it is only a matter of time before it will be accepted everywhere.

By citing "political courage" and "political will," Drucker implies in the second quotation that the necessary reforms must be undertaken by strong leaders despite popular resistance. What he has attributed to Central Europe surely would apply even more so to the Third World. If he sees any inconsistency between this proposed courage and democracy, he does not mention it.

Both quotations together reflect an oft-repeated theme of this book: that Western society believes in a *liberal* economic system that may be imposed (in other countries) by an *interventionist* power. The present book, however, argues that economic development so orchestrated contravenes the examples of the West and Japan and will not endure for centuries.

Reform from on Top: Structural Adjustment

The triumph of liberalism at the dawn of the twenty-first century is exemplified in the policies of the International Monetary Fund (IMF) and the World Bank, as well as the governments of Western countries. But if "political courage" is required to implement them in eastern Europe and the less-developed zones, then the dynamo of power diffusion has not been started. Because these societies are not culturally ready, the reforms are likely to fail just as historic reforms have failed when similarly mandated by the rulers of Russia, Turkey, China, Iran, and the Middle East, and by the colonial governments in Africa and Asia.

When the IMF began operations in 1947, its purpose was to create an orderly international monetary system. To do so, it would help countries with balance of payments deficits. One of the ways was to lend foreign exchange.[4] The IMF reasoned that if the borrowing governments continued the monetary, fiscal, and exchange policies that had caused their deficits, those deficits would also continue and the borrowed foreign exchange would also be lost. Therefore, it insisted on corrective measures, to be agreed on by the government and the IMF. Typically, these included balanced budgets, market exchange rates, and a rein on the money supply. Since loans would be made only if proposed measures were accepted by the IMF, this requirement became known as *conditionality*.

Over the years, the IMF has increasingly intervened in decisions of borrowing governments. Instead of requiring only an overall balanced budget or balanced international payments, it has stipulated ways to achieve these results: specific budget lines to be cut, the end of multiple exchange rates, revisions of price and wage controls, and others.

In the early 1970s, sudden increases in the price of oil destabilized the balance of payments of non-oil-producing Third World countries.[5] To compensate, their governments borrowed heavily from the IMF. Commercial banks in Europe and the United States also accommodated them, as a way to recycle the moneys deposited by newly rich governments of oil-producing countries. Even governments of oil-producing countries, such as Mexico, Venezuela, Nigeria, and Indonesia, borrowed on the expectation of repayment to be made possible by greater oil revenues in the future. When oil prices tapered off in the 1980s, many governments could not service their debts. In the face of this crisis, Western governments and international agencies agreed to stretch out payment terms or even forgive portions of the debt—provided that inefficient, even corrupt, state enterprises in the borrowing countries were privatized and market and production controls liberalized.

Believing that "it is virtually impossible to have a good project in a bad policy environment,"[6] in the mid-1970s, the World Bank began making "structural adjustment" loans to assist in reforms to improve the environment for their projects. These reforms required moves toward balanced budgets, free markets, and market exchange rates.

In 1985, the United States government proposed the Baker Plan, by which commercial banks would increase their lending to the fifteen biggest debtor countries. Since these banks were reluctant to "send good money after bad," the IMF and World Bank would participate to increase the creditworthiness of the borrowers. Borrowing governments in return would "adopt economic policies—deregulation and privatization of state-owned industries, removing barriers to private and foreign investment."[7] The plan died two years later when commercial-bank losses became too severe. Foreign debt owed to them was selling on the market for a fraction of its face value.

This debt became a reason for further intervention both by Western governments and international agencies. In 1986, the IMF opened a Structural Adjustment Facility. Loans would be made to governments agreeing to IMF constraints on their "financial aggregates such as domestic credit, the public sector borrowing requirements, and external debt, as well as key elements of the price system, and—in some cases—the prices of commodities that bear significantly upon the country's public finances and foreign trade."[8]

International agencies intervened in internal economic structures in other ways as well. For example, in 1989, the World Bank encouraged the Philippine central bank to promote mergers to eliminate smaller banks, much to the righteous indignation of the latter.[9] This interference seems preposterous, coming from a culture that professes liberal democracy. In 1989, through the Brady Plan, the United States government "offered to forgive debt to countries willing to undertake tough reforms intended to foster a market-oriented economy."[10] Commercial banks were asked also to exchange part of their loans for new bonds or shares of Third World enterprises.[11]

What started as IMF conditionality therefore turned into structural adjustment directed by international agencies, Western governments, and commercial banks. What started as policy packages to improve government finance became directives for radical change in economic structures. What started as simple economic policy changes turned into political levers by which Western governments have tried to reshape the economic structures of the Third World in their own images. The debt crisis proved to be a convenient handle for this pressure.

This experience then supplied a model for Western governments and the International Monetary Fund also to pressure for change in the countries of the former Soviet Union. In 1992, these countries and the IMF proposed $24 billion of assistance to Russia, provided its government would implement President Boris Yeltsin's program of privatization of state enterprises and economic liberalization.[12] In a remarkable irony, therefore, foreign governments and international agencies are insisting on less economic intervention by Third-World and Soviet-successor governments, but on strong political intervention to make this happen.

This is history déjà vu. It is reminiscent of Peter the Great, who would restructure Russia along Western lines. It recalls the Tanzimat sultans, who with Western advice tried to make Turkey a European nation in the nineteenth

330 Centuries of Economic Endeavor

century. It brings to mind the colonial powers in Africa, Britain in India, and France in Vietnam, trying to convert those areas into imitations of themselves. *Per se, there is nothing wrong with "imitations of themselves."* Western countries and Japan are the models of economic development; the free market has proved its worth; sound government finance and realistic exchange rates are economic boons. What is forgotten is *how these came about in the West*.

Even in this forgetfulness is history repeated. Having "forgotten" how they had ended feudalism in their own country, the British appointed the East India Company as the equivalent of an Indian feudal lord in the eighteenth century. They "forgot" it again when they put governments in Egypt under their tutelage in the nineteenth century. The French "forgot" their democratic revolutions of 1789, 1830, and 1848 when they inflicted government from Paris on their African colonies and Vietnam. The Germans "forgot" their struggle to become a nation when they imposed themselves on Tanganyika, Namibia, and Togo. The Italians "forgot" their wars against Spanish, French, and Habsburg overlords as they seized Eritrea, Ethiopia, and Libya.

In all these cases—as we have seen in earlier chapters—the colonial occupiers enhanced the power of local rulers who were already too powerful, in exchange for those rulers submitting themselves to European sovereignty and adopting European organizations. The restructuring succeeded organizationally, but not institutionally, while the enhanced power remained after independence. Thus the colonial masters contributed to the underdevelopment, inefficiency, corruption, violence, and fraud being committed in those countries today, though they did not cause them. Appendix 23.1 provides selected references to power and economic distortions in the Third World today.

This is the history being repeated today with structural adjustment for the Third World and the plans to modernize the former Soviet countries. However honest their intentions and however correct the economic policies, the power ambiance in these areas will inhibit their rulers from carrying out all their promises to Western governments and international agencies. Their "success" would depend on thousands of common people behaving, in response to commands, in the ways that Westerners have *agreed* to behave for mutual benefit. Also, these rulers or their successors may subvert the organizations they have founded, just as Latin American governments like Mexico and the Dominican Republic subverted the Congress and other political organizations they had copied from the United States. In the process, power may be enhanced for those who are already too powerful, just as happened in the eighteenth and nineteenth centuries in India and Africa. The beneficent objectives of liberalization, privatization, and a market economy will perish, and only the power concentration will remain. Other references to structural adjustment, including its interventionist nature, are listed in appendix 23.2.

The Conventional Scenario

What will the twenty-first century bring the Third World and eastern Europe? The conventional scenario has an economic and a political part. According to the first, economic development consists in the cumulative growth of gross domestic product caused by increased investment and improved technology and labor skills. Labor flows from agriculture into industry, while the productivity of the remaining farm workers is increased to compensate for its loss. With greater income, population increase tapers off, ultimately to zero. Why the free market has not brought this about for so long before the present day is not explained. The political part, typified by Fukuyama, is that liberal democracy comes with economic development. Democracy is presumed to be accelerated if politicians with liberal market policies are kept in power. This description is brief and shorn of its usual qualifications, for the conventional scenario requires no elaboration here.

If History Repeats: Another Scenario

In the belief that liberalism requires political leaders who favor it, Westerners are biased by our own institutions. A society that already possesses a modern monetary system, an independent legal system, and free pricing has great flexibility in adjusting its fiscal, trade, and monetary policies as well as its laws. A society that lacks these institutions may appear to change policies or laws abruptly, but when the reverberations die down, the new resembles the old in critical respects. This happens regardless of who is in power. In the less developed world, political leaders are forced into policies and laws reflecting the dominant power balance, regardless of promises made to Western governments or international agencies. Therefore, no lasting benefit will come to Western leaders for favoring one politician, such as Yeltsin in Russia, rather than another.

The following is only one of many possible scenarios for the twenty-first century. Assume a country in either the Third World or eastern Europe. As food, housing, and other necessities become short because of corruption and inefficiency, a politician arguing for a free market seizes power. He is immediately supported by Western governments, in their belief that his is the most likely energy to bring about liberalism.

In exchange for foreign financial assistance, this ruler orders government-owned firms to be privatized. Competing groups now have access to resources. Let us suppose—as one among many—that labor unions demand that stock of some enterprises be sold to them at a preferential price. After some bloody strikes, they win. As new managers, the union leaders increase

wages, running their firms at a loss until working capital is exhausted. (Yugo-
slavia before its breakup is a model.) To stave off bankruptcy, the workers
riot, threaten violence, and set up roadblocks until the government grants
subsidies. Heavy inflation ensues, the exchange rate is depreciated, and foreign reserves flow out. The international agencies complain that the government has not lived up to its structural-adjustment agreement, but they cannot
force it to do so. Indeed, it *cannot* do so and survive.

Other enterprises are sold or given to former ministers who had managed them in the state apparatus. They operate them as private monopolies,
based on privileges, price controls, and purchase agreements similar to those
of the erstwhile state monopolies. State farms are sold, leased, or otherwise
made available to farmers, who may now sell their crops on the free market.
However, their inputs—fertilizer, seed, and machinery—are available only
from newly privatized monopolies whose prices are extortionary and deliveries irregular. Although agricultural output increases at first, after a few years
it languishes.

The governing clique reforms its organizations along Western lines,
with Western advice: the central bank, the development bank, a banking code,
commercial laws, labor unions, local governments, stock and commodities
exchanges, and others, along with multiple-party democracy. Price controls
are removed. However, the government cannot successfully command millions of people at lower levels suddenly to reverse their behavior of centuries.
Political bosses, clans, and *caudillos* who manage virtual fiefs are able to
thwart central-government commands. They demand special attention, without which they will at best refuse to cooperate and at worst rebel violently.[13]
The development bank lends for questionable projects of the governing clique;
the central bank creates unlimited reserves for both the development bank and
others supporting the dominant party. Interest rates are kept artificially low
while bank credit is rationed to privileged people. Laws are bent or not enforced. The dominant party absorbs other parties.

The governing clique sets up private food-distributing monopolies.
Prices on the commodities exchange are arranged to favor these distributors.
The parliament is a rubber stamp for the government's bidding. To avoid wage
competition, labor unions limit their membership to long-time political supporters. The ministry of labor supervises wage negotiations, tilting decisions
in favor of the unions. Using the leverage of their informal alliance with the
governing clique, unions achieve wages for their members of five times the
earnings of nonunion workers employed elsewhere.

While a single intervention in the economy, such as price controls,
may yield the results foreseen by the powerholders, normally there are un-
foreseen side effects such as the proliferation of black markets and smug-

gling. These call for another intervention, then another and yet another, each intended to offset the adverse impacts of earlier ones. They pile up cumulatively until the powerholders are caught in such a web of inefficiencies and graft that they cannot extricate themselves. At this point the whole government may be removed by military coup. But the military is caught in the same web as before, and the cycle is repeated.

In all these ways the new wine (organizations) is poured into old bottles (institutions). The aforementioned events may happen with a set of political and economic organizations and rules identical to those in Japan, the United States, France, Germany, Britain, or other Western.

Many workers—those not in unions—are left out. As a simplified model, assume only two groups: a governing clique allied with unions on the one hand and supernumerary peasants or slum dwellers on the other ("supernumerary" means that their marginal product is very low).

Some development theorists of the 1950s and 1960s proposed that low-marginal-product labor was a hidden resource for less-developed zones,[14] to be drawn on in development plans. For example, farm surplus labor would be employed in urban industries. But none of these theories explained why this shift had not already occurred through the play of the market. A free-market scenario presumes either that supernumerary workers form their own enterprises or that firms employ them because of their low wages. The historic universality of entrepreneurship and trade supports this expectation, but history itself does not.

In discussions of the sectioned society in chapter 17, two obstacles were suggested that might block the assimilation of the out-group. First, although in-group and out-group would both benefit from doing business with each other, the former does not trust the latter. Commercial banks refuse credit to small-scale farmers even though their projects and credit reputations are unblemished. Second, the governing clique precludes enterprises not in their control, that might dilute their power. In Peru they pushed entrepreneurs underground, in ways revealed by de Soto's research.

Before liberalization, the power group appropriated material wealth for itself in two ways. The first was to nationalize enterprises, both farm and business, and pay their profits to the state, which in turn would pay them to its favorite supporters. The second was through price and production controls placed on private enterprise. For example, governments would require farmers to sell their crops to state marketing boards at low prices and to buy their inputs from state monopolies at high prices. In an earlier writing, my co-author and I documented this activity for twenty-six Third World countries.[15]

If the agreement with Western governments and international agencies requires that these *institutions* be abandoned, in this scenario they survive through new *organizations*. Private monopolies replace nationalized, with the same managers now becoming owners. Farmers still may be limited in where they can buy their inputs or sell their outputs, and price controls continue. Disillusioned because liberalization has not brought the promised benefits, consumers riot frequently. Students strike, universities close. While many persons advocate general or millennial solutions, at first no group has a focused idea of its specific demands and what it would concede in exchange.

This scenario is only a sample; others are possible depending on power distributions. In one form or another, economic inefficiency and disorders continue for decades, perhaps for a century. This or another grim scenario continues until the survival crisis is reached. When violence and hunger so threaten the social order that government cannot rule, for its own survival it begins to negotiate with private groups. Only then is the power-diffusion process set into motion.

In the meantime, the weakness of government has permitted interest groups to form. The first to liberate themselves from central control are money changers, known as black marketers. Using small amounts of capital saved or borrowed from friends and neighbors, they acquire foreign currency and lend it out. Foreign money replaces the valueless national currency. In addition, money changers issue promissory notes of their own, as do businesses wanting to acquire inventories and working capital. In this way small-scale production of necessities—textiles, shoes, and housing—is revived.

Circumventing an impotent government, about the middle of the twenty-first century, producer associations meet to set private rules of economic interchange. They carve out monopoly markets and protect their prices. Disillusioned with bribes paid to the ministry of labor and the scanty favors bestowed by government, unions start to bargain directly with employers. Refusing to buy from and sell to state agencies or private monopolies, farmers form cooperatives to acquire inputs wholesale and to demand monopoly stalls in town markets. These cooperatives set prices favorable to farmers.

Only as enterprises grow and use modern technology do groups bargain with each other for mutual price reductions or exceptions to monopoly. These negotiations are reminiscent of reciprocal trade agreements among Western governments. As they continue over decades, monopolies diminish and the free market is gradually approached.

When negotiations become cumbersome because of the numbers involved—perhaps by the beginning of the twenty-second century—the groups elect delegates to congresses, and then to a parliament. At first, parliament is biased toward large enterprises and landowners, but gradually ethnic and tribal minorities and other disadvantaged producers force their way into parliamentary representation, on the strength of their products and lower prices. Their demands first are voiced through bloody battles, but over time, all parties recognize the positive sums arising out of face-to-face negotiation. Private groups agree on a system to enforce contracts, which is ultimately adopted by public courts. The money changers and note departments of businesses become banks, and eventually the central bank is revised or replaced to serve financial institutions impartially.

For those who wish to resolve all problems in one's own lifetime (or one's term of office), this scenario is intolerably slow. But all history is intolerably slow. Attempts to collapse it have only lengthened it.

This one of many possible scenarios is also history déjà vu. But the Western and Japanese experiences need not be repeated exactly. Rather, a well-known general characteristic recurs in a modern setting: that the governing clique and its successors persistently fail, over decades, to restore prosperity and order, despite their good intentions and despite foreign advice, support, and pressure. Only the interaction of many interest groups, none overly powerful, succeeds.

One pessimistic qualification remains. Suppose modern technology creates a sectioned society, in which unskilled labor is superfluous,[16] because in the future only skilled workers can supply all human needs. Some indications exist that the elasticity of substitution between labor and capital may be decreasing in some industries.[17] For example, no number of workers could replace the rocket that can hurl a person to the moon; thus the elasticity of substitution of labor for rocket is zero. Now suppose that the number of productive activities with zero elasticity of substitution is increased to the point where most essential production requires little labor, all of it skilled. It is, let us suppose, cheaper to dispense with unskilled labor altogether than to educate it, or else the cost of mistrust is too great to employ it. Unable to acquire skills or to instill trust, the abundant labor force becomes marginalized. Marx's prediction of a reserve army of unemployed laborers becomes realized, although not in the way he foresaw.

Unlike the peasants in medieval Europe and Japan, supernumerary laborers could not form alliances with upper groups and exert leverage, because they would have nothing to offer, nor would marginalized workers possess the material wealth to acquire arms for revolution. Their only leverage would be through the charity of those who take pity on them or through their "nuisance value" as robber bands or other disruptive forces.

The eleven examples cited in appendix 23.3 indicate a likelihood that already in the United States labor proportions are shifting from unskilled to skilled. The empirical evidence is not fully clear, however.

But suppose it is true, and the transfer of technology from more-developed to less-developed zones renders their unskilled labor superfluous, in addition to being deemed "untrustworthy" because of ethnic or other biases. The ability of governing elites to manage without any assistance from unemployed workers would reinforce the deficit in trust and the vast communications gap. Of course, this condition is one of degree: elasticity of substitution may be low if not zero, and it may affect a greater or lesser number of activities. But if this tendency, now only speculative, should be confirmed in the next few decades, the turnaround for sectioned societies might be a long time away. The survival crisis, when it comes, would be bloody.

Power Diffusion in the Third World

To seek hopeful signs in the Third World, we do not examine increased gross domestic product or investment, as conventional economics does. Increases in these do not necessarily last over centuries, nor do they always affect all persons, especially in a sectioned society. Instead, we look for the survival crisis, however painful that may be, and signs of pluralism, leverage, and diffusion of power.

The South African Example

In South Africa, where the first black president assumed office just before this book went to press, reform-minded groups had long been forming from below: people's committees, black labor unions and chambers of commerce, the United Democratic Front which linked some 650 antiapartheid organizations,[18] the African National Congress (ANC), the Pan-African Congress of Azania, the black People's Convention, and the Zulu group Inkatha. The ANC, strongest of these groups politically, began serious negotiations with the white government after the release from prison of its leader, Nelson Mandela, in 1989. The following year the ANC renounced its earlier policy of violence, and both Mandela and the government expressed their willingness to compromise. In 1992, the white electorate voted 2-to-1 to endorse President F.W. de Klerk's policies leading toward political and economic equality for blacks and whites (though previous deficiencies in skills and lower income and wealth will inhibit true equality for a long time to come). In 1993 an interim committee was set up, including blacks, to plan election for a universal government. This committee presented a new constitution, totally abolishing apartheid, which was approved at the end of 1993. Fears on the part of the Zulu leader, Mangosuthu Buthelezi, that the new government would overly centralize power and be just as dictatorial and interventionist as those of many African states, were presumably overcome when Mandela, elected as the first black president, appointed Buthelezi to his unity cabinet in May 1994. The "honeymoon" may not last, however, since deep intellectual differences divide these powerful leaders, and a serious problem still exists over whether land confiscated from blacks decades ago will be returned.

A list of reforms already undertaken prior to the new constitution appears in appendix 23.4. It is not possible to associate any of these with specific bargaining. Furthermore, counter-reform thrusts and violence also occurred. Yet the cumulative action of the many pressure groups just cited, rather than outside pressure, was surely the major cause of change. The reforms already were gaining momentum before international economic sanctions were applied in 1985-86. However, the threat of sanctions may also have been at work, so their impact relative to that of domestic groups is debatable.

If the newly-constituted society possesses checks on the arbitrary power of any group, including government, then the *concept* of power will have been depreciated, and durable economic development will be advanced. If on the other hand a small black elite should come to dominate instead of the white elite—as Buthelezi has feared—the power concentration may resemble that of other African states. If so, another cycle may be enacted. Success of the power-diffusion process depends on no group dominating others, but on all groups compromising because only thus will they survive.

Formation of Lower-Level Groups

Some have argued that lower-level interest groups do not form easily in the Third World. After a study of Manizales, Colombia, Drake concluded that "the ongoing voluntary associations . . . effectively represent only the interests of the ruling class . . . the cards are stacked against the development and survival of organizations that could possibly serve as a force for expressing the interests of the 'gente popular.'"[19]

But there is other evidence that lower-level groups have been forming in the Third World during the twentieth century, or even earlier. They fall into three classes: First are those that negotiate with the dominant groups, usually from an independent power position and sometimes with results that are mutually advantageous. Second are groups that are either destroyed or co-opted by the power group. Third are unfocused groups, which make millennial or undefined demands, such as for "democracy" with no clear idea of what it is. Sometimes the third type rebels out of frustration against real but poorly defined repressions, as in the Taiping Rebellion in China in the mid-nineteenth century and the centuries-long Tutsi-Hutu massacres in Rwanda and Burundi, in which tens of thousands died in 1994.

Sometimes leverage is applied by the first of these three types, in alliance—formal or otherwise—with more powerful groups. Before the 1994 constitution, South African businesspeople were pressuring to modify apartheid.[20] An arrested activist was released in Haiti after bishops had raised a protest.[21] In Peru, "the Government has been forced to turn its attention to the sierras because the Shining Path guerrillas got there first, exploiting the desperate poverty of the Indians . . . [T]he traditional neglect of the Andean Indians by Lima-based governments has become the rebels' greatest asset."[22]

Sometimes potential leverage is visible in the second type ("unsuccessful groups") but is not used. In El Salvador before the end of civil war in 1992, both government and rebels tried to improve the conditions of peasants[23] when not destroying their villages, but in either case, the peasants did not appear to participate much in decisions on their own behalf.

Co-opted groups are typified by Saudi Arabia. There the power of the royal family is so great that all other groups in alliance could not match it. "[P]ublic loyalty to the Sauds springs largely from a lack of alternatives . . . [O]ver the years the rulers have demonstrated extraordinary ability to juggle factions in society—tribes, traders, technocrats, religious leaders, and the military—so that grievances don't coalesce. Religious leaders . . . have been largely co-opted by a royal family that yields to them on social issues in exchange for exclusive political control."[24] Another group might replace the Sauds in a coup, but it would not spread the power. The combination of crown, nobility, and church in sixteenth-century Spain and Portugal was similar.

The Chinese students who protested in Tiananmen Square in 1989 represent the third type of group—unfocused.

Additional historical and current examples of all three types of groups are listed in appendix 23.5.

Past, Present, and the Twenty-First Century

The hindsight with which we have viewed northwestern Europe and Japan runs the risk of appearing too neat, too sequenced. Only as we examine the present, with all its uncertainties, qualifications, and options, is our attention drawn to similar uncertainties, qualifications, and options at all points in history.

No world area need follow the exact pattern of any that has preceded it. It would be folly to suppose that contract feudalism—so important to medieval northwestern Europe and Japan—would be repeated today. It would be equally folly to suppose that land shortage and a geography unsuitable to international trade would initiate the power-diffusion process, as I speculate that they did for medieval northwestern Europe and Japan. Instead, we must seek modern counterparts to these. Where the survival crisis earlier comprised pressures among kings, nobles, land barons, peasants, workers, and bourgeois, today it is waged by presidents and bureaucracies, military and civilian controllers of resources, large corporations, and small independent producers, workers and farmers. Each time history repeats itself, it does so a little differently. If these differences accumulate, might they approach a threshold, beyond which prior patterns would no longer predict future events? For example, the information superhighway and other modern technology might change the nature of those who pressure the ruling elites or of the elites themselves. The widespread economic hardships heaped upon unfocused corporate categories might impel them into demands, peaceful or violent, so threatening that power groups will bring about liberalizing economic reform on their own, even without the vertical negotiation and leverage of history. Structural adjustment advocates are hoping so.

This seems unlikely. Had we not seen the pattern of unfocused groups before, many times, we might believe results would be different now. In the past, power groups that have enacted reforms when pressured to do so by unfocused corporate categories have retained their power—or another power group has overthrown them, to enact its own reforms. The generic power *class* has been reinforced, just with different members, and the survival crisis has been postponed.

Two polar scenarios appear possible for the twenty-first century, with many others in between. In the worst-case scenario, economic growth occurs in elite sectors of sectioned societies, but fear and mistrust widens the gulf between them and the out-groups. The perceived risk-cost to the elites of associating with these "lower" classes becomes prohibitive. Entrepreneurship may abound in either section, but the institutions of economic development are captured by the powerful and diverted to their benefit. Chronic growth becomes a sterile mirror of more developed zones, but grotesque, inefficient, and lacking vitality. Break-the-system is a repeated feature. Multitudes live in destitution in the slums, violence remains endemic, and gross domestic product increases slowly.

But the best-case scenario is alternatively possible for any society. In it, durable economic development depends on the tension among many autonomous corporate groups, not just corporate categories. These groups are already forming in eastern Europe and in many parts of the Third World. The free market in institutions consists in their jockeying back and forth, while exercising leverage through vertical alliances. The free market in goods and services—the most powerful force for durable development—emerges not as the dictate of the powerful, but as the second, only attainable, choice of each group. A precarious balance of pressures, as portrayed in the "balloon" analogy of chapter 1 (page 7) sustains the structure. If any small number of groups becomes too powerful, even the strongest of liberal economies may become derailed. But the balance *might* hold and become institutionalized.

If societies are—as I have speculated—so obdurate that only a survival crisis will budge them in the direction of durable economic development, then we must look for such a crisis to determine which of the many scenarios a given society will follow. In whichever is chosen, the future will probably be little different from the past, of the same or some other society.

Notes

1. Fukuyama 1989:3.
2. Drucker, Peter, "Junk Central Europe's Factories and Start Over," *Wall Street Journal*, 07/19/90.
3. "Chronocentric," not in the dictionary, means an exaggerated importance placed on one's own era.
4. Technically, the IMF did not lend currency; it paid foreign exchange to buy the deficit country's local currency with a repurchase agreement. Since the deficit government could create its own local currency, the transaction was identical to a loan of a foreign currency.
5. The impact on Third World balance of payments was much more severe than on the industrial world, because oil-producing countries tended both to keep their reserves and to invest in Europe and the United States. I performed a quantitative analysis of the directions of these flows in Powelson 1977.
6. Michalopoulos, Constantine, "World Bank Lending for Structural Adjustment," *Finance and Development*, June 1987:7.
7. Kilborn, Peter T., "Death of 'Baker Plan' on Debt Seen," *New York Times*, 5/26/87.
8. "Conditionality: Financing and Adjustment Should Work in Tandem, According to Fund Policy," *IMF Survey*, 9/1/86.
9. Tiglao, Rigoberto, "World Bank Presses Reform on the Philippines: Loan Tied to Changes," *Business Affairs*, 7/6/89.
10. Farnsworth, Clyde H., "U.S. Falls Short on Its Debt Plan for Third World," *New York Times*, 1/9/89.
11. Farnsworth, Clyde H., "World Bank and I.M.F. Approve Plan to Cut Debt of Poorer Lands," *New York Times*, 4/5/89.
12. Greenhouse, Steven, "I.M.F. Endorses Russian Plan for Economy, Clearing Way for Aid and Membership," *New York Times*, 4/1/92.
13. For Brazil, see Brooke, James, "Even Brazil is Shocked: State is One Family's Fief," *New York Times*, 11/12/93. For China, see WuDunn, Sheryl, "China is Sowing Discontent with 'Taxes' on the Peasants," in *New York Times*, 5/19/93. Other references to local bosses abound in the media.
14. For example, Lewis 1954, and Fei and Ranis 1969.
15. Powelson and Stock 1990.
16. See chapter 17, section on Guatemala.
17. Zero elasticity means that either a machine or a laborer is indispensable, and neither can substitute for the other.
18. Banks 1989:552.
19. Drake 1973:11.
20. Mufson, Steve, "Businessmen Pressure South Africa's Botha to Modify Apartheid," *Wall Street Journal*, 9/13/85.

21. Ricks, Thomas E., "The Pope Visits Haiti Just as Church There is Challenging Regime." *Wall Street Journal*, 3/7/83.
22. Riding, Alan, "In the Incas' Land, a War is Fought to Win over Impoverished People," *New York Times*, 11/18/86.
23. Chavez, Lydia, "El Salvador's Military Trying to Win Peasants and Battles," *New York Times*, 8/26/84.
24. House, Karen Elliott, "Saudis Find Stability in the Royal Family, but Frustrations Rise," *Wall Street Journal*, 6/16/81.

Appendixes

Each chapter contains only the examples I have deemed necessary to illustrate the thesis of that chapter. Many more historical and current citations are necessary to convince the skeptic that the power-diffusion process is credible; these are listed here, beginning with appendix 2.1. Obviously, no number of examples will *prove* any point, but an abundance is necessary to be convincing.

In these appendixes, LDC refers to less-developed countries and MDC to more-developed countries.

Appendix 1.1: Institution Theory in Modern Economics

The grandfather of institutional economics is John R. Commons, who in 1934 described the economic system in terms of the institutions through which it functioned.[1] His work was grounded in the history of economic thought. However, it did not make much impact on the mainstream, and later work on institutional economics takes off from a different point.

Two sets of authors have contributed to the more recent understanding of the institutions to be negotiated in a pluralist society. The first of these —public choice economists —tackled the question of which goods ought to be produced publicly and which privately. The second —theorists of transaction costs and the firm —engaged the question of criteria for the scale and shape of cooperative activity: What is the optimal size, construction, and composition of the firm, such that transaction costs will be minimized and resources used jointly will produce more than they would separately and individually.

Buchanan and Tullock[2] and others in public choice address these further questions: Under what contractual arrangements should public goods be produced? Who should benefit and who should pay the costs?

In a review of Buchanan's contributions, Thomas Romer[3] describes the problem as follows:

> Imagine a group of persons gathered to enact rules to govern future collective decisions. They may foresee that different rules will have different distributional consequences, and so there will be conflicting interests about what rules to adopt. But suppose they recognize that the rules they are selecting are to apply far into the future —sufficiently so that everyone's expectations about future positions are essentially the same. Or alternatively, just assume directly that people at this stage make deci-

- 343 -

sions under a "veil of ignorance" about their own future positions. Then it is more likely that there will be consensus on general rules for collective choice.

Public choice economists have criticized contemporary economic theory for assuming that the government is a "benevolent despot" acting in some "public interest" whose existence they do not accept. Rather, all interests are private, including those of government officials. In a context reminiscent of Rawls,[4] on how a "just" society is defined, they assume that individuals are capable of determining rules for the public sector totally apart from their *own* interests. But such a group of individuals may be as difficult to find as a "benevolent despot."

Williamson[5] set forth the kinds of contract, expected behavior, laws, and composition of the firm that make possible complex economic activity. In addition, a set of moral standards is required, which Alchian and Woodward[6] refer to as follows:

> That contracts are not sufficiently well-enforced by resort to the law is emphasized by Williamson. Unique parties who would expropriate dependent quasi-rents resist the temptation, in part, because "it isn't right." Social opprobrium and the feeling of guilt may operate.

One does not assume from this that more-developed societies have "more" morality than less-developed. Every society has its own morality. Rather, the economic morality of more-developed societies, and the institutions of cooperation and corporate activity, are *different* from those of the less-developed, and presumably these differences have something to do with the degree of development.

The contributions of both sets of writers are stimulating and innovative. But neither intended to study the historical process by which a society may approach the capability that Buchanan and Tullock attribute to the "wise people" or that Coase, Williamson, and others attribute to those who form modern firms. Rather, they have sought theoretical constructs to specify the definition of an efficient and just public sector or private firm.[7] By contrast, this book purports to show how a society may allocate rights and responsibilities over time with the result that—*given relative balance of power*—durable development is promoted and *incidentally* an efficient and just public sector or private firm. Kaempfer and Lowenberg and Mueller[8] supply a good review of the literature on public choice.

In addition to these institutionalists, I am indebted to other authors who have preceded me. North,[9] North and Thomas,[10] and Weber[11] have written on the evolution of institutions. Their contributions are discussed in chapters 4 and 6. At the same time as this book was being written, North was writing his *Institutions, Institutional Change, and Economic Performance* (1990), with ideas overlapping those presented here. The relationship between that book and this one is discussed in chapter 5.

Still others are Bauer,[12] whose advocacy of the free market as a means to development pre-dated the current mode in that direction, and Boulding, a wide-ranging institutionalist whose views do not conform to the modes of public choice or transaction cost. His *The Three Phases of Power*[13] follows lines that might have inspired parts of the power-diffusion process. Since he and I frequently conversed about these questions before his death in 1993, it is difficult to know exactly how much his thinking has influenced mine. In addition, Boulding broadened the field of economics far beyond any of our contemporaries; his general line of thought has inspired me immensely.

Reuven Brenner emphasized the role of trust in the modern economy.[14] E. L. Jones (1988) wrote about intense spurts of growth, such as the Industrial Revolution, occurring in the ancient world, Asia, and elsewhere. He also emphasized the centuries-long continuity of economic development. Furthermore, he recognized Japan as an independent progenitor of economic development even before the Meiji restoration. He describes the culture and manner of early Japanese growth. In recognizing the need for "relative interconnectedness of society,"[15] Jones comes tantalizingly close to the concept of the interlocking society. His proposition that rent-seeking is one explanation of failure to grow is surely related to the distribution of power. But power is a consumption good as well as a rent-earning one.

Only after completing this manuscript did I read Singer and Wildavsky, *The Real World Order* (1993). Here I found some sympathetic overlap with my book. But their presentation is intuitive/political, while mine is more analytical/historical. Some of the historical grounding for the intuitions expressed in *The Real World Order* will be found in the present book.

Appendix 1.2: Game Theory[16]

Game theory presents in formal, rigorous (often mathematical) logic the manner in which people move from noncooperative to cooperative economic behavior. Prisoner's dilemma is the prototype. Noncooperative behavior leads to a mutually suboptimal outcome (see note 5 to chapter 1). Although each prisoner would be better off if neither defected, nevertheless each fears that the other will do so. To avoid the "worst" outcome of being charged with both crimes, X and Y, each decides to report on the other. As a result, both are forgiven for the less serious crime, X, but they are both convicted of the more serious one, Y.

Extensions of this game move from this suboptimal outcome to an optimal one. They show how persons can achieve a cooperative solution that would leave each one better off than the uncooperative one. In repeated plays, each defecting player may be penalized in the next round. Predictions of these penalties provide each with a basis for trust that one's own cooperation will evoke the same from the other. Social conventions enshrine this behavior in ethical terms, making opportunistic deviations infrequent. Another variant allows monetary rewards for good behavior or penalties for defection. Institutions will be established to monitor compliance and administer the rewards and punishments.

Thus institutions become the key elements in establishing the trust necessary to move from individually rational (opportunistic) behavior with socially suboptimal results to a cooperative solution in which each party is, in the long run, better off than otherwise.

Appendix 2.1: Historical References to the Weakening Power of the Shogun during the Tokugawa Era (1603-1868)

1. Merchants repeatedly made loans to the shogun, to his retainers (*hatamoto*), and to the daimyo and their samurai. Why did not these borrowers pull their rank to demand this money as gift or tax? Why did they not default? They did both, but to insist on this privilege too often would kill the goose of the golden eggs. After defaulting, they could not borrow more without making concessions that improved merchant freedom and control over business practices. Thus power shifted from a military and/or religious base to one based on capabilities—the ability to produce and sell.

2. The exclusion of foreigners from 1635 to 1868 was intended, among other things, to bolster the power of the shogun relative to the western daimyo, particularly those of Satsuma and Choshu, who were in the best position to trade abroad. Hall[17] writes that "seclusion was merely the culminating step in the Tokugawa effort to deny the western daimyo access to profits from foreign trade." But widespread smuggling confirmed the relative power of these daimyo. Takekoshi[18] relates an episode in which merchants hid a smuggler while the shogun was trying to arrest him.

3. Many shogunal decrees were repeated time and again, an indication that they could not be enforced. Fearing the corruption of the samurai, the shogunate issued numerous decrees against marriage for money. To preserve the system of the samurai, many times it pronounced these offices hereditary; sons were required to assume them. Decree after decree outlawed rice speculation. Takekoshi[19] describes the abundant ways in which the mer-

chants outdid the shogun in maneuvering around his orders. "In spite of the Shogunate issuing countless statutes prohibiting the combination of merchants and tonyas [guilds], when we note these underhand methods of the business men, we cannot but realize their ingenuity and the power of wealth."

4. The shogun attempted repeatedly to establish a gold standard instead of a silver one, when the latter was more popular in the trading center of Osaka. Often he failed. An attempt at a bimetallic standard in the 1760s failed because the shogun did not have the officials to enforce it and because he tried to fix an exchange rate in favor of gold, while merchants traded these precious metals at market price. A new coin issued by the shogun failed despite threats of punishment for those who would not accept it. Nor did the shogun succeed in suppressing private coinage, so that he might profit more readily from debasement.

5. When ordered by the shogun to open an office in Yokohama to keep trade in Japanese hands, the Mitsui house at first refused.[20] Finally, in compromise, it opened a branch there.

6. Many peasant rebellions were settled on terms the shogunate would not have favored. Between 1765 and 1800 the shogun tried to institute a uniform system of punishments for peasants. But his law was repeatedly broken.[21]

7. The shogunate had little military power west of Osaka.[22]

8. The custom of primogeniture, which had become law, strengthened the power of the house (family landownership) while also sending younger sons to the cities where they enhanced the power of guilds. Increases in the power of both house and guild decreased relatively the power of the shogun, who was often their adversary.

9. Many of the price controls declared by the shogunate were ignored. For example, in 1742 a number of decrees were issued, but prices continued to rise.[23]

10. The ninth Tokugawa shogun, Iyeshige (r.1744-63), was a paralytic who had difficulty speaking. That he was allowed to take office shows that the shogun was by then a figurehead.[24] Many shoguns thereafter were personally weak.

Other references to the weakening power of the Tokugawa shogun are found in Bix 1986:109; Hall 1970:167, 206; Takekoshi 1930:125, 354, 363, 499; and Wigmore 1969:90.

Appendix 4.1: Historical References to Vertical Alliances and the Use of Leverage by Groups in Europe other than Peasants

1. In 1376, the English House of Commons, previously an institution only to collect taxes, gathered its political forces to attack the idea of purveyance, or the king's right to commandeer supplies while traveling. In doing so, it sought the support of the House of Lords, which contained a rival faction to John of Gaunt, the power behind the throne. The complaint was soon intermixed with charges of corruption. In this interchange, parliament established its ability to impeach officers of the crown.[25]

2. "Every town [in western Europe] had a putative lord —a king, count, bishop, or pope —and these figures, maintaining some tenuous or quite real rights in the town, were hence in the enviable position of entertaining appeals against the tyranny of the commune. For example, a guild might make an end run around the town government and attempt to secure justice or recognition from the lord."[26]

3. De Tocqueville observed that "by reason of the political freedom obtaining in England, the aristocracy and the lower orders were obliged to maintain contact with each other so as to be able to join forces if and when the need arose. [This demonstrated] the skill with which the English nobility, in order to safeguard their position, were quite ready, whenever it seemed advisable, to fraternize with the common people and to profess regard for them as equals."[27]

4. "Urban guilds tried to enhance their prospects by attacking rural industry, but rural townspeople and villagers were capable of finding allies of their own, occasionally the count of Flanders, to defend their right to make a living."[28]

5. Tuchman tells how, in the fourteenth century, the petty bourgeois on the one hand and the masters and merchants ruling in French towns on the other would appeal to the working classes for support in their struggles with each other.[29]

6. In medieval towns, popular participation by all groups tended to be valued by any one group, whether rich or poor, since the hard-won liberties of the commune could be sustained only by the harmony of all classes within it. Black[30] cites Clemens Jaeger of Augsburg, who wrote about 1500-61: As "God gives his graces to rich and poor alike, using both as overseers of his church, so too is it only just that, 'following God's ordinance in regard to vocation to city government,' all those endowed by God with 'understanding, wisdom, and honesty' should be eligible for office."

7. Nevertheless, Jews were often discriminated against in those towns. Frequently, however, they would call upon the crown or the pope to support them against the oppression of the city government.[31] Jews were also defended in court cases by Christians whom they had treated honestly and reasonably.[32]

8. The Merchant Adventurers bargained with both Antwerp and Bergen-op-Zoom at the turn of the sixteenth century, to locate in the city that offered it more privileges.[33]

9. Mary I of England (r.1553-58) gave more latitude to parliament, increasing its prestige, in order to gain support for her proposed (but unsuccessful) reconciliation with the pope.[34]

10. Promises of official recognition of the Scottish Presbyterian Church were made by both sides in the English civil war (1640-49). The sweeping reforms accepted by Charles I included limitations to his own power in Scotland. Parliament agreed to reforms in English church government favorable to the Scots.[35]

11. When the Estates General met in Versailles in 1789, in the months preceding the French Revolution, a first question was whether the three estates would vote separately, so that the first two (nobles and clergy) might outvote the third (commoners), or whether they would vote by head, with the third estate holding an amount of votes (six hundred) equal to the other two combined (three hundred each). With only a few defections from the other two estates, the third might win a vote. Louis XVI favored the former. But the latter was agreed upon after parish priests had supported the third estate against the more privileged.

12. Dennis Smith[36] attributes Birmingham's lead over Sheffield in post-industrial-revolution economic development to its more complex pattern of shifting alliances and the more sophisticated way in which organized interest groups negotiated with each other.

Appendix 4.2: Historical References to Power Enhancement through Bargaining by Weaker Groups in Europe without Use of Leverage

1. In England, the House of Commons, with some support from the Lords, refused to pass a subsidy to finance the Hundred Years' War in 1376 until the king redressed 146 grievances.[37] The war was considered a project of the king rather than a vital emergency affecting all citizens.

2. In England and the Netherlands, and later in France, trading agglomerations increased the power of entrepreneurs relative to nobility and kings. Merchants of the Staple and Merchant Adventurers carried elements of

sovereignty on to the European continent. Companies such as the East India Company did the same in the sixteenth century and thereafter. The goods they could bring to the upper classes, such as tea, and the service they provided in war, such as piracy against Spain in the sixteenth century, brought them greater prestige and bargaining ability. The growth of financial institutions further decentralized economic power.

3. "In France [in the seventeenth century], there were limits to the burdens which peasants would bear without revolting and to the amount the crown could squeeze out of its officials without seriously disrupting tax collections and law enforcement. . . . In England, the king could not press JPs and militia officers too hard, or he would meet obstruction and resignations from office. The collection of money, especially ship money, depended on taxpayers' willingness to pay."[38]

4. Although the French monarchy was well centralized by the time of Louis XIV (r.1643-1715), nevertheless he was neither capricious nor absolute. France then enjoyed many federal principles, for outlying provinces retained their own customs. "Having issued its orders, the [king's] council often found difficulty in having them obeyed. Local officials delayed and equivocated; the intendants tried to make them act, but they could not be everywhere."[39]

5. By the seventeenth century, the power of local *parlements* (which combined judicial and administrative functions) was entrenched in France. By the eighteenth century, orders passed on by the king to local authorities were increasingly ignored, and the *lit de justice*, earlier a principal form of issuing such orders, fell into disuse.[40]

6. Governmental offices were often sold to replenish the state treasury, especially in France. However, each time this occurred the king would lose a little power to the officeholder. He no longer could hire and fire at will, for if he fired someone who had bought an office, the process would lose credibility.[41]

7. Before the nineteenth century, European governments from time to time substituted regular taxation for arbitrary exactions. Almost always this happened at the behest of the bourgeoisie, sometimes in armed revolt. Rarely did it occur on the volition of the government.[42]

Appendix 5.1: Historical References to Vertical Alliances, Negotiation, Cooperation, and Compromise in Economics and Trade in Europe

1. The compromises of Edward I included the Statute of Quia Emptores (1290), which allows free alienation of land but prevents subinfeudation. Hence the new tenant becomes a vassal of the original lord and not, as heretofore, the vassal of the lord's vassal. Thus the feudal chain is not lengthened. This was a positive-sum move, wanted by both king—to keep better track of his vassals and his taxes—and the barons, who did not want intermediate responsibility for lands they had passed on to others. This law, according to some historians, facilitated the subsequent demise of feudalism, although the parties who drew it up had not so intended.[43]

The Statute of Merchants (1285) was a compromise between the interests of parties to foreclosure. Although a merchant would receive seisin (a medieval term implying rights similar to ownership) over lands of a debtor in bankruptcy, the debtor might still arrange for the subsequent sale of these lands, provided he compensated the merchant (creditor) for improvements in the meantime. This law would protect both the debtor, who might fear that the land would be sold at a price no greater than his debt, leaving no residual compensation for him, and the creditor, whose claims would be satisfied to the full extent of the land value. Historians attribute these achievements mainly to Edward's advisors, and particularly to Burnell, his chancellor. When Burnell died in 1292, this period of creativity came to an end, and the latter part of Edward's reign (1292-1307) saw a return to destructive warfare that nearly crippled the monarchy. I have described the negotiations and compromises in these and others of Edward's land laws in greater detail in an earlier writing.[44]

2. Large-scale production and wholesaling in the thirteenth century required pooling of products by cooperating masters.[45] Evolution was step by step: they did not jump at once into large companies of unified management.

3. Edward III "established a harmonious relationship with his nobility, who eagerly joined his enterprises, and the Commons in Parliament, to whose self-importance Edward pandered in taxation and legislation."[46]

4. In sixteenth-century England, new leaseholding arrangements forged a partnership between "innovating landlords" and "innovating tenants." Tenants demanded and received greater proportional shares in income as a price of their participation.[47] "[I]n particular, the displacement of the traditionally antagonistic relationship in which landlord squeezing undermined peasant initiative, by an emergent landlord/tenant symbiosis brought mutual co-operation in investment and improvement."[48] In historical accounts of the agricultural revolution, the role of landlords has probably been exaggerated and that of tenants underestimated.

5. "Since they had to live together, the Dutch towns [in the seventeenth century] could not escape the need for joint action. 'Their interests,' as Pieter de la Court says, 'are intertwined one with another.'"[49]

6. The Union of England and Scotland in 1707 was negotiated after a crisis precipitated by England. The Aliens Act of 1705 provided that the Scots would be treated as foreigners and subject to import duties unless they agreed to the Hanoverian succession, which would produce George I as king of a united country in 1714. Both sides agreed, presumably to their mutual benefit.

Appendix 5.2: Historical References to Vertical Alliances, Negotiation, Cooperation, and Compromise on Jurisdiction and Power in Europe

Gilles (1986:82-83) shows how the relationship between parlements and king was worked out in France. Tuchman (1978:298-99) writes of the compromises between England and France in the Hundred Years' War. Many compromises went into the formation of the Swiss Confederacy (Holborn 1959:51). Elizabeth I made many compromises concerning religion and other political matters (Miller 1987:18). European wars of the seventeenth and eighteenth centuries were increasingly resolved by compromise.

Twenty-five specific references follow.

1. The English civil war between Stephen and Matilda ended in a compromise treaty in 1153, by which Stephen would remain king for life, but Matilda's son, Henry, would become his heir. (Matilda had died in 1151.)

2. Despite the increased power of the barons relative to the English king and their temporary renouncement of allegiance, Magna Carta was an exercise in which barons, ecclesiastics, town burghers, and King John (r.1199-1216) all participated, each group to defend its own interests. Stephen Langton, Archbishop of Canterbury, was a principal advisor to the barons, but his main aim was to protect the interests of the church while also preserving royal prerogative.[50]

3. In 1216, the barons chose William Marshall, earl of Pembroke, as regent for the young Henry III. He "had already served under three English kings, and he enjoyed the confidence of Guala, the papal legate, who worked closely with him in a program designed to [end] civil war. . . . A generous amnesty brought disaffected subjects back to their allegiance to the crown. Within a year William had persuaded Louis of France to give up all hope of obtaining the kingship of England and to return to Paris."[51]

Momentarily, it seemed that both barons and king were satisfied. By 1260 several barons had defected from their leader, Simon de Montfort, who wanted to continue the assault upon the king. However, the Provisions of

Oxford affronted Henry's majesty. Taking advantage of baronial disunity, he stopped enforcing them, and in 1260 the pope absolved him from having to do so. Unwilling to accept the Papal decision, the barons restored the Provisions in 1263, and the civil war continued. Louis IX of France (later St. Louis, noted for his fairness) was called on to arbitrate the quarrel. In the Mise of Amiens of 1264, Louis annulled the Provisions of Oxford and restored the full authority of the king.

The barons were defeated and Simon killed in 1265. Naturally, the ensuing settlement favored the king. Persuaded by Edward's uncle Richard and other advisors to be moderate, however, Henry and Edward did not press for the baronial humiliation they might have wanted. The rather mild Dictum of Kenilworth, which finally repealed the Provisions of Oxford, reflected "a concern for the proper administration of the law, the proper use of royal writs, and the appointment of disinterested judges."[52]

4. Despite the fact that he had defeated Henry III of England militarily, Louis IX of France compromised with him in the Treaty of Paris in 1259. Henry renounced his claims to Normandy, Maine, Anjou, Touraine, and Poitou but kept his title to lands in Guyenne.

5. The thirteenth and early fourteenth centuries are known as the eras of French centralization, with sovereignty over the provinces assumed especially by Philip II (r.1180-1223) and Philip IV (r.1285-1314). But from Philip IV on, we sense a tension over jurisdiction between king and local authorities, both nobility and parlements.

In principle, the ancient precept prevailed: "What pleases the prince has the force of law." But in fact, power was shared through various devices. The king might issue an ordinance that the local authorities would register but not enforce unless the king came in person to request it. A parlement might declare a royal regulation "incomplete," to be implemented only when "completed" locally. Thus the nominal powers of the king, local nobility, and parlements were worked out informally on the basis of the relative real power of each. Since none of these wanted a violent showdown —although that occurred from time to time —each ended up respecting the others. The result was a compromise not ratified formally but informally allowed to evolve:[53] again a free market in institutions.

6. Many times during the Hundred Years' War, the British and French negotiated. Tuchman[54] describes an unsuccessful effort in 1377: "Offers and counteroffers and intricate bargains were discussed concerning Scotland, Castile, Calais, a proposed new dynasty for Aquitaine under a son of Edward III who would renounce his ties to England, or failing that, a partition, or an exchange of fiefs as complicated as a game of jackstraws. As always since the war began, nuncios of the pope added their intensive efforts at mediation."

7. Tuchman[55] tells how the Austrians compromised with the Sire de Coucy of France: they signed a treaty "by which they ceded to him the fief of the deceased Count of Nidau, including the town of Buren, in return for his renouncing his other claims."

8. She also writes of another compromise between Coucy and the Habsburgs: "In . . . 1385-86, Coucy attended the wedding at Dijon of his Habsburg relative and recent enemy. . . . [I]t may be that Coucy's presence at Dijon was connected with the Habsburgs' desire for his support. In any event, his quarrel with his mother's family was apparently made up. 'They ended always by accommodating,' in the words of the discoverer of the document."[56] Already we see a shift from conflict over who has the power toward a concept of power sharing.

9. When Genoa and France jointly attacked the Barbary Coast in 1390, during the Great Schism, which papal representative should bless the departing fleet? Genoa recognized one pope, France the other. So two priests officiated, one representing each pope.[57]

10. The formation of the Swiss Confederacy required numerous compromises. One example among many: In 1491, Zurich and Lucerne opposed the admission of Friborg and Solothurn, which was favored by the other cantons. Civil war was threatened. The compromise, worked out by "Bruder Klaus" (Nikolas von der Flühe) affirmed the sovereignty of member states, with a renewal of contract every five years and other provisions. Under these terms, the admission of the two states became acceptable.

11. "The Swiss ruled themselves by councils [in the sixteenth century], in war as in peace. No single general commanded the Swiss armies, but the captains of the individual units would go into a huddle before issuing the orders of the day."[58] This cooperation was precarious, however. For almost three centuries after Zwingli's death in 1531, religion so divided them that the confederation nearly fell apart.

12. To settle the wars of the Roses and unite the warring houses, Henry VII, Lancastrian, married Elizabeth of York in 1486.

13. Elizabeth I of England offered an alliance to Ivan IV of Russia "only if Ivan agreed to attempt third-party mediation of disputes before hostilities were declared—'thinking it requisite,' she wrote in a letter, 'both in Christianity, and by the law of nations, and common sense not to profess enmity, or enter into effects of hostility against any prince or potentate, without warning first given.'"[59] She was thinking in particular of Ivan's war with Sweden. But Ivan refused the offer.

14. "For much of Elizabeth's reign, the reality of government was not too removed from this ideal image of harmonious cooperation. In its dealings with local governors, the council showed tact and a willingness to listen and to change its mind."[60]

15. Despite military victories over Austria in the War of the Polish Succession (1733-36), Cardinal Fleury of France (allied with Sardinia and Spain) proposed a compromise peace, to avoid possible intervention of England and Holland on the side of Austria. The French objective was met: that Lorraine be given to Stanislas Leszczynski, father-in-law of Louis XV, in compensation for relinquishing his claim as king of Poland. Lorraine would be ceded to France upon his death. France agreed to the Pragmatic Sanction of Charles VI, that his daughter Maria Theresa would become heiress to the Habsburg lands. Austria received Parma and Piacenza in compensation for Naples and Sicily, which it ceded to Spain. Francis Stephen, now displaced from Lorraine but soon to become the husband of Maria Theresa, became Grand Duke of Tuscany. Augustus II of Saxony, the Austrian and Russian candidate, became king of Poland. This agreement illustrates the complex compromise, which was becoming more usual in Europe. It contrasts with the simple occupation of territory by the victor.

16. In the Declaration of Breda in 1660, Charles II issued a general pardon, to relieve the fears of parliamentarians and others who had opposed the king. He did not immediately reclaim crown or church lands that had been sold after the civil war; their settlement would be left to parliament. He also promised religious liberty.[61]

17. By the end of the seventeenth century, the British king could achieve little without the cooperation of parliament. "Wise kings had always operated within the limits imposed by the need to maintain the co-operation of their leading subjects; now the need for that co-operation became more obvious."[62] Dickering behind the scenes between William III's ministers and members of parliament was common.

18. By contrast in foreign relations, the British demanded the politically impossible of Louis XIV of France: that he withdraw support from his grandson Philip as king of Spain, to end the War of the Spanish Succession in 1709. This confrontational position was widely criticized at home, an indication perhaps that the British public was more prone to compromise in international affairs than was its government. But the new Tory government that began to negotiate peace in 1710 agreed that Philip V would remain king of Spain provided the French Bourbons would renounce any further claims on the Spanish crown. In return, Philip would renounce, for himself and descendants, any claim to the throne of France.

19. The treaties of Utrecht (1713) and Rastatt (1714), which affirmed this agreement, were one grand compromise in which complex exchanges of territories took place. Most important among these, the Spanish Netherlands (now Belgium) was given to the United Provinces (now Netherlands), to be

passed on to the Habsburg emperor, Charles VI, as soon as he agreed to set up a "Dutch barrier" to protect the United Provinces from invasion, and to continue closing the River Scheldt, to reduce competition with Dutch cities.

20. In re-forming political units in France after the revolution, the controversy lay between départements drawn in rectangular blocs each with a capital city within a day's journey by horse from any interior location versus the ancient provinces. Those in favor of the former argued that for a clean slate: delegates from départements should represent the nation, not the special interests of centuries. Those for the latter wanted to preserve local cultural ties and languages. The compromise was to form départements but to draw boundaries that would respect, as far as possible, provincial and other historic lines of demarcation.[63]

21. The Peace of Campo Formio (1797) was also a compromise, albeit in France's favor. Austria ceded its Netherlands (now Belgium) and Lombardy in exchange for Venice and Venetia. Secretly, the entire left bank of the Rhine was promised to France, except for Prussian possessions.

22. The Congress of Vienna (1815) was Europe's crowning effort in complex compromise. France had been defeated, but it had not lost all power. Instead, Tallyrand was skilled in playing upon the divisions of the victors to acquire reasonable terms. Compromises were possible because all delegates wanted a balance of power, or a "Concert of Europe," for peace managed by the great powers. Castlereagh of England proved to be a consummate mediator.

23. The Congress of Vienna also decided that Neuenberg, which belonged to the king of Prussia, should become a member of the Swiss Federation even though the king remained sovereign. For the moment, Prussia seemed content. In 1852, however, royal supporters in Neuenberg were defeated in an attempted coup and were imprisoned. Prussian King Frederick William IV demanded their immediate release and threatened invasion. In a compromise of 1857, he gave up all his rights except claim to a shadow title, and his supporters in Neuenberg were amnestied.[64]

24. Besides sovereignty, the two major Irish grievances, early in the nineteenth century, were that Catholic peasants were paying heavy tithes to an official Protestant Church, and that many Catholic farmers were tenants of wealthy English Protestant landowners. The first was overcome by the disestablishment of the Irish (Protestant) Church in 1861. Gladstone's early compromises on the second grievance dissatisfied both the Land Leaguers on the one side and Queen Victoria and the House of Lords on the other, though the latter two finally yielded.

The debate over Irish Home Rule and the "Irish Land War" combined intransigence and compromise throughout the nineteenth century but finally ended in peaceful settlement. Repeal of the Union had become an almost holy cause for members of Young Ireland, with intransigence on both sides. Nevertheless, "O'Connell was prepared to compromise with the British government and seek more modest, but more obtainable objectives than repeal."[65]

Charles Parnell, Irish Member of Parliament, alienated the hard-line Fenians by cooperating with Gladstone to hammer out new land laws promising improved rights for tenants. But ownership became overwhelmingly Irish only after the Land Act of 1903, by whose terms English landlords were bought out and their properties sold to Irish tenants at prices attractive to each, with the government subsidizing the difference and lending money to the purchasers.

Home rule came in 1921 after some violent skirmishes often called the Irish war. Final resolution is still evasive, however, for violence continues in northern Ireland. Here it resembles earlier European history, in which religion blended with mistrust and the search for power: belief that a proper society demanded sovereignty for one's own group.

25. Many of the military compromises in Europe occurred as a result of exhaustion, when no side could win. Then only negotiated settlements were possible. The Peace of Cambrai ended the Italian Wars in 1517, with Francis I of France, Emperor Maximilian, and Charles I of Spain agreeing to settle their differences and undertake a crusade against the Turks. In the French-Habsburg Wars, impending bankruptcies brought both sides to the negotiating table at Cateau-Cambrésis in 1559, which stabilized relationships among European states until the next century. But the Thirty Years' War repeated the exhaustion, calling for new negotiations at Westphalia in 1648. The wars of Louis XIV (Devolution, Dutch War, League of Augsburg, and Spanish Succession) also ate into the social and economic fabrics of Europe, requiring the treaties of Utrecht and Rastatt, also complex compromises. By 1739, however, the lessons had been forgotten again, and a new round—the wars of Jenkins' Ear, Austrian Succession, and Seven Years'—repeated the history of exhaustion and compromise. Yet all these wars and all these treaties contributed to the shift in philosophic emphasis from simple conquest to complex compromise, which was so manifest in the Congress of Vienna.

Appendix 5.3: Historical References to Negotiation, Cooperation, and Compromise on Religious Questions in Europe

During Stephen's reign (1135-54) in England, ecclesiastical courts had assumed jurisdiction which under Henry I had belonged to lay courts. In an effort to return to the former balance, Henry II issued the Constitutions of Clarendon of 1164, affirming royal rights over the church. While many historians believe he overshot his mark, and while these constitutions were a principal cause of the break between Henry II and Thomas Becket, nevertheless they contained one element of compromise. Disputes over whether land had been granted in church or lay jurisdiction would be decided by a jury.

The roles of priests were constantly under dispute. Gratian examined the arguments, pro and con, on whether priests should read profane literature. In compromise, he concluded that they might read it for instruction but they should not enjoy it.[66]

To heal the Great Schism of 1378-1417, the Western Church called on the conciliar theory of earlier writers such as Marsilius of Padua and William of Ockham, according to which a general council of the church has greater authority than the pope. The Council of Constance in 1414 dismissed one pope, received the resignation of another, and deposed a third, thus preparing the way for compromise reunification of the church under a single pope.

Elizabeth I's Religious Settlement of 1559 "preserved the traditional system of church government, based on bishops, and introduced a form of worship somewhere between Catholicism and full-blooded Protestantism."[67] Elizabeth feared that Catholicism might challenge her authority as it had the sovereigns of France and Holland. All English were required to attend Anglican services, but Catholics might avoid this by paying a one-shilling fine. Otherwise, they were left alone, and they might conduct mass privately.[68]

Although James I (r.1603-25) insisted on religious conformity with himself as head of the church, nevertheless he was relatively tolerant of other faiths. His "declared intention was to heal divisions and to avoid extremes, which was seen most clearly in his ecclesiastical policy. . . . For most of his reign, the church enjoyed an unaccustomed peace, as James held the balance between its disparate elements."[69]

In 1610, a coalition of England, France, and the Netherlands was poised to oust the Habsburg rulers of Julich-Cleves in Germany. The threatened opposition by the Catholic League would doubtless have meant war. But the death of Henry IV of France enabled his widow, Marie de Medici, to reverse his plan to invade Spanish Milan. Instead, she sought compromise and peace with Spain, and the war was avoided.[70]

The Netherlands became tolerant of religious diversity because "it was compelled to be tolerant, obliged to take all the men it needed, from wherever they came."[71] Only thus would such a small nation acquire a sufficient labor force with the skills to compete economically with the powers surrounding it.

Sweden's alliance with France in 1631, during the Thirty Years' War, required Protestant Gustavus Adolphus to agree that the Catholic religion would be protected wherever it was found in conquered territories.[72]

In the 1790s, the Irish used England's war with France as a lever to move toward civil and political rights for Catholics ("Catholic Emancipation"). Various concessions were made during the decade. A severe Irish rebellion in 1798, along with a French invasion, persuaded Pitt that the two kingdoms should unite.[73] The Irish agreed, on condition of full emancipation. Union was effected in 1801.

Appendix 7.1: Historical References to Africa as a Trading Continent

1. "[T]he organization of the more northerly West African peoples was not solely tribal [in the fourteenth century]. They had considerable towns and cities that were supported by a developed agriculture. They had organized networks of markets and trade and a developed system of monarchical government."[74]

2. West African monarchies discovered by the Arabs of the tenth century were located not in the well-watered Niger Valley or Lake Chad but north of these in less hospitable territory. This observation would "suggest that the evolution of these monarchies was the influence of long-distance trade."[75]

3. "The Keita clan [later royalty in Mali] seem originally to have been traders from lower down the Niger."[76]

4. In the Aksumite Empire, second through ninth centuries CE, "the intense maritime traffic in the southern Red Sea . . . brought ships of all origins to Ethiopian ports."[77]

5. Whereas Iraq and Tunisia had been flourishing centers for trade both within the Muslim world and with European countries, during the Fatimid dynasty (969-1171) Egypt became the commercial hub for the Mediterranean and the East.[78]

6. "[A]lthough the Latin West closed the Mediterranean to them, the Moslems of North Africa were able to compensate by expanding trade and contacts along Saharan caravan routes."[79]

"7. African societies to the north of the river had been trading directly with coastal merchants in ivory and other products at various locations along the Zambezi since about AD 1400."[80]

"8. Takrur, Ghana, and Gao . . . became commercial entrepots and political centres [by the fourteenth century]. Their rulers endeavored to extend their authority in order to achieve an effective control over trade."[81]

9. "Between the 11th and 15th centuries some 37 new towns were founded along the [Sofala/Kilwa] coast, and there were trade routes between the coast and the gold-producing areas of Penhalonga and Inyanga in present-day Rhodesia [Zimbabwe]."[82]

10. "Linked by the Niger waterway, Timbuktu and Jenne had developed simultaneously as important centres of trade and Islam [in the seventeenth century]. . . . Jenne was the hub of an extensive network of trade routes."[83]

11. "[S]everal rulers in the central Sudan [in the seventeenth century showed] a concern for the proper organization of trade—weights and measures, regulation of markets, and policing of roads."[84]

12. "Foreign commerce, particularly across the Sahara, was in every period of great importance. . . . From the Fezzan, corn and dates supplied Ghadames and the mountains beyond on the way to Tripoli; dates from Kawar went south. Raiding supplemented trade."[85] Great pilgrimage caravans from West Africa to Mecca via Egypt were elements of this trade.

13. "[The Fezzan in the seventeenth century] was a junction of many trade routes across the Sahara. . . . [It] was also a granary for parts of the barren hinterland of the *Maghrib al-Adna*."[86]

14. "[T]he Arabs, while they lived on the [eastern] coast [in the seventeenth century] and organized their business in the ports, were yet dependent on caravans which they sent inland for supplies of gold, ivory, and all the other goods which they needed for export."[87]

15. "Accra policy at this time [about 1600] was directed to creating for themselves a middleman role in trade between the European merchants on the coast and the 'Akanist' traders from the interior, by confining the former to the beaches while preventing the latter crossing the northern border."[88]

16. "[The orientation of the coastal city states in east Africa in the sixteenth century] was exclusively seaward, dependent equally on Asia and the Near East for their manufactured goods—and for the markets which had called them into being as entrepots on the African coast."[89]

17. " [T]he trade with Bornu [in the seventeenth century] was so lucrative that the Pasha of Tripoli was anxious to secure a personal monopoly of it."[90]

18. "The internal circulation and consumption of African mineral products [about 1600] continued to have a wide economic significance, sometimes supporting exchanges over enormous distances."[91]

19. "[L]ike the Dyula of West Africa, . . . these explorers [Yao, Bisa, Tsonga, Kamba, and Nyamwezi] began to construct great commercial arteries [in the seventeenth century]. In the nineteenth century, these were to be uti-

lized first by Arabs and then by Europeans, but again the vital initiative had come in this earlier period not from outside Africa but from within."[92]

20. "Numerous markets were dotted all over the Aja [Yoruba] region. Some four or five miles outside the town of Ba, there was a daily market which attracted residents from all over Allada, who brought a variety of commodities for exchange. Nearby, a major fair was held every four years for dealers in salt, some of which was transferred to Oyo."[93]

21. "Iboland was dotted with four-day and eight-day markets. . . . River ports . . . gained their reputations in the period when they served as staging points for a commerce that was externally oriented. However, their first stages of growth pre-dated their massive involvement with European trade."[94]

22. Loango, in the seventeenth century, "had an important market at its inland capital, and the peoples of the [central Atlantic] coast appear to have been active traders before the Europeans arrived on the scene. Their economy was already partially geared for marketing and export."[95]

23. "One can reasonably suppose that by the latter half of the seventeenth century the long-distance trade paths [in the Lunda Empire, central Africa] were beginning to carry such foreign merchandise as European hardware, Brazilian alcohol and tobacco, and Asian textiles. Many of these paths were not newly created for the purpose of foreign trade but pre-dated the arrival of European and Indian manufactures from Luanda."[96]

24. In the seventeenth century, "the annual fair of Berbera [Ethiopia], attended by tens of thousands of Somali tribesmen, attracted caravans from Harar, Shoa and southern Ethiopia and merchants from Arabia and India."[97]

25. "But by 1616 . . . the Yao were already developing those impressive commercial skills which were to dominate the trade of the southern interior of East Africa until the imposition of colonial rule."[98]

26. "Trade was an important stabilizing factor in the economy of the pastoral Tuareg, and it mainly involved the exchange of Saharan salt from the agricultural products of the Sudan. The Tuareg also levied tolls on the trans-Saharan caravans in return for abstaining from attacking them."[99]

27. "Although trans-Saharan trade lost its monopoly with the opening of alternative outlets on the coast, it continued to operate successfully during the seventeenth and eighteenth centuries."[100]

28. "Throughout the seventeenth and eighteenth centuries the Xhosa had been involved in an extensive trading network, which mounted in importance as the eighteenth century wore on. Even at the end of the sixteenth century, Portuguese sources report copper ornaments worn by chiefs along the coast, and red beads from the Indian Ocean trading network had reached as far south from Delagoa Bay as the Umzimvubu."[101]

29. "A great deal of the trade oriented towards the Atlantic [in the upper Guinea coast, seventeenth century] had its origins in the deep hinterland, sometimes passing along well-established trade routes and at other times percolating slowly through the many intervening societies."[102]

30. The Lunda royal messengers "supervised caravans, escorted foreign travellers, safeguarded royal monopolies, and punished subjects who evaded tolls and tariffs. From the court's point of view they formed an efficient administrative cadre. For the people, their activities were often burdensome and even violent."[103]

31. By the beginning of the seventeenth century, Madagascar "had long participated in the commerce of the Indian Ocean, and Arab traders continued to visit the north-western coast. where they established flourishing settlements on small islands."[104]

32. "By 1750 at least, an extensive trading network and commercial system had developed around the salt works of Katwe and Kisenyi in the Lake George-Lake Edward region of what is today south-western Uganda ... a variety of other products was exchanged in a string of markets around the shores of the lakes and at inland market centres."[105]

33. "From the second century at least, Arabs from the south of Arabia and the Persian Gulf had been trading to East Africa. . . . They transacted their business in the ports and went back with the trade winds to India or beyond. By the eighteenth century, however, Arab settlers were penetrating inland, where they cooperated with Nyamwezi traders to carry ivory to the coastal ports. "With capital borrowed from the Indian commercial houses in Zanzibar, coastal traders led caravans of porters laden with a variety of goods, including cloth of various sizes and qualities, beads, copper wire, hats, guns and gunpowder, into the interior in search of ivory."[106]

34. "[In the Maghrib in the eighteenth century], marble came from Genoa for sumptuous building, tiles from Malta together with Maltese craftsmen to lay them, wood for graves and coffins from Venice—such supplies came to Tripoli, stricken with plague, even while Venice was at war with neighboring Tunis—and many other commodities."[107]

35. "Along with the intensification of ivory hunting [in the early nineteenth century] came an expansion both of the areas within which Africans traded and the scale of their commercial organization. This was particularly the case among the Nyamwezi, the Kamba, and the Shambaa. . . . By the 1860s the trade had become such an integral part of their life that porterage had even become one of the tests of manliness."[108]

36. "The Kano [Nigeria] market, in the mid-nineteenth century, was partly supplied by copper from mines south of Darfur [Sudan], carried west by traders from Wadai [Sudan]."[109]

37. "Down to the nineteenth century the distribution of incomes from foreign trade had been very uneven [in the West African states], and purchasing power had been concentrated in a relatively few, large units. With the development of exports of vegetable oils, earnings from overseas commerce began to be spread over many small units of consumption, and incomes achieved greater equality."[110]

38. "There was ... a great deal of commercial activity [in Algiers before the French occupation of 1830]. The variety of agricultural production gave rise to extensive exchanges, organized in a complicated manner. ... Particular regions had their specialties, and the production of certain textile goods was often the result of an extensive division of labour, which has sometimes been compared to a form of industrial capitalism."[111]

39. "Traders, chiefs, and lineage heads were the main beneficiaries of the growing international trade in the central Zaire basin [in the early nineteenth century]."[112]

Appendix 7.2: Historical Reference to African State Domination over Trade, Land, and other Resources

1. According to Horton,[113] African states formed through "common residence on a defined tract of land and common submission to the laws sanctioned by the spirit of the land." Thus the principles of political and of economic integration were the same, and there was no clear distinction between sovereignty over land and the right to use it as a factor of production.

2. Also according to Horton,[114] in stateless societies the "hiring of labour for large-scale agricultural operations is an option that does not arise." Nor may land be owned except by the group. Instead, economic resources are mustered by the settlement with closely-related kin. The authors term this the "segmentary lineage system," which occurs "where a society is organized from top to bottom in terms of a single, embracing genealogical scheme, and where this scheme provides the sole or the dominant principle of social organization." Given a slight change in the balance of power, the stateless society may turn into the ministate,[115] in which kinship, economic, and political organization are bound into a single entity.

3. Gold mining in West Africa began in the fifteenth century, with rulers either controlling the mines directly or taxing the independent producers heavily.[116]

4. In the Mossi states of West Africa, 1500-1800, agricultural "surpluses passed, by various forms of taxation, to the local chiefs, who were able to maintain courts, often small-scale replicas of that of the king, and to equip and train a number of their kin as cavalrymen who could be mobilized in time

of war."[117] While these surpluses covered the ordinary expenses of government, they also enabled the court both to live luxuriously and to become the principal traders.

5. "In 1750 a well-informed governor of Sena reported that the *changamire*'s subjects were forbidden on pain of death to mine gold on their own account, and the 1769 [Portuguese] embassy recounted how three detachments of his troops had been sent to punish some miners for not having reported the discovery of new mines."[118] (The *changamire* was ruler of Butua, an empire in southern Africa in the hinterland of Mozambique.) Apparently in Butua, once the royal court's needs were satisfied, no one was allowed to industrialize further, possibly to reduce any threat to the ruler.

6. "The Lozi kings [southern Africa, seventeenth century], like the Kongo kings, maintained an economic balance between the various parts of their empire. The woodland peoples surrounding the valley supplied game, hides, iron, woodwork, cloth and honey as their tribute. The valley people supplied fish, grain, baskets, and pastoral produce. The court, after consuming many of these goods, acted as the centre of exchange for the remainder. This economic role of the king was further enhanced by the distribution among his followers of captured cattle and slaves. The cattle were held on trust from him. The slaves attached to the land as serfs and were rarely, if ever, sold outside."[119]

7. "The Rozvi expeditions to Zumbo [trading center on the Zambezi, frequented by Portuguese] were *embassies* not trading caravans [italics mine], and the only permitted intermediaries in the gold trade were the *va-shambadzi*, the influential indigenous agents, even if technically armed slaves, of the traders and Dominicans at Zumbo."[120]

8. Rwanda's emergence as a kingdom at the end of the eighteenth century was accompanied by a concentration of wealth in the ruling class, "a rigid class difference, with all political power and social worth belonging to Tutsi, and the Hutu becoming little more than serfs."[121]

9. Trade was an important part of the superiority gained by Buganda over Bunyoro at the turn of the nineteenth century. "Already by the third quarter of the eighteenth century, plates, cups, saucers and glass imports were reaching the court of the Ganda king of that period, Kyabaggu; and his second son to rule after him, Semakokiro, seems to have moved wholeheartedly to exploit and expand this trade. The trade was a royal monopoly, and Semakokiro himself employed hunters . . . and then had the ivory transported to the south of Lake Victoria to be exchanged for imported manufactures, among which cotton cloth gained increasing favour."[122]

10. The northern Nguni chiefs monopolized the cattle and ivory trade in the nineteenth century, selling primarily in ports such as Durban. Because

the ivory trade required social organization, the Xhosa chiefs were able to control it in their region. But the cattle trade escaped them, because its individual nature lent itself to smaller units of production, and the land frontier with the whites facilitated smuggling.[123]

11. "The transformation of small local chiefs, constantly fighting and robbing one another, into Muslim heads of state [at the end of the eighteenth century] seems to have been encouraged by the commercial role of Bundu [on the west African coast], which lay on the route which led from gold-producing Bambuk to the European trading posts of the Gambia."[124]

12. "[I]n the later eighteenth century and early nineteenth, when Asante was at the height of its power, [the government] brought into being an appointive bureaucracy directly responsible to the king, and charged with the running of all agencies of central government: taxation and general finance, *the management of state enterprises*, the administration of the provinces, the conduct of foreign affairs, and the maintenance of internal security."[125] (Italics are mine, to emphasize that the administration of enterprises was part of a major bureaucracy.)

13. In the Lunda Empire of Central Africa in the eighteenth century, "control of the country's external economy became a central function of royal authority."[126]

14. Among the Ngonde (south of Lake Tanganyika), in the eighteenth century the ruler of the Kyungu dynasty "served as the representative of his people in the initial dealings with the traders . . . Steadily he increased his economic power through the control of the export trade in ivory and his resultant ability to distribute its proceeds among his followers."[127]

15. Hopkins writes of professional and long-distance traders, presumably nongovernment, among the Dioula and the Hausa in the early nineteenth century. But there were also "official traders, who transacted business on the part of the state. . . . [I]n Dahomey royal rights over trade were delegated to a group of quasi-official merchants in return for a share of the profits; and in the Mossi states large caravans were organized by senior officials. Public enterprise had access to the capital needed for long distance trade, and it was also in a position to secure privileges which . . . gave official traders a competitive advantage over private merchants."[128]

16. Mohammed Ali, Ottoman viceroy of Egypt in the early nineteenth century, "tried to organize the commercial exploitation of Egyptian agriculture and to concentrate it in the hands of the government. . . . His general policy was to prohibit sales to merchants and to require the delivery of all crops to government at prices fixed by government. By this means he was able to make considerable profits selling Egyptian wheat to the armies engaged in the Peninsular and other Napoleonic wars."[129]

17. For the caravans between the east coast and the interior, traders needed protection from constant banditry and slave raiding. "They had therefore [in the early nineteenth century] to reach some sort of understanding with the rulers of the African communities considered powerful enough to offer them protection. Sayyid Sai'd of Zanzibar is known to have entered into agreements with a number of interior rulers and to have exchanged gifts with them in the attempt to secure the safety of coastal caravans."[130] Surely these agreements left the African rulers with considerable power over trading movements, or the profits from them.

18. "The more slaves a chief owned [Loango, nineteenth century], the more land it was possible to cultivate and the higher his economic and social standing became. [But] the development of trade had meant that officers such as the Mafouk, who were responsible for trade negotiations, had become enormously powerful, usually at the expense of the monarchy. . . . [P]ower shifted in fact, if not in theory, to the commercial officials and slave-owning aristocrats."[131]

19. For the Tswana of the early nineteenth century: "As elsewhere in southern Africa, the chief held supreme religious, judicial, legislative and executive power over his people, and controlled trade. In carrying out these functions, he was aided by a small council of his close relations and trusted advisers, which was enlarged when necessary into a council or *pitso* of the whole nation, a feature shared also by other Sotho groups."[132]

Appendix 8.1: Precolonial Slavery in Africa

1. In West Africa of the eighteenth century: "Each household approximated to the optimum size for the conditions in which it operated. A large household could divide itself into several smaller units, though without necessarily breaking up the family too. The household was also capable of expanding. . . . Many of the 'slaves' recorded by foreign visitors may have been . . . loyal, if subordinate, citizens of the state, while others, though formally of slave status, were in practice integrated into the household and were virtually indistinguishable from free men. . . . At the same time . . . some slaves were bought, sold and otherwise used like the chattel slaves of the Americas."[133]

2. Among the Bobangi in the Upper Zaire, nineteenth century: "A slave called his master 'father,' and whichever of the master's wives had been chosen to take care of him was called 'mother.' Slaves of the same age as well as freeborn children were called 'brother and sister.'"[134]

3. Chanock criticizes the tendency among Western writers to describe African slavery as benign, which he attributes to our own guilt about Ameri-

can slavery. These apologist authors "generally pointed to the slave as 'part of the family,' living happily and in terms of virtual equality with the rest of society."[135] But the real subordination lay within the family. The father was often deemed to "own" his wife and children as well as the slaves. Marrying a slave rather than a free woman would give him greater control, for a slave wife had lost the home family that might otherwise protect her against her husband's cruelty.

Instead of Africans treating their slaves as members of the family it might be equally accurate to say that they treated members of the family as slaves. As in England before the Industrial Revolution, families were business enterprises in which the distinction between member of the family and employee was often vague. Since families differed in their moral sensibilities, the treatment of a slave/employee ran the gamut from benign to cruel and despotic.

4. A husband could obtain greater rights over his bride, relatively to her original family, by paying a higher bride-price. If high enough, she was virtually his slave.[136]

5. "Slaves came into the main markets of the central Sudan [in the seventeenth century] in three principal ways: through raids and kidnaping; as tribute; and in trade."[137] They were also acquired as settlement for debt.

6. Similarly, in the Upper Zaire basin in the nineteenth century: "[T]he violent separation of a person from his lineage was accomplished in three ways: warfare, raiding, and kidnapping. Slaves were by-products of the small-scale wars that plagued the area."[138]

7. "The domestic demand for slaves, within the central Sahara and Sudan, may well have been even more of a stimulus to slave raiding than was the trans-Saharan trade [for export to the Americas]. The number of slaves in the central Sahara and Sudan was considerable. In the nineteenth century, when fairly accurate estimates first become available, very wealthy individuals in Bornu might own thousands of slaves, while people of modest means owned two or three."[139]

8. About the Chewa in Central Malawi, reported by a Chewa author: "[P]owerful lineages took advantage of weaker ones to acquire dependents. In the event of a legal dispute the weaker side would be forced to surrender a child in addition to the normal compensation in goats and hoes."[140]

9. The Lunda [in Central Africa, seventeenth century] did not lack land; they lacked people. So they raided their neighbors, not for territorial aggrandizement, but to capture slaves.[141]

10. Harms reports that in the Upper Zaire in the nineteenth century wages were sometimes paid, but only in kind, and usually for young men working for fathers or uncles.[142]

Appendix 8.2: The Transition from Slavery to Cash Labor in Africa

1. The Bobangi considered that abolition of slavery by the French in the early colonial period was theft of capital.[143]

2. Hopkins associates the end of slavery in the colonial period with the growth of export markets, such as in groundnuts and cocoa, which required greater mobility of labor.[144] But this explanation is not consistent with the fact that earlier export markets, such as in gold, ivory, cloths, and hides, which also required mobile labor, were conducted with slaves and family members.

3. Marques records a case in which free labor was converted into virtual slavery. Portuguese plantation owners in the second half of the nineteenth century hired free workers from West African countries and even China to work in São Tomé. Gradually they restricted the rights of these workers. Protests by other European powers led to a halfhearted attempt by Lisbon to correct the practice, but with little power to enforce even that.[145]

4. "The development of the market [in the twentieth century] was pushing people towards contractual relationships, the struggle for control of things —money, land, crops, cattle —rather than people. Yet there was often insufficient profit to hire labour, and farmers had to squeeze kin labour for market purposes, leading to an emphasis on traditional occupations for one purpose, at precisely the time they were being ignored for other purposes."[146]

Whether activities moved to a market economy would seem to have depended on the relative strengths of two forces: the return earned from the market versus the power of houses to retain their family and slave labor. Growth of the former may have weakened the latter.

5. Chanock describes the difficulties of shifting from a slave to cash labor system in Central Africa in the immediate pre-colonial period: "The central issue was . . . the use and control of labour in the new venture [cash cropping]. . . . The loss of control over the labour of slaves, the potential competition for male labour of the mining sector, and the gradual replacement of kinship obligations by cash payments, all meant that the mobilisation of labour resources for cash-crop farming was taking place in an unfavourable environment (though of course not all these factors were contemporaneously present in all areas). Family head producers could not respond to the market by intensifying their exploitation of slaves, and it was now harder to manipulate 'traditional' labour obligations to the increased disadvantage of younger men. . . . [Slavery] could not simply be abolished when . . . British colonialism ceased to give legal recognition to slave status. For patterns of residence, and patterns of dependence and control, were slow in changing. And even

while they are changing they remain a habitual and meaningful way in which people conceive and conduct relationships."[147]

6. The supreme chief of the Lozi resisted abolition even into the 1920s, declaring that slaves who wished to remain among the Lozi must keep their status. If they refused, they would be expelled "to places from which they had been carried off as children, and where they were now strangers."[148]

7. "Forms of servitude and consciousness of servile status continued to exist even if last-resort legal power to enforce them had been taken away. Turner found that slavery had been clung to tenaciously long after its abolition; that in the late 1920s cases in which people were trying to repurchase relatives were still continuing which were kept from the Boma [British district government], that feelings against recalcitrant slaves ran high in the 1920s and 1930s, and that slaves were being compelled to remain in their owners' villages."[149]

8. As many as 100,000 slaves, probably the world's largest slave population, are laboring in Mauritania [in 1981], according to a report under study by the United Nations Human Rights Commission.[150]

Appendix 9.1: Centralization of Power in Post-Colonial Africa and its Capricious Use (in alphabetical order by country name)

Algeria. In response to anti-government riots in 1988, President Chadli Benjedid admitted that the problem was "how to strip the encrusted 250,000 or so people who control the top of the party of their overwhelming control of every facet of power and politics."[151] In 1991, the decline of socialism everywhere had its impact on Algeria, so that Ibrahim could report "an astonishing flowering of political diversity." But when an Islamic fundamentalist movement won initial elections, the old-line parties suspended further democracy, leaving Algeria in a state of uncertainty that must have inhibited economic or entrepreneurial propensities.

However "correct" the policies may be from the viewpoint of economists, nevertheless frequent changes, with the risk that they may be reversed, reduce economic activity. Not knowing what kind of state will be formed—Muslim, Christian, or nonsectarian—or how stable it will be can also be unsettling.

Botswana. Land boards took over the traditional functions of tribal chiefs after independence.[152] The land boards themselves seem to be decentralized, however.

Equatorial Guinea. In 1979, President Francisco Macias Nguema was overthrown in a coup. He had been "widely recognized as a paranoid despot, [who] destroyed his nation's economy by expelling the entire Spanish population of 7,000 or forcing into exile about one-third of the African population."[153]

Ghana. In 1979, "soldiers demolished stalls and goods in one of the market places in this rundown capital [Accra]. . . . [T]he action was taken because the market women were selling goods at prices above those set by the Government."[154]

Ivory Coast. From its independence in 1960 until 1989, this country was looked upon as an economic miracle. The government of President Houphouët-Boigny welcomed foreign capital, mainly French, and followed liberal market policies, with a high level of economic growth. In 1989, with the decline in the price of cocoa, the internal weaknesses of his paternalistic regime were revealed. The government had vastly overspent its budget; the President had constructed a palace in his birth town[155] and the largest Catholic cathedral in the world—with his own funds, he said (where did they come from?)—and the country was heavily in debt. The Ivory Coast is a classic model of a government commanding the right economic policies but without the institutional base to hold the power groups in check.[156]

Kenya. As the third economic plan was about to go to parliament in 1974, President Kenyatta was asked at a public meeting whether the tax on taxis would be reduced. "This tax is abolished forthwith," was the President's instant reply. That week, the Ministry of Finance and Planning had to revise the fiscal projections for the next five years.[157]

Liberia. "Although the party of General [Samuel K.] Doe easily gained legal status to engage in politics, opposition parties have become frustrated in their attempts to become registered. . . . General Doe has promulgated a decree empowering security forces to arrest anyone 'found spreading rumors, lies and misinformation' about it."[158] Business executives complain that Doe's government is unpredictable in both its policies and the enforcement of laws.[159]

Libya and Morocco. Without consulting anyone else, in 1984, Colonel Muammar Qadhafi, de facto head of state of Libya, and King Hassan II of Morocco declared a federation of their two countries. The uncertainties for businesspeople and farmers—who surely pondered the effect on price controls, commercial law, and tariffs—must have been enormous.[160]

Mozambique. In 1980, President Machel complained that "government bureaucracy has paralyzed the economy."[161]

Nigeria. Pluralism does not arise in situations where one group (government) is so powerful that it may demolish all competing groups. With no competition among the powerful, weaker groups are unable to make alliances to lever their power upward. For example: "In a crackdown on dissent, the Government this year disbanded the National Trade Union Council, the National Students' Union and the National University Professors' Union. Thirty universities were temporarily closed. Journalists have been detained. Magazines have been seized."[162] Another example: According to a 1987 report, the government rejected a loan offered by the International Monetary Fund, and then adopted a "structural adjustment" program that was far more radical than what the Fund would probably have imposed.[163] Growing Islamic fundamentalism has strained religious tolerance. Fundamentalist leaders have called for making Nigeria an Islamic state and for imposing shari'a, or Islamic law, throughout the land.

São Tomé. "[T]he government, which occupies the first 10 pages of the island's 20-page telephone directory, has trouble digesting the foreign aid largesse."[164]

Tanzania. President Nyerere cited African tradition in defense of the single-party state. He mentioned "the notions of free discussion, on the basis of individual, rather than party, opinions, as being a traditional feature of African life that could be preserved in an adapted form in a modern constitution."[165] By 1962, however, the National Assembly had withdrawn all political, administrative, and judicial authority from tribal chiefs and centered it in the government at Dar es Salaam.

Uganda. With a change of government in 1987, controlled agricultural prices were boosted 500 percent.[166] Sudden changes of such magnitude must upset the economic projections of purchasers and sellers.

Zaire. The arbitrary use of power and the corruption in this almost-bankrupt country have been often reported: President Mobutu Sese Seko's palace, "Versailles in the Jungle;"[167] his speech to schoolchildren after women had demonstrated against him: if they ever saw women demonstrating, the children should "beat them, kick them;"[168] his banishment of political opponents to internal exile;[169] and many more.[170] "Corruption is rampant, and harassment, imprisonment, torture and execution have taught most Zairians not to protest."[171]

Zambia. "As Zambia's economic troubles have worsened, [President Kenneth] Kaunda has branded his critics, from churchmen to business leaders, as traitors to the country and has moved to stifle dissent. 'There has been an erosion of the freedom of the judiciary and of parliamentary dissent,' one diplomat said. "As the pressures have increased, toadyism has increased. Kaunda sees fewer people and is increasingly cut off.'"[172] In Zambia government wage scales are increased by irregularly constituted salary review commissions. . . .[173] Leading figures in the army, politics, and the economy are frequently shifted around between the nation's top posts, a maneuver that lessens political risk but prevents an accumulation of expertise.[174] (President Kaunda was defeated for re-election in 1991 and peacefully relinquished his office.)

Appendix 9.2: Citations of Recent African Wars and Their Consequences

1. The western Sahara has been an area of endemic wars among tribal groups for centuries.[175]

2. A conference of the United Nations and Africa Network on Protection against Child Abuse reported in 1987:

> The death rate of this continent's children, from bullets and preventable diseases, is soaring, and the toll exacted by conflict is felt in other serious ways: Children often lose their homes and clothing and, because of the protracted chaos, cannot attend school. Many have seen their parents killed or have been separated from their families. With anxiety and depression as uncompromising companions, they wander toward a future that seems to offer more despair than promise.[176]

3. A thriving agriculture in Angola has reverted to subsistence. "Coffee, diamond, and food production has been largely destroyed."[177] After 27 years of war, Angolans find 'peace' has lost its meaning."[178]

4. The government of Ethiopia moved "enemy" populations en masse to southern areas where presumably they would find more fertile land with rainfall. But they were not supplied with housing or agricultural implements, and many perished. The government was charged with preventing foreign relief supplies from reaching rebel areas.[179]

In addition to outright wars, a tendency toward personal violence remains in some parts of Africa, as is shown by the following list of references:

1. In the past twenty-five years, more than seventy leaders in twenty-nine African countries have been deposed by assassinations, purges or coups.[180]

2. Massacres, which have taken place for more than a century, are still frequent between Tutsi elite and Hutu peasants in Burundi.[181]

3. Violence and lack of freedom of speech are reported in Lesotho.[182]

4. Masses of Liberian refugees flee rebellion and reprisal killings.[183]

5. Continued violence occurs between Muslims in northern Nigeria and Christians in the south. "Rivalries among the country's 250 ethnic groups often parallel religious rivalries." In a conflict reminiscent of the jihads of earlier centuries, Hausa and Fulani Muslims have attacked Yoruba and Ibo.[184]

6. In South Africa, clan warfare breaks out regularly among the Zulus. Fighting between the Inkatha organization and the African National Congress is frequent.[185]

7. Ruinous violence continues in Uganda. Murders and disappearances are rife as various factions fight with one another.[186]

8. Essentially, the violence in Matabeleland [Zimbabwe] stems from tribal enmities that were translated into political terms during the long guerrilla war for independence. In that war, two guerrilla forces formed, largely but not entirely on tribal lines, often feuding and plotting. A truce of sorts was arranged on the eve of Zimbabwe's birth in April 1980 and it unraveled shortly afterward.[187]

Appendix 10.1: Historical References to Endemic Low-Level Violence in India

1. The so-called imperial Pallavas, who were believed to have dominated peninsular India by 600 CE, were, in fact, little more than plunderers, using their urban fortresses to store wealth they looted from most of Tamilnad. Their Chola rivals were equally adept at plunder, and thanks to their seafaring capability, they expanded the horizons of their predatory raids to Southeast Asia as well.[188]

2. "In southern India [in the twelfth century] the final destruction of the Chola realm by feudalized Pandya and Hosala warriors [was] a triumph of militarized, feudalized society over more peaceful elements which had characterized the preceding century . . . a divided southern India composed of a number of warring states."[189]

3. The Delhi Sultanate was probably the most powerful Indian regime to date. In 1246, Balban, one of the forty counselors of the preceding sultan, took power. "Employing assassins to poison all of his former comrades among the Forty, Balban ended his reign with no friends to remind him of his former status. . . . In his constant dependence on spies and his enhancement of the espionage arm of the sultanate, Balban was employing traditional Indian techniques, reaching back to the *Arthashastra* for prescriptions of how to retain power."[190]

4. "Two centuries of rampant military competition after 1330 increased the regional power of specialized military men" in southern India.[191]

5. Tales of the Maravas of southern India in the fourteenth century "all revolve around military competition, battles with Muslims, Kallars, and Kurumbars (hunters); and all cite authoritative grants of territory from obscure later Pandyan kings."[192]

6. "Between the fall of the Madurai Pandyas to Malik Kafur in the early 1300s and the rise of Madurai Nayaka kings in the later 1500s, rampant military competition produced political chaos in Tirunelveli."[193]

7. "Needless to say, everyone accepted violence as a legitimate means to establish authority in poligar territory, and struggles by those below to resist demands from above were constant features of order itself."[194] (Poligars were lesser royal authorities under the Nayaka dynasty in southern India, about 1600.)

8. Toward the end of the Mughal Empire (1707-64), succession struggles among the sons of each emperor led to almost continuous warfare.[195]

9. Particularly in Western Malwa and Khandesh [about 1750], it seems to have been customary for dissatisfied nobility to burn and loot *their own villages* to deny revenue to government, until their demands were met. Equally often, these local nobility took the field against the villages of a rival branch of the family.[196]

10. In Khandesh and Malwa during Mughal and Maratha times, tribes occupying the hills repeatedly raided agricultural settlements. "The country is often disturbed by Bheels, who sometimes in hundreds come to plunder the village. [T]he simplest village response was fight or flight."[197]

11. "Again in the eighteenth century, the capital [Madurai] broke open with war, as it had in the tenth, twelfth, fourteenth, and sixteenth centuries. Again armies vied for the throne. When the Nayakas disappeared as the pinnacle of authority in the regional system of tributary payments, competition ensued that altered the rules of political negotiations throughout the countryside."[198]

Appendix 11.1: Historical References to China's Despotism and Centralization of Power

During virtually all of its history, the Chinese Empire/Republic/People's Republic has kept a tight control over business enterprise, either monopolizing it, denigrating and insulting it, taxing it heavily, or organizing it centrally. The only exception is perhaps the Republic (1912-49), with even more liberalism by its successor on Taiwan. There, financial control has centered on a small number of investors rather than the government.

Out of 143 historical references that I have placed in my computer, below are a few representative, in chronological order by centuries:

1. "[T]he Western Chou kings [beginning 1028 BCE] exercised very powerful control over a remarkably wide territory. [T]he king and his officials could and sometimes did intervene in the affairs of feudal states."[199]

2. "[T]he goal of the Legalists' action [fourth century BCE] was to solve a major crisis in Chinese society, a situation of growing anarchy, by using an all-powerful State to create a social order of which the functioning would be perfectly controllable and predictable. No social mobility would be allowed."[200]

3. "The factories of Suzhou are part of the system of offices assigned to the supply of goods necessary to the life of the imperial court, and in particular of the section for the supplies of textiles and ceremonial dresses. This system goes back to the Qin and perpetuated itself under various names during the whole imperial period."[201]

4. The Yunmeng texts [third century BCE] show that "the agricultural overseer was rewarded when on the occasion of the four annual inspections the oxen used in agricultural work were in good condition, and punished if they were thin."[202]

5. In his book, *The Chinese Emperor*, Jean Lévi evokes the atmosphere in the third century BCE "of an archaic and murderous bureaucratic state that destroys the individual in its search for an impossible precision where all deviance from the state's norms will be obliterated."[203]

6. "[N]ot only was the conduct of trade in the towns bound by regulations [in the second century BCE], for instance, for the concentration of shops or the official supervision of markets; restrictions were also imposed on the free export of certain wares. . . . At the northwest frontier a sharp watch was maintained to prevent the export of contraband goods and specially controlled markets were established for dealing with foreign traders."[204]

7. "[W]ithin the urban centres, economic activity was tolerated only if strictly regulated. By the time of the T'ang Dynasty a Director of Markets, with a number of assistants, regulated the area, time, and prices of all market activities."[205]

8. "The ruler in China had the ethical right and duty, in order to secure economic justice, to intervene in the activities of the market. The urban centres (cities and towns, but not villages) were economically and otherwise fully under his control. Thus the free township, with a corporate charter and independent activity, did not arise in China. In Japan however, as in western Europe, the freedom of the market and the formation of independent corporate towns were distinctive features of feudal economic life."[206]

9. "Chu's [first Ming emperor] conception of an emperor was that of an absolute monarch, master over life and death of his subjects; it was formed by the Mongol emperors with their magnificence and the huge expenditure of their life in Peking."[207]

10. "The Hongwu Emperor (1368-98), who came from the lowest levels of China's agrarian world, did inaugurate the tone of despotism. He grew from village hunger through warlord experience to an imperial pride of universalistic style."[208]

11. The Ming and Qing imperial factories were "dependent on the ordinary tax revenue both for expenses and for the purchase of raw materials, such as yarn."[209]

12. "High officials used to sit with the emperor during the Tang; they stood in front of the sitting emperor during the Song; and they had to prostrate themselves and kneel in front of the emperor during Ming and Qing."[210]

13. In the sixteenth century "an agreement was arrived at with [Mongol ruler] Anda for state-controlled markets to be set up along the frontier, where the Mongols could dispose of their goods against Chinese goods on very favourable terms."[211]

14. Yuan (first President of the Chinese Republic, 1912) "was unprepared by experience or tradition to countenance a 'loyal opposition'."[212]

The following are twentieth-century newspaper reports of decisions made centrally in China which, in more-developed countries, would have been made largely in a free market. In China, they may have created inefficiencies in the allocation of resources or end products.

[The Chinese newspaper *Chungkuo Chingnien Pao* reported that] Peking intends to have "more and more young people" go directly to college or into jobs in factories or offices, [so that] the number to be resettled in rural areas "will inevitably diminish.". . . However, "some young people will still be settled in the countryside," at least for temporary periods.[213]

[The *People's Daily* demanded that all projects] "should be stopped where buildings will not have necessary supplies of fuel, raw materials, or water or where there will not be means of transport on completion."[214] [Presumably these projects should not have been started in the first place.]

Professor [Nicholas] Lardy says that official grain figures that showed steady growth during the 60s and 70s were misleading. They obscured the fact that peasants were ordered to concentrate on planting grain and neglected other important food, including meat, edible oils and peanuts.[215]

"[H]igh forced savings . . . were plowed into heavy industry, like steel, and produced glamorous statistics of rapid increases in the gross national product. Peking found it had neglected other important areas, especially energy, transportation, housing and consumer goods. China had millions of tons of steel that couldn't be transported and no one could use it."[216]

[Prior to 1983, the government took all the profits from state-owned enterprises, leaving no incentive for managers to improve production. To correct this condition, the government decided in 1983 to take only half the profits.][217]

A woman living with relatives in Sichuan province recalls how commune officials swooped down last year, demanding that villagers immediately buy new furniture because a foreign delegation would be passing through. In a letter to the English language *China Daily*, writer Chan Yunhao complains of officials requiring peasants to buy television sets and painting village girls with rouge and lipstick to impress foreigners.[218]

[P]rices for many Chinese products have remained unchanged since the 1950s and 1960s. Because of constant shortages, these administrative prices are generally lower than market prices would be. The gap is particularly wide for coal, iron ore, and other raw materials."[219]

[In response to rampant inflation in 1988, the government announced sweeping cuts in investment.] The current situation is a result of Beijing's success in decentralization. Given a freer hand, factory managers began investing in plants geared to growing consumer demand. . . . But central planners contend that these industries are creating bottlenecks in energy and raw materials.[220] [In another country, the factory managers might have been restrained by the interest rate. In China, only the central planners could hold them back, and only by fiat.]

Beijing announced that to save scarce resources, manufacturers of soft drink cans must immediately cease production.[221]

In a sweeping nationwide crackdown on nonstate enterprises, China has shut down more than a million rural industrial collectives and forced the demise of 2.2 million private enterprises, the Government announced today.[222]

Appendix 11.2: Historical References to the Abundance of Land, Migratory Nature of Labor, and Small Amount of Communication among Social Classes in China

1. In the early Chou dynasty, around the tenth century BCE, the territory was "enormous," with foot paths connecting settlements. Cultivation was shifting. Serfs worked on one field for a year or more and then moved to others.[223]

2. "There was [around the third century BCE], in spite of the growth of population, still much cultivable land available. Victorious feudal lords induced farmers to come to their territory and to cultivate the wasteland. This is a period of great migrations, internal and external. It seems that from this

period on not only merchants but also farmers began to migrate southwards into the area of the present provinces of Kwangtung and Kwangsi and as far as Tonking."[224]

3. In the Early Han dynasty, "institutions were found to operate sponsored agricultural settlements at the periphery of the empire."[225]

4. "To maintain itself, the central government [of the Later Han dynasty] was forced to levy increasingly heavy taxes on the dwindling number of tax-paying peasants in North China. The burden eventually became unbearable, and many peasants fled to the less rigorously taxed South or into the estates of the great landowners, where the rents were less crushing than the taxes on free peasants."[226]

5. "[Toward the end of the Han dynasty] huge numbers of Chinese, naturally, attempted to escape the depredations of the 'barbarians' and the generally chaotic conditions in North China, fleeing southward to the safety of Szechuan and the area south of the Yangtze. As a result, the Chinese populations in the South multiplied several times over between the third and fifth centuries, and the absorption of the non-Chinese peoples of the area was accelerated."[227]

6. "The massacres [9-23 CE] had so reduced the population that there was land enough for the peasants who remained alive. Moreover, their lords and the money-lenders of the towns were generally no longer alive, so that many peasants had become free of debt. . . . During the period of Wang Mang's rule and the fighting connected with it, there had been extensive migration to the south and south-west. Considerable regions of Chinese settlement had come into existence in Yunnan and even in Annam and Tongking, and a series of campaigns . . . added these regions to the territory of the empire."[228]

7. In return for armed aid, nineteen tribes of Hsiung-Nu were settled in Shansi between 180 and 200 CE.[229]

8. "So long as there was still more land potentially available than the labour that could work it," no size limit was imposed on individual holdings, in the second century CE.[230]

9. To support soldiers on duty away from home, the Later Han officials established sponsored farms, or military colonies.[231]

10. In the third century CE, "the south lay relatively open, but at that time there were few Chinese living there."[232]

11. The southern state of Shu Han, in the third century CE, did not maintain a population large enough to withstand incursions by the northern Wei dynasty. To secure manpower it raided the native tribes in present-day Yunnan. It also encouraged immigration from the north.[233]

12. During the period of the three kingdoms (220-265 CE), "a wave of non-Chinese nomad dynasties poured over the north, in the south one Chinese clique after another seized power, so that dynasty followed dynasty."[234]

13. After a general disarmament in 280 CE, "many Chinese soldiers, though not all by any means, went as peasants to the regions in the north of China and beyond the frontier." They were welcomed by the Hsiung-nu and the Hsien-pi, who needed them as farmers.[235]

14. As war raged around the capital in the early fourth century CE, "there took place a mass migration of Chinese from the centre of the empire to its periphery," which remained relatively quiet. "This process . . . is one of the most important events of that epoch."[236]

15. In the seventh century, the Tang adopted a land-equalization system developed earlier by the Toba and also used by the Sui dynasty. In this, small farms were allocated to all males between eighteen and sixty years of age.[237] Eberhard argues that the purpose of these allotments was to prevent further migration of farmers and to raise production and taxes.[238]

16. In 629-30 "eastern Turks were settled in the bend of the Hwang-ho. . . . More than a million Turks were settled in this way, and many of them actually became Chinese."[239]

17. From the late eighth century until the early eleventh, "a gradual shift of China's center of gravity [took place] toward the south and southeast, since now it was in the Yangtze valley and along the southern coasts that considerable economic expansion was taking place."[240]

18. In the early Sung period (mid-tenth century), as the army was demobilized, peasants were settled in regions depopulated by the war, or in newly opened areas.[241]

19. Many new Sung estates "came into origin as gifts of the emperor to individuals or to temples, others were created on hillsides on land which belonged to the villages. . . . Some tenants were probably the non-registered migrants, [who] depended on the managers who could always denounce them to the authorities, which would lead to punishment"[242]

20. As provincial capitals shifted from place to place during the early Sung dynasty, "a complete reorganization appeared: landlords and officials gave up their properties, cultivation changed, and a new system of circles began to form around the new capital. . . . [T]he thinly-populated province of Shensi in the north-west . . . had no large landowners, no wealthy gentry, . . . only a mass of newly settled small peasants' holdings."[243]

21. During the Liao (Kitan) dynasty in the north (937-1125), "the army commanders had been awarded large regions which they themselves had conquered. . . . [I]n order to feed the armies . . . the frontier regions were settled, the soldiers working as peasants in times of peace."[244]

22. In 1239, Southern Sung officials appointed a "high commissioner for colonization" who built reservoirs in the Hubei plain, where he settled peasants. "This is said to have resulted in the creation of 170 'domains' and 20 'colonies' . . ."[245]

23. In addition to their forces in the north, the Ming rulers kept armies in south China. To supply them, they "resorted to the old system of military colonies, which seems to have been invented in the second century B.C. and is still in use even today (in Sinkiang). Soldiers were settled in camps. . . . They worked as state farmers."[246]

24. In the mid-seventeenth century, "in spite of laws which prohibited emigration, Chinese also moved into South-East Asia." At the same time, gentry families were sending "surplus" sons to Kwantung and Kwangsi to sell Chinese products to local peoples or to new settlers.[247]

25. A great popular uprising was under way in western China when the Qing dynasty began in 1644. "[W]hen it was ultimately crushed by the Manchus the province of Szechwan, formerly so populous, was almost de-populated, so that it had later to be resettled."[248]

26. In 1655, artisans fled from Suzhou and dispersed themselves over the countryside when the state factories did not have enough funds to pay them.[249]

Beginning with the eighteenth century, references to internal migrations diminish in Chinese histories. At the end of the twentieth century, China is "totally" populated, and virtually all farms consist of only a few acres.

Appendix 12.1: Historical References to China's Legal System

State Power

1. "The purpose of legal procedures, in Western Chou times [1122-771 BCE], appears to have had nothing to do with maintaining cosmic harmony; they were designed, rather, to uphold the authority of the government and to maintain order and tranquillity among the people. These were also the ends that law, as conceived by the Legalists, was calculated to achieve."[250]

2. Creel "sees the Legalists as preaching a philosophy conducive to the construction of a centralized government over widely dispersed and diverse peoples who had yet to become a nation."[251]

3. Discovery of the Yunmeng texts in a tomb in 1975 reveals that "in the third century B.C. the Qin state possessed an extensive corpus of administrative and criminal law, handled by a complex hierarchy of officials . . . a considerable body of laws must have existed before Shang Yang. . . . The genesis of these laws will have coincided, I believe, with the creation of the centralizing and increasingly bureaucratic states in the course of the eighth and seventh centuries before our era."[252]

Criminal, Civil, and Commercial Law

1. "Chinese written law ... was basically criminal and administrative law. Large areas which fall into civil law, or trade law were never codified. Cases of this type were solved by processes of arbitration or mediation between the partners or, more often, between the families involved."[253]

2. "Foreign trade, especially the junk trade, was always extensive, ... [but] all this clandestine activity was *institutionally* illegal; hence any assertion of economic power based on this trade was an admission of crime."[254]

3. In the Qing code, "the impact of the legal system on local commerce was further limited by a general tendency in Chinese legal administration to be flexible in the application of existing laws. It was felt that achieving justice in the circumstances of an individual case was more important than rigid adherence to the letter of the law."[255]

4. "There were no statutes of any kind [on the law of sales], however incoherent. The case law was underdeveloped and, in any event, had no binding force. It was the joint product of individual traders, guild regulations, and local customs. It depended for adherence not on the enforcement power of the state, ... but rather on its acceptance by the merchants and the public. ... Because there was no national or even regional body to legislate rules, the trade practices tended to be localized geographically and to specific trades."[256]

Appendix 12.2: Some Decisions Made by the Government of the People's Republic without Much Consultation with Those Affected

"In 1949 Mao proclaimed a 'shift to the cities' and the need to learn from the Soviet example in industrialization."[257] Industrialists and farmers, who were being or were about to be displaced as owners and operators, did not bargain for this change. Indeed, they had no say about it. In 1950, "the entire fiscal administration was reorganized to give the central government control over formerly local taxes, to eliminate the handling of official funds by private banks, and generally to reduce expenditures."[258] There were no vehicles by which local governments or private banks might protest or even express their views on how their lives and economies might be affected.

In the Great Leap Forward of 1958-60, the rulers mandated communes, communal dining halls, women in the fields instead of taking care of children, and the construction of "tens of thousands of reservoirs, thousands of hydroelectric power stations, hundreds of miles of railways, bridges over the great rivers, new canals and highways, more mines, more irrigated land.

But this all-out effort at instant growth led to massive errors, such as the salinization of newly irrigated land, and a tremendous waste of manpower, which was withdrawn from agriculture."[259]

During the Great Leap, the government ordered farmers to build backyard steel mills and to operate them, even as grain lay rotting on the fields for want of harvesters.

[In] one *hsien* [county] in Kwantung province . . . 20,000 people starved to death. Nationwide, the mortality rate doubled from 1.08 percent in 1957 to 2.54 percent in 1960. In that year the population actually *declined* by 4.5 percent. Anywhere from 16.4 to 29.5 million extra people died from the leap, because of the leap.[260]

The ensuing Cultural Revolution of 1967 reflected a power contest between Mao and those who criticized him for the Great Leap and other errors. In this "revolution," students and others in the Red Guards ravaged buildings, destroyed libraries, tortured intellectuals and forced political foes into exile in the country, so they would experience how peasants lived. But twenty years later: "As mature adults, these people should be the backbone of China's modernization. But millions left school to wage revolution, and many never went back. Now, without skills or education, they watch their younger brothers and sisters leapfrog them to the top."[261]

Many more examples have appeared in recent newspapers, but space limits the number that can be cited.

Appendix 12.3: Reports of Inefficiencies in the Chinese Economy

1. The Beijing newspaper, *Kwangming Jih Pao*, described a mercury mine in Kweichow province in which skilled technicians had been relegated to menial jobs where they were not using their training; construction materials, always in short supply, had been acquired through illegal barter rather than normal purchase. Workers seeking eggs had to pass through "five layers of governmental purchasing agencies between the commune and the capital. In the process over 20 percent were spoiled."[262]

2. *Jenmin Jih Pao* reported "poor management and shoddy products [such that] of the $4 billion worth of farm machinery stored in China, one-third was unsalable because of low quality."[263]

3. "In the 1970s, Tibetans had to obey Mao Zedong's arbitrary order to 'take grain as the key link' and grow more wheat and less barley. Their preference for barley, which is ground with yak butter, tea and salt for the

traditional zampa that Tibetans eat, was ignored. So was the cold, windy climate. Winter wheat fared poorly in the high altitude. It needed too much water, used up fertilizer and leached the soil. . . . [T]ens of thousands of Tibetans were pushed to the brink of starvation."[264]

4. "Productivity remains stifled by the 'iron rice bowl,' a job tenure that pays workers however badly they perform."[265]

5. "China's factories are inefficient; over 15 percent of them lost money last year, many because of state-administered prices that don't reflect their cost of production. Meanwhile, factories that benefit from outdated pricing churn out big profits."[266]

6. "Western economists estimate that subsidies amount to 40 percent to 50 percent of government spending."[267]

7. "Enterprises commonly pay four different prices for the same raw material: one price for the 30 percent supplied by the central government, another for the 30 percent supplied by the provincial government, a third for the 10 percent supplied by the city, and yet another for the last 30 percent obtained in barter deals from customers."[268]

8. "So far, China's leaders have been reluctant to [allow] truly free decision making or prices, fearing chronic production imbalances and urban unrest over higher food prices."[269]

9. "A desperate shortage of cash has left some local governments unable to pay farmers for their crops and may force many state-owned factories to close."[270]

10. "A national austerity program has made working capital virtually unattainable. Skewed pricing policies create crippling shortages of raw materials and energy. Shifting political winds mean sharp swings in economic policy. . . . [I]t is still personal connections, not business skills, that matter most in running an enterprise."[271]

Appendix 12.4: Government-Mandated Decisions for a Freer Economy in China

Following is a list of newspaper reports on decisions made by the central government to free the economy. Although these may be the "correct" decisions for economic efficiency, nevertheless they were not bargained for by the groups concerned. Thus, the beneficiaries do not have enough power, or leverage through vertical alliances, to assure that they are not revised or violated. For reports of reversals already occurring, see the next appendix.

1. At a meeting of the National People's Congress in 1980, Deputy Prime Minister Yao Lin declared: "Regulation of the economy through the market will be carried out under the guidance of the state plan." He called for

experiments to "give expression to the principle of regulation through planning combined with the regulation of the market."[272]

2. Since taking power in 1978, Deng has "opened China to foreign technology and investment, restored family farming in the countryside, and encouraged modern management in industry."[273]

3. "Private enterprise, which is now encouraged nationwide in China, is being hampered by local authorities who have arbitrarily imposed crippling taxes on many successful small businessmen."[274]

4. "But once a producer has sold the assigned quotas at fixed prices, he is to be free to sell the surplus at flexible prices. Factories that fail to meet assigned goals are to be fined or to have their allotment of raw materials and electric power reduced."[275]

5. In October 1984, the Chinese government announced sweeping changes in economic controls. Many prices would be de-controlled. "The decision called for each plant director to assume responsibility for his enterprise and to link wage increases and bonuses to higher productivity by the workers."[276]

6. "At first, investment opportunities were restricted to four special economic zones along China's southeast coast. Last May preferential treatment was extended to 14 other coastal cities and the island of Hainan. The more backward Chinese interior has complained about being left out, so now provinces like Qinghai are being permitted to seek their own outside contracts."[277]

7. "China plans to halt state purchases of grain, produce."[278]

8. "In agriculture [in Tibet], the household had been restored as the basic unit of production and 90 percent of agricultural families have been given leases over their lands for between 30 and 50 years. This is double the most generous leases in the rest of China."[279]

9. "For the first time in the four decades of Communist rule, constitutional protection will be accorded to private enterprise and the right of people to buy and sell the right to use land in what amounts to the re-emergence of private property."[280]

10. "A law intended to strip grass-roots Communist Party committees of much of their power and concentrate decision-making in the hands of technocratic managers was approved by China's legislature."[281]

11. In 1988, Hainan Island was selected as an enclave of capitalism, experimental beyond what would be permitted on the mainland. "Private enterprise . . . is to constitute the economic underpinning of Hainan's economy. Much of the island's land will be able to be bought and sold. . . . Foreign investors . . . are to have extraordinary discretion in operating their enterprises, in hiring and firing, in repatriating profits and in negotiating con-

tracts."[282] But in an atmosphere in which the rules may be changed by the supreme power at any time, there would be some question as to whether private enterprise would respond.

12. "China is determined to adopt far-reaching reforms, including a partially convertible currency early next year, to speed its transition to a market economy, says Vice Premier Zhu Rongji, the nation's economic czar."[283]

Appendix 12.5: Reports of Reversals of Liberalizing Policies in China

1. In an emergency conference in February 1985, Prime Minister Zhao defended but then cut back "a package of liberalizing urban measures that had been hit by a wave of irresponsible bank-borrowing and corruption only months after they were announced."[284] It is not clear whether "irresponsible" and "corruption" are words of the reporter or of the government. But such statements, to throw the blame on others, are characteristic of governments that rescind decisions as soon as they run into political opposition.

2. The policy of free hiring announced in 1986 would affect only new employees. Others would fall under "an arrangement that locks workers into their jobs and has helped paralyze industry and keep China on starvation rations during the great post-World War II expansion enjoyed by so much of the rest of the world."[285]

3. In 1987, Chinese newspapers "carried numerous articles on central planning, the slowness of consumer spending and a return to the ethic of hard work and thrift—a retreat from the policies propounded by Mr. Deng and party aides known as 'reformers.'"[286]

4. "A proposed law that would prevent Communist Party officials from interfering with the operations of China's state factories and enterprises appears to have become the latest casualty in the crackdown on Western influences here."[287]

5. Chairman Peng Zhen of the National People's Congress "urged a reassertion of some traditional socialist economic practices, such as a renewed emphasis on central planning."[288]

6. "The Chinese Government, in an effort to reassert control over the country's economy, has imposed a series of stringent measures in the last week intended to reduce sharply the role of the free market and local decision-making in economic affairs."[289]

7. Prime Minister Li Peng called for the spirit of centralization to replace that of liberalization.[290]

Appendix 13.1: Historical Citations on the Ulozhenie (1649) as an Instrument of Absolutism in Russia

1. The *Ulozhenie* was "a benchmark in the transition of Russia from feudalism to absolutism."[291]
2. "*Ulozhenie* put the finishing touches on a system which made every subject of the tsar a potential victim of false accusation. This system operated on the principle that every citizen had the duty to denounce: he was legally required, under pain of 'death without mercy,' to act as informer whenever disloyal words or conduct came to his attention."[292]
3. The *Ulozhenie* "sealed the fate of the seignorial peasantry, once free renters of land belonging to members of the upper classes, and now converted into the serfs of their erstwhile landlords."[293]
4. "The 1649 *Ulozhenie* threatened with disgrace (*opala*) landholders who aliened land; persons removing taxpayers from rolls by receiving them as residents; boyars' peasants and other nontaxpaying subjects who purchased commercial establishments or engaged in trade in taxpaying settlements; and Russians who sold dwellings to foreigners in restricted sections of Moscow."[294] Disgrace constituted a legal status by which privileges of one's usual status were denied and penalties exacted.
5. "In the judicial realm, acts of private law (such as contracts of sale and exchange) as well as public law (such as convocations of synods, measures of ecclesiastical discipline, and religious ordinances issued by the patriarch or metropolitans) enjoyed the same status as acts of the tsar."[295]

This last quotation, by Raeff, might seem to indicate an equality of church, urban/commercial, and monarchical law, such as was evolving in the West. Not so. Raeff goes on to explain how "the idea of Moscow as the Third Rome, whereby the tsar, as heir to the legacy of Rome and Byzantium, claimed the legitimate right to rule [meant that] the tsar could be approached only in an attitude of fervent devotion."[296] Thus the "equality" of different laws derived only from their equal subordination to a despotic tsar. It congealed Russian society in a rigid hierarchy, a feudalism depending not on contract as in the West but on the immutable status of every person. Possibilities of vertical alliance and leverage were frozen out.

Appendix 13.2: References to Interest-Groups Arising after the Collapse of the Soviet Union

1. "Two months after they led the largest industrial walkout this country has seen since the 1920s, independent coal miners this week took the first steps in a campaign to seize control of the official local workers' union."[297]

2. "Another sign [of a lower level of fear] is the birth of genuine interest groups to defend the promised changes. These include not only the popular fronts in the Baltic and other republics, but associations of private entrepreneurs organized to protect their new niche in the Soviet economy."[298]

3. "Scores of political upstarts who triumphed in last month's elections have begun to join forces in what promises to be the first independent bloc in the Soviet Government since Lenin's time. . . . Like-minded deputies in Moscow, the Baltic Republics and elsewhere have begun forming committees, establishing links, and drafting plans to increase their leverage in the new Congress."[299]

4. "Alternative political parties have popped up like mushrooms, feeding on the decay of the communist apparatus. These parties arise in turn from the thousands of active organizations and civic clubs that have emerged in recent years. These voluntary organizations are the embryos of a civil society."[300]

5. In the Ukraine in 1989 (now simply "Ukraine"), at least three new political-action groups were formed: the Movement of Ukraine for Restructuring, by writers advocating radical change; the Shevchenko Ukrainian Language Society, to demand official status for the Ukrainian language; and the Ukrainian Memorial Society, dedicated to expose Stalinist crimes against the Ukrainian nation.[301]

6. ". . . the *neformaly*, the thousands of voluntary associations that have successfully defined the political agenda in virtually every republic and are now seedbeds for the country's emerging political parties."[302]

7. Sajudis, the leading independent reform association in Lithuania, is "an umbrella organization for dozens of smaller organizations, including a Hyde Park-like speakers' association, a temperance group and parties that go so far as to endorse a shift to democratic capitalism." It has helped form "the Lithuanian Workers' Association, a group that supports the rise of Solidarity-type independent labor unions."[303]

8. "Before the end of the Soviet Union, farmers in Uzbekistan organized to keep for themselves the crops demanded by the central government, which they sold privately in foreign markets."[304]

Appendix 14.1: Historical References to the Abundance of Land Relative to Labor in Russia

1. "Throughout the medieval period the relative abundance of all but the most suitable land, and the fact that agricultural implements could easily be made, combined to make peasant flight at least a possibility."[305]

2. "In the age of Kiev life was primitive, but there was as yet land for all and the black earth was fruitful."[306]

3. The peasants "who colonized the Northeast [about the thirteenth century] were confronted with a land of dense forests, great marshes, and many rivers and streams. So they sought out the high, dry places or the narrow open stretches that sometimes lay between forest edge and river land."[307]

4. "In those days [fourteenth century], as again recently, many Russian monks worked the land to keep themselves alive, and their efforts to find ever more remote 'wildernesses' in which to cultivate the land and lead a godly life produced a great movement of colonization."[308]

5. In the fourteenth century, "the worst tyrannies were abated by the acknowledged right of peasants to leave their masters."[309]

6. ". . . that perpetual evil of the Russian land, the physical lack of people, the disproportion of the population to the area of the enormous state."[310]

7. During the Livonian War under Ivan IV, hardships were so great that "in gradually increasing numbers, commoners had begun to 'flee the frontiers' into the wilds."[311]

8. "Individual or group flights of the serfs from their lords [in the seventeenth century] was one of the most widespread forms of peasant protest. . . . The obligation to find and return fugitive serfs to their lawful owners was placed on the state (after 1649). Thus a continuous manhunt was under way on the territory of Russia, primarily in its eastern provinces, which attracted oppressed peasants from the more densely populated areas of central Russia."[312]

9. In the seventeenth century, "Russia had some of the best land in the world waiting to be settled as soon as she could master the black earth steppe and Siberia."[313]

10. "Driven to desperation by these exactions [of Peter the Great], many peasants fled across the borders of Muscovy and villages became empty, as they had a hundred years before."[314]

Appendix 14.2: Historical References to the Authoritarian Nature of the Russian State

The Sixteenth Century and Earlier

1. The Mongol khan "ruled over many clans, and he demanded absolute and unqualified obedience from all his subjects."[315]

2. Contradicting a tradition that already had been weakening—that servitors of tsar or nobility had a right to move to other masters—in the sixteenth century, both Ivan III and Vasilii III insisted that their servitors bind

themselves for life. "If a member of the *kniazhata* [serving princes] tried to leave the service for that of another ruler he was arrested and charged with treason and apostasy."[316]

3. Berman finds that religion did dampen the autocratic character of the tsar, but not significantly. Not, it would seem to me, as much as it leavened the power of monarchs in western Europe. "[T]he religious character of the empire had a certain limiting effect upon the activities of the tsar. This was manifest in a semi-legal conception of the right of high dignitaries of the church to intercede in behalf of the victims of the tsar's displeasure or to beg the tsar to reform that which was incompatible with the Christian religion. Such intervention by the church could be made only in the form of petitions. The decision lay with the tsar and nothing of a legal character could be done to alter that decision."[317]

4. "The Muscovy tsardom established a State Orthodoxy, hostile to opposition and dissent in matters of belief."[318]

5. Ivan IV convoked a National Assembly (*Zemsky Sobor*) in 1549 to gain support for his war objectives. "But it was not democratic. . . . All of its 374 members were Muscovite officials, selected by the crown, and obliged to deliberate on subjects of the sovereign's choice. They were not there so the tsar could learn their opinions. . . . They were expected to proclaim their support and transmit the will of the government to localities."[319]

The Seventeenth Century

6. "The ease with which the extension of central authority overwhelmed all other political and social forces [in the seventeenth century] is to be explained by the frailty of local institutions and by the absence of independent ecclesiastical or social authority."[320]

7. Under Peter the Great, "the influence of the administration over economic life was gradually extended to every sector of the economy and every region of the empire."[321]

The Eighteenth Century

8. "Catherine [the Great] believed that the autocratic state had important functions; she had no intention of relinquishing or limiting her authority." Her agricultural settlements in newly conquered territories transported Russian political structures into areas of different cultures. To operate them, Russian officials had to be sent in, "strengthening uniformity and centralization in contradiction to the professed aim of furthering autonomy in local affairs."[322]

9. In the eighteenth century, imperial restrictions were placed on the number of horses a person might have, which varied according to the individual's rank.[323]

10. Government attempted to stop peasants from going into crafts, in the eighteenth century, by issuing decrees, or urban controls, or threats of punishment such as whipping. Usually these attempts did not succeed completely.[324]

The Nineteenth Century

11. "Russian absolutism was able to withstand the years of the French Revolution and Napoleon relatively unscathed."[325]

12. "The introduction of the peasantry into commercial-money relationships [was] by no means entirely welcome to the government [in the early nineteenth century], which attempted to keep them under its control, with the primacy of agriculture, and the maintenance of serfdom, or at least restriction of the pace of its dissolution, firmly in mind."[326]

13. With reference to the Russian government in the early nineteenth century, "the well-ordered police state was most successful where the government was able to harmonize the activities of a centralized bureaucracy with the work of local institutions."[327]

14. Again with reference to Russia in the early nineteenth century: "No longer is the sovereign merely a judge or ultimate arbiter. . . . He has become the active proponent of a deliberate, methodical policy, the purpose of which is to maximize his country's productive potential, increase its wealth and power, and promote its material well-being."[328]

15. "Centralization of responsibility [under Alexander I and Nicholas I] meant slowness of decision, and delays of many years were not unusual; death often provided the answer."[329]

16. "After putting down the Decembrist uprising, the government of the young Emperor, Nicholas I, energetically reasserted its control over the country. Every aspect of life in the empire was subject to close scrutiny."[330]

Appendix 14.3: Historical References to the Quest for and Concentration of Power in Russia

1. In the twelfth century, Prince Vladimir Monomakh "admonishes his children to live dangerously, . . . not to delegate power but to rule and judge in person."[331] In this, he was not much different from Western kings and princes of that time. The difference is that this type of admonition continued much longer in the East than it did in the West.

2. In the sixteenth century, the Muscovite rulers "knew that to reach their final goal they had to destroy the power of the princes and of the nobility in the lands they annexed."[332]

3. "[A] mighty—and insane—drive by the tsar [Ivan IV] to wipe out all resistance to his bid for absolute power."[333]

4. In the sixteenth century, the tsar had the power to declare disgrace (*opala*) on any of his subjects. Disgrace "could entail a variety of penalties: banishment from court, confinement to one's town residence or country estate, appointment to a distant and/or undesirable post, removal from service, loss of *mestnichestvo* standing, partial or complete confiscation of property, arrest, imprisonment, or exile, forced entry into a monastery, or execution, depending upon the person disgraced and the reasons for his disfavor."[334]

5. "In Muscovy [in the sixteenth century], rulership by divine right had managed to combine the pious absolutism of the Byzantine aristocrat with the arbitrary despotism of the Mongol khan."[335]

6. When Ivan IV wanted to marry an English aristocratic woman, he asked Elizabeth I to order the marriage. Elizabeth explained that she had no power to do so. Ivan found this incredible.[336]

Appendix 15.1: Historical References to Power of Iberian Monarchs and the State

1. "[A]ll Spanish kings considered themselves lawful heirs and descendants of the old Visigothic monarchs. Consequently, every piece of land they could take from the infidel was theirs legitimately."[337]

2. Under Ferdinand and Isabella, "feudal castles were destroyed, private wars were declared illegal, the *adelantados*, or frontier governors, were displaced, and the great officers of the crown were reduced to precise and limited functions and deprived of all influence in government and the formulation of policy."[338]

3. "The reduction of the three estates—nobility, clergy, and towns— . . . in Castile . . . was no problem, for its *cortes* were utterly dependent on the crown, which controlled their composition and even the right of representation, and summoned or ignored them at its will."[339]

4. Under Afonso V, king of Portugal, 1438-81: "Gradually, the people gave up their right to control the government or even try to advise on its acts. Gradually, the king forgot the benefits of periodical dialogue with his people. Between the two, contacts ceased to be direct and tended to rely on a developing bureaucracy alone."[340]

5. King Manuel of Portugal pleaded with the pope for the establishment of the Inquisition in 1515. "His real purpose was to secure one more weapon to achieve centralization and royal control."[341]

6. In the sixteenth century, "the Spanish system of justice oppressed its subjects pretty equally: the hand of the dynast, bureaucrat, and tax gatherer fell upon all without much distinction in that ruined and exhausted kingdom, which the riches of the Indies only succeeded in impoverishing."[342]

7. From the fifteenth century on, "Portuguese activity and commerce were stringently regulated by the crown, functioning under the monopolies of the Casa da Guine and the subsequent Casa da India established for the eastern trade."[343]

8. "The reigns of Charles V [i.e. Charles I of Spain] and Philip II are the development of this absolutism. . . . The Councils of government continued to exist, in a purely advisory capacity and knowing only what he [Philip] wanted them to know. . . . When literally everything had to be approved by the king, nothing could happen at all quickly."[344]

9. "Madrid's policy [during the dual kingdoms, 1580-1640] indeed tended to centralize administration, gradually reducing the autonomy of the various political units that made up Spain—Portugal as well as Catalonia, Aragon, Navarre, etc."[345]

10. "Thwarted in their attempt to share the legislative power with the crown, the Castilian people lost all effective mediation in the control of taxation, and they could do nothing but watch the painful process of exploitation in the interests of a policy which was hardly their own."[346]

11. The aristocracy in the sixteenth century "had surrendered its feudal role to the demands of absolute monarchy and was now content to serve the crown in the subordinate fields of war, diplomacy, and viceregal administration."[347]

12. The wool industry in the sixteenth century "was strangled by over-regulation, which tended to remove *decision and initiative* from the producer"[348] (italics mine). In *two ways*, therefore, market efficiency was impaired.

13. "The backbone of commercial empires like those of Venice, Genoa, and later Holland had always been the existence of a strong middle class of enterprising bourgeois. . . . Such a middle class . . . was lacking in Portugal. Instead of private initiatives supported or encouraged by the state, the essence of the Portuguese expansion was a state enterprise, to which private interests or initiatives were applied."[349]

14. "In 1563 Cadiz complained that rising impositions were ruining its commerce. In 1571 the *cortes* blamed the disturbing rise in prices not on American treasure but . . . 'it is due to these taxes and the high cost of all the necessities of life.'"[350]

15. "[I]t was only in the service of the state that capital could be used."[351]

16. "The Richelieu and Olivares regimes [in France and Spain respectively, early seventeenth century] were both reserving to the crown vast discretionary powers which they justified by an emergency of their own defining. It was under these discretionary powers that Paris and Madrid brushed aside the constitutional objections of parliaments and corporate bodies, raising money by every device at their disposal and bringing the most intense pressures to bear on harassed populations."[352]

17. Spanish agriculture steadily declined in the seventeenth century. "The principal factor was probably the enormous weight of taxation on peasant agriculture in Castile."[353]

Appendix 15.2: Historical References to the Quantity of Land Relative to Labor in Iberia

1. "Poor peasants from Catalonia were brought over [to Mallorca in the fourteenth century] to work the empty fields for the new overlords, at first on fairly favorable terms."[354]

2. "[T]hroughout southern and central Spain there were vast tracts of untilled land. The main reason why it was not given over to farming was that its use was monopolised by the owners of livestock, especially that of the flocks of migrant merino sheep in which Spain abounded."[355]

3. "To the sixteenth-century observer, the most striking feature of the Spanish landscape was its emptiness. . . . Much of Spain was indeed deserted, and if its land was ill-cultivated it was partly because it was under-populated."[356]

4. "[T]he dominant feature of the agrarian regime in Spain was the existence of vast latifundia, held in rigid entail and mortmain and worked by a rural proletariat."[357]

5. "To fill the vacuum created by this immense migration [of Moriscos from Granada in 1584-85], the empty lands were confiscated by the crown and offered on favourable terms . . . to colonists recruited in Galicia, Asturias, and the regions of León and Burgos. . . . [T]he Alpujarras and neighbouring coastal districts were much less peopled than they had been and thus continued to provide a problem of internal security." [358]

6. "Towards 1575-80 Castile began to experience a reversal of the demographic trend, and by 1600 depopulation was notorious. The primary cause was rural migration, which peasants attributed to 'lack of land'; some of them went to the Indies; others . . . sought their El Dorado in neighbouring towns or in Madrid."[359]

Appendix 15.3: Historical References to the Weakness
of Vertical Alliances, Pluralism and Leverage in Iberia

1. In Asturias in the tenth century, "rulers were able to maintain control over both their border fortresses and their warrior nobility, and so avoided the feudalism that took hold in northern France."[360] Without the ruler-noble division, and without contract feudalism, peasants missed the opportunity for vertical alliances and leverage.

2. Whereas in northwestern Europe the investiture controversy was settled by compromise, in Iberia it was won by the monarchy.[361] As a result the church, with its separate courts and protection, was knocked out as a contender for leverage-making alliances, in a result quite different from northwestern Europe.

3. Land taken from the Moors was doled out among their conquerors, and on several occasions after the conquest remaining Moriscos were expelled. Each time vast new land became available, but each time there was no mechanism for negotiating mutually profitable arrangements between tenants and lords.[362]

4. "While Ferdinand and Isabella distrusted the higher aristocracy and sought to curb them, they favoured and promoted the lower nobility, . . . who came to occupy an important role in the administration, the army and local government."[363]   But the upper nobility made a comeback during the period of weak monarchy, 1504-17, and the lower nobles were rejected by Charles I, who came to power in 1517. In 1520, many joined the *comuneros* (smaller merchants and manufacturers) in revolt. Upon their defeat, the lesser nobility ceased to be an important class; the merchants were ignored, and the upper nobility closed ranks with the crown. Thus a possible split among the nobility, which might have been exploited for leverage by lower classes, was sealed, and the way was paved for close relations between upper nobility and monarchy.

5. Possibilities of peasant leverage were also stifled in Valencia after the expulsion of the Moriscos in 1609, with the consolidation of upper groups. Village organizations such as those cited in chapter 4, from Hilton and others, for northwestern Europe could not arise: "The peasants had no representation in regional institutions: the lay and ecclesiastical nobility controlled two of the three estates of the *cortes* of Valencia, and they also dominated the *Diputación*."[364]

6. "[T]he united monarchy [of Spain and Portugal, 1580-1640] followed a dual policy toward the aristocracy: while reducing it to political obedience on the one hand, the crown fully ratified its social and economic predominance on the other."[365] Hence there was no possibility for leverage by peasants or merchants.

Appendix 15.4: Historical References to Guilds and Corporations in Iberia

1. "The classic medieval guild system never developed fully in Castile, where it was restricted by royal law."[366]

2. "From about 1480 Ferdinand encouraged the extension of gilds which were then stifled with a surfeit of regulations."[367]

3. "Throughout the Middle Ages, Castilian towns had resisted the formation of guilds, their lower level of production requiring less organization, but the Catholic kings favored guilds in order to regulate the urban population more precisely. The Castilian towns of the sixteenth century thus developed an archaic guild system at the very time that such a pattern was tending to die out . . . in the most economically progressive regions of Europe."[368]

4. "[A] corporative [guild] system did not arise in Portugal before the late Middle Ages . . . because of strong interference and control by the king and rigidly organized municipalities."[369]

5. "As in Castile, the corporations [that is, guilds] did not arise in Portugal before the later 1440's. . . . The breakdown of their political power, along with the centralizing spirit of the century, made them ready for stricter royal control and for other class tutelage. In 1487 the king ordered each craft to accept two representatives or deputies (*vedores*) as judges in economic and professional matters."[370]

6. "There was an extraordinary development of craft gilds in Spain in the sixteenth and seventeenth centuries, and their over-regulated and antiquated methods dominated manufacturing process."[371]

7. "Urban government was organized under the general principle of hierarchy [in the eighteenth century], and urban guilds were also brought under stricter supervision."[372]

8. "Great concern was shown by merchants and artisans for guild rights. Gremios [guilds] continued to expand but their rigidity was more of a restraint on production than ever, and edicts of the 1770s and 1780s reduced their authority."[373]

Appendix 15.5: Historical References to Peasant Organizations and Peasant Rebellions in Iberia

Many references to peasant uprisings are found, but few or none reflect the kinds of organization found in northwestern Europe and Japan. Encountering citations such as the following, one receives the impression that peasant rebellions in Iberia were not accompanied by as much negotiation, bargaining, and compromise as occurred in their counterparts in northwestern Europe and

Japan. To be scientifically sure of this, it would be necessary to compare peasant rebellions in detail in the three areas, with this particular focus in mind. I do not know of any historian who has done that.

1. "In Catalonia, . . . one also finds increased legislation by the *Corts* . . . to limit peasant movement and decrease personal freedom. . . . But [this legislation] provoked in response a high level of peasant organization and, in particular, the assembling of mass peasant armies. Only a series of violent bloody confrontations ultimately assured peasant victory. Armed warfare ended finally in 1486 with the Sentence of Guadalupe by which peasantry were granted in full their personal freedom."[374]

2. "In 1462, the Council of the Generalitat raised an army to put down rebellious remences [redemption peasants] [that] quickly expanded into civil war against the crown, lasting ten long and bloody years. The conflict ranged the urban oligarchy and most of the aristocracy and clergy on one side against the crown, most of the peasants, and part of the Catalan aristocracy, on the other."[375]

3. "The only major social revolt in Castile during the fifteenth century was the rebellion of the peasant *irmandades* (brotherhoods) of Galicia. . . . Formation of irmandades of Galician peasants and townspeople of the third estate had been authorized by Enrique IV in 1465 to check the overweening power of the Galician aristocracy. The irmandades were reasonably well organized by districts, and in some areas into groups of one hundred. . . . The irmandade revolt was put down."[376]

4. "The Aragonese variant of the Hispanic social revolts of the period—several small peasant uprisings between 1507 and 1517—were simply suppressed."[377]

5. "Hatred of the 'exactions' of a foreign soldiery erupted in general revolt in the north Catalan countryside in May 1640, as peasants attacked Spanish troops throughout the district. . . . Poor peasants rose against their overlords, the laborers and unemployed in the towns took over the streets, and bandit gangs reasserted themselves in many parts of the countryside." The Catalans called upon the French for assistance and submitted to a French government, which turned out to be as oppressive as the Spanish. The Spanish returned in 1651, pledging "a general amnesty and preservation of the laws of Catalonia."[378]

6. "A semiclandestine peasants' league was founded in the Jativa region [of Valencia], and in 1693 its members refused to pay seigneurial dues. . . This rebellion was put down rather easily."[379]

7. In 1702, "the Habsburg candidacy [in the War of the Spanish Succession] took full advantage of social tensions [in Aragon] and encouraged a peasant revolt against the seigneurial control of the aristocracy. . . . [In Aragon

and Valencia] the cause of the Habsburg pretender was embraced particularly by peasants and village clergy."[380] But the peasants gained no leverage from this, since the Bourbon candidate triumphed at the Peace of Utrecht in 1713.

8. "On more than one occasion, in Andalucia in the 1650's and in Valencia later in the century, peasant unrest exploded into violence, but the alliance between the crown and aristocracy was too close and the forces of law and order were too solid to leave any opening for social revolution."[381]

Appendix 17.1: Newspaper References to Centralization and Power Concentration in Modern Mexico

1. "When necessary, Mexico's regime can be crudely repressive. In 1968, for example, a massive anti-government protest led by leftist students was crushed with the loss of more than 300 lives. In the early 1970s, several leftist guerrilla groups emerged and were duly wiped out, with more than 500 persons disappearing in the process. And when anti-government trade unions began agitating in 1977, their leaders were quickly arrested. In the countryside, the government uses the army as its police force, but it also maintains its own highly efficient security apparatus, which carefully monitors opposition movements and leftist exiles from Latin America."[382]

2. "In order to drive a truck for hire in the state of Jalisco, you must have commercial license plates issued by the PRI-controlled state government. [PRI is the dominant political party.] To get those plates, you must join the union. . . . The state leader of the union is a PRI congressman, and the national leader is a PRI senator. Of course, nothing in the union by-laws says one must be a PRI member in order to belong. It just happens that way."[383]

3. "'Nearly everyone has been co-opted by the P.R.I. in one way or another, admittedly not always by legitimate means,' said a Government official. 'If you arrange to get taxi plates for someone, no matter how, that man will vote for you for life, because you've given him his way of making a living.'"[384]

4. "Checks of the voting rolls showed instances of fictitious names listed by the hundreds, and other names—including one opposition mayoral candidate—had been purged. In Nuevo León, the local congress did not even bother to wait for the official results before declaring the governing party candidate the winner."[385]

5. "When peasants organize land takeovers, the patrones work with the PRI to form a co-opted group of peasants, which then receives the support of the police to kick out the genuine organizers. . . . In virtually every major and medium-sized town in the south, well-compensated PRI loyalists in unions, town councils and even health centers make sure that independent movements do not grow to the point where they threaten the PRI's base of control."[386]

6. In 1980, President Lopez-Portillo announced a "Mexican Food System," designed to increase agricultural production through central control. "The key to the Mexican Food System appears to be the coordination of all aspects of the cycle, from credit for seeds, fertilizer and machinery, through technical assistance for planting and harvesting, to improved transportation and storage facilities, nationwide marketing and occasional price subsidies. The Government, according to the President, will 'share the risks of the peasantry.'"[387]

7. "It happens again and again: A non-PRI labor movement springs up, then gets beaten down. Last fall, Mexico City garment workers unionized outside the PRI labor confederations; now, the courts are challenging their certification. In 1983, the nation's nuclear workers struck; the government shut down the whole uranium industry. This fall, Mexico City trolley drivers tried to strike without PRI permission; riot police and attack dogs dispersed the picketers after just one day."[388]

8. Often the law is capriciously enforced to convict a political foe. Whereas many labor leaders have been armed, illegally but with impunity, in 1989 the law against holding arms was capriciously enforced against a powerful labor leader, Joaquín Hernandez. Hernandez had been accusing the national oil company, Petróleos Mexicanos (Pemex) of corruption in order to embarrass the President. Since the unions themselves have been beds of corruption, the accusation had a clear political base. So did the President's "law enforcement:" Hernandez was convicted and imprisoned.[389]

Appendix 17.2: Newspaper References to Lack of Accountability in Modern Mexico

1. Some Mexicans see "rampant corruption" as "a natural consequence of a political system that lacks checks and balances on the enormous power of the executive branch and, particularly, of the President. . . . [T]he oil boom enabled the government to postpone many of the fundamental reforms needed to modernize the economy. As a result, inefficiencies remained hidden by state subsidies, uncompetitive domestic industry was protected by tariff barriers, an antiquated tax system was able to survive and huge public deficits were covered by foreign borrowing."[390]

2. "Between 1970 and 1980, federal spending in Mexico City 'far exceeded the worth of the entire existing plant in the city,' according to Gustavo Garza, a noted urbanologist at the Colégio de México."[391]

3. President "Lopez Portillo could have tried to harness these [oil] riches to fundamental development. Instead he let the economy take off on a

headlong boom, indulging inflation, piling up debt and fertilizing high-level corruption."[392]

4. After the earthquake of 1985, "while volunteers clawed for survivors under tons of cement and steel, top officials tried to preserve an image of self-reliance by refusing specialized foreign help. 'They sacrificed concrete lives for abstract ideas,' says Enrique Krauze, a historian."[393]

5. "The government owns hundreds of enterprises, and about half lose money. . . . La Libertad is one of eight state-owned sugar mills that government reformers tried to close. . . . [W]ork stopped but the workers didn't. They come each day and collect their pay each week. . . . Sugar workers don't have cars, so they wouldn't be able to get to work if the government stopped sending the bus. That would be tantamount to a layoff, and in Mexico businesses must pay severance pay when they lay off workers. . . . So the mills keep losing money, production fell and Mexico spends millions of dollars to import sugar."[394]

6. "If you decide to be an activist, you have to decide that you may, at some point, confront naked force with no constitutional balances against it," says Lorenzo Mayer, a political scientist at the Colégio de México."[395]

7. "Between 1977 and 1982, according to the Government, state enterprises accounted for half of a swelling public-sector deficit."[396]

8. Critics argue that by reserving certain oil operations for Pemex, the government makes oil production more costly. "Pemex . . . has its own rigs and drilling crews. However, the private drilling companies have always been more efficient. Says a manager of one of the private firms, who, like every other private rigger interviewed for this story, agreed to talk only if his name would not be used: 'In the time it takes a Pemex operation to produce oil from a well, a private company can begin pumping under the same conditions in approximately half the time.'"[397]

Appendix 17.3: Newspaper References to Land, Lack of Accountability, and Break-the-System in Nicaragua

Land

Proposition: Land, historically always subject to confiscation, continued to be so under both Somoza and Sandinista governments.

1. Domingo Sánchez Salgado, candidate for the presidency, reported that his "parents were of Indian ancestry and held title to a modest farm . . . but were pushed out by soldiers after President Anastasio Somoza García decided to give their land to one of his supporters."[398]

2. "Pasqual, a small grower, can't get a loan from the [Sandinista] state-owned bank because he won't join a co-op. The farm of Jaime, who was a medium-sized grower, was expropriated. Another grower would like to sell out but fears that if he asked permission, it will simply be seized."[399]

3. To gather support for a forthcoming election, "dozens of trucks were mobilized [by the Sandinista government] to bring farm laborers to Matagalpa so they could receive titles to work on cooperative farms."[400]

4. To bring the Contra war to an end, the rebels were promised that if they laid down their arms, they would be given land. When the land was not distributed as expected, they seized a cooperative and again called for war. (Apparently, they still had arms).[401]

Lack of Accountability and Pluralism

Proposition: Power over economic matters is concentrated in the government, and disputes tend to be met by confrontation, or stonewalling, rather than by negotiations.

1. "Entrepreneurs are forbidden to send their profits abroad, and their businesses can be confiscated if the Government decides they are "decapitalizing" by refusing to modernize them. They cannot raise prices, or even wages, without Government consent. Thus, many businessmen have concluded that the economy is closer to being state-run than it appears on the surface."[402]

2. "Tomas Borge, [Sandinista] Minister of the Interior: 'Class struggle can be seen either from the point of view of hate or from the point of view of love. State coercion is an act of love.'"[403]

3. "The [coffee] growers must sell to the state, instead of exporting directly. The government gets dollars for their coffee, pays the growers in local currency and cheats on the exchange rate."[404]

4. "A former Maryknoll nun . . . calmly accused Nicaragua's Sandinista leaders of aligning themselves with the Soviet bloc, assassinating government opponents, massacring Indians and generally betraying the democratic spirit of the 1979 revolution."[405]

5. "[E]ssentials are in short supply, are sometimes refused to those who object to the government's policies."[406]

6. "A private businessman complained that 'his primary competitor, a state-run outfit, undersells him and hogs the best-quality raw materials for itself. . . . [T]he Central Bank rarely provides . . . enough foreign exchange. . . . [T]he government fixes wages, prices and frequently even what an enterprise can or can't produce.'"[407]

7. "'They began to bother me three years ago because I wouldn't join their cooperative,' Mr. Martinez said of the Sandinistas [explaining why he had joined the Contra army]. 'I refused because I knew they formed the cooperatives to have us all controlled.'"[408]

8. "[T]he habit of rule from above dies hard. The new [Violeta Chamorro] Government's pluralistic exterior has given way to the familiar image of a closed, even secretive group of leaders, pursuing its vision of Nicaragua's future with little attention—or even advance notice—to its allies and the public."[409]

Break-the-System

Proposition: Significant elements of the political system are so lightly held that they are willingly sacrificed to win individual points.

1. Arturo Cruz, opposition candidate, refused to register for elections, unless the government agreed to have a dialogue with the rebels.[410] He knew that his refusal would threaten the *system* of elections, which he was willing to put on the line in order to gain his point.

2. Crippling or destroying an economy, such as when Salvadoran rebels destroyed village electricity or shot mayoral candidates, is frequently a ploy by an out-group to gain a particular point. After losing the elections in 1990, the Sandinistas refused to give up patronage government jobs or control of the army, and the new (Chamorro) government lacked the power to force them. Sandinista leaders declared their intention to "rule from below" despite their defeat. In the ensuing struggle, Sandinista-controlled unions declared strikes that would paralyze key economic sectors.[411] Finally, the Chamorro government yielded, "by agreeing to double wages and suspend a decree that gave her Government wide powers to dismiss workers."[412] There might be some debate as to whether this incident should be classified as break-the-system or as a legitimate strike, since the boundary is not clear. The argument for break-the-system is that the system was one of elections, but the results were partially voided when, through economy-crippling measures, the new government was not allowed to assume power in strategic areas.

Appendix 18.1: References on State Power and Lack of Accountability in Peru

References on state power and deficient government accountability from historical sources bear a strong resemblance to those appearing in newspapers today. For comparison, they are combined into a single section, in roughly chronological order.

1. In the sixteenth century, corregidores "prohibited outside merchants from trading in their jurisdictions and then brought in goods themselves which they forced the natives to buy at inflated prices, whether the goods were of any use to the purchasers or not."[413]

2. Spanish economic policies of the seventeenth century were designed to squeeze resources out of Peru as Spain's own needs increased, mainly with wars on the European continent: increased taxes, trade prohibited which might compete with Spain, offices sold.[414]

3. In 1646, Fray Buenaventura reported that corregidores "take as much as they can because they doubt that they will have an office again."[415]

4. "If Spain could not kill Peruvian production and trade, it could limit them by increasing the amount of bribery necessary to carry on a profitable operation and by increasing the number of laws and officials charged with its suppression."[416]

5. "The problem of resuscitating the mines was complicated by the fact that loans raised to benefit South America, both public and private, failed to reach the continent, through mismanagement on the part of the fund raisers"[417]

6. "What does it matter," President Echenique asked in 1853, "that a few have enriched themselves whose wealth has remained in the country and contributed to the development of these benefits?"[418]

7. In 1868, the new president, General Díaz Conseco, "wanted a railroad between his city [Arequipa] and Lima (to reward it for supporting him in the revolution)." This was constructed at a price that far exceeded the cost. The British railroad builder reported to an author that "the only way to get on with successive governments in Peru was to let each sell itself for its own price. He then added that the contract price includes the sums required by the President and the President's friends, . . . to keep all rivals at a distance."[419]

8. "[In 1893] payments were made according to the will of the Minister who ordered them and of the Minister of Finance who could want to order their payment, or of the treasury cashier who wished to execute the order. As a result, not all the payments were honored. . . . These [orders of payment] were sold at a low price and later paid according to the circumstances."[420]

9. "[A] law passed in 1900 gave the government the right to expropriate real estate by simple declaration; in 1903 entail (*manos muertas*) was abolished."[421] (In England and Europe, the abolition of entail was negotiated piecemeal and decided in the courts and parliaments over centuries. In Peru, by contrast, it was done by a single decree).

10. In studying an agrarian reform cooperative in the 1960s, Guillet found that the sense of trust and loyalty to the group did not carry over from

tribal society. Bringing together peasants from different communities increased tensions. But above all, the peasants resented the usurpation of decision making by a new level of national bureaucrats.[422]

11. "So far [1985], only a few conservatives have publicly warned of the perils of the enormous popularity and highly centralized power enjoyed by [the new president] Mr. García, with the weekly magazine Oiga drawing an analogy with the personal style of Juan Domingo Perón, the late Argentine leader, and noting that 'demagogy is governing the country.'"[423]

12. Relative values placed on power versus policy/ideology are exemplified by the 180-degree shift of the political party APRA in 1980. Although dedicated to agrarian and social reform, it joined right-wing parties to deny another party, Acción Popular, the funds to carry out the reforms that both of them favored. Thus APRA preferred to forgo its principles rather than allow them to be implemented by someone else. Power rather than reform was the dominating force.[424]

13. Price controls have been used by every government since 1969, despite their manifest inability to limit inflation and their distortion of production. Upon taking office in 1985, President García announced "an emergency program to double minimum wages, freeze the price of basic goods, tighten exchange controls and raise gasoline prices to increase Government revenues."[425]

14. "'We realize we have mismanaged our affairs in a gross manner and we are paying the price,' said Manual Ulloa, a former Prime Minister from Peru." [He was referring to the debt crisis.][426]

15. One of the effects of centralized power is extreme or capricious actions. The resulting inability to predict wages and prices make business decision-making difficult. For example: "The Government increased the price of gasoline by 400 percent and of most food by 100 to 200 percent, devalued the currency by around 100 percent and increased the minimum wage by 150 percent. It then gave the private sector 10 days in which to adjust its prices, after which there was to be a 120-day across-the-board price freeze. . . . But many businesses raised their prices to anticipate inflation through January, immediately putting the prices of their products beyond the reach of most consumers and throwing the economy into a sudden and violent recession."[427]

16. There have been many reports of mismanagement and embezzlement from state enterprises and cooperatives. For example: "In many cooperatives, charges of corruption were also leveled against managers, particularly when peasants found their wages docked to cover outstanding debt."[428]

Appendix 18.2: References on State Power and Lack of Accountability in Brazil

1. In 1888, credit to agriculture "began the inflationary process known as the 'encilhamento.' . . . [This term] indicates distrust of the government's role in the inflation, since it refers to the part of a race track where horses are girthed, and shady bets were placed if the race itself was not fixed."[429]

2. Under the Consolidated Labor Code of 1943, local organizations were "grouped into state federations which, in turn, were united into national federations. By means of this device, [President Getúlio] Vargas was able to create an organized national labor movement where virtually none had existed before. More important still from the perspective of statist development, that movement was malleable and dependent, and constituted a political tool in the hands of the government."[430]

3. "But even many Brazilian businessmen are concerned about Brazil's ambitious drive toward economic power, arguing that it has sharply increased the powers of the central government."[431]

4. "Brazil is one of the most notarized, sealed, beribboned, stamped, authenticated, photocopied, docketed, registered and cross-filed countries on earth. Lines of citizen supplicants waiting to have their papers inscribed with some official emblem are as much a part of the local landscape as Sugar Loaf Mountain."[432]

5. "Seventy percent of food moves by highway, thanks to the nation's commitment in the 1960's to create its own automobile industry and concentrate on road building. Left unattended by Government choice were the railways and the world's richest river network, two resources that, had they been developed, could have cut transportation costs. . . . Thus far, the Government has favored agribusiness with its subsidy and credit provision programs, bringing rapid improvements to productivity but leaving unattended long-range social problems posed by the continuing movement of small farmers to the overcrowded cities."[433]

6. "The upper echelons of the state-run enterprise were filled with retired military officers, and the frills they offered ranking employees were generous and imaginative. Employees received bonuses simply for faithfully showing up at work, and officials shared in annual profits even of state corporations that were not profitable."[434]

7. "[T]he country's giant state enterprises . . . accounted for billions of dollars of the borrowing. So much money has disappeared into the trio of steel and glass towers that some people have taken to calling the area [Rio de Janeiro] the Bermuda Triangle. . . . The military-run government has relied, with apparent justification, on the conditioning of the Brazilian public over

two decades to take orders. . . . [T]he Government remains centralized and authoritarian. Local administrations have virtually no revenue-raising authority, and Congress has no say in the principal budgetary decisions."[435]

8. "An explosion of government borrowing has kept interest costs here sky-high and is crowding out many small borrowers. Working capital costs so much that it often exceeds what businessmen can make from selling their products. Price controls are strangling business and particularly business investment without noticeably curbing inflation, which has doubled to 227 percent a year. So . . . business investment remains flat."[436]

9. "Horror stories of bureaucratic arbitrariness abound. It took a year for Petrobras—the powerful oil monopoly —to clear through SEI [Special Secretary of Information] a license to import an IBM 3090 mainframe."[437]

10. The World Bank criticized Brazil's welfare program because its funds were "badly managed by highly centralized government agencies and . . . their distribution is often influenced by political interests." Referring to the problem of "ghost" employees, the Bank noted that "when one northeast state recently tried to verify the 14,000 teachers on the state education payroll, it found that 6,000 individuals regularly collecting salaries could not be located."[438]

11. Forests in Brazil are being destroyed because the government gives sizable tax breaks to cattle ranchers, whose activity is "inherently uneconomic. . . . The tragedy is that the forest could be preserved even as its resources are tapped. Permanent crops like coffee bushes do less damage than annual cropping or cattle."[439]

12. "An inefficient state sector, rife with overmanning, corruption, and money-losing industries, continues to squander the nation's resources."[440]

13. "20 percent to 40 percent of Brazil's output occurs in the informal economy, which operates outside of government purview in order to avoid taxes and regulation."[441]

14. "If I was able to end the misery of 45 million people; get milk into the mouths of starving Brazilians; eradicate the illiteracy of eight million people; end external debt repayments of 4.5 percent of GNP in a country which is growing at only 0.5 percent per year . . . If I could do these things I would be making the greatest revolution on the continent."[442] I include this quotation by a presidential candidate for two reasons. First, it appears in the first person singular, perhaps indicating a belief in the enormous power of a president; and second, it cites broad, sweeping goals to combat all the perceived social ills, without attention to the microsteps, the political coordination, the moderation of conflicting interests, the cooperation of diverse groups, and the length of time that would be required before it might be implemented.

Appendix 18.3: References to Confrontation and Break-the-System in Argentina

1. When challenged by the Organization of American States on the torture and executions in the "dirty war," Argentina "threatened to quit the assembly and perhaps the regional organization if the 27-nation body adopts a resolution naming Argentina as a violator of human rights."[443]

2. "Argentina's largest party, the Peronists, are even more deeply divided [than the Radical Party], with about a dozen factions. Members have ranged from the extreme leftists who assassinated policemen in the mid-1970s to extreme rightists who assassinated the leftists."[444]

3. Political parties "have had a poor record of espousing wild-eyed populism, engaging in corruption and goading the military into coups against competitors."[445]

4. "Two weeks ago about 10,000 Peronist workers marched in front of Congress to protest the government's labor policies. Carrying banners, beating drums, singing and chanting obscene insults, they denounced President [Raúl] Alfonsín as a 'dictator' and 'gorilla' and succeeded in interrupting the debate on the new labor law for several hours."[446]

5. "The Peronist party has been hopelessly fractured since Peron's death—riven by personal jealousies, its populism ranging from left-wing nationalism to right-wing ultra-Catholicism. As a party, it can obstruct the Government but cannot get together on a minimum agenda."[447]

6. "A general of the army, accused of involvement in the 'dirty war,' brandished a knife against demonstrators who taunted him outside a television studio in Buenos Aires."[448]

7. By calling a 24-hour strike in 1984, the General Confederation of Labor "halted what had been painstaking negotiations for a national accord on wages, labor laws and long-term economic policy." When the government called on business and union leaders to discuss the matter, Peronist CGT leaders refused to attend.[449]

8. From a professor of law at the University of Buenos Aires: "Protest is essential to democracy. But demonstrations and slogans do not contribute to the dialogue necessary among all sectors to overcome grave problems. Uncritical repetition of outdated catchwords turned into dogma must be replaced by analysis and imaginative solutions."[450]

9. In 1985, President Alfonsín imposed a sixty-day state of siege as "a move to free the Government's hand to combat a sharp increase in violence widely attributed to right-wing terrorists."[451]

10. In 1985, differences within the Peronist party on whether to elect officers by direct vote or by delegates, and the personal dislike of an officer,

caused the party to split into two parts. It is the inconsequentiality—to outside observers—of the reasons behind this split that draws our attention: "This month two groups, each claiming to be the real Peronist party, held separate congresses, a development analogous to two wings of the Democratic Party in the United States holding competing national conventions."[452]

11. From César Jaroslavsky, Radical Party leader in the Chamber of Deputies: "This is an impossible debate in Argentina between the military and civilians . . . because the military are never going to understand or admit that they violated human rights and that no cause justified that. They want the vindication of their fight, and for us, the civilians, to render them homage."[453]

12. "The channeling of demands through the military involved a very real threat of ouster to the government. This danger was evident in the numerous *planteos* (demands from the military backed by the threat of force if they were denied), as well as in the many coups and attempted coups between 1955-66. . . . By promoting social unrest, as well as by paralyzing production through strikes and the occupation of factories, they could make a government appear unable to maintain even minimum levels of law and order, and thus put it in immediate danger of being ousted."[454]

Appendix 18.4: Newspaper References to State Power and Lack of Accountability in Argentina

1. The Ministry of the Economy "is so archaic in its methods that no one knows the real size of the budget deficit."[455]

2. "The underground economy in Argentina has the same causes as everywhere else: high taxes, excessive regulations and government intervention. It is an indicator not of a sick society that evades its political duties, but of a society seeking freedom from bureaucratic distortion."[456]

3. "Argentina is struggling with an old problem—the lack of a strong and constructive opposition. . . . Opposition parties simply have never gotten going in Argentina. They have been banned under the frequent periods of military rule—28 of the last 55 years—and co-opted or crushed electorally by populist *caudillos* such as the late Gen. Juan Peron who have formed massive political movements."[457]

4. The following was written about an Argentine industrial engineer whom the president had appointed to promote a national privatization drive. "He resigned in despair several months later, [complaining that] past loans from [international lending institutions], rather than inducing substantive, free-market changes in the economy, have often maintained and even strengthened the status quo. . . . [Several examples are mentioned, of which the following is one]: Road building and maintenance is nationally controlled by *Viabilidad*

Nacional. Its bureaucrats are notorious opponents of toll systems; a private company running a toll system would strip them of power. They have even 'liberated' existing toll charges."[458]

5. "The state-owned corporations that provide public services are so mismanaged that they have been running annual deficits that make up the bulk of the nation's fiscal deficit."[459]

6. "These elephantine companies, the products of a past that saw the state as the primary engine of development, dominate the region's economic activity. Performing poorly, burdened with obsolete equipment and bloated by featherbedding, many of the enterprises have been targeted for sale or reorganization. . . . A study by a government auditing agency found that state enterprises in Argentina lack passable financial records, and some—including the telephone company and railroads—do not even have complete inventory lists. . . .' For each important decision in ENTEL,' says Nicolas Gallo, who quit in August after eight months as the company's head, 'one has to consult the ministers of economy and public works, the secretaries of communication, industry and foreign trade, the director of public enterprises, four unions, the business chambers and some important suppliers.'"[460]

7. "The national railroads need about $750 million a year from the treasury for their operating deficit. . . . The telephone company has two to four times more employees per line than similar companies around the world. Aerolíneas Argentinas has twice the number of employees per plane."[461]

8. "Last year, Ferrocarriles Argentinos, as the state-owned [railroad] company is known, lost $700 million following a loss of almost $1 billion in 1987. That, economist Lisandro Bril estimates, represented close to 20 percent of the state deficit in both years. The deficit is widely seen as the central factor in Argentina's persistent inflationary scourge."[462]

9. Jeffrey Sachs of Harvard reported on the temporary success of command development under Perón (1946-55). But as early as 1948, "the Perón prosperity fell apart."[463]

10. "Today, the list of troubles adding up to what President [Carlos Saúl] Menem calls 'the long sickness of the Argentine economy' includes fiscal deficits that typically exceed 10 percent of the gross national product, tax evasion as a way of life, low productivity, a bloated state payroll and heavy dependence on the state by private enterprise."[464]

11. "State-owned companies are losing billions of dollars, yet their labor unions are resisting job dismissals or privatization; tax evasion is so rampant that more than half of economic activity may have gone underground; only 7% of industrial output is sold abroad; and agrarian exports, the main source of government revenue, are stagnating. [A] give-and-take-away sys-

tem of subsidies and taxes has discouraged producers from investing or raising exports."[465]

12. "[U]niversal free medical care has long become irrelevant because the public hospital system has virtually collapsed under the weight of corruption and fiscal deficits. . . . Argentines are notorious for avoiding taxes . . . partly because of the conviction that too much of public funds are siphoned off by bribes, thefts, and layers of middle men."[466]

13. "[D]espite major rate increases telephone and electrical utilities have had to borrow to meet costs."[467]

14. "Yacimientos Petrolíferos Fiscales [YPF] is Argentina's state oil company, and it has run up a debt of $4.5 billion, or 10 percent of the country's entire $45 billion debt. Yet in contracting this debt, YPF got its hands on just $300 million of it, a mere 6 percent, company officials say. The remaining $4.2 billion was used by the previous military government to subsidize extremely low gasoline prices, to buy arms and to finance Argentine tourists traveling abroad.[468]

15. Maximo Flugelman, a leading Argentine banker, calls the country a "study in the impoverishment linked to the outrageous refusal to compete."[469]

16. The final affront to accountability is the manner in which the military has escaped responsibility for the "dirty war."[470] Not being an "economic" matter, this question has avoided the purview of foreign critics, except the human-rights agencies.

Appendix 19.1: References to Concentration of Power in the Middle East

1. "The Byzantine state regulated the economy in a way that Diocletian would have envied; this aspect of the law remained in full force and seems in fact to have become more rigorous. The prefect kept lists of members of the guilds and supervised the admission of new ones."[471]

2. "Justinian, authoritarian by character and convinced of his mission to recreate the Christian Roman Empire . . ."[472]

3. "For Justinian the wealth of his subordinates and the splendour of their way of life merely increased their dependence upon him. So long as his power remained undisputed, a nod could divest them of their palaces, their lands, their private armies and their throngs of servitors and dispatch them in chains to a wretched exile in some dismal corner of his empire."[473]

4. "[T]he self-governing rights of the Byzantine village [about the seventh century] were of a very limited nature, for nothing took place in a

Byzantine village without government supervision and even the most trivial matters of daily life were controlled by the government officials."[474]

5. "Byzantium had no interest in a free commerce which flowed into and out of its empire from neighboring regions or in a powerful merchant class. . . . Nor was it willing to allow its large or small landowners to become so involved in the world of trade and finance that they ignored what it felt were their primary functions; namely, to serve as soldiers, sailors, or diplomats at the disposal of the empire."[475]

6. [In contrast with Europe] "the eastern [Byzantine] idea [was] that a ruler was not the first among equals, but sovereign and even divine."[476]

7. "Government in Muslim society . . . was never, or almost never, anything other than superimposed; never, or almost never, the emanation or expression of that society."[477]

8. "Machiavelli cited the Ottoman empire as the prime example of a government 'by a prince and his servants,' in modern terms a bureaucratic empire, as opposed to a government 'by a prince and his barons,' a feudal state exemplified by the France of his day."[478]

9. "The thought of extreme centralization of the administration seems to have been intoxicating [in the Ottoman empire, at the end of the nineteenth century]."[479]

10. "*Osmanli* (pertaining to the House of Osman, Ottoman) or *askeri* (military) . . . served the sultan, from whom their power derived, and only secondarily served his subjects. . . . [W]hile in other societies wealth or status might become the basis for claims to political power, the kind of patrimonial domination seen in the Ottoman Empire made any such claims practically impossible."[480]

11. 'The powers of the sultan were immense [at the turn of the nineteenth century]; the governance of the empire was largely dependent on his personal discretion. And yet his powers were far from being without limit. Some of the restrictions were of a practical kind, related to factors such as the capabilities of the administrative and military apparatus. . . . Other limits were ones of principle, derived from the conception of the society as the fulfillment of a divinely appointed and thus invariable plan, and the consequent necessity of the sultan to maintain the legitimacy of his rule through performance of religiously valued functions."[481]

12. In Iraq in the nineteenth century, the Turks "saw that in the alienation of lands to the tribes and particularly to tribal sheiks, the government would forfeit a weapon which if retained would still be of great value for the control of the tribes and their chiefs. Hence in subsequent years they lost no opportunity to exploit the principle of state landownership."[482]

13. In an example of command development, Richmond cites the manner in which Ibrahim Pasha of Egypt in the 1830s broke the power of nomad tribes in order to extend agriculture in Syria. Ibrahim personally led army troops "on one occasion into battle against an army of locusts."[483]

14. The mid-nineteenth century was a period "of extreme political imbalance [in the Ottoman Empire]—of practically unfettered dominance by the civil-bureaucrat politicians."[484]

15. "One of the results of the reign of Riza shah [in Iran] and his policy of centralization was for the countryside to be invaded by a horde of government officials. At best they live on the country and at worst they look upon office as an opportunity to grow wealthy. . . . Moreover, the tendency to extortion is one of the factors, though perhaps not the most important one, making for absenteeism. Tradition demands that hospitality should be offered to all comers on as lavish a scale as possible: anything else would not be consistent with the dignity and status of the landowner. Consequently many feel that the only way of avoiding such impositions is to remain away."[485]

16. "The king ran [Kuwait] in the old-fashioned tribal way, with a benevolent paternalism. . . . Members of the Sabah family, like other royal families in the Gulf region, fill many of the major posts in the Government, the army, the police and in the private sector."[486]

17. "To a large extent, the material progress in the kingdom [Saudi Arabia] . . . has been forced by the Government, to which petroleum revenues flow. . . . Government policies . . . have spawned hundreds of new companies in the past five years. . . . The two huge new industrial cities —Jubail on the east coast and Yanabu on the west coast —are Government initiatives. Government has also been the impetus behind the eightfold rise in the kingdom's electrical generating capacity in the last five years, as well as the tripling in the number of roads. . . . The result has been an explosion in the number of private factories. . . . The Government is creating new private companies through divesting itself of large chunks of its interest in public projects. . . . The Government is also trying to create a work ethic."[487] NOTE: Although Saudi Arabia is largely a "private" economy, this economy was created and is overseen by a benevolent government. The status is reminiscent of medieval city-states in Europe. But the Europeans had to overcome these institutions before proceeding on a power-diffusion path.

18. "Real power [in Syria] lies with an inner circle consisting of [President] Assad, his brother Rifaat, the commander of his Special Forces, and the heads of the political and military intelligence. All are Alawites. . . . The most serious danger to the Assad regime has come from the Moslem Brotherhood . . . [whose] tracts reveal three basic grievances —lack of politi-

cal freedom, government intrusion into economic areas traditionally dominated by Sunnis, and the influence of "atheist" Alawites at Sunni expense."[488]

19. "[In Iran] Ayatollah Khomeini never disguised his intention to
establish a regime based on clerical supremacy and Islamic law. . . . The human rights record has been abysmal. As many as 10,000 men and women
have passed before the firing squads. The prisons remain full. Islamic dress
and codes of moral behavior are imposed by force. The obsession with ideological conformity has left little room for dissent. One by one, the opposition
parties have been eliminated."[489]

20. "Iraq is virtually a sealed society [in the 1990s], secured by an
organized party structure, an interlocking system of police, internal security
and neighborhood organizations unrivaled in the Middle East."

21. "Every Iraqi military unit, every bazaar, every office, every fac-
tory, is infiltrated by members of the ruling Baath party or its supporters. At
Baghdad University, . . . it is not permitted to talk politics in a history class.
. . . The classroom does not belong to [the professor]."[490]

Appendix 19.2: Historical References to State Control over Guilds and Corporations in the Middle East

1. Under the Emperor Justinian (r.527-65) guilds—one for every
trade—reported to the city prefect. Guild price controls were superficially
similar to those found later in Europe and Japan. But "established in the first
place perhaps for the protection of the producers, these had over the centuries
been adapted by the state to the protection of the consumers and through them
the security of the government."[491]

2. In the seventh century, guild rules in Constantinople rested "on the
assumption that the prosperity of the capital depended upon wise and careful
state intervention. The state intended to regulate the guilds down to the smallest detail. 'Any spinner [of silk] . . . showing himself to be gossiping, a boaster,
troublesome, or noisy, shall be expelled from the corporation with blows and
insults, to prevent his selling the silk.' . . . No ruler in the West had a city the
size of Constantinople, a ready bureaucracy, or a level of economic activity
comparable to the east, so the system of state-supervised artisan and professional associations survived, with some fundamental changes, only in the
east."[492]

3. "Byzantium grouped its merchants and artisan classes into guilds
. . . under strict government control. This included an extensive system of
price fixing, especially as regards foodstuffs necessary to provision the capital."[493]

4. "In Islamic cities no true merchant guilds seem to have appeared by the tenth century. . . . [There was] a tendency for governmental authorities to group merchants and workers alike under heads or leaders who could be held responsible for their activities."[494]

5. "[S]ervile elitism [in the Ottoman Empire] . . . meant that the ruling class was in principle deprived of corporate autonomy, and thus was in a position radically different from that of the estates or privileged corporate bodies of medieval or early modern Europe."[495]

6. The Ottomans [of the eighteenth century] opposed the development of autonomous organizations intermediary between the individual and the state. In this they resembled other Middle Eastern states and found support in the Islamic religious-legal tradition. Where the emergence of such bodies could not be prevented, the state attempted to dominate them and use them to maintain or extend its own power.[496]

7. In the Ottoman Empire in the fifteenth century, the state used guilds as conduits for "collecting taxes, controlling prices, policing the market place, outfitting and supplying the army, and eventually limiting the number of shops in a given craft through a kind of licensing system."[497]

8. In the Ottoman Empire in the nineteenth century: "[S]tate dominance over the differentiation and validation of distinctions of social status, and so to the restriction of possibilities of the emergence of classes, estates, or even smaller types of corporate organizations independent of government control."[498]

9. In the nineteenth century in Iran, town elites and guild elders jointly possessed many of the powers held by the state in the Byzantine and Ottoman Empires. "The structure of the craft guilds shows profound inequality in the property rights enjoyed by their members." Town elders intervened in many guild functions; for example they "saw to it that the master craftsmen gave proper instruction to the apprentices" and took an active role in selecting masters. In "order to limit competition, each master worked and sold his goods in a strictly defined place."[499]

Appendix 22.1: Historical References to Vertical Alliances, Pluralism, and Leverage in Germany During the High Period of the Estates, sixteenth to eighteenth centuries

Examples of vertical alliances, negotiation, and compromise among estates, princes, and emperor are so numerous that it is not practical to list them all, even in an appendix. The most complete history of them that I know of is Carsten (1959), but other histories of Germany (for example, Barraclough

1947 and Holborn's three-volume treatise, 1959, 1964, 1969) also contain instances. Those listed here are illustrative only.

1. "[C]onflicts with other rulers, above all the Elector Palatine, Frederick I, forced Ulrich [Count of Württemberg] to consult his knights, prelates, and towns [in 1457]. These took the side of the native nobility; grievances were raised; in the end Ulrich had to promise that he would in future govern with the advice of his Three Estates, to his benefit and theirs. It does not seem, however, that he kept his promise, for two years later the Estates complained that he was not governing with the help of his councillors from the native nobility."[500]

2. "After an initial refusal of Duke Eberhard [of Württemberg], his councillors summoned a diet which met in March 1498. . . . Eberhard was invited to attend. If he failed to do so, they informed him, they would nevertheless proceed. . . . [The Duke] left the country and sought refuge in the Free City of Ulm, from where he appealed to the Emperor Maximilian. . . . Maximilian decided in favor of the rebels: Eberhard was deprived of his principality on account of his manifold bad and disorderly practices."[501]

3. "In 1422 the Emperor Sigismund confirmed this privilege of the [Bavarian] Estates to conclude unions with the nobility of other German territories and with his towns and those of the Empire, because the nobility were much oppressed and suffered much injustice in Germany."[502]

4. "[L]ong feuds occurred between the hostile brothers [Louis II and Henry of Hesse], [so] the Estates had to act as arbiters between them. . . . [T]he continuous division of Hesse strengthening their position."[503]

5. "[T]he treaty of Passau [1552] had established a religious peace in the Empire, for [Catholic] King Ferdinand . . . needed Protestant support against the Turks."[504]

6. "[In 1512, Duke William of Bavaria] fulfilled a demand of the Estates to confirm their privileges] only because of his pressing debts, and because his brother Louis, disregarding the treaty of 1506 and the principle of primogeniture, demanded a partition of the duchy. [The Estates decided that] the two dukes should rule together."[505]

7. "In the secularized duchy of Prussia [1570s] the Estates emerged as the decisive power. They considered Lutheran orthodoxy and the *Corpus Doctrinae Prussicae* their most cherished privileges. They dominated the church and the administration and made the duke completely dependent on themselves, playing him off against the king of Poland and becoming the real masters of the country."[506]

8. "The Emperor also managed to recover some of his power through the renewal of hitherto neglected perquisites. Among these was the privilege of protecting the subjects of the Empire from the arbitrary rule of the territo-

rial authorities. . . . [In 1755, he] supported the estates of Mecklenburg in their successful effort to curb the absolute rule of the duke."[507]

9. "In short, the Empire provided the framework for a diplomacy of countervailing intervention, in which each prince could involve himself in his neighbor's internal affairs in order to protect the local 'liberties' of his neighbor's subjects."[508]

Appendix 22.2: Historical References to the Accountability of Princes and Dukes Demanded by the German Estates

1. "Frederick [IV of Saxony] tried to win the support of the Estates and in 1446 he summoned a diet and requested a new tax to pay off his debts. To this the Estates agreed, but they demanded to be informed of how he had incurred such debts. [If Frederick's son should succeed to the throne as a minor] the government should be exercised by his mother and sixteen members of the Estates, eight of the nobility, four of the clergy, and four burghers; they should appoint all officials and receive an audit of the accounts."[509]

2. "In Cleves and Mark John III neglected his promises of 1486 and 1489 and aroused new opposition by his arbitrary and belligerent policy. In 1499 the Estates refused to pay the second installment of the tax which they had granted to redeem the prisoners taken in the war with Gülders, because it was used for other purposes."[510]

3. "Joachim II [of Brandenburg, r.1531-71] was recklessly extravagant. He could never balance his budget. As a result he several times asked the town and country estates to assume his debts, and this they did in return for the right to assess and collect their own taxes, raise their own troops and otherwise run their own domestic affairs."[511]

4. "Anna [of Mecklenburg] reached an agreement with the majority of the Estates. The union of 1509 was revoked and a new one concluded which severely limited her power. The Estates were granted the power of the purse; they were to be consulted before a war or feud was begun and in other important affairs. If they found fault with her government, this was to be remedied with their 'advice and will.'"[512]

5. "[F]or the rendering of accounts [in Hesse, mid-sixteenth century] some burghers were associated with [the landgraves], so that they could not only see 'what came in, but also to what useful purposes the money was put'."[513]

6. In Saxony in 1540, a committee was appointed to deal with sequestered religious lands. "The members of the religious orders should be provided for, the surplus should be administered by the Estates, and yearly

accounts should be rendered in the presence of ducal councillors. Again Henry conceded most of these wishes."[514]

7. When the Estates of Bavaria voted a tax in 1514, they "elected eight of their members to keep records of revenues and expenditures."[515]

Many, many more examples are found in the general histories. Once again, Carsten (1959) is a rich source.

Appendix 23.1: Selected References to Power and Economic Distortions in the Third World Today

Although I have collected many similar illustrations, only one or occasionally two are reported for any one Third World country. Countries are listed in alphabetical order:

Algeria: "President Houari Boumedienne . . . built steel mills and petrochemical plants only to find a world glut of steel and petrochemicals. He also pushed through a plan to collectivize farms, . . . that encouraged young people to move to the cities [turning] Algeria, once nearly self-sufficient in foodstuffs, into a huge importer." [516]

Argentina: "[F]iscal deficits . . . typically exceed 10 percent of the gross national product, tax evasion as a way of life, low productivity, a bloated state payroll and heavy dependence on the state by private enterprise . . . poor quality of manufactured goods protected by high tariffs, the large amount of business that is done off the books. . . . [The President] plans to reduce the state's role in the economy [and] intends to 'privatize private enterprise,' an allusion to the custom of the Government's guaranteeing markets and profits for private businesses."[517]

Bolivia: "[C]ontrols keep a long list of essential items at prices well below production costs. . . . Many Bolivians have become ingenious smugglers, buying goods at home and slipping them into neighboring countries to sell at a handsome profit."[518]

Brazil: "[President Fernando] Collor's deflationary plan . . . was to freeze all bank accounts and change the currency. . . . As the Brazilian economy went into shock and prices crashed, those with any cash at all . . . were in a position to take advantage of such opportunities as a stock market that lost 60 percent of its value, or to purchase state enterprises for sale at 30 percent of their value."[519]

Burma (Myanmar): "At least 5,000 Burmese are being forced to move from Myanmar's cities to new, ill-prepared outlying towns where malaria and hepatitis are rampant. . . . Once in their new areas, which can be up to 50 miles away, the Burmese are required to buy land and secure and pay for Government permits to rebuild."[520]

Dominican Republic: "The State Sugar Council owns and manages 12 large sugar plantation factories, which were the property of the dictator Rafael Trujillo. . . . Trujillo institutionalized the use of cheap Haitian migratory labor. . . . By 1983 the Dominican Government was paying the Government of the Haitian dictator Jean-Claude Duvalier as much as $2,250,000 a year under the arrangement." Even after the overthrow of Duvalier, Haitian workers are recruited with the promise of well-paying jobs. When they arrive at the border, "they are seized by the army and taken by truck to one of the 280 or so plantation villages."[521]

Equatorial Guinea: President Francisco Nguema, "a paranoid despot, destroyed his nation's economy by expelling almost the entire Spanish population of 7,000 and killing or forcing into exile about one-third of the African population. The population is now 300,000."[522]

Egypt: In a cotton factory, "a lot of the problems can be traced to the government, including state-produced cotton yarn that breaks on the loom and the 34 official signatures it sometimes takes to ship an order. . . .The price [of underwear] is set by government-owned spinning companies, which have a monopoly on the production of yarn from raw cotton and have deficit problems of their own. Importing cheaper cotton yarn is no solution because Egypt would only tack on customs duties of up to 65 percent to protect state companies."[523]

Ethiopia: "Villagization was heralded by President Mengistu [as] the answer to the many difficulties of the . . . peasantry. By being grouped together, the argument went, peasants would be able to produce more and have easier access to such services as schools and health clinics. . . . Unspoken, but more to the point, in the view of many Ethiopian and Western researchers, villagization was an effort to increase the power of the state by marshaling people in more easily controlled groups."[524]

Ghana: "[S]oldiers demolished stalls and goods in one of the market places in this rundown capital. . . . [T]he action was taken because the market women were selling goods at prices above those set by the government. . . . The new Rawlings Government barred the women from selling certain essential commodities, including milk, sugar and textiles."[525]

"Information percolates up in Ghana through a hierarchy of fear. Everyone must report anyone who seems suspicious or he himself becomes suspect."[526]

Haiti: Leslie Delatour, the minister of finance, "has stanched the hemorrhaging of public funds, closing, amid enormous protest, two large state enterprises . . . that had helped serve as conduits from the public treasury to private pockets. He has reduced the tariffs that protected the monopolies making up Haiti's structure of 'crony capitalism' and slashed export taxes on coffee and other commodities."[527]

Honduras: "Cohbana, the state agency charged with exporting bananas, loses more than $3 million a year. Meanwhile, Honduran banana exports lag behind those of other banana-exporting countries. Cohdefor, a state enterprise with a monopoly on the lumber industry, has lost $290 million since its inception. . . . Graft plays a large part in these losses."[528]

"The Government began legal proceedings today aimed at jailing all 53 members of Congress who supported" the appointment of the Chief Justice of the Supreme Court, jailed in a political struggle, on charges of treason and plotting against the existing political system.[529]

India: "India's planning apparatus might be Adam Smith's vision of hell. Businesses must obtain permission to enter markets or leave them, to build new factories or close old ones, to import or export. Opening a tourist hotel requires 43 licenses, which take years and millions of under-the-table rupees. Much industry is government-owned —often with dreary results. . . . Labor, of course, is not free, and state enterprises use lots of it. In Calcutta, the bus company employs 35 people for every vehicle it owns."[530]

Indonesia: "Massive amounts of capital are wasted by being poured into protected industries. One Jakarta-based economist says that more than $3 billion has been sunk in the projected steel works at Cilegon, in West Java, an investment that he notes 'can't possibly pay.'. . . When the Indonesian newspaper Sinar Harapan referred forthrightly to Suharto family monopoly interests last fall, it was closed."[531]

Iraq: "Iraq's government is essentially a family affair and army politics became bizarrely entwined with family politics. . . . Problems exist elsewhere in the repressive apparatus that keeps the regime in power."[532]

Kenya: A report discusses "the Kenya Government's decision to build a 60-story prestige building . . . [costing $200 million, which] can be put to much better purposes, like assisting the credit-starved agrarian sector." [533]

Liberia: A report cites "President Doe's growing appetite for government-subsidized extravagances. He owns a small fleet of luxury automobiles and is said to spend lavishly on clothes and jewelry. . . . "Well-connected senior Government workers have also grown wealthy through lucrative business opportunities, obtained through the executive mansion."[534]

Mexico: "[A] labyrinth of regulations encourages many legitimate business innovators to remain in the underground. The alternative can mean months or years of delays and costly legal assistance."[535]

Morocco: "[A]t the bottom of Morocco's troubles lies . . . the defeat of a true market economy by the concentration of power and wealth in a bloated network of bureaucrats and well-connected families ultimately controlled by the monarch."[536]

Nigeria: "In a crackdown on dissent, the Government this year disbanded the National Trade Union Council, the National Students' Union and the National University Professors' Union. Thirty universities were temporarily closed. Journalists have been detained. Magazines have been seized. . . . Keeping officers happy involves allowing as many officers as possible a chance for power and personal enrichment."[537]

Pakistan: "Some ministers and top officials are said to have made fortunes out of kickbacks on contracts with government-owned steel and flour mills, and from deals in which government land worth millions of dollars was obtained for as little as $20,000, then quickly resold."[538]

Peru: "[O]nly 1 percent of Peruvian laws emanate from the body created to make them: Parliament. The other 99 percent derive from the executive . . . with no interference, no debate, no criticism and, often enough, without the knowledge of those affected by them."[539]

Senegal: A report points out that "27 companies completely operated by the state and 75 quasi-public concerns, all of which together employ 25,000 people, four times the manpower that some critics say is needed in these enterprises. . . . an economy under very tight control."[540]

Sierra Leone: "Economists attribute the rice shortage largely to the low prices paid to producers in Sierra Leone's overvalued currency. . . . [I]mporting rice spins off more money than growing it. . . . Lack of foreign exchange has meant that spare parts are now scarce. That, in turn, has led to frequent power outages. . . . There is no longer a functioning railroad. . . . A farmer who does manage to bring in a good crop may not be able to get it to market."[541]

Sudan: "[A] wave of political terror has claimed doctors, lawyers, journalists, poets and trade unionists. Hundreds have been detained and scores executed for the crime of dissent. . . . [T]he press has been shackled, trade unions abolished and political parties stripped of their property by military rulers."[542]

Syria: "Because of the atmosphere of pervasive insecurity, anyone who is anyone in Syria has his team of bodyguards. These men prey on the populace at large, stopping cars and breaking into homes with impunity."[543]

Tanzania: "[A]ccording to World Bank dictates, the Government raised the producer price of cotton two years ago. The cotton growers, responding as they were supposed to, worked harder and harvested twice the amount of cotton as they had in the past. But the roads to the cotton farms were so poor, trucks were unable to get to the harvest, much of the cotton went bad in storage and the farmers were left unpaid. Some cotton farmers persevered for a second season, but with the same results."[544]

Turkey: "[T]orture is still being used by the Turkish police in nearly every case of arrest."[545]

Venezuela: "Down here, powerful families with close ties to government often control whole industries nearly by themselves. . . . Near monopolies are common, as in much of Latin America. . . . [F]riends in politics are almost a requirement for business success here."[546]

Zaire: "Some of [President] Mobutu's overseas real estate holdings are public knowledge. They include chateaus in Spain and Belgium, a townhouse in Paris, a villa near Monte Carlo, an estate in Switzerland, a horse ranch in Portugal and a villa in the Ivory Coast."[547]

Zimbabwe: "[I]nvestment is being undermined partly by the foreign-exchange crisis but also by price controls and labor regulations, that have deterred entrepreneurs from expanding capacity. . . . Zimbabwe is . . . establishing new parastatals and new interlocking, and even duplicative, state organizations to manage its economy."[548]

Appendix 23.2: Selected References to Structural Adjustment

1. In 1984, the World Bank proposed a special fund to "make low-interest loans to the poorest black African countries if they agreed to adopt domestic economic policies that the World Bank and most aid-giving nations deem sensible. These would include adopting realistic exchange rates for their currencies and setting food prices at levels that would encourage farmers to increase production."[549]

2. "The Administration wants the [Inter-American Development Bank] to make its loans conditional upon market-oriented policy shifts."[550]

3. A report by Richard Feinberg, president of the Overseas Development Council, called for the World Bank "to make a much greater percentage of its loans as 'structural adjustment,'" with the IMF and the Bank "assuming the lead role at the country level." This cooperative effort would "follow a line of thinking among some Treasury officials."[551]

4. In 1987, James Bovard wrote that the "structural adjustment program has been a dismal failure. . . . SALs [structural adjustment loans] are often used to perpetuate government control rather than to induce pro-market reforms. . . . In the Ivory Coast the SAL was used to pay the debts of floundering government enterprises. In Senegal, the SAL bankrolled the budgets of government-owned agricultural companies. In Pakistan, bank aid was used to

'rationalize' state-owned companies, but auditors concluded that efficiency had not been increased. . . . [T]he companies are still losing money."[552]

5. In 1987, the International Monetary Fund created an \$8.4 billion facility for long-term, low-interest loans to countries "that undertake strong three-year programs to improve their balance of payments position and to foster growth."[553] This move marked a fundamental shift from the Fund as short-term lender to finance temporary balance of payments difficulties to a longer-term lender to finance structural change.

6. In 1988, a proposal by James D. Robinson circulated in Washington, for an Institute of International Debt and Development (known as I2D2), which would buy debts of less-developed countries to banks at a deep discount, cancelling them in exchange for government securities from the borrowing countries. But the conditions would be "tougher than the structural adjustment conditions. . . . Participant nations would be required to open their borders to trade and foreign investment and privatize state industries."[554]

7. In 1989, Hernando de Soto argued that the structural adjustment policies advocated by international lending agencies and governments of more-developed countries would alternatively be negotiated by private groups in the less-developed countries. "Truly effective structural adjustment must well up from the bottom, not be imposed by international institutions and foreign governments. . . . Recent events in Peru attest to a groundswell of support for the same types of policies that would have been required by the IMF. . . .[I]nformal transportation operators in Peru successfully lobbied the government for the enactment of a package of measures that included the reduction of taxes and tariffs and the removal of duties on tire imports."[555]

Appendix 23.3: Skilled versus Unskilled Labor in the United States

1. Drucker found in 1987 "a steady shift from labor-intensive to knowledge-intensive industries." He wrote that "as a proportion of the working population, blue-collar workers in manufacturing have already decreased to less than a fifth of the American labor force from more than a third."[556]

2. "The labor pool of younger workers who historically fill entry-level jobs is declining both in numbers and in quality, for reasons ranging from the demographic to the social, while the jobs waiting for them require ever more knowledge and skill. . . . Also, more people who once went into entry-level jobs after high school now go to college." At the same time, "entry-level jobs are growing more complex and demanding." Therefore, companies increasingly finance education and training programs to promote job skills.[557]

3. William Wilson[558] wrote of "the disappearance over the last quarter-century of hundreds of thousands of low-skill jobs, mainly involving physical labor." Reubens, however, argued that Wilson had noted not so much a decline in low-skill jobs as their migration from the North and East to the South and West.[559]

4. In 1988, Drucker argued that "blue-collar labor no longer accounts for enough of the total costs to give low wages much competitive advantage" for low-wage countries competing with United States industry.[560]

5. "Worker skills are sadly lacking, employers increasingly complain. . . . A high-school diploma no longer means the grad 'can read and write or add and subtract,' an AmeriFirst Bank official says."[561]

6. A 1988 study by the Commission on Youth and America's Future[562] argued that "America's highly competitive technological society places great emphasis on educational attainment. . . . 'Those with less education must scramble for good jobs in a sea of part-time, low-paying, limited-future employment opportunities.'"[563]

7. A survey of business executives in 1989 indicated that United States students "are not being educated fast enough and at sophisticated enough levels to keep pace with the advances and upgrading in jobs."[564]

8. Uchitelle argues, however, that the reputed shortage of skilled workers in the United States is a myth. Rather, the oversupply of college graduates has resulted in unskilled jobs being offered to them instead of to less educated applicants. "The college degree, or even the evidence of having participated in college, has become the nation's major form of job certification," since a high-school graduation alone does not imply the required amount of discipline or functional literacy.[565]

9. Supporting the trend indicated in preceding reports, a study by Bluestone and Harrison in 1987 showed that although employment has been increasing, most of the new jobs are in low-paying unskilled occupations.[566]

10. But Brookes pointed out that by using the wrong deflator, Bluestone and Harrison "dramatically understated constant-dollar wage scales." Relying on Labor Department data, he argued that "this whole low-pay jobs thesis is largely a statistical fraud resulting from careful selection of unrepresentative years. . . . The notion that the U.S. economy is producing mostly low-paying, unskilled jobs is an economic fiction."[567]

11. In June, 1994, however, a commission of the U. S. Departments of Labor and Commerce, headed by Professor John T. Dunlop of Harvard University, issued a report detailing "the development of an underclass of low-paid and unskilled workers unable to compete in a complex marketplace."

In commenting on this report, Robert Reich, Secretary of Labor, declared: "A society divided between the haves and have-nots or the well-educated and the poorly-educated can not be a stable society over time."[568]

Appendix 23.4: Political and Economic Reforms in South Africa during the 1980/1990s.

This list was compiled partly from Jerry B. Eckert's articles in *Christian Science Monitor*, "Economics can Defeat Apartheid," 28 March 1989, and "Rethinking South Africa," 21 April 1989, and partly from current news sources.

1978: Eating places, theaters, rest rooms, public parks desegregated.

1979: Government began investing millions in job training for black productivity and incomes. In the most recent twelve years [1977-89], real black income rose 65 percent, while real white income declined 5 percent.

1980: Beginning of massive investment in black education. Fifteen classrooms per working day are built. Expenditure on black schooling has grown 30 percent per year. Aim is to bring black education up to white before desegregation.

1981: Black and mixed-race unions legalized. Strikes for higher wages, some successful. Sports integrated.

1984: Uniform tax laws for all races. Universities desegregated.

1985: Mixed marriages act and Morality act repealed. Job reservations acts (reserving specific jobs for whites) largely bypassed and not enforced.

1986: Racial barriers removed for "international" hotels. South African citizenship restored to citizens of homelands. Pass laws abolished. Government announced it would no longer enforce Group Areas Act (which placed areas off limits for black homes). "Gray areas" (mixed-race residences) appearing in Johannesburg, other major cities. Sales of liquor allowed to all races. Separate systems of courts removed. U.S. Congress imposes Federal sanctions on South Africa.

1987: Job Reservations Acts repealed.

1987 and 1989: Dutch Reformed Church states that segregation is a sin.

1989: Free Settlement Areas Act permits residential areas to apply for and be granted exemptions from Group Areas Act, thus becoming nonracial. National Party adopts "black vote in five years" as party platform for September elections. Johannesburg desegregates swimming pools and recreation centers. All beaches opened to persons regardless of color.

1990: Buses in Johannesburg open to all races.

1991: Apartheid land laws abolished. Law defining people by race repealed. President George Bush lifts most US Federal sanctions; those of many localities in U.S. remain.

1992: Whites in referendum overwhelmingly approve negotiations to end minority rule.

1993: African National Congress accepts the idea of power-sharing with white elements. Parliament adopts laws giving blacks participation in government; elections are called in which a black president would be possible. Nelson Mandela calls for ending of sanctions. Other countries and U.S. localities start to comply. New constitution abolishes apartheid.

1994: Nelson Mandela elected the first black president.

Appendix 23.5: References to Groups and Emerging Pluralism in the Third World

I. Groups with Promise of Becoming Bargaining Agents

1. In British East Africa in colonial times, "with increasing urbanization, immigrants to the towns often formed associations which, in addition to fulfilling other functions, settled disputes between members, applying the customary rules of behaviour as best they might in the new situations which arose."[569]

2. Working class organization began in Egypt about 1908. In 1922, a Commission on Commerce and Industry was set up, which became the Egyptian Federation of Industry in 1924.[570]

3. In West Africa in the early twentieth century, "just as wage-earners established trade unions, so, too, the indigenous distributive system spawned new commercial organizations, . . . such as the Ivory Coast Transporters' Association, which grew up in the 1950s."[571]

4. "[A] new Movement of the Landless is gaining momentum throughout Brazil and, with strong support from activist sectors of the Roman Catholic Church, it has so far set up 42 similar camps. . . . Its immediate objective is to insure that the Government carries out a law . . . with the intention of distributing 100 million acres of land to 1.4 million families through 1989. . . . [T]he group is trying to mobilize the peasantry to resist the mounting political offensive of those opposed to land redistribution."[572]

5. "Under the leadership of Verghese Kurien, a champion of India's producer cooperatives, peanut farmers in Bhaunagar and four other districts of Gujarat began banking together in 1979 in an effort to break the hold of the area's powerful oil millers and traders on the peanut industry. . . . The cooperative is part of a growing network of village units that are seeking to restructure the region's economy, which revolves around peanut production."[573]

II. Corporate Groups Co-opted by the Power Group

1. "In the 1950s a voluntary cooperative movement grew beyond traditional functions [in Tanzania] and spread rapidly in the coffee and cotton regions. It did not come because of a swelling of mass participation, as Nyerere had envisioned, but in response to perceived opportunity. [These unions] were initiated, organized, and controlled by African traders and farmers."[574] However, they ran counter to the Nyerere government's plans for socialist villages. In 1967, the Government took control of sixteen regional cooperative unions.

2. In Mexico, the Plan de Ayala group, taking its name from Zapata's revolutionary manifesto, "has successfully coordinated dozens of peasant protests in southern Mexico in recent years, often with violent results. . . . Last month, about 10,000 peasants affiliated with the Plan de Ayala chapters converged on the capital to publicize land complaints."[575] No agreement was reached, and such peasant protests—common throughout Mexican history—have generally failed.

3. Again in Mexico, "a group of peasant farmers (*campesinos*) . . . decided to petition for title to the land. . . . [The] petition [was] denied because of lack of corroborating documents. Some 35 pages of details apparently did not satisfy certain federal bureaucrats. No wonder campesinos are driven by such bureaucratic obfuscation to informal land seizures."[576]

III. Groups with Unfocused Objectives

1. "A crowd of 15,000 chanting, jeering protesters marched through Managua today to dramatize their grievances against the Nicaraguan Government . . . . [T]he march provided a narrow slice of common ground between groups that agree on little beyond their distaste for the Sandinistas [the government]."[577]

2. Before the overthrow of the Duvalier government in Haiti in 1986, demonstrations broke out in several towns, thousands of students boycotted classes, and anti-government flyers were circulating.[578] While the points of discontent were clear—mainly unemployment, inflation, and government profligacy—nevertheless no specific set of demands was advanced, that the government might have been capable of undertaking.

3. During June 1987, protesters in South Korea had made specific demands, including direct presidential elections, release of political prisoners, and restoration of civil rights to dissidents, but the reports of these did not contain any information on protesters and government negotiating directly. On July 1, the government granted these demands. Yet the protest continued,

with no agenda other than the overthrow of the government—"down with dictatorship" and "down with America"—which could hardly have been accomplished by these means.[579]

Notes

1. Commons 1934.
2. Buchanan and Tullock 1962.
3. Romer 1988:170.
4. Rawls 1971.
5. Williamson 1985.
6. Alchian and Woodward 1988:77.
7. The Coase theorem—which contributed to its author's winning the Nobel Prize in 1991—might be applied to the distribution of pollution rights under the Clean Air Act of 1990. Assume that at any time and place, a certain amount of pollution is acceptable, because the wind will blow it away or air dissolve it. Companies with noxious emissions are awarded a limited number of marketable rights to pollute, set so that total pollution is no more than the acceptable level. A company whose clean-up costs are less than the market value of its rights will gain by selling them to a company whose cleanup is more costly. The total amount of pollution is contained at the acceptable level in the least costly manner. According to Coase's theorem, the final distribution of rights after trading would be the same no matter what the initial distribution. The market is therefore an efficient allocator.

   But the Coase theorem leaves many questions unanswered, as Coase himself would agree. How do we decide on the original distribution of rights? Why should a company be awarded the right to pollute just because it is already polluting? The power-diffusion process, while not necessarily adjudicating pollution rights, provides a framework to consider how *any* rights— over land, capital, labor, or other economic good—are allocated historically, and how the institutions of trading, financing, and adjudicating those rights are evolved. Thus we call on historical evolution rather than a round table of "wise people."
8. Kaempfer and Lowenberg 1992: chapter 3 and Mueller (1989). Other introductions are found in Brennan (1990), Buchanan (1979, 1984), Mueller (1990), Sandmo (1990), and Wagner and Gartney (1988).
9. North 1981, 1990.
10. North and Thomas 1973.
11. Weber 1958, 1964.
12. Bauer 1972.
13. Boulding 1990.
14. Brenner, Reuven 1983.
15. E.L. Jones 1988:128.
16. Kenneth B. Powelson assisted me in the preparation of this appendix.
17. Hall 1970:206.
18. Takekoshi 1930:2:354.
19. Takekoshi 1930:2:499.
20. Wigmore 1969:90.
21. Bix 1986:109.
22. Hall 1970:167.

23. Takekoshi 1960:2:363.
24. Takekoshi 1930:3:125.
25. Tuchman 1984:290-96.
26. Epstein 1991:55.
27. de Tocqueville 1856/1955:97.
28. Epstein 1991:245-46.
29. Tuchman 1984:370.
30. Black 1984:115.
31. Berman 1983:394.
32. Shatzmiller 1990.
33. Braudel 1979:448.
34. Cannon 1988:334.
35. Cannon 1988:380.
36. Smith, Dennis 1982
37. Tuchman 1984:284.
38. Miller 1987:129.
39. Miller 1987:214.
40. Sicard 1986:217ff.
41. de Tocqueville 1856/1955:109.
42. Rosenberg and Birdzell 1986:122.
43. Kolbert and Mackay 1977:56-57; Hogue 1966:217-18.
44. Powelson 1988: chapter 7 (pp.67-75).
45. Epstein 1991:129.
46. Cannon and Griffiths 1988:225.
47. Brenner 1985:49.
48. Brenner 1985:51.
49. Braudel 1979:180.
50. Hogue 1966:52.
51. Hogue 1966:57-58.
52. Hogue 1966:67.
53. Gilles 1986:82-83.
54. Tuchman 1978:298-99.
55. Tuchman 1978:280-81.
56. Tuchman 1978:423-24.
57. Tuchman 1978:471.
58. Holborn 1959:51.
59. Bobrick 1987:329.
60. Miller 1987:18.
61. Miller 1987:179.
62. Miller 1987:246.
63. Ozouf 1989:494-503.
64. Craig 1988:90.
65. Bottigheimer 1982:182.
66. Berman 1977:926.
67. Miller 1987:29.
68. Hibbert 1987:187.
69. Miller 1987:29-30.
70. Holborn 1959:299-300.

71. Braudel 1984:185.
72. Holborn 1959:340.
73. Cannon and Griffiths 1988:526.
74. EBMa 1974:19:761.
75. EBMa 1974:19:762.
76. EBMa 1974:19:763.
77. EBMa 1974:6:1007.
78. EBMa 1974:6:490.
79. Lewis 1988:187.
80. Alpers 1975:517.
81. Levtzion 1976:116.
82. EBMa 1974:.
83. Levtzion 1975:160-61.
84. Fisher 1975:64.
85. Fisher 1975:85-86.
86. Fisher 1975:129.
87. Shinnie 1965:142.
88. Wilks 1976:435.
89. Alpers 1975:527.
90. Adeleye 1976:573.
91. Gray 1975:7.
92. Gray 1975:11.
93. Rodney 1975:234.
94. Rodney 1975:257.
95. Birmingham 1975:344.
96. Birmingham 1975:371.
97. Abir 1975:553.
98. Alpers 1975:524.
99. Levtzion 1975:168.
100. Levtzion 1975:216.
101. Marks and Gray 1975:436.
102. Rodney 1975:280.
103. Birmingham 1975:373-74.
104. Marks and Gray 1975:458.
105. Unomah and Webster 1976:289.
106. Unomah and Webster 1976:270-77.
107. Fisher 1975:121.
108. Unomah and Webster 1976:284.
109. Fisher 1975:141.
110. Hopkins 1973:127.
111. Johnson 1976:102.
112. Harms 1981:43.
113. Horton 1976:106.
114. Horton 1976:76-77.
115. Horton 1976:110.
116. Wilks 1976:427; Hopkins 1973:47.
117. Wilks 1986:421.

118. Marks and Gray 1975:400.
119. Birmingham 1975:381, who cites Mainga 1973.
120. Marks 1975:400.
121. Alpers 1975:478.
122. Alpers 1975:480-81.
123. Marks and Gray 1975:438.
124. Suret Canale and Barry 1976:504.
125. Wilks 1976:449.
126. Birmingham 1975:372.
127. Alpers 1975:514.
128. Hopkins 1973:62.
129. Richmond 1977:63.
130. Unomah and Webster 1975:303.
131. Birmingham 1976:260-61.
132. Marks and Gray 1975:417.
133. Hopkins 1973:21-23.
134. Harms 1981:151.
135. Chanock 1985:160.
136. Harms 1981:35, 177.
137. Fisher 1975:101.
138. Harms 1981:35.
139. Fisher 1975:97.
140. Chanock 1985:163, attributed to M. Phiri, "Chewa History in Central Malawi and the Use of the Oral Tradition," Ph.D. thesis, Wisconsin, 1975.
141. Birmingham 1975:372.
142. 1981:169.
143. Harms 1981:224.
144. Hopkins 1973:225.
145. Marques 1976:89.
146. Chanock 1985:235.
147. Chanock 1985:13-15.
148. Chanock 1985:169.
149. Chanock 1985:170.
150. *New York Times*, 8/25/81.
151. Ibrahim, Youssef M., in *New York Times*, 11/27/88.
152. University of Wisconsin, Land Tenure Center *Newsletter* No. 68.
153. Brooke, James in *New York Times*, 11/01/87.
154. Rule, Sheila, in *New York Times*, 06/09/85.
155. Cowell, Alan, in *New York Times*, 04/21/82.
156. See also articles in the *New York Times*,11/2/83, 11/15/87, 11/19/89, 2/25/90, and 3/3/90.
157. As Senior Economic Advisor at the Ministry, I participated in preparing the revisions.
158. Rule, Sheila, in *New York Times*, 6/5/85. See also articles in *New York Times*, 6/10/84, 6/11/84, 6/5/85, 7/3/85, 4/13/86, 8/15/89, and 1/31/90.
159. May, Clifford, *New York Times*, 6/11/84.
160. Ibrahimn, Youssef M., "In Algeria, Hope for Democracy but not Economy," *New York Times*, 7/26/91.
161. *Wall Street Journal*, 12/30/80.

162. Brooke, James, in *New York Times*, 8/11/88. See also articles in *New York Times* on 11/21/82, 2/12/83, 1/8/84, 10/2/85, 3/4/86, 6/22/88, 6/4/89, 8/11/88, and 1/14/90.

163. Brooke, James, in *New York Times*, 11/23/87.

164. Brooke, James, in *New York Times*, 3/6/88.

165. Morris and Read 1976:264.

166. *New York Times*, 8/19/87.

167. Brooke, James, in *New York Times*, 09/29/88

168. Greenhouse, Steven, in *New York Times*, 05/24/88.

169. Greenhouse, Steven, in *New York Times*, 05/04/88.

170. See *New York Times*, 08/09/81, 08/10/81, 08/16/81. 08/30/81, 06/18/82, 06/06/83 (article on torture), 10/06/83, 10/25/83, 04/13/86, 12/14/86, 02/04/87, 02/08/87, for a small sample.

171. Editorial in *New York Times*, 12/15/86.

172. Moseley, Ray, in *Chicago Tribune*. From *Boston Globe*, 09/25/81.

173. World Bank 1977:82.

174. *New York Times*, 10/15/81.

175. Markham, James M., "King Hassan's Quagmire," *New York Times Magazine*, 4/27/80.

176. Rule, Sheila, in *New York Times*, 7/13/87.

177. Brooke, James, in *New York Times*, 1/31/86.

178. Thurow, Roger, in *Wall Street Journal*, 9/12/88.

179. May, Clifford, in *New York Times*, 9/165/87; Hardin, Blaine, in *Washington Post Weekly*, 1/18/88; and Rule, Sheila, in *New York Times*, 4/29/88.

180. *Time Magazine*, 1/16/84.

181. Perlez, Jane, *New York Times Magazine*, 11/6/88.

182. *New York Times*, 9/17/81 and 9/30/81.

183. Noble, Kenneth B., *New York Times*, 1/31/90.

184. Brooke, James, *New York Times*, 3/22/87.

185. Battersby, John D., *New York Times*, 11/9/87; Wren, Christopher, *New York Times*, 1/29/89.

186. Lescaze, Lee, *Wall Street Journal*, 7/24/85.

187. Kaufman, Michael, *New York Times*, 9/26/83. Other *New York Times* references to intertribal violence in Zimbabwe occur on 7/24/80, 7/25/80, 11/16/80, 10/8/81, 6/11/84, 3/3/85, 12/21/87, and 12/23/87.

188. Wolpert 1977:99.

189. Lewis 1988:164.

190. Wolpert 1977:110.

191. Ludden 1985:44.

192. Ludden 1985:49-50.

193. Ludden 1985:59.

194. Ludden 1985:72.

195. Wolpert 1977:168ff.

196. Gordon 1979:65.

197. Gordon 1979:66.

198. Ludden 1985:97.

199. Creel 1980:28.

200. Billeter 1985:165.

201. Santangelo 1985:269.

202. Hulsewe 1985:221-22.

203. Spence 1987:1.

204. Loewe 1985:259.
205. Jacobs 1958:31.
206. Jacobs 1958:30.
207. Eberhard 1977:253.
208. Grimm 1985:28.
209. Santangelo 1985:274.
210. Grimm 1985:34.
211. Eberhard 1977:274.
212. Fairbank, Reischauer and Craig 1978:752.
213. Butterfield, Fox, "China Eases Policy of Sending Youth to Countryside," *New York Times*, 12/5/78.
214. Butterfield, Fox, *New York Times*, 3/27/79.
215. Butterfield, Fox, "China's Liberalized Farm Rules Pay Off for Peasants," *New York Times*, 4/5/80.
216. Butterfield, Fox, "China Trades the Little Red Book for a Little Adam Smith," *New York Times*, 9/7/80.
217. Wren, Christopher S., "China Offers Output Incentive," *New York Times*, 3/23/83.
218. Bennett, Amanda, "Despite Deng's Quest for a Credible China, Truth Remains Elusive," *Wall Street Journal*, 7/30/85.
219. Shirk, Susan L., "Still Moving Toward Market Socialism," *New York Times*, 9/29/85.
220. Leung, Julia, "Beijing Orders Sweeping Cuts in Investment," *Wall Street Journal*, 10/10/88.
221. Kristof, Nicholas D., "Beijing Authority Being Challenged by Local Powers," *New York Times*, 12/11/88.
222. WuDunn, Sheryl, "China Cracks Down on Private Work," *New York Times,* 11/08/89.
223. Eberhard 1977:24-26.
224. Eberhard 1977:50.
225. Loewe 1985:240.
226. Fairbank, Reischauer and Craig 1978:78.
227. Fairbank, Reischauer and Craig 1978:82.
228. Eberhard 1977:95-6.
229. Eberhard 1977:101.
230. Loewe 1985:250.
231. Loewe 1985:252.
232. Eberhard 1977:111.
233. Eberhard 1977:112-13.
234. Eberhard 1977:109.
235. Eberhard 1977:118.
236. Eberhard 1977:122.
237. Powelson 1988:164.
238. 1977:144.
239. Eberhard 1977:181.
240. Lewis 1988:8.
241. Eberhard 1977:212.
242. Eberhard 1977:214.
243. Eberhard 1977:216.
244. Eberhard 1977:226.
245. Will 1985:302.

246. Eberhard 1977:254.
247. Eberhard 1977:286-87.
248. Eberhard 1977:277.
249. Santangelo 1985:278.
250. Creel 1980:46.
251. Cohen 1980:10.
252. Hulsewe 1985:213.
253. Eberhard 1977:79.
254. Jacobs 1958:35.
255. Brockman 1980:89.
256. Brockman 1980;106.
257. Fairbank, Reischauer and Craig 1978:907.
258. Fairbank, Reischauer and Craig 1978:907.
259. Fairbank, Reischauer and Craig 1978:919.
260. MacFarquhar 1983:330.
261. Bennett, Amanda, "In Today's New China, Red Guards of the '60s Are a Lost Generation," *Wall Street Journal*, 1/4/85.
262. "Chinese, in a Flush of Candor, Say Things Aren't All Working Right," *New York Times*, 11/11/78.
263. Butterfield, Fox, "China's Road to Progress is Mostly Uphill," *New York Times*, 2/4/79.
264. Wren, Christopher S., "Chinese Trying to Undo Damage in Tibet," *New York Times*, 5/3/83.
265. Wren, Christopher S., "China Reagan Will Visit Unlike That Nixon Saw," *New York Times*, 4/24/84.
266. Bennett, Amanda, "China Plans a Transformation of Economy to Unpeg Prices, Reduce State Planning Role," *Wall Street Journal*, 10/11/84.
267. Sterba, James P., and Bennett, Amanda, "Peking Turns Sharply Down Capitalist Road in New Economic Plan," *Wall Street Journal*, 10/25/84.
268. Drucker, Peter F., "No Jobs for the Millions is China's Nemesis," *Wall Street Journal*, 11/19/87.
269. Ignatius, Adi, "Despite Recent Gains, China is Again Facing a Shortage of Grain," *Wall Street Journal*, 1/19/88.
270. Kristoff, Nicholas D., "Chinese Local Powers Facing Cash Shortage," *New York Times*, 4/15/89.
271. Ignatius, Adi, "For China's Managers, Keeping Plants Going is a Daily Struggle," *Wall Street Journal*, 4/13/90.
272. Sterba, James P., "Peking Congress Meets to Adopt Economic Change, New Leaders," *New York Times*, 8/31/80.
273. Ignathius, David, "Reagan to find a China Considerably Changed by Deng's Pragmatism," *Wall Street Journal*, 4/23/84.
274. Wren, Christopher S., "Chinese Take 'Free' Out of Enterprise," *New York Times*, 9/15/84.
275. Wren, Christopher S., "China's Cities to Get More Capitalism," *New York Times*, 11/14/84.
276. Wren, Christopher S., "Chinese Announce Sweeping Changes in their Economy," *New York Times*, 10/21/84.
277. Wren, Christopher S., "China's Forgotten Corner Dreams of Days to Come," *New York Times*, 11/23/84.
278. *Wall Street Journal*, 1/2/85.
279. Wang, David, "Tibet's Proud People Chafe Under Chinese Rule," *Wall Street Journal*, 9/9/85.
280. Gargan, Edward A., "Chinese Official Urges Moderation," *New York Times*, 3/26/88.
281. Gargan, Edward A., "China Gives Managers Greater Control in Industry," *New York Times*, 4/14/88.

282. Gargan, Edward A., "The Short March to Capitalism Takes a Great Leap," *New York Times*, 4/22/88.
283. House, Karen Elliott, "Beijing Vice Premier Vows to Press Reform on Nation's Economy," *Wall Street Journal,* 12/10/93.
284. Burns, John F., "Citing Declines in Grain, China Defers on Policy," *New York Times*, 1/1/86.
285. Editorial, *Wall Street Journal*, 9/8/96.
286. Gargan, Edward A., "Opposition Astir over Economy in China," *New York Times*, 2/1/87.
287. Gargan, Edward A., "China Halts Plan for Curb on Party," *New York Times*, 3/23/87.
288. Gargan, Edward A., "Chinese Premier, in Major Speech, Adopts Hard Line," *New York Times*, 3/26/87.
289. Gargan, Edward A., "China Reining in Economy's Shift to a Free Market," *New York Times*, 10/17/88.
290. Kristof, Nicholas D., "China Again Moves Central Planning to Center Stage," *New York Times*, 3/21/89.
291. Butler 1977:68.
292. Dewey 1977:61-2.
293. Blum 1961:262.
294. Kleimola 1977:30.
295. Raeff 1984:4.
296. Raeff 1984:4-5.
297. Keller, Bill, "Soviet Miners Seek Control of Union," *New York Times*, 9/17/89.
298. Keller, Bill, "Gorbachev's Grand Plan: Is It Real or a Pipe Dream?" *New York Times*, 12/5/88.
299. Keller, Bill, "Soviet Progressive Seek to Form an Independent Bloc," *New York Times*, 4/23/89.
300. Starr, S. Frederick, "The Disintegration of the Soviet State," *Wall Street Journal*, 2/6/90.
301. Solchanyk, Roman, "Red Storm Rising in the Ukraine," *Wall Street Journal*, 6/6/89.
302. Starr, S. Frederick, "Scenes from a New Revolution," in a book review of *The New Russians*, by Hedrick Smith, *New York Times Book Review*, 12/9/90.
303. Remnick, David, "Lithuania and Goliath," *Washington Post Weekly*, 8/21-27/89.
304. Clines, Francis X., "Defiance of Kremlin's Control is Accelerating in Soviet Asia," *New York Times*, 7/1/90.
305. Smith, R.E.F., 1971:1966.
306. Lawrence 1978:43.
307. Blum 1961:94.
308. Lawrence 1978:86-87.
309. Lawrence 1978:85.
310. From S.M. Solov'ev, quoted by Bartlett 1974:4 and by Dukes 1977:108.
311. Bobrick 1987:202.
312. Kahan 1989:160.
313. Lawrence 1978:122.
314. Lawrence 1978:154.
315. Berman 1963:195.
316. Blum 1961:140.
317. Berman 1963:199-200.
318. Berman 1963:223.
319. Bobrick 1987:208.
320. EBMa 1974:16:48.

321. Raeff 1984:63.
322. EBMa 1974:16:54.
323. Braudel 1973:424.
324. Braudel 1973:408.
325. Dukes 1977:106.
326. Dukes 1977:110.
327. Raeff 1984:29.
328. Raeff 1984:31.
329. EBMa 1974:16:58.
330. Raeff 1984:147.
331. Lawrence 1978:42.
332. Blum 1961:139.
333. Blum 1961;143.
334. Kleimola 1977:35.
335. Bobrick 1987:77.
336. Bobrick 1987:329.
337. Marques 1972:79.
338. Payne 1973:1:5.
339. Payne 1973:1:8.
340. Marques 1972:189.
341. Marques1972:206.
342. Wilson 1967:494.
343. Payne 1973:224.
344. Melko and Hord 1984:42.
345. Marques 1972:317-18.
346. Lynch 1981:1:63.
347. Lynch 1981:1:112.
348. Lynch 1981:1:124.
349. Marques 1972:265.
350. Lynch 1981:1:137.
351. Lynch 1981:1:141.
352. Elliott 1984:137.
353. Payne 1973:293.
354. Payne 1973:101.
355. Lynch 1981:1:16.
356. Lynch 1981:1:109.
357. Lynch 1981:1:119.
358. Lynch 1981:1:230.
359. Payne 1981:2:2.
360. Lewis 1988:84.
361. Lynch 1981:7-8.
362. Payne 1973:59.
363. Lynch 1981:1:43.
364. Lynch 1981:2:281.
365. Payne 1973:270.
366. Payne 1973:157.
367. Lynch 1981:1:18.

368. Payne 1973:273.
369. Marques 1972:95.
370. Marques 1972:184-5.
371. Lynch 1981:1:124.
372. Payne 1973:356.
373. Payne 1973:384.
374. Brenner 1985:35.
375. Payne 1973:166.
376. Payne 1973:175.
377. Payne 1973:176.
378. Payne 1973:313-4.
379. Payne 1973:323.
380. Payne 1973:352.
381. Lynch 1981:2:153.
382. Riding, Alan, "Getting Mexico Moving Again," *New York Times Magazine*, 07/04/82.
383. Ulman, Neil, "Mexicans Feel Pinch of Austerity Measures but are Stoic About it," *Wall Street Journal*, 11/15/85.
384. Meislin, Richard J., "Mexico's Perpetual Political Machine," *New York Times*, 6/30/85.
385. Meislin, Richard J., "Mexico's Election: Nation's Image May Have Lost," *New York Times*, 7/16/85.
386. Asman, David, "The PRI's 'Cure' in Southern Mexico," *Wall Street Journal*, 3/3/87.
387. Riding, Alan, "Mexican President Emphasizes Farming," *New York Times*, 4/9/80.
388. Walsh, Mary Williams, "Poor People of Mexico, Afraid of Protesting, Endure Much Injustice," *Wall Street Journal*, 12/29/86.
389. Rohter, Larry, "Battleground in Mexico: Union Power," *New York Times*, 1/12/89; Moffett, Matt, "Mexico's President Asserts his Authority." *Wall Street Journal*, 1/12/89.
390. Riding, Alan, "The Crisis in Mexico," *New York Times*, 8/23/82.
391. Kandell, Jonathan, "Mexico City's Growth, Once Fostered, Turns into Economic Burden," *Wall Street Journal*. 10/04/85.
392. "In the Shadow of the Dollar," editorial in *New York Times*, 8/25/82.
393. Frazier, Steve, "Earthquake Aftermath Points up Weaknesses of Mexican Leadership," *Wall Street Journal*, 10/15/85.
394. Walsh, Mary Williams, "When Mill in Mexico is Closed, It Can Take Some Time to Shut," *Wall Street Journal*, 10/13/86.
395. Walsh, Mary Williams, "Poor People of Mexico, Afraid of Protesting, Endure Much Injustice," *Wall Street Journal*, 12/29/86.
396. Rohter, Larry, "Divestment Efforts in Mexico Debated," *New York Times*, 4/13/87.
397. Asman, David, "Has the Mexican Government Rigged the Oil Business?" *Wall Street Journal*, 2/6/87.
398. Kinzer, Stephen, "One Marxist's Mission: To Outvote Sandinistas," *New York Times*, 10/7/84.
399. Lowenstein, Roger, "Sandinistas Stir Up Much Dissatisfaction Among Rich and Poor," *Wall Street Journal*, 6/20/84.
400. Kinzer, Stephen, "Sandinista is Favored but Runs Hard," *New York Times*, 10/30/84.
401. Gruson, Lindsey, "Ex-Contras, Citing Broken Promises, Seize Land and Talk Again of War," *New York Times*, 10/29/90.
402. Kinzer, Stephen, "Nicaragua: The Beleaguered Revolution," *New York Times Magazine*, 3/28/83.

403. *Time*, 4/16/84. Also quoted in Powelson and Stock 1990:323.
404. Lowenstein, Roger, "Sandinistas Stir Up Much Dissatisfaction Among Rich and Poor," *Wall Street Journal*, 6/20/84.
405. Lange, Timothy, "Former Nun Roasts Sandinista Government," *Colorado Daily* (Boulder, Colorado), 11/30/84.
406. Asman, David, "Despair and Fear in Managua," *Wall Street Journal*, 3/25/85.
407. Krauss, Clifford, "How One Businessman Manages to Survive Nicaraguan Sandinistas," *Wall Street Journal*, 10/8/85.
408. LeMoyne, James, "Along the Honduran Border, the Peasant Refugees Rally to the Contras, *New York Times*, 3/4/87.
409. Uhlig, Mark A., "In the Democracy of Nicaragua, Control is Still from the Top, *New York Times*, 9/23/90.
410. Kinzer, Stephen, "Sandinistas Seek to Win Credibly," *New York Times*, 7/29/84.
411. Uhlig, Mark A., "Strikes Testing Chamorro's Rule," *New York Times*, 5/16/90; other articles by Uhlig 4/24, 5/18, 5/30, 7/11, 7/12, and 7/13/90.
412. Gruson, Lindsey, "In Managua, Chamorro Takes Hold," *New York Times*, 6/17/90.
413. Rowe 1957:161-3, cited in Randall 1977:4:30.
414. Randall 1977:4:54.
415. Randall 1977:4:32.
416. Randall 1977:4:55.
417. Randall 1977:4:76.
418. Randall 1977:4:84.
419. Randall 1977:4:101.
420. From a senate commission; cited by Randall 1977:4:129.
421. Randall 1977:4:140.
422. Guillet 1978.
423. Riding, Alan, "Garcia Asks for Change and Peruvians Say Sí!" *New York Times*, 12/25/85.
424. de Onis, Juan, "Peru's New Chief Won by Shrewd Use of Military Issues," *New York Times*, 5/21/80.
425. Riding, Alan, "In Peru, a New Personality Attracts a Cult," *New York Times*, 8/4/85.
426. Gilpin, Kenneth N., "A Consensus on Latin Debt," *New York Times*, 9/10/83.
427. Riding, Alan, "Peru, in Economic Disarray, Directs its Anger at the President," *New York Times*, 10/20/88.
428. Riding, Alan, "Family Farming Replaces Collectivization in Peru," *New York Times*, 12/11/88.
429. Randall 1977:3:140.
430. Cehelsky 1979:25-6.
431. McDowell, Edwin, "Brazil Alters its Export Mix," *New York Times*, 1/7/79.
432. Hoge, Warren, "Brazil is Seeking to Untangle Itself from Red Tape," *New York Times*, 10/2/79.
433. Hoge, Warren, "Brazil Hopes to Make a Semi-Desert Bloom," *New York Times*, 5/18/80.
434. Hodge, Warren, "Brazil's Economy After the Miracle," *New York Times*, 7/17/83.
435. Hoge, Warren, "As the Fortunes of Brazil Founder, Jobless Make a Profession of Peddling," *New York Times*, 7/22/83.
436. Pine, Art, "Brazil's Foreign Debt Seems Under Control As Domestic Ills Grow," *Wall Street Journal*, 12/5/85.
437. Campos, Roberto (former Minister of Finance), "A Protectionist Monster Threatens Brazil's Development," *Wall Street Journal*, 1/29/88.
438. Riding, Alan, "Improving Brazilian Social Welfare Proves Far Easier Said than Done," *New York Times*, 8/9/88.

439. Editorial, *New York Times*, 8/29/88.

440. Cohen, Roger, "Brazil's Price Spiral Nears Hyperinflation, Could Ruin Economy," *Wall Street Journal*, 12/8/88.

441. Bridges, Tyler, "Brazil Attacks Capital Flight, but What of its Causes?" *Wall Street Journal*, 1/20/89.

442. Cockburn, Alexander, "Brazil's Poor Get Hungrier on Bare-Bones IMF Menu," *Wall Street Journal*, 3/23/89.

443. de Onis, Juan, "O.A.S. Meeting to Focus on Human Rights Violations," *New York Times*, 11/16/80.

444. Schumacher, Edward, "Argentina's Jubilant Rebirth of Politics," *New York Times*, 7/21/82.

445. Schumacher, Edward, "Argentina's Jubilant Rebirth of Politics," *New York Times*, 7/21/82.

446. Ulman, Neil, "Argentine Democracy Faces Debt Problems, Trouble from Unions," *Wall Street Journal*, 2/24/84.

447. Schumacher, Edward, "Defending Argentina's New Democracy," *New York Times Magazine*, 6/10/84.

448. *New York Times*. 8/23/84.

449. Diehl, Jackson, "Alfonsín's Political Cure for Argentina's Economy Isn't Working," *Washington Post*, 9/17/84.

450. Cardenas, Emilio J., "Argentine Politics Must Cool Down," *New York Times*, 11/20/84.

451. Chavez, Lydia, "Leader Imposes a State of Siege on Argentina," *New York Times*, 10/26/85.

452. Chavez, Lydia, "Perón's Movement Splits Wide Open," *New York Times*, 2/13/85.

453. Christian, Shirley, "The Argentina Leadership is Shaken by Setbacks," *New York Times*, 11/29/87.

454. O'Donnell 1978:138.

455. Schumacher, Edward G., "Defending Argentina's New Democracy," *New York Times Magazine*, 6/10/84.

456. Helguera, Eduardo, "Argentina's Ghost-Chasers Stalk the Economy," *Wall Street Journal*, 2/15/85.

457. Hatch, George, "Argentine Election Lacks Credible Opposition Party," *Wall Street Journal*, 10/31/85.

458. Tanoira, Manuel J., "Confessions of an Argentine Privatizer," *Wall Street Journal*, 5/29/87.

459. Christian, Shirley, "Argentina's Woeful Services," *New York Times*, 10/13/87.

460. Graham, Bradley, "Don't Dial for Me, Argentina," *Washington Post Weekly*, 2/15-22/88.

461. Tanoira, Manuel, "U.S. Bailout of Argentina: More of the Same Poison," *Wall Street Journal*, 8/12/88.

462. Cohen, Roger, "Argentine Trains, Economy Spin Wheels," *Wall street Journal*, 3/2/89.

463. National Bureau of Economic Research paper no. 2897, as described by Clark, Lindley H., "Argentina Has Plenty to Cry About," *Wall Street Journal*, 5/24/89.

464. Christian, Shirley, "Another Crisis in Argentina is Prompting Radical Ideas," *New York Times*, 2/12/90.

465. Kandell, Jonathan, "Argentines, as Usual, See Country Averting Plunge into Poverty," *Wall Street Journal*, 6/22/89.

466. Christian, Shirley, "Argentines See Spread of Poverty's Pain, and Start to Believe It," *New York Times*, 7/22/90.

467. de Onis, Juan, "Argentina's Economic Skid Mars the Junta's Record," *New York Times*, 8/17/80.

468. Schumacher, Edward, "Argentine Debt: A Case Study," *New York Times*, 3/12/84.

469. Cohen, Roger, "After a Long Decline, Argentina is Striving to Revive Economy," *Wall Street Journal*, 11/12/86.

470. "Argentina Acts to Acquit Military," Reuters, *New York Times*, 12/23/86; "Justice Diluted in Argentina, editorial, *New York Times*, 2/25/87.
471. Epstein 1991:46.
472. Browning 1971:61.
473. Browning 1971:42.
474. Ostrogorsky 1966:212.
475. Lewis 1988:55-56.
476. Finley, Smith, and Duggan 1987:57.
477. Cahen 1970:530.
478. Kunt 1983:31.
479. Findley 1980:121-22.
480. Findley 1980:13-15.
481. Findley 1980:7.
482. Haider 1966:169.
483. Richmond 1977:56.
484. Findley 1980:152.
485. Lambton 1953:385.
486. Editorial, "Sketches of the Iraqi and Kuwaiti Leaders," *New York Times*, 8/3/90.
487. Martin, Douglas, "Saudi Arabia's New Capitalism," *New York Times*, 2/21/82.
488. Reed, Stanley, "Syria's Assad: His Power and His Plan," *New York Times Magazine*, 2/19/84.
489. Bakhash, Shaul, "Iran, 5 Years Later, Divided and in Conflict," *New York Times*, 2/10/84.
490. Sciolino, Elaine, "The Big Brother: Iraq Under Saddam Hussein," *New York Times Magazine*, 2/3/85.
491. Browning 1987:34.
492. Epstein 1991:46-47. The inner quotation is from Boak 1928:609.
493. Lewis 1988:57.
494. Lewis 1988:30-31.
495. Findley 1980:14.
496. Findley 1980:19.
497. Findley 1980:27.
498. Findley 1980:39.
499. Issawi 1971:288-89.
500. Carsten 1959:6.
501. Carsten 1959:9,
502. Carsten 1959:353.
503. Carsten 1959:150.
504. Carsten 1959:217.
505. Carsten 1959:359.
506. Carsten 1959:431.
507. Gross 1974:15-16.
508. Rose 1974:67.
509. Carsten 1959:198-99.
510. Carsten 1959:266.
511. Melko and Hord 1984:31.
512. Carsten 1959:155-56.
513. Carsten 1959:169.
514. Carsten 1959:208.
515. Carsten 1959:362.

516. Greenhouse, Steve, "Algerians' Misfortune: 'Quick Blow' From Oil," *New York Times*, 10/12/88.

517. Christian, Shirley, "Another Crisis in Argentina is Prompting Radical Ideas," *New York Times*, 2/12/90.

518. Martin, Everett G., "Bolivian's Difficulties Have Them Worrying About the Next Coup," *Wall Street Journal*, 3/2/84.

519. Cockburn, Alexander, "Piggies at Market: The Brazilian Paradigm, *Wall Street Journal*, 4/12/90.

520. Erlanger, Steven, "Burmese Military is Forcing Mass Migration from Cities," *New York Times*, 3/21/90.

521. French, Howard W., "Sugar's Bitter Harvest: Slave Labor?" *New York Times*, 4/27/90.

522. Brooke, James, "African Nation Opens Door to French," *New York Times*, 11/1/87.

523. Rosewicz, Barbara, "Factory Owner Joins Egypt's Export Push but Runs Into Hurdles," *New York Times*, 11/11/85.

524. Perletz, Jane, "Ethiopians Driven From Good Earth," *New York Times*, 9/12/89.

525. Rule, Sheila, "Ghana's Women Maintain their Corner on the Marketplace," *New York Times*, 6/9/85.

526. Kouril, Kathleen, "Fear and Crumbling in Rawlings's Ghana," *New York Times*, 4/17/87.

527. Danner, Mark D., "The Struggle for a Democratic Haiti," *New York Times Magazine*, 6/21/87:59.

528. Primorac, Max, "New Honduran Game Plan Depends on Follow-Through," *Wall Street Journal*, 3/23/90.

529. Kinzer, Stephen, "Honduran Judge, in Jail, Ponders Quality of Justice," *New York Times*, 4/2/85.

530. Passell, Peter, "India's Slow-Growth Path," *New York Times*, 3/18/87.

531. Rosett, Claudia, "Indonesia Vote Marks Development Crossroad," *Wall Street Journal*, 4/20/87.

532. Mylroie, Laurie, "Saddam Was in Desperate Trouble," *Wall Street Journal*, 8/10/90.

533. Kilson, Martin, and Cottingham, Clement, "In Africa, Democracy Needs Some Help," *New York Times*, 2/2/90.

534. Noble, Kenneth B., "Doe Lives High as Liberian Economy Erodes," *New York Times*, 3/26/90.

535. Alisky, Marvin, "Tapping the Resources of Mexico's Underground Economy," *Wall Street Journal*, 12/30/88.

536. Schwartz, Ethan, "Morocco's Plutocracy Strangles Capitalism," *Wall Street Journal*, 8/17/89.

537. Brooke, James, "An Agile Nigerian President Keeps Troubles at Bay and Himself at Top," *New York Times*, 8/11/88.

538. Crosette, Barbara, "Bhutto Finds New Era Is Still an Elusive Goal," *New York Times*, 11/08/89.

539. Vargas Llosa, Mario, "In Defense of the Black Market," *New York Times Magazine*, 2/27/87:45.

540. Gupte, Pranbay B., "Senegal, Once France's Star Colony, Sees Glory Dim," *New York Times*, 9/17/80.

541. May, Clifford D., "In Sierra Leone, Diamonds and Decay," *New York Times*, 6/21/84.

542. Editorial, *New York Times*, 6/18/90.

543. Reed, Stanley, "Syria's Assad: His Power and His Plan," *New York Times Magazine*, 2/19/84:57.

544. Perlez, Jane, "Tanzanian Economy Is Still Limping Despite Outside Money," *New York Times*, 3/18/90.

545. Laber, Jeri, "Cruel and Usual Punishment," *New York Review*, 7/20/89:34.

546. Lowenstein, Roger, "In Venezuela, Name of Cisneros Connotes Wealth and Influence," *New York Times*, 2/21/85.

547. Brooke, James, "Two Vultures in Zaire: Corruption and Neglect," *New York Times*, 2/4/87.

548. Hawkins, Tony, "Illusionary Prosperity in Zimbabwe," *New York Times*, 11/08/88.

549. Lewis, Paul, "World Bank Plan for Aid to Africa Divides Members," *New York Times*, 9/16/84.

550. Kilborn, Peter P., "Shifts Sought at Latin Bank," *New York Times*, 5/26/86.

551. Rosen, Hobart, "Conable's World Bank," *Washington Post National Weekly Edition*, 7/14/86.

552. Bovard, James, "World Bank Confidentially Damns Itself," *Wall Street Journal*, 9/23/87.

553. Pearson, David G., and Lachica, Eduardo, "IMF Creates $8.4 Billion Facility For Poorest Nations, Marking Shift," *Wall Street Journal*, 12/30/87. Also, IMF Press Release, 12/29/87, reported in *IMF Survey*, 1/11/88.

554. Melloan, George, "I2D2's Problem: Empires Usually Strike Back," *Wall Street Journal*, 3/8/88.

555. de Soto, Hernando, "A Latin American View of the Brady Plan," *Wall Street Journal*, 5/19/89.

556. Drucker, Peter F., "The Rise and Fall of the Blue Collar Worker," *Wall Street Journal*, 4/22/87.

557. Simpson, Janice C., "A Shallow Labor Pool Spurs Businesses to Act to Bolster Education," *Wall Street Journal*, 9/28/87.

558. Wilson, William, 1987.

559. Reubens, Edwin P., "Low-Skill Jobs have Migrated, not Vanished," Letter to the Editor, *New York Times*, 12/9/87.

560. Drucker, Peter F., "Low Wages No Longer Give Competitive Edge," *Wall Street Journal*, 3/16/88.

561. Labor Letter, *New York Times*, 8/16/88.

562. "The Forgotten Half: Pathways to Success for America's Youth and Young Families." *New York Times*, 11/19/88.

563. "Many in U.S. Face Bleak Job Outlook," *New York Times*, 11/19/88.

564. Fiske, Edward B., "Impending U.S. Jobs 'Disaster': Work Force Unqualified to Work," *New York Times*, 9/25/89.

565. Uchitelle, Louis, "Surplus of College Graduates Dims Job Outlook for Others," *New York Times*, 6/18/90.

566. Bluestone, Barry, and Harrison, Bennett, "The Grim Truth About the Job MIracle," *New York Times* 2/1/87.

567. Brookes, Warren T., "Low-Pay Jobs: The Big Lie," *Wall Street Journal*, 3/25/87.

568. Manegold, Catherine S., "Study Warns of Growing Underclass of the Unskilled," *New York Times*, 6/3/94.

569. Morris and Read 1972:186.

570. Richmond 1977:200.

571. Hopkins 1973:253.

572. Riding, Alan, "Brazilians Still Await Land Grant," *New York Times*, 4/8/86.

573. Hazarika, Sanjoy, "India's Farmers Seek to Share in the Peanuts," *New York Times*, 2/5/84.

574. Powelson and Stock 1990:63-4.

575. Orme, William A., Jr., "Mexico's Promised Land: After 70 Years, Peasants Still Fight," *Washington Post Weekly*, 5/27/85.

576. Alisky, Marvin, "Tapping the Resources of Mexico's Underground Economy," *Wall Street Journal*, 12/30/88.

577. Uhlig, Mark A., "15,000 Opponents of Sandinistas Hold Protest March in Nicaragua," *New York Times*, 1/16/89.

578. Treaster, Joseph E., "Protests Resume in Haiti, Posing New Challenge to Duvalier Regime," *New York Times*, 1/9/86.

579. Haberman, Clyde, "Fury and Turmoil: Days that Shook Korea," *New York Times*, 7/6/87; and Kristof, Nicholas D., "Seoul Protesters Fight Government with Huge Rally," *New York Times*, 7/9/87.

Bibliography

This bibliography contains only works cited in the text. Space does not permit the listing of all works consulted.

Articles in anthologies are listed by author of the article, with reference to the editor(s) under whose names the anthologies are listed elsewhere in this bibliography.

Abir, M. "Ethiopia and the Horn of Africa," in Gray, 1975.

Aceña, Pablo Martín. "Development and Modernization of the Financial System," in Sanchez-Albornoz, 1987.

Adeleye, R.A. "Hausaland and Borno 1600-1800," in Ajayi and Crowder, 1976.

Adelman, Irma, and Morris, Cynthia Taft. *Economic Growth and Social Equity in Developing Countries*, Stanford, CA, Stanford University Press, 1973.

Adelman, Irma, and Morris, Cynthia Taft. *An Anatomy of Income Distribution Patterns in Developing Countries*, Washington, DC, International Development Association, 1971.

Afrika Institut. *The Future of Customary Law in Africa,* Leiden, Universitaire Pers, 1956.

Ajayi, J. F. A., and Crowder, Michael, eds. *History of West Africa*, volume 1, New York, Columbia University Press, 1976.

Alagoa, E. J. "The Niger Delta states and their neighbours to 1800," in Ajayi and Crowder, 1976.

Alchian, Armen A., and Woodward, Susan. "The Firm is Dead; Long Live the Firm," *Journal of Economic Literature*, March 1988.

Allmand, Christopher. *Henry V,* Berkeley, University of California Press, 1992.

Alpers, Edward A. "Eastern Africa," in Gray, 1975.

Amsden, Alice H. *Asia's Next Giant: South Korea and Late Industrialization*, New York, Oxford University Press, 1989.

Anderson, James N.D. "Customary Law and Islamic Law in British African Territories," in Afrika Institut, 1956.

Anderson, Philip W.; Arrow, Kenneth J.; and Pines, David, eds. *The Economy as an Evolving Complex System,* Reading MA, Addison Wesley, 1988.

Arnold, Arthur Z. *Banks, Credit, and Money in Soviet Russia*, New York, Columbia University Press, 1937.

Arthur, W. Brian. "Self-Reinforcing Mechanisms in Economics," in Anderson, Arrow, and Pines, 1988.

Asakawa, Kanichi. "The Life of a Monastic Sho in Medieval Japan," *Annual Report of the American Historical Association for 1916*, Washington, DC, 1916.

Asakawa, Kanichi. "The Early Sho and the Early Manor: A Comparative Study," *Journal of Economic and Business History*, volume L, no. 2, London, January 1929.

Asakawa, Kanichi. "The Founding of the Shogunate by Minamoto no Yoritomo," *Seminarium Kondakovianum: Receuil d'Etudes Archéologie. Histoire d'Art. Etudes Byzantines.* VI, Prague, 1933.

Asakawa, Kanichi. "The Origin of the Feudal Land Tenure in Japan," *The American Historical Review*, volume 20, no. 1, October 1914.

Aspe, Pedro. *Economic Transformation the Mexican Way*, Cambridge MA, MIT Press, 1993.

Aston, T. H., and Philpin, C. H. E. *The Brenner Debate: Agrarian Class Structure and Economic Development in Pre-Industrial Europe,* Cambridge University Press, 1985.

Babinger, Franz. *Mehmed the Conqueror and His Time,* Bollingen Series XCIV, Princeton University Press, 1978.

Bairoch, Paul. "Agriculture and the Industrial Revolution," in Cipolla, 1973.

Bak, Janos, and Benecke, Gerhardt, eds. *Religion and Rural Revolt*, Manchester, Manchester University Press, 1984.

Baklanoff, Eric N. *The Economic Transformation of Spain and Portugal*, New York, Praeger, 1978.

Balassa, Bela, and Williamson, John. *Adjusting to Success: Balance of Payments Policy in the East Asian NICs*, Washington, DC, Institute for International Economics, 1987.

Banerjee, Anil Chandra. *The Agrarian System of Bengal*, volume 1: 1582-1793, Calcutta, K. P. Bagchi, 1980.

Banks, Arthur, et al, eds. *Political Handbook of the World: 1990*. Government and Inter-Governmental Organizations as of June 1, 1990, Binghamton, NY, CSA Publications, 1990.

Banks, Arthur, et al, eds. *Political Handbook of the World*, 1989, Binghamton, NY, CSA Publications, 1989.

Barber, Malcolm. *The Two Cities: Medieval Europe, 1050-1320*, London, Routledge, 1992.

Barnes, J.A. *Politics in a Changing Society*, Manchester, Manchester University Press, 1967.

Barraclough, Geoffrey, ed. *The Times Atlas of World History*, London, Times Books, 1984.

Barraclough, Geoffrey. *The Origins of Modern Germany*, Second Revised Edition, paperback 1979, New York, Paragon Books, 1947.

Barraclough, Geoffrey. *The Crucible of Europe: The Ninth and Tenth Centuries in European History,* Berkeley, CA, University of California Press, 1976.

Barthelemy, Dominique. "The Aristocratic Households of Feudal France: Kinship," in Duby, 1988.

Bastid, Marianne. "The Structure of the Financial Institutions of the State in the Late Qing," in Schram, 1985.

Bauer, P.T. *Dissent on Development: Studies and Debates in Development Economics,* Cambridge, MA, Harvard University Press, 1972.

Bauer, P.T. *The Development Dilemma: Reality and Rhetoric*, Cambridge, MA, Harvard University Press, 1984.

Benecke, Gerhard. "The Westphalian Circle, the County of Lippe and Imperial Currency Control," in Vann and Rowan, 1974.

Bergier, Jean-François. "From the Fifteenth Century in Italy to the Sixteenth Century in Germany: A New Banking Concept?" in California University, 1979.

Berliner, Joseph S. *Soviet Industry from Stalin to Gorbachev,* Ithaca, NY, Cornell University Press, 1988.

Berman, Harold J. *Law and Revolution: The Formation of the Western Legal Tradition*, Cambridge, MA, Harvard University Press, 1983.

Berman, Harold J. "The Origins of Western Legal Science," *Harvard Law Review,* March, volume 90, No. 5, 1977.

Berman, Harold J. *Justice in the U.S.S.R.: An Interpretation of Soviet Law,* Cambridge, MA, Harvard University Press, 1963.

Biebuyck, Daniel, ed. *African Agrarian Systems*, Oxford, Oxford University Press, 1963.

Bierwirth, Henry Christian. "Peddlers, Merchants and Middlemen: Lebanese Entrepreneurs in West Africa," student paper at University of Colorado, unpublished, 1963.

Birmingham David. "The Forest and the Savanna of Central Africa," in Flint, 1976.

Birmingham David. "Central Africa from Cameroun to the Zambezi," in Gray, 1975.

Birnbaum, Henrik. *Lord Novgorod the Great: Essays in the History and Culture of a Medieval City-State*, Columbus, OH, Slavica Publishers, 1981.

Bix, Herbert P. *Peasant Protest in Japan, 1590-1884*, New Haven and London, Yale University Press, 1986.

Black, Antony. *Guilds and Civil Society in European Political Thought from the Twelfth Century to the Present*, Ithaca, NY, Cornell University Press, 1984.

Blakemore, Harold. "José Manuel Balmaceda," in Delpar, 1974.

Bloch, Marc. *Feudal Society*, London, Routledge and Kegan Paul, 1966.

Bloch, Marc. *Feudal Society*, volumes 1 and 2, University of Chicago Press, 1961.

Blomquist, Thomas W. "The Dawn of Banking in an Italian Commune: Thirteenth Century Lucca" in California University, 1979.

Blum, Jerome. *The End of the Old Order in Rural Europe*, Princeton University Press, 1978.

Blum, Jerome. *Lord and Peasant in Russia: From the Ninth to the Nineteenth Century*, Princeton, NJ, Princeton University Press, 1961.

Blum, Jerome. "The Rise of Serfdom in Eastern Europe," *American Historical Review*, volume LXII, 1957.

Boak, A.E.R. "The Book of the Perfect," *Journal of Economic and Business History*, volume 1 (1928-9):597-619, 1928.

Bobrick, Benson. *Fearful Majesty: The Life and Reign of Ivan the Terrible,* New York, G.P. Putnam's Sons, 1987.

Bodde, Derk. *Essays on Chinese Civilization,* Princeton University Press, 1980.

Bohannan, Paul. "'Land,' 'Tenure,' and 'Land Tenure,'" in Biebuyck, 1963.

Bolin, Sture. "Scandinavia," in Postan, 1966.

Borton, Hugh. *Peasant Uprisings in Japan of the Tokugawa Period*, New York, Paragon Book Reprint, 1968.

Bottigheim, Karl S. *Ireland and the Irish*, New York, Columbia University Press, 1982.

Boulding, Kenneth E. *Three Faces of Power,* Newbury Park, CA, Sage Publications, Inc., 1990.

Bowman, Alan K. *Egypt After the Pharaohs, 332 B.C. - A.D. 642*, Berkeley, University of California Press, 1986.

Boxer, C.R. *The Golden Age of Brazil, 1695-1750: Growing Pains of a Colonial Society,* Berkeley, University of California Press, 1984.

Bozeman, Adda B. *Conflict in Africa: Concepts and Realities*, Princeton University Press, 1976.

Braudel, Fernand. *The Perspective of the World, volume 3, Civilization and Capitalism, 15th-18th Century,* New York, Harper and Row, 1984.

Braudel, Fernand. *The Wheels of Commerce, volume 2, Civilization and Capitalism, 15th-18th Century,* New York, Harper and Row, 1982.

Braudel, Fernand. *The Structures of Everyday Life, volume 1, Civilization and Capitalism, 15th-18th Century,* New York, Harper and Row, 1981.

Braudel, Fernand. *La Méditerranée et le Monde Méditerranéen à l'Epoque de Phillipe II*, two volumes, Paris, Librairie Armand Colin, 1979.

Braunthal, Gerard. *The Federation of German Industry in Politics*, Ithaca, NY, Cornell University Press, 1965.

Brennan, Geoffrey. "James Buchanan's Public Economics: One Proposition, Two Speculations, and Three Queries," *Constitutional Political Economy*, Spring/Summer, volume 1, 1990.

Brenner, Reuven. *History—The Human Gamble*, University of Chicago Press, 1983.

Brenner, Robert. "Agrarian Class Structure and Economic Development in Preindustrial Europe," *Past and Present*, no. 70, February 1976, reprinted in Aston and Philpin, 1985.

Brewer, John, and Styles, John, eds. *An Ungovernable People: The English and Their Law in the Seventeenth and Eighteenth Centuries*, New Brunswick, NJ, Rutgers University Press, 1980.

Broadhead, Philip. "Rural Revolt and Urban Betrayal in Reformation Switzerland: the Peasants of St. Gallen and Zwinglian Zurich," in Bak and Benecke, 1984.

Brockman, Rosser H. "Commercial Contract Law in Late Nineteenth-Century Taiwan," in Cohen, Edwards, and Chang Chen, 1980.

Browning, Robert. *Justinian and Theodora*, revised edition, London, Thames and Hudson, 1987.

Bruce, John W., and Dorner, Peter W. "Agricultural Land Tenure in Zambia: Perspectives, Problems and Opportunities," Land Tenure Center, Madison, WI, unpublished, September 1982.

Bruguière, Marie Bernard; Gilles, Henri; and Sicard, Germain. *Introduction à l'Histoire des Institutions Françaises*, Toulouse, Editions Privat, 1986.

Buchanan, James M. *What Should Economists Do?* Indianapolis, Liberty Press, 1979.

Buchanan, James M., and Tollison, Robert D., eds. *The Theory of Public Choice*, Ann Arbor, University of Michigan Press, 1984.

Buchanan, James M., and Tullock, Gordon. *The Calculus of Consent*, Ann Arbor, University of Michigan Press, 1962.

Burmeister Larry L. "The South Korean Green Revolution: Induced or Directed Innovation?" *Economic Development and Cultural Change*, July 1987.

Burke, Peter. "Mediterranean Europe, 1500-1800," in Bak and Benecke, 1984.

Bury, J.B.; Gwatkin, H.M.; and Whitney, J.P., eds. *The Cambridge Medieval History*, Cambridge University Press, 1964.

Butler, William E. "Foreign Impressions of Russian Law to 1800: Some Reflections," in Butler, 1977.

Butler, William E., ed. *Russian Law: Historical and Political Perspectives*, Leiden, A.W. Sijthoff, 1977.

Byrd, William. *China's Financial System: The Changing Role of Banks*, Boulder, CO, Westview Press, 1983.

California University = Center for Medieval and Renaissance Studies, University of California, Los Angeles, *The Dawn of Medieval Banking,* New Haven, CT, Yale University Press, 1979.

Cahen, Claude. "Economy, Society, Institutions," in Holt, Lambton, and Lewis, 1970.

Cannon, John, and Griffiths, Ralph. *The Oxford Illustrated History of the British Monarchy*, Oxford University Press, 1988.

Cantor, Norman F. *The Civilization of the Middle Ages*, New York, Harper Collins, 1993.

Carreras, Albert. "An Annual Index of Spanish Industrial Output," in Sanchez-Albornoz, 1987.

Carsten, F.L. *Princes and Parliaments in Germany: From the Fifteenth to the Eighteenth Century*, Oxford, Clarendon Press, 1959.

Castan, Yves. "Politics and Private Life," in Chartier, 1989.

CEHE = *Cambridge Economic History of Europe*: volume 1, see Postan, 1966; volume 2, see Rich and Wilson, 1967; volume, 3, see Postan, Rich, and Miller, 1971; volume 4, see Rich and Wilson, 1967; volume 5, see Rich and Wilson, 1977; volume 6, see Habakkuk and Postan, 1965; volume 7, see Mathias and Postan, 1978.

Cehelsky, Marta. *Land Reform in Brazil: The Management of Social Change*, Boulder, CO, Westview Press, 1979.

Chanock, Martin. *Law, Custom and Social Order: The Colonial Experience in Malawi and Zambia,* Cambridge University Press, 1985.

Chartier, Roger. "Introduction," in Chartier, 1989.

Chartier, Roger, *A History of Private Life*, volume 3, Cambridge MA, Belknap, Harvard. 1989.

Chang Chen, Fu-mei. "The Influence of Shen Chih-Ch'i's Chi-Chu Commentary Upon Ch'ing Judicial Decisions," in Cohen, Edwards, and Chang Chen, 1980.

Chaudhuri, K. N. *Trade and Civilization in the Indian Ocean: An Economic History from the Rise of Islam to 1750,* Cambridge University Press, 1985.

Cheung, Steven. "Privatization vs. Special Interests: The Experience of China's Economic Reforms," *Cato Journal*, winter 1989.

Chevalier, François. *Land and Society in Colonial Mexico: The Great Hacienda,* Berkeley, University of California Press, 1963.

CIA (U.S. Central Intelligence Agency). *Soviet Gross National Product in Current Prices, 1960-80,* Washington, DC. Central Intelligence Agency, 1983.

Cipolla, Carlo M. *Before the Industrial Revolution: European Society and Economy, 1000-1700,* Second Edition, New York, Norton Press, 1980.

Cipolla, Carlo M., *The Fontana Economic History of Europe*, volume 3, Glasgow, Fontana/Collins, 1973.

Cipolla, Carlo M. "The Italian and Iberian Peninsulas," in Postan, Rich, and Miller, 1971.

Clark, Samuel. *Social Origins of the Irish Land War*, Princeton University Press, 1979.

Clark, Ronald J. *Land Reform and Peasant Market Participation on the Northern Highlands of Bolivia*, Land Tenure Center Research Paper No. 42, Madison, WI, University of Wisconsin, LTC, 1968.

Clendenning, Philip H. "The Economic Awakening of Russia in the Eighteenth Century," *Journal of European Economic History*, Sept-Dec 1985.

Cohen, Jerome A.; Edwards, R. Randall; and Chang Chen, Fu-mei, eds. *Essays on China's Legal Tradition*, Princeton University Press, 1980.

Cole, David C. and Lyman, Princeton N. *Korean Development: The Interplay of Politics and Economics*, Cambridge, MA, Harvard University Press, 1971.

Colton, Timothy J. *The Dilemma of Reform in the Soviet Union*, New York, Council of Foreign Relations, 1986.

Conquest, Robert. *Harvest of Sorrow: Soviet Collectivization and the Terror-Famine*, Oxford University Press, 1986.

Corbo, Vittorio; Krueger, Anne; and Ossa, Fernando, eds. *Export-Oriented Development Strategies: The Success of Five Newly Industrializing Countries*, Boulder, CO, Westview Press, 1985.

Cotler, Julio. "The New Mode of Political Domination in Peru," in Lowenthal, 1975.

Coulson, Noel J. *Commercial Law in the Gulf States: The Islamic Legal Tradition*, London, Graham and Trotman, 1984.

Coulson, Noel J. "Islamic Law," in Derrett, 1968.

Crawcour, Sydney. "The Development of a Credit System in Seventeenth-Century Japan," *Journal of Economic History*, volume 21, 1961.

Creel, Herlee. "Legal Institutions and Procedures during the Chou Dynasty," in Cohen, Edwards, and Chang Chen, 1980.

Curtin, Philip D. "The Atlantic Slave Trade 1600-1800," in Ajayi and Crowder, 1976.

David, Paul. *Technical Choice: Innovation and Economic Growth*, Cambridge University Press, 1975.

Davis, David L. "Ikki in Late Medieval Japan," in Hall and Mass, 1974.

Davison, Roderic S. *Reform in the Ottoman Empire: 1856-1876*, Princeton University Press, 1963.

de la Roncière, Charles. "Tuscan Notables on the Eve of the Renaissance," in Duby, 1988.

de Soto, Hernando. "Constraints on People: The Origins of Underground Economies and the Limits on their Growth," unpublished paper, 1988.

de Soto, Hernando. *The Other Path: The Invisible Revolution in the Third World,* New York, Harper and Row, 1989a.

de Soto, Hernando. *Technical and Statistical Compendium to The Other Path,* New York, Harper and Row. 1989b.

de Vries, Jan. *The Economy of Europe in an Age of Crisis, 1600-1750,* Cambridge University Press, 1976.

Deere, Carmen D. "The Worker-Peasant Alliance in the First Year of the Nicaragua Agrarian Reform," *Latin American Perspectives,* issue 29, spring 1981.

Delpar, Helen, *Encyclopedia of Latin America,* New York, McGraw-Hill, 1974.

Derrett, J. Duncan M. *History of Indian Law (Dharmasastra),* Leiden/Köln, E.J. Brill, 1973.

Derrett, J. Duncan M., *An Introduction to Legal Systems,* New York, Praeger, 1968.

Desai, A.R. *Social Background of Indian Nationalism,* Bombay, G. R. Bhaktai, 1954.

Deschamps, Hubert. "Tradition and Change in Madagascar, 1790-1870," in Flint, 1976.

Dewey, Horace W. "Morality and the Law in Muscovite Russia," in Butler, 1977.

Dietz, Henry A. *Poverty and Problem-Solving Under Military Rule: The Urban Poor in Lima, Peru,* Austin, University of Texas Press. 1980.

Dietz, Henry A., and Moore, Richard J. *Political Participation in a Non-Electoral Setting: The Urban Poor in Lima, Peru,* Papers in International Studies, Latin America Series No. 6, Ohio University Center for International Studies, Latin America Program, Athens, Ohio University, 1979.

Divekar, V.D. *Planning Process in Indian Polity,* Bombay, Popular Prakashan, 1978.

Dollinger, Philippe. *The German Hansa,* Stanford University Press, 1964.

Domar, Evsey D. *Essays in the Theory of Economic Growth,* Oxford University Press, 1957.

Domar, Evsey D. "The Causes of Slavery or Serfdom: A Hypothesis," *Journal of Economic History,* volume 30, 1970.

Dorn, James A. "Economic Reform in China," *Cato Journal,* winter 1989.

Drake, George F. "Elites and Voluntary Associations: a Study of Community Power in Manizales, Colombia," Land Tenure Center Research Paper No. 52, Madison, WI, Land Tenure Center, June 1973

Duby, Georges. *A History of Private Life,* volume II, Cambridge, MA, Belknap Press, 1988.

Duby, Georges. "Introduction: Private Power, Public Power," cited as Duby 1988a, in Duby, 1988.

Duby, Georges. "The Aristocratic Households of Feudal France: Communal Living," cited as Duby 1988b, in Duby, 1988.

Duggan, Lawrence G. "The Church as An Institution of the Reich," in Vann and Rowan, 1974.

Dukes, E. "Catherine II's Enlightened Absolutism and the Problem of Serfdom," in Butler, 1977.

Duus, Peter. *Feudalism in Japan*, New York, Alfred A. Knopf, Inc., 1969.

Dyster, Barrie. "Argentine and Australian Development Compared," *Past and Present*, August 1979.

Easton, David. *Varieties of Political Theory,* Englewood Cliffs, NJ, Prentice Hall 1966.

Eberhard, Wolfram. *A History of China*, Richmond, CA, University of California Press, 1977.

EBMa or EBMi. *Encyclopedia Britannica.* Ma=Macropedia; Mi=Micropedia, Chicago, Encyclopedia Britannica, 1974.

Encyclopedia Britannica. *The Arabs: People and Power*, New York, Bantam Books, 1978.

Epstein, Steven A. *Wage and Labor Guilds in Medieval Europe*, Chapel Hill, University of North Carolina, 1991.

Etzioni, Amitai, ed. *Social Change: Sources, Patterns, and Consequences,* New York, Basic Books. 1964.

Fairbank, John K.; Reischauer, Edwin O.; and Craig, Albert M. *East Asia: Tradition and Transformation*, Boston, MA, Houghton Mifflin Company, 1978.

Fei, John C.H. *Development of the Surplus Economy*, New Haven, Yale University Press, 1964.

Fei, John C. H., and Ranis, Gustav. *Economic Development in Historical Perspective*, New Haven, CT, Yale University Press, 1969.

Fei, John C.H.; Ranis, Gustav; and Kuo, Shirley Y. W., *Growth with Equity: The Taiwan Case*, New York, Oxford University Press, 1979.

Feldbrugge F.J.M. "The Law of Land Tenure in Kievan Russia," in Butler, 1977.

Findley, Carter V. *Bureaucratic Reform in the Ottoman Empire: The Sublime Porte, 1789-1922*, Princeton University Press, 1980.

Finley, M. I.; Smith, Mack; and Duggan, Christopher. *A History of Sicily,* New York, Elizabeth Sifton Books, Viking Press, 1987.

Fisher, H. J. "Egypt, the Funj and Darfur," in Gray, 1975.

Fitzgerald E.V.K. *The State and Economic Development: Peru Since 1968*, Cambridge University Press, 1976.

Flint, John E., *The Cambridge History of Africa,* volume 5, from c.1790 to c.1870, Cambridge University Press, 1976.

Fogel, Robert W. and Engerman, Stanley. *Time on the Cross: The Economics of American Slavery*, Boston, Little Brown, 1974.

Ford, Thomas R. *Man and Land in Peru*, Gainesville, University of Florida Press, 1962.

Frankel, Francine R. "Compulsion and Social Change: Is Authoritarianism the Solution to India's Economic Problems?" in Kohli, 1979.

Friedman, Milton. "Using the Market for Social Development," *Cato Journal*, winter 1989.

Fryde, E.B., and Fryde, M.M. "Public Credit, with Special Reference to North-Western Europe," in Postan, Rich, and Miller, 1963.

Frykenberg Robert E. *Land Control and Social Structure in Indian History,* Madison, WI, University of Wisconsin Press, 1969.

Fukuyama, Francis. "The End of History?" *The National Interest*, September, 1989.

Furet, François, and Ozouf, Mona, eds. *A Critical Dictionary of the French Revolution*, Cambridge, MA, The Belknap Press of Harvard University Press, 1989.

Gang, Dai. "Searching for the Keys: Economists Talk About China's Decentralization," *Beijing Review*, October 24-30, 1988.

García Delgado, José Luís. "Economic Nationalism and State Intervention," in Sanchez-Albornoz, 1987.

Geiger, Theodore. *Tales of Two City-States: The Development Progress of Hong Kong and Singapore*, New York, National Planning Association, 1973.

Genicot, Leopold. "Crisis: From the Middle Ages to the Modern World," in Postan, 1966.

Gilles, Henri. "La France Médiévale," in Bruguières et al., 1986.

Gillis, Malcolm; Perkins, Dwight H.; Roemer, Michael; and Snodgrass, Donald R. *Economics of Development, Second Edition*, New York, W. W. Norton & Company, 1987.

Gluckman, Max. *The Judicial Process among the Barotse of Northern Rhodesia,* Manchester University Press, 1955.

Gluckman, Max. *The Ideas in Barotse Jurisprudence*, Manchester University Press, 1972.

Gold, Thomas B. *State and Society in the Taiwan Miracle*, London, Sharp, East Gate Book, 1986.

Goldman, Marshall. *U.S.S.R. in Crisis: The Failure of an Economic System*, New York, McLeod, 1983.

Goodell, Grace E. "The Philippines," in Powelson and Stock, 1990.

Goodell, Grace E. *The Elementary Structures of Political Life: Rural Development in Pahlavi Iran,* Oxford University Press, 1986.

Goodell, Grace E. "From Status to Contract: The Significance of Agrarian Relations of Production in the West, Japan and in 'Asiatic' Persia," *Archives Européenes de Sociologie,* volume XXI, no. 2, December 1980.

Gordon, Stewart. Comment in "Recovery from Adversity in 18th Century India: Rethinking 'Villages,' 'Peasants,' and Politics in Pre-Modern Kingdoms," *Peasant Studies,* no. 4, 1980.

Granott, A. *The Land System in Palestine: History and Structure,* London, Eyre and Spottiswoode, 1952.

Grant, Michael. *A Social History of Greece and Rome,* New York, Scribner's, 1992.

Gray, Richard. *The Cambridge History of Africa,* volume 4, from c.1600 to c.1790, Cambridge, Cambridge University Press, 1975.

Gregg, Pauline. *Black Death to Industrial Revolution: A Social and Economic History of England,* New York, Barnes and Noble, 1976.

Gregg, Pauline. *Free-born John: A Biography of John Lilburne,* Westport, CT, Greenwood Press, 1961.

Gregory, Paul R. and Stuart, Robert C. *Soviet Economic Structure and Performance,* third edition, New York, Harper and Row, 1986.

Griffeth, Robert, and Thomas, Carol G., eds. *The City-State in Five Cultures,* Santa Barbara, CA, ABC-Clio, 1981.

Grimm, Tilemann. "State and Power in Juxtaposition: An Assessment of Ming Despotism," in Schram, 1985.

Gross, Hanns. "The Holy Roman Empire in Modern Times: Constitutional Reality and Legal Theory," in Vann and Rowan, 1974.

Grossberg, Kenneth A. *The Laws of the Muromachi Bakufu,* Tokyo, Sophia University, 1981.

Grunwald, Joseph. "The Structuralists' School on Price Stability and Development: The Chilean Case," in Hirschman, 1961.

Habakkuk, H. J. "The Economic History of Modern Britain," *Journal of Economic History,* volume 18, 1958.

Habakkuk, H. J., and Postan, M.M., *The Industrial Revolutions and After: Incomes, Population, and Technological Change,* Cambridge Economic History of Europe, volume 6 (in two parts), Cambridge University Press, 1965.

Habib, Irfan. "Northern India under the Sultanate: The Agrarian Economy," in Raychaudhuri and Habib, 1982.

Haejoang, Cho. "A Study of Changing Rural Communities in Korea," *Korea Journal,* June 1981.

Hagen, Everett E. *The Economics of Development,* Homewood, IL, Richard D. Irwin Inc., 1975.

Hagen, Everett E. *On the Theory of Economic Change*, Homewood, IL, Dorsey Press, 1962.

Hall, John W. *Japan: From Prehistory to Modern Times*, New York, Dell, 1970.

Hall, John W., and Takeshi, Toyoda, eds. *Japan in the Muromachi Age*, Berkeley, University of California Press, 1977.

Hall, John W., and Mass, Jeffrey P., eds. *Medieval Japan: Essays in Institutional History*, New Haven, Yale University Press, 1974.

Hallam, Elizabeth, ed. *Four Gothic Kings: The Turbulent History of Medieval England and the Plantagenet Kings—Seen Through the Eyes of Their Contemporaries,* New York, Weidenfeld and Nicholson, 1987.

Hamilton, Clive. *Capitalist Industrialization in Korea*, Westview Special Studies Series, Boulder, CO, Westview Press, 1986.

Hanley, Susan B., and Yamamura, Kozo. *Economic and Demographic Change in Preindustrial Japan, 1600-1868,* Princeton University Press, 1977.

Hanley, Susan B. "A High Standard of Living in Nineteenth-Century Japan: Fact or Fantasy?" *Journal of Economic History,* March, 1983.

Harms, Robert W. *River of Wealth, River of Sorrow: The Central Zaire Basin in the Era of the Slave and Ivory Trade, 1580-1891*, New Haven, CT, Yale University Press, 1981.

Harootunian Harry. "Ideology as Conflict," in Najita and Koschmann, 1982.

Harrison, Joseph. *An Economic History of Modern Spain*, New York, Holms and Meier, 1978.

Harrod, Roy F. "An Essay in Dynamic Theory," *Economic Journal*, volume 49, 1939

Harrod, Roy F. *Towards a Dynamic Economics*, London, Macmillan, 1948.

Harvey, P.D.A., ed. *The Peasant Land Market in Medieval England*, Oxford, Clarendon Press, 1984.

Hasan, Parvez. *Korea: Problems and Issues in a Rapidly Growing Economy*, Baltimore, MD, Johns Hopkins University Press, 1976.

Hasan, Saiyid N. *Thoughts on Agrarian Relations in Mughal India,* New Delhi, People's Publishing, 1973.

Haskell, T.L. "Capitalism and the Origins of the Humanitarian Sensibility," *American History Review*, Part 1 in April, Part 2 in June, 1985.

Hayami, Yujiro, and Ruttan, Vernon W. *Agricultural Development: An International Perspective,* Baltimore, MD, John Hopkins University Press, 1971.

Hayami, Yujiro; Ruttan, Vernon W.; and Southworth, Herman, eds. *Agricultural Growth in Japan, Taiwan, Korea, and the Philippines*, Honolulu, HA, University of Hawaii, 1979.

Hazard, John N. "Soviet Law: The Bridge Years, 1917-1920," in Butler, 1977.

Henderson, Dan Fenno. "Chinese Influences on Eighteenth-Century Tokugawa Codes," in Cohen, Edwards, and Chang Chen, 1980.

Herlihy, David. "Family and Property in Renaissance Florence," in Miskimin, Herlihy, and Udovitch, 1977.

Herr, Elizabeth B. "Lübeck, the Hanseatic League, and Florence: A Comparison,*" Boulder CO, unpublished student paper, 1988.

Herrick, Bruce, and Kindleberger, Charles P. *Economic Development*, New York, NY, McGraw-Hill, 1983.

Hewett, Ed A. *Reforming the Soviet Economy: Equality versus Efficiency*, Washington, DC, The Brookings Institute, 1988.

Hewett, Ed A. "Economic Reform in the Soviet Union," Washington, DC, *The Brookings Review*, spring 1984.

Hibbert, Christopher. *The English: A Social History, 1066-1645*, New York, W. W. Norton and Company, 1987.

Hickok, Susan, and Gray, Clives S. "Capital Market Controls and Credit Rationing in Mali and Senegal," *Journal of Modern African Studies*, 1981.

Hill, Polly. "The History of Migration of Ghana Cocoa Farmers," *Transactions of the Historical Society of Ghana*, 4:1959.

Hilton, Rodney H. "Agrarian Class Structure and Economic Development in Pre-Industrial Europe," *Past and Present*, August 1978.

Hilton, Rodney H. *Bond Men Made Free*, London, Temple Smith, 1973.

Hirschman, Albert O. *Journeys Toward Progress: Studies of Economic Policy-Making in Latin America*, New York, Twentieth Century Fund, 1963.

Hirschman, Albert O. *Latin American Issues*, New York, Twentieth Century Fund, 1961.

Hirschmeier, Johannes. *The Origins of Entrepreneurship in Meiji Japan*, Cambridge, MA, Harvard University Press, 1964.

Hobsbawm, Eric J. "Peasant Land Occupations," *Past and Present*, February 1974.

Hofstede, G. *Culture's Consequences: International Differences in Work-Related Values*, Beverly Hills, Sage, 1980.

Hogue, Arthur H. *Origins of the Common Law*, Bloomington, Indiana University Press, 1966.

Holborn, Hajo. *A History of Modern Germany, 1840-1945*, Princeton University Press, 1968.

Holborn, Hajo. *A History of Modern Germany, 1648-1840*, Princeton University Press, 1964.

Holborn, Hajo. *A History of Modern Germany: The Reformation*, Princeton University Press, 1959.

Holleman, F.D. "The Recognition of Bantu Customary Law in South Africa," in Afrika Institut, 1956.

Holt, J. C.; Lambton, Ann K.S.; and Bernard, Lewis. *The Cambridge History of Islam*, volumes 1 and 2, Cambridge University Press, 1970.

Hong Kong Institute of Science. *The Crisis in Economics and the Hong Kong Response,* Fremont, CA, Victoria Press, 1984.

Hopkins, A.G. *An Economic History of West Africa,* New York, Columbia University Press, 1973.

Horton, Robin. "Stateless Societies in the History of West Africa," in Ajayi and Crowder, 1976.

Hou, Chi-ming, and Yu, Tzong-Shian, eds. *Agricultural Development in China, Japan, and Korea,* Seattle, WA, University of Washington Press, 1983.

Hsiao, Frank S. T., and Hsiao, Mei-chu W. "Taiwanese Economic Development and Foreign Trade, in Kuark, John Y. T., *Comparative Asian Economics,* forthcoming, 1994 (?).

Hsiao, Katharine H. *Money and Monetary Policy in Communist China,* New York, Columbia University Press, 1971.

Hsu, Cho-yun. *Ancient China in Transition: An Analysis of Social Mobility,* Stanford University Press, 1965.

Hulsewe, Anthony. "The Influence of the 'Legalist' Government of Qin on the Economy as Reflected in the Texts Discovered in Yunmeng County," in Schram, 1985.

Hunter, John M. "Cocoa Migration and Patterns of Land Ownership in the Densu Valley near Suhum, Ghana," in Prothero, 1972.

Hunwick, John. "Songhay, Borno and Hausaland in the Sixteenth Century," in Ajayi and Crowder, 1976.

Hutchings, Raymond. *Soviet Economic Development,* New York University Press, 1982.

Huxley, Elspeth. *Red Strangers: A Story of Kenya,* London, Chatto and Windus, 1964.

Imaz, José Luis. *Los Que Mandan (Those Who Rule),* New York, State University of New York Press, 1964.

Ishii, Ryosuke. *Nihon Hoseishi Gaieytsu,* Sobunasha, 1971.

Issawi, Charles, ed. *The Economic History of Iran,* 1800-1914, University of Chicago Press, 1971.

Jacobs, Norman. *The Origin of Modern Capitalism and Eastern Asia*, Hong Kong, Cathay Press, 1958.

Johnson, Douglas. "The Maghrib," in Flint, 1976.

Jones, E.L. *Growth Recurring: Economic Change in World History,* Oxford University Press, 1988.

Jones, E.L. *The European Miracle: Environments, Economies, and Geopolitics in the History of Europe and Asia,* second edition, Cambridge University Press, 1987.

Jones, E.L. *Environments, Economies and Geopolitics in the History of Europe and Asia,* Cambridge University Press, 1981.

Ka, C.M., and Seldon, M. "Original Accumulation, Equity and Late Industrialization: The Cases of Socialist China and Capitalist Taiwan" *World Development,* October/November 1986.

Kahan, Arcadius. *Russian Economic History: The Nineteenth Century,* University of Chicago Press, 1989.

Kaiser, Daniel H. *The Growth of the Law in Medieval Russia,* Princeton University Press, 1980.

Kakar, S. *The Inner World: A Psycho-Analytic Study of Childhood and Society in India, Second Edition,* Delhi, Oxford University Press, 1981.

Kaser, M.C. "Russian Entrepreneurship," in Mathias and Postan, part 2, 1978.

Kaempfer, William H., and Lowenberg, Anton D. *International Economic Sanctions: A Public Choice Perspective,* Boulder CO, Westview Press, 1992.

Kennedy, Paul. *Preparing for the Twenty-First Century,* New York, Random House, 1993.

Kiley, Cornelius. "Estate and Property in the Late Heian Period," in Hall and Mass, 1974.

Kim, Hyong Chun. "Korea's Export Success," *Finance and Development,* March 1971.

Kim, Kwang Suk. *Growth and Structural Transformation: Studies in the Modernization of the Republic of Korea, 1945-1975,* Cambridge, MA, Harvard University Press, 1979.

Kindleberger, Charles P. *A Financial History of Western Europe,* London, Allen and Unwin, 1984.

Kirsch, Henry W. *Industrial Development in a Traditional Society: The Conflict of Entrepreneurship and Modernization in Chile,* Gainesville, University of Florida, 1977.

Kleimola, Ann M. "The Muscovite Autocracy at Work: The Use of Disgrace as an Instrument of Control," in Butler, 1977.

Knight, Peter T. "New Forms of Economic Organization in Peru: Toward Workers' Self- Management," in Lowenthal, 1975.

Koebner, Richard. "The Settlement and Colonization of Europe," in Postan, 1966.

Kohli, Atul. *The State and Development in the Third World,* Princeton University Press, 1979.

Korb, J.G. *Diary of an Austrian Secretary of Legation at the Court of Czar Peter the Great,* reprint edition 1968, London, 1863.

Koschmann, J. Victor. "Action as a Text: Ideology in the Tengu Insurrection," in Najita and Koschmann, 1982.

Kriedte, Peter. *Peasants, Landlords and Merchant Capitalists: Europe and the World Economy 1500-1800*, Cambridge University Press, 1983.

Kumar, Dharma, ed. *The Cambridge Economic History of India,* volume 2, Cambridge University Press, 1982.

Kunt, I. Metin. *The Sultan's Servants: The Transformation of Ottoman Provincial Government, 1550-1650,* New York, Columbia University Press, 1983.

Kuo, Shirley W. *The Taiwan Economy in Transition,* Boulder, CO, Westview Press, 1983.

Kuo, Shirley W.; Ranis, Gustav; and Fei, John. *The Taiwan Success Story: Rapid Growth with Improved Distribution in the Republic of China,* Boulder, CO, Westview Press, 1981.

Lambton, Ann K. S. *Landlord and Peasant in Persia: A Study of Land Tenure and Land Revenue Administration,* Oxford University Press, 1953.

Landes, David S. *The Unbound Prometheus: Technological Change and Industrial Development in Western Europe, 1758-Present,* Cambridge University Press, 1969.

Laroui, Abdallah. *The History of the Maghrib, An Interpretive Essay*, Princeton University Press, 1977.

Lawrence, John A. *A History of Russia*, New York, New American Library, 1978.

Lee, Soo-Ann. *Assault on Poverty in Singapore*, Los Angeles, University of Southern California Press, 1979.

Leeming, Frank. "The Earlier Industrialization of Hong Kong," in *Modern Asian Studies,* volume 9, no. 3, July 1975.

Lefebvre, Georges. *The Coming of the French Revolution,* Princeton University Press, 1947.

Leibenstein, Harvey. *General X-Efficiency Theory and Economic Development*, Oxford University Press, 1978.

Lenczowski George. *Iran Under the Pahlavis*, Stanford, CA, Hoover Institute Press, 1978.

Le Roy Ladurie, Emmanuel. "Agrarian Class Structure and Economic Development in Pre-Industrial Europe," *Past and Present,* May 1978.

Le Roy Ladurie, Emmanuel. "L'Histoire Immobile," in *Annales, Ecole des Sciences Politiques*, volume 19, Paris, 1974.

Le Roy Ladurie, Emmanuel. *Les Paysans de Languedoc*, Paris, S.E.V.P.E.N., 1966.

Levtzion, Nehemia. "The Early States of the Western Sudan to 1500," in Ajayi and Crowder, 1976.

Levtzion, Nehemia. "North-West Africa: from the Maghrib to the Fringes of the Forest," in Gray, 1975.

Lewin, M. *Russian Peasants and Soviet Power: A Study of Collectivization,* New York, W. W. Norton, Inc., 1968.

Lewis, Archibald R. *Nomads and Crusaders, A.D. 1000-1368,* Bloomington, IN, Indiana University Press, 1988.

Lewis, W. Arthur. *Selected Economic Writings of W. Arthur Lewis,* New York, Columbia University Press, 1983.

Lewis, W. Arthur. "A Review of Economic Development," *American Economic Review,* volume LV, no. 2, May 1965.

Lewis, W. Arthur. *The Theory of Economic Growth,* London, G. Allen 1955.

Lewis, W. Arthur. "Economic Development with Unlimited Supplies of Labour," *The Manchester School,* May 1954.

Li, Kou-Ting. *The Evolution of Policy Behind Taiwan's Development Success,* New Haven and London, Yale University Press, 1988.

Li, Yu-Ning, ed. *Shang Yang's Reforms and State Control in China,* White Plains, NY, M.E. Sharpe, Inc., 1977.

Lim, Chong-Yah. *Policy Options for the Singapore Economy,* New York, McGraw-Hill, 1988.

Lin, W. Y. *The New Monetary System of China: A Personal Interpretation,* University of Chicago Press, 1936.

Linz, Juan J., and Stepan, Alfred, eds. *The Breakdown of Democratic Regimes: Latin America,* Baltimore, Johns Hopkins University Press, 1978.

Linz, Susan J., and Moskoff, William, eds. *Reorganization and Reform in the Soviet Economy,* Armonk, NY, Sharpe, 1988.

Loehr, William, and Powelson, John P. *The Economics of Development and Distribution,* New York, Harcourt Brace Jovanovich, 1981.

Loewe, Michael. "Attempts at Economic Coordination during the Western Han Dynasty," in Schram, 1985.

Lopez, Robert S. *The Commercial Revolution of the Middle Ages, 950-1350,* Cambridge University Press, 1979.

Lowenthal, Abraham, *The Peruvian Experiment: Continuity and Change under Military Rule,* Princeton University Press, 1975.

Lucas, Robert E.B. *The Indian Economy: Recent Development and Future Prospects,* Boulder, CO, Westview Press, 1988.

Ludden, David. *Peasant History in South India,* Princeton University Press, 1985.

Luzzatto, Gino. *An Economic History of Italy from the Fall of the Roman Empire to the Beginning of the Sixteenth Century,* London, Routledge, Kegan Paul, 1961.

Lynch, John. *Spain Under the Habsburgs: Second Edition,* volume I: *Empire and Absolutism, 1516-1598,* volume II: *Spain and America: 1598-1700,* New York University Press, 1981.

Mabogunje, Akin. "The Land and Peoples of West Africa," in Ajayi and Crowder, 1976.

MacFarquhar, Roderick. *The Origins of the Cultural Revolution: The Great Leap Forward 1958-1960,* New York, Columbia University Press 1983.

MacFarquhar, Roderick. *The Origins of the Cultural Revolution: Contradictions Among the People, 1956-1957.* New York, Columbia University Press, 1974.

Maitland, Frederic W. *Roman Canon Law in the Church of England.* London, 1898.

Marks, Shula, and Gray, Richard. "Southern Africa and Madagascar," in Gray, 1975.

Marques, A.H. de Oliveira. *History of Portugal:* volume I: *From Lusitania to Empire.* New York, Columbia University Press, 1972.

Marques, A.H. de Oliveira. *History of Portugal:* volume II: *From Empire to Corporate State,* New York, Columbia University Press, 1976.

Mason, Edward S. *The Economic and Social Modernization of the Republic of Korea,* Cambridge, MA, Harvard University Press,. 1980.

Mass, Jeffrey P. *Warrior Government in Early Medieval Japan: A Study of the Kamakura Bakufu, Shugo, and Jito,* New Haven, CT, Yale University Press, 1974.

Mathias, Peter, and Postan, M.M. *The Industrial Economies: Capital, Labour, and Enterprise,* Cambridge Economic History of Europe, volume 7 (in two parts), Cambridge University Press, 1978.

Matienzo, José N. *El Gobierno Representativo en la República Argentina,* Madrid, Editorial América, 1917.

Matthews, Mervyn. *Poverty in the Soviet Union: The Life-Styles of the Underprivileged in Recent Years,* Cambridge University Press, 1986.

Maurois, André. *History of France,* New York, Minerva Press, 1948.

McClelland, David C. *The Achieving Society,* Princeton, NJ, D. Van Nostrand Co., 1961.

Meijer, Marinus J. "Slavery at the End of the Ch'ing Dynasty," in Cohen, Edwards, and Chang Chen, 1980.

Melko, Matthew, and Hord, John. *Peace in the Western World,* Jefferson, NC, McFarland and Company, Inc., 1984.

Mensah-Brown, A.K. *Introduction to Law in Contemporary Africa,* New York, Conch Magazine Ltd., 1976.

Metcalf, Thomas R. *Land, Landlords, and the British Raj: Northern India in the Nineteenth Century,* Berkeley, University of California Press, 1979.

Meyer, Jean. "The Cristiada: Peasant War and Religious War in Revolutionary Mexico, 1926-9," in Bak and Benecke, 1984.

Miers, Suzanne, and Kopytoff, Igor, eds. *Slavery in Africa: Historical and Anthropological Perspectives,* Madison, University of Wisconsin Press, 1977.

Miller, John. *Bourbon and Stuart: Kings and Kingship in France and England in the Seventeenth Century,* New York, Franklin Watts, 1987.

Milner-Gul Robin. *Cultural Atlas of Russia and the Soviet Union,* New York, Oxford University Press, 1989.

Mirza, Hafiz. *Multinationals and the Growth of the Singapore Economy*, New York, St. Martin's Press, 1986.

Miskimin, Harry A.; Herlihy, David; and Udovich, Abraham L. *The Medieval City*, New Haven, CT, Yale University Press, 1977.

Miskimin, Harry A. *The Economy of Early Renaissance Europe, 1300-1460,* Cambridge University Press, 1975.

Mitsuru, Hashimoto. "The Social Background of Peasant Uprisings in Tokugawa Japan," in Najita and Koschmann, 1982.

Miyazaki, Ichisada. "The Administration of Justice During the Sung Dynasty," in Cohen, Edwards, and Chang Chen, 1980.

Morgan, John. *Godly Learning: Puritan Attitudes Towards Reason, Learning and Education,* 1560-1640, Cambridge University Press, 1986.

Morris, Henry F. and Read, James S. *Indirect Rule and the Search for Justice: Essays in East African Legal History,* Oxford University Press, 1972.

Mousnier, Roland. *The Institutions of France under the Absolute Monarchy 1598-1789: Society and the State*, University of Chicago Press, 1974.

Mueller, Dennis C. *Public Choice II,* Cambridge University Press, 1989.

Munting, Roger. *The Economic Development of the USSR,* New York, St. Martin's Press, 1982.

Nadal, Jordi. "A Century of Industrialization in Spain," in Sanchez-Albornoz, 1987.

Nadal, Jordi. *El Fracaso de la Revolución Industrial en España, 1814-1913,* Barcelona, Editorial Ariel, 1975.

Najita, Tetsuo. "Introduction: A Synchronous Approach to the Study of Conflict in Japanese History," in Najita and Koschmann, 1982.

Najita, Tetsuo. *Hara Kei in the Politics of Compromise, 1905-1915,* Cambridge, MA, Harvard University Press, 1967.

Najita, Tetsuo, and Koschmann, J. Victor, eds. *Conflict in Modern Japanese History: The Neglected Transition,* Princeton University Press, 1982.

Neale, Walter C., "Land is to Rule," in Frykenberg, 1969.

Newman, Katherine S. *Law and Economic Organization: A Comparative Study of Preindustrial Societies,* Cambridge University Press, 1983.

Nicholls, David. *"Religion and Peasant Movements in Normandy during the French Religious Wars,"* in Bak and Benecke, 1984.

North, Douglass C. *Institutions, Institutional Change and Economic Performance,* Cambridge University Press, 1990.

North, Douglass C. *Structure and Change in Economic History*, New York, W.W. Norton & Company, 1981.

North, Douglass, and Thomas, Robert P. *The Rise of the Western World: A New Economic History,* Cambridge University Press, 1973.

O'Donnell, Guillermo. "Permanent Crisis and the Failure to Create a Democratic Regime," in Linz and Stepan, 1978.

Obayemi, Ade. "The Yoruba and Edo-speaking Peoples and their Neighbours before 1600," in Ajayi and Crowder, 1976.

Ofer, Gur. "Soviet Economic Growth: 1928-1985," *Journal of Economic Literature,* December 1987.

Ohkawa, Kazushi, and Rosovsky, Henry. "Capital Formation in Japan," in Mathias and Postan, 1978.

Ohkawa, Kazushi. *Japanese Economic Growth: Trend Acceleration in the Twentieth Century,* Stanford University Press, 1973.

Oldham, John R., ed. *China's Legal Development,* Armonk, N.Y., M.E. Sharpe, Inc., 1986.

Olson, Mancur. *The Rise and Decline of Nations: Economic Growth, Stagflation, and Social Rigidities,* New Haven, CT, Yale University Press, 1982.

Omer-Cooper, J. D. "The Nguni outburst," in Flint, 1976.

Ong, Wee Hock. *The Economics of Growth and Survival,* Singapore, National Trades Union Congress, 1978.

Ostrogorsky, Georg. "Agrarian Conditions in the Byzantine Empire in the Middle Ages," in Postan, 1966.

Ozment, Steven. *The Age of Reform, 1250-1550,* New Haven, CT, Yale University Press, 1980.

Park, Chong Kee. *Human Resources and Social Development in Korea,* Seoul, Korea Development Institute, 1980.

Parry, V.J. *A History of the Ottoman Empire to 1730,* Cambridge University Press.

Patrick, Hugh, and Rosovsky, Henry, eds. *Asia's New Giant: How the Japanese Economy Works,* Washington, DC, Brookings Institution, 1976.

Payne, Stanley G. *A History of Spain and Portugal,* two volumes, Madison, University of Wisconsin Press, 1973.

Paz, Octavio. *One Earth, Four or Five Worlds: Reflections on Comparative History,* San Diego, CA, Harcourt Brace Jovanovich, 1985.

Peisker, T. "The Asiatic Background," in Bury, Gwatkin, and Whitney, 1964.

Perlin, Frank. "Money-use in Late Pre-colonial India and the International Trade in Currency Media," in Richards, 1987.

Petro, Nicolai. "Toward a New Russian Federation," *Wilson Quarterly,* Summer 1990.

Phillips, Arthur. "The Future of Customary Law in Africa," in Afrika Institute, 1956.

Pinto, Aníbal. *Inflación: Raices Estructurales, Ensayso,* Mexico, Fondo de Cultura Económica, 1973.

Pinto, Aníbal. *Inflación: Raices Estructurales,* Mexico, Fondo de Cultura Económica, 1960.

Poblete Troncoso, Moíses, and Burnett, Ben G. *The Rise of the Latin American Labor Movement,* New York, Bookman Associates, 1960.

Poirier, J. "L'avenir du Droit Coutumier Negro-Africain," in Afrika Institut, 1956.

Poly, Jean and Bournazel, Eric. *The Feudal Transformation, 900-1200,* New York, Holmes and Meier, 1991.

Postan, M. M. *Essays on Medieval Agriculture and General Problems of the Medieval Economy,* Cambridge University Press, 1973.

Postan, M. M. *The Medieval Economy and Society: An Economic History of Britain,* Berkeley, CA, University of California Press, 1972.

Postan, M. M. *The Medieval Economy and Society: An Economic History of Britain in the Middle Ages*, London, Weidenfield and Nicholson, 1972.

Postan, M. M., ed. *The Agrarian Life of the Middle Ages,* Cambridge Economic History of Europe, volume 1, second edition, Cambridge University Press, 1966.

Postan, M. M. "The Medieval Agrarian Economy in its Prime: England," in Postan, 1966.

Postan, M. M. and Hatcher, John. "Agrarian Class Structure and Economic Development in Pre-Industrial Europe," *Past and Present,* February 1978.

Postan, M. M., and Miller, Edward, eds. *Trade and Industry in the Middle Ages*, Cambridge Economic History of Europe, volume 2, second edition, Cambridge University Press, 1987.

Postan, M. M., Rich, E.E., and Miller, Edward, eds. *Economic Organization and Policies in the Middle Ages,* Cambridge Economic History of Europe, volume 3, Cambridge University Press, 1963.

Powelson, John P. "The Land Grabbers of Cali," *The Reporter*, January 1964.

Powelson, John P. *Latin America: Today's Economic and Social Revolution*, New York, McGraw-Hill Book Company, 1964.

Powelson, John P. "The Oil Price Increase: Impacts on Industrialized and Less-Developed Countries," *Journal of Energy and Development,* volume II, no. 1, 1977.

Powelson, John P., *The Story of Land*, Cambridge MA, Lincoln Institute of Land Policy, 1988.

Powelson, John P. and Stock, Richard. *The Peasant Betrayed: Agriculture and Land Reform in the Third World*, revised edition, Washington, DC, Cato Institute, 1990.

Prado Junior, Caio. *The Colonial Background of Modern Brazil*, Berkeley, University of California Press, 1967.

Prakash, Om. "Foreign Merchants and Indian Mints in the Seventeenth and Early Eighteenth Century," in Richards, 1987.

Prothero, R. Mansell ed. *People and Land in Africa South of the Sahara: Readings in Social Geography*, Oxford University Press, 1972.

Rabin, Matthew. "Incorporating Fairness into Game Theory and Economics," *American Economic Review*, December 1993.

Rabushka, Alvin. *Hong Kong: a Study in Economic Freedom*, Chicago, IL, University of Chicago, 1979.

Raeff, Marc. *Understanding Imperial Russia*, Irvington, NY, Columbia University Press, 1984.

Randall, Laura. *A Comparative Economic History of Latin America, 1500-1914*, volumes I-IV, New York, University Microfilms International, 1977.

Raychaudhuri, Tapan, and Habib, Irfan, eds. *The Cambridge Economic History of India*, volume 1: c.1200-c.1750, Cambridge, Cambridge University Press, 1982.

Reynolds, Clark W. *The Mexican Economy: Twentieth Century Structure and Growth*, New Haven, CT, Yale University Press, 1970.

Ricardo, David. *On the Principles of Political Economy and Taxation*, New York, Penguin Books, 1971, original in 1817.

Rich, E. E., "Colonial Settlement and its Labour Problems," in Rich and Wilson, 1967.

Rich, E. E., and Wilson, C.H., eds. *The Economic Organization of Early Modern Europe*, Cambridge Economic History of Europe, volume 5, Cambridge University Press, 1977.

Rich, E. E., and Wilson, C.H., eds. *The Economy of Expanding Europe in the 16th and 17th Centuries*, Cambridge Economic History of Europe, volume 4, Cambridge University Press, 1967.

Richards, John F., ed. *The Imperial Monetary System of Mughal India.*, Delhi, Oxford University Press, 1987.

Richet, Denis. "Revolutionary Assemblies," in Furet and Ozouf, 1989.

Richmond, J.C.B. *Egypt, 1798-1952, Her Advance Towards A Modern Identity*, New York, Columbia University Press, 1977.

Roberts, Andrew. *History of Zambia: New Edition*, New York, NY, Holmes and Meier, 1979.

Robertson, Priscilla. *Revolutions of 1848: A Social History*, Princeton University Press, 1952.

Rodan, Garry. *The Political Economy of Singapore's Industrialization: National, State, and International Capital*, New York, St. Martin's Press, 1989.

Rodney, Walter. "The Guinea Coast," in Gray, 1975.

Romer, Paul. "Endogenous Technological Change," *Journal of Political Economy*, October 1, 1990, Supplement, no. 5, 1990.

Romer, Paul. "Nobel Laureate: On James Buchanan's Contributions to Public Economics," *Journal of Economic Perspectives*, Fall 1988.

Rosenberg, Nathan, and Birdzell, L.E. *How the West Grew Rich*, New York, Basic Books Inc., 1986.

Rostow, W. W. *The Stages of Economic Growth: A Non-Communist Manifesto*, Cambridge University Press, 1961.

Rouche, Michel. "The Early Middle Ages in the West," in Veyne, 1987.

Rowan, Steven. "A Reichstag in the Reform Era: Freiburg in Breisgau 1497-98," in Vann and Rowan, 1974.

Rozman, Gilbert. *Urban Networks in Ch'ing China and Tokugawa Japan*, Princeton University Press, 1973.

Rubenson, Sven. "Ethiopia and the Horn," in Flint, 1976.

Sanchez-Albornoz, Nicolas. *The Economic Modernization of Spain, 1830-1930*, New York University Press, 1987.

Sandmo, Agnar. "Buchanan on Political Economy: A Review Article," *Journal of Economic Literature*, March 1990.

Santangelo, Paolo. "The Imperial Factories of Suzhou: Limits and Characteristics of State Intervention during the Ming and Qing Dynasties," in Schram, 1985.

Schacht, Joseph. "Law and Justice," in Holt, Lambton, and Lewis, 1970.

Schapera, I. "The Development of Customary Law in the Bechuanaland Protectorate," in Afrika Institut, 1956.

Schram, Stuart R. ed. *The Scope of State Power in China,* London, St. Martin's Press, 1985.

Schumpeter Joseph A. *The Theory of Economic Development: An Inquiry into Profits, Capital, Credit, Interest, and the Business Cycle*, Cambridge, MA, Harvard University Press. 1936.

Scott, Maurice Fitzgerald. *A New View of Economic Growth*, Oxford University Press, 1989.

Sen-Gupta, Nares Chandra. *Evolution of Ancient Indian Law*, London, Arthur Probsthain, 1953.

Seward, Desmond. *Henry V: The Scourge of God*, Middlesex, England, Viking Penguin Inc., 1987.

Shapiro, Barbara J. *Probability and Certainty in Seventeenth-Century England,* Princeton University Press, 1983.

Shelvankar K.S. *The Problem of India,* 1940.

Sicard, Germain. "La France Moderne," in Bruguière et al, 1986.

Simon, Denis F. *Taiwan, Technology Transfer, and Transnationalism*, Boulder, CO, Westview Press, 1983.

Singer, Max, and Wildavsky, Aaron. *The Real World Order: Zones of Peace / Zones of Turmoil*, Chatham, NJ, Chatham House Publishers, 1993.

Smith, Abdullahi. "The Early States of the Central Sudan," in Ajayi and Crowder, 1976.

Smith, M. G. "A Structural Approach to Comparative Politics," in Easton, 1966.

Smith, Thomas C. *The Agrarian Origins of Modern Japan*, Stanford, CA, Stanford University Press, 1970.

Smithies, Arthur. "Argentina and Australia," *American Economic Review*, May 1965.

Snow, Peter G. *Argentine Radicalism: The History and Doctrine of the Radical Civil Union,* Iowa City, IA, University of Iowa Press, 1965.

Solow, Robert M. "Economic History and Economics," *American Economic Review*, May 1985.

Solow, Robert M. *Growth Theory*, Oxford University Press, 1970.

Spence, Jonathan. "Review of Jean Levi, The Chinese Emperor," *New York Times Book Review*, October 4, 1987.

Stein, Burton. "Integration of the Agrarian System of Southern India," in Frykenberg, 1969.

Strayer, Joseph R. *The Albigensian Crusades*, Ann Arbor, University of Michigan Press, 1992.

Suh, Suk Tai. *Import Substitution and Economic Development in Korea,* Seoul, Korea Development Institute. Paper, 1975.

Sunkel, Osvaldo. "La Inflación Chilena: Un Enfoque Heterodoxo," *Trimestre Económico*, No. 100, October/December 1958.

Suret-Canale, Jean, and Barry, Boubacar. "The Western Atlantic Coast to 1800," in Ajayi and Crowder, 1976.

Takekoshi, Yosoburo. *The Economic Aspects of the History of the Civilization of Japan*, volumes 1,2, and 3, New York, Macmillan, 1930.

Thaxton, Ralph. "Land Rent, Peasant Migration, and Political Power in Yao cun, 1911-1937," *Modern Asian Studies (Cambridge)*,16, part 1, 1982.

Théry, Edmond. *La Transformation Economique de la Russie*, Paris, 1912.

Tocqueville, Alexis de. *The Old Regime and the French Revolution*, Garden City, NY, Doubleday & Company, 1955. Original edition, 1858.

Todaro, Michael P. *The Struggle for Economic Development: Readings in Problems and Policies,* New York, Longman Inc., 1983.

Todaro, Michael P. *Economic Development in the Third World, Second Edition*, New York, Longman Inc., 1981.

Todaro, Michael P. *Economic Development in the Third World, Second Edition*, New York, Longman Inc., 1981.

Todaro, Michael P. *Development Planning: Models and Methods*, New York, Oxford University Press, 1971.

Todaro, Michael P. "A Model of Labor Migration and Urban Unemployment in Less Developed Countries," *American Economic Review*, March 1969.

Tolz, Vera. *The USSR's Emerging Multiparty System*, New York, Praeger, 1990.

Tortella, Gabriel. "Agriculture: A Slow-Moving Sector, 1830-1935," in Sanchez-Albornoz, 1987.

Totman, Conrad. "From Reformism to Transformism: Bakufu Policy, 1853-1868," in Najita and Koschmann, 1982.

Tsuchiya, Takao. "An Economic History of Japan," in *The Transaction of the Asiatic Society of Japan*, second series, volume 15, 1937.

Tuchman, Barbara W. *The March of Folly, From Troy to Vietnam*, New York, Alfred A. Knopf, 1984.

Tuchman, Barbara W. *A Distant Mirror: The Calamitous Fourteenth Century*, New York, Alfred A. Knopf, 1978.

Tun Wai, U. "Financial Markets in Development," *Finafrica Bulletin*, 1976.

Tun Wai, U. "A Revisit to Interest Rates Outside the Money Markets of Under-Developed Countries," *Banca Quarterly Review*, no. 122, 1977.

UCLA, See California University.

Udovitch, Abraham L. "Bankers without Banks: Commerce, Banking and Society in the Islamic World of the Middle Ages," in California University, 1979.

Unomah, A. C., and Webster, J. B. "East Africa: the Expansion of Commerce," in Flint, 1976.

van den Berg, G.P. "Elements of Continuity in Soviet Constitutional Law," in Butler, 1977.

Van Velsen J. *The Politics of Kinship*, Manchester University Press, 1957.

Van Werveke, H. "The Rise of the Towns," in Postan, Rich, and Miller, 1963.

Vandermeersch, Leon. "An Enquiry into the Chinese Conception of the Law," in Schram, 1985.

Vann, James A., and Rowan, Stephen W., ed. *The Old Reich: Essays on German Political Institutions, 1495-1806*, Brussels, Librairie Encyclopédique de Luxembourg, 1974.

Veyne, Paul, ed. *A History of Private Life*, volume 1, Cambridge, MA, Belknap Press, 1987.

Wade, Robert. *Village Republics, Economic Conditions for Collective Action in South India*, Cambridge University Press, 1988.

Wadekin, Karl-Eugen. *Agrarian Policies in Communist Europe: A Critical Introduction*, Totowa, NJ, Rowman & Allanheld, 1982.

Wagner, Richard E., and Gwartney, James D. "Public Choice and Constitutional Order," in Wagner and Gwartney, 1988.

Wagner, Richard E., and Gwartney, James D., eds. *Public Choice and Constitutional Economics*, Greenwich CT, JWI Press, 1988.

Wagner, William G. "Tsarist Legal Policies at the End of the Nineteenth Century: A Study in Inconsistencies," *Slavic and East European Review,* July 1976.

Wang, Joseph E. *Outline of Modern Chinese Law: Studies in Chinese Government and Law,* Arlington, VA, University Publications, 1934.

Watson, W. *Tribal Cohesion in a Money Economy,* Manchester University Press, 1958.

Webb, Richard. *Government Policy and the Distribution of Income in Peru, 1963-1973,* Cambridge, MA., Harvard University Press, 1977.

Webber, Carolyn, and Wildavsky, Aaron. *A History of Taxation and Expenditure in the Western World,* New York, Simon and Schuster, 1986.

Weber, Max. *The Theory of Social and Economic Organization,* New York, Free Press, 1964, original in 1922.

Weber, Max. *The Protestant Ethic and the Spirit of Capitalism,* New York, Charles Scribner's, 1958, original in 1904-05.

White, Stephen D. "Pactum regem vincit et amor judicium, The Settlement of Disputes by Compromise in Eleventh-Century Western France," *American Journal of Legal History*, volume 22, 1978.

Wigmore, John H., ed. *Law and Justice in Tokugawa Japan,* ten volumes, Tokyo, Japan Cultural Society, 1969.

Wiles, Peter, ed. *The Soviet Economy on the Brink of Reform: Essays in Honor of Alec Nove,* Boston, MA, Unwin Hyman, 1988.

Wilks, Ivor. "The Mossi and the Akan states to 1800," in Ajayi and Crowder, 1976.

Will, Pierre-Etien. "State Intervention in the Administration of a Hydraulic Infrastructure: The Example of Hubei Province in Late Imperial Times," in Schram, 1985.

Williamson, Oliver E. *The Economic Institutions of Capitalism: Firms, Markets, Relational Contracting,* New York, Free Press, 1985.

Wilson, C.H. "Trade, Society, and the State," in Rich and Wilson, 1967.

Wilson, James Q. *The Moral Sense,* Oxford University Press, 1993.

Wilson, P.R.D. *Export Instability and Economic Development—A Survey, Part 2: The Empirical Work,* Coventry, University of Warwick, 1977.

Wilson, William. *The Truly Disadvantaged: The Inner City, the Underclass, and Public Policy*, University of Chicago Press, 1987.

Winterstee, Prescott B. "The Early Muromachi Bakufu in Kyoto," in Hall and Mass, 1974.

Wolf, Eric R. *Europe and the People Without History*, Berkeley, CA., University of California Press, 1982.

Wolpert, Stanley. *A History of India*, Oxford University Press, 1977.

World Bank. *The East Asian Miracle*, Washington, DC, World Bank, 1993.

World Bank, *Developing Economies in Transition*, volume 2, Washington, DC, World Bank, 1990a.

World Bank, *India: Recent Developments and Medium-Term Issues*, Washington, DC, World Bank, 1990b.

World Bank. *Sub-Saharan Africa: From Crisis to Sustainable Growth*, Washington, DC, World Bank, 1989.

World Bank. *Tanzania Agricultural Sector Report*, no. 4052-TA, Washington, DC, World Bank, 1983.

World Bank. *Zambia: A Basic Economic Report*, Washington, DC, World Bank, 1977.

Wu, Jianfan. "Building China's New Legal System," in Oldham, 1986.

Wunder, Heidi. "Peasant Organization and Class Conflict in East and West Germany," *Past and Present*, February 1987.

Yan Meng. "Review of Law in Traditional China: I and II," unpublished papers prepared as part of special study at University of Colorado, Boulder, CO, 1988.

Yang, Lien-shing. *Money and Credit in China: A Short History*, Cambridge, Harvard University Press, 1952.

Yasuba, Yasukichi. "Standard of Living in Japan Before Industrialization: From What Level Did Japan Begin? A Comment," *Journal of Economic History*, March 1986.

Index

To save space, items have been omitted from this index if they appear frequently in the text and can be readily found in their expected places. These would include countries of Europe, found in chapters 4 and 5, and the dynasties of China, found in chapters 11 and 12. Items in the appendixes are also omitted, since they can readily be found by the titles to the appendixes.

Louis of Hungary, 321
Louis VI of France, 49
Louis XI of France, 78
Louis XIII of France, 83, 85
Louis XIV of France, 49, 65, 83, 85
Loyang, 155
Lozi, 101, 120
Luba, 92-93, 102, 105
Lübeck, 320, 323
Ludden, David, 138
Lunda, 92-93, 101, 102, 110, 111
Lusignan, Hughes de, 53

Machiavelli, 307
Madagascar, 110
Maghrib, 101, 102, 108
Magna Carta, 60
Magyar invasions, 61
Mahmud II, 289
Maitland, Frederic, 64, 78
makhtabi, 296
Malawi, 101, 110, 111, 119, 126
Malaysia, 310
Mali, 92, 101
Malthus, Thomas R., 3
Mambwe, 99
Mamluks, in Egypt, 95
Manchuria, 169
Mandara, 109
Mandela, Nelson, 336-37
Manizales, Colombia, 337
manufacturing, in Japan, 33
Mao Zedong, 169, 178, 186
Marathan rebellions, 139
Marcos, Subcomandante, 251
Maria Theresa of Austria, 314
Marks and Gray, 101
Masai, 109
Mass, Jeffrey P., 2
Matapa, 111
Mauritius, 124
Maximilian I, Emperor, 317
Maynard, John, 84
Mazarin, Jules, 225
McClelland, David, 92
McIntyre, Robert, 218
McKee, Margaret, 215

McKinnon, Donald I., 217
Medici family, 307, 309
Mehmed II, 281
Meiji Restoration, 18, 26, 31, 37
Mensah-Brown, A.K., 120, 145
mercantilism, 228
Merchant Adventurers, 61
Mesta, 225, 238
Metternich, Fürst von, 324
Mexico, 246-52
mfecane, 110
Middle East, definition, 279
Milan, 306
Mill, John Stuart, 3
millets, 282
Minamoto family, 14
Minamoto Yoritomo, 14, 82
ministeriales, 325
mir, 214
miras, 137
Mito fief, 17
Mitsui Hachiroemon, 28
Miyazaki, Ichisada, 179
Mabogunje, Akin, 96, 100
Mobutu Sese Seko, 4, 128
Mohammed Ali, 101, 110
Mohammed Reza Shah, 290-91
Mohenjo-dara, 134
Mombasa, 109
monasteries, Buddhist in China, 181
  in China, 155
  in Japan, 17
money, in Africa, 95-96, 116-17
  in China, 181-84
  in Germany, 322-24
  in Iberia, 232-34
  in India, 145-47
  in Japan, 26
  in Middle East, 285-86
  in northwestern Europe, 56
  in Russia, 199-203
moneylenders, in Africa, 117
Mongols, in Russia, 195, 203, 210
Montezuma (Moctezuma), 246
Montoneros, 271
Morocco, 110, 111, 130
Morris and Read, 145